MACROMEDIA Flash MX Studio

Dennis Baldwin
Jamie Macdonald
Keith Peters
Jon Steer
David Tudury
Jerome Turner
Steve Webster
Alex White
Todd Yard

Flash MX Studio

© 2002 friends of ED

First Printed July 2002

Trademark Acknowledgements

Published by friends of ED

30-32 Lincoln Road, Olton, Birmingham.
B27 6PA. UK.
Printed in USA

ISBN 1-903450-026-8

Flash MX Studio

Credits

Authors
Dennis Baldwin
Jamie Macdonald
Keith Peters
Jon Steer
David Tudury
Jerome Turner
Steve Webster
Alex White
Todd Yard

Additional Material
Kristian Besley

Commissioning Editor
Jim Hannah

Graphic Editor
Ty Bhogal

Editors
Adam Dutton
Caroline Robeson
James Robinson
Gavin Wray

Author Agent
Chris Matterface

Project Manager
Simon Brand

Technical Reviewers
Sally Cruikshank
Steve Kirby
Steve McCormick
Mike Pearce
Jon Steer
Steve Webster
Steven Williams

Indexer
Fiona Murray

Proofing
Cathy Succamore

Managing Editor
Ben Huczek

Alex White: Coming from a Fine Art background, Alex once did 'arty' things with Director and obscure Mac 3D modelling programs, before selling out and moving to the big city making fancy Flash web sites for companies who could afford it. He has recently combined creative forces with fellow 'Messenger Buddy' Jez Turner for their 'ground-breaking' Flatpack Media venture.

Thanks go out to Jez at the 'Poole office', Claire for the countless hearty meals, and mum for her moral support.

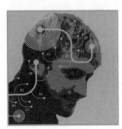

David Tudury: David discovered Flash while interning in San Francisco three years ago. Since then he's worked in advertising, plug-in development, and online-gaming. The volatile economy quickly added some breadth to his experience. He's used Flash for simple animations, web sites, video games, and as a presentation layer for N-tier web applications. Mostly though, he just likes playing with it (**www.outmoded.com** is his playground).

"I need to thank Aaron Piland of **www.apakstudio.com** for the terrific portrait, Michael Montagna for helping with possible XML examples, Adam Dutton who edited (fixed) this chapter, Keith Peters who got me this opportunity, the other good folks at **www.were-here.com**, and Regina, my fiance, for understanding that computer people aren't supposed to sleep at night."

Dennis Baldwin: Dennis' main focus is to stay on top of technology and find exciting new ways to push the envelope of web development. He currently maintains a couple of online resources for Flash and ColdFusion developers at **www.flashcfm.com** and **www.devmx.com**. He is also the lead developer for Eternal Media (**www.eternal-media.com**), a web and multimedia firm that offers technology solutions for ministries and non-profit organizations. When he's not in front of the computer screen, Dennis mainly spends time with his wife Jamie or can be found skating around the streets of Dallas with his friends.

Jamie Macdonald; Jamie Macdonald works at Relevare in London. When he finds time he updates his own site **www.nooflat.nu**.

Author Biographies

Jerome Turner: comes from Leighton Buzzard where his first cinematic experience was watching Tom and Jerry beat the hell out of each other on his parent's woodchip wallpaper. He then studied Art at Bedford College where he learnt that photography was cool because you could visit the Fine Art department whilst your films were drying. Following this he travelled to Exeter, wouldn't touch the cider, but did wander off with a degree in Media Arts/Visual Arts, which involved a lot of photocopying and pointing cameras at people who didn't really enjoy being filmed.

Since then he's moved to Poole with his long-suffering partner Claire and worked on a number of film and video productions as a production assistant, camera operator, script writer, boom operator, 1st AD, runner, producer, and director. Sometimes when he's very bored he goes to the boating lake to film Canadian geese.

Jon Steer: Jon has been working as a web developer for nearly five years after graduating from Durham University with a degree in Economics. He is Technical Director of Durham Associates Ltd (**www.da-group.co.uk**), a marketing communications company in the north-east of England and admits to being far happier working with code than with pretty pictures! His main focus is server-side technologies, especially PHP and mySQL, and is always looking for different ways to put these to work. Jon lives near Durham with his wife and two daughters to whom special thanks go for their enormous support and encouragement.

Keith Peters: lives in Lynn, Massachusetts with his wife Kazumi. He's been using Flash on and off for nearly three years now, but far more heavily in the last year. His personal site, **www.bit-101.com**, launched in August 2001 and he strives to keep up with the experiment-a-day schedule. It features fairly simple graphics, usually relying on math and scripting to build complex forms and movements.

Steve Webster: propeller beanie hat firmly in place, spends most of his time tinkering with scripting, backend, and Flash technologies, or writing about tinkering with scripting, backend, and Flash technologies. Being clearly masochistic in nature, he's been programming since he was knee-high to a grasshopper and can currently be found plotting his route to world domination. Mwahahaha...

As always, I owe a great debt to my girlfriend Nicki for her saint-like patience while I was once again "that bloke locked away upstairs". Thanks also to the fantastic team at friends of Ed – you rock!

Todd Yard: After studying and working for seven years as an actor, Todd was introduced to Flash in 2000 and was quickly taken by how it allowed for both stunning creativity and programmatic logic application – a truly left-brain, right-brain approach to production – and has not looked back. He now works as Creative Director for Daedalus Media in New York City, which specializes in the creation of Flash-based corporate presentations, primarily for clients in the investment banking industry. His more frivolous work and experimentation can be found at his personal web site **www.27Bobs.com**.

Table of Contents

section 3: Rich Media   463

chapter 12: Dynamic Graphics   467

chapter 13: Video   493

chapter 14: Audio   531

Introduction

Macromedia Flash MX: The Lay of the Land

With the release of a new version, Flash has grown up. In the heady days of the late 1990s, designers were trying their hand at anything and everything they could lay their hands on. Nowadays, the marketplace is seriously focused, and the serious Flash designer has to know exactly what they're doing and why.

Flash MX allows users to create distinctive web experiences and interfaces that do not just replicate standard approaches to web design, but push in different directions. With all the new features of Flash MX – the rich component set and the improved environment for application development – it would be easy to become distracted, so this book has been structured to equip readers for real world Flash design experiences. It homes in on the subject areas that have become Flash's role to fulfill, meeting the needs of even the most demanding sites.

Flash MX Studio: not for the faint-hearted

This book has been broken into four sections to address the most common needs of the Flash designer. First off, Jamie McDonald provides five chapters on site presentation and the principles of web design. These opening chapters take a look at how to create slick, professional-level site features, involving Flash MX's new drawing and motion capabilities, and interactive ActionScripting techniques.

The second section takes these techniques, and concentrates on evolving the keen user's ActionScript capabilities. Flash's resident coding environment is crucial to master, and taps into Flash's great strength – creating intuitive and interactive applications. Keith Peters and Todd Yard have buddied up on this section, and examine some of the most advanced ActionScript techniques around. Be warned – this section is not for the faint-hearted!

Section three takes a look at Flash MX's greatly improved visual, audio, and multimedia capabilities. Its three chapters, written by Jez Turner and Alex White, concentrate on building a single site specifically designed for displaying rich media content.

The final section is devoted to expounding a few myths about dynamic content using Flash. Its four chapters talk about dynamic principles, before focusing in on specific areas, including introductions to PHP and XML, together with a look at Macromedia's brand new ColdFusion MX.

What's on the CD?

The accompanying CD contains full support for the book's content. It includes all the example files used in (or created in) the book, so you can compare your work to that of the authors. You may even choose to cut a few corners if you like! The CD also contains chapters from other friends of ED books you may find useful.

Layout conventions

We've tried to keep this book as clear and easy to follow as possible, so we've only used a few layout styles to avoid confusion. Here they are:

- When you first come across an important word it will be in **bold** type, then in normal type thereafter.

- We'll use a different font to emphasize `code` and `file names`. We'll also use this font when we want you to type in `some text`.

- Menu commands are written in the form **Menu > Sub-menu > Sub-menu**.

- Interesting or important points will be highlighted like this:

  This is very important stuff – don't skip it!

- Practical exercises will appear under headings in this style...

Start building this movie

...and where we think it helps the discussion, they'll have numbered steps like this:

1. Do this first

2. Do this second

3. Follow this with another step

- When we're showing ActionScript code blocks that should be typed into the Script pane of the Actions panel, we'll use this style:

```
pos = {x:0, y:0};
stageWidth = Stage.width;
stageHeight = Stage.height;
```

- Where a line of ActionScript is too wide to fit on the page, we'll indicate that it runs over two lines by using an arrow-like 'continuation' symbol:

```
drawObj.moveTo(shape.anchorPoints[0][0],
➥shape.anchorPoints[0][1];
```

Lines like this should be typed as a single continuous statement.

- When we discuss ActionScript in the body of the text, we'll put statements such as `stop` in a code-like style too.

- When we add new code to an existing block, we'll highlight it like this:

```
square.lineStyle(2, 0x333333, 100);
square.beginGradientFill("linear", colors, alphas, ratios, matrix);
square.lineTo(100, -100);
```

- Pseudo code will appear in this style:

```
if (we win the world cup) then {
have a big party
} else {
cry
}
```

- In the text, symbol names, layer names, labels, and web site addresses will be in **bold**.

3

Support

If you have any questions about the book or about friends of ED, check out our web site (**www.friendsofed.com**). There is a range of contact e-mail addresses there, or you can just use the generic address: **feedback@friendsofed.com**.

There is also a host of other features up there on the site: interviews with renowned designers, samples from our other books, and a message board for you to post your own questions, discussions, or answers. If you have any comments or problems whatsoever, just write us; it's what we're here for and we'd love to hear from you.

section 1: Site Presentation

chapter 1: **Motion**

One of the fundamental features of Flash is its ability to make things move; we can add motion to anything that we've created in Flash. In this chapter, we're going to go through some of the various ways that Flash MX lets us create different types of motion.

For some readers, the principles of this may be familiar already, but we'll also explore the new features of Flash MX that allow us to achieve motion in a much simpler and efficient way than before. To give you a feel for Flash's flexibility, we'll look at some of the different types of motion you might like to incorporate into your projects and how to implement them. In particular, we will use ActionScript to achieve the following types of motion:

- Easing out: adding deceleration to movement.
- Swing: adding acceleration and friction to movement.
- Frame based motion: achieving constant motion across a number of frames.

We'll look first at how we can use these types of motion to move an object along the x and y axes, implementing trails behind the object to help illustrate the way that the types of motion work. We'll also look at how to implement this motion for other properties, such as the scale of an object.

As well as the motion itself we'll look at different ways of implementing the motion with ActionScript, how to trigger motion with a mouse click and also how best to handle the motion: how to initiate it and how to terminate it when it has finished.

We'll finally embark on a case study exercise where we'll have several pictures that shift into a viewing area when you click a button. Techniques covered in the exercise include creating a mask with ActionScript as well as dynamically attaching a button.

So, now we've got the pleasantries out of the way, let's make a start by looking at frame based motion.

Easing out

The first type of motion I'm going to cover is easing out. This is where an object begins its movement fairly quickly and gradually slows down to a halt as it reaches its target. This kind of motion is probably the simplest type of motion to achieve – we basically have to calculate how far an object is from its target and then move the object towards the target by a fraction of the distance. So, if an object is 100 pixels from its target, we can move it half that distance and it will then be 50 pixels from the target, then 25, then 12.5, and so on. The motion has quite a nice organic feel, as we are more used to seeing objects slow to a halt than stopping abruptly.

The diagram below shows this in action, with each line representing a frame as an object moves across 200 pixels.

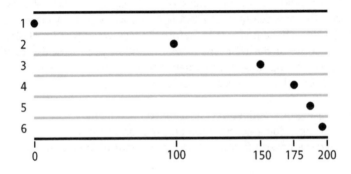

The distance the object moves is halved eaach frame. In frame 1 the object moves 100 pixels, in frame 2 it moves 50 pixels frame 3 it moves 25 pixels, then 12.5 pixels, then 6.25 pixels, then 3.125 pixels and so on and so on.

Let's now see how this can be employed practically by making an object follow the mouse. While this is nothing particularly new or exciting, it will help to clearly illustrate the principle.

Making a movie clip move with easing

1.   Open a new Flash file with default stage dimensions (550 x 400). In the Property inspector, set the background color to white and the frame rate to 31 fps. (We'll use these settings whenever we create a Flash file in this section of the book.)

2. Draw a black circle on the stage, convert it to a movie clip symbol (F8) and then give the movie clip a name.

3. Open the Property inspector and give the movie clip an instance name 'ball_mc'.

   We're using the suffix '_mc' in the name here as this follows the naming conventions set out by macromedia. Using this has two advantages; firstly it helps differentiate different types of object in one's code, and secondly it means that the correct type of code hint will appear when you are typing the code in the authoring environment.

   That's the basic set-up. Now we need to add the actions.

4. As it's generally best to keep actions on a separate layer from your content, insert a new layer beneath your current one. It's generally good practice to name all layers you use. We've simply named ours circle and script.

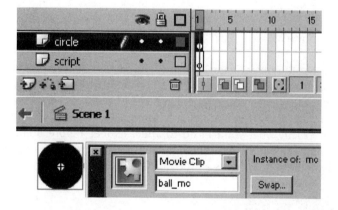

5. Select the first frame of the new layer and open the Actions panel. Click the little white options icon on the top right of the panel and make sure that **Expert Mode** is checked. The best way to get familiar with code is by typing it in, which may be a pain in the short term, but will reap dividends in the long term.

6. OK, now for the code. We need to assign an action to our movie clip that makes it check each frame to see where the mouse is, and then move itself towards that point. In Flash 5 the most straightforward way of doing this would be to select the movie clip and attach an onClipEvent (enterFrame).

   With the new event model in Flash MX, we no longer need to do this. We can dynamically attach clipEvents to movie clips, giving us a couple of benefits; it allows us to keep all or most of our code in one place, and also allows us to manipulate these events at runtime, such as turning them on and off or altering the functionality.

We achieve this by assigning a function to the movie clip's `onEnterFrame` handler. If a movie clip has a function assigned to its `onEnterFrame` handler, it will execute that function every frame.

Enter the following code into frame 1 of your `script` layer:

```
ball_mc.onEnterFrame = function() {
    this._x += (this._parent._xmouse-this._x)/4;
    this._y += (this._parent._ymouse-this._y)/4;
};
```

This code basically creates a function, which it assigns to the `onEnterFrame` handler of the movie clip 'ball_mc'. The code inside the function first calculates how far away the object is from the mouse and then adds a fraction of that amount to the movie clip's position. If you wanted to write it out longhand the first line would read, 'calculate the difference between the X position of the mouse and my X position, then increment my X position by a quarter of this value'.

7. Save your movie as `ball motion_01.fla` and test it.

You'll see that the object happily follows the mouse, behaving similarly to what we saw in the original diagram – moving quickly at first and then slowing down. At this point it would be valuable to try different numbers in place of the 4 above to see the different qualities of motion that result. If you're going to employ this type of motion it's important to have a grasp of exactly what you can do to affect its feel. Before doing this it's worthwhile to take the number out of the function itself and define it as a variable, which will make plugging in different numbers a little quicker.

Adding a speed variable

To make it easier to change the speed of the object in our movie, we can add a speed variable (the lower the speed value, the faster the motion):

1. Using the same setup as the previous examples, use the Actions panel to add the following code to frame 1 of your **script** layer:

```
var speed = 4;

ball_mc.onEnterFrame = function() {
    this._x += (this._parent._xmouse-this._x)/speed;
    this._y += (this._parent._ymouse-this._y)/speed;
};
```

Note that within the onEnterFrame function 'this' refers to the movie clip that we have named ball_mc, so when we refer to the speed variable from within the function, we have to use, this._parent.speed, to take us to the level the movie clip is in; the _root level, where the speed variable is defined.

2.   Save your movie as ball motion_02_speed var.fla and test it. It's the same effect, but the code is now easier to change.

Initiating motion with a mouse click

We're now going to modify the code slightly to make the movie clip move to wherever the user clicks with their mouse. In a similar way to how we have assigned an onEnterFrame function to our movie clip, we can assign an onMouseDown function. This function will be triggered whenever the user clicks the mouse anywhere in the root movie.

So, when the user clicks we first want to set the movie clip's target positions to the location of the click, before setting the onEnterFrame function to move to that point:

1.   Using the same setup as the previous examples, use the Actions panel to add the following code to frame 1 of your script layer:

```
var speed = 4;
// set up target variables
ball_mc.targetx=0
ballmc.targety=0

ball_mc.moveToMouse = function() {
    this._x += (targetX-this._x)/speed;
    this._y += (targetY-this._y)/speed;
};

triggerMotion = function() {
    // reset target variables on click
    targetX = _xmouse;
    targetY = _ymouse;
    // set the movieclip in motion
    this.onEnterFrame = this.moveToMouse;
}
ball_mc.onMouseDown = triggerMotion;
```

You can see that this ActionScript differs from our previous ActionScript in one major way. Whereas before we were attaching the function directly to the onEnterFrame handler, this time we are defining a function first – moveToMouse – so when the user clicks the mouse, this.onEnterFrame points to this function and calls it every frame. The function itself works exactly the same as before, except that we are no longer moving to the position of the mouse, but to targetX and targetY, which are two variables for the mouse position that are set whenever the user clicks the mouse.

This approach seems more efficient because we only have to define the function once, and we can then point onEnterFrame to it when we want it activated. If we want to turn the motion off later we can do so by deleting this.onEnterFrame.

2.   Save your movie as ball motion_03_click to move.fla and test it.

You'll see that the object moves to where you have clicked and then comes to a halt, perhaps giving a clearer example of motion compared to when the ball was continually following the mouse.

Adding a trail to an object's motion

One further thing we can do to make the pattern of the motion clearer is to leave a trail of where the movie clip has been. For our purposes here this is useful to help us see how the easing works, but trails like this can obviously be implemented in other circumstances as well, whether as an amusement while waiting for something to load, or for a kind of motion blur effect. We can create such trails simply by duplicating the movie clip each frame using the duplicateMovieClip function. We only need to add one line of code to do this, which increments the depth of value of _root and then duplicates the current movie clip.

The duplicate is placed by default at the same position as the original movie clip. In fact, the duplicate will have all the same properties as the original, such as alpha, xscale, yscale, etc. but will not have the same onEnterFrame functions or any variables that the original movie clip might contain. This is different from Flash 5, where if you duplicated a movie clip with a clipEvent attached to it, that clipEvent would also be duplicated and run on the duplicate. We place each duplicate at one level higher than the previous, introducing a depth variable for '_root' which we will increment each frame.

You might want to think of duplicateMovieClip as producing a duplicate that is cosmetically identical to the original, but with none of the original's behavior. In our case then, the duplicates do not start following the mouse, they're just left where they're duplicated.

1.   Once again, use the same setup as the previous examples, and add the following ActionScript to your movie:

```
var speed = 4;

ball_mc.moveToMouse = function() {
```

```
        this._x += (this.targetX-this._x)/this._parent.speed;
        this._y += (this.targetY-this._y)/this._parent.speed;
        this.duplicateMovieClip("dupe"+this._parent.depth,
        ➥this._parent.depth++);
    };
    ball_mc.onMouseDown = function() {
        this.targetX = this._parent._xmouse;
        this.targetY = this._parent._ymouse;
        this.onEnterFrame = this.moveToMouse;
    };
```

2. Save your movie as `ball motion_04_click for trail.fla`. If you now test the movie, you'll see very clearly how this easing works in the way that we saw in the original diagram:

Start position   Target

As you click to a new position, the duplicates are at first distributed widely, before gradually getting closer together and becoming more clustered as they approach the target. However, the number of objects here continues to increase as the movie runs and would eventually begin to bog down, so to avoid this, it would be ideal if each duplicate gradually shrank and faded away. We'll do exactly that in the next example.

Making the trail fade

To prevent the movie becoming laden with too many duplicates of the same object, we can assign each duplicate its own `enterFrame` function, which will tell the duplicates to get smaller each frame and then remove themselves once they get to a certain size.

As we're going to be doing more with each duplicate, it seems sensible to give `ball_mc` it's own `duplicate()` function. Here's the code, with the new parts highlighted:

```
    var speed = 4;

    ball_mc.moveToMouse = function() {
        this._x += (this.targetX-this._x)/this._parent.speed;
        this._y += (this.targetY-this._y)/this._parent.speed;
        this.duplicate();
    };
    ball_mc.duplicate = function() {
```

continues overleaf

```
                var dupe = this.duplicateMovieClip("dupe"+this._parent.depth,
                ➥this._parent.depth++);
                dupe.onEnterFrame = this._parent.diminish
        };
        ball_mc.onMouseDown = function() {
            this.targetX = this._parent._xmouse;
            this.targetY = this._parent._ymouse;
            this.onEnterFrame = this.moveToMouse;
        };
            function diminish(){
                // reduce scale gradually
                this._xscale = this._yscale-=2;
                //remove movieclip when scale goes below zero
                if (this._xscale <= 0) {
                    this.removeMovieClip();
                }
            }
```

So, we've added a call to the duplicate() function and inside it, we've changed the duplicateMovieClip call slightly, putting, var dupe= in front of it. Although the ActionScript dictionary states that duplicateMovieClip does not return any value, it does in fact return a reference to the movie clip that has been created.

What we're doing here is taking that value and then placing it in the dupe variable. We've declared the variable using var so that this value only lasts as long as the function is executing – after that, it disappears – we don't need it any more.

Now we can use dupe to refer to our newly duplicated movie clip and to assign it an onEnterFrame function, the diminish function that we have defined on the _root. In diminish we subtract in increments of two from both the xscale and yscale every frame, and once it reaches zero, we remove the movie clip.

When you run the movie now there's a lot less clutter and dead movie clips because each clip is taking care of itself.

Making it more efficient

That's all working fairly well now, with the number of movie clips kept to a reasonable level. However, you might have realized that the movie clip keeps moving and producing duplicates of itself even when it has reached its target. We can't see the motion because it is so fractional and you can't see the duplicates because they are at the same position as the original ball instance. If you want to see that they're there, list variables or list objects when you're in test movie mode. There's no need for it to do this, so what we need to do is check when the movie clip has reached the target and then turn it off. The fact that this movie clip is continually trying to move isn't really that big an issue, but if we were using this as a menu of some kind and we had other objects moving as well, the number of actions being performed becomes crucial in terms of how much processing power they use collectively, so it's important to avoid any redundant actions.

So, as the movie clip moves, it needs to check whether it is at the target, and if it is it should stop moving. This seems like it would be a simple question of seeing whether the movie clip's x position is equal to the target y position, etc. In actual fact, when you look at the way this easing works, you'll see that the movie clip actually never reaches its target, but just gets closer and closer to it until the difference is negligible.

If we go back to the original example of an object moving from 0 to 200, halving the distance each time – here are the positions for each frame: 100, 150, 175, 187.5, 193.75, 196.875, 198.4375, 199.21875, 199.609375, 199.8046875. This is due to something called Zeno's paradox, which deals with the fact that if an object always moves half, (or any other fraction), of its distance towards a given point, it will never actually hit that point, merely getting closer and closer and closer to it. Since there's no such thing as a fraction of a pixel, the image is essentially still, but the ActionScript doesn't know that. Rather than checking if the clip is actually at its target, we check whether it is *near* its target and that the distance between the object and its target is below a certain figure. When it gets near its target we can then stop it moving by deleting the onEnterFrame handler.

Starting with our previous code, we add a new checkDistance function to check if the distance is below a certain amount. The movie clip then snaps to its target and the function assigned to the onEnterFrame handler is deleted. Add the following code after the code we already have:

```
ball_mc.checkDistance = function() {
    // check movieclip is within 0.2 pixels of target
    if (Math.abs(this.targetX-this._x)<0.2 &&
    ➥Math.abs(this.targetY-this._y)<0.2) {
        this._x = this.targetX;
        this._y = this.targetY;
        delete this.onEnterFrame;
    }
};
```

First of all we have the conditional statement that checks if the movieclip is within 0.2 pixels of the target. In the code, `this.targetX-this._x` represents the distance from the movie clip to the target on the X axis, and we use `Math.abs` to convert this value to a positive, because it doesn't matter whether the movie clip is 0.2 to the left or the right of the target, as long as it is between −0.2 and +0.2. Finally, in the `moveToMouse` function, we add a call to the `checkDistance` function:

```
ball_mc.moveToMouse = function() {
    this._x += (this.targetX-this._x)/this._parent.speed;
    this._y += (this.targetY-this._y)/this._parent.speed;
    this.duplicate();
    this.checkDistance();
};
```

When you run this code it will appear to behave exactly the same as our previous file. However, if you select **Debug > List Variables** while in **Test Movie** mode after the movie clip has stopped moving you'll see that there are no duplicates and the `ball_mc` movie clip has no `onEnterFrame` function. Effectively, nothing is happening in our movie – it is just waiting for another mouse click to activate again.

Let's now move on to see how we can create time-based constant motion.

Frame-based motion

Let's start by achieving motion with a constant speed. We'll instruct a movieclip to move from point A to point B over a certain number of frames, moving the same distance within each frame. This kind of motion is useful when you need to have something happen over a certain amount of time. It doesn't have the fluidity of the easing method, but is a lot more precise – you know that the object will reach its target after the specified number of frames. The motion feels a lot more solid.

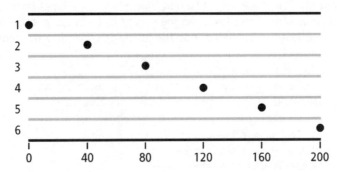

The distance the object moves is the same each frame. The distance moved equivalent to the total distance divided by the total number of frames, in this case 200 pixels divided by 5 frames = 40 pixels each frame.

Constant velocity

You'll see that the distance moved is the same in each frame. In order to trigger the motion, we need to know how far the clip has to move, and how many frames it has to do it in. Calculating the distance per frame simply involves dividing the distance by the total number of frames.

1. Follow the same steps as the previous example until you are ready to add your ActionScript in the Actions panel.

2. OK, now for the code. We need to assign an action to our movie clip that makes it check each frame to see where the mouse is, and then move itself towards that point. In Flash 5 the most straightforward way of doing this would be to select the movie clip and attach an `onClipEvent(enterFrame)`.

3. First of all, we set a variable for the number of frames that the motion will take. Then we set an `onMouseDown` function for `ball_mc`. This function will calculate the total distance on the x- and y-axes and then divide that number by the frames variable to calculate how much the movie clip should move each frame.

4. We also set a counter variable `frameNum`, which is used to keep track of how far the movie clip has moved – we'll add one to it for each frame and when it equals the frames value, we'll know to disable the motion.

```
this.frames = 30;

ball_mc.onMouseDown = function() {
    this.frameNum = 0;
    // calculate how far to move each frame on the x and y axes
    this.xStep = (this._parent._xmouse-this._x)
    ➡/this._parent.frames;
    this.yStep = (this._parent._ymouse-this._y)
    ➡/this._parent.frames;
    this.onEnterFrame = moveToMouse;
};
```

5. We then have to write a `moveToMouse` function, which will first add our `xStep` and `yStep` values, add a duplicate, and then check if it has reached its target:

```
moveToMouse = function() {
    // add the step value each frame
    this._x += this.xStep;
    this._y += this.yStep;
```

17

```
        this.duplicate();
    this.checkTime();
    };
```

6. The duplicate and diminish functions are exactly the same as the ones we've just been using.

7. The final addition to our code is the `checkTime` function, which adds one to the `frameNum` variable and then disables the motion when it reaches its target, the number of frames that we specified at the start:

```
ball_mc.checkTime = function() {
    this.frameNum++;
    if (this.frameNum == this._parent.frames) {
        delete this.onEnterFrame;
    }
};
```

8. Save your movie as `frame based motion.fla` and then test it. When you run this code you'll see that the duplicates are distributed completely evenly and the movie clip hits its target precisely.

Target 1

Target 2

Target 3

The quality of motion in this example is very different to what we'll look at next. Let's move straight on and look at incorporating **acceleration and friction** into simple motions.

Swinging motion

This type of motion reflects that of somebody on a bungee cord on the ground. Imagine somebody running towards the point where the cord is anchored intending to get as far as they can past the anchor . The movieClip (the person tied to the cord) calculates its difference from its target (the anchor for the cord) and then adds a fraction of this value to a speed variable. The movie clip will speed up as it approaches its target (as the runner accelerates), and then as it goes beyond the target, it will be pulled back again and slow down.

In each frame, we multiply the `speed` variable by a fraction to reduce the speed. The diagram below shows how the motion continues beyond the target and then swings back.

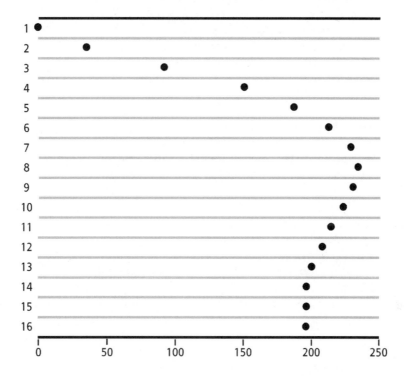

The object's speed increases in proportion to ho far away it is from its target. We see here that it accelerates quickly at first, overshoots its target and is then pulled back. The magnitude of its oscillation about the target slowly diminishes.

There are a lot of different effects that can be achieved with this kind of motion because there are two parameters involved:

1. The fraction of the distance from its target, which is added to the speed.
2. The fraction by which the speed is to be multiplied in order to reduce it.

The final effect can vary between a quite pronounced oscillation back and forth around the target to a much more subtle ease out, or a shuddering snap effect.

1. Once again, this exercise will use the same basic setup as those previous, with a movie clip placed on stage called `ball_mc` and a separate layer for the code. We can also reuse some

of the code we used earlier as well (the functions that check the distance, create the trails and listen for the mouseDown) – it is only the motion itself that we'll need to change.

```
ball_mc.checkDistance = function() {
    if (Math.abs(this.targetX-this._x)<0.2 &&
    ➥Math.abs(this.targetY-this._y)<0.2) {
        this._x = this.targetX;
        this._y = this.targetY;
        delete this.onEnterFrame;
    }
};

ball_mc.duplicate = function() {
    var dupe = this.duplicateMovieClip
    ➥("dupe"+this._parent.depth, this._parent.depth++);
    dupe.onEnterFrame = this._parent.diminish
};

function diminish(){
    // reduce scale gradually
    this._xscale = this._yscale-=2;
    //remove movieclip when scale goes below zero
    if (this._xscale <= 0) {
        this.removeMovieClip();
    }
}

ball_mc.onMouseDown = function() {
    this.targetX = this._parent._xmouse;
    this.targetY = this._parent._ymouse;
    this.onEnterFrame = this.moveToMouse;
};
```

2. The only part we need to write over is the moveToMouse function, implementing the speed variables, etc. The first thing we need to do is define our two parameters, which we'll call acceleration and friction. Initially, we'll set them at 12 and 0.8, although we'll be able to vary them later for different effects. Add these two lines above the function definitions, at the top of the code:

```
var acceleration = 12;
var friction = 0.8;
```

OK, acceleration will be the value that we divide the distance by before we add it to the speed of our movie clip, and friction will be the value that we multiply the speed of each frame by in order to reduce its motion.

We'll step through the code for the motion on the x-axis before putting it all together into our moveToMouse function.

3. First of all we create a temporary variable to contain the distance between our movieClip and its target. The following code goes into the moveToMouse function.

```
var xdif=this.targetX-this._x
```

4. We then add a fraction of this value to our xspeed value (the variable representing the movie clip's speed on the x-axis):

```
this.xspeed+=xdif/this._parent.react
```

5. We then multiply the speed variable by our friction variable to reduce the speed. If we didn't do this, our movie clip would oscillate around its target without getting any closer. This multiplication means the orbit diminishes each time. If you were to remove this line from our finished example, the movie clip would not home in on its target, but continue moving back and forth at the same rate.

```
this.xspeed*=this._parent.friction
```

6. Finally, we update the movie clip's position, adding its speed value to its x position:

```
this._x+=this.xspeed
```

Now we integrate all of this into our moveToMouse function, also adding calls to duplicate and checkDistance. Here's the full code, for both the x- and y-axis:

```
ball_mc.moveToMouse = function() {

    // calculate difference on x and y axes
    var xdif = this.targetX-this._x;
    var ydif = this.targetY-this._y;

    // increment speed values
    this.xspeed += xdif/this._parent.acceleration;
    this.yspeed += ydif/this._parent.acceleration;

    // dampen speed values
    this.xspeed *= this._parent.friction;
    this.yspeed *= this._parent.friction;

    // add speed values to x and y properties
    this._x += this.xspeed;
    this._y += this.yspeed;
```

continues overleaf

```
            // create duplicate
            this.duplicate();
            // check if the movieclip has reached its target
            this.checkDistance();
      };
```

7.   Save your movie as `swing.fla` and test it. You'll see the oscillation effect, with the movie clip almost orbiting its target:

Changing the values for `acceleration` and `friction` will have a dramatic effect on the quality of the motion. Experiment and try changing them and get a feel for how they affect the motion.

In general, the lower the `acceleration` value, the faster the movie clip will move at first, and the closer the friction gets to 1, the more the movie clip will swing back and forth. Some values can make this very similar to the 'easing out' example we looked at first. For example, try `acceleration = 17;` and `friction = 0.4;` and save your movie as `swing02.fla` The difference in using this swing effect is that because we have a speed variable that persists across frames, the movie clip doesn't change direction instantly as with our original easing, or the frame based motion, but changes direction more gradually.

This is all working fine, but there's one more thing we need to change. Whereas previously with the 'easing out' example, it was appropriate that the movie clip should stop once it reached a certain distance from the target, with this method the movie clip could conceivably pass directly over the target before carrying across to the other side. This means that we need to change our `checkDistance` function to make sure that the movie clip's speed is also below a certain amount so that it doesn't stop suddenly by mistake.

This is a fairly simple matter – all we need to do is insert another `if` statement into our function, checking that the speed is low enough after confirming that the distance is within range:

```
      ball_mc.checkDistance = function() {
            // check that distance is within range
            if (Math.abs(this.targetX-this._x)<0.2 &&
```

```
➥Math.abs(this.targetY-this._y)<0.2) {

    // check that speed is nearly zero
    if(Math.abs(this.xspeed)<0.2 && Math.abs(this.yspeed)
    ➥<0.2){
        this._x = this.targetX;
        this._y = this.targetY;
        delete this.onEnterFrame;
    }
    }
};
```

The script above, contained within `swing3.fla` has now safeguarded against any unforeseen circumstances.

You can take these principles in different directions by controlling the object's speed in different ways. At the moment the speed is influenced by a target position, a kind of magnetism, but you could for example have a key press on the right cursor key add 5 to the `xspeed`. This would push the object slightly to the right before it slows down and stops

If you're interested in ways of creating further kinds of motion, I'd recommend that you take a look at the easing equations at **www.robertpenner.com**. Using these equations you can specify the number of frames that you want the motion to last for, and the movieclip will ease in and out from point a to b. Additionally, you can see an implementation of these equations at **www.gizma.com/easing**. If you're interested in these equations, Chris Andrade from **www.fifthrotation.com** has posted a document going into how they are derived here: **http://www.fifthrotation.com/u2/parabolic_ease.zip**

Scale in motion

So far we've looked at different kinds of easing applied to motion on the x and y-axes, but there's no reason that their use be confined to these properties. It's possible to bring one value towards another value, and create motion in a scalable way – making objects bigger or smaller.

In this exercise, we're going to employ the springy motion we've just looked at. What we're going to do is capture the co-ordinates of a mouse click and use them to determine the size that our movie clip will scale to.

1. Create a movie file the same as the previous examples, with a movie clip named `ball_mc` except this time, position `ball_mc` with an X value of 275 and a Y value of 200 (near the middle of the stage).

2. Once again we'll start by defining our `mouseDown` function. We'll add the X and Y co-ordinates of the mouse pointer together, then multiply by two and use that to determine our movieClip's target scale. If the user clicks in the top left corner, the movie should scale to zero and if the user clicks in the bottom right corner it should scale to 1900, or (550 + 400)*2.

```
ball_mc.onMouseDown=function(){
    this.targetScale=(this._parent._xmouse+this._parent._ymouse)
    ➥*2
    this.onEnterFrame=this.scaleMe
}
```

So we've taken this value and placed it in the `targetScale` variable in the movie clip.

3. We now have to define our `scaleMe` function, which will take the movie clip from its current size towards its target size. We'll achieve this by employing a similar approach to moving towards a specific point on the x- or y-axis, like we did earlier. The only difference is that we're affecting the _xscale and _yscale properties rather than _x and _y. As we want _xscale to equal _yscale, we can perform all our calculations using _xscale and set _yscale to be the same after we've finished:

```
    this.acceleration = 12;
    this.friction = 0.8;
    ball_mc.scaleMe = function() {
        var scaleDiff = this.targetScale-this._xscale;
        this.scaleSpeed += scaleDiff/this._parent.acceleration;
        this.scaleSpeed *= this._parent.friction;
        this._yscale = this._xscale += this.scaleSpeed;
        this.checkScale();
    };
```

The first three lines of the function are the same as before – they calculate the difference between actual scale and target scale, and add a fraction of the difference to scaleSpeed. The speed variable is then reduced – multiplying it by our friction constant.

You might notice something different with the next line, which is that we're assigning two things in one line. This is just an annotated way of doing the following:

```
this._xscale += this.scaleSpeed;
this._yscale = this._xscale;
```

> When Flash hits a line of code like the one we've chosen to use in this example, it starts on the right-hand side and works left. It first adds the speed variable to _xscale and after that, sets _yscale to equal _xscale).

4. Save your movie as scale.fla and test it – your movie clip should now spring to various sizes depending on where you click.

5. The final thing to do is add the checkScale function. This is more or less the same as the checkDistance function we had before and checks that the movie clip's scale is more or less the same as the target scale, and that its speed is almost equal to zero:

```
ball_mc.checkScale = function() {
    if (Math.abs(this.targetScale-this._xscale)<0.2) {
        if (Math.abs(this.scaleSpeed)<0.2) {
            this._xscale = this._yscale=this.targetScale;
            delete this.onEnterFrame;
        }
    }
};
```

While we've used this technique for scaling an object, it can also easily be extrapolated for `_alpha, _rotation` or whatever movie clip property you want.

Managing the motion

You should now be getting a fairly good handle on how these different methods of scripted motion work. We'll now move on to look at different ways of implementing this motion. The method we've used up to now entails quite a few different stages, and we've set it up specifically for one movie clip.

It would be more preferable if we could point to any specific movie clip and write `myMovieClip.slideTo(100,200)` so the movie clip would move to that point and stop, without us having to manually assign a clipEvent handler to the movie clip, or assign a function to check that it has reached its target, etc.

In this section we'll look at various scripting methods that we can use to initiate motion. We won't advocate any particular best way of doing this, but rather show you some of the different possibilities so that you can choose what you feel most comfortable with in relation to your projects.

Slide to

1. Open a new movie and place an instance of `ball_mc` on the stage.

2. In a separate script layer on your timeline, the first thing we'll do is add the call to our slideTo function, which will happen whenever the user clicks their mouse.

3. We'll pass the `slideTo` function three parameters; an x position, a y position and a third value, which will specify the speed of the slide:

    ```
    _root.onMouseDown = function() {
        ball_mc.slideTo(this._xmouse, this._ymouse, 4);
    };
    ```

4. We now need to create the actual `slideTo` function, which will need to do two separate things:

    ● Set the `targetX` and `targetY` values within the movie clip.

    ● Set the `enterFrame` handler of the movie clip to make it slide towards the target.

    Rather than define this function for a particular movie clip as we did with the previous functions `ball_mc.checkDistance`, with this one we're going to put it in

MovieClip.prototype. Any functions within MovieClip.prototype are available to all movieclips equally. The built in movieclip methods such as goToAndPlay, etc, all reside in movieclip.prototype. When we call the function it behaves as though it is within the movieclip.

```
MovieClip.prototype.slideTo = function(x, y, speed) {
    // set up targets and speed variable
    this.targetX = x;
    this.targetY = y;
    this.speed = speed;

    // create onEnterFrame function
    this.onEnterFrame = function() {
        // take care of motion
        this._x += (this.targetX-this._x)/this.speed;
        this._y += (this.targetY-this._y)/this.speed;

        // check if near target
        if (Math.abs(this.targetX-this._x)<0.2 &&
        ➡Math.abs(this.targetY-this._y)<0.2) {
            this._x = this.targetX;
            this._y = this.targetY;
            delete this.onEnterFrame;
        }
    };
};
```

The first three lines of the function take the parameters that are passed to it and store them in variables inside the movie clip. We then assign an onEnterFrame function, which moves the movie clip and also checks to see if it has reached its target.

5. Save your file as issueCommand1.fla and test it. When you click the mouse, the movie clip will slide to it.

6. We can also try the same approach with two movie clips – make a copy of the original ball_mc movie clip and give it an instance name ball_mc2 using the Property inspector.

7. Drag the instance of ball_mc2 onto the stage and then open the Actions panel to change the onMouseDown code to the following:

```
_root.onMouseDown = function() {
    ball_mc.slideTo(this._xmouse, this._ymouse, 4);
    ball_mc2.slideTo(this._xmouse+19, this._ymouse, 1);
};
```

8.   Save this movie as `issueCommand1b.fla` and test it. You'll notice that the second movie clip moves slightly to the right of the mouse and at a slightly slower speed.

So, the movie appears to work exactly how we want it to, but some closer scrutiny suggests that there are in fact a few problems with this method of doing things. The most apparent problem is that any movie clip can only have one function assigned to its `onEnterFrame` handler: If the movieClip in question already had a function assigned to its `onEnterFrame` handler and we assigned another one, the first one would simply be overwritten. This might occur if the movie clip was fading in or scaling up or for any number of reasons.

The other problem is that we're putting variables inside the movie clip such as `targetX`, `targetY` and `speed`, which may be already be used for another purpose in the movie clip. Again, we would simply overwrite them, resulting in drastic affects on the functionality of the movie clip. Though we like to think we can remember names we have assigned in our ActionScript, it's good practice to employ intuitive and descriptive naming conventions.

Using empty movie clips

We'll now look at a way around any potential problems raised by this issue by creating an empty movie clip inside the existing one. We'll use the inner movie clip as a container for all the variables, and as the target onto which we can attach our `onEnterFrame` handler without fear of disrupting any pre-existing functionality.

The `mouseDown` handler is set up as before:

```
_root.onMouseDown = function() {
    ball_mc.slideTo(this._xmouse, this._ymouse, 4);
};
```

Now our `slideTo` function will appear largely the same as before, the main differences being that before the movie clip was controlling itself, whereas now a movie clip inside it executes the actions. This manifests itself in a change of scope from 'this' to 'this._parent' when accessing or altering the X and Y properties. Our controller clip accesses and manipulates the properties of its parent clip, the clip that we want to move.

```
MovieClip.prototype.slideTo = function(x, y, speed) {
    // create controller movieclip
    var control_mc = this.createEmptyMovieClip
    ➡("slideControl", this.depth++);
    control_mc.targetX = x;
    control_mc.targetY = y;
    control_mc.speed = speed;

    control_mc.onEnterFrame = function() {
        // this._parent is the movieclip we're moving
```

continues overleaf

```
this._parent._x += (this.targetX-this._parent._x)
➡/this.speed;
this._parent._y +=
➡(this.targetY-this._parent._y)/this.speed;

if (Math.abs(this.targetX-this._parent._x)<0.2 &&
➡Math.abs(this.targetY-this._parent._y)<0.2) {
    this._parent._x = this.targetX;
    this._parent._y = this.targetY;
    this.removeMovieClip();
}
};
};
```

As with the `duplicate` function we created earlier, we're using the reference returned by the `createEmptyMovieClip` function to refer to the newly created movieClip. One possible pitfall of this method using `createEmptyMovieClip` is that one might overwrite another movie clip already present at that depth. To a certain extent this is something you have to be aware of when managing your movie; you should have some mechanism of being aware at what depth objects and symbols are placed. Employing a depth variable for each timeline is a useful way to do this, incrementing this as each movieclip is added. Another approach might be to have a global depth variable for all timelines, but I think it's probably better to have one for each timeline to prevent the value getting out of hand. Ultimately it's down to personal preference.

You could use `addProperty` to make depth increment automatically whenever it is accessed, but you would have to set this up for each movie clip individually, so a static variable that increments with each addition seems a fair solution. The other possible solution would be to loop through the entire movie clips in a particular location and use `getDepth()` on each of them in turn to find out which depths have been taken, but this seems a somewhat extreme approach, involving a lot of ultimately unnecessary action calls.

Save your movie as `issueCommand2.fla`. If you test the movie at this point, you'll notice it will become paralyzed if you click successively and quickly. If you go to **Debug > List Variables**, it quickly becomes apparent that the reason for this is because there is more than one instance of `slideControl` inside our movie clip – each one pulling in a different direction. So, we need to implement something that will ensure we only have one instance of this control clip inside our movie clip at any time.

A possible solution is to have the `slideControl` clip duplicated to the same depth every time so that it automatically overwrites any previous instance. However, it's best to avoid this approach because it breaks the depth scheme we've just implemented. Additionally, if we were using the swing method to move our movie clip, we wouldn't want to overwrite any speed variables inside the clip and have it stop – we would want that data to persist until the movie clip stops.

A more measured solution would be to just check and see if the `slideControl` movieClip is already present. If it isn't we go ahead and create it, if it is we overwrite its X and Y target variables and its `onEnterFrame` event.

Both have the same end result. The part that's changed is highlighted bold:

```
MovieClip.prototype.slideTo = function(x, y, speed) {
    var control_mc
    if (this.slideControl) {
        //if slideControl already exists
        control_mc = this.slideControl;
    }
    else {
        //if slideControl doesn't exist then create it
        control_mc = this.createEmptyMovieClip
        ➡("slideControl", this.depth++);
    }
    control_mc.targetX = x;
    control_mc.targetY = y;
    control_mc.speed = speed;
    control_mc.onEnterFrame = function() {
        this._parent._x +=
        ➡(this.targetX-this._parent._x)/this.speed;
        this._parent._y +=
        ➡(this.targetY-this._parent._y)/this.speed;
        if (Math.abs(this.targetX-this._parent._x)<0.2 &&
        ➡Math.abs(this.targetY-this._parent._y)<0.2) {
            this._parent._x = this.targetX;
            this._parent._y = this.targetY;
            this.removeMovieClip();
        }
    };
};
```

Save your file as `issueCommand3.fla` and when you test the movie you'll find that it now behaves in the way we want.

However, this solution is still slightly lacking in a practical situation because it gives us no indication when the movie clip has reached its target position. The motion does indeed stop, but often we would want some other action to be triggered when the motion finishes. At the very least, it would be nice to keep track of when a movie clip is moving and when it is not.

To address this issue we're going to implement a kind of callback function. This will work in the same way as some of the components work – you provide them with a function to call when a value is changed or something is updated. When the motion stops it calls the function that we specify. So, first of all we'll create the function that should be called when the movie clip finishes moving. At the moment it's sufficient for it to just trace a message in the Output window, giving the name of the movie clip whose motion has finished, which we'll pass to it as a parameter.

```
function slideDone(mc) {
    trace("movieClip "+mc+" has finished moving");
}
```

Basically, when the movie clip has finished moving it will call this function `slideDone` on the `_root`. When we call the `slideTo` function, we need to add two more parameters: `callBackObj` and `callBackFunc`. `callBackObj` is the location of the function to be called (`_root` in our case) and `callBackFunc` is the name of the function to be called, which in this case is `slideDone`. So, first of all we revise our function to include these two extra parameters:

```
_root.onMouseDown = function() {
    ball_mc.slideTo(this._xmouse, this._ymouse, 4,
    ➥_root, "slideDone");
};
```

We then need to adjust the `slideTo` function to accept these extra parameters and store them in the `slideControl` movie clip (the areas highlighted in bold in the following ActionScript):

```
MovieClip.prototype.slideTo = function(x, y, speed,
➥callbackObj, callbackFunc) {
    var control_mc
    if (this.slideControl) {
        control_mc = this.slideControl;
    }
    else {
        control_mc = this.createEmptyMovieClip("slideControl",
        ➥this.depth++);
    }
    control_mc.targetX = x;
    control_mc.targetY = y;
    control_mc.speed = speed;
    control_mc.callBackObj = callBackObj;
    control_mc.callBackFunc = callBackFunc;
};
```

Finally, we need to know how to call `_root.slideDone` using the two variables `callBackObj` and `callBackFunc`. This is actually fairly simple – it's done in more or less the same way as when you access a value in an array, or dynamically create a reference to a movie clip:

```
this.callBackObj[this.callBackFunc](this._parent)
```

The part before the square brackets is the location of the function (_root). The square brackets mean, 'find the value corresponding to this string' (slideDone in our case), and the value in brackets is then passed as a parameter. The value we pass here is a reference to the movieclip that we've been moving, this._parent, our ball_mc. So, our finished function looks like this.

```
MovieClip.prototype.slideTo = function
➡(x, y, speed, callbackObj, callbackFunc) {
    var control_mc
    if (this.slideControl) {
        control_mc = this.slideControl;
    }
    else {
        control_mc = this.createEmptyMovieClip
        ➡("slideControl", this.depth++);
    }

    control_mc.targetX = x;
    control_mc.targetY = y;
    control_mc.speed = speed;
    control_mc.callBackObj = callBackObj;
    control_mc.callBackFunc = callBackFunc;

    control_mc.onEnterFrame = function() {
        this._parent._x += (this.targetX-this._parent._x)
        ➡/this.speed;
        this._parent._y += (this.targetY-this._parent._y)
        ➡/this.speed;

        if (Math.abs(this.targetX-this._parent._x)<0.2 &&
        ➡Math.abs(this.targetY-this._parent._y)<0.2) {
            this._parent._x = this.targetX;
            this._parent._y = this.targetY;
            this.callBackObj[this.callBackFunc](this._parent);
            this.removeMovieClip();
        }
    };
};
```

Save your movie as issueCommand004.fla and when you test the movie, you'll see that the Output window reports, **"movieClip _level0.mc has finished moving"** every time the movie clip comes to a halt.

You could change the contents of the slideDone function to do whatever you wanted with that information. For example, you could have an array containing whichever movie clips are moving and then only execute the next stage of a project once they have all finished moving.

The `callback` function provides us with important feedback. We can trigger the movie clip to move to a certain spot and leave it to do that on its own, knowing that when it has finished it will report back that it has finished. The next step with this would be to set up a function that we can pass whatever properties we want altered in a movie clip and then the movie clip would alter all these properties simultaneously. We'll come back to this in a later chapter.

The techniques in action

As we mentioned at the start of the chapter, we'll now revisit some of the techniques we have encountered so far. What we've covered so far may have seemed a little dry, but we'll now construct a simple example, that utilizes some of the techniques in order to create a navigable Flash page.

Picture navigator

We're going to have a layout of several photographs so that when the user clicks a button, the photographs will shift beneath a mask and move so that the correct one appears in a target area. Let's get to work.

1. Open a new movie with (550 x 400 pixels), and in the Property inspector, set the fps to 31.

2. Import the photographs found in the source files for this book (`001.jpg` – `009.jpg`) and convert each into a movie clip with a top left-hand corner registration point, naming them 001 – 009 respectively.

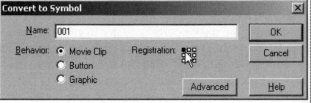 

3. We now need to name all of our picture movieclips. Using the Property inspector to give them instance names `c1` through to `c9`.

4. Arrange the pictures adjacent to each other in a 3 x 3 grid and with all the pictures selected, convert your selection into a movie clip called `holder`, giving it a top left registration point.

`holder` movie clip containing movie clips c1 to c9

OK, we now have an instance of `holder` on the stage in the root timeline. We'll implement motion by moving the `holder` movie clip underneath the mask until the correct picture is in position.

5. With the `holder` movie clip selected, use the Property inspector to give it an instance name `holder` and set its X and Y values to 0,0. This will place holder's registration point at the top left corner of the stage. Finally, name the layer that this is on 'pictures'.

6. We will need to create a mask, so add a new layer above the `pictures` layer and label it mask.

7. Draw a 200 x 200 pixel square of any color and use the Property inspector to give it X and Y values of 180,89.

8. With the square still selected, convert it to a movie clip called `maskSquare`, again making sure that the registration point is at the top left-hand corner. Finally, use the Property inspector to give `maskSquare` an instance name, `maska`.

9. We now need to add some code to make the square into a mask. Create a new layer called `scripts` and inside the new layer, open the Actions panel to add the following code:

```
holder.setMask(maska);
```

This sets the movie clip within the brackets (`maska`) to act as a mask for the movie clip the method has called for (`holder`). If you test the movie now, you'll see that the only parts of `holder` (our grid of nine pictures) that show through are those beneath `maska` – everything else has been obscured.

10. We'll now create a frame for the area that shows through simply by adding two new layers that contain squares slightly bigger than one another. Add two new layers beneath your existing layers called `background1` and `background2`. The layers in your timeline should now look like this:

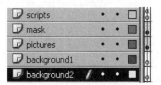

11. Next, on the background1 layer, draw a light gray square with 202 x 202 dimensions and use the Property inspector to give it X and Y values of 179,88. Now on the background2 layer, draw another gray square – darker in color than the one you just placed on background1, and give this square 204 x 244 dimensions with X and Y values of 178,87. This will serve as a border for our movieclips

    You can add any other graphics that you like to the background layers.

12. To make the holder clip move, we're going to use the slide function we created earlier. Add the following in our scripts layer, above the line of code you just added:

```
speed = 4;
MovieClip.prototype.slideTo = function(x, y, speed, callbackObj,
➥callbackFunc) {
    Var mc_control
    if (this.slideControl) {
        mc_control = this.slideControl;
    }
    else {
        mc_control = this.createEmptyMovieClip
        ➥("slideControl", this.depth++);
    }
    mc_control.targetX = x;
    mc_control.targetY = y;
    mc_control.speed = speed;
    mc_control.callBackObj = callBackObj;
    mc_control.callBackFunc = callBackFunc;

    mc_control.onEnterFrame = function() {
        this._parent._x += (this.targetX-this._parent._x)
        ➥/this.speed;
        this._parent._y += (this.targetY-this._parent._y)
        ➥/this.speed;
        if (Math.abs(this.targetX-this._parent._x)<0.2 &&
        ➥Math.abs(this.targetY-this._parent._y)<0.2) {
            this._parent._x = this.targetX;
            this._parent._y = this.targetY;
            this.callBackObj[this.callBackFunc](this._parent);
            this.removeMovieClip();
        }
    };
};
function slideDone(mc) {
    trace("movieClip "+mc+" has finished moving");
}
```

To trigger this we're going to create some buttons. Rather than dynamically creating the buttons using `createEmptyMovieclip` and `createTextField` (we'll look at these techniques later), we're going to create a symbol manually and then attach it dynamically.

13. Create a new movie clip and name it `butt`. Select the clip in the Library and click the white menu icon at the top of the Library title bar. From the menu, select the **Linkage...** option to open the **Linkage Properties** window.

14. Check the **Export for ActionScript** box, give the symbol the identifier `butt` and hit OK.

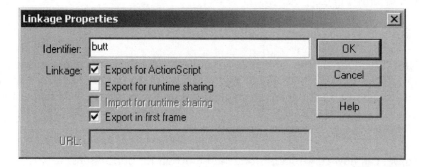

15. You'll now be in the root of the `butt` movie clip. Place a Dynamic Text field inside the movie clip and using the Property inspector, give it the instance name `tf`. Ours is size 9 Arial without embedded fonts.

16. To attach the buttons dynamically, we now need to add the following code to the `scripts` layer of our root timeline (beneath the already existing code):

```
holder.setMask(maska);
for (var i = 1; i<=9; i++) {
    var mc_control = _root.attachMovie("butt", "butt"+i, i);
    mc_control._x = 175+i*9;
    mc_control._y = 295;
    mc_control.mc = this.holder["c"+i];
    mc_control.tf.text = i;
}
```

This loops once for each of the photo movie clips and attaches a button. It uses the iterator 'i' to set the text value of the text field 'tf' so that the numbers 1 to 9 appear inside it. Additionally, it uses the 'i' value to set a target movie clip for each button (although `butt` is a movie clip, it will be behaving as a button because we will be giving it an `onPress` event). It's also worth noting that the 9 at the end of the fourth line of code controls the spacing between each button movieclip.

Before we assign the onPress event we need to work out exactly what we want the button press to do, as well as how we're going to work out where holder needs to slide to display each photograph correctly beneath the mask.

A good way to figure out this kind of thing is to look at one particular case. For example, if we had a movie clip at 300,300 within holder, where would holder need to be placed for it to display properly beneath the mask? If we placed holder at the same position on stage as the mask, whatever was at 0,0 within holder would show through. Based upon that, we can say that if we wanted whatever was at 300,300 within holder to display through the mask, we would have to move holder 300 to the left and 300 up. In code we would write this as:

```
(maska._x-300, maska._y-300);
```

Now if we look up the _x and _y co-ordinate of any of our photo movie clips, that will return the movie clip's co-ordinates within holder. We can therefore say that for any movie clip to be positioned directly underneath the mask, we need holder to move to:

```
(maska._x-mc._x, maska._y-mc._y);
```

17. So, we can now construct our onPress function for our buttons.

```
for (var i = 1; i<=9; i++) {
    var mc_control = _root.attachMovie("butt", "butt"+i, i);
    mc_control._x = 175+i*9;
    mc_control._y = 295;
    mc_control.mc = this.holder["c"+i];
    mc_control.tf.text = i;
    mc_control.onPress = function() {
        var x = this._parent.maska._x-this.mc._x;
        var y = this._parent.maska._y-this.mc._y;
        this._parent.holder.slideTo(x, y, this._parent.speed,
        ➥this._parent, "slideDone");
    };
}
```

We've called our slideTo function as before, using the calculation we showed above to specify the X and Y co-ordinates to slide to. Once again, we don't really need to put the X and Y values in variables, so we can get rid of that part and perform the calculations inside the function call. The annotated code is highlighted in bold:

```
for (var i = 1; i<=9; i++) {
    var mc_control = _root.attachMovie("butt", "butt"+i, i);
    mc_control._x = 175+i*9;
    mc_control._y = 295;
```

```
        mc_control.mc = this.holder["c"+i];
        mc_control.tf.text = i;
        mc_control.onPress = function() {
            this._parent.holder.slideTo(this._parent.maska.
            ➥_x-this.mc._x, this._parent.maska._y-this.mc._y,
            ➥this._parent.speed, this._parent, "slideDone");
        };
    }
```

Save your movie as `pictureMask.fla` and when you test it you'll see that as each picture slides into position, it traces in the Output window. For now we're not doing anything with that, but later on we'll look at how we can use it to trigger some other event, such as a text effect. That's just one possible application, but this kind of trigger could also be used to bring in a piece of explanatory text if the photos were the background to an interface, or to start off an animation. The important thing is that we're in control of the motion that we're initiating. We know when it starts and we can be notified when it ends, meaning that it can become part of a chain of events.

Summary

Hopefully at this point you'll have a solid grasp of the different ways we can make an object move with script in Flash and the different types of motion this achieves. We'll build on this work in later chapters and look at making things more dynamic and automating things that we've done by hand so far, like for instance creating buttons and drawing graphics. We'll also be returning to these motion effects throughout.

section 1: Site Presentation

chapter 2: **Formatting Text**

One of the big new features in Flash MX is the far greater degree of control we have over text. Previously, if we wanted to change the font in a text field, we needed to format the text as HTML, but fortunately, now we have the `textFormat` object. This avoids the need to have tags strewn throughout our variables if we want to display them in any other way than plain text.

We can now specify a certain part of our text and set the format independently from the text itself. We can now also manipulate the height and width of specific pieces of text, affording us more control over position and layout. The text field can now be treated much like a movie clip – we can now create text fields dynamically, set their X and Y positions, and assign listeners to them so that events are triggered when their content is altered.

In this chapter we'll go through a series of exercises that will have a varying degree of practical use. We'll first work with the `textField` and `textFormat` objects, to familiarize ourselves with their operation and to look at what effects can be achieved with them. Some of the effects will be useful in terms of their practical application, while other exercises help to illustrate the capabilities of these new objects. We'll then move on to look at how we can use the ability to find out the width and height of different text content in order to create dynamic text effects with proper positioning, without the need for third party tools.

Creating our own text effects

The first effect we're going to look at is a standard typewriter effect, where the text inside a text field appears as though it were being typed manually. We're going to go through a couple of different ways of creating the typewriter effect. First of all we'll work on the basic mechanics of the effect.

We want slightly more of our text string to appear in the text field with every frame. We can achieve this by having a counter variable that will increment each frame and then use this counter to extract a longer section of the text each frame before placing it in the text field. In Flash 5 we had to make text appear in a text field by assigning a variable to the text field. Whenever that variable was updated, the text field would update accordingly. In Flash MX, the text field is now an object, which has a property `text`. To make text appear in the text field we assign the piece of text to the `text` property of the text field.

Note that there is still a place to enter a variable for a text field (**Var**), but we won't be using this, as it seems to be included mainly as a legacy feature for working with Flash 5 files.

Variable field

Creating a typewriter effect

1. Open a new Flash file and place a text field on stage at (50,50). Now drag out the text field handle to make its size around 360 pixels wide and 150 pixels high.

> *It's always better to resize Dynamic Text fields by dragging the text field's handle. If you adjust the text field's dimensions by entering W and H values in the Property inspector, your text will become distorted.*

2. Set the font to Verdana, the size to 9 and the color to black. Set the text field to **Dynamic Text**, then from the Line Type drop-down select **Multiline**. Make sure **Selectable** is unchecked and finally give the text field the instance name `tf_txt`. (Selectable is a feature that determines whether the user can highlight and select text for cut and paste purposes when they view the movie.) Your Property inspector should now look like this:

3. Now add a new `scripts` layer and enter the following ActionScript in frame 1. First of all we'll just assign some text to the text field:

    ```
    tf_txt.text = "When a vibrating source of waves is
    ➡approaching an observer, the frequency observed is higher
    ➡than the frequency emitted by the source. When the source is
    ➡receding, the observed frequency is lower than that emitted.
    ➡This is known as the Doppler effect, or Doppler's
    principle.";
    ```

4. Test the movie and you'll see that Flash has placed the text inside our text field. At this point it's worth selecting the **Debug > List Variables** menu option to see what's going on with the text field. You should see something like this in the **Output** window:

    ```
    Output                                                                    ⌧
                                                                       Options ◢
    Level #0:
    Variable _level0.$version = "WIN 6,0,21,0"
    Edit Text: Target="_level0.tf_txt"
        variable = null,
        text = "When a vibrating source of waves is approaching an observer, the frequency observ
        htmlText = "When a vibrating source of waves is approaching an observer, the frequency ob
        html = false, textWidth = 98, textHeight = 340, maxChars = null,
        borderColor = 0x000000, backgroundColor = 0xFFFFFF, textColor = 0x000000, border = false,
        background = false, wordWrap = true, password = false, multiline = true,
        selectable = false, scroll = 1, hscroll = 0, maxscroll = 26,
        maxhscroll = 0, bottomScroll = 2,
        type = "dynamic",
        embedFonts = false, restrict = null, length = 276, tabIndex = undefined,
        autoSize = "none",
        condenseWhite = false
    ```

    That gives you an idea of exactly what's going on with a text field. Every Dynamic or Input text field you put on stage contains all these properties and all these properties can be accessed or manipulated at run-time.

5. So far we've entered the whole chunk of text at once, but we now want to add one character at a time. To achieve this, we'll take our piece of text and assign it to a variable rather than the `text` property of the text field. Simply replace `tf_txt.text` with `text_str`:

    text_str="When a vibrating source...

    Now we create an `enterFrame` function to add characters to the text field one-by-one using the `substr` method of the string object. This method is generally passed two arguments – the first allows us to specify a start point and the second specifies the number of characters. The method will then retrieve that portion of the string. So, with the text string we've been using up until now, take a look at the following ActionScript.

```
text_str.substr(0, 6);
```

This will retrieve "When a", the first six characters of the string. With our typewriter effect, the first argument passed will always be zero because we always want the text displayed to start at the beginning of the string, while the second argument (the length of the string retrieved) will increase each time, displaying gradually more of our string.

6. Enter the following ActionScript below the scripts layer's existing code:

```
this.onEnterFrame = function() {
// assign the portion of the string from 0 to count to the
// textField.
    tf_txt.text = text_str.substr(0, count);
    count += 2;
};
```

7. Save your movie as typeWriter001.fla and test it. You can make the text appear faster by increasing the amount that count is incremented by each frame. One slightly undesirable effect is the way that the text wraps – it begins to appear on one line and when it hits the end of the line is pushed down to the next, which a typewriter would obviously not do. We can get around this by adding our own new line (\n) characters in the text string to force them onto the next line. The new line characters in the text string below are highlighted in bold:

```
text_str="When a vibrating source of waves is approaching
➥an\nobserver, the frequency observed is higher than\nthe
➥frequency emitted by the source. When the source is
➥receding, the observed frequency is lower than
➥that\nemitted. This is known as the Doppler effect,
➥or\nDoppler's principle."
```

8. Save your file as typeWriter001b.fla and when you test it now, you'll see that the text appears on a new line at each place where we've added a \n.

When a vibrating source of waves is approaching an observer, the frequency observed is higher than the frequency emitted by the source. When the source is receding, the observed frequency is lower than that emitted. This is known as the Doppler effect, or Doppler's principle.	When a vibrating source of waves is approaching an observer, the frequency observed is higher than the frequency emitted by the source. When the source is receding, the observed frequency is lower than that emitted. This is known as the Doppler effect, or Doppler's principle.
Without newline characters	**With newline characters**

While this effect works as it is, it's really not ideal because it's never going to stop running – count will continue incrementing forever. Additionally, we have to set an onEnterFrame function on our root level to control the effect; it would really be much better if we could have the text field take care of itself.

The ideal situation would be if we had a text field set up and could just say myTextField.typeIn("some text to type in") and let it do its business. In previous versions of Flash, we did this with a movie clip by setting an onEnterFrame function for it, or by attaching a controller movie clip inside it that would execute its actions. The textField object unfortunately has no onEnterFrame handler, so we have to take a different approach.

The method we'll use is setInterval. It allows us to repeat a specified function after every number of milliseconds. setInterval is not necessarily tied to the frame rate the movie is running at. Let's put together a quick file to look at how this works.

Repeating specified functions with SetInterval

To do this we are going to animate two movie clips. One will use the onEnterframe, and the other will use the setInterval method.

1. Open a new Flash file and set the frame rate to 20 fps.

2. Draw a graphic and convert it to a movie clip – we've opted for a small circular ball shape. Place two instances of it on stage and call one obja_mc, and the other obja2_mc.

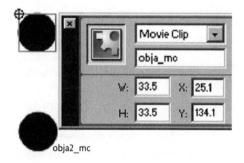

3. Now add a scripts layer to the main timeline and add the following code – we're creating one function to run onEnterFrame and another to run controlled by setInterval:

```
_root.onEnterFrame = function() {
    obja_mc._x++;
    trace("on enter frame");
};
function inter() {
    obja2_mc._x++;
    trace("interval function");
}
setInterval(inter, 50);
```

45

We've used `setInterval` here by just passing it two arguments – the function to call and the interval between each call. Our function `inter` will be called every 50 milliseconds. We've chosen 50 milliseconds because this should correspond to the frame rate – there are 1000 milliseconds in a second and our movie is updating 20 times every second, or once every fifty milliseconds.

4. Save your file as `setInterval1.fla` and test it – you'll notice that the balls are moving at more or less the same speed, but that the distance between them seems to grow slightly as they move across the screen.

   The two should remain in sync, but if you look at the Output window you'll see that on enter frame and `interval function` generally alternate, as they should, although every second instance of `interval function` is traced twice in a row:

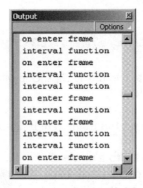

   To see the way that the distance alters, put this code in one of the functions; it will produce a trace of the distance between the two movie clips:

   ```
   trace(obja2_mc._x-obja_mc._x);
   ```

   The distance does not stay constant. Altering the interval to 51 or 49 doesn't help either – with one, `obja_mc` moves faster, while `obja2_mc` moves faster with the other. It's important not to think that setInterval doesn't work or is useless, but just that if we want events to be synchronized perfectly, it is best to pick either `onEnterFrame` or `setInterval` to control our motion rather than a mixture of both. If precise synchronization is not essential for a particular application then it seems fine to use both.

5. To see another issue, alter the frame rate of the movie to 1 fps. Now our interval function is called every 50 milliseconds, but the stage only updates every 1000 milliseconds.

   As you'll see when you test the movie, every second when the stage updates, `obja_mc` moves 1 pixel and `obja2_mc` jumps 10 or 11 pixels because the `setInterval` function has been called 10 or 11 times in the gap between the stage updating.

6. Replace the code in the scripts layer with the following and save your file as setInterval2.fla. We'll use it to force the stage to update by using updateAfterEvent().

```
_root.onEnterFrame = function() {
    trace("on enter frame");
    obja_mc._x++;
    trace(obja2_mc._x);
};
function inter() {
    obja2_mc._x += 3;
    trace("interval function called");
    updateAfterEvent();
}
setInterval(inter, 30);
```

updateAfterEvent is a method called to update the stage independently of the frame rate. It will only work as part of a clipEvent handler or within a function assigned to setInterval. A common use of this method is to create a smoother drag when dealing with draggable objects. In this case, we use it within an onMouseMove handler so that the new position of the draggable object is displayed instantly rather than at the beginning of the next frame. It's better to exercise caution regarding using this too much though, because you can see how jerky the motion is when we use it with setInterval. To compare, switch the frame rate back to 30 and you'll see the difference. Ultimately, the answer is not to try and force setInterval to go faster than the frame rate (although this is possible to an extent). Just because Flash allows us to do it, it doesn't always mean it's a good idea.

Creating a text field dynamically

Now we're familiar with how setInterval works, we can employ it to rebuild our typewriter effect. This time, rather than placing the text field from on stage manually, we're going to create it dynamically.

We use the createTextField method to do this:

```
this.createTextField("tf_txt", 1, 50, 50, 360, 150);
```

The arguments in the brackets specify (respectively) the name, depth, X, Y, width and height of the new text field. This creates a basic text field with the default font, point size, etc. We now need to turn word wrap on and stop the text field being selectable:

```
tf_txt.wordWrap = true;
tf_txt.selectable = false;
```

We then create our own `textFormat` object to apply our chosen attributes to the text field. There are two ways to do this – the first way is to create the new `textFormat` object and then give it the properties we require as in the following ActionScript.

```
myTform = new textFormat();
// set properties of textFormat object
myTform.font = "Verdana";
myTform.size = 9;
myTform.color = 0xff3300;
```

The second approach is to pass the properties as arguments when we create the object. This way is more compact, but slightly more complicated because it requires knowing what order the arguments have to be passed in (there's no code hint for this, which doesn't help). Here's the order they have to be passed in:

```
new textFormat(font, size, color, bold, italic, underline,
➥ url, target, align, leftMargin, rightMargin, indent,
➥leading);
```

Although all of these arguments are optional, in order to set any particular parameter, we must include all the arguments preceding it. If we want to leave out any of these arguments, then pass the value null to the method. For example, if we want to specify italic, but not bold, then we would write:

```
new textFormat("Arial", 10, 0xff0000, null, true);
```

So for our `textFormat`:

```
myTform = new textFormat("Verdana", 9, 0xff3300);
```

Finally, we apply the `textFormat` object to the text field object:

```
tf_txt.setNewTextFormat(myTform);
```

Note that we use `setNewTextFormat` rather than `setTextFormat` because the latter only takes effect on characters already present in the text field and not new characters that are added. To see the effect, add this line to the end of your ActionScript:

```
tf_txt.text = "quick test";
```

If you use `setNewTextFormat` it will appear in red Verdana; if you use `setTextFormat` it will appear in black Times New Roman.

So, this is the full code used to create our text field, set up how we want it:

```
this.createTextField("tf_txt", 1, 50, 50, 360, 150);
tf_txt.wordWrap = true;
tf_txt.selectable = false;
myTform = new textFormat("Verdana", 9, 0xff3300);
// apply the textFormat to the textField
tf_txt.setNewTextFormat(myTform);
```

It's rather a lot of effort isn't it? In most situations it's probably easier to just drag a text field on stage and set the properties with the Property inspector. It's useful to know how all this works though, as there are situations where this is useful, such as when you are creating layout on the fly for example. Even here it has allowed us to set the size of the text field precisely, although we could just have done:

```
tf_txt._width = 360;
tf_txt._height = 150;
```

Typing in

That's the set up complete and we'll use it as the basis to create our next effect. Before we create the function, we'll create the call to the function so that we know what we're aiming to achieve.

1. Keep the five lines of code from the previous exercise and place the following below it; first the declaration of a variable to hold our string and then a call to a function to type the string into the text field:

```
text_str = "When a vibrating source of waves is approaching an
➡observer, the frequency observed is higher than the
➡frequency emitted by the source. When the source is
➡receding, the observed frequency is lower than that emitted.
➡This is known as the Doppler effect, or Doppler's
➡principle.";
this.tf_txt.typeIn(text_str);
```

For this we're going to need to have the typeIn function as a method to the textField object. There are two ways we can define the function – by attaching it to the property of an object:

```
tf_txt.typeIn = function(texta) {
    //etc. etc.
};
```

or inside TextField.prototype:

```
TextField.prototype.typeIn = function(texta) {
    //etc. etc.
};
```

With the first method, every text field we want to use the function with has to have the function defined for it individually, whereas with the second approach, the method will be available to all instances of the `TextField` object, which is probably preferable, as it allows us to use it for any text field without modifying the code.

2. Now that we've ascertained where the function is going to be put on the root timeline, we need to work out what it's going to do exactly. Basically, the functionality will be the same as we had earlier. We'll take the `texta` argument that is passed to the function and store that in the text field. We'll then gradually add to the text field's text property until text is the same as `texta`. So, first of all we store the text in the `TextField` – add the following code to the top of the existing code:

```
TextField.prototype.typeIn = function(texta) {
    this.texta = texta;
};
```

3. We then need to create a function that will run at an interval to increment a counter variable and alter the text property accordingly:

```
TextField.prototype.typeIn = function(texta) {
    this.texta = texta;
    this.controlType = function() {
        this.count++;
        this.text = this.texta.substr(0, this.count);
    };
};
```

This is similar to what we had before – adding one to a counter and then using that value to extract a portion of `this.texta` using the `substr` method.

4. All we need to add now is the `setInterval` to make this command repeat itself. Earlier on when we used `setInterval`, we just gave it the name of a function to call. This time we need to give it the name of the method and a reference to the object it needs to call the method for:

```
setInterval(this, "controlType", 30);
```

The finished code to get the whole thing working is this:

```
TextField.prototype.typeIn = function(texta) {
    this.texta = texta;
```

```
        this.controlType = function() {
            this.count++;
            this.text = this.texta.substr(0, this.count);
        };
        // call the controlType function every 30 milliseconds
        setInterval(this, "controlType", 30);
    };

    this.createTextField("tf_txt", 1, 50, 50, 300, 150);
    tf_txt.wordWrap = true;
    tf_txt.selectable = false;
    myTform = new textFormat("Verdana", 9, 0xff3300);
    tf_txt.setNewTextFormat(myTform);

    text_str = "When a vibrating source of waves is approaching an
    observer, the frequency observed is higher than the frequency emitted
    by the source. When the source is receding, the observed frequency is
    lower than that emitted. This is known as the Doppler effect, or
    Doppler's principle.";
    // initialize typeIn effect
    this.tf_txt.typeIn(text_str);
```

5. Save your file as typeWriter002.fla and test it. You'll see the same effect as our previous examples, but this time the text field is attached dynamically.

Splitting the method in two: initialization and control

One initial thing we could change here is that every time the typeIn method is called, our controlType function is redefined, which is not really necessary. Alternatively, we could change our method into two separate methods – one to initialize the typing and another to control it:

```
    TextField.prototype.typeIn = function(texta) {
        this.count = 0;
        this.texta = texta;
        setInterval(this, "controlType", 30);
    };
    TextField.prototype.controlType = function() {
        this.count++;
        this.text = this.texta.substr(0, this.count);
    };
```

This (typeWriter003.fla) isn't as compact as our previous version because it's two functions rather than one, although probably a little clearer to follow. You may have noticed that we haven't actually done anything to stop the function running yet, so that's our next step.

Stopping the function from running

Once a function has been set using `setInterval`, it will continue calling that function until `clearInterval` is called for that function. When `setInterval` is called in the first place it returns a unique id number, which you must use when you want to clear the interval again. We haven't made use of this so far, but now we will.

For this exercise, we've reverted to just having the text field placed manually on stage:

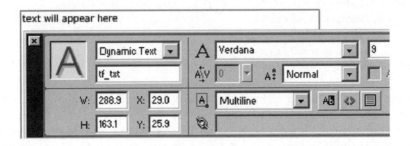

1. To set the interval we add the following line of highlighted code:

```
TextField.prototype.typeIn = function(texta) {
    this.count = 0;
    this.texta = texta;
    this.myTypeID = setInterval(this, "controlType", 30);
};
```

2. To clear the interval and stop the interval timer calling the function, we add the following:

```
clearInterval(this.myTypeID);
```

3. To build this in, we'll add another method, `typeDone`, which will clear the function call and then get rid of any temporary variables that we've been using:

```
TextField.prototype.typeDone = function() {
    delete this.count;
    delete this.texta;
    // clear the interval that calls controlType
    clearInterval(this.myTypeID);
    delete this.myTypeID;
};
```

4. We then have to add the call to this function, which should occur when the `count` variable has reached the length of `texta`:

```
TextField.prototype.controlType = function() {
```

```
        this.count++;
        this.text = this.texta.substr(0, this.count);
// if we reach the end of the string call typeDone
        if (this.count>=this.texta.length) {
            this.typeDone();
        }
};
```

5. The final piece of ActionScript for this example contains the text that we want to appear:

```
text_str = "When a vibrating...
// rest of text goes here
...or Doppler's principle.";
this.tf_txt.typeIn(text_str);
```

6. Save your movie as `typeWriter004.fla` and test it. If you select the **Debug > List Variables** menu option after the typing has finished, you'll see that we've left no variables or anything within the text field object. You could add a trace statement within the `controlType` function to see when the action stops.

Further refinements to our typing in effect

There are a couple more refinements we could make to this set of functions.

1. First of all we might add extra parameters to trigger the `typeIn` function that sits on the last line of our ActionScript. It would be nice if we could pass it numbers for how many characters to add each frame, and how often the `setInterval` runs, like this:

```
this.tf_txt.typeIn(text_str, 3, 30);
```

So, 3 would be the number of characters to add each frame and it would be called every 30 milliseconds. This is fairly easily done – we first have to add these parameters to our `typeIn` function; the new code is highlighted in bold:

```
TextField.prototype.typeIn = function(texta, typeSpeed,
➡interval) {
        this.count = 0;
// store the typeSpeed inside the textField
        this.typeSpeed = typeSpeed;
        this.texta = texta;
        this.myTypeID = setInterval(this, "controlType", interval);
};
```

2. We then alter our `typeControl` function to make use of the `typeSpeed` variable:
    ```
    TextField.prototype.controlType = function() {
    ```

```
            // increase the amount of text displayed by typeSpeed
            this.count += this.typeSpeed;
            this.text = this.texta.substr(0, this.count);
            if (this.count>=this.texta.length) {
                this.typeDone();
            }
        };
```

3. Finally, we get rid of our extra variable in the typeDone function:

```
TextField.prototype.typeDone = function() {
    delete this.count;
    delete this.texta;
    delete this.typeSpeed;
    clearInterval(this.myTypeID);
    delete this.myTypeID;
};
```

4. Save your file as typeWriter005.fla. We can easily change the way our typeIn function behaves, simply by passing it different values. You might like to try:

```
this.tf.typeIn(tex, 30, 60);
or
this.tf.typeIn(tex, 30, 30);
```

5. Essentially, we want as much control as possible over the behavior of the typing in without having to go into our function and change the internal code. This makes the method a lot more flexible and powerful.

Adding a callback function

Finally, we'll add the ability to pass the function a callback function that will trigger when the typing effect finishes. To do this, we'll add two more parameters to the function, which we'll place at the end so that if we don't need to have this callback, we don't have to use it.

1. Add the new parameters to the typeIn function. They are highlighted here in bold:

```
TextField.prototype.typeIn = function(texta, typeSpeed,
➥interval, obja, func) {
    this.obja = obja;
    this.func = func;
    this.count = 0;
    this.typeSpeed = typeSpeed;
    this.texta = texta;
    this.myTypeID = setInterval(this, "controlType", interval);
};
```

2. So here we've stored two new variables, obja and func. We need to call them when the typing is finished, so we place them in our typeDone function. You'll probably remember the format from the previous chapter – the new code is highlighted in bold:

```
TextField.prototype.typeDone = function() {
    delete this.count;
    delete this.texta;
    delete this.typeSpeed;
    clearInterval(this.myTypeID);
    delete this.myTypeID;
    // execute callback function
    this.obja[this.func]();
    delete this.obja;
    delete this.func;
};
```

3. To test this we need to create a function to receive the callback and then alter our initial call. Place the following code below the existing functions:

```
function allDone() {
        trace("type done");
    }
```

4. Finally, we need to pass some additional values to our typeIn function. Add the following highlighted code to the last line of ActionScript:

```
this.tf_txt.typeIn(text_str, 1, 30, _root, "allDone");
```

5. Save your movie as typeWriter006.fla. When you run the movie, after all the text has appeared on the screen, you'll see the words **type done** appear in the Output window because allDone is called after the typing has finished.

When a vibrating source of waves is approaching an observer, the frequency observed is higher than the frequency emitted by the source. When the source is receding, the observed frequency is lower than that emitted. This is known as the Doppler effect, or Doppler's principle.

A note on prototypes

When placing functions or properties in the prototypes of objects, there's one thing we need to be wary of. If we use a `for..in` loop to enumerate the properties and methods of an instance of that object, the new methods and properties of the object will show up. Take a look at the following code by way of an example:

```
_root.createEmptyMovieClip("blah", 1);
blah.myVariable = 20;
for (var i in blah) {
     trace(i+" : "+blah[i]);
}
```

The trace that this produces in the Output window shows up as **myVariable : 20**. Now if we add a function to the `Movieclip` prototype that will also show up in the individual movie clip instance...

```
MovieClip.prototype.yada = function() {
};
_root.createEmptyMovieClip("blah", 1);
blah.myVariable = 20;
for (var i in blah) {
     trace(i+" : "+blah[i]);
}
```

...the trace should now be the following:

yada : [type Function]
myVariable : 20

The function `yada`, which we have defined for all movie clips, shows up in the instance `blah`. There's no reason for this to be a problem, especially if we're aware that this behavior will occur. However, certain situations may arise when this does become a problem, such as if you're using someone else's code that iterates through `MovieClip` properties and methods expecting certain results.

To circumvent this we can use the `AsSetPropFlags` method. It's not officially supported by ActionScript, so it's perhaps best not to rely on it, but it does allow us to 'hide' any extra properties or methods we add from a `for..in` loop. The way we do this is to call `AsSetPropFlags`, passing it the name of the object whose property we want to hide, the name of the property or method and the number 1, like this:

```
ASSetPropFlags(MovieClip.prototype, "yada", 1);
```

So, if we put this into our previous code and run it, the method yada will no longer be shown by the loop:

```
MovieClip.prototype.yada = function() {
};
ASSetPropFlags(MovieClip.prototype, "yada", 1);
_root.createEmptyMovieClip("blah", 1);
blah.myVariable = 20;
for (var i in blah) {
    trace(i+" : "+blah[i]);
}
```

This is actually one of several things that AsSetPropFlags can achieve, such as protecting properties from being overwritten, and so on. You can find out more at **http://chattyfig.figleaf.com/flashcoders-wiki/index.php?ASSetPropFlags**

Working with textFormat

We're now going to employ the textFormat object to build on the principles we've just been working on. We mentioned earlier that we could use the textFormat object to alter the formatting of certain sections of text – we're now going to produce something that will do so character-by-character rather than all at once. We'll then look towards using this to produce a function that picks out all instances of a certain word and displays them in a different format, a larger size or a different color.

Using setTextFormat

We'll begin by looking briefly at how to use setTextFormat in isolation. As we mentioned earlier, the textFormat object contains all the formatting data for a text field. Even if we don't set a textFormat object for a text field, it has one by default, which can be retrieved by using TextField.getTextFormat(). When we've used textFormat before, we've used it to set the formatting for the whole textField – we're now going to use it to set the formatting to a certain section of the text field.

1.   Open a new movie and create a text field like the ones in our previous examples:

In this text field, set the text color to red and don't forget to name your instance in the Property inspector (`tf_txt`).

2. We want to highlight a certain section of text, so first we'll define what the text is and how we want it to be formatted. Add a new `scripts` layer and place the following code inside its first frame:

```
this.tf_txt.text = "The eidophor system is a projection
➥television system, i.e. it enables enlarged television
➥pictures to be projected on to a screen. An ordinary
➥television picture derives its brightness from the
➥fluorescence of a screen bombarded by electrons; with the
➥eidophor system, on the other hand, a very powerful source
➥of light is controlled by the television signal picked up by
➥the receiver.";
// create textFormat object
myForm = new TextFormat();
myForm.color = 0x00000;
myForm.font = "Verdana";
myForm.size = 9;
```

3. So, we've created a `textFormat` object called `myForm` and now we'll apply it to the text field. Let's focus on the word 'eidophor', whose first character is at 4 and whose last character is at 12. We pass these two values as arguments to the `setTextFormat` method, along with our `myForm` object. Add the following line of code beneath your existing code:

```
// apply textformat to characters 4 to 12
this.tf_txt.setTextFormat(4, 12, myForm);
```

4. Save your movie as `setTextFormat.fla` and when you run it, you'll see the word 'eidophor' picked out in black. Whatever you change in the `textFormat` object will be displayed in the text. For instance, if you add the following above the `setTextFormat` line, our target word will be bold as well as black:

```
myform.bold = true;
```

One thing that's useful to know about `textFormat` is that if the `textFormat` object doesn't have a particular property within it when it is applied to a `textField` object, it will use the value that is already present. We'll try that now.

5. Change all our `textFormat` code to the following:

```
myForm = new TextFormat();
myForm.color = 0x000000;
```

There is no information for font or font size here, but when it is applied to the text field object, it just uses the formatting that was already there (9pt Verdana). When you test the movie, if you choose the **Debug > List Variables** menu option, you'll see that the myForm object has a lot of values set to null:

```
Output                                                          ▼
                                                       Options ◢
Variable _level0.myForm = [object #1, class 'TextFormat'] {  ▲
    getTextExtent:[function],
    font:[getter/setter] null,
    size:[getter/setter] null,
    color:[getter/setter] 0x000000,
    url:[getter/setter] null,
    target:[getter/setter] null,
    bold:[getter/setter] null,                               ▼
◄                                               ►
```

When the textFormat object is applied using textField.setTextFormat, all these null values are simply discarded and replaced with whatever's already there.

6. Add the following line of code. We'll use the getTextFormat method to retrieve the textFormat of the section of text we just set:

```
// retrieve the textFormat for characters 4 to 12 in the text field
post = this.tf_txt.getTextFormat(4, 12);
```

7. Save your movie as setTextFormat(post).fla, and when you test it this time and select the **Debug > List Variables** menu option, you'll see that all the values are present in post – even the ones we hadn't set in myForm:

```
Output                                                          ▼
                                                       Options ◢
Variable _level0.post = [object #3, class 'TextFormat'] {  ▲
    getTextExtent:[function],
    font:[getter/setter] "Verdana",
    size:[getter/setter] 9,
    color:[getter/setter] 0x000000,
    url:[getter/setter] ,
    target:[getter/setter] ,
    bold:[getter/setter] false,                            ▼
◄                                               ►
```

Now we've got a grasp of how to use setTextFormat, we'll start on making our method, to gradually change the textFormat. We'll be setting this up much as we did previously with the typeID function. We'll pass the function a number of parameters including a textFormat object, a start point, an end point, a speed and an interval. We'll also set it up to accept a callback function that we'll put to use in the second part of this example.

8. Here's what the call to the function will look like. Add it to the bottom of the ActionScript, below the `myForm` lines of code:

   ```
   this.tf_txt.nooTextFormat(myForm, 4, 11, 1, 30);
   ```

   At the moment, your ActionScript should look like this:

   ```
   this.tf_txt.text = "The eidophor system...by the receiver.";
   myForm = new TextFormat();
   myForm.color = 0x000000;
   this.tf_txt.nooTextFormat(myForm, 25, 43, 1, 30);
   ```

9. The basic shell of the function should be familiar to you from before. Add the following ActionScript above the existing code (we'll add the rest of the code for `nooTextFormatControl` and `cleanNooTextFormat` in a moment.

   ```
   TextField.prototype.nooTextFormat = function(tForm, begin,
   ➥end, speed, interval, obja, func) {
   // store parameters in text field
       this.begin = this.current= begin;
       this.end = end+1;
       this.speed = speed;
       this.end = end;
       this.obja = obja;
       this.func = func;
       this.nooTform = tForm;
    // set interval to call nooTextFormatControl
       this.myNooText = setInterval(this, "nooTextFormatControl",
       ➥interval);
   };
   TextField.prototype.nooTextFormatControl = function() {
   };
   TextField.prototype.cleanNooTextFormat = function() {
   };
   ```

   We're doing the same thing as before – putting copies of all the arguments passed to the argument in the text field itself. We set `this.end` to equal `end+1` because the second argument passed to `setTextFormat` refers to the character after the last character affected by the format change, whereas the value we are passing refers to the last character we want affected.

   For our `nooTextFormatControl` function we're going to gradually increment the `this.current` variable and increase the span of text that we apply the `textFormat` to. We start `current` off at the value of `begin` and carry on incrementing it until it reaches the value of `end`.

10. Add the following highlighted code to nooTextFormatControl:

```
TextField.prototype.nooTextFormatControl = function() {
    this.current += this.speed;
    if (this.current>this.end) {
        this.setTextFormat(this.begin, this.end,
            ➡this.nooTform);
        this.cleanNooTextFormat();
    } else {
        this.setTextFormat(this.begin, this.current,
            ➡this.nooTform);
    }
};
```

Every time the function is called we add speed to the value of our current variable. If this value is less than the end of the area we want to affect, then we set the textFormat of our text from begin to current. If it is at or beyond the end (it might be beyond if we were adding 3 or 4 to current each time), we set the text format using the begin and end values we passed at the start and then call our cleanUp function.

11. The final thing to do is add the following highlighted code to cleanNooTextFormat:

```
TextField.prototype.cleanNooTextFormat = function() {
    delete this.current;
    delete this.nooTform;
    delete this.begin;
    delete this.end;
    clearInterval(this.myNooText);
    delete this.myNooText;
    this.obja[this.func]();
};
```

12. Save your new file as switchTextFormat1.fla. Like before, this function gets rid of any variables or properties that we're not using any more.

Application of technique

We're now going to get into a practical application of the technique we've just looked at. We'll create a small application that will locate all instances of a specific piece of text within a larger piece of text, and then highlight them in turn. This is where you'll see the value of the callback functions that we've been adding.

To start with we're going to need a function to look through text and return the positions of a string that we specify. As this function deals with strings we're going to create this as a method of the string object. Following that approach, using findInstances on its own looks like this:

```
myString.findInstances(str);
```

To find an instance of a string within another string, we can use indexOf. When used on its own indexOf is written like this:

```
var pos = myString.indexOf(str);
```

Written like this, indexOf returns the index number of the first instance of str. We now need to find every instance of str and for this purpose we can implement a different way of using indexOf, where we specify an index number to start looking at:

```
var pos = myString.indexOf(str, startIndex);
```

So, our function will need to contain a loop. As it finds one instance of the string it will take the index number of the first instance of str found and then use this as the start point for the next indexOf operation. The loop will keep repeating until str is no longer found, at which point indexOf will return -1 and we'll break out of the loop and return an array of the values we've found:

```
String.prototype.findInstances = function(str) {
    var foundAt = [];
    var nextFound = 0;
    // while there are still instances of the string
    while (nextFound != -1) {
        nextFound = this.indexOf(smallStr, nextFound);
        if (nextFound != -1) {
            foundAt.push({begin:nextFound,
            ➡end:nextFound+str.length});
            nextFound++;
        }
    }
    // return the array of beginning and end values
    return foundAt;
};
```

Let's go through it line-by-line. First we set our currIndex to zero, which is where we'll start looking. Next, we create an array foundAt, which is where we'll put all our values to return. We then declare a variable nextFound, which is what we'll use to hold the value that is returned. We then use var to declare this because we only want the variable to persist as long as the function is running.

For setting up the loop we use `while(nextFound!=-1)` because we want the loop to terminate when no more instances of the string are found. The first line in the loop gives us the index number of the next instance of the search string in the larger string, after the point specified by `currIndex`.

```
nextFound = this.indexOf(str, currIndex);
```

If `nextFound` is not -1, it means we have found an instance of the string and the statements inside the conditional will be executed, adding the next instance to the string and incrementing `nextFound`, so that it carries on through the text:

```
if (nextFound != -1) {
    foundAt.push({begin:nextFound,
    ➥end:nextFound+smallStr.length});
    nextFound++;
}
```

We add this as an object containing a start and end value, so that we can specify a beginning and end point for the span of text:

```
foundAt.push({begin:nextFound, end:nextFound+str.length});
```

If there are no more instances of the search string, `nextFound` will equal -1 and the `while` loop will stop running. We then return all the values we've found and terminate the function:

```
return foundAt;
```

To try this method out we'll create a new file. Add the method we defined above and following that:

```
text_str="The eidophor system is a projection television
➥system, i.e. it enables enlarged television pictures to be
➥projected on to a screen. An ordinary television picture
➥derives its brightness from the fluorescence of a screen
➥bombarded by electrons; with the eidophor system, on the
➥other hand, a very powerful source of light is controlled by
➥the television signal picked up by the receiver."
vals=text_str.findInstances("television")
```

If you run the code and list variables you'll see that `vals` contains an array with four objects – one for each instance of the word 'television' in the string above. However, there's a change we need to make before it will work in all situations.

Converting Strings

1. With our current set up, if the case (upper/lower) of our search string does not match the instance in the text, they will not register as a match. To overcome this we convert both strings to lower case before using them. Here are the adjustments, again highlighted in bold:

```
String.prototype.findInstances = function(str) {
    var foundAt = [];
    var nextFound = 0;
 // change both strings to lower case
    var largeStr = this.toLowerCase();
    var smallStr = str.toLowerCase();
    while (nextFound!=-1) {
        nextFound = largeStr.indexOf(smallStr, nextFound);
        if (nextFound != -1) {
            foundAt.push({begin:nextFound,
            ➥end:nextFound+smallStr.length});
            nextFound++;
        }
    }
return foundAt;
};
```

    This will now work for finding all instances of any string within any larger string.

2. We'll now deploy this. Open switchTextFormat1.fla and retain the text field on stage and the three functions, nooTextFormat, nooTextFormatControl and cleanNooTextFormat. Add our findInstances method after these. Now we create the functions to find the instances of a string and highlight them. We'll first need a function to initialize, which will call findInstances and put the result in an array. Once it has done this, it will call the function doNext.

```
function nooFindAndReplace(textObj, str) {
    this.indices = textObj.text.findInstances(str);
    this.doNext();
}
```

    doNext will use the array method shift to extract the first pair of indices from the indices array, and then pass them to nooTextFormat. We are passing doNext as the callback function so that when the format has changed for one word doNext is called again and we move on to the next word.

```
function doNext() {
// if there is another string
    if (indices.length>0) {
        var nexta = this.indices.shift();
        this.tf_txt.nooTextFormat(myForm, nexta.begin,
        ➥nexta.end, 1, 30, this, "doNext");
    }
}
```

3. Finally, we define a string to search in, and then a call to the function:

```
this.tf_txt.text = "The eidophor system is a projection
➥television system, i.e. it enables enlarged television
➥pictures to be projected on to a screen. An ordinary
➥television picture derives its brightness from the
➥fluorescence of a screen bombarded by electrons; with the
➥eidophor system, on the other hand, a very powerful source
➥of light is controlled by the television signal picked up by
➥the receiver.";
myForm = this.tf_txt.getTextFormat();
myForm.color = 0x000000;
myForm.size = 9;
myForm.bold = true;
// trigger find and replace
nooFindAndReplace(this.tf_txt, "television", myForm);
```

The completed code looks like this:

```
TextField.prototype.nooTextFormat = function(tForm, begin,
➥end, speed, interval, obja, func) {
    this.begin = this.current=begin;
    this.end = end+1;
    this.speed = speed;
    this.end = end;
    this.obja = obja;
    this.func = func;
    this.nooTform = tForm;
    this.myNooText = setInterval(this,
    ➥"nooTextFormatControl", interval);
};
TextField.prototype.nooTextFormatControl = function() {
    this.current += this.speed;
    if (this.current>this.end) {
        this.setTextFormat(this.begin, this.end, this.nooTform);
        this.cleanNooTextFormat();
```

65

continues overleaf

```
        } else {
            this.setTextFormat(this.begin, this.current, this.nooTform);
        }
    };
    TextField.prototype.cleanNooTextFormat = function() {
        delete this.current;
        delete this.nooTform;
        delete this.begin;
        delete this.end;
        clearInterval(this.myNooText);
        delete this.myNooText;
        this.obja[this.func]();
    };
    String.prototype.findInstances = function(str) {
        var foundAt = [];
        var nextFound = 0;
        var largeStr = this.toLowerCase();
        var smallStr = str.toLowerCase();
        while (nextFound!=-1) {
            nextFound = largeStr.indexOf(smallStr, nextFound);
            if (nextFound != -1) {
                foundAt.push({begin:nextFound,
                ➥end:nextFound+smallStr.length});
                nextFound++;
            }
        }
    return foundAt;
    };
    function nooFindAndReplace(textObj, str) {
        this.indices = textObj.text.findInstances(str);
        this.doNext();
    }
    function doNext() {
        if (indices.length>0) {
            var nexta = this.indices.shift();
            this.tf_txt.nooTextFormat(myForm, nexta.begin,
            ➥nexta.end, 1, 30, this, "doNext");
        }
    }
    this.tf_txt.text = "The eidophor system is a projection television
    system, i.e. it enables enlarged television pictures to be projected
    on to a screen. An ordinary television picture derives its brightness
    from the fluorescence of a screen bombarded by electrons; with the
    eidophor system, on the other hand, a very powerful source of light
    is controlled by the television signal picked up by the receiver.";
```

```
myForm = this.tf_txt.getTextFormat();
myForm.color = 0x000000;
myForm.size = 9;
myForm.bold = true;
nooFindAndReplace(this.tf_txt, "television", myForm);
```

4. Save your file as `switchTextFormat2.fla` and test it. You'll see the four instances of the word 'television' turn from black to red:

The eidophor system is a projection **television** system, i.e. it enables enlarged **television** pictures to be projected on to a screen. An ordinary **television** picture derives its brightness from the fluorescence of a screen bombarded by electrons; with the eidophor system, on the other hand, a very powerful source of light is controlled by the **televis**ion signal picked up by the receiver.

We can achieve a variety of effects using this method. For instance, we can simply change some of the values in the `textFormat object`, as well as varying the speed, and so on.

There are some minor improvements we could make to further enhance this approach. For example, the `doNext` function is written with a specific text field object and `textFormat` object in mind. Ideally we would have the text object and text format object passed to it as arguments. We can accomplish that by passing these values to the text field at the beginning, and then when each word is done it would pass these arguments to `doNext` for use in its next call. While we don't have space to go into this here, the source file `switchTextFormat3.fla` contains some comments to help point you in the right direction. It's basically just an extension of our callback function to pass arguments.

Advanced text effects

So far we've looked at text effects within the bounds of the text field object and while these can be useful, they do have their limitations. Flash MX also helps us out with creating larger text effects dynamically. In creating a text effect we will generally have each letter placed in a movie clip and then dynamically position that at (or move it to) a specific position. With Flash 5 it was impossible to retrieve the width of text dynamically and thus position individual characters effectively. To achieve such effects in Flash 5, it was necessary to use a third party tool – the string width calculator from www.swfx.org.

Flash MX gives us two ways of calculating the width of a string so that we can figure out where each character should be positioned. The first uses `textFormat.getTextExtent(str)`. With this method you can pass it a string and it will return an object containing the width and height of that piece of text as though it were all laid out in a single line. Although this is very convenient, the approach does have some discrepancies, which we'll go into in a moment. The second way to work out the width of a string is to put the string in a text field (with the required formatting), and then use the text field's textWidth property. While this method is more cumbersome because we have to create a text field to employ it, it is more accurate than using getTextExtent when using embedded fonts. Let's test this now to show the difference.

Calculating the width of a string

1. Open a new Flash movie and put a Dynamic Text field on the stage – make it so that its length covers most of the stage. Make sure the fonts are embedded – we'll use Verdana.

2. In the Property inspector, name the instance tf_txt. Next, create a scripts layer and add the following code:

    ```
    myTForm = new TextFormat();
    myTForm.size = 24;
    myTForm.font = "Verdana";
    str = "a piece of test text to check widths";
    tf_txt.text = str;
    tf_txt.setTextFormat(myTForm);
    // retrieve width with getTextExtent
    a = myTForm.getTextExtent(str).width;
    // retrieve width with textWidth
    b = tf_txt.textWidth;
    trace(a+" : "+b);
    ```

3. Test your file and you'll get a result in the Output window. Ours is **407 : 416**. 407 represents the width for getTextExtent and 416 represents textWidth.

    We've drawn two bars on stage so that you can compare the two. The file is textWidthTest.fla:

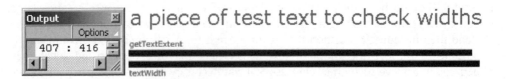

The problem here is likely attributable to kerning information – if we position text using getTextExtent, the characters seem to be placed exactly next to each other with no spacing. Either way, textWidth is the best option to choose for really accurate positioning.

Obtaining character positions

Now we've decided that we need to use `TextField.textWidth` to determine character positioning, we need to write a function to calculate this for any given `textFormat` object (for a particular font and point size, for instance). It would be a lot more straightforward to do this using `textFormat.getTextExtent`, because we wouldn't have to create a text field to measure the width, but as we decided this approach was more accurate, we'll stick with it.

Once we've obtained the positions for the characters we'll be able to use this information to position movie clips for each character, allowing us greater flexibility to scale, move, and so on.

We want to be able to pass the function a `textFormat` object and a string, like this:

```
function charPositions(tFormat, str, depth) {
    ...
}
```

We're also including a `depth` parameter so we can specify that from outside and avoid overwriting any other objects.

Obtaining further chararcter data

1. Create a (dummy) Dynamic Text field, placed somewhere off the stage. Set the font of this text field to Arial.

2. Add a new `scripts` layer and attach the following code to it:

```
function charPositions(tFormat, str, depth) {
    _root.createTextField("temp", depth, 0, -300, 100, 400);
    temp.embedFonts = true;
    temp.autoSize = true;
    temp.setNewTextFormat(tFormat);
    temp.text = str;
}
```

We've set `autoSize` to true so the text field will expand to fit whatever text we put in it. We've also set `embedFonts` to true, and `textFormat` to `tFormat`. We also need to assign our str variable to the text field's `text` property.

One thing to note when setting a text field's `embedFonts` property to true is that you need to have exported the font you wish to use with the movie. This is basically why we need to have a dummy Dynamic Text field off the stage somewhere. We also need to ensure that we have checked the **Embed Font Outlines For All Characters** option from the **Character Options** dialog:

3. To open the **Character Options** dialog, simply click on the **Character...** button when you're adjusting text attributes in the Property inspector. It's also worth noting that if you wish to use bold or italic formatting, you need another text field set to bold or italic. You could also accomplish the same thing using a font symbol.

4. Next, we create a temporary array to hold our position values and then we're ready to loop and determine the string widths:

```
function charPositions(tFormat, str, depth) {
    _root.createTextField("temp", depth, 0, -300, 100, 400);
    temp.embedFonts = true;
    temp.autoSize = true;
    temp.setNewTextFormat(tFormat);
    temp.text = str;
    var arr = [];
}
```

5. To determine the position of each character, we're going to start with the width of the entire string, and then the position of each character will be equivalent to the total width of the string minus the width of the string from that point on. For example, if our string is 'In the manufacture', the position of the 'm' in 'manufacture' is equal to the width of 'In the manufacture' minus the width of 'manufacture'. So for our loop, we need to add the following highlighted code:

```
function charPositions(tFormat, str, depth) {
    _root.createTextField("temp", depth, 0, -300, 100, 400);
    temp.embedFonts = true;
    temp.autoSize = true;
```

```
        temp.setNewTextFormat(tFormat);
        temp.text = str;
        var arr = [];
        //the total width of the text
        var totalWidth = temp.textWidth;

        for (var i = 0; i<str.length; i++) {
            temp.text = str.substr(i);
            // calculate the difference between the width to this point
            // and the total width
          arr[i] = totalWidth-temp.textWidth;
        }
    }
```

For each iteration of the loop, we move one character further into the string and place the string from that character into our temporary text field `str.substr(i)`. We then measure that width, subtract it from the total width, and place the value in our array.

6. We then need to remove the text field we created and return the array:

```
function charPositions(tFormat, str, depth) {
    _root.createTextField("temp", depth, 0, -300, 100, 400);
    temp.embedFonts = true;
    temp.autoSize = true;
    temp.setNewTextFormat(tFormat);
    temp.text = str;
    var arr = [];
    var totalWidth = temp.textWidth;
    for (var i = 0; i<str.length; i++) {
        temp.text = str.substr(i);
        arr[i] = totalWidth-temp.textWidth;
    }
    temp.removeTextField();
    return arr;
}
```

7. Finally, we call the function:

```
mt = new TextFormat();
mt.font = "Arial";
mt.size = 45;

str = "In the manufacture of safety matches, softwood logs
➥are peeled into a thin continuous shaving, or veneer, about
➥one tenth of an inch thick. The ribbon of wood is then cut
```

71

continues overleaf

➥up into splints at a rate of about two million per hour.
➥These splints are soaked in a bath of sodium silicate,
➥ammonium phosphate or sodium phosphate and then dried. This
➥impregnation prevents afterglow.";

```
posArray = charPositions(mt, str, 1);
```

Save your movie as `obtainCharPos.fla` and test it. If you select the **Debug > List Variables** menu option, you'll see that `posArray` contains a value for each letter in our string.

```
Output                                                              ☒
                                                        Options ◢
  Variable _level0.str = "In the manufacture of safety matches, softwood logs are
  Variable _level0.posArray = [object #4, class 'Array'] [
      0:0,
      1:12,
      2:37,
      3:50,
      4:62,
      5:87,
      6:112,
      7:125,
```

So, now we have a big list of X positions. The next thing is to do something with this information.

Using the character positions

We're now going to create a simple text effect using the positions we just retrieved. It's going to be fairly simple because once we have the positions where each character needs to end up, most of the hard work's done – it's up to us how we choose to get them there.

We're going to have each letter fade in one-by-one. The first problem that we have to deal with is that our positions array has all of the characters on one line, whereas we're more likely to have them displayed on more than one line. An easy way to overcome this would be to have our text divided into lines beforehand. We could either split the lines manually or break the string up using `string.split()` with a special delimiter or just the new line character as the point to split it at.

Having done that, we could get the character positions of each line in turn. What we're going to do here though is split the text up automatically. We'll specify a width for our text area and then once the text goes past that width we'll push it back to the beginning of a new line. We'll create a function, `setUpText` which will get the positions for the text, then go through that array and divide it into different lines, putting the results and all of the individual characters into a new array.

First of all we retrieve the character positions. Then we determine the height of each line using `getTextExtent` (accuracy is not so important here). We then create a variable, `currentLine` to keep track of what line we're on and an array, `finalPositions` to contain all of our final coordinates:

Using our character data for a text fade

1. Add the following ActionScript beneath the `charPositions` function in `obtainCharPos.fla`.

```
function setUpText(str, forma, lineLength) {
    var positions = charPositions(forma, str, 1000);
    var currentLine;
    var lineHeight = forma.getTextExtent(str).height;
    var finalPositions = [];
}
```

Next, we add a loop to go through each entry in the positions array. As it does this it will check whether the X position is greater than `lineLength`. If it is, we need to shunt it back to zero and add one to our `currentLine` variable to ascertain the Y position. We keep track of how far we have to push it back because all the subsequent characters will also be pushed back by the same amount. We'll put this value in a variable called `subtracta`.

2. For example, if we have a character at 510 and the `lineLength` is 500, we have to push it and all subsequent characters back by 510. If a character's X position is greater than 510 plus the length of the line, we shunt that back to zero and add the amount it was shunted back to our `subtracta` variable, thus keeping track of the cumulative total. Add the following highlighted code to the `setUpText` function:

```
function setUpText(str, forma, lineLength) {
    var positions = charPositions(forma, str, 1000);
    var currentLine;
    var subtracta;
    var lineHeight = forma.getTextExtent(str).height;
    var finalPositions = [];
    for (var i = 0; i<positions.length; i++) {
    // if the current position is off the right edge
        if (positions[i]>(lineLength+subtracta)) {
            subtracta = positions[i];
            currentLine++;
        }
        var x = positions[i]-subtracta;
        var y = lineHeight*currentLine;
        finalPositions[i] = {char:str.charAt(i), x:x, y:y};
    }
    return finalPositions;
}
```

We've added two further things here. The first is that we've calculated the Y position by multiplying the currentLine value by the lineHeight; we're pushing down the page by the height of the text for every added line of text. You'll also see that we've put our character values and positions into the array as an object. That way, when we return the array we'll be able to use it without knowing what the string is; it's now just a list of characters.

3. We now create a small initialize function to call our setUpText function:

```
function init(str, tForm, lineLength) {
    // retrieve character positions
    charPos = setUpText(str, tForm, lineLength);
    this.count = 0;
    // set drawNext to be called every frame
    this.onEnterFrame = drawNext;
}
```

We'll pass that all the relevant information and it will retrieve the character positions for the string. Once that's accomplished, we set an enterFrame function for _root, drawNext. This will take care of drawing each letter in turn, using the count variable to keep track.

4. Next, we add a drawNext function, which is fairly simple. Basically, every frame it is called it will look up the next character in the array and retrieve its position. It will then duplicate a movie clip at that position and create a text field inside it, set to the relevant character with the correct formatting. It will set the movie clip's alpha to 30 and give it an onEnterFrame function to increase the alpha gradually. This should all be clear from the code we've covered so far. Add the following code to the movie:

```
function drawNext() {
    var noo = this.createEmptyMovieClip
    ➥("lett"+count, count);
    var nextObj = charPos[this.count];
    // a reference to the object in the array
    noo._x = nextObj.x;
    noo._y = nextObj.y;
    noo.createTextField("tex", 1, 0, 0, 100, 100);
    noo.tex.text = nextObj.char;
    noo.tex.embedFonts = true;
    noo.tex.selectable = false;
    noo.tex.setTextFormat(mt);
    noo._alpha = 30;
    noo.onEnterFrame = function() {
        // increase alpha until 100 is reached
        this._alpha += 5;
```

```
            if (this._alpha>=100) {
                delete this.onEnterFrame;
            }
        };
        count++;
        if (count>charPos.length) {
            delete this.onEnterFrame;
        }
    }
}
```

5.   Finally, we set up our text formats and add a call to the `init` function:

```
mt = new TextFormat();
mt.font = "Arial";
mt.size = 24;
str = "In the manufacture of safety matches, softwood logs
➥are peeled into a thin continuous shaving, or veneer, about
➥one tenth of an inch thick. The ribbon of wood is then cut
➥up into splints at a rate of about two million per hour.
➥These splints are soaked in a bath of sodium silicate,
➥ammonium phosphate or sodium phosphate and then dried. This
➥impregnation prevents afterglow.";
init(str, mt, 530);
```

6.   Save your file as `useCharPos.fla` and test it. Remember, for it to work correctly, you need a text field off stage set to the font you're using – Arial in the case of this exercise. You'll see the letter gradually fade into their full color as they appear:

You may have noticed that the method we have used to calculate where the end of each line is and move on to the next line can split words in the middle. We're not going to go into this here, but it would be possible to change the method to ensure that words are not split. We could do this by first going through the string, calculating the widths of each individual word and then adding these values together to find where they go beyond our right-hand boundary. When this happens we would move on to the next line.

Further possibilities

We're now going to create another file based on the previous one to show how easy it is to manipulate things once we have achieved the basics, and we'll bring the characters in at random rather than in order.

Creating a random fade

1. The only difference in this file will be in the drawNext function. So let's open useCharPos.fla and modify it.

    We need drawNext to pick a character at random from the array and draw it. It should then remove it from the array, leaving only the characters that still need to be drawn. The code to do this is simple. First we pick a random number between 0 and the number of entries in the array. Then we store that entry from the array in a temporary variable. Then we remove the item from the array using the splice method:

    ```
    var next = Math.floor(Math.random()*charpos.length);
    var nextObj = charPos[next];
    charPos.splice(next, 1);
    ```

2. The rest of the function is more or less the same as before – it is only the way we pick which character to duplicate that differs:

    ```
    function drawNext() {
        this.count++;
        // pick a random character
        var next = Math.floor(Math.random()*charpos.length);
        var nextObj = charPos[next];
        charPos.splice(next, 1);
        var noo = this.createEmptyMovieClip
        ➥("lett"+this.count, this.count);
        noo._x = nextObj.x;
        noo._y = nextObj.y;
        noo._alpha = 30;
        noo.onEnterFrame = function() {
            this._alpha += 5;
            if (this._alpha>=100) {
                delete this.onEnterFrame;
            }
        };
        noo.createTextField("tex", 1, 0, 0, 100, 100);
        noo.tex.text = nextObj.char;
        noo.tex.embedFonts = true;
    ```

```
        noo.tex.selectable = false;
        noo.tex.setTextFormat(mt);
        if (charPos.length == 0) {
            delete this.onEnterFrame;
            return;
        }
    }
}
```

3. We can make this run faster by putting the whole thing in a loop, duplicating more letters each frame:

```
function drawNext() {
    for (var i = 0; i<4; i++) {
        this.count++;
        var next = Math.floor(Math.random()*charpos.length);
        var nextObj = charPos[next];
        charPos.splice(next, 1);
        var noo = this.createEmptyMovieClip
        ➡("lett"+this.count, this.count);
        noo._x = nextObj.x;
        noo._y = nextObj.y;
        noo._alpha = 30;
        noo.onEnterFrame = function() {
            this._alpha += 5;
            if (this._alpha>=100) {
                delete this.onEnterFrame;
            }
        };
        noo.createTextField("tex", 1, 0, 0, 100, 100);
        noo.tex.text = nextObj.char;
        noo.tex.embedFonts = true;
        noo.tex.selectable = false;
        noo.tex.setTextFormat(mt);
        if (charPos.length == 0) {
            delete this.onEnterFrame;
            return;
        }
    }
}
```

This code will run fine if you replace the previous drawNext function with it. Save your movie as useCharPosFurther.fla and test it. You'll see that this time, the letters fade in at random to compose the text string:

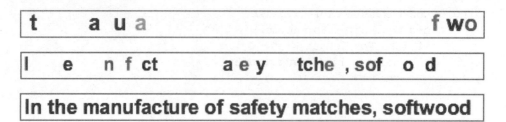

With this basis established, it's fairly easy to go on and create quite advanced text effects – you could for example implement our `slideTo` function with this to have the letters slide into place one-by-one, or swing into place.

Once we know where each letter has to end up, we can do whatever we want with each letter movie clip before putting it in its final position. There are three extra source files included with this chapter, illustrating the kind of effects that can be achieved just by changing a few lines of code. The first file, `useCharPosSwingTo.fla` places each letter slightly offset from its proper position and uses the swing motion from the first chapter to move each letter into place. The second file, `useCharPosScaleTo.fla` introduces each letter at an increased scale and offset slightly, scaling them down to normal size and moving into position gradually. The third file, `useCharPosScaleTo2.fla` works on the same principle, but brings in the letters in order, rather than randomly.

η t e a fa tur o f s f atches **S** wo d lo s ar p e in o n co tinu o **S** g, or v e r	In the manufacture o f safety matches , s o f wo**d**
useCharPosScaleTo.fla	**useCharPosScaleTo2.fla**

Enhancing the picture navigation interface

What we're going to do now is rework the example we put together in Chapter 1. We're going to start again from scratch using different photographs. This time we're going to make it a little more dynamic, so we don't have to place all the photos manually, and we're also going to add a text effect, which will be triggered when the photo slides into place. Although this is a new file we will be using some of the code from the earlier exercise.

In the final chapter of this section, we'll look at how we can load in the images dynamically, but for now we're going to import them into the Flash file. We're going to place each image in its own movie clip and then attach them to the stage dynamically.

Dynamically positioning images and adding text effects

1. To start with, import all of the images (pic1.jpeg to pic8.jpeg from the CD) and place them in movie clips. Name them "pic1" to "pic8" and in the linkage dialog, set to export for ActionScript, again with the names "pic1" to "pic8", also make their **Registration** top left.

2. Now on the main stage we'll set up some basic variables for the movie. This is information about the size of the movie and the size of the images. We'll use this information to center the images on stage:

   ```
   stageWidth=550;
   stageHeight=400;
   imageWidth=410;
   imageHeight=308;
   speed=3;
   ```

   Including all this information as variables means that if we wanted to use the code again with different sized images or a different sized stage, the transition would be relatively painless. We've also added a speed variable to control the speed of the slide.

3. From the stageWidth and stageHeight variables we can calculate where the image must be placed, to be centered on stage. If your clips are center aligned, you can calculate the left-hand side of the image by subtracting the width of the image from the width of the stage and then dividing it by two. stageWidth minus imageWidth will be the amount of space on either side of the image so dividing this space by two ensures equal space on either side of the image:

   ```
   topPos=(stageHeight-imageHeight)/2;
   leftPos=(stageWidth-imageWidth)/2;
   ```

4. We're going to set up the movie with the picture centered on stage, and a row of text buttons underneath the picture. We need a textFormat object for these buttons and another textFormat object for the text effect that will appear on top of the image:

   ```
   buttonTextFormat=new TextFormat("_sans",9,0x87A7E2,true);
   captionTextFormat=new TextFormat("Arial",30,0xffffff,true);
   ```

5. We're going to embed the Arial font, but not the _sans, so put a text field offstage, set the font to Arial, set it to dynamic text and embed all characters as we did before. Make sure

bold is checked as we've specified this in our `TextFormat` object. It doesn't have to be the font I've specified, I've just used Arial as everybody should have it, as long as the font in the string matches the font onstage everything should work fine.

6. Next we'll define an array containing the linkage identifiers of the pictures we want to add and the title we want to go with each of them. We create each element of the array as an object containing two properties, link and title:

```
images=[{link:"pic1",title:"MAY 15 2002"},
        {link:"pic2",title:"MARCH 12 2002"},
        {link:"pic3",title:"JANUARY 23 2002"},
        {link:"pic4",title:"APRIL 30 2001"},
        {link:"pic5",title:"JUNE 07 2002"},
        {link:"pic6",title:"JULY 12 2002"},
        {link:"pic7",title:"AUGUST 25 2002"},
        {link:"pic8",title:"DECEMBER 01 2002"}
        ]
```

Now to place the images on stage we need to create a function. As in the **Chapter 1** example we're going to have all of the images inside one movie clip and move that to slide the images to the correct position. So in the function we first need to create an empty movie clip, "imageHolder", which we'll place at the `leftpos` and `topPos` coordinates we calculated above. Now to attach the images we'll loop through our images array and use the link property to pull the respective movie clips from the library. We place a reference to the newly created movie clip in our images array as an extra property "mov", so that we have all this information in one central register. As we attach each movie clip we'll increment a variable `currx` by `imageWidth`. We use this value to set the X position of each movie clip, ensuring that they are adjacent:

```
function populateImages(imageArr,imageWid){
  _root.createEmptyMovieClip("imageHolder",++this.depth)
  imageHolder._x=leftpos;
  imageHolder._y=topPos;
  var currx=0;
  for(var i=0;i<imageArr.length;i++){
    imageHolder.depth++;
    //attach image movieclip at currx
    imageArr[i].mov=imageHolder.attachMovie(imageArr[i].link,
    ➡"image"+i,imageHolder.depth,{_x:currx,_alpha:102});
    //increase currx
    currx+=imageWidth;
  }
}
```

Note that we've used the ability to pass values with `attachMovie` to set the movie clips' X position and alpha:

```
imageArr[i].mov=imageHolder.attachMovie(imageArr[i].link,
➥"image"+i,imageHolder.depth,{_x:currx,_alpha:102})
```

We've set the movie clips' alpha to 102 to cure the image-shifting problem that can occur when moving images in Flash. I'm not sure why that works, but it does. You can try removing it when we've finished and you'll see the difference. If you run the code now you'll see at least two of the movie clips sitting on stage next to each other.

7.   Next we create the buttons:

```
function createButtons(imageArr,tF){
  _root.createEmptyMovieClip("buttonHolder",++this.depth)
  buttonHolder._x=leftPos+10;
  buttonHolder._y=topPos+imageHeight+5;
  var currx;
  for(var i=0;i<images.length;i++){
    // attach empty movieclip for button to sit in
    var nooButton=buttonHolder.createEmptyMovieClip
    ➥("button"+i,i);
    // place button at currx
    nooButton._x=currx;
    nooButton.item=imageArr[i];
    nooButton.createTextField("texta",1,0,0,1,1);
    nooButton.texta.autoSize=true;
    var caption = i>9 ? i+1 :"0"+(i+1);
    nooButton.texta.text=caption;
    nooButton.texta.setTextFormat(tF);
    nooButton.onPress=function(){
       _root.centerPic(this.item)
    }
    currx+=nooButton.texta.textWidth+5
  }
}
```

We create another blank movie clip, "buttonHolder" to hold each of the individual buttons. We place this movie clip just to the right of the left edge of the images and slightly below the bottom (`topPos+imageHeight`):

```
_root.createEmptyMovieClip("buttonHolder",++this.depth);
buttonHolder._x=leftPos+10;
buttonHolder._y=topPos+imageHeight+5;
```

We then loop through the image array again, adding a button for each element in the array, i.e. one for each picture. Inside each button we create a variable "item" which contains a reference to the element in the image array that it corresponds to. We can use this to access the other information about the image, e.g. the movie clip that represents it. Next we add a textField inside each variable, using the TextFormat object we created above. We use the value of i to set the text in the TextField. If the value of i is less than one character, we put a 0 in front of it. While at the moment this is irrelevant as we only have 8 images, it allows for future expansion:

```
var caption = i>9 ? i+1 :"0"+(i+1);
nooButton.texta.text=caption;
```

We set an onPress function in the button to call a function centerPic, passing the "item" variable that we created earlier. This function will be what moves the pictures.

```
nooButton.onPress=function(){
    _root.centerPic(this.item)
}
```

Finally we take care of positioning, incrementing the value of the current X position by the width of the TextField plus a little extra to ensure everything's even.

8. Next we need to create the motion. We'll use the slideTo function that we created earlier to manage this:

```
MovieClip.prototype.slideTo=function(x,y,speed,callbackObj,
➥callbackFunc){
    if(this.slideControl){
        var noo=this.slideControl
    }else{
        var noo=this.createEmptyMovieClip
        ➥ ("slideControl",++this.depth)
    }
    noo.tx=x;
    noo.ty=y;
    noo.speed=speed;
    noo.callBackObj=callBackObj;
    noo.callBackFunc=callBackFunc;
    noo.onEnterFrame=function(){
        this._parent._x+=(this.tx-this._parent._x)/this.speed;
        this._parent._y+=(this.ty-this._parent._y)/this.speed;
        if(Math.abs(this.tx-this._parent._x)<0.2 &&
            ➥Math.abs(this.ty-this._parent._y)<0.2){
            this._parent._x=this.tx;
            this._parent._y=this.ty;
```

```
            this.callBackObj[this.callBackFunc](this._parent)
            this.removeMovieClip ()
        }
    }
}
```

9. Now we add the function to trigger this, `centerPic`:

```
function centerPic(item){
    // if the picture is not already centered
    if(item!=_root.currentPicture){
        _root.currentPicture =item;
        var mov=item.mov;
        var x=leftPos-mov._x;
        var y=imageHolder._y;
        imageHolder.slideTo(x,y,speed,this,"triggerText");
        clearText();
    }
}
```

In this function we need to check whether the picture we're trying to center is already centered, we keep track of this in a variable, `_root.currentPicture`. If it isn't, we set it to be `_root.currentPicture` and then set about moving it. We extract the movie clip from the item passed (this was an entry in the images array, so we use the `mov` property). We then work out the position that `imageHolder` needs to move to as we did earlier (`leftPos` minus the movie clips's X position) and call `slideTo` to move it there. When we call `slideTo` we pass it a function "`triggerText`" which will trigger the text effect when the movie clip reaches its target. Finally we'll need to clear any text, which may already be there. To that end we'll call `clearText`.

10. If you run the code now, you should find that the pictures into position properly. Next we need to create a mask to hide the pictures around the chosen picture. We could do this using the drawing api, but for now we'll use a movie clip from the library. Create a new movie clip, "`square`" with its linkage set to "`square`" and inside it draw a 100x100 pixel square with its registration point at the top left corner.

11. Then add the following to your code:

```
function createMask(targ,x,y,wid,high){
// create init object containing values for scale and //position
    var obj={_x:x,_y:y,_xscale:wid,_yscale:high};
    _root.attachMovie("square","maska",++depth,obj);
    targ.setMask(maska);
}
```

Something I noticed when doing this, which may be of interest is that if we try to set the _width and _height of a movie clip when attaching it using the initObj as we do here, it will fail and you won't see the movie clip. This makes sense as it seems like the values passed are set before anything else happens in the movie clip and thus it doesn't know what's inside the movie clip to be able to set the width or height of.

12. Now we deal with the text effect element. First off all we calculate the characters and character positions from each image. We loop through the images array and call a charPositions function for each element, storing the results as characterArr within each image object:

```
function setCharPositions(imageArr,tF){
  for(var i in imageArr){
    imageArr[i].characterArr=charPositions
    ➡ (tf,imageArr[i].title,10000)
  }
}
```

13. The charPositions function has been slightly modified from what we looked at earlier. I've highlighted the parts that have been changed. There are two main differences. The first difference is that it uses the textWidth and textHeight of the TextField object to work out where the whole piece of text needs to be placed. This is added to the X and Y coordinates as an offset. The second difference is that now the array that it returns now contains objects, each with properties for the X and Y coordinate and the relevant character:

```
function charPositions(tFormat,str,depth){
  _root.createTextField("temp",depth,0,-300,100,400);
  temp.autoSize=true;
  temp.embedFonts=tru;e
  temp.setNewTextFormat(tFormat);
  temp.text=str;
  var arr=[];
  var totalWidth=temp.textWidth;
  var leftEdge=(stageWidth-totalWidth)/2;
  var height=temp.textHeight;
  var topEdge=(stageHeight-height)/2;
  for(var i=0;i<str.length;i++){
    temp.text=str.substr(i);
    var xp=totalWidth-temp.textWidth;
    arr[i]={x:xp+leftEdge,y:topEdge,char:str.charAt(i)};
  }
  return arr;
}
```

14. So at this point, we have an extra entry for each image in our images array containing the positions for all of the characters. Next we have to create the `triggerText` function, which we'll use to position the letters. The bulk of this will be familiar from earlier. We're picking a character at random from the caption and fading it in. There are several things of note that I've highlighted.

```
function triggerText(){
  depth++
  latestText=_root.createEmptyMovieClip
  ➡("textHolder"+depth,depth);
  latestText.characters=currentPicture.characterArr.slice();
  latestText.movs=[];
  latestText.onEnterFrame=function(){
    this.count++;
    var next=Math.floor(Math.random()*
    ➡this.characters.length);
    var nextObj=this.characters[next];
    this.characters.splice(next,1);
    var noo=this.createEmptyMovieClip
    ➡("lett"+this.count,this.count);
    noo._x=nextObj.x;
    noo._y=nextObj.y;
    noo._alpha=30;
    noo.onEnterFrame=function(){
      this._alpha+=5;
      if(this._alpha>=100){
        delete this.onEnterFrame
      }
    }
    noo.createTextField("tex",1,0,0,100,100);
    noo.tex.text=nextObj.char;
    noo.tex.embedFonts=true;
    noo.tex.selectable=false;
    noo.tex.setTextFormat(_root.captionTextFormat);
    this.movs.push(noo);
    if(this.characters.length==0){
      delete this.onEnterFrame;
      return;
    }
  }
  latestText.remove=function(){
    var next=Math.floor(Math.random()*this.movs.length);
    this.movs[next].removeMovieClip();
    this.movs.splice(next,1);
    if(this.movs.length==0){
```

continues overleaf

```
        this.removeMovieClip();
    }
  }
}
```

The first thing to notice is that we've created a separate movie clip for the text effect. This acts both as a holder movie clip for the individual letter movie clips and as a control clip, first creating the letters and then removing them again when we switch photos. We store the latest textHolder movie clip in a variable, latestText. When we switch photographs the text in latestText should be cleared. When we create the holder movie clip we need to know what all the letters are and where they should go and we use the characters array of the current picture to get this information. As we're going to be removing elements of this array, we use slice to create a copy of the array in the movie clip so that we don't touch the original. The slice method is used generally to return elements from an array between two points, so arr.slice (2,5) would return a copy of elements 2 to 5 of the array. When you call it without any arguments it returns a copy of the whole array.

```
latestText.characters=currentPicture.characterArr.slice()
```

15. The final section of the function defines a function "remove" to be called onEnterFrame to remove all the letters from the clip and then itself when it's done. To complete things we add a function clearText to initiate this:

```
function clearText(){
   _root.latestText.onEnterFrame=_root.latestText.remove
}
```

16. The final lines of code we add are the calls to the functions we have defined, to put the images on stage, create the buttons, calculate the character positions, create the mask and finally center the first image.

```
populateImages(images,imageWidth);
createButtons(images,buttonTextFormat);
setCharPositions(images,captionTextFormat);
createMask(imageHolder,leftPos,topPos,imageWidth,imageHeight);
centerPic(images[0]);
```

That completes our enhanced picture interface. Save it and give it a test – everything should run perfectly.

01 02 03 04 05 06 07 08

Summary

In this chapter we've seen how the textFormat object works, how to use the properties of the TextField object and how to use these capabilities to create text effects, both on their own and integrated into a larger interface. There are a number of ways to take this further and create more advanced text effects. From the basics, we've established it would be fairly easy to allow the user to enter the text to be used in the text effect and to integrate more complex motion, such as using sine waves or circular motions, and so on. Once the final position for the letters has been established, how you get them there is up to you.

In the next chapter we'll look at the drawing API, get to grips with its methods and employ it in conjunction with shared objects to create a basic drawing application.

section 1: Site Presentation

chapter 3: Drawing API

In this chapter we're going to look at the drawing API – a new feature to Flash MX that lets you create new graphical content on the fly. We'll start by covering some of its basic methods and how they work, before moving on to see how we can extend the power of the drawing API – writing additional methods to draw squares, for example.

In particular, we will look at using the drawing API to:

- Draw straight and curved lines.

- Draw curved lines through a specified point.

- Fill an area with a solid color or gradient.

- Use shared objects to create a sketchpad that lets us save pictures locally.

Drawing a straight line

There are two things we need to know about the drawing API before we look at how to draw a straight line:

1. Each movie clip has a current drawing position, which we can set using the `moveTo` function. Each movie clip is initialized at its default drawing position, which is (0,0).

2. Each movie clip has a `lineStyle` property, which determines the appearance of any lines drawn inside the movie clip. If we don't set the `lineStyle`, any lines we draw will not appear. (This is sometimes useful though, as we'll see when we move on to adding fills.)

So, to draw a straight line – open the Actions panel and place the following code into frame 1 of your new movie, and then test it.

```
this.lineStyle(3, 0x000000);
this.lineTo(200, 100);
```

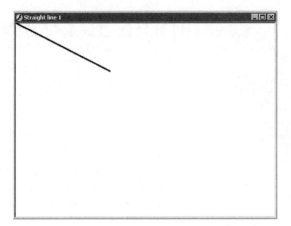

This draws a line from the top left corner of the stage to (200,100). Using the `lineStyle` function, we've set the line to be three pixels wide and black. You can also include an optional third argument to set the alpha of the line – this defaults to 100 if you don't include it. If you don't specify a color a black line is drawn.

If we want the line to start somewhere else we use the `moveTo` function:

```
this.lineStyle(3, 0x000000);
this.moveTo(200, 0);
this.lineTo(200, 100);
```

As you can see, `moveTo` relocates the drawing position without drawing a line, whereas `lineTo` draws a line and moves the drawing position:

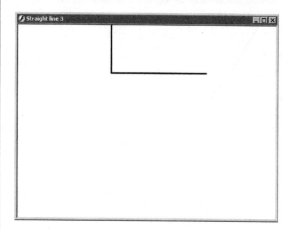

```
this.lineStyle(3, 0x000000);
this.moveTo(200, 0);
this.lineTo(200, 100);
this.lineTo(400, 100);
```

That's all it takes to draw a straight line, although we'll also use the `lineTo` function to define the edge of a filled area in a moment.

Drawing a curved line

A curved line works in a similar way, but we have to specify two sets of points:

```
this.curveTo(controlX, controlY, anchorX, anchorY);
```

The line will be drawn from the current drawing position to anchorX, anchorY, with the value of controlX and controlY determining the way in which the line curves. One way to understand how the controlX and controlY values affect the curve is to imagine this as a third point that acts almost like a magnet, bending the line towards it. For example, try the following:

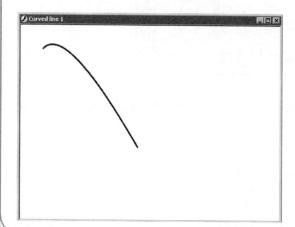

```
this.lineStyle(3, 0x000000);
this.moveTo(50, 50);
this.curveTo(100, 0, 250, 250);
```

...and then compare it to this, with different control points:

```
this.lineStyle(3, 0x000000);
this.moveTo(50, 50);
this.curveTo(200, 300, 250,
➡250);
```

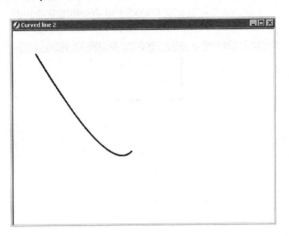

To help visualize the way the control point affects the curve, we'll put together a quick movie with three draggable handles – one for each end of the line and the third representing the control point.

1. Open a new Flash file and draw a simple shape like a circle. Next, convert it to a movie clip with a center registration point and name it `point`.

2. Select the movie clip in the Library and click the white menu icon. From the menu, select the **Linkage...** option to bring up the **Linkage Properties** dialog window. Check the **Export for ActionScript** option and set the linkage **Identifier** to `point`:

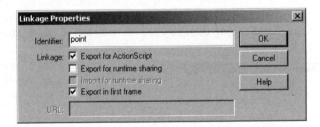

3. Delete your instance of `point` from the stage and add the following code to the main timeline:

```
_quality = "LOW";
this.attachMovie("point", "start_mc", 1);
this.attachMovie("point", "end_mc", 2);
this.attachMovie("point", "control_mc", 3);
```

This has given us three instances of point on stage, named start_mc, end_mc, and control_mc. We now need to set each point up so that we can drag them around and redraw the curve to fit the points.

4. To achieve this, we need an onPress function to start the drag, an onRelease function to stop the drag, and an onMouseMove function to execute the drag and redraw the curve. Add the following ActionScript beneath what you've already included:

```
function dragOn() {
// sets the mousemove handler of the movieclip to 'dragMe'
    this.onMouseMove = dragMe;
}
function dragOff() {
// clears the mousemove handler of the movieclip.
    delete this.onMouseMove;
}
function dragMe() {
// moves the movieclip to the position of the mouse
    this._x = _root._xmouse;
    this._y = _root._ymouse;
// calls the redraw function in the parent clip ie the _root
    this._parent.reDraw();
}
```

5. We now need to assign these functions to the event handlers of our movie clips and there are two options available to us. Here's the most obvious choice:

```
start_mc.onPress = dragOn;
end_mc.onPress = dragOn;
control_mc.onPress = dragOn;
```

However, there's actually a better way to do this. In Flash MX, the attachMovie method has a very useful piece of extra functionality that allows us to pass an object when we're attaching the new movie clip. As the movie clip is attached, all of the properties of this object are copied into the new movie clip.

6. So, we'll create an object containing all the information for onPress, onRelease and onMouseMove, which we'll pass in the attachMovie function so that all the assignments are taken care of for us. We pass the object to attachMovie as the fourth argument – here's the new code, highlighted in bold:

```
_quality = "LOW";
// set up an init object
initObj = {onPress:dragOn, onRelease:dragOff,
```

```
⮕onReleaseOutside:dragOff, useHandCursor:false};
// pass the init object when we call attachMovie
this.attachMovie("point", "start_mc", 1, initObj);
this.attachMovie("point", "end_mc", 2, initObj);
this.attachMovie("point", "control_mc", 3, initObj);
```

If you run this code now you'll be able to drag and drop the movie clips.

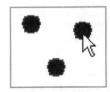

7. Our final task is to define the function for drawing the curve. First, we call `this.clear()`, which clears any lines or fills already drawn in the current scope. Next, we set the `lineStyle` to black and draw the curve form `start_mc` to `end_mc`, using `control_mc` as the anchor point for the curve. Finally, we draw a red line with an alpha of 30 from `end_mc` to `control_mc`, and from `control_mc` to `start_mc`.

```
function redraw() {
    this.clear();
    this.lineStyle(2, 0x000000);
    this.moveTo(start_mc._x, start_mc._y);
    this.curveTo(control_mc._x, control_mc._y, end_mc._x,
    ⮕ end_mc._y);
    this.lineStyle(2, 0xFF5555, 30);
    this.lineTo(control_mc._x, control_mc._y);
    this.lineTo(start_mc._x, start_mc._y);
}
```

8. Save your movie as `Curve with anchor.fla` and test it.

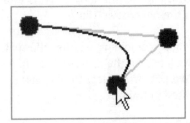

9. You'll now be able to clearly see the effect that a differing anchor point has on the trajectory of the curve. We'll come back to the precise characteristics of the curve after looking at fills and how to make a curve pass through a certain point.

Adding fills

Drawing a number of lines to create a path creates a fill. The general way to create a fill is by first calling beginFill and then drawing lines. Note that a lineStyle does not have to be specified. If no lineStyle is specified, the fill will be created with no outline. Here's the ActionScript for drawing a filled square:

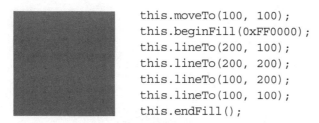

```
this.moveTo(100, 100);
this.beginFill(0xFF0000);
this.lineTo(200, 100);
this.lineTo(200, 200);
this.lineTo(100, 200);
this.lineTo(100, 100);
this.endFill();
```

We can add an outline by adding a lineStyle call:

```
this.moveTo(100, 100);
this.lineStyle(2, 0x000000);
this.beginFill(0xFF0000);
this.lineTo(200, 100);
this.lineTo(200, 200);
this.lineTo(100, 200);
this.lineTo(100, 100);
this.endFill();
```

Note that although the ActionScript dictionary doesn't mention this, it's possible to clear a lineStyle once it is set by calling lineStyle without any parameters. So, here we can have an outline for just half of our square:

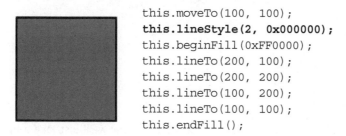

```
this.moveTo(100, 100);
this.lineStyle(2, 0x000000);
this.beginFill(0xFF0000);
this.lineTo(200, 100);
this.lineTo(200, 200);
this.lineStyle();
this.lineTo(100, 200);
this.lineTo(100, 100);
this.endFill();
```

With this approach, the `lineTo` functions take the drawing position back to where it started. In actual fact, `endFill` closes the path anyway and draws a straight line back to the start position. So, it's possible to trim a line of code and still draw a red square like this:

```
this.moveTo(100, 100);
this.beginFill(0xFF0000);
this.lineTo(200, 100);
this.lineTo(200, 200);
this.lineTo(100, 200);
this.endFill();
```

Fills also work with `curveTo` and we can draw a bowed square like this:

```
this.moveTo(100, 100);
this.beginFill(0xFF0000);
this.curveTo(150, 50, 200, 100);
this.curveTo(250, 150, 200, 200);
this.curveTo(150, 250, 100, 200);
this.curveTo(50, 150, 100, 100);
this.endFill();
```

Adding gradient fills

We'll be coming back to gradient fills a little later in the book, so for now we'll just take a brief look at one of the ways we can use the `beginGradientFill` function. `beginGradientFill` requires a number of parameters – we must pass arrays containing the different colors to be used, the alphas for the colors, the ratios of the colors, and finally an array containing values for the X and Y coordinates as well as the width and height of the gradient. Here's what `beginGradientFill` looks like in the ActionScript dictionary:

```
myMovieClip.beginGradientFill(fillType, colors, alphas, ratios,
➥matrix);
```

With the first method of using the function, the `matrix` argument refers to a 3 x 3 matrix that is used to control the appearance of the gradient, skewing, scaling, rotating and translating the gradient. We're going to leave this version of the function for now, as it is covered in detail later on in the book.

Using the simpler method, the matrix object that we pass contains width, height, starting X and Y positions and a rotation value. It also contains a final property `matrixType` which must always be set to `box`. When we define the gradient with width and height, the area specified is where the gradient takes effect. For example, if we define a linear gradient with X=100, Y=100, width=100 and height=100, the gradient will be in effect from 100 to 200 on the x-axis. The right and left of the gradient area will simply be flat color.

If you look at the following code, the gradient's X position is 120 and it is 60 wide. The shape we draw displays from 100 to 200 on the x-axis, meaning that from 100 to 120 we have flat pink and from 180 to 200 we have flat orange.

```
this.moveTo(100, 100);
colors = [0x 0xFFE4E1, 0xFF6600];
alphas = [100, 100];
ratios = [23, 255];
matrix = {matrixType:"box", x:120, y:30, w:60, h:10, r:0};
beginGradientFill("linear", colors, alphas, ratios, matrix);
this.curveTo(150, 50, 200, 100);
this.curveTo(250, 150, 200, 200);
this.curveTo(150, 250, 100, 200);
this.curveTo(50, 150, 100, 100);
this.endFill();
```

The best way to get a feel for the way gradient fills are implemented is to play around with the values and note the effects. For example, in the matrix line in the ActionScript above, change r to equal Math.PI. You'll see that it rotates the gradient by 180 degrees (**pi radians**).

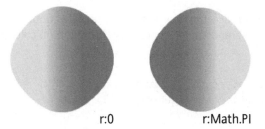

r:0   r:Math.PI

It's also interesting to move the X and Y position. Here, we have moved a radial fill up to the tip of our shape:

```
this.moveTo(100, 100);
colors = [0xFFE4E1, 0xff6600];
alphas = [100, 100];
ratios = [23, 255];
matrix = {matrixType:"box", x:100, y:30, w:100, h:100, r:1};
beginGradientFill("radial", colors, alphas, ratios, matrix);
this.curveTo(150, 50, 200, 100);
this.curveTo(250, 150, 200, 200);
```

continues overleaf

```
this.curveTo(150, 250, 100, 200);
this.curveTo(50, 150, 100, 100);
this.endFill();
```

The method appears intimidating at first sight but becomes a lot more intuitive once you get a feel for what the numbers do. You might try creating an enterFrame function that would vary these values. With a little experimentation, it's possible to achieve some quite subtle effects.

A draw square function

While the drawing methods provided are useful, it's helpful to create wrapper functions that combine different aspects of their functionality. For example, if we want to draw a square we don't want to have to go through the same procedure every time of setting the fill color and the lineStyle, moving the drawing position, drawing the lines, and closing the fill again. So, we create a function where we can pass all the parameters so that the square will be drawn for us.

When creating a function like this, the first thing to do is outline all the parameters we might need. For this we'll need X and Y coordinates, width, height, fill color and alpha, line color, weight and alpha:

```
MovieClip.prototype.drawSquare = function(x, y, w, h, fillCol,
➡fillAlpha, lineCol, lineWeight, lineAlpha) {

};
```

The order we choose to place the parameters in the function definition is important. For example, we might want to regularly draw a square without a line around the edge. Instead of creating a separate function to draw a square without an outline, we can put all of the parameters for the line style at the end of our function definition and omit them when we call the function. If this is the case, the values for lineCol, lineWeight and lineAlpha will show up as 'undefined', and we'll know not to draw an outline.

So, inside the function we're first going to need to set the `lineStyle` and fill color, and move the drawing position to the (X, Y) position we have specified:

```
MovieClip.prototype.drawSquare = function(x, y, w, h, fillCol,
➡fillAlpha, lineCol, lineWeight, lineAlpha) {
    this.moveTo(x, y);
    // check if a line colour has been specified
    if (lineCol) {
        this.lineStyle(lineWeight, lineCol, lineAlpha);
    } else {
        this.lineStyle();
    }
    this.beginFill(fillCol, fillAlpha);
};
```

So we check if the `lineCol` argument has been passed. If it has, we set the `lineStyle` accordingly. If not, we call `lineStyle` with no parameters to clear any `lineStyle` that might already have been set in the movie clip.

Another decision we make is based on whether the user doesn't pass a `lineAlpha` argument (`lineAlpha` will default to zero if not). We might, though, want to legislate against this, and change the function to default to 100 if `lineCol` has been passed, but `lineAlpha` has not. Again, we just have to test if `lineAlpha` is undefined and act accordingly:

```
MovieClip.prototype.drawSquare = function(x, y, w, h, fillCol,
➡fillAlpha, lineCol, lineWeight, lineAlpha) {
    this.moveTo(x, y);
    if (lineCol != undefined) {
        if (lineAlpha == undefined) {
            lineAlpha = 100;
        }
        this.lineStyle(lineWeight, lineCol, lineAlpha);
    } else {
        this.lineStyle();
    }
    this.beginFill(fillCol, fillAlpha);
};
```

Now we have to draw the lines to delineate the area for our fill. We're starting at the top left and we'll then move around the square in a clockwise direction, drawing a line to each corner in turn. It might be useful to work out how we specify the coordinates:

Top left: (X, Y)
Top right: (X + width, Y)
Bottom right: (X + width, Y + height)

Bottom left:(X, Y + height)

Now we just need to draw a line to each of these points in turn and then end the fill:

```
MovieClip.prototype.drawSquare = function(x, y, w, h, fillCol,
➥fillAlpha, lineCol, lineWeight, lineAlpha) {
    this.moveTo(x, y);
    if (lineCol != undefined) {
        if (lineAlpha == undefined) {
            lineAlpha = 100;
        }
        this.lineStyle(lineWeight, lineCol, lineAlpha);
    } else {
        this.lineStyle();
    }
    this.beginFill(fillCol, fillAlpha);
    // top right
    this.lineTo(x+w, y);
    // bottom right
    this.lineTo(x+w, y+h);
    // bottom left
    this.lineTo(x, y+h);
    // top left.
    this.lineTo(x, y);
    // end the fill
    this.endFill();
};
```

and finally, we need to call this:

```
_root.drawSquare(100, 100, 200, 100, 0xFF0000, 100, 0xdddddd, 20,
➥50);
```

You'll notice that the outline created with the `lineTo` is centered on top of the edge of the square, so if we have an outline twenty pixels wide, then the square will be ten pixels wider on each side. The corners of the outline are also rounded, which might not be what you want. If you wanted to avoid this you could change the method to first draw a square for the outline and then draw a square on top of it for the fill.

Ultimately, how you set up a method like this is determined by how you intend to use it. For example, you might prefer to specify values for left, right, top and bottom rather than X, Y, width and height (as you may want to use it with the values returned by the `Movieclip.getBounds` function for instance). That's a fairly easy thing to implement.

```
MovieClip.prototype.drawSquare = function(left, right, top, bottom,
```

```
➡fillCol, fillAlpha, lineCol, lineWeight, lineAlpha) {
    this.moveTo(left, top);
    if (lineCol != undefined) {
        if (lineAlpha == undefined) {
            lineAlpha = 100;
        }
        this.lineStyle(lineWeight, lineCol, lineAlpha);
    } else {
        this.lineStyle();
    }
    this.beginFill(fillCol, fillAlpha);
    this.lineTo(right, top);
    // top right
    this.lineTo(right, bottom);
    // bottom right
    this.lineTo(left, bottom);
    // bottom left
    this.lineTo(left, top);
    // top left.
    this.endFill();
};
```

...and to call it:

```
// a square with left edge at 100, right edge at 200, top at
// 200 and bottom at 300:
this.drawSquare(100,200,200,300,0xff0000,100)
```

Finally, you could build in other things like a default color, or a default alpha for the fill, etc. It all depends on how you intend to most commonly use the method; there's no right or wrong way to do it – just a matter of tailoring it to suit your needs.

A draw circle function

We're going to look now at a method that allows us to draw circles with the drawing API. This method was written by Den Ivanov from **www.cleoag.com**, and is rather clever. Many methods for drawing circles depend on using curveTo to form a circle by drawing arcs. Den's method works on the basis that when Flash draws a line, it gives it rounded ends. So, if we draw a line that has a line weight of 100, it can be used to create a circle with a radius of 100 – in Den's function he draws 0.15 pixels from the current drawing position, which creates a perfect circle.

The parameters passed to the function are the X and Y coordinates of the center of the circle, and `cWidth` is the width of the outline:

```
function drawCircle(x, y, radius, cWidth) {
    mc = _root.createEmptyMovieClip("circle"+cnt,++cnt);
    mc.lineStyle(radius, 0x000000, 100);
    mc.moveTo(x, y);
    mc.lineTo(x, y+.15);
    mc.lineStyle(radius-cWidth, 0xffffff, 100);
    mc.moveTo(x, y);
    mc.lineTo(x, y+.15);
}
drawCircle(100, 100, 100, 20);
```

With this method, the outline is indented from the outside of the circle – it is included in the total radius. Note that we also create a movie clip in which to draw the circle.

We'll convert this to work the way we've had our other functions working and then add the ability to specify colors:

```
MovieClip.prototype.drawCircle = function (x, y, radius, cWidth) {
    this.lineStyle(radius, 0x000000, 100);
    this.moveTo(x, y);
    this.lineTo(x, y+.15);
    this.lineStyle(radius-cWidth, 0xffffff, 100);
    this.moveTo(x, y);
    this.lineTo(x, y+.15);
};
drawCircle(100, 100, 100, 20);
```

Now we'll add colors:

```
MovieClip.prototype.drawCircle = function(x, y, radius,
➥cWidth, innerCol, outerCol) {
    this.lineStyle(radius, outerCol, 100);
    this.moveTo(x, y);
    this.lineTo(x, y+.15);
    this.lineStyle(radius-cWidth, innerCol, 100);
    this.moveTo(x, y);
    this.lineTo(x, y+.15);
};
drawCircle(100, 100, 100, 10, 0xff0000, 0x000000);
```

We could also play with the order of the parameters here so that we could first specify fill color and radius before specifying outline width and outline color. You could also alter the function to allow variable alpha for the fill and outline, if you required that, for example if you wanted a circle with an outline but no fill.

Drawing a curve through a specified point

As we've seen, the way that the curveTo function is set up, we specify a start point, end point and a control point. Sometimes, though, it might be more convenient to have the curve pass through a specified point, so we'll write a function now to help us achieve this.

The curveTo function in Flash draws what's known as a quadratic bezier. Before Flash MX, curved lines had to be drawn by plotting a series of points on a curve and then duplicating line movie clips between those points, which was achieved by using an equation for a Bezier curve.

With this equation, we specify an end point, control point and a start point. The variable in this equation is t, which varies between 0 and 1, from the start of the curve to the end. We can plug in various values of t to arrive at the coordinates for any specific point on the curve.

Quadratic Bezier

x	x position that the curve passes through at t
x0	x position of the start point of curve
x1	x position of the control point of curve
X2	x position of the end point of curve
y	y position that the curve passes through at t
Y0	y position of the start point of curve
Y1	y position of the control point of curve
Y2	y position of the end point of curve
t	time

Here's the equation:

```
x = x0*t*t + x1*2*t*(1-t) + x2*(1-t)*(1-t)
y = y0*t*t + y1*2*t*(1-t) + y2*(1-t)*(1-t)
```

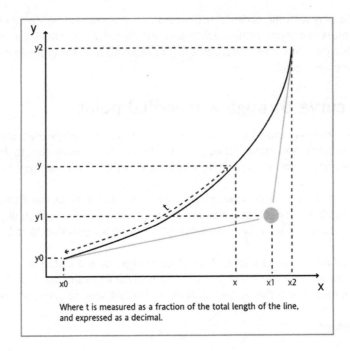

Where t is measured as a fraction of the total length of the line, and expressed as a decimal.

This equation is useful to find the specific position that the curve passes through at any point, t, from 0 to 1, i.e. from the beginning to the end of the curve. We plug in the start point, control point, end point and t to arrive at the position (X,Y) (where the curve passes through at this point).

We need to alter the function so that we can specify values for the start point (x0,y0), the end point (x2,y2) and the specific point (X,Y), and arrive at the necessary control point (x1,y1). In other words, we need to rework the function so that it looks something like this:

x1= whatever multiplied by x0, x2, x and t
y1= whatever multiplied by y0, y2, y and t

This is a reasonably simple matter. We'll work this out for the X equation and then duplicate our results, switching X for Y as the two equations are identical. First of all, we need to get the values of x1 and y1 on the left-hand side of the equation. We do this by subtracting from both sides:

x - x1*2*t*(1-t) = x0*t*t + x1*2*t*(1-t) + x2*(1-t)*(1-t) - x1*2*t*(1-t)

The values for plus and minus x1*2*t*(1-t) on the right-hand side cancel each other out:

x - x1*2*t*(1-t) = x0*t*t + ~~x1*2*t*(1-t)~~ + x2*(1-t)*(1-t) ~~- x1*2*t*(1-t)~~
x - x1*2*t*(1-t) = x0*t*t + x2*(1-t)*(1-t)

We now subtract x from both sides:

x - x1*2*t*(1-t) - x = x0*t*t + x2*(1-t)*(1-t) – x

~~x~~ - x1*2*t*(1-t) ~~- x~~ = x0*t*t + x2*(1-t)*(1-t) – x

-x1*2*t*(1-t) = x0*t*t + x2*(1-t)*(1-t) – x

-1*x1*2*t*(1-t) = x0*t*t + x2*(1-t)*(1-t) – x

Now multiply the -1 by the 2 on the left side of the equation:

x1*-2*t*(1-t) = x0*t*t + x2*(1-t)*(1-t) – x

Next, we divide both sides of the equation by (-2*t*(1-t)):

x1*(-2*t*(1-t)) / (-2*t*(1-t)) = (x0*t*t + x2*(1-t)*(1-t) – x) / (-2*t*(1-t))

On the left-hand side we have (-2*t*(1-t)) / (-2*t*(1-t)), which equals 1 so we can get rid of that:

x1 ~~(*-2 * t * (1-t))~~ / ~~(-2 * t * (1-t))~~ = (x0*t*t + x2*(1-t)*(1-t) – x) / (-2*t*(1-t))

x1 = (x0*t*t + x2*(1-t)*(1-t)–x) / (-2*t*(1-t))

That is the equation we need to find x1, so the equation for y1 will be:

y1 = (y0*t*t + y2*(1-t)*(1-t)–y) / (-2*t*(1-t))

We can now use this to create a function which we will pass values for x, y, x0, y0, x2, y2 and t in order to draw a curve from (x0,y0) to (x2,y2) that passes through (x,y) at the point on the curve specified by t.

The precise role of t will be clearer once you start plugging in numbers as it has a large effect on the shape of the curve. Within our function, we'll rename the values a, b and c for clarity. We'll call the function aToBThroughC to remind us what the significance of each value is. Here's the equation with a, b and c inserted:

```
controlX = (ax*t*t + bx*(1-t)*(1-t)–cx) / (-2*t*(1-t))
controlY = (ay*t*t + by*(1-t)*(1-t)–cy) / (-2*t*(1-t))
```

Now onto the function itself – we'll assume that we've set a lineStyle before the function to allow for ease of use:

```
MovieClip.prototype.aToBThroughC = function (ax, ay, bx, by, cx, cy,
➡t) {
    var controlX = (ax*t*t+bx*(1-t)*(1-t)-cx)/(-2*t*(1-t));
    var controlY = (ay*t*t+by*(1-t)*(1-t)-cy)/(-2*t*(1-t));
    this.moveTo(ax, ay);
    // for security
    this.curveTo(controlx, controly, bx, by);
};
```

Finally, to test this add:

```
this.lineStyle(27, 0xff0000);
this.aToBThroughC(100, 100, 250, 100, 200, 350, 0.5);
```

Save your file as AtoBthroughC.fla, and test it. You'll see that we've created quite a severely curved line:

To demonstrate that this is working properly we'll open up the curve with anchor.fla file we created earlier, and change it so that the third draggable point is the point that the curve passes through rather than the control point. The code that has been changed is highlighted in bold:

```
_quality = "LOW";
MovieClip.prototype.aToBThroughC = function(ax, ay, bx, by, cx, cy,
➡t) {
    var controlX = (ax*t*t+bx*(1-t)*(1-t)-cx)/(-2*t*(1-t));
    var controlY = (ay*t*t+by*(1-t)*(1-t)-cy)/(-2*t*(1-t));
    this.moveTo(ax, ay);
    // for security
    this.curveTo(controlx, controly, bx, by);
};
initObj = {onPress:dragOn, onRelease:dragOff,onReleaseOutside:dragOff,
```

continues overleaf

```
➥useHandCursor:false};
this.attachMovie("point", "start_mc", 1, initObj);
this.attachMovie("point", "end_mc", 2, initObj);
this.attachMovie("point", "control_mc", 3, initObj);
function dragOn() {
    this.onMouseMove = dragMe;
}
function dragOff() {
    delete this.onMouseMove;
}
function dragMe() {
    this._x = _root._xmouse;
    this._y = _root._ymouse;
    this._parent.reDraw();
}
function reDraw() {
    this.clear();
    this.lineStyle(2, 0xFF5555, 100);
    this.aToBThroughC(start_mc._x, start_mc._y, end_mc._x, end_mc._y,
    ➥control_mc._x, control_mc._y, 0.5);
}
```

You'll see that as you drag the points this time, the curve always passes through the third point:

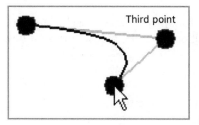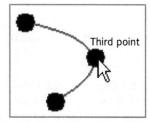

If you change the value of t you'll see the differing effect on the shape of the curve:

```
this.aToBThroughC(start_mc._x, start_mc._y, end_mc._x, end_mc._y,
➥control_mc._x, control_mc._y, 0.1);
}
```

t can be any value between 0 and 1, so as you can see there are a very large number of curves that will pass through our point c – one for every value between 0 and 1.

Making a sample application

In this section we're going to create a sample application where we can draw pictures and save the results to be viewed later. We'll do this in three stages:

- Allowing the user to draw with the mouse.

- Looking at how shared objects work to store information.

- Combining both together so that pictures can be stored and retrieved later.

While this application is hardly innovative, it will be instructive in terms of methodology and will give us an opportunity to look at how shared objects work; a powerful new feature of Flash MX.

Drawing

A simple drawing application is amazingly easy. We can do it with just thirteen lines of code – here's the procedure:

- When the user clicks, we move the current drawing position to the position of the mouse. We keep track of when the user moves the mouse, and when it is moved; we draw a line from where it was in the previous frame to where it is now.

- When the user releases, we end the line, stop tracking the mouse position, and stop drawing.

So, for this we need three functions – one for when the user clicks, one for when the user releases, and one for tracking the mouse position while the mouse button is down:

```
function drawOn() {
    this.lineStyle(1, 0x000000);
    this.moveTo(this._xmouse, this._ymouse);
    this.onMouseMove = addPoint;
}
function addPoint() {
    this.lineTo(this._xmouse, this._ymouse);
}
function drawOff() {
    delete this.onMouseMove;
}
this.onMouseDown = drawOn;
this.onMouseUp = drawOff;
```

That's it; all the code we need. With onMouseDown we set the lineStyle and move the drawing position to where the mouse is, as well as setting onMouseMove to addPoint.

Whenever the user moves the mouse we draw a line to the new mouse position. When the user releases the mouse button, we clear the onMouseMove handler.

Simply type the code into the Actions panel of a new movie, save it as doDrawing.fla and test it:

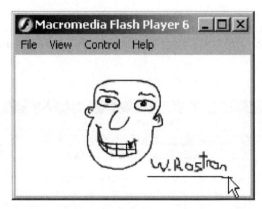

There you have it – a simple drawing interface with just thirteen lines of code.

OK – we'll now move on to look at how we can store and reproduce the drawing. To do this, we need to put the coordinates that constitute the drawing into an array. We'll also need to keep track of when the user has moved the mouse without drawing a line. For that purpose, we'll add a special value, "break", which will indicate that the pen has been picked up and moved elsewhere. The new code is highlighted in bold:

```
function drawOn() {
    this.lineStyle(1, 0x000000);
    this.moveTo(this._xmouse, this._ymouse);
    // add the new point to the array
    tempArr.push({x:_root._xmouse, y:_root._ymouse});
    this.onMouseMove = addPoint;
}
function addPoint() {
    // add the new point to the array
    tempArr.push({x:_root._xmouse, y:_root._ymouse});
    this.lineTo(_root._xmouse, _root._ymouse);
}
function drawOff() {
    // the pen is lifted so we add the value "break" to the array
    tempArr.push("break");
    delete this.onMouseMove;
}
tempArr = [];
```

continues overleaf

```
        this.onMouseDown = drawOn;
        this.onMouseUp = drawOff;
```

We've created an array `tempArr` to store all of our coordinates, in objects containing X and Y properties.

Save your movie as `doAndStoreDrawing.fla`. If you run the movie and select the **Debug > List Variables** menu option, you'll see all of the coordinates in the **Output** window for anything you may have drawn:

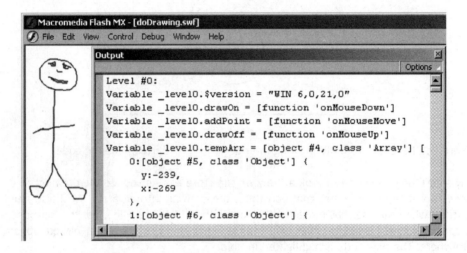

Before we look at how to redraw the picture from these coordinates, we'll look at how we can use shared objects to store the values.

Shared objects

Shared objects allow us to store data locally, on a user's hard drive in a controlled way. Basically, shared objects are like cookies for Flash. They enable us to store any data from our Flash movies locally, and they work from all browsers as well as the local Flash Player.

So, we've already mentioned that shared objects can be used to save data that represents artwork produced in a paint application created by the drawing API. Other potential uses for shared objects would be inside online forms, where they remember users' previous entries and auto-complete their names and addresses, etc. It would also be possible to produce a custom page on a shopping site, based on the user's previous buying habits.

Using a shared object

We're not going to go into huge detail about shared objects here, but we'll learn how to create a shared object and put it to work. If you want to learn more about shared objects and their application it's worth looking at this link (as the various properties and methods are not covered in the ActionScript dictionary provided with Flash):

www.macromedia.com/support/flash/action_scripts/local_shared_object

We're going to start with a very simple application:

1. Create a new movie, put a static text field on stage and write visit number inside it.

2. Now place a dynamic text field next to it and give it the instance name visited.

We're going to use the shared object to store the number of times we've viewed the page; it's a basic application, but covers just about all we need to know to continue with our drawing application.

3. Now create a new script layer so that we can begin to add the code to our basic application.

4. First of all we retrieve the sharedObject using SharedObject.getLocal. This retrieves the object if it's already been created and if it hasn't been created, it creates it for you. Put the following code into the Actions panel:

```
mySharedObj = SharedObject.getLocal("visits");
```

We now have a copy of the sharedObject in the variable mySharedObj. mySharedObj is an object that you can give properties to like any other, whether they're variables or arrays, etc. The parameter "visits" that we've passed is the name of the shared object, allowing you to have more than one shared object for each project.

5. We're now going to increment a variable visitCount and put its value in the text field we created. Add the next two new lines of ActionScript:

```
mySharedObj = SharedObject.getLocal("visits");
```

111

continues overleaf

```
//we increment a variable "visitCount" inside "data" where
//all the data resides in a shared object
mySharedObj.data.visitCount++;
visited.text = mySharedObj.data.visitCount;
```

6. We finally update the `sharedObject` – synchronizing it if you like, using the `flush` method, which basically puts everything from `mySharedObj` back into the actual sharedObject. Add the last line of script to your Actions panel:

```
mySharedObj = SharedObject.getLocal("visits");
mySharedObj.data.visitCount++;
visited.text = mySharedObj.data.visitCount;
mySharedObj.flush();
```

7. Save your movie as `sharedObj basics.fla`. If you run the movie multiple times you'll see the number increasing, (unless you deny the security request, and in a real situation we would want to take notice of this and act upon it).

visit number 6

Saving our picture data

OK – after going through that simple exercise, it should now be apparent that saving picture data from our drawing application will be a simple matter of storing the array of data in a shared object. We're going to create an interface that will list all the pictures that have been saved locally, and then give you the option to either draw a new picture or view an old one.

Here's a representation of what we will want:

Main Page:
Features:
```
Panel containing scrollable list of drawings
retrieved from sharedObject
```
Options:
```
Pick an existing drawing - go to redraw page
Do a new drawing - go to compose page
```

Redraw Page:
Features:
```
Previous drawing being redrawn
```
Options:
```
Go back to main page
```

Compose Page:
    Features:
```
    Ability to draw with mouse
```
    Options:
```
    Save current picture - save picture in sharedObject -
    go to main page
    Return - go back to main page
```

So, we can see that basically we have three states to our application: menu, drawing and redrawing. It's possible for us to sketch out some functions that we'll need as well:

Function name	Purpose
init	Set up some basic button handlers and then call drawPanel.
drawPanel	Retrieve data from sharedObject and turn off the back button and save button. Will call listDrawings and initScrollers.
listDrawings	Will populate the text field in the menu.
initScrollers	Will set the visibility of the scrollers for the text field.
initDraw	Will turn off the menu, turn on the back button and save button, and set the event handlers for onMouseDown and onMouseUp to enable drawing. Will also set up the lineStyle and create a temporary array in which to store the points.
drawOn	Will start drawing a line, setting onEnterFrame to addPoint.
addPoint	Will draw a line and add the current point to an array.
drawOff	Will turn addPoint off.
save	Will add the current array of points to the sharedObject and call backToMain.
backToMain	Will remove all frame/mouse events on the _root. Will also call drawPanel.
redraw	Will turn off the menu and turn on the back button. Will also set onEnterFrame.
drawNextPoint	Will draw the next point in the current drawing.

The fully functioning drawing application

Let's now get to work on our fully functional draw and save drawing application.

1. First of all we have some basic setup things to do. Create two button symbols, which we'll use to save our drawings and to go back through our eventual cache of pictures. It's up to you how you create your buttons – we've simply written 'Save' and 'Return' inside ours, with the text field set to 'use device fonts' and placed them in the bottom right-hand corner of the main stage.

Save   Return

2. Next, give the **Save** button an instance name of saverButton using the Property inspector, and give the **Return** button an instance name of backButton.

3. Create a movie clip symbol and name it listingsPanel. Inside the movie clip, create a new layer called textfield and insert a dynamic text field on this layer. Using the Property inspector, label the text field lista:

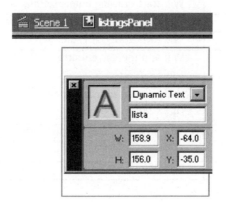

4. Create a new layer called background and draw a rectangle (ours is a pale gray, #F5F5F5) that's slightly bigger than the dynamic text field you just created. Underneath that I've drawn another rectangle, slightly darker (#E8E8E8) to make it stand out slightly. Then, drag the **background** layer beneath the **textfield** layer:

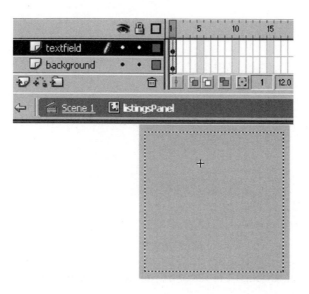

5. Still inside the **listingsPanel** movie clip, create a layer called new above the textfield layer. Inside the **new** layer, create a button symbol and give it the instance name newButton using the Property inspector. You can see that we've simply inserted the relevant text inside our button and placed it at the foot of the dynamic text field:

New

6. Create two new layers called upscroll and downscroll. Create a button symbol for scrolling up and another for scrolling down. I've just used text fields with the greater than and less than characters for mine. Place the symbol for scrolling up on the **upscroll** layer and using the Property inspector, give it an instance name upScroll. Place the other button symbol on the **downscroll** layer and give it an instance name downScroll. It's pretty self-explanatory which button is which – we've placed ours below the text field to the left of the **new** button:

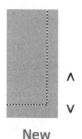

We could have used a component to achieve this simple scrolling functionality, but since we're dealing with components in the next chapter, we'll hold fire until then. That's our movie clip almost finished – the last thing to do is give it some sort of informative label. We created a new layer called `title` and inserted a static text field with the words 'List of drawings':

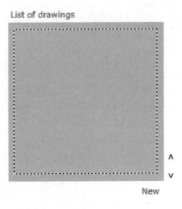

List of drawings

New

7.   That's the movie clip created. Now drag it on stage and name the instance `listingsPanel`.

We'll now step through the functions we outlined above, one by one, explaining the less obvious areas.

```
function drawPanel() {
    // turn off the back button and the save button
    backButton._visible = false;
    saverButton._visible = false;
    // make the menu panel visible
    this.listingsPanel._visible = true;
    // retrieve the shared object
    myPictureObj = SharedObject.getLocal("pictures");
    // list any drawings
    listDrawings(myPictureObj.data.arrays);
    // check if we need to turn on the scrollers
    initScrollers();
}
```

Here, we've initialized the shared object and stored it in `myPictureObj` as well as setting the visibility of some stage elements. Next, we call `listDrawings` to look through `myPictureObj` and retrieve how many drawings there are. We're going to store our arrays of points in an array called arrays in the `sharedObject` and we'll pass this array to the `listDrawings` function. There will be one array inside arrays for each drawing. Rather than creating a button for each drawing, we're going to use `asfunction`, which allows us to have a piece of HTML text behave as a link to an ActionScript function. Here's the format, of this is below:

```
asfunction:functionName, parameter;
```

8. We're going to use it to call `_root.redraw` and pass it the number of the array entry:

```
function listDrawings(pictureArray) {
    listingsPanel.lista.htmlText = "";
    // loop through the picture array
    for (var i = 0; i<pictureArray.length; i++) {
    // for each entry in the picture array add another line
    // to the text in the textfield
    var nexta = "<A HREF='asfunction:_root.redraw,"+i+"'>"+"
    ➡Drawing Number "+(i+1)+"</A><b/>";
        listingsPanel.lista.htmlText += nexta;
    }
}
```

9. Now we make the second function called by `drawPanel`. This simply sets the visibility of the scroll buttons depending on whether we are at the top or bottom of the text field and whether there are more lines of text than will fit inside it. We use `with` to switch our scope to inside the `listingsPanel` movie clip. We set `downScroll`'s `visible` property to `on` if the scroll value is less than the maximum possible scroll value. We set `upScroll`'s `visible` to `on` if the text field has been scrolled at all:

```
function initScrollers() {
    with (this.listingsPanel) {
        downScroll._visible = lista.scroll<lista.maxscroll;
        upScroll._visible = lista.scroll>1;
    }
}
```

Our list in actions should look something like this:

List of drawings

Drawing Number 2
Drawing Number 3
Drawing Number 4
Drawing Number 5
Drawing Number 6
Drawing Number 7
Drawing Number 8
Drawing Number 9
Drawing Number 10
Drawing Number 11
Drawing Number 12
Drawing Number 13
Drawing Number 14

10. Now we'll add the functions to draw, which should be largely familiar from before. First we have `initDraw`, which will be called when the user clicks the **new** button:

```
function initDraw() {
    // turn on the back and save buttons
    backButton._visible = true;
    saverButton._visible = true;
    // turn off the menu
    _root.listingsPanel._visible = false;
    // create an array for the points
    tempArr = [];
    _root.lineStyle(1, 0x000000);
    // set up out mouse event handlers
    _root.onMouseDown = drawOn;
    _root.onMouseUp = drawOff;
}
```

All that should be familiar – setting the visibility of the stage elements to leave the **back** button and the **save** button visible, then setting the `lineStyle` and creating an array for our points.

11. Finally, we assign the `onMouseDown` and `onMouseUp` handlers to trigger the drawing. These functions are exactly as we had earlier:

```
function drawOn() {
    this.moveTo(this._xmouse, this._ymouse);
    tempArr.push({x:this._xmouse, y:this._ymouse});
    this.onMouseMove = addPoint;
}
function addPoint() {
    tempArr.push({x:this._xmouse, y:this._ymouse});
    this.lineTo(this._xmouse, this._ymouse);
}
function drawOff() {
    tempArr.push("break");
    delete this.onMouseMove;
}
```

12. The next thing to do is create the function so that we can save the picture. This will be called when the `save` button is pressed and will save the `tempArr` in the sharedObject. Before we save the array we remove the last object, because a point object is placed in the array when the user clicks the button to save it (as `onMouseDown` is triggered). If we don't discard this, we may have problems with a stray line at the end of the picture.

```
function save() {
```

continues overleaf

```
// remove final element
tempArr.pop();
if (!myPictureObj.data.arrays) {
// if our array for pictures has not yet been created,
// create it
    myPictureObj.data.arrays = [];
}
// put the current picture array into the array
// containing all pictures
myPictureObj.data.arrays.push(tempArr);
// update the shared object
myPictureObj.flush();
// return to the menu screen
_root.backToMain();
}
```

Note that it first checks if the arrays array exists and if not, it creates it. It then pushes our tempArr to the end of this array and calls flush to save it in the object. After it has done this, it calls backToMain, which clears all the event handlers, and all drawing in the clip, before taking us back to the start:

```
function backToMain() {
    delete _root.onEnterFrame;
    delete _root.onMouseMove;
    delete _root.onMouseDown;
    delete _root.onMouseUp;
    _root.clear();
    _root.drawPanel();
}
```

13. Now for the final part – redrawing. We need two functions: redraw to start the redrawing and another drawNextPoint to continue each frame. The redrawing will work by moving through the array of points, drawing a line from the previous point to the current point each frame. When it hits break it will move to the point instead of drawing a line:

```
function redraw(num) {
    backButton._visible = true;
    this.listingsPanel._visible = false;
    // set count to zero, used to keep track of current point
    this.count = 0;
    // the array which we are redrawing
    this.currentArr = myPictureObj.data.arrays[num];
    this.lineStyle(1, 0x000000);
    this.moveTo(this.currentArr[0].x,this.currentArr[0].y);
    // every frame we draw the next point
```

continues overleaf

```
        this.onEnterFrame = drawNextPoint;
    }
```

14. So, this is the trigger function that retrieves the array of the target drawing and moves the drawing position to the first position in the array. It resets the count variable, which will be used to keep track of out position in the array, and finally sets the enterFrame function to drawNextPoint:

```
function drawNextPoint() {
    this.count++;
    // nextEntry is the next point object in the array
    var nextEntry = this.currentArr[this.count];
    if (nextEntry != "break") {
        this.lineTo(nextEntry.x, nextEntry.y);
    } else {
        // if the nextEntry is "break", we increment count
        // and move to the next point.
        this.count++;
        var nextEntry = this.currentArr[this.count];
        this.moveTo(nextEntry.x, nextEntry.y);
    }
    if (this.count>this.currentArr.length) {
        // we have drawn all available points
        delete this.onEnterFrame;
    }
}
```

So, with drawNextPoint we're incrementing our counter and setting a variable, nextEntry, to point to the next entry in the array. We check if this value equals "break" and if it does, we increment count and move to the next position in the array using moveTo. If it doesn't equal "break", we draw a line to the new position. Finally, we check if we've reached the end of the array – if so, we delete the onEnterFrame function and stop executing the action.

15. The final function is an initialize function, which will just set up handlers for the buttons, set the textField in listingsPanel to HTML text, and draw the panel for the first time:

```
function init() {
    this.saverButton.onPress = this.save;
    this.backButton.onPress = this.backToMain;
    with (this.listingsPanel) {
        newButton.onRelease = this.initDraw;
        // enable html text in the textfield
        lista.html = true;
        downScroll.onPress = function() {
```

continues overleaf

```
                    // scroll the textfield down
                    lista.scroll++;
                    // check if the scrollers should still appear
                    _root.initScrollers();
                };
                upScroll.onPress = function() {
                    lista.scroll--;
                    _root.initScrollers();
                };
            }
            drawPanel();
        }
```

16. We also add a call to this function to initialize the application:

```
init()
```

You can find the full code listing in the `drawingapp.fla`.

It would of course be possible to create all of this with code and that's something you might like to try, though it's useful to see how everything's going to lay out in the authoring environment.

Summary

We now have a decent handle on the way the drawing API works and how we can use it, as well as a grasp of the usefulness of shared objects. You could take the exercises in this chapter a lot further. For example, you could create a more fully featured drawing application, allowing the user to specify line color and weight, and add fills and maybe other graphical primitives. The drawing API also becomes useful when dealing with 3D and, in fact, anything when you want to move beyond stretching and skewing movie clips, to actually specifying points to create your own shapes. It's useful to note that once you've drawn in a movie clip with the drawing API, that that movie clip can then be used as a mask – the source of some very interesting effects. The shared object is also something with truly great potential. What it ultimately means is that we're no longer restricted to Flash as a discrete phenomenon. Flash movies or applications can now evolve over time, reacting and changing according to the user's behavior.

In the next chapter we'll be looking at another powerful new feature of Flash MX components, building on some of the work we've done this chapter. We'll be creating a tooltip component, and also going back to the site we created in the second chapter creating button components.

section 1: Site Presentation

chapter 4: **Components**

Components are one of the most powerful new features of Macromedia Flash MX. They allow us to create compact, reusable objects such as those included with Flash MX, such as scrollbars, drop-down menus and radio buttons. The ability to build components is a very useful skill, and the approaches we take to make our components flexible and self-contained can be applied to other areas of Flash. We can use the same approach whenever we want to create self–contained objects with their own internal logic that can be slotted into larger systems. When creating a component, we are basically creating a new class, a template from which we can instantiate objects with their own methods and properties. When we drag a component on stage we create an instance of this class. The component is a movie clip, but it is also part of the new class that we're defining; the new class inherits from the movie clip class, which means that it also has access to all the properties and methods of an ordinary movie clip.

The components included with Flash MX also inherit from another class called **FUIComponentClass**, providing each individual component with the methods to enable us to set broad behavioral features, text styles, colors, and so on, across all of the components. This adds a lot of flexibility to the way we can use Flash MX's components, but it also makes it somewhat difficult to learn how to make our components because you'll find there is a large amount of extra code intertwined with their core functionality. Combined with the lack of documentation on how to create **live previews** for components (so that their appearance updates on stage as its parameters are altered), creating components can be quite an involved task.

In this chapter we'll navigate through some of the mist and look at how to create a useful component from scratch, with a live preview on stage and a certain degree of flexibility. We'll gain an insight into the mechanics of a component and also consider what can be gained by employing a kind of 'object-oriented' scripting approach within Flash. All too often one finds the same examples of creating custom objects, a square object, a circle object, and so on, which are fine in terms of communicating the principles, but not necessarily the possible applications. In this chapter we'll gain more of an idea of the usefulness of such an 'object-oriented' approach in a practical situation, and we'll start by walking through the creation of a tooltip component.

The guts of a component

There are five things that almost every component will have, which will always need to be placed in the same order:

- An `initclip` statement

- The class definition

- An `Object.registerClass` statement

- Assignment of properties and methods

- An `endinitclip` statement

So, here's the basic framework for any component:

```
#initclip 0
// constructor
function tooltip() {
    this.init();
}
// set to inherit from MovieClip
tooltip.prototype = new MovieClip();
// register the class
Object.registerClass("tooltipMc", tooltip);
// definitions of properties & methods here
#endinitclip
```

Let's now examine each of these elements in turn:

The `initclip` and `endinitclip` statements enclose our class definition and designate it as a component definition. The code inside will be executed once, after the movie is initialized to define our class. The number 0 after the `initclip` statement is used to stipulate the order in which the component's classes are initialized, which can be important if one component depends on another. For example, with the components included with Flash MX, `FUIComponentClass` must be initialized before any of the components that inherit from it. So, `FUIComponentClass` has #initclip 0, where the individual component classes have #initclip 1. Our tooltip component will not be inheriting from any other component classes, so we can just leave it as #initclip 0. It doesn't matter if there is more than one component with the same #initclip number as long as the components do not have to inherit from each other.

After the `initclip` statement we have our constructor function, which will be called whenever a tooltip movie clip is instantiated – whether it is dropped on stage or attached dynamically. After the constructor we have the line that ensures our tool tip class inherits all of the properties and methods of a movie clip:

```
tooltip.prototype = new MovieClip();
```

It's essential that this statement precedes the definition of any properties or methods for our new class, or they'll be overwritten. The next statement associates a certain movie clip linkage with the tooltip class that we're creating:

```
Object.registerClass("tooltipMc", tooltip);
```

So in this case, any movie clip that has the linkage ID `tooltipMc` will automatically be a part of our tooltip class – this can be the movie clip in which we define the component or some other movie clip.

The `initclip` means that the class is created globally rather than just inside the movie clip, and is only defined once in each movie. When a movie clip that's registered with this class is placed on stage, we're effectively creating a new instance of this class; the constructor function is called as though it were inside the movie clip. After we've registered a movie clip with the class, we create all of the properties and methods for our class before finally closing our statement block with `endinitclip`.

Tooltip basics

Before we look at how we want the tooltip to operate – when it will appear, how to activate it and so on, we'll just look at how to create a tooltip graphic that we can put on stage and then specify its text and size and so on, using the **Component Parameters** panel.

1.   To start with we'll set up the basic framework, so create a new movie clip, name it `tooltip`, and place the following code on the first frame:

```
#initclip 1
function tooltip() {
    this.init();
}
tooltip.prototype = new MovieClip();
Object.registerClass("tooltipMc", tooltip);
#endinitclip
```

2. With the movie clip selected in the Library, right-click and choose the **Linkage...** option from the context-sensitive menu. In the **Linkage Properties** dialog box, select the **Export for ActionScript** checkbox and enter `tooltipMc` in the **Identifier** field. This will ensure that all instances of this movie clip are associated with the `tooltip` class.

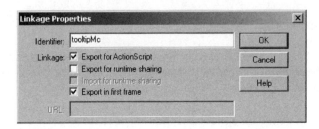

We now have to decide which parameters we want to define for the tooltip. At this stage, we only really need three parameters: a text value, then a Boolean value to specify whether fonts should be embedded or not, and finally a value for maximum width – if the text extends beyond this width, it should wrap onto the next line. Finally, we'll add a fourth value to specify whether or not to display the live preview.

3. To set these values as parameters for our component we need to use the **Component Definition** dialog box. With the **tooltip** movie clip selected in the Library, click the Library window's white menu icon and select the **Component Definition...** menu option to bring up the **Component Definition** dialog box:

You'll notice that the dialog box has four columns:

- The **Name** column contains the names of the parameters that we see in the Component Parameters panel (the Property inspector, when we have a component selected).

- The **Variable** column contains the variable names for the parameters; these are what will be available to us within the movie clip. If you like you can just specify a variable, or just specify a name – in which case the value entered will be both displayed in the Component Parameters panel and used as the variable name.

- The **Value** column contains the default values for each parameter.

- The **Type** column specifies the type of parameter, enabling access to the font list or color picker, as well as various types of drop-down.

Here are the values we need to add for our tooltip component. We can add values by clicking the button with the '**+**' icon, shown below:

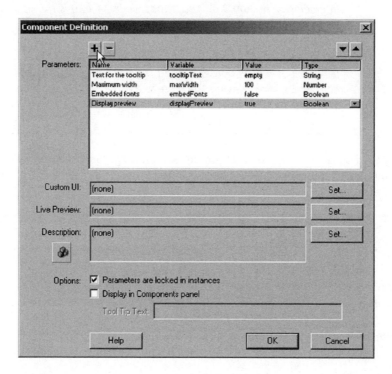

4. Enter the values as you see them in the screenshot above, and then click OK to confirm your choices.

You'll now see that the icon for the movie clip in the Library has changed to the component icon:

As a brief side note, it is possible to create your own icon for the component. To do this, create a graphic, 24 x 20 pixels, which can be a PNG, GIF or JPEG, although PNG is probably best as you can have the icon appear transparent. Import the graphic into the Flash file. Find the graphic in the Library and place it inside a new folder called fCustomIcons*. Once it's inside this folder, give it the same name as the component, 'tooltip' in this case, removing any file extension it may have. The icon is automatically associated with the component, and the Library symbol for the component should update immediately. It should be noted that while 24 x 20 is the size you use for the image file, so that the icon centers properly, the other icons that appear in the Library are probably no bigger than 20 x 20 pixels. When creating your icon it's best to leave a 2 or 3 pixel border around the edge of any graphical content to avoid having the icon touch the left edge of the Library panel.*

If you drag an instance of the component on stage and select it, you'll see that the Component Parameter panel will appear in the Property inspector and allow us to alter the values:

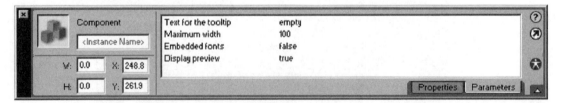

Note how we've hidden our variable values (maxWidth, tooltipText, embedFonts and displayPreview), and have the friendlier parameter names instead.

The next step is to make use of these parameters. As soon as the movie clip is initialized, all of these values are available as variables inside it, unlike the way in which we would normally call a constructor function with a number of parameters:

```
function tooltip(maxWidth, tooltipText,
embedFonts, displayPreview) {
}
new tooltip(300, "some text", false);
```

Here we have something more like the following:

```
this.maxWidth = 300;
this.tooltipText = "some text";
this.embedFonts = false;
this.displayPreview = true;
function tooltip() {
}
new tooltip();
```

5. Now it's time to create some functions to use these values. We now need to create an `init` function, which will be called when the constructor function is invoked. Name the layer with your code on it `scripts` in your **tooltip** movie clip, and attach the following bold ActionScript below the code you've already added but before `#endinitclip`:

```
#initclip 1
function tooltip() {
    // call initialize function
    this.init();
}
tooltip.prototype = new MovieClip();
Object.registerClass("tooltipMc", tooltip);
tooltip.prototype.init = function() {
    // call the draw function
    this.draw();
};
#endinitclip
```

6. Our `draw` function will first create a text field and set its `text` property to the value of our `tooltipText` variable. Again add this code after the `init` function, but as with all of this code, before the `#endinitclip`:

```
tooltip.prototype.draw = function() {
    // create textfield
    this.createTextField("myText", 3, 14, 2, this.maxWidth, 10);
    // set text options
    this.myText.autoSize = true;
    this.myText.embedFonts = this.embedFonts;
    this.myText.wordWrap = true;
    this.myText.condenseWhite = true;
```

continues overleaf

```
        this.myText.html = true;
        this.myText.htmlText = this.tooltipText;
        this.myText.selectable = false;
    };
```

We're assigning the `tooltipText` variable to the `htmlText` property, as this is the easiest way of taking care of the text formatting. We could set the tooltip up to use `textFormat` objects, but this seems a more straightforward way to accomplish text formatting; the user can enter HTML text straight into the **Component Parameters** panel and have this show up with all the correct formatting in the tooltip. You'll also notice that we're using our `maxWidth` variable to set the width of the text field when we create it. Having it set up like this allows us to use the `textWidth` and `textHeight` parameters, as the text will wrap around to the next line when it reaches the maximum width.

7. After we've created the text field we need to call another function to draw the tooltip graphic. We'll pass this function the relevant width and height values that we've retrieved from the text field. The new code to add is highlighted in bold:

```
tooltip.prototype.draw = function() {
    this.createTextField("myText", 3, 14, 2, this.maxWidth, 10);
    this.myText.autoSize = true;
    this.myText.embedFonts = this.embedFonts;
    this.myText.wordWrap = true;
    this.myText.condenseWhite = true;
    this.myText.html = true;
    this.myText.htmlText = this.tooltipText;
    this.myText.selectable = false;
    // set width and height of graphic
    var w = this.myText.textWidth+32;
    var h = this.myText.textHeight+7;
    // call drawGraphic function
    this.drawGraphic(w, h);
};
```

At the moment you'll see we're hard coding the numbers for the amount of padding around the text. This could of course also be defined by parameters, but for now we'll leave it. It's something that you might want to try adding yourself if you feel it would be useful. There will probably be other areas where you'd maybe like the tooltip to work differently, and by the end of the chapter you'll have the confidence to experiment and do this yourself.

The next bit of code then, is the function to draw the tooltip background. Here we're expanding upon the `drawSquare` method we created last chapter. Instead of creating it as a method of the MovieClip object we create it as a method of the toolTip object, as not all movie clips necessarily need it and it might possibly conflict with some user defined drawSquare method. The drawGraphic method basically draws 3 rectangles, a black one for the background, another black one for a shadow on the right-hand side, and finally an off-white one for the face of the tooltip:

```
tooltip.prototype.drawGraphic = function(w, h) {
    // clear any existing drawing
    this.clear();
    // draw three squares to make the background graphic
    this.drawSquare(0, 0, w+2, h+3, 0x000000, 100);
    this.drawSquare(w+2, 3, 1, h, 0x00000, 100);
    this.drawSquare(1, 1, w, h, 0xf3f3f3, 100);
};

tooltip.prototype.drawSquare = function(x, y, w, h, fillCol,
➥fillAlpha) {
    this.moveTo(x, y);
    this.lineStyle();
    this.beginFill(fillCol, fillAlpha);
    this.lineTo(x+w, y);
    this.lineTo(x+w, y+h);
    this.lineTo(x, y+h);
    this.lineTo(x, y);
    this.endFill();
};
```

Again, you might like to create the different colors we specify here as parameters of the tooltip component, but for now we'll leave them hard-coded.

So here's our complete code to this point:

```
#initclip 1
    function tooltip() {
        this.init();
    }
    tooltip.prototype = new MovieClip();
    Object.registerClass("tooltipMc", tooltip);
    tooltip.prototype.init = function() {
        this.draw();
    };
    tooltip.prototype.draw = function() {
        this.createTextField("myText", 3, 14, 2, this.maxWidth, 10);
        this.myText.autoSize = true;
        this.myText.embedFonts = this.embedFonts;
        this.myText.wordWrap = true;
        this.myText.condenseWhite = true;
```

continues overleaf

```
            this.myText.html = true;
            this.myText.htmlText = this.tooltipText;
            this.myText.selectable = false;
            var w = this.myText.textWidth+32;
            var h = this.myText.textHeight+7;
            this.drawGraphic(w, h);
    };
    tooltip.prototype.drawGraphic = function(w, h) {
            this.clear();
            this.drawSquare(0, 0, w+2, h+3, 0x000000, 100);
            this.drawSquare(w+2, 3, 1, h, 0x00000, 100);
            this.drawSquare(1, 1, w, h, 0xf3f3f3, 100);
    };
    tooltip.prototype.drawSquare = function(x, y, w, h, fillCol,
    ➥fillAlpha) {
            this.moveTo(x, y);
            this.lineStyle();
            this.beginFill(fillCol, fillAlpha);
            this.lineTo(x+w, y);
            this.lineTo(x+w, y+h);
            this.lineTo(x, y+h);
            this.lineTo(x, y);
            this.endFill();
    };
    #endinitclip
```

8. Save your movie as `justGraphic.fla`, ensure that you have an instance of the component dragged into the main part of the movie, and test it. You'll see a tooltip graphic on stage, with the text '**empty**' in the standard 12 point Times New Roman:

    empty

Try changing some of the parameters such as setting the `maxWidth` to `140` and, in the text variable field, adding:

```
<font face="verdana" size="10" color="#ff0000">
    <b>A TITLE</b>
    <br/>
</font>
<font face="arial"   size="10"> and a larger piece of body text
</font>
```

You'll see that the tooltip will alter size to accommodate the text:

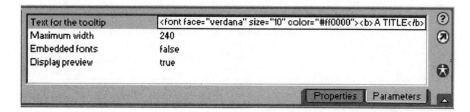

Note that if you set the embedFonts parameter to true, then as with dynamic text fields in general, you'll need to have the font embedded somewhere else in the movie. This is inconvenient, as it would be nice to have the component completely self-contained, but it's unfortunately something we have to live with.

Live preview

Before we move on to creating the core functionality of our tooltip, we're going to quickly look at how to set up a live preview. To see the effect of the changes we make to the tooltip parameters, we currently have to test the movie. Live preview enables us to view changes live on stage as they happen. It's fairly simple to create a live preview, but there are a few peculiarities we need to be aware of.

The basic thing we have to do to set up a live preview is to create a new Flash file that will receive all the values that are set in the Component Parameters panel. Whenever a value in the Component Parameters panel is changed, the onUpdate function is called in the live preview file.

All of the component's parameters are set inside an object called xch. This is an object that is created automatically in a live preview movie; there is no need for us to create it ourselves. When onUpdate is called we're going to need it to redraw our tooltip using the values that are set inside xch, such as xch.maxWidth and xch.tooltipText, for example.

Scaling is one particular peculiarity associated with live previews, and there is potential for a lot of problems if the live preview movie is not the same size as the **tooltip** movie clip. The way we had it set up with no graphics inside would generate problems when we create the live preview, such as the preview movie first not showing up at all before appearing, but horribly stretched. There's no documentation concerning this, but it's possible to solve the problem by placing a graphic inside the tooltip.

It's essential that we do this because in Flash MX, components that have nothing on stage inside them will not work. It's worth knowing, because problems like this can be very hard to troubleshoot.

Setting up a live preview

So, before we create the live preview we need to modify a couple of things in our tooltip component – adding in a placeholder movie clip.

1. Open up the tooltip component and draw a rectangle, 150 pixels wide and 50 pixels high.

2. Convert it to a movie clip and give it a top left registration point, naming the symbol bg_mc, then delete that instance.

3. We next add a line of code (highlighted in bold) in our init function to make this invisible when the movie clip is initialized:

    ```
    tooltip.prototype.init = function() {
        // turn off the bg placeholder
        this.bg_mc._visible = false;
        this.draw();
    };
    ```

4. We're now ready to create the live preview movie. Save the current movie as graphic+livePreview.fla and then save it again as tooltipPreview.fla.

5. Now in tooltipPreview.fla, change the stage size to 150 x 50 pixels. Make sure there is only one instance of the tooltip component on stage and place it on its own layer named tooltip at (0,0). Next, use the Property inspector to give it an instance name tt_mc.

6. Now create another layer beneath **tooltip** and name it bg. On this layer drag an instance of the **bg_mc** movie clip on to the stage and, using the Property inspector, name the instance bg_mc.

7. Now create a scripts layer for our onUpdate function. The onUpdate is called whenever our component's parameters are changed on stage and will update the tooltip component in the preview movie with these values, which it will pull from the xch clip:

```
function onUpdate() {
    // if displayPreview is true turn off bg_mc and vice versa
    this.bg_mc._visible = !_root.xch.displayPreview;
    // if displayPreview is true turn on tt_mc and vice versa
    this.tt_mc._visible = _root.xch.displayPreview;
    // do not embed fonts
    this.tt_mc.embedFonts = false;
    // retrieve values frrom xch and set as values inside tt_mc
    this.tt_mc.maxWidth = _root.xch.maxWidth;
    this.tt_mc.tooltipText = _root.xch.tooltipText;
    // call tt_mc's draw method
    this.tt_mc.draw();
}
```

You'll notice that here we're using the `displayPreview` parameter to set the visibility of the tooltip clip and the `bg_mc` clip. If `displayPreview` is true, `bg_mc` is invisible and `tt_mc` is visible – if it's false then `bg_mc` is visible and `tt_mc` is invisible.

We're also setting `embedFonts` here to false regardless of the value in `xch`. This is because there's no way of getting all possible fonts embedded in the preview movie. If you were using this for your own purposes and wanted to have an embedded font show up in the preview with its antialiasing on, then you could do this by embedding the particular fonts within the preview SWF. As it is, any fonts you want to use will show up fine, but not antialiased.

8. Test the movie so that we have a SWF for it and then save the file. The next step is to set the SWF we've created as the preview SWF for the tooltip.

9. Open `graphic+livePreview.fla` and with the **tooltip** component selected in the Library, click the white menu icon and select the Component Definition... menu option to open the Component Definition dialog box.

10. Click the **Set...** button adjacent to the **Live Preview** row, and the **Live Preview** dialog box will appear:

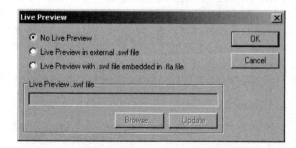

You have two options here – you can either set a path to the SWF, in which case you'll be able to work on the preview SWF and see the changes in the interface, or you can choose to embed the preview SWF.

11. We'll do the latter here and click the third radio button to embed the SWF in the FLA as we've got what we're looking for, and it saves hassle when moving the file around. If you intend to distribute the component, this is definitely the way to go as it keeps everything neatly packaged.

12. Back inside the `graphic+livePreview.fla`, double-click on the **tooltip** component in the Library, so that you're actually inside it. We now need to drag in an instance of the **bg_mc** movie clip inside of the **tooltip** component. Using the Property inspector, position it at (0,0) and give it an instance name `bg_mc`.

    If you look on stage now you should see the tooltips in all their glory according to the parameters we've set:

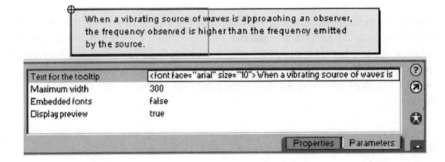

Now if you change the properties, add new text, alter the width and so on, the tooltip's appearance on stage will update to reflect this, transmitting these values to the `xch` object in our preview SWF and calling the `onChanged` function.

What we want our tooltip to do

Now that we have the graphic element sorted out, we move on to the tricky part – how our tooltip is going to function. Let's list some of our requirements – although the list may seem excessive, it's best to cater for as many eventualities as possible. If we imagine all the situations where we might want to use a component now, it will save us time later. So, what we want is for:

- The tooltip to become associated with a movie clip when we drop the tooltip onto the movie clip.

- The tooltip to attach itself to the mouse, and also be able to specify an offset from the mouse.

- The tooltip to appear after a short delay when the user rolls over the movie clip that's associated with the tooltip.

- The tooltip to disappear when the user rolls out of its associated movie clip.

- The text appearing on a tooltip to be changed at any time, and have it update accordingly.

- The tooltip to be disabled and enabled at any time.

- The tooltip to be completely removed at any time.

- The tooltip to have a movie clip attached at run-time.

- The target movie clip of any tooltip to be changed at run-time.

- The tooltip function to be attached to a button without interfering with the normal functionality of that button.

Now that we have a list of basic requirements, we can suggest a more final list of parameters we need to include:

- Text to be displayed

- Maximum width

- Embedded fonts

- Target Movie clip

- X offset from mouse

- Y offset from mouse

- Milliseconds delay before appearing

- Tooltip enabled

- Display preview

We can also suggest some functions that we might need to define. Some of the functions we require will need to:

- Set the tooltip text and redraw the background to fit.

- Reveal the tooltip.

- Hide the tooltip.

- Set the target movie clip of the tooltip.

- Enable the tooltip.

- Disable the tooltip.

- Trigger the tooltip.

- Delete the tooltip.

OK – we've now got a considerable outline of requirements to help assess the scope of what we need to do, which will hopefully save us some time later.

Making a tooltip appear on rollover

The first thing we need to consider here is how the tooltip will relate to the movie clip it's associated with. We need to be able to drop the tooltip onto a movie clip and have it create an association automatically, like the way that the scrollBar component picks up on and snaps to the nearest text field. It's pretty simple to achieve this, and all we have to do is add a parameter to the component parameter list with the variable name `_targetInstanceName`. We'll do that now and while we're doing so, we may as well add the extra parameters that we mentioned above.

1. Open the `graphic+livePreview.fla` and save it as `tooltipProper.fla`. With the **tooltip** component selected in the Library, click on the white menu icon and select the **Component Definition...** menu option.

2. Open the **Component Definition** dialog for the tooltip and add the following parameters. We've added five new parameters including `Target Movieclip`, which is highlighted along with the four beneath it in the screenshot opposite.

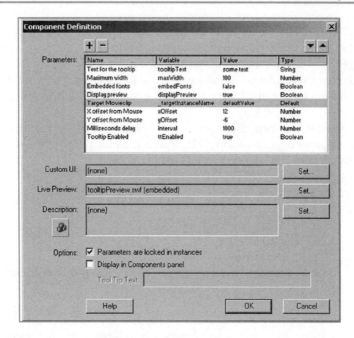

3. Now create a movie clip with any kind of graphic in it (we've opted for a small black circle with no fill). Name it `targ_mc`. Next, drag a copy on stage and using the Property inspector, give it an instance name `targ_mc`.

4. Now take an instance of the **tooltip** component and drag that on top of the **targ_mc** movie clip. You should see that it now snaps into position and that the **Target Movieclip** field in the Component Parameters panel has now changed to read `targ_mc`.

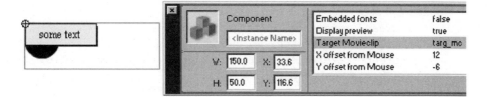

Note that we could just input this value manually if we wanted – like if we wanted to leave our tooltips offstage, for example.

Now we can look at implementing the functionality for our tooltip. We need to trigger the tooltip when the user rolls over the target movie clip, which we could do by having a defined hit area for the tooltip. We could then place the tooltip over the target movie clip and stretch it so that it covers the desired rollover area. When we roll over the target area, we would trigger the rollover function of the target movie clip and then trigger the tooltip. While this seems like a fairly satisfactory solution, we'd have trouble keeping the hit area consistent for complex shapes.

Another problem would be if we had a button with a rollover state. While we can put a button on top of another button and call the lower button's rollover function, we cannot trigger its rollover state. As we want to keep the button as flexible as possible, we'll have to discount this solution. What we're going to try instead is to set the rollover function of the movie clip to call a function inside the tooltip to tell it to wait and then display itself.

5. So, in order to create the onRollOver function in our target movie clip, we're going to create a setTarget function. First of all we add a call to the setTarget function in our init function. The new code is highlighted in bold:

```
tooltip.prototype.init = function() {
    this.bg_mc._visible = 0;
    // hide tooltip to start with
    this._visible = 0;
    // call setTarget
    this.setTarget(this._parent[this._targetInstanceName]);
    this.draw();
};
```

We're passing the setTarget function a reference to the target movie clip. In the setTarget function we need to create a reference to the **tooltip** component for ease of use, and then we need to set functions for the rollOver, rollOut and dragOut handlers.

6. The rollOver function will initialize a delay, after which the tooltip will be displayed. The onRollOut and onDragOut functions will both be the same – clearing the delay in case the tooltip has not yet displayed, and then calling a function to clear the tooltip. Now add the following code above the original draw function:

```
tooltip.prototype.setTarget = function(mc) {
    // create reference to target movieclip
    this.targetMovie = mc;
    // create reference to tooltip inside target movieclip
    this.targetMovie.toolTip = this;
    this.targetMovie.onRollOver = function() {
    // create an interval after which to display tooltip
     this.toolTip.wait = setInterval(this.toolTip, "displayToolTip",
     ➥this.tooltip.interval);
    };
    this.targetMovie.onRollOut = function() {
    // on rollOur clearInterval in case tooltip has not yet
    // appeared
        clearInterval(this.toolTip.wait);
        this.toolTip.clearToolTip();
    };
    this.targetMovie.onDragOut = this.targetMovie.onRollOut;
};
```

Note that although we're defining the handler functions inside the tooltip, when executed they will behave as if they were inside the target movie clip, and so to refer to the tooltip we use `this.tooltip`.

7.   Next, we create the `displayTooltip` and `clearTooltip` methods. These are both fairly self-explanatory; the `displayTooltip` method will first clear the interval that called it and then set a `mouseMove` function for the tooltip `putMeByMouse`, which will move the movie clip to the position of the mouse:

```
tooltip.prototype.displayTooltip = function() {
    // clear interval so the method is not called again
    clearInterval(this.wait);
    // show tooltip
    this._visible = 1;
    // set mouseMove function
    this.onMouseMove = this.putMeByMouse;
    // put tooltip by mouse
    this.putMeByMouse();
};
```

The `clearTooltip` method will delete the `mouseMove` handler and set the tooltip's visibility to zero:

```
tooltip.prototype.clearTooltip = function() {
    delete this.onMouseMove;
    this._visible = 0;
};
```

All we have to do now is create the `putMeByMouse` method and we'll have a functional tooltip. This method is fairly simple; it retrieves the mouse's X and Y position and then use the `globalToLocal` method to convert these global coordinates to local coordinates.

The reason we do this is because the tooltip could be inside another movie clip that is at (400,400). If it just took the mouse co-ordinates and used them as they were, it would end up far too much to the right of where it should be. In other words – the same distance from (400,400) as the mouse is from (0,0).

The `globalToLocal` method translates the global coordinates of the mouse to the local coordinates of the current movie clip. The method basically answers the question "Whereabouts inside this movie clip should I place my movie clip so that it is at the specified set of co-ordinates on the root?" To make `globalToLocal` work, we pass it an object with an X property and a Y property. It then transforms the global coordinates specified inside the object to the local coordinates relative to the movie clip specified – in this case, _parent.

```
tooltip.prototype.putMeByMouse = function() {
// create point object
    var point = {x:_root._xmouse+this.xOffSet,
    ➡y:_root._ymouse+this.yOffset};
// translate co-ordinates inside point to local co-ordinates
    this._parent.globalToLocal(point);
    this._x = point.x;
    this._y = point.y;
    updateAfterEvent();
};
```

8.   Save your movie as `finalTooltipBasic.fla` and when you test it, you'll see a basic functioning tooltip:

When you rollover the object the tooltip appears and when you roll out it goes away again. You can change the delay in the Component Parameters panel, as well as the X and Y offset from the mouse position to get different effects.

Dynamically changing the text inside the tooltip

There are still a lot of things that we still have to achieve from the list we set out at the beginning. We'll now concentrate on being able to change the text that displays inside the tooltip.

1.   Inside your new `finalTooltipBasic.fla`, add a new `scripts` layer to the main timeline and put in the following ActionScript:

```
targ_mc.onPress = function() {
    this.tooltip.tooltipText += "<font face='arial'
    ➡size='10'> oh</font>";
};
```

As you can see when you run the code, this does absolutely nothing. This is because the only time that we update the text field is when we call the `draw` function. If we knew what was going on inside the tooltip, we could of course do this:

```
targ_mc.onPress = function() {
    this.tooltip.tooltipText += "<font face='arial'
    ➡size='10'> oh</font>";
```

```
        this.tooltip.draw();
};
```

That's not really ideal though. We want to allow interface with the component in a relatively simple way, so it would be much better if we could change `tooltipText` and have the tooltip update automatically. One of the new methods in Flash MX that allows us to do this is `addProperty`. What `addProperty` allows us to do is add a property that behaves as a normal variable, but in fact when accessed and set, calls special functions to set the variable and retrieve the variable – a 'getter' and a 'setter'.

The property created with an `addProperty` statement is known as a getter/setter and indeed shows up when you list variables with `[getter/setter]` after the variable name. So, for the tooltip we're going to set up `tooltipText` as a getter/setter.

2. First of all we include an `addProperty` statement in the `init` function. This specifies the name of the property, the function called to retrieve (or 'get') the property, and the function called to set the property. The new statement is highlighted in bold:

```
tooltip.prototype.init = function() {
    this.bg_mc._visible = 0;
    this._visible = 0;
    this.setTarget(this._parent[this._targetInstanceName]);
    // add tooltipText as a getter / setter property
    this.addProperty("tooltipText", this.getText, this.setText);
    this.draw();
};
```

> *If you ever have any problems using* `addProperty`, *make sure you have the getter and setter functions the right way round, as it fails completely otherwise. You can generally tell if this is happening if the value shows up as undefined when you list variables. Another way to check this is to put the entire* `addProperty` *statement inside a trace – if the property is defined it will* `trace` *true otherwise it will trace* `false`.

3.   Now we create the functions getText and setText. The getText function simply returns the value of tooltipText.

```
tooltip.prototype.getText = function() {
    return this.tooltipText;
}
```

Whenever the setter function is included, it's passed a single argument specifying the new value that the property is being set to. We take this value and put it in the tooltipText variable and then call the draw function. Add the following ActionScript above the getText function:

```
tooltip.prototype.setText = function(newVal) {
    this.tooltipText = newVal;
    this.draw();
};
```

If you changed the code on your main timeline earlier, now change it back to:

```
targ_mc.onPress = function() {
    this.tooltip.tooltipText += "<font face='arial'
    ➥size='10'> oh</font>";
};
```

4.   Save your movie as finalTooltipbasicAddText.fla and test it – you'll see that everything works properly now, with the tooltip updating every time you click the mouse:

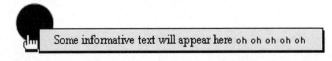

Though this isn't a real application, it provides us with a good proof of concept. Let's now move on to add an enabled property.

Adding an enabled property

We'll use the same approach to add an enabled property.

1.   Add the following highlighted code to the ActionScript for your tooltip component:

```
tooltip.prototype.init = function() {
    this.bg_mc._visible = 0;
```

```
        this._visible = 0;
        this.setTarget(this._parent[this._targetInstanceName]);
        this.addProperty("tooltipText", this.getText, this.setText);
        // add ttEnabled as a getter / setter property
        this.addProperty("ttEnabled", this.getEnabled,
        ➥this.setEnabled);
        this.draw();
    };
```

2. Next we add the getter and setter methods. Add a setEnabled and a getEnabled function below our setText and getText functions:

```
tooltip.prototype.setEnabled = function(newval) {
    this.ttEnabled = newval;
    if (!this.ttEnabled) {
        this.clearTooltip();
    }
};
tooltip.prototype.getEnabled = function() {
    return this.ttenabled;
};
```

So if ttEnabled is set to false, we're setting the variable and after that, clearing the tooltip if it's already displayed by calling the clearTooltip method.

3. The one thing we have to add is a check if the tooltip is enabled in the displayTooltip function, highlighted in bold:

```
tooltip.prototype.displayTooltip = function() {
    clearInterval(this.wait);
    // check if tooltip enabled before displaying
    if (this.ttEnabled) {
        this._visible = 1;
        this.onMouseMove = this.putMeByMouse;
        this.putMeByMouse();
    }
};
```

4. In order to test this, we add some code on the main timeline to toggle the enabled state of our tooltip:

```
targ_mc.onPress = function() {
    this.tooltip.ttEnabled = !this.tooltip.ttEnabled;
};
```

5. Save your movie as `finalTooltipbasicAddEnabled.fla` and test it. If you click the mouse while the tooltip is displayed, it will disable the tooltip until you roll over the movie clip again.

Attaching the tooltip dynamically to a movie clip

Another requirement we mentioned for our tooltip was that we should be able to attach it dynamically and have it apply to a movie clip. This is relatively simple because components are set up to initialize in the same way whether attached or dragged on stage.

The only thing to consider is getting the parameters into the movie clip. We can do this by passing an initialization object when we call `attachMovie`, containing all of the parameters. These values would be available to the tooltip when it initializes in the same way that the values from the Components panel are.

1. Delete the tooltip from the stage and add the following code on the main timeline:

```
obj = {
    ttEnabled:true, _targetInstanceName:"targ_mc",
    ➥tooltipText:"whatever text you reckon", maxWidth:150,
    ➥interval:50, xOffset:6, yOffset:-12
    }
_root.attachMovie("tooltipMc","tt_mc",1,obj)
```

If you run this, you'll see that it works fine, but it's hardly user friendly. For one thing it's a lot of typing, and also, if we miss out any of the parameters, it will fail. So, we need to build in some insulation in our `init` function. If any of the parameters are undefined we should set them to their default values.

2. Add the following highlighted code inside the **tooltip** component's `init` function:

```
tooltip.prototype.init = function() {
    this.bg_mc._visible = 0;
    this._visible = 0;
    // with all of the following we check if the property
    // is defined and if not set a default value
    if (this.tooltiptext == undefined) {
        this.tooltiptext = "empty";
    }
    if (this.interval == undefined) {
        this.interval = 500;
    }
    if (this._parent[this._targetInstanceName]) {
```

```
            this.setTarget(this._parent[this._targetInstanceName]);
        }
        if (this.maxWidth == undefined) {
            this.maxWidth = 500;
        }
        if (this.xOffset == undefined) {
            this.xOffset = 12;
        }
        if (this.yOffset == undefined) {
            this.yOffset = -6;
        }
        if (this.ttEnabled == undefined) {
            this.ttEnabled = true;
        }
        this.setTarget(this._parent[this._targetInstanceName]);
        this.addProperty("tooltipText", this.getText, this.setText);
        this.addProperty("ttEnabled", this.getEnabled, this.setEnabled);
        this.draw();
    };
```

We also only call the `setTarget` function if we have a `_targetInstanceName`, otherwise we'll wait until it's called manually.

3. Now change the text on the main timeline to the following:

```
_root.attachMovie("tooltipMc", "tt_mc", 1);
tt_mc.setTarget(targ_mc);
tt_mc.tooltipText = "a piece of text";
```

Save the movie as `finalTooltipbasicAttach.fla`. This approach just uses the default values, but we could just as easily pass it an initialization object like we did before to set the maximum width, and so on. If the values are there, it uses them – if not, it uses the defaults.

Preserving the original button actions

So far this all works fine and does more or less what we want it to, although we do have a problem.

1. Delete the code on the main stage and drag a new instance of the tooltip onto the stage above our `targ_mc` movie clip. Now add this code on the main timeline:

```
targ_mc.onRollOver = function() {
    this._alpha = 50;
};
targ_mc.onRollOut = function() {
    this._alpha = 100;
};
```

When you run the code, you'll see that the alpha of the movie clip is set as expected, but our tooltip doesn't appear. The reason for this is that we've overwritten the movie clip's `onRollOver` handler, which triggered the tooltip. We could get around this by attaching the tooltip to the movie clip, but then the function to trigger the tooltip would overwrite the `alpha` function. This would go against one of our stated aims, which was not to interfere with the operations of the target movie clip – which may already have a rollover function. We're going to have to work out a way around this.

What we're going to need to do is have the tooltip store any functions that the target movie clip may already have in its `onRollOver`, `onRollOut` and `onDragOut` handlers. We will then assign new functions to these handlers, which will first call the old functions and then take care of our tooltip business.

We also need to ensure that if the user were to assign different functions to these handlers, this would again update to perform both the new function and the tooltip trigger function. To accomplish this, we can use another new method available in Flash MX: `Object.watch`.

`Object.watch` works in a similar way to `addProperty`, allowing us to keep a watchful eye on the value of a property or method, and letting us call a specified function whenever the property is altered. We can use this to catch the value of the movie clip's `rollOver` function and then assign it a new function, which will first call this new function and then trigger the tooltip.

2. Add the following highlighted code to our `setTarget` function. Note that we have removed the previous definitions of the button handlers for our target movie clip and replaced them with the watch statements:

```
tooltip.prototype.setTarget = function(mc) {
    this.targetMovie = mc;
```

```
        this.targetMovie.toolTip = this;
        // set watch points on the button actions of the target
        this.targetMovie.watch("onRollOver", this.addToRollOver);
        this.targetMovie.watch("onRollOut", this.addToRollOut);
        this.targetMovie.watch("onDragOut", this.addToDragOut);
        this.targetMovie.onRollOut = this.targetMovie.onRollOut;
        this.targetMovie.onRollOver = this.targetMovie.onRollOver;
        this.targetMovie.onDragOut = this.targetMovie.onDragOut;
    }
```

We first set the watch points for our various handlers (we'll create the actual functions in a moment) and then we redefine all the handlers for the target movie so that the watch functions will be called at the start. We do this in case the target movie already has these handlers defined and we need to add our tooltip trigger to them.

3. We'll start with the method to store the movie clip's rollOver function:

```
tooltip.prototype.addToRollover = function(id, oldVal, newVal) {
    // store the new rollover value in oldRollover
    this.tooltip.oldRollOver = newVal;
    // define the function that will be returned to the
    // target movieclip as its new rollOver function
    return function () {
        // call the old Rollover function
        this.tooltip.oldRollover.call(this);
        // trigger the tooltip
        this.tooltip.wait = setInterval(this.tooltip,
        ➡"displayTooltip", this.tooltip.interval);
    };
};
```

Let's go through this line-by-line, starting with the function definition:

```
tooltip.prototype.addToRollover = function(id, oldVal, newVal) {
```

A function called by `Object.watch` is passed three arguments: `id`, `oldVal` and `newVal`. `id` refers to the property that's being watched, `oldVal` is the previous value assigned to the property, and `newVal` is the new value assigned to the property.

```
        this.tooltip.oldRollOver = newVal;
```

Here we store the new function that `onRollOver` is set to, or that the user has tried to set it to, in a variable named `oldRollOut` inside our tooltip. Basically, what we're doing is intercepting this value. We could store this in the target movie clip, but it's better to avoid putting things in the target as much as possible.

We now return the function that will actually be set as the onRollOver of the target movie clip:

```
return function () {
    this.tooltip.oldRollover.call(this);
    this.tooltip.wait = setInterval(this.tooltip, "displayTooltip",
    ➥this.tooltip.interval);
```

The first line of this calls the oldRollover function and the second sets the interval to call displayTooltip exactly as we did earlier. You should notice that the first line of code uses call to call the function. The reason for this is that the oldRollover function is inside the tooltip, but we want it to behave as though it were in the target movie clip. Our original method of having oldRollOver inside the target movie clip meant that we could just have:

```
this.oldRollover();
```

Because oldRollover is inside the tooltip and not the target clip we can't do this. Instead, we use function.call – another new addition to Flash MX, which allows us to call a function that's in one location as though it were actually located somewhere else. If you look at the rollover definition you'll see that the scope in which the code executes is the target movie clip. In other words, this refers to the target movie clip.

```
return function () {
    this.tooltip.oldRollover.call(this);
    this.tooltip.wait = setInterval(this.tooltip, "displayTooltip",
    ➥this.tooltip.interval);
};
```

When we use function.call to call a function, we pass an argument (in front of any other arguments we might have), specifying the scope in which we want the function to run: this in our case. Essentially, what this statement says is "call the function oldRollover inside the tooltip movie clip, but have it execute as though it were on my own timeline".

4. We can now create the functions for all three of the rollOver handlers. The other two do broadly the same thing, calling clearTooltip instead of setting an interval to display the tooltip:

```
tooltip.prototype.addToRollover = function(id, oldVal, newVal) {
    this.tooltip.oldRollOver = newVal;
    return function () {
        this.tooltip.oldRollover.call(this);
        this.toolTip.wait = setInterval(this.toolTip,
        ➥"displayToolTip", this.tooltip.interval);
    };
};
```

```
tooltip.prototype.addToRollOut = function(id, oldVal, newVal) {
    this.tooltip.oldRollOut = newVal;
    return function () {
        this.tooltip.oldRollOut.call(this);
        clearInterval(this.toolTip.wait);
        this.toolTip.clearToolTip();

    };
};

tooltip.prototype.addToDragOut = function(id, oldVal, newVal) {
    this.tooltip.oldDragOut = newVal;
    return function () {
        this.tooltip.oldDragOut.call(this);
        clearInterval(this.toolTip.wait);
        this.toolTip.clearToolTip();
    };
};
```

5. Save your movie as `finalTooltipbasicWatch.fla`. When you test the movie, you'll see that the rollover now changes both the alpha of the movie clip *and* generates a tooltip.

If we look back at our original list of features you'll see we only have a few left to cover:

Tooltip Requirement	Achieved
The tooltip to become associated with a movie clip when we drop the tooltip onto the movie clip.	✔
The movie clip to attach itself to the mouse, and also be able to specify an offset from the mouse.	✔
The tooltip to appear after a short delay when the user rolls over the movie clip that's associated with the tooltip.	✔
The tooltip to disappear when the user rolls out of its associated movie clip.	✔
The text appearing on a tooltip to be changed at any time, and have it update accordingly.	✔
The tooltip to be disabled and enabled at any time.	✔
The tooltip to be completely removed at any time.	✘
The tooltip to have a movie clip attached at run-time.	✔
The target movie clip of any tooltip to be changed at run-time.	✘
The tooltip function to be attached to a button without interfering with the normal functionality of that button	✔

So, the requirements we still have to achieve are to do with removing the tooltip and switching it from one movie clip to another, which are related to each other. Currently, the user could just remove the movie clip using `tooltip.removeMovieClip()`. This would work, but when the tooltip is removed it would also remove any `onRollOver` handlers and leave a reference to the tooltip in the target movie clip.

We need a function that will be called to remove all traces of the tooltip and reset the target movie clip's event handlers. We'll also call this function in our `setTarget` function if a target movie already exists and we're thus switching from one movie clip to another. We need to do a number of things in this function:

- Remove the reference to the tooltip.
- Remove the watch points that we set on `onRollOver`, `onRollOut` and `onDragOut`.
- Restore the `rollOver`, `rollOut` and `dragOut` to their previous values.
- If there were no functions defined for these handlers, then we remove the handlers altogether.

Adding the final requirements for the tooltip

1. So, there are three sections to our function, which we'll add above our `clearTooltip` function. First we delete the `tooltip` property from the target movie clip and then we `unwatch` the event handlers. Finally, we check through `oldRollOver`, `oldRollOut` and `oldDragOut` – either deleting the handlers if the old function was undefined (there was no `rollOver` function), or resetting it to the old function:

```
tooltip.prototype.clearTooltipInfo = function() {
    // delete reference to tooltip
    delete this.targetMovie.tooltip;
    // stop watching the button handlers
    this.targetMovie.unwatch("onRollOver");
    this.targetMovie.unwatch("onRollOut");
    this.targetMovie.unwatch("onDragOut");
    // if the button handlers are undefined delete them
    if (this.oldRollOut == undefined) {
        delete this.targetMovie.onRollOut;
    } else {
        this.targetMovie.onRollOut = this.oldRollOut;
    }
    if (this.oldDragOut == undefined) {
        delete this.targetMovie.onDragOut;
    } else {
        this.targetMovie.onDragOut = this.oldDragOut;
    }
```

```
        if (this.oldRollOver == undefined) {
            delete this.targetMovie.onRollOver;
        } else {
            this.targetMovie.onRollOver = this.oldRollOver;
        }
    };
```

2. We could create a custom `deleteTooltip` method to call this and then remove the tooltip, but instead we'll just let the user use `removeMovieClip`, as this seems more intuitive. Whenever a movie clip is removed, it calls its `unload` handler, so that's what we'll use here, above the `clearTooltipInfo` function we've just added:

```
tooltip.prototype.onUnload = function() {
    this.clearTooltipInfo();
};
```

3. Finally, we'll also need to call `clearTooltip` if a `targetMovie` is already defined when we call `setTarget`. The new code is highlighted in bold:

```
tooltip.prototype.setTarget = function(mc) {
    // if targetMovie is already defined, disassociate the
    // tooltip from it
    if (this.targetMovie) {
        this.clearTooltipInfo();
    }
    this.targetMovie = mc;
    this.targetMovie.tooltip = this;
    this.targetMovie.watch("onRollOver", this.addToRollOver);
    this.targetMovie.watch("onRollOut", this.addToRollOut);
    this.targetMovie.watch("onDragOut", this.addToDragOut);
    this.targetMovie.onRollOut = this.targetMovie.onRollOut;
    this.targetMovie.onRollOver = this.targetMovie.onRollOver;
    this.targetMovie.onDragOut = this.targetMovie.onDragOut;
};
```

To test that this is working, remove the tooltip from the stage, leaving just the **targ_mc** movie clip, and add the following code to the root timeline:

```
targ_mc.onRollOver = function() {
    this._alpha = 50;
};
targ_mc.onRollOut = function() {
    this._alpha = 100;
};
targ_mc.onPress = function() {
```

continues overleaf

```
                        this.tooltip.removeMovieClip();
                };
                _root.attachMovie("tooltipMc", "nootool", 2);
                _root.nootool.setTarget(targ_mc);
```

4.   Save your movie as `finalTooltipDone.fla`. When you test the code, you'll see that the tooltip works fine until you click on `targ_mc`, at which point it disappears. If you select the **Debug > List Variables** menu option, you'll see that we've removed all trace of it and that our rollover still works fine.

There's a little too much code to include it as a reference here in the book, but you can reference the full code in the source file `finalTooltipDone.fla`. There's also an additional FLA (`finalTooltipImplemented.fla`) with several implementations of the tooltip, which are dynamically created, attached on stage, and attached to a nested movie clip.

There are still things you could add to the movie. You might want to manipulate the color for example, which would be added in the same way as the `text` property, or you could add parameters to specify the depth of the shadow on the tooltip and its alpha.

You could also turn `tooltipText` into a property of the target movie so that the user could say `myMovie.tooltiptext` rather than `mymovie.tooltip.tooltiptext`, which you could do with either `watch` or `addProperty`. You could turn `maxWidth` into a getter/setter if you wanted to manipulate that at run-time, and you might also want to build in something to make sure that if the movie clip the tooltip is inside is scaled, then the tooltip is scaled inversely to maintain its proportions. If we were going to use that approach, it might be better to have the tooltip created on the main stage rather than inside the movie. Overall, what we've learned here is the approach to create a component – the final product itself is by no means perfect, but a good base for experimentation.

As a final exercise you might want to have the tooltip component appear in the Components panel. This is a simple process. Create a new FLA with just the tooltip component inside it. Open the Component Definition dialog box and check **Display in Components Panel**. You then need to place this FLA inside the folder where Flash looks for components when it starts up. This will be something like **Program Files/Macromedia/Flash MX/First Run/Components**. When you close Flash and reopen it the component should appear in the Components panel. Note that you can place more than one component inside an FLA in which case they will appear as a set (in the same way that the Flash UI components appear as a set).

Returning to the site

We're now going to return to the version of the site we completed in the last chapter. So far, the buttons that we've created execute the actions but nothing else – they have no rollover states and no indication that the user has visited each section. We're now going to create a button class that will change the brightness of the buttons depending on whether we have visited each link, as well as creating rollover and active states.

Extra button interactivity: retrieving alpha and brightness settings with Color.setBrightness

The first thing we're going to have to do is create a method of the Color object to set the brightness of the buttons. As we discovered earlier, we can set a tint or brightness on stage and then retrieve the settings from the **Advanced Effect** panel to reproduce the tint or brightness dynamically using setTransform.

Before we move on to this, let's briefly remind ourselves of some of the values we'll be dealing with: OK – **rgb** is for Red, Green and Blue, while **a** and **b** refer to alpha and brightness. So **ra** will refer to the red alpha setting while **gb** is the green brightness setting.

So, we need to look at the effect that changing the brightness of a movie clip has on the individual entries for the colorTransform object and try to see if there's a pattern. We have a few settings recorded below:

Brightness:	100	50	25	70	-50	-25
ra:	0	50	75	30	50	75
ba:	0	50	75	30	50	75
ga:	0	50	75	30	50	75
aa:	100	100	100	100	100	100
rb:	255	128	64	179	0	0
gb:	255	128	64	179	0	0
bb:	255	128	64	179	0	0
ab:	0	0	0	0	0	0

The first thing to note is that the values for **aa** and **ab** are the same throughout – 100 and 0, respectively. You'll also notice that **ra**, **ga** and **ba**, and **rb**, **gb** and **bb** always contain the same values.

Let's first look at the brightness values; **ra**, **ga** and **ba** are fairly obvious and each contains 100 minus the brightness value. The **rb**, **gb** and **bb** values may take a little more thought. At 100 they are 255 and at 50 they are 128, so it's a fair guess that multiplying 255 by the brightness value and then dividing by 100 determines their value, before the figure is rounded up. You can check this hypothesis by plugging in some other brightness values. For example, **rb** is 179 with 70% brightness. 255 multiplied by 70 and divided by 100 is 178.5, which when rounded up is indeed 179! For negative brightness the **rb**, **gb** and **bb** values are zero whatever the brightness is, so that's fine. **ra**, **ga** and **ba** seem to be 100 plus the brightness value, or indeed minus the absolute value of brightness (the brightness value ignoring the negative).

Now we can attempt to write a method to use this. We'll check whether the brightness is negative or positive and act accordingly, calculating values for all of the **a** transform values and all of the **b** transform values:

```
color.prototype.setBrightness = function(bright) {
    if (bright<0) {
        var aNum = 100-Math.abs(bright);
        var bNum = 0;
    } else {
        var aNum = 100-bright;
        var bNum = Math.ceil(255*bright/100);
    }
    this.setTransform({ra:aNum, ga:aNum, ba:aNum, aa:100, rb:bNum,
➥gb:bNum, bb:bNum, ab:0});
};
```

After looking at the code, it becomes apparent that we can simplify it. We can actually perform the same calculation for aNum, whether or not brightness is negative, because Math.abs(bright) will be equivalent to bright if bright is greater than 0.

```
color.prototype.setBrightness = function(bright) {
    var aNum = 100-Math.abs(bright);
    if (bright<0) {
        var bNum = 0;
    } else {
        var bNum = Math.ceil(255*bright/100);
    }
    this.setTransform({ra:aNum, ga:aNum, ba:aNum, aa:100, rb:bNum,
➥gb:bNum, bb:bNum, ab:0});
};
```

We can also get rid of the if...else statement using the ternary operator. If you're not familiar with this, it's a way of compacting brief if...else statements and works like this:

```
var whatever = conditionalStatement ? returnIfTrue : returnIfFalse;
```

When Flash comes across the question mark, it evaluates the statement before it. If the statement is true, it executes the statement between the question mark and the colon. If it is false, it executes the statement after the colon. This can be used in many situations – there's no need for it to be used to assign variables and it can trigger functions as well. In our case, we want the conditional to be brightness<0. If that's true we want to return 0, and if it's false we return Math.ceil(255*bright/100). Here's the statement then:

```
var bNum = bright<0 ? 0 : Math.ceil(255*bright/100);
```

Our completed method, which is a lot more compact than the first attempt, now looks like this:

```
color.prototype.setBrightness = function(bright) {
    // values for a properties
    var aNum = 100-Math.abs(bright);
    // values for b properties
    var bNum = bright<0 ? 0 : Math.ceil(255*bright/100);
    this.setTransform({ra:aNum, ga:aNum, ba:aNum, aa:100, rb:bNum,
    ➥gb:bNum, bb:bNum, ab:0});
};
```

Building our own button component

We're not actually going to create the button as a component, but we'll be constructing it in the same way as a component, and creating it as its own class. It would be easy however, to make this into a component just by adding parameters in the Components panel. Before we start it's best to consider what methods and properties our button needs:

- Brightness values for active, visited and rollover states.
- Methods to return width and height.
- A textFormat object.
- A text variable.
- Whether or not the font is embedded.
- Methods to set the button as active and visited.
- Actions for the various states.
- Methods to set the button actions and to clear them for when the button is active.

1. We start off as we did before. Open `roller.fla` and put the `Color.setBrightness` method below all of the existing code on the root timeline.

2. Create a new movie clip, named `nooButton`. With the symbol selected in the Library, click the Library's white menu icon and select the **Linkage...** menu option. Check the **Export for ActionScript** option and type `nooButtonMc` in the **Identifier** field:

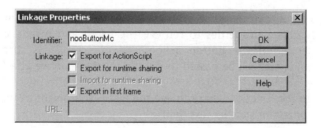

3. Place a dynamic text field inside the movie clip and name the instance `texta`. We've included a light colored background so that later on when we click the buttons, it will be easier to tell if they've been clicked or not, depending on their alpha settings:

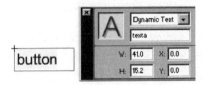

4. Create a new `scripts` layer inside the movie clip and add the standard code for a component:

```
#initclip
function nooButton() {
    this.init();
}
nooButton.prototype = new MovieClip();
Object.registerClass("nooButtonMc", nooButton);
```

5. Then we add the `init` function:

```
nooButton.prototype.init = function() {
    // set up a new color object
    this.col = new Color(this);
    this.texta.autosize = true;
    this.texta.embedfonts = this.embedFonts;
    this.texta.text = this.myText;
    this.texta.setTextFormat(this.tf);
    // add getter / setter properties for width and height
    this.addProperty("width", this.getWidth, null);
    this.addProperty("height", this.getHeight, null);
    this.setButtonActions();
};
```

We're doing a number of things here; creating a Color object for the movie clip, setting up the text field, adding properties to retrieve the width and height, and finally calling a function to set all of the button actions. All of the values such as `this.myText`, `this.embedFonts`, etc. will be passed to the movie clip when we attach it.

6. Next, we create the functions that retrieve the width and height of the button, which are based on the dimensions of the text field:

```
nooButton.prototype.getWidth = function() {
```

```
        return this.texta.textWidth;
    };
nooButton.prototype.getHeight = function() {
        return this.texta.textHeight;
    };
```

7. We're now going to set the button actions as we did before – allowing an object, a function
    and arguments for each:

```
nooButton.prototype.setButtonActions = function() {
    this.onPress = function() {
    this.setActive();
    this.obj[this.pressFunction](this.pressArgs);
    };
    this.onRelease = function() {
    this.obj[this.releaseFunction](this.releaseArgs);
    };
    this.onRollOver = function() {
        this.setCol(this.rollOverBright);
        this.obj[this.rollOverFunction](this.rolloverArgs);
    };
    this.onDragOut = function() {
        this.setCol(this.defaultBright);
        this.obj[this.dragOutFunction](this.dragOutArgs);
    };
    this.onRollOut = function() {
        this.setCol(this.defaultBright);
        this.obj[this.rollOutFunction](this.rollOutArgs);
    };
};
```

You'll notice that as well as these functions, we're also calling another internal method. The
first of these is setCol, which just calls setBrightness for the color object:

```
nooButton.prototype.setCol = function(bright) {
    this.col.setBrightness(bright);
};
```

Then for the press function we call setActive, which will disable all button actions and
then store a reference to itself in a global variable nooActive. The movie clip already inside
nooActive has its setInactive method called. In other circumstances, you might want to
create some kind of special callback for this, to create smaller groups of buttons, but for
our purposes this is fine:

```
nooButton.prototype.setActive = function() {
```

continues overleaf

```
        this.clearButtonActions();
        // deactivate the button that is currently active
        nooActive.setInactive();
        _global.nooActive = this;
        this.setCol(this.activeBright);
    };
nooButton.prototype.clearButtonActions = function() {
        // delete all button handlers
        delete this.onPress;
        delete this.onRelease;
        delete this.onRollOver;
        delete this.onDragOut;
        delete this.onRollOut;
    };
```

The `setInactive` method resets the button actions and then calls `setVisited`. `setVisited` in turn sets the default brightness value for the button as the visited brightness value, so that when `rollOut`, etc. are called they will restore the button to the visited brightness rather than the original brightness we had:

```
nooButton.prototype.setInactive = function() {
        this.setButtonActions();
        this.setVisited();
        this.setCol(this.defaultBright);
    };
nooButton.prototype.setVisited = function() {
        this.defaultBright = this.visitedBright;
    };
```

8. To implement this, we return to our `createButtons` function on the root timeline. We can just use `attachMovie` as usual, passing an initialization object containing all of the parameters we want to set:

```
function createButtons(imageArr, tF) {
        _root.createEmptyMovieClip("buttonHolder", ++this.depth);
        buttonHolder._x = leftPos+10;
        buttonHolder._y = topPos+imageHeight+5;
        var currx;
        for (var i = 0; i<images.length; i++) {
            var caption = (i+1).toString().length>1 ? i+1 : "0"+(i+1);
            var obj = {myText:caption, _x:currx, obj:_root,
            ➡defaultBright:0, rollOverBright:30, visitedBright:60,
            ➡activeBright:-10, pressFunction:"centerPic",
            ➡pressArgs:imageArr[i], tf:buttonTextFormat,
            ➡embedFonts:true}; var nooButton = buttonHolder.attachMovie
```

```
       ⮑("nooButtonMc", "noob"+i, i, obj);
       currX += nooButton.width+5;
     }
   }
```

9.   `textFormat` has also been changed to better demonstrate the effect:

```
buttonTextFormat = new TextFormat("Arial", 15, 0xdddddd, true);
```

Save your movie as `rollerNooButton.fla` and test it. There are many ways that we could add to this component, such as methods to disable the button or to switch the text. You could also create different graphical states for the buttons using frames and `gotoAndStop` actions. Hopefully you now have a decent enough grounding to go away and create your own code, modifying what we've already created.

Summary

This chapter should have given you a solid understanding of how to go about building your own components and the kind of issues you will come across. It's worth taking time to plan and create components to be as versatile as possible. This initial outlay will be very worthwhile in terms of the time saved in implementation later. It's also a good idea to try and dissect the built-in components as these have been constructed to allow for almost all possibilities, and all situations in which you might wish to deploy the component. They offer insight into the methodologies used to achieve this versatility and are great examples for further study.

section 1: Site Presentation

chapter 5: Taking Things Further

In this chapter we're going to build upon what we've looked at so far. The central example here will be another image–viewing interface. We're going to work on a number of things that will improve what we've already built. We'll look at loading images dynamically and also keep the list of images external to the Flash movie so we can modify the site without reopening the FLA.

As we'll be loading the images dynamically we'll also look at how to create a preloader for them. We'll look at how to deal with different sized pictures, extending the slideTo prototype we created earlier so that we can also scale the viewing area. We'll also employ the newly added Stage object to arrange our interface, taking advantage of all the available space. Finally, we'll look at how we can use shared objects so that the interface can store the file names of the images to load for a certain amount of time, before putting it all together to create an improved interface for viewing our photos.

The Stage object

The Stage object is one of the most powerful additions to Flash MX. It allows us to access the space around the stage area, be it the browser window or the standalone player, to ascertain its dimensions and make use of the space. We can assign events to react to any change in available space and rearrange elements accordingly. This allows us to achieve the kind of fluid layouts that are possible with HTML. To make use of the Stage object we have to set up the HTML in a particular way. Generally when publishing a movie, there are two options.

With the first option, the Flash movie is displayed at its actual size and the movie dimensions define the space it takes up, forming a hard border around which we have an HTML page. To achieve this setting, open the **Publish Settings** dialog window (**File > Publish Settings**) and select the **HTML** tab. Set the **Dimensions** drop-down menu to **Match Movie** and the **Scale** drop-down menu to **Default (Show all)**.

Dimensions: Match Movie

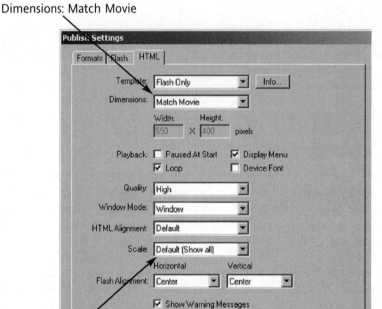

Scale: Default (Show all)

The second option allows us to set the Flash movie to stretch and fill the available space by setting the **Dimensions** to 100% whilst maintaining a default **Scale** mode:

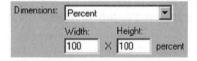

Resizing the stage with the Stage object

Flash MX allows us another option when setting our Publishing Settings, which enables the user to adjust the size of the browser or Flash player window and the objects on the stage will adjust accordingly. We'll look at how we can achieve this now.

1. Open a new Flash movie with default stage dimensions (550 x 400), and in the Publish Settings dialog window set **Dimensions** to 100% and the **Scale** mode to **No scale**.

2.   Now draw some random stuff on the stage area and also in the work area, off the stage:

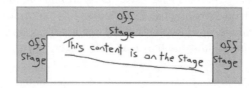

When you open the movie in your browser or the standalone Flash Player, you'll see that we're able to see not only the area on stage, but also a certain amount of the content in the work area, depending on how large your browser window is.

> We have to set up the HTML this way whenever we want to use the Stage object.

We'll now look at how to take advantage of this extra space. The Stage object is fairly minimal in terms of the properties and methods that it has available. We can access the width and height of the stage and we can also assign listeners to receive notifications that the stage size has changed. It's important to realize that Stage.Width and Stage.Height do not refer to the dimensions that we've set for the movie, but to the actual size that's available to us: the size of the standalone Player window or the size of the browser window. On its own, this information is relatively useless, so we need to know how big our stage was to begin with to do anything meaningful with it.

3.   In order to access this information we need to temporarily switch the scale mode of the stage back to showAll – in this mode the stage dimensions will be as we entered them in the movie Properties dialog. Clear everything from the stage of the movie we just created and add the following code to a new scripts layer:

```
fscommand("allowscale", "false");
// switch to showAll mode
Stage.scaleMode = "showAll";
Stage.originalWidth = Stage.Width;
Stage.originalHeight = Stage.Height;
// switch back to noScale
Stage.scaleMode = "noScale"
```

We've now added two additional properties to the Stage object; originalWidth and originalHeight. We've also added the allowscale = false fscommand so that our movie doesn't stretch in preview mode.

Before we go farther, it's important to understand exactly what's going on with the extra space that we have. When we have extra space around the movie, the top left corner is no longer (0,0). Instead, the original (stage) area of our movie maintains its coordinates, floating in the middle, and any extra space around it is relative to these coordinates. The following diagram should make things a little clearer:

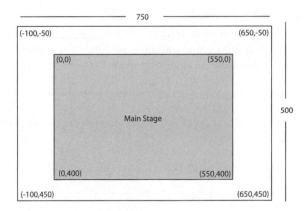

The gray area is the main stage, measuring 550 x 400 pixels, with the coordinates of each corner marked accordingly. The larger box around the edge represents the window in which the movie sits, currently sized at 750 x 500 pixels. This is 200 pixels wider than our original movie and 100 pixels taller. The extra pixels are distributed evenly on either side of the stage, so the left edge of the viewable area is at -100 pixels (0-100), the right edge at 650 (550+100), the top edge at -50 (0-50) and the bottom edge is at 450 (400+50).

It's these edges that are important to us if we want to place movie clips in relation to them, so we'll write some new methods for the Stage object to return them for us. First of all we'll work out how to calculate the values:

- **Left Edge:** 0 minus half of `Stage.Width` minus the original width.
- **Top Edge:** 0 minus half of `Stage.Height` minus the original height.
- **Right Edge:** The original width plus half of `Stage.Width` minus the original width.
- **Bottom Edge:** The original height plus half of `Stage.Height` minus the original height.

4.   We can now write that as ActionScript:

```
//define methods to retrieve boundaries
Stage.getLeft = function() {
    return -1*(this.width-this.originalWidth)/2;
};
Stage.getTop = function() {
```

```
        return -1*(this.height-this.originalHeight)/2;
};
Stage.getRight = function() {
        return this.originalWidth+(this.width-this.originalWidth)/2;
};
Stage.getBottom = function() {
        return this.originalHeight+(this.height-this.originalHeight)/2;
};
```

5. We'll now create some movie clips to use these values. We'll use four brackets, like picture corners, for each corner of the stage. We've called them tl, tr, br and bl, and the graphics in each are 50 x 50 pixels, with the registration point in the top left corner. The bracket movie clips are available with the source files on the CD.

6. Drag the four on stage, and also name the instances tl, tr, br and bl using the Property inspector, and place each in their respective corners of the stage. We've also put some text in the middle of the stage to indicate the middle of the movie. Your stage should now look something like this:

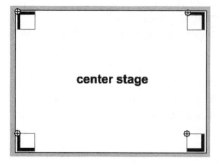

To have these movie clips move into their respective corners when the stage resizes, we have to create listeners for them, which is a fairly simple concept to grasp. Basically, the Stage object has a list of objects and/or movie clips that are registered with it to receive notification when the stage is resized. Whenever the stage is resized, the Stage object will call the onResize event in any objects that are registered with it. So, first we need to register our movie clips with the Stage object and then create an onResize method for each of them to put them into place.

7. To add listeners we just have to call the addListener method of the Stage object, passing the names of the movie clips as arguments. Add the following to your existing ActionScript:

```
// register four movie clips to receive notification of onResize
Stage.addListener(tl);
Stage.addListener(tr);
```

```
Stage.addListener(bl);
Stage.addListener(br);
```

8. Next, we have to create the `onResize` methods. Note that we have to take account of the fact that the registration points of our movie clips are not necessarily on the correct side, so for the bottom right clip for example, we have to put it at the right edge minus its width and the bottom edge minus its height:

```
// top left
tl.onResize = function() {
    this._x = Stage.getLeft();
    this._y = Stage.getTop();
};
// top right
tr.onResize = function() {
    this._x = Stage.getRight()-this._width;
    this._y = Stage.getTop();
};
// bottom left
bl.onResize = function() {
    this._x = Stage.getLeft();
    this._y = Stage.getBottom()-this._height;
};
// bottom right
br.onResize = function() {
    this._x = Stage.getRight()-this._width;
    this._y = Stage.getBottom()-this._height;
};
```

Here's the complete code:

```
fscommand("allowscale", "false");
Stage.scaleMode="showAll";
Stage.originalWidth = Stage.Width;
Stage.originalHeight = Stage.Height;
Stage.scaleMode="noScale"
Stage.getLeft = function() {
    return -1*(this.width-this.originalWidth)/2;
};
Stage.getTop = function() {
    return -1*(this.height-this.originalHeight)/2;
};
Stage.getRight = function() {
    return this.originalWidth+(this.width-this.originalWidth)/2;
};
```

```
Stage.getBottom = function() {
    return this.originalHeight+(this.height-this.originalHeight)/2;
};
Stage.addListener(tl);
Stage.addListener(tr);
Stage.addListener(bl);
Stage.addListener(br);
// top left
tl.onResize = function() {
    this._x = Stage.getLeft();
    this._y = Stage.getTop();
};
// top right
tr.onResize = function() {
    this._x = Stage.getRight()-this._width;
    this._y = Stage.getTop();
};
// bottom left
bl.onResize = function() {
    this._x = Stage.getLeft();
    this._y = Stage.getBottom()-this._height;
};
// bottom right
br.onResize = function() {
    this._x = Stage.getRight()-this._width;
    this._y = Stage.getBottom()-this._height;
};
```

9. Save your movie as `stageObject.fla` and when you run it, you'll see that it is putting the movie clips in the correct corners, as expected. It is slightly more accurate in the standalone Player than in the browser as there is a small gutter around the Flash movie in the HTML page:

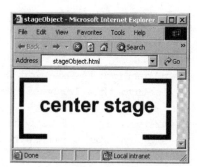

This works as it is, but it's slightly inefficient. Every time we need to find the left coordinate of the stage we're calling the `Stage.getLeft` function, whereas the only actual time this value changes is when the stage size changes.

More efficient resizing

It would be better if these were static values, calculated only when the stage size changes. This is best accomplished inside the Stage object itself, so we'll set the properties `Stage.left`, `Stage.top`, `Stage.right` and `Stage.bottom` whenever it's resized. According to the ActionScript dictionary, the Stage object has a built-in `onResize` handler to which we should be able to assign a function and have it work. Unfortunately, this doesn't seem to work and the only way of making it work is to add the Stage object as a listener to itself, which might seem slightly strange, but it works.

So, for our `Stage.onResize` function we have the code below, calling each of our four `get` functions and placing the results in properties inside the Stage object.

1. Add the following code above the `get` functions:

```
Stage.onResize = function() {
    this.left = this.getLeft();
    this.top = this.getTop();
    this.right = this.getRight();
    this.bottom = this.getBottom();
};
```

2. While we're doing this we'll make a slight modification to our `get` functions. As we're calculating left and top first we can have right equal left plus width and bottom equal top plus height:

```
Stage.getLeft = function() {
    return -1*(this.width-this.originalWidth)/2;
};
Stage.getTop = function() {
    return -1*(this.height-this.originalHeight)/2;
};
Stage.getRight = function() {
    return this.left+this.width;
};
Stage.getBottom = function() {
    return this.top+this.height;
};
```

3.   Then we add the stage listener:

```
Stage.addListener(Stage);
Stage.addListener(tl);
Stage.addListener(tr);
Stage.addListener(bl);
Stage.addListener(br);
```

Note that the listeners are notified of the resize event in the order that they are added, so in this case, Stage is first, then tl, tr, bl and finally br. This is important here as we have to be sure that the values for left, right, and so on are set before we access them from the movie clips.

4.   We now have to rewrite the movie clips' onResize functions to use these new values:

```
// top left
tl.onResize = function() {
    this._x = Stage.left;
    this._y = Stage.top;
};
// top right
tr.onResize = function() {
    this._x = Stage.right-this._width;
    this._y = Stage.top;
};
// bottom left
bl.onResize = function() {
    this._x = Stage.left;
    this._y = Stage.bottom-this._height;
};
// bottom right
br.onResize = function() {
    this._x = Stage.right-this._width;
    this._y = Stage.bottom-this._height;
};
```

5.   Save your movie as stageObject2.fla. Here's the complete code, which works exactly the same as before, but is somewhat tidier:

```
fscommand("allowscale", "false");
Stage.scaleMode="showAll";
Stage.originalWidth = Stage.Width;
Stage.originalHeight = Stage.Height;
Stage.scaleMode="noScale";
Stage.onResize = function() {
```

continues overleaf

```
            this.left = this.getLeft();
            this.top = this.getTop();
            this.right = this.getRight();
            this.bottom = this.getBottom();
        };
        Stage.getLeft = function() {
            return -1*(this.width-this.originalWidth)/2;
        };
        Stage.getTop = function() {
            return -1*(this.height-this.originalHeight)/2;
        };
        Stage.getRight = function() {
            return this.left+this.width;
        };
        Stage.getBottom = function() {
            return this.top+this.height;
        };
        Stage.addListener(Stage);
        Stage.addListener(tl);
        Stage.addListener(tr);
        Stage.addListener(bl);
        Stage.addListener(br);
        // top left
        tl.onResize = function() {
            this._x = Stage.left;
            this._y = Stage.top;
        };
        // top right
        tr.onResize = function() {
            this._x = Stage.right-this._width;
            this._y = Stage.top;
        };
        // bottom left
        bl.onResize = function() {
            this._x = Stage.left;
            this._y = Stage.bottom-this._height;
        };
        // bottom right
        br.onResize = function() {
            this._x = Stage.right-this._width;
            this._y = Stage.bottom-this._height;
        };
```

Applying motion when the stage is resized

We'll now quickly demonstrate how we can build in some motion here, taking the rearrangement of the layout further than the way it works with standard HTML by having the corners slide into place. To do this we need to copy across our `slideTo` function that we first created in Chapter 1.

1. Add the following code above the `onResize` functions:

```
MovieClip.prototype.slideTo = function(x, y, speed, callbackObj,
➥callbackFunc) {
    var noo
    if (this.slideControl) {
        noo = this.slideControl;
    } else {
        noo = this.createEmptyMovieClip("slideControl",this.depth++);
    }
    noo.tx = x;
    noo.ty = y;
    noo.speed = speed;
    // store callback object / method (not used yet)
    noo.callBackObj = callBackObj;
    noo.callBackFunc = callBackFunc;
    noo.onEnterFrame = function() {
        this._parent._x += (this.tx-this._parent._x)/this.speed;
        this._parent._y += (this.ty-this._parent._y)/this.speed;
        if (Math.abs(this.tx-this._parent._x)<0.2 && Math.abs(this.ty
        ➥this._parent._y)<0.2) {
            this._parent._x = this.tx;
            this._parent._y = this.ty;
            // execute callback (we're not using this yet)
            this.callBackObj[this.callBackFunc](this._parent);
            this.removeMovieClip();
        }
    };
};
```

2. Next, we have to alter the `onResize` calls to instead trigger the `slideTo` function, with the X and Y values as targets to slide to:

```
tl.onResize = function() {
    var x = Stage.left;
    var y = Stage.top;
    this.slideTo(x, y, 5);
};
```

continues overleaf

```
tr.onResize = function() {
    var x = Stage.right-this._width;
    var y = Stage.top;
    this.slideTo(x, y, 5);
};
bl.onResize = function() {
    var x = Stage.left;
    var y = Stage.bottom-this._height;
    this.slideTo(x, y, 5);
};
br.onResize = function() {
    var x = Stage.right-this._width;
    var y = Stage.bottom-this._height;
    this.slideTo(x, y, 5);
};
```

3. Save your movie as `stageObject3.fla` and when you test it, you'll see the corner brackets fade into position and slide into position whenever the browser or Flash Player window is resized. Here's the complete code:

```
fscommand("allowscale", "false");
Stage.scaleMode="showAll";
Stage.originalWidth = Stage.Width;
Stage.originalHeight = Stage.Height;
Stage.scaleMode="noScale";
Stage.onResize = function() {
    this.left = this.getLeft();
    this.top = this.getTop();
    this.right = this.getRight();
    this.bottom = this.getBottom();
};
Stage.getLeft = function() {
    return -1*(this.width-this.originalWidth)/2;
};
Stage.getTop = function() {
    return -1*(this.height-this.originalHeight)/2;
};
Stage.getRight = function() {
    return this.left+this.width;
};
Stage.getBottom = function() {
    return this.top+this.height;
};
Stage.addListener(Stage);
Stage.addListener(tl);
```

```
Stage.addListener(tr);
Stage.addListener(bl);
Stage.addListener(br);
MovieClip.prototype.slideTo = function(x, y, speed, callbackObj,
➥callbackFunc) {
    var noo
    if (this.slideControl) {
        noo = this.slideControl;
    } else {
        noo = this.createEmptyMovieClip("slideControl",this.depth++);
    }
    noo.tx = x;
    noo.ty = y;
    noo.speed = speed;
    noo.callBackObj = callBackObj;
    noo.callBackFunc = callBackFunc;
    noo.onEnterFrame = function() {
        this._parent._x += (this.tx-this._parent._x)/this.speed;
        this._parent._y += (this.ty-this._parent._y)/this.speed;
        if (Math.abs(this.tx-this._parent._x)<0.2 &&Math.abs(this.ty
        ➥this._parent._y)<0.2) {
            this._parent._x = this.tx;
            this._parent._y = this.ty;
            this.callBackObj[this.callBackFunc](this._parent);
            this.removeMovieClip();
        }
    };
};
tl.onResize = function() {
    var x = Stage.left;
    var y = Stage.top;
    this.slideTo(x, y, 5);
};
tr.onResize = function() {
    var x = Stage.right-this._width;
    var y = Stage.top;
    this.slideTo(x, y, 5);
};
bl.onResize = function() {
    var x = Stage.left;
    var y = Stage.bottom-this._height;
    this.slideTo(x, y, 5);
};
br.onResize = function() {
    var x = Stage.right-this._width;
```

continues overleaf

```
            var y = Stage.bottom-this._height;
            this.slideTo(x, y, 5);
    };
```

> *Using this technique of having an expandable stage means the Flash Player has a much larger area to deal with. If there's a lot of motion going on, especially with transparencies, the Flash Player may get bogged down – worth considering if you're thinking of using this.*

Scaling an object

We have already created a slideTo method to move an object from one location to another. We're now going to modify the slideTo method a little to create a scaleTo method, which we'll employ in conjunction with the Stage object to create a scalable background panel that will scale with the movie and sit underneath our centered title.

1. Open the stageObject3.fla and save it as resize001.fla. Now draw a 100 x 100 pixel gray square and convert it to a movie clip with a central registration point.

2. Delete the new movie clip from the stage, but drag an instance of it onto a new layer called background panel, which you should place beneath the layer containing the 'center stage' caption.

3. Using the Property inspector, name the instance of the movie clip bg and scale it up so that it's 500 pixels wide and 350 pixels high. Using the **Align** panel, center the movie clip horizontally and vertically by pressing the relevant buttons while the **To Stage** button is selected. Your stage and timeline should look like this:

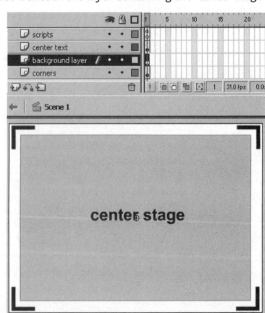

4. We're going to create some code for this movie clip that will keep it 25 pixels from the edge of the movie on all sides no matter how much the movie is resized. First of all we'll just have it change scale straight away. Add a listener for the movie clip below the other listeners:

```
Stage.addListener(bg);
```

5. Next, add an onResize listener for the movie clip below the other onResize listeners, and then resave your movie and test it.

```
bg.onResize = function() {
    this._xscale = Stage.width-50;
    this._yscale = Stage.height-50;
};
```

Animating the scaling

That works fine, but our corner pieces are sliding into position and so it would be nice if we could have the background also scale up gradually. We'll accomplish that next. Save your movie here as resize002.fla

1. To do this we need to create a scaleTo method, which can be achieved fairly easily by modifying our slideTo method, substituting _xscale and _yscale for _x and _y. Place the following code below the slideTo function:

```
MovieClip.prototype.scaleTo = function(xsc, ysc, speed,callbackObj,
➥callbackFunc) {
    var noo;
    if (this.scaleControl) {
        noo = this.scaleControl;
    } else {
        noo = this.createEmptyMovieClip("scaleControl",
        ➥this.depth++);
    }
    noo.txsc = xsc;
    noo.tysc = ysc;
    noo.speed = speed;
    noo.callBackObj = callBackObj;
    noo.callBackFunc = callBackFunc;
    noo.onEnterFrame = function() {
        this._parent._xscale += (this.txsc-this._parent._xscale)
        ➥/this.speed;
        this._parent._yscale += (this.tysc-this._parent._yscale)
```

177

```
          ➥/this.speed;
          if (Math.abs(this.txsc-this._parent._xscale)<0.2 &&
          ➥Math.abs(this.tysc-this._parent._yscale)<0.2) {
     this._parent._xscale = this.tx;
     this._parent._yscale = this.ty;
     //execute callback (not used yet)
     this.callBackObj[this.callBackFunc](this._parent);
     this.removeMovieClip();
          }
     };
};
```

2. This works in exactly the same way as `slideTo`, but using scale. Now we just change the
    `onResize` function to call this method, passing it the target scale values:

    ```
    bg.onResize = function() {
        var xsc = Stage.width-50;
        var ysc = Stage.height-50;
        this.scaleTo(xsc, ysc, 5);
    };
    ```

3. When you test this in your browser you'll see that the gray background now scales gradually
    as you resize your browser window.

This works perfectly, although it seems somewhat irritating to have different methods to affect
different properties. If we wanted to change the alpha we would have to add another, and so on.
It would be better if we had a single method for shifting a set of values inside a movie clip towards
a target set of values.

Using a single method to alter the properties

There is in fact a way of doing this, which we'd accomplish by passing the method an object
containing a set of all the values that we want to affect. We then loop through every value in the
target object and gradually push the corresponding value in our movie clip towards this value.
When the values become close together we snap the movie clip's value to the target value and
remove this value from the `targets` object. So, for moving an object to a point we'd pass it an
object like this:

```
var obj = {_x:50, _y:100};
this.tweenTo(obj, 5);
```

The beginning of the method will be the same as with the `slideTo` method, creating a controller
movie clip if there isn't one already and then setting values inside it.

1. Replace the previous `slideTo` and `scaleTo` functions with the following code:

```
MovieClip.prototype.tweenTo = function(targetsObj, speed,
➡callbackObj, callbackFunc) {
var noo;
    if (this.tweenControl) {
        noo = this.tweenControl;
    } else {
    noo = this.createEmptyMovieClip("tweenControl", this.depth++);
    }
    // store the object containing target properties and values
    noo.targetsObj = targetsObj;
    noo.speed = speed;
    noo.callBackObj = callBackObj;
    noo.callBackFunc = callBackFunc;
    noo.onEnterFrame = function() {
    var count;
    // as its an object we can't check length.
    }
}
```

2. We then have to set up the loop to go through and change all the values. To iterate through the values in an object we use a `for ... in` loop, like this:

```
for (var prop in this.targetsObj) {
    this._parent[prop]+=(this.targetsObj[prop]this._parent[prop])
    ➡/this.speed;
}
```

As we loop, `prop` will refer to the name of each property we loop through, and so the next line of code brings the value of this property in the movie clip closer to the value of this property in the `targets` object.

3. We also have to check to see if the movie clip property has reached the target property, in which case we snap to it and then delete it from the `targets` object. The new code is highlighted in bold:

```
for (var prop in this.targetsObj) {
    this._parent[prop] += (this.targetsObj[prop]
    ➡this._parent[prop])/this.speed;
    // if property has reached target value
    if (Math.abs(this.targetsObj[prop]- this._parent[prop])<0.4) {
        this._parent[prop] = this.targetsObj[prop];
        delete this.targetsObj[prop];
```

```
            }
        }
```

4. The final thing we need to do is put in some kind of check to see when the `targets` object is empty. Unlike an array object, a generic object like we're using here has no length property. So, to determine when it's empty, we'll have to keep count of how many properties are looped through. As each movie clip property reaches the corresponding target property, the target property is removed from `targetsObj`. When all of the movie clip properties have reached the target properties, there will be no properties left in `targetsObj` and `count` will remain at zero as there are no properties left to loop through. When `count` equals zero we can terminate the control movie clip and call our callback function.

```
MovieClip.prototype.tweenTo = function(targetsObj, speed, callbackObj,
➥callbackFunc) {
    var noo;
    if (this.tweenControl) {
        noo = this.tweenControl;
    } else {
        noo = this.createEmptyMovieClip("tweenControl",
        ➥this.depth++);
    }
    noo.targetsObj = targetsObj;
    noo.speed = speed;
    noo.callBackObj = callBackObj;
    noo.callBackFunc = callBackFunc;
    noo.onEnterFrame = function() {
        var count;
        // as it's an object we can't check length.
        for (var prop in this.targetsObj) {
            this._parent[prop] += (this.targetsObj[prop]-
            ➥this._parent[prop])/this.speed;
            if (Math.abs(this.targetsObj[prop]
            ➥this._parent[prop])<0.4) {
                this._parent[prop] = this.targetsObj[prop];
                delete this.targetsObj[prop];
            }
            count++;
        }
    if (!count) {
        this.callBackObj[this.callBackFunc](this._parent);
        this.removeMovieClip();
        }
    };
};
```

5. So, to implement this new method of controlling motion we have to alter our `onResize` listeners. Here's one for the bottom right corner, affecting _x and _y:

```
br.onResize = function() {
    // define targets
    var obj = {_x:Stage.right-this._width, _y:Stage.bottom
    ➥this._height};
    this.tweenTo(obj, 5);
};
```

...and here's one for the background, affecting _xscale and _yscale:

```
bg.onResize = function() {
    var obj = {_xscale:Stage.width-50, _yscale:Stage.height-50};
    this.tweenTo(obj, 5);
};
```

Here's the complete code where the other `onResize` functions have been changed as well, highlighted in bold at the bottom:

```
fscommand("allowscale", "false");
Stage.scaleMode="showAll";
Stage.originalWidth = Stage.Width;
Stage.originalHeight = Stage.Height;
Stage.scaleMode="noScale";
Stage.onResize = function() {
    this.left = this.getLeft();
    this.top = this.getTop();
    this.right = this.getRight();
    this.bottom = this.getBottom();
};
Stage.getLeft = function() {
    return -1*(this.width-this.originalWidth)/2;
};
Stage.getTop = function() {
    return -1*(this.height-this.originalHeight)/2;
};
Stage.getRight = function() {
    return this.left+this.width;
};
Stage.getBottom = function() {
    return this.top+this.height;
};
```

continues overleaf

```
Stage.addListener(Stage);
Stage.addListener(tl);
Stage.addListener(tr);
Stage.addListener(bl);
Stage.addListener(br);
Stage.addListener(bg);
MovieClip.prototype.tweenTo = function(targetsObj, speed,
➥callbackObj, callbackFunc) {
    var noo;
    if (this.tweenControl) {
        noo = this.tweenControl;
    } else {
        noo = this.createEmptyMovieClip("tweenControl",this.depth++);
    }
    noo.targetsObj = targetsObj;
    noo.speed = speed;
    noo.callBackObj = callBackObj;
    noo.callBackFunc = callBackFunc;
    noo.onEnterFrame = function() {
        var count;
        // as its an object we can't check length.
        for (var prop in this.targetsObj) {
            this._parent[prop] += (this.targetsObj[prop]-
            ➥this._parent[prop])/this.speed;
            if (Math.abs(this.targetsObj[prop]-
            ➥this._parent[prop])<0.4) {
                this._parent[prop] = this.targetsObj[prop];
                delete this.targetsObj[prop];
            }
            count++;
        }
        if (!count) {
            this.callBackObj[this.callBackFunc](this._parent);
            this.removeMovieClip();
        }
    };
};
tl.onResize = function() {
    var obj = {_x:Stage.left, _y:Stage.top};
    this.tweenTo(obj, 5);
};
tr.onResize = function() {
    var obj = {_x:Stage.right-this._width, _y:Stage.top};
    this.tweenTo(obj, 5);
};
```

continues overleaf

```
bl.onResize = function() {
    var obj = {_x:Stage.left, _y:Stage.bottom-this._height};
    this.tweenTo(obj, 5);
};
br.onResize = function() {
    var obj = {_x:Stage.right-this._width, _y:Stage.bottom
    ➥this._height};
    this.tweenTo(obj, 5);
};
bg.onResize = function() {
    var obj = {_xscale:Stage.width-50, _yscale:Stage.height-50};
    this.tweenTo(obj, 5);
};
```

6. Save your movie as `resize003.fla` and test it. It will work exactly the same as the previous file, but is a lot more compact.

We could do more with it if we wanted. For example, we could set the alpha of the background panel depending on how large the stage is:

```
bg.onResize = function() {
    var obj = {_alpha:100*(Stage.Width/Stage.originalWidth),
    ➥_xscale:Stage.width-50, _yscale:Stage.height-50};
    this.tweenTo(obj, 5);
};
```

You'll see the effect better if you change the color of the square in the movie clip from gray to a red or a blue. If you make the stage really small, the background will almost fade out entirely (`resize004.fla`).

It should be noted that while here we are creating `tweenTo` as a method of the MovieClip object, we could create a separate tween class, inheriting from the MovieClip class. This might be appropriate if only a certain number of movie clips needed access to these tween methods. You could set it up something like this:

```
function tweenable() {
}
tweenable.prototype = new Movieclip();
Object.registerClass("tweenableMc", tweenable);
tweenable.tweenTo = function() {
    var noo;
    if (this.tweenControl) {
        noo = this.tweenControl;
    } else {
        noo = this.createEmptyMovieClip("tweenControl",this.depth++);
```

183

continues overleaf

```
        }
        noo.targetsObj = targetsObj;
        noo.speed = speed;
        noo.callBackObj = callBackObj;
        noo.callBackFunc = callBackFunc;
        noo.onEnterFrame = function() {
            var count;
            // as it's an object we can't check length.
            for (var prop in this.targetsObj) {
                this._parent[prop] += (this.targetsObj[prop]
                ➥this._parent[prop])/this.speed;
                if (Math.abs(this.targetsObj[prop]
                ➥this._parent[prop])<0.4) {
                    this._parent[prop] = this.targetsObj[prop];
                    delete this.targetsObj[prop];
                }
                count++;
            }
            if (!count) {
                this.callBackObj[this.callBackFunc](this._parent);
                this.removeMovieClip();
            }
        };
};
```

You would use `Object.registerClass` to associate any particular movie clip symbol with this class. You could then add extra methods to this class to add properties to the tween like this:

```
tweenable.prototype.addToTween = function(obj) {
    //loop through and add properties to targetsObj
    for (var prop in obj) {
        this.tweenControl.targetsObj[prop] = obj[prop];
    }
};
```

You could also add individual speeds for each property, individual callbacks for when each property reaches its target, or passing an argument with the property name and the value reached. It all depends on how you want to use it. You might also think back to the way we set up a watchpoint on the `rollOver` event with the tooltip component – it may be that you could work out something similar here, to allow normal `onEnterFrame` events to run at the same time as the `tweenTo` function and avoid the need to add a controller movie clip.

This kind of event management is quite an extensive topic, which not everybody will be interested in. For those of you who are interested though, hopefully these suggestions will have given you some scope for pursuing this area further.

XML

We're now going to start work on putting together a final version of our site. If we're going to bring the pictures in dynamically, it makes sense to store a list of pictures external to the Flash movie, which we can bring in at the start to determine what pictures to load.

It could also provide us with some basic information concerning the pictures that we can use in the movie, such as width, height and a caption. The best way to do this is to use XML. In the application that we'll develop here, we'll concentrate simply on loading the XML data for our purposes. Chapter 17 takes more of an extensive look at using XML with Flash MX, and will also teach you some of the more general rules and considerations that are important when using XML data. If you're completely new to XML then it might be helpful for you to read the first few pages of Chapter 17 before continuing to get a stronger grasp of the subject.

OK – we can describe our list of pictures very simply with XML. Each picture will have its own node, containing attributes for its file name and name. Each node will look something like this:

```
<picture file="denim001.jpg" name="whatever"/>
```

You'll see that the XML above contains information about the image's file name, its width and height, as well as a designated image name, if it has one. The < sign indicates the beginning of a node in the same way as it does in HTML, and in the same way that the /> at the end indicates that this node is closed. `picture` simply indicates the type of node that this is, in the same way that `b` indicates bold in HTML.

The completed XML file will consist of a few of these picture elements all nested in a root element, `pictures`. Type this text into a text file and save it as `pictures.xml`.

```
<pictures>
    <picture file="denim001.jpg" name="whatever"/>
    <picture file="denim002.jpg" name="whatever"/>
    <picture file="denim003.jpg" name="whatever"/>
    <picture file="denim004.jpg" name="whatever"/>
    <picture file="denim005.jpg" name="whatever"/>
    <picture file="denim006.jpg" name="whatever"/>
    <picture file="denim007.jpg" name="whatever"/>
    <picture file="denim008.jpg" name="whatever"/>
</pictures>
```

You've just created a simple XML file. If you open `pictures.xml` inside your Internet browser, you'll see a depiction of the hierarchy of information:

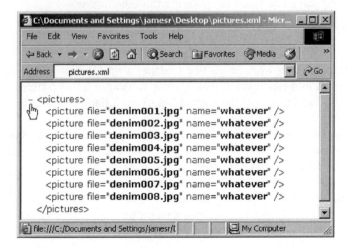

Notice that there's a **+/–** icon that you can click to open/close the document structure and bring out the nested data. On its own, this document can't really do much for us. XML data only really becomes useful when it is processed by some other application.

So, let's look at how we can bring this data into Flash and actually make some use of it.

Bringing XML data into Flash

We have our XML structure laid out, so we now need to import it into Flash and then convert the information into data that we can use – an array of picture objects.

1. First we have to create a new object into which we'll load the XML document:

    ```
    myXml = new Xml();
    myXml.load("pictures.xml");
    ```

    This will bring in the XML document OK, but we need to trigger a function once the document has loaded fully.

2. To trigger a function once the XML document has been fully loaded, we can use the XML object's `onLoad` handler. As with the movie clip event handlers, we can define a function to be called when this event is triggered:

    ```
    myXml = new Xml();
    ```

```
// call parseMe once xml has loaded
myXml.onLoad = parseMe;
myXml.load("pictures.xml");
function parseMe() {
}
```

3. Before we create the parseMe function we have to add one more line of code, to ensure that any white space in the XML source (such as carriage returns or tabs) are ignored:

```
myXml = new Xml();
myXml.ignoreWhite = true;
myXml.onLoad = parseMe;
myXml.load("pictures.xml");
function parseMe() {
}
```

4. We want the parseMe function to extract the relevant information from each picture node and store it, so we'll also create an array to store the data in:

```
pictureObjects = [];
myXml = new Xml();
myXml.ignoreWhite = true;
myXml.onLoad = parseMe;
myXml.load("pictures.xml");
function parseMe() {
}
```

5. When we call the parseMe function, the scope is inside the XML object, so if we trace this, we'll get a listing of the entire document: Place this under the existing code:

```
function parseMe() {
    trace(this);
}
```

If you save your movie in the same folder as where you stored pictures.xml and test it, you'll see a string in the Output window that contains all of the information inside pictures.xml.

There's a lot more to the XML object than that, though. When Flash brings in an XML document, it parses it itself and creates an object structure from it, with each node having references to its child nodes, its siblings and its parents as well as attributes that the node may have.

6.   If you want to see all of this you can create a loop to iterate through all the properties of the object:

```
function parseMe () {
}
function parseMe () {
    for (var i in this) {
        trace ("property - "+i+" : value - "+this[i]");
    }
}
```

...which will return this result in the Output window:

```
Output                                                                    ⊠
                                                                  Options
  property - previousSibling : value - null
  property - parentNode : value - null
  property - nodeValue : value - null
  property - nodeType : value - 1
  property - nodeName : value - null
  property - nextSibling : value - null
  property - lastChild : value - <pictures><picture file="denim001.jpg"
  property - firstChild : value - <pictures><picture file="denim001.jpg"
  property - childNodes : value - <pictures><picture file="denim001.jpg"
  property - attributes : value -
  property - toString : value - [type Function]
  property - hasChildNodes : value - [type Function]
  property - appendChild : value - [type Function]
  property - insertBefore : value - [type Function]
  property - removeNode : value - [type Function]
  property - cloneNode : value - [type Function]
  property - xmlDecl : value -
  property - status : value - 0
  property - loaded : value - true
  property - ignoreWhite : value - true
```

So with our parseMe function, we need to navigate to our pictures node and loop through its child nodes (the picture nodes), extracting the attributes of each picture and storing them in our array.

When we call parseMe we are inside the XML document at the document root – a level above the pictures node.

To refer to our pictures node, we write:

```
this.firstChild;
```

This refers to the first child of the main node. Now the nodes for each individual picture are stored within the `childNodes` array of the `pictures` node. These are the nodes that exist within the `pictures` node in the hierarchy, as we saw above. To refer to this array we write:

```
this.firstChild.childNodes;
```

7.   That's the array we need to loop through so we set up a loop like this:

```
function parseMe() {
    var pictures = this.firstChild.childNodes;
    // loop through child nodes
    for (var i in pictures) {
        populate the array
    }
}
```

8.   Inside the loop, each individual picture node will be `pictures[i]`. The information we want to extract is held within the `attributes` object of the `picture` node. This object is a standard object with a property for each of the attributes, so we can just copy this straight across into our array, using `Array.push` to append it to the end of the array:

```
function parseMe() {
    var pictures = this.firstChild.childNodes;
    for (var i in pictures) {
        var obj = pictures[i].attributes;
        pictureObjects.push(obj);
    }
}
```

9.   We can cut this down:

```
function parseMe() {
    var pictures = this.firstChild.childNodes;
    for (var i in pictures) {
        pictureObjects.push(pictures[i].attributes);
    }
}
```

One problem with this is that we're not creating a new object in the array, but just creating a reference to the `attributes` object in the XML object. If the `attributes` object in the XML node changes, so does the object in our array.

10. For example, look at the following and adjust your code to match it:

```
function parseMe() {
    var pictures = this.firstChild.childNodes;
    for (var i in pictures) {
        pictureObjects.push(pictures[i].attributes);
    }
    // add an attribute "hello" to the first childNode
    this.firstChild.childNodes[0].attributes.hello = true;
}
```

11. Now run the code and select the **Debug > List Variables** menu option. You'll see that the `hello` value shows up in our array:

12. To avoid this, we'll iterate through the `attributes` object and copy across all the properties:

```
function parseMe() {
    // this is the entire document
    // this.firstChild is the first node, ie our pictures node
    // this firstChild.childNodes is the list of individual documents
    var pictures = this.firstChild.childNodes;
    for (var i in pictures) {
        var obj = {};
        // loop through and copy attributes
        for (var j in pictures[i].attributes) {
            obj[j] = pictures[i].attributes[j];
        }
        pictureObjects.push(obj);
    }
    this.firstChild.childNodes[0].attributes.hello = true;
}
```

13. Save your file as `bringInXML.fla`, and now when you test it and **List Variables**, you'll see that `hello` does not show up in the array:

```
Output                                                            ×
                                                        Options ▾
      7:[object #10, class 'Object'] {
        file:"denim001.jpg",
        name:"whatever"
      }
    ]
 Variable _level0.myXml = [object #11, class 'XMLNode'] {
```

This is not really terribly important here, as we're not going to be manipulating the XML document any further, but it is important to understand when objects are defined by reference to another object and not on their own terms. Originally our array merely contained a pointer to the attributes object in the XML node so instead we copied all of the properties across. Another way of dealing with it here would be to delete the `myXml` object as this would destroy the original `attributes` object and leave the value in the array as the only reference to that object.

An XML loader

As the interface we're creating will be incorporated into a site, it would be a good idea to add a loader for the XML data. We're just going to create a simple text status indicator, showing what percent of the data is loading, which will also display a message if the XML fails to load. This is where we're going to start creating our interface in earnest, so we need to include the code for the `tweenTo` method, the `setBrightness` method from the previous chapter, as well as the `Stage` object that we created.

Rather than putting all this code in manually we're going to store the code externally in `.as` files and use `include` statements to bring them in:

```
#include "tweento.as"
#include "brightness.as"
#include "stage.as"
```

This is generally good practice if you have such chunks of code that you use across projects. When Flash comes across an `include` statement when compiling an SWF, the effect is as if the contents of the file specified were pasted in place of the `include` statement. Note that you may encounter problems if the last line of your AS file does not have a semi-colon at the end of it. One new feature of Flash MX is a global `include` path. Normally when using an `include` statement we must ensure that the AS files are placed in the same directory as the Flash file that is including them. This can be somewhat tiresome and the global include path gives us a place to store any AS files and have them accessible to all movies. On a PC the path to this is **C:\Program Files\Macromedia\Flash MX\Configuration\Include** – you may have to create the `include` directory yourself. Now when Flash encounters an `include` statement it will first look in the local directory and if it does not find the AS file there it will then look into the global `include` directory for it.

We have three files to include here, with the ActionScript for each included below. However, if you don't want to type them out again or copy from previous files, the AS files are included in the source files for this chapter.

Here are the contents for each of the three files:

Including code stored externally: tweenTo.as

```
MovieClip.prototype.tweenTo = function(targetsObj, speed, callbackObj,
➥callbackFunc) {
    var noo
    if (this.tweenControl) {
        noo = this.tweenControl;
    } else {
        noo = this.createEmptyMovieClip("tweenControl",this.depth++);
    }
    noo.targetsObj = targetsObj;
    noo.speed = speed;
    noo.callBackObj = callBackObj;
    noo.callBackFunc = callBackFunc;
    noo.onEnterFrame = function() {
        var count;
        // as its an object we can't check length.
        for (var prop in this.targetsObj) {
            this._parent[prop] += (this.targetsObj[prop]-
            ➥this._parent[prop])/this.speed;
            if (Math.abs(this.targetsObj[prop]-
            ➥this._parent[prop])<0.9) {
                this._parent[prop] = this.targetsObj[prop];
                delete this.targetsObj[prop];
            }
            count++;
        }
        if (!count) {
            this.callBackObj[this.callBackFunc](this._parent);
            this.removeMovieClip();
        }
    };
};
```

Including code stored externally: brightness.as

```
Color.prototype.setBrightness = function(bright) {
    var aNum = 100-Math.abs(bright);
    var bNum = bright<0 ? 0 : Math.ceil(255*bright/100);
    this.setTransform({ra:aNum, ga:aNum, ba:aNum, aa:100, rb:bNum,
    ➥gb:bNum, bb:bNum, ab:0});
};
```

Including code stored externally: stage.as

```
fscommand("allowscale", "false");
Stage.scaleMode="showAll";
Stage.originalWidth = Stage.Width;
Stage.originalHeight = Stage.Height;
Stage.scaleMode="noScale"
Stage.onResize = function() {
    this.left = this.getLeft();
    this.top = this.getTop();
    this.right = this.getRight();
    this.bottom = this.getBottom();
};
Stage.getLeft = function() {
    return -1*(Stage.width-this.originalWidth)/2;
};
Stage.getTop = function() {
    return -1*(Stage.height-this.originalHeight)/2;
};
Stage.getRight = function() {
    return this.left+this.width;
};
Stage.getBottom = function() {
    return this.top+this.height;
};
Stage.addListener(Stage);
// ensure onResize is called at start
Stage.onResize();
```

Building the XML loader

OK, now we have our external ActionScript files set up, let's concentrate on the code to go into the movie.

1. Add a new `scripts` layer. First of all we create a function to display a status movie clip, containing our status text. We need to start with a `TextFormat` object for the text, which we'll add beneath our `include` statements.

```
statusTf = new TextFormat("Arial", 40, 0x4375A6);
statusTf.align = "center";
statusTf.leading = -5;
```

Your current code should look like this:

```
#include "tweento.as"
#include "brightness.as"
#include "stage.as"

statusTf = new TextFormat("Arial", 40, 0x4375A6);
statusTf.align = "center";
statusTf.leading = -5;
```

2. On your other layer, add a dynamic text field just off the top of the stage – we'll position it using our ActionScript. With the text field selected, embed all characters for Arial (or whatever font you want to use) by clicking the **Character...** button in the Property inspector. In the **Character Options** dialog window, choose the **All Characters** option before hitting **Done**:

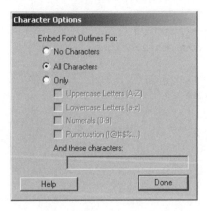

3. Using the Property inspector, name the text field embedder, and add the following highlighted code to make it invisible:

```
embedder._visible = 0;
statusTf = new TextFormat("Arial", 40, 0x4375A6);
statusTf.align = "center";
statusTf.leading = -5;
```

4. We also add a filename variable (highlighted in bold) to signify the XML file we want to load. We don't have to use a variable here, but it makes easier to change the file name if necessary.

```
_root.filename = "pictures.xml";
embedder._visible = 0;
statusTf = new TextFormat("Arial", 40, 0x4375A6);
statusTf.align = "center";
statusTf.leading = -5;
```

5. We'll now add a createStatusMovie function to create a text field, set the text format and set the text to the value we pass to the function:

```
function createStatusMovie(tex) {
    _root.createEmptyMovieClip("statusClip", 1);
    statusClip.createTextField("statusText", 1, 0, 0, 550, 100);
  //set properties of textfield
    statusClip.statusText.embedFonts = true;
    statusClip.statusText.selectable = false;
    statusClip.statusText.setNewTextFormat(statusTf);
    statusClip.statusText.text = tex;
    statusClip._x = 0;
    statusClip._y = (Stage.originalHeight-
    ➥statusClip.statusText.textHeight)/2-50;
}
```

Note that we're using the Stage object to place the text field slightly above the center vertically, and setting the alignment of the text field to center to center it horizontally. The createStatus function will be called when we first import the XML. We can also use the same function to create a loader for the individual pictures.

6. To create the XML preloader, we use the getBytesLoaded and getBytesTotal methods of the XML object. If we divide getBytesLoaded by getBytesTotal and then multiply by 100 it gives us the percentage of the XML that has been loaded. We're going to create a function, updateXmlStatus, which will calculate the percentage and display the result in the text field. We use setInterval to have this function called regularly.

Some of the following code for the `importXml` function will be familiar from the previous section where we first brought our XML data into Flash. The new code is highlighted in bold:

```
function importXml() {
    pictureObjects = [];
    myXml = new XML();
    myXml.ignoreWhite = true;
    // method to update display
    myXml.updateXmlStatus = function() {
        var percent = Math.round(this.getBytesLoaded()/
        ➥this.getBytesTotal()*100);
        if (percent<=0) {
            percent = "0";
        }
        _root.statusClip.statusText.text = "PICTURE DATA LOADING
        ➥\n"+percent+"%";
    };
    // use setInterval to call updateXmlStatus every 20
    //milliseconds
    myXml.updater = setInterval(myXml, "updateXmlStatus", 20);
    myXml.onLoad = parseMe;
    myXml.load(_root.filename);
    _root.createStatusMovie("PICTURE DATA LOADING");
}
```

Let's look at the `updateXmlStatus` function on its own:

```
myXml.updateXmlStatus = function() {
    var percent = Math.round(this.getBytesLoaded()/
    ➥this.getBytesTotal()*100);
    if (percent<=0) {
        percent = "0";
    }
    _root.statusClip.statusText.text = "PICTURE DATA LOADING
    ➥\n"+percent+"%";
};
```

First of all we calculate the percentage value and round it to get rid of decimals. When a call to load the XML is first executed (before Flash has time to contact the sever or retrieve any information about the file), `getBytesTotal` returns `undefined`. The percent value would then be equal to 0 divided by `undefined`, which obviously won't work, and returns NaN (not a number).

To avoid having this value show up as the percentage we run a check on `percent`. As NaN is seen by Flash as less than zero, we check if percent is less than zero and if so, just set percent to zero. In the final line we update the display text, adding a new line after PICTURE DATA LOADING.

7. We'll now move on to look at how to display a message if something goes wrong, which we'll achieve by slightly modifying our parseMe function. When a function is assigned to an XML object's onLoad handler, it is passed a single parameter when the onLoad event is fired. If the XML loads successfully, it passes true – if not, it passes false. So, we alter our previous parseMe function to check this value and act upon it. The new code is highlighted in bold:

```
function parseMe(success) {
    // if the xml has loaded successfully
    if (success) {
        var pictures = this.firstChild.childNodes;
        for (var i = 0; i<pictures.length; i++) {
            var obj = {};
            for (var j in pictures[i].attributes) {
                obj[j] = pictures[i].attributes[j];
            }
            pictureObjects.push(obj);
        }
        // stop calling the display update function
        clearInterval(this.updater);
        _root.pictureDataComplete();
        this.updateXmlStatus();
        //statusClip.removeMovieClip()
    } else {
        _root.statusClip.statusText.text = "FAILED TO LOAD DATA";
        clearInterval(this.updater);
    }
}
```

If the load is not successful, we change the statusText to read FAILED TO LOAD DATA. Whether successful or not, the interval calling updateXmlStatus is called. When we actually use the code we'll remove the status clip once the load is completed, but for now we'll leave it to see that the status call is working properly – otherwise, the message would disappear almost instantly.

8. Finally we'll add the function pictureDataComplete which is called when the XML has loaded, and an init function to trigger the XML load. Here's the complete code, with the pictureDataComplete and init functions highlighted in bold:

```
#include "tweento.as"
#include "brightness.as"
#include "stage.as"
_root.filename = "pictures.xml";
```

continues overleaf

```
            embedder._visible = 0;
            statusTf = new TextFormat("Arial", 40, 0x4375A6);
            statusTf.align = "center";
            statusTf.leading = -5;
            function createStatusMovie(tex) {
                _root.createEmptyMovieClip("statusClip", 1);
                statusClip.createTextField("statusText", 1, 0, 0, 550, 100);
                statusClip.statusText.embedFonts = true;
                statusClip.statusText.selectable = false;
                statusClip.statusText.setNewTextFormat(statusTf);
                statusClip.statusText.text = tex;
                statusClip._x = 0;
                statusClip._y = (Stage.originalHeight-
                ➥statusClip.statusText.textHeight)/2-50;
            }
            function importXml() {
                pictureObjects = [];
                myXml = new XML();
                myXml.ignoreWhite = true;
                myXml.updateXmlStatus = function() {
                    var percent = Math.round(this.getBytesLoaded()/
                    ➥this.getBytesTotal()*100);
                    if (percent<=0) {
                        percent = "0";
                    }
                    _root.statusClip.statusText.text = "PICTURE DATA LOADING
                    ➥\n"+percent+"%";
                };
                myXml.updater = setInterval(myXml, "updateXmlStatus", 20);
                myXml.onLoad = parseMe;
                myXml.load(_root.filename);
                _root.createStatusMovie("PICTURE DATA LOADING");
            }
            function parseMe(success) {
                if (success) {
                    var pictures = this.firstChild.childNodes;
                    for (var i = 0; i<pictures.length; i++) {
                        var obj = {};
                        for (var j in pictures[i].attributes) {
                            obj[j] = pictures[i].attributes[j];
                        }
                        pictureObjects.push(obj);
                    }
                    clearInterval(this.updater);
                    _root.pictureDataComplete();
```

```
            this.updateXmlStatus();
            //statusClip.removeMovieClip()
        } else {
            _root.statusClip.statusText.text = "FAILED TO LOAD DATA";
            clearInterval(this.updater);
        }
    }
}
function pictureDataComplete() {
    trace("picture data loaded");
}
function init() {
    importXml();
}
init();
```

If you test the file without saving it, you'll correctly get a FAILED TO LOAD DATA message because the FLA and pictures.xml are not stored in the same folder. Save the movie as xmlLoader.fla and test it again. This time, we get the PICTURE DATA LOADING 100% message as planned, so everything is working fine:

PICTURE DATA LOADING
100%

Storing the XML locally

One of the great things about shared objects is that we can store any kind of data inside them. Leading on from this, rather than importing the XML containing the picture file names every time we run the file, we can store the array of pictures locally. We can also build in an expiry date for the shared object, after which we re-import the XML in case of any changes.

The methodology for this is fairly simple. Before we import the XML, we check to see if we've already created a shared object for the movie, using sharedObject.getLocal. If we haven't created a shared object, or if the shared object is older than a certain date, then we go ahead and import the XML. After we've imported and parsed the XML, we store the pictureObjects array plus the current time in the shared object. If we do already have a shared object, then we retrieve the pictureObjects array from the shared object instead of from the XML.

1. First, let's create the function to save the array in the shared object. We add a call to this function when the XML has been loaded successfully and also uncomment the line of code to remove statusClip:

```
function parseMe(success) {
    if (success) {
        var pictures = this.firstChild.childNodes;
        for (var i = 0; i<pictures.length; i++) {
            var obj = {};
            for (var j in pictures[i].attributes) {
                obj[j] = pictures[i].attributes[j];
            }
            pictureObjects.push(obj);
        }
        _root.refreshSharedObj();
        clearInterval(this.updater);
        statusClip.removeMovieClip();
        _root.pictureDataComplete();
    } else {
        _root.statusClip.statusText.text = "FAILED TO LOAD DATA";
        clearInterval(this.updater);
    }
}
```

2. In the refreshSharedObj function we need to first retrieve the shared object using sharedObject.getLocal. We then put our pictureObjects array inside the shared object:

```
mySharedObj = sharedobject.getLocal("denim");
mySharedObj.data.pictureObjects = pictureObjects;
```

3. We then need to create our timestamp. The simplest way to do this is to use the getTime method of the Date object. The method returns the number of milliseconds elapsed since midnight January 1, 1970, providing us with a straightforward numerical value to deal with. To use this we first create a new instance of the Date object and then call its getTime method, finally storing the value as timeStamp in the shared object:

```
var dat = new Date();
mySharedObj.data.timeStamp = dat.getTime();
```

4. The complete function includes all of the code from steps 2 and 3, plus a call to the flush method of the shared object to save the information. Place the refreshSharedObj function beneath the parseMe function:

```
function refreshSharedObj() {
    mySharedObj = sharedobject.getLocal("denim");
```

```
    mySharedObj.data.pictureObjects = pictureObjects;
    var dat = new Date();
    // store the timestamp in the shared object
    mySharedObj.data.timeStamp = dat.getTime();
    mySharedObj.flush();
}
```

5. The next function we create is `checkShared`. We're going to call this from our `init` function and use the value returned from the function to determine whether or not we call the `importXml` function. If the function returns true, it will indicate that the data has been found in the shared object and we don't need to import the XML – if it returns false, we do import the XML. So basically, our function only needs to return true if it finds the shared object with the array of pictures inside it, and the difference between the current time and the time it was created is below a certain amount. Here's what our `init` function will look like now:

```
function init() {
    // if the checkShared function returns true
    if (!checkShared()) {
        importXml();
    }
}
```

6. The first thing to accomplish in `checkShared` (which we'll place beneath the `refreshSharedObj` function), is to retrieve the shared object:

```
function checkShared() {
    mySharedObj = sharedobject.getLocal("denim");
}
```

7. We then check if `mySharedObj` has an array called `pictureObjects` in its `data` object:

```
function checkShared() {
    mySharedObj = sharedobject.getLocal("denim");
    if (mySharedObj.data.pictureObjects) {
        ...
    }
}
```

8. If it does, then we already have the data we need – we just need to check the dates, so we create a `new Date` object:

```
function checkShared() {
    mySharedObj = sharedobject.getLocal("denim");
    if (mySharedObj.data.pictureObjects) {
```

continues overleaf

```
                    var dat = new Date();
          }
     }
```

9. To compare the current date with the date the shared object was saved as, we can do the following:

```
dat.getTime()-mysharedObj.data.timeStamp;
```

This will give us the number of milliseconds between the current time and the time the shared object was set. A reasonable amount of time to load the XML again would be about once a week, so we check if this value is less than 1000 * 60 * 60 * 24 * 7 = 604800000.

If it is less, we return true – if not, nothing will be returned – the equivalent of returning false. We also call the same `pictureDataComplete` function that we created for when the XML loading was finished. Here's the new code, highlighted in bold:

```
function checkShared() {
     mySharedObj = sharedobject.getLocal("denim");
     if (mySharedObj.data.pictureObjects) {
          var dat = new Date();
          if (dat.getTime()-mysharedObj.data.timeStamp<604800000) {
     // retrieve the array from the sharedObject
               _root.pictureObjects = mySharedObj.data.pictureObjects;
               pictureDataComplete();
               return true;
          }
     }
}
```

Finally, here's the completed code:

```
#include "tweento.as"
#include "brightness.as"
#include "stage.as"
_root.filename = "pictures.xml";
embedder._visible = 0;
statusTf = new TextFormat("Arial", 40, 0x4375A6);
statusTf.align = "center";
statusTf.leading = -5;
function createStatusMovie(tex) {
     _root.createEmptyMovieClip("statusClip", 1);
     statusClip.createTextField("statusText", 1, 0, 0, 550, 100);
     statusClip.statusText.embedFonts = true;
     statusClip.statusText.selectable = false;
```

```
                  statusClip.statusText.setNewTextFormat(statusTf);
                  statusClip.statusText.text = tex;
                  statusClip._x = 0;
                  statusClip._y = (Stage.originalHeight-
                  ➡statusClip.statusText.textHeight)/2-50;
         }
         function importXml() {
                  trace("data imported from xml");
                  pictureObjects = [];
                  myXml = new XML();
                  myXml.ignoreWhite = true;
                  myXml.updateXmlStatus = function() {
                           var percent = Math.round(this.getBytesLoaded()/
                           ➡this.getBytesTotal()*100);
                           if (percent<=0) {
                                    percent = "0";
                           }
                           _root.statusClip.statusText.text = "PICTURE DATA LOADING
                           ➡\n"+percent+"%";
                  };
                  myXml.updater = setInterval(myXml, "updateXmlStatus", 20);
                  myXml.onLoad = parseMe;
                  myXml.load(_root.filename);
                  _root.createStatusMovie("PICTURE DATA LOADING");
         }
         function parseMe(success) {
                  if (success) {
                           var pictures = this.firstChild.childNodes;
                           for (var i = 0; i<pictures.length; i++) {
                                    var obj = {};
                                    for (var j in pictures[i].attributes) {
                                             obj[j] = pictures[i].attributes[j];
                                    }
                                    pictureObjects.push(obj);
                           }
                           _root.refreshSharedObj();
                           clearInterval(this.updater);
                           statusClip.removeMovieClip();
                           _root.pictureDataComplete();
                  } else {
                           _root.statusClip.statusText.text = "FAILED TO LOAD DATA";
                           clearInterval(this.updater);
                  }
         }
         function refreshSharedObj() {
```

continues overleaf

```
            mySharedObj = sharedobject.getLocal("denim");
            mySharedObj.data.pictureObjects = pictureObjects;
            var dat = new Date();
            mySharedObj.data.timeStamp = dat.getTime();
            mySharedObj.flush();
        }
    function checkShared() {
            mySharedObj = sharedobject.getLocal("denim");
            if (mySharedObj.data.pictureObjects) {
                var dat = new Date();
                if (dat.getTime()-mysharedObj.data.timeStamp<604800000) {
                    trace("data found in shared object");
                    _root.pictureObjects = mySharedObj.data.pictureObjects;
                    pictureDataComplete();
                    return true;
                }
            }
        }
    function pictureDataComplete() {
            trace("picture data loaded");
        }
    function init() {
            importXml();
        }
    function init() {
            if (!checkShared()) {
                    importXml();
            }
        }
    init();
```

10. Save your file as `xmlInShared.fla` and test it. Here's the result you'll get in the Output window with the current code:

You'll see we've added two `trace` statements (highlighted in bold) just for testing purposes, to indicate whether the data is loaded from the XML or the shared object. You might want to play with this to see what's happening – try changing the number of milliseconds before the shared object expires. You could also clear the shared object entirely by doing this:

```
function checkShared() {
    mySharedObj = sharedobject.getLocal("denim");
    // loop through properties and delete them
    for (var i in mySharedObj.data) {
        delete mySharedObj.data[i];
    }
}
```

In which case, the Output window will state that the data has been imported from the XML.

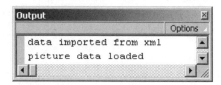

This technique of storing XML parsed into an object structure is useful here, but would be particularly helpful if dealing with larger structures or using complicated parsing routines. In those circumstances, saving the results from parsing the XML allow us to skip what can be a time - consuming step (both loading the data and interpreting it) by saving it locally and bringing it in as data that Flash understands natively.

Preloading the pictures

Once we've loaded the data for the pictures, we'll want to preload the pictures one by one. We'll trigger this in the pictureDataComplete function, which we'll accomplish by loading the pictures into an empty movie clip placed offstage one by one. It's better to do it this way rather than loading them all at once because multiple calls to loadMovie at one time can cause problems in certain browsers.

1. In pictureDataComplete we first create a new status movie and create the movie clip to load the pictures into. We then set the enterFrame of _root to checkPreload, which will update the status and check if each picture is loaded. Finally, we call loadNext to trigger the first picture loading. We have a variable picLoading to help ascertain which picture is currently being loaded. We replace the trace statement that we previously placed in the pictureDataComplete function with the following:

```
function pictureDataComplete() {
    _root.createStatusMovie("PICTURES LOADING");
    _root.createEmptyMovieClip("picturePlacebo", 2);
    picturePlacebo._x = 1000;
    picLoading = 0;
    // check how much is loaded on enterFrame
```

continues overleaf

```
        this.onEnterFrame = checkPreload;
        loadNext();
    }
```

2. loadNext will check if there are any pictures left to load in the pictureObjects array (if picLoading is less than the length of the array). If there is a picture left to load, it will load it into the offstage movie clip – if not, it will remove the offstage movie clip and set the statusClip to fade out using tweenTo.

    When the fade is done, it will call setUpStage – the function that will set up the interface to view the pictures. Here's the code, which we've placed beneath our pictureDataComplete function:

```
function loadNext() {
    if (picLoading<pictureObjects.length) {
    // Load the next picture using the file property
    picturePlacebo.loadMovie(pictureObjects[picLoading].file);
    } else {
        delete this.onEnterFrame;
        var obj = {_alpha:0};
        picturePlacebo.removeMovieClip();
        _root.statusClip.tweenTo(obj, 9, _root, "setUpStage");
    }
}
```

3. The checkPreload function works much as our XML loader did. It creates a percent variable and sets it based on the getBytesLoaded of the offstage movie clip, and then displays the percentage in the status movie clip. When the picture has fully loaded (when percent equals 100), it first stores the width and height of the movie clip (which is the same as that of the picture inside the movie clip) in our pictureObjects array. It then increments the picLoading variable and calls loadNext. We've placed this function beneath loadNext:

```
function checkPreload() {
    var percent = Math.round(picturePlacebo.getBytesLoaded()
    ➥/picturePlacebo.getBytesTotal()*100);
    if (percent<=0) {
        percent = "0";
    }
    _root.statusClip.statusText.text = "PICTURE "+(picLoading+1)+"
    ➥LOADING \n"+percent+"%";
    if (percent == 100) {
    // store picture's width and height
        _root.pictureObjects[picLoading].width =_root.picturePlacebo.
        ➥_width;
```

```
        _root.pictureObjects[picLoading].height =
    ➥_root.picturePlacebo._height;
        picLoading++;
        loadNext();
    }
}
```

Here's the completed code:

```
#include "tweento.as"
#include "brightness.as"
#include "stage.as"
_root.filename = "pictures.xml";
embedder._visible = 0;
statusTf = new TextFormat("Arial", 40, 0x4375A6);
statusTf.align = "center";
statusTf.leading = -5;
function createStatusMovie(tex) {
    _root.createEmptyMovieClip("statusClip", 1);
    statusClip.createTextField("statusText", 1, 0, 0, 550, 100);
    statusClip.statusText.embedFonts = true;
    statusClip.statusText.selectable = false;
    statusClip.statusText.setNewTextFormat(statusTf);
    statusClip.statusText.text = tex;
    statusClip._x = 0;
    statusClip._y = (Stage.originalHeight
    ➥statusClip.statusText.textHeight)/2-50;
}
function importXml() {
    trace("data imported from xml");
    pictureObjects = [];
    myXml = new Xml();
    myXml.ignoreWhite = true;
    myXml.updateXmlStatus = function() {
        var percent = Math.round(this.getBytesLoaded()/
        ➥this.getBytesTotal()*100);
        if (percent<=0) {
            percent = "0";
        }
        _root.statusClip.statusText.text = "PICTURE DATA LOADING
        ➥\n"+percent+"%";
    };
    myXml.updater = setInterval(myXml, "updateXmlStatus", 20);
    myXml.onLoad = parseMe;
    myXml.load(_root.filename);
```

continues overleaf

```
                _root.createStatusMovie("PICTURE DATA LOADING");
        }
        function parseMe(success) {
            if (success) {
                var pictures = this.firstChild.childNodes;
                for (var i = 0; i<pictures.length; i++) {
                    var obj = {};
                    for (var j in pictures[i].attributes) {
                        obj[j] = pictures[i].attributes[j];
                    }
                    pictureObjects.push(obj);
                }
                _root.refreshSharedObj();
                clearInterval(this.updater);
                statusClip.removeMovieClip();
                _root.pictureDataComplete();
            } else {
                _root.statusClip.statusText.text = "FAILED TO LOAD DATA";
                clearInterval(this.updater);
            }
        }
        function refreshSharedObj() {
            mySharedObj = sharedobject.getLocal("denim");
            mySharedObj.data.pictureObjects = pictureObjects;
            var dat = new Date();
            mySharedObj.data.timeStamp = dat.getTime();
            mySharedObj.flush();
        }
        function checkShared() {
            mySharedObj = sharedobject.getLocal("denim");
            if (mySharedObj.data.pictureObjects) {
                var dat = new Date();
                if (dat.getTime()-mysharedObj.data.timeStamp<604800000) {
                    trace("data found in shared object");
                    _root.pictureObjects = mySharedObj.data.pictureObjects;
                    pictureDataComplete();
                    return true;
                }
            }
        }
        function pictureDataComplete() {
            _root.createStatusMovie("PICTURES LOADING");
            _root.createEmptyMovieClip("picturePlacebo", 2);
            picturePlacebo._x = 1000;
            picLoading = 0;
```

```
            this.onEnterFrame = checkPreload;
            loadNext();
    }
    function loadNext() {
        if (picLoading<pictureObjects.length) {
            picturePlacebo.loadMovie(pictureObjects[picLoading].file);
        } else {
            delete this.onEnterFrame;
            var obj = {_alpha:0};
            picturePlacebo.removeMovieClip();
            _root.statusClip.tweenTo(obj, 9, _root, "setUpStage");
        }
    }
    function checkPreload() {
        var percent = Math.round(picturePlacebo.getBytesLoaded()/
        ➥picturePlacebo.getBytesTotal()*100);
        if (percent<=0) {
            percent = "0";
        }
        _root.statusClip.statusText.text = "PICTURE "+(picLoading+1)+"
        ➥LOADING \n"+percent+"%";
        if (percent == 100) {
            _root.pictureObjects[picLoading].width =
            ➥_root.picturePlacebo._width;
            _root.pictureObjects[picLoading].height =
            ➥_root.picturePlacebo._height;
            picLoading++;
            loadNext();
        }
    }
    function init() {
        if (!checkShared()) {
            importXml();
        }
    }
    init();
```

4. Save your file as `preloadPictures.fla` and when you test it, you'll see the following message:

```
PICTURE 3 LOADING
100%
```

Additionally, if you select the **Debug > List Variables** menu option, the **Output** window will also show that all of the pictures have indeed been loaded:

```
Output                                                          ×
                                                      Options
Variable _level0.mySharedObj = [object #12, class 'SharedObject'] {
        data:[object #13, class 'Object'] {
            pictureObjects:[object #14, class 'Array'] [
              0:[object #15, class 'Object'] {
                file:"denim001.jpg",
                name:"whatever",
                width:467,
                height:336
              },
              1:[object #16, class 'Object'] {
                file:"denim002.jpg",
                name:"whatever",
                width:467,
                height:336
              },
```

We'll now turn our attention to putting the final touches to our interface, which involves setting up the stage so that the photos can be displayed, before considering exactly how we'll display them.

Setting up the stage

To display the photographs we're going to have each appear in the center of the stage and have a mask move across from left to right, revealing the picture gradually. As the mask for one photograph comes across and reveals it, the mask for the previous photograph will also move across, hiding it simultaneously and giving the effect of a film wipe.

1. The first thing that we need to do when `setUpStage` is called, is remove the `statusClip`. We'll then create a row of buttons to trigger the relevant photos, before the first photo is triggered:

```
function setUpStage() {
    _root.statusClip.removeMovieClip();
    // create the buttons
    createButtons();
    // trigger the first photo
    triggerPhoto(0);
}
```

2. To create the buttons, we're going to use the nooButton component we created in the last chapter, so make sure there's a copy in the Library (you can grab it from the completed version of this exercise named finalVersion.fla). We'll add a textFormat object for the buttons at the top of our code. Here's the new line of code, highlighted in bold:

```
#include "tweento.as"
#include "brightness.as"
#include "stage.as"
_root.filename = "pictures.xml";
embedder._visible = 0;
buttonTf = new TextFormat("Arial", 20, 0x4375A6);
statusTf = new TextFormat("Arial", 40, 0x4375A6);
```

3. The bulk of the createButtons function (which we've placed beneath setUpStage) will be familiar from the previous chapter. We're creating an object to set the properties of the new button, its appearance and its behavior. This time we're assigning the function triggerPhoto to the press event handler, which will pass the number of the photo to the function:

```
function createButtons(imageArr, tF) {
    _root.createEmptyMovieClip("buttonHolder", 100000);
    var currx;
    for (var i = 0; i<pictureObjects.length; i++) {
        _root.buttonHolder.depth = i+1;
        var caption = (i+1).toString().length<2 ? "00"+(i+1)
        ➡: "0"+(i+1);
        var obj = {myText:caption, _x:currx, obj:_root,
        ➡defaultBright:0, rollOverBright:30, visitedBright:60,
        ➡activeBright:-30, pressFunction:"triggerPhoto",
        ➡pressArgs:i, tf:buttonTf, embedFonts:true};
        var nooButton = buttonHolder.attachMovie("nooButtonMc",
        ➡"noob"+i, i, obj);
        currX += nooButton.width+5;
    }
    // set the first button to active
    buttonHolder.noob0.setActive();
    buttonHolder._x = (Stage.originalWidth-buttonHolder._width)/2;
    buttonHolder._y = Math.round(Stage.bottom)-buttonHolder._height;
    // move to the bottom of the stage onResize
    buttonHolder.onResize = function() {
        var y = Math.round(Stage.bottom)-30;
        this.tweenTo({_y:y}, 3);
    };
    Stage.addListener(buttonHolder);
    Stage.onResize();
```

continues overleaf

```
                buttonHolder.onResize();
         }
```

If we test the movie at this point, the buttons load in at the bottom of the stage:

001 002 003 004 005 006 007 008

We've done several new things in the second half of the createButtons function, so we'll have a closer look at those now.

First of all we're calling the setActive method of the first button. This is the button corresponding to the first picture loaded, so needs to be disabled at the start:

```
buttonHolder.noob0.setActive();
```

We then use the Stage object to set the position of the buttonHolder clip so that it's centered horizontally and sits just above the bottom vertically:

```
buttonHolder._x = (Stage.originalWidth-buttonHolder._width)/2;
buttonHolder._y = Math.round (Stage.bottom)-buttonHolder._height;
```

We're going to keep the buttons at the bottom of the browser/Flash Player window, so we add an onResize function, triggering a tween to the correct spot:

```
         buttonHolder.onResize = function() {
              var y = Math.round(Stage.bottom)-30;
              this.tweenTo({_y:y}, 3);
         };
         Stage.addListener(buttonHolder);
```

Finally, we've added calls to Stage.onResize and buttonHolder.onResize to make sure these are both up to date when the buttons are created. This shouldn't really be necessary, but without it, the Stage values don't seem to update properly and the positioning gets messed up. The inclusion of this, however, fixes the problem.

We're now ready to build the final part of our interface and set it up so we can view the photographs on the stage, as well as deciding the manner in which they will be displayed.

Displaying the photographs

To implement our masking mechanism when displaying the photographs, we're going to create pairs of movie clips. When we trigger a new photograph we create a movie clip to contain the photograph and a mask to sit on top of it. As the photo is triggered, the mask will scale across the top of it so it's fully revealed. At the same time, the mask that was sitting on top of the previous photograph will move across the stage to unmask (hide) it. When the mask is entirely off stage and the photo entirely hidden, the old mask and photo will be removed.

1. Each pair of photographs is going to be created beneath the previous pair so we add a depth variable after our include statements that will start at 1000 and gradually be reduced:

    ```
    #include "tweento.as"
    #include "brightness.as"
    #include "stage.as"
    _root.depth = 1000;
    _root.filename = "pictures.xml";
    ```

2. Now create a movie clip that we'll use for the mask. Call it mask and inside it draw a 100 x 100 pixel square.

3. Next, right-click on **mask** in the Library and select **Linkage...** from the menu to display the **Linkage Properties** dialog window. Select the **Export for ActionScript** option and set the **Identifier** to mask:

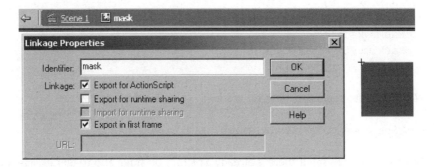

4. The triggerPhoto function will take care of several things.

    ```
    function triggerPhoto(currentPicture) {
    ```

    It will first ascertain the picture object that is to be used, looking in the pictureObjects array for the value passed to the function:

```
function triggerPhoto(currentPicture) {
    var nextPicObj = pictureObjects[currentPicture];
```

It will then create an empty movie clip to hold the picture. We then create another movie clip inside that where we'll actually load the picture. We do this because when a movie clip has a picture or another SWF loaded into it, a lot of things are erased, such as onEnterFrame handlers and – more pertinently in our case – masking data.

We position the movie clip at center stage using the width and height information when we preloaded the images, and we scale the movie clip up slightly to cure the bitmap shift issue:

```
_root.depth--;
var noopic = createEmptyMovieClip("picClip"+depth, depth);
noopic.createEmptyMovieClip("inner", 1);
noopic.inner.loadMovie(nextPicObj.file);
nooPic._xscale = nooPic._yscale = 101;
nooPic.inner._x = (Stage.originalWidth-nextPicObj.width)/2;
nooPic.inner._y = (Stage.originalHeight-nextPicObj.height)/2;
```

After this we create the mask, which will be placed at the left edge of the stage and stretched to the height of the movie. Inside the mask we place a reference to its corresponding picture movie clip so that when the mask is removed the picture can be removed as well:

```
_root.depth--;
var nooMask = _root.attachMovie("mask", "mask"+depth, depth);
nooMask._x = 0;
nooMask._yscale = Stage.originalHeight;
nooMask._xscale = 1;
nooMask.myPic = nooPic;
nooPic.setMask(nooMask);
```

We're going to scale the mask up gradually to cover the whole stage:

```
nooMask.tweenTo({_xscale:Stage.originalWidth+200}, 15);
```

The next step is to see if there is already a picture on stage and trigger its maskOut function if there is:

```
if (_root.latestMask) {
    maskOut();
}
```

We then set latestMask to be the current mask, indicating that it is the next to be removed:

```
_root.latestMask = nooMask;
```

Finally, we check if depth has fallen below 900, in which case we move it back up to 1000 to avoid overwriting anything else on stage:

```
if (_root.depth<900) {
        _root.depth = 1000;
    }
```

Here's the complete function:

```
function triggerPhoto(currentPicture) {
    var nextPicObj = pictureObjects[currentPicture];
    _root.depth--;
    var noopic = createEmptyMovieClip("picClip"+depth, depth);
    noopic.createEmptyMovieClip("inner", 1);
    noopic.inner.loadMovie(nextPicObj.file);
    nooPic._xscale = nooPic._yscale=101;
    nooPic.inner._x = (Stage.originalWidth-nextPicObj.width)/2;
    nooPic.inner._y = (Stage.originalHeight-nextPicObj.height)/2;
    _root.depth--;
    var nooMask = _root.attachMovie("mask", "mask"+depth, depth);
    nooMask._x = 0;
    nooMask._yscale = Stage.originalHeight;
    nooMask._xscale = 1;
    nooMask.myPic = nooPic;
    nooPic.setMask(nooMask);
    nooMask.tweenTo({_xscale:Stage.originalWidth+200}, 15);
    if (_root.latestMask) {
        maskOut();
    }
    _root.latestMask = nooMask;
    if (_root.depth<900) {
        _root.depth = 1000;
    }
}
```

5. We now have to create the `maskOut` that will tween the previous mask offstage. Note that we're moving this movie clip to the same position (`Stage.originalWidth+200`) that the first mask is scaled to. This helps to ensure that the revealing mask and the hiding mask wipe in and out at roughly the same speeds:

```
function maskOut() {
    _root.latestMask.tweenTo({_x:Stage.originalWidth+200},
    ➥15, _root, "remove");
}
```

6. When this movie clip reaches its target it will call `remove` which will remove it along with its corresponding picture:

```
function remove(maskMc) {
    maskMc.myPic.removeMovieClip();
    maskMc.removeMovieClip();
}
```

That's the code finished – there's now a little too much code to display it in its entirety here in the book, but here's the major additions that we've made in the last two sections, highlighted in bold:

```
#include "tweento.as"
#include "brightness.as"
#include "stage.as"
_root.depth = 1000;
_root.filename = "pictures.xml";
embedder._visible = 0;
buttonTf = new textFormat("Arial", 20, 0x4375A6);
statusTf = new TextFormat("Arial", 40, 0x4375A6);

//rest of code goes here

function createButtons(imageArr, tF) {
    _root.createEmptyMovieClip("buttonHolder", 100000);
    var currx;
    for (var i = 0; i<pictureObjects.length; i++) {
        _root.buttonHolder.depth = i+1;
        var caption = (i+1).toString().length<2 ? "00"+(i+1)
        ➥: "0"+(i+1);
        var obj = {myText:caption, _x:currx, obj:_root,
        ➥defaultBright:0, rollOverBright:30, visitedBright:60,
        ➥activeBright:-30, pressFunction:"triggerPhoto",
        ➥pressArgs:i, tf:buttonTf, embedFonts:true};
        var nooButton =
```

```
          ➡buttonHolder.attachMovie("nooButtonMc", "noob"+i, i, obj);
          currX += nooButton.width+5;
     }
     buttonHolder.noob0.setActive();
     buttonHolder._x = (Stage.originalWidth-buttonHolder._width)/2;
     buttonHolder._y = Math.round(Stage.bottom)-buttonHolder._height;
     buttonHolder.onResize = function() {
          var y = Math.round(Stage.bottom)-30;
          this.tweenTo({_y:y}, 3);
     };
     Stage.addListener(buttonHolder);
     Stage.onResize();
     buttonHolder.onResize();
}
function triggerPhoto(currentPicture) {
     var nextPicObj = pictureObjects[currentPicture];
     _root.depth--;
     var noopic = createEmptyMovieClip("picClip"+depth, depth);
     noopic.createEmptyMovieClip("inner", 1);
     noopic.inner.loadMovie(nextPicObj.file);
     nooPic._xscale = nooPic._yscale=101;
     nooPic.inner._x = (Stage.originalWidth-nextPicObj.width)/2;
     nooPic.inner._y = (Stage.originalHeight-nextPicObj.height)/2;
     _root.depth--;
     var nooMask = _root.attachMovie("mask", "mask"+depth, depth);
     nooMask._x = 0;
     nooMask._yscale = Stage.originalHeight;
     nooMask._xscale = 1;
     nooMask.myPic = nooPic;
     nooPic.setMask(nooMask);
     nooMask.tweenTo({_xscale:Stage.originalWidth+200}, 15);
     if (_root.latestMask) {
          maskOut();
     }
     _root.latestMask = nooMask;
     if (_root.depth<900) {
          _root.depth = 1000;
     }
}
function maskOut() {
     _root.latestMask.tweenTo({_x:Stage.originalWidth+200}, 15, _root,
     ➡"remove");
}
function remove(maskMc) {
     maskMc.myPic.removeMovieClip();
```

continues overleaf

```
        maskMc.removeMovieClip();
}
function init() {
    if (!checkShared()) {
        importXml();
    }
}
init();
```

7.   Save your file as `finalVersion.fla` and test it – you'll first see the message telling us that the pictures are loaded. This then fades out before the buttons appear as the first picture is masking in:

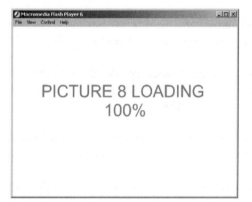

Picture loading complete

Picture 1 masking in while buttons tween into position

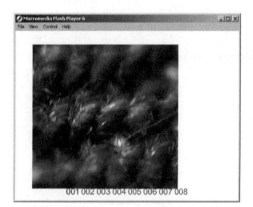

Stage setup almost complete

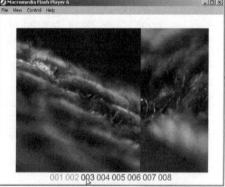

Picture 1 masking out and picture 3 masking in

So with this interface we've gone quite a lot further than with the other two. Here the images are loaded dynamically and by using XML we can also change which images are loaded without modifying the FLA. We've also minimized the initialization time of the piece by using `sharedObjects` to cache the array we create from parsing the XML. The interface will still work with different sized pictures even though the ones we have used here are all the same size. You'll notice that the interface is quite robust; even if you click multiple buttons quickly, the images just continue to slide across. With the system of callbacks we have in place, it would be fairly easy to modify the way the masks work and you could have one photo appear only after the other has been masked out, for instance. You might also want to use the caption data we included in the XML to include some kind of titling to go with the images.

Summary

In this chapter then we've created a fairly dynamic interface. In the first approach we placed the images manually, in the second we placed them dynamically, but had to import them into Flash, whereas here we are both importing and placing the images dynamically. I think the main advantage of this is ease of maintenance. There is no need to go back into the Flash file to make changes to the content. If we want to add an image, we simply add another node to our XML document. If we want to change the images entirely, we just change the file names; the interface should work fine whatever size the new images are. We could add other information to the XML document as well, for instance the color for the text buttons or the font size. Taking this further, you might want to have the images divided into different types. You would then set up the XML so that beneath the pictures node you have several "imageType" nodes and then place the individual pictures within these nodes. This would of course require modifications to the interface as well, adding a sub-menu of some kind to switch between image types.

section 2: ActionScript Interfaces

chapter 6: Introduction to Events and Handlers

One of the most important changes in Flash MX is the new event handler model. This totally changes the way we are able to code animation and interaction with the keyboard and mouse. You already learned a bit about this earlier in the book, but now we are going to get into them in a bit more depth.

We'll cover a few of the more important events here, as they relate to basic animation and interactivity, and develop a good model for a code-based movie structure. We'll also delve into some related features, such as setInterval and watches.

Some basic definitions

An **event** is something that happens in a movie while it is running. There are specific events that are defined. Certain objects in the movie are able to perceive these events and react to them. Some of the more commonly used events are those that occur when a movie enters into a new frame, the mouse is moved, a mouse button or keyboard key is pressed or released.

An **event handler** or event handler method is a function that is executed when a particular event occurs.

A **listener** or listener object is an object that can perceive and respond to specific types of events with an event handler.

Since you are already familiar with onEnterFrame, let's take that as an example. First create a movie clip. Nothing fancy, just a small shape or something. Name its instance mc1_mc. The first thing we should know is that a movie clip, by default, is a listener for the enterFrame event. Whenever Flash enters a new frame, the enterFrame event occurs, and our mc1_mc is duly informed of the fact. Right now it doesn't do much about it, because we haven't defined an event handler to handle the event, but be assured that it is aware of the event and is ready to act if we tell it to.

Now let's define a function to use as a handler. Put this in frame 1 of the movie:

```
function move() {
    this._x++;
}
```

Now this is just a function called move. It takes whatever object, calls this function and moves it one pixel to the right. Pretty simple function. We can now assign this function to mc1_mc's onEnterFrame handler like so:

```
mc1_mc.onEnterFrame = move;
```

You should pay very close attention to the keyword, this, in the above code. When you use a property or variable by itself – without a path – it is assumed to belong to the current timeline. If we left out the this in the above block of code, _x would be evaluated to _root._x and our function would move not mc1_mc, but the entire movie!

When you specify this in a function, it refers to whatever object called that function. In this case, the move function is being called by mc1_mc, therefore this._x is evaluated instead to mc1_mc._x, which does what we want.

When this is run, mc1_mc gets the enterFrame event at the beginning of each new frame, which causes its onEnterFrame method – now the function, move() – to execute, which slowly slides the movie clip across the stage.

I know this has been largely covered earlier in the book, but let's take a deeper look at what is happening here. When you define a variable, such as name="Keith", Flash is setting aside a spot in your computer's memory and putting the value, "Keith" in that memory location. If you later say, name="Todd", it replaces the value in memory with this new string. A similar thing happens when you define a function.

When we say,

```
function move() {
    this._x++;
}
```

Flash sets aside a spot in memory to store whatever commands are contained in the function. If you now issue the command move() with the two parentheses, Flash will go to that memory location and execute whatever statements it finds there. This may be pretty obvious, but what is less well known, yet very important in handling events, is that the function name, without the parentheses, also has quite a bit of meaning.

The name of a function itself can be thought of as a variable that holds the memory address of the function. You might imagine a mailroom with a wall full of those little metal post office boxes. Each one has a number, which is its location, and has some contents, the mail. A function name is like a slip of paper with the box number on it. It tells you where your function is located. The technical way of saying it is that the variable move contains a reference to the function. Now just as you can assign a value to a variable and then pass that value onto another variable, you can pass function references around in the same way. Take a look at the following code:

```
function hello() {
    trace("hi there");
}
```

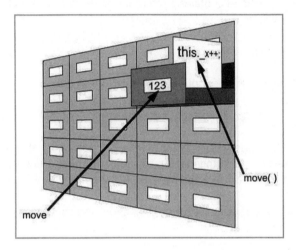

We've created a function in memory. The variable hello contains a reference to that function. Any variable which contains a function reference can be used to execute that function by adding a pair of parentheses.

```
hello();
```

Now we can pass that reference onto another variable:

```
greeting = hello;
```

Here, the variable greeting is given the reference to the function. Both variables now contain a reference to the same function. Now you can execute the function by saying:

```
greeting ();
```

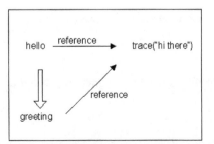

This even works for built in functions and special objects in Flash. For example, we have the `Math` object, which contains the `random()` method. It's just a function in memory. The variable `random` in the `Math` object contains a reference to that function. We can grab this reference and store it anywhere we like:

```
myRand = Math.random;
```

Now `myRand` contains a reference to the function that will return a random number. You can call it by saying:

```
myRand();
```

Notice that this is quite different from saying:

```
myRand = Math.random();
```

In this case, the function name is followed by the parentheses, which causes the function to execute. It will then return a random number and pass it to `myRand`. Not at all what we want, but I guarantee you will make this mistake many times. I still do!

So, getting back to our original code, you should have a more complete view of what is going on here.

```
function move() {
    this._x++;
}
mc1_mc.onEnterFrame = move;
```

We create a function in memory, `move` gets a reference to this function and passes that reference onto `mc1_mc.onEnterFrame`. It's important to get this idea down. So many people make the initial mistake of typing:

```
mc1_mc.onEnterFrame = move();
```

You should now understand why this doesn't work and what actually occurs when you do this.

You may have also run into the shorthand method of defining event handlers:

```
mc1_mc.onEnterFrame = function() {
    this._x++;
};
```

You can look at this as creating a function without a name.

```
function _____ () {
    this._x++;
}
```

While the reference to the function is not passed onto a variable, the above statement itself results in a reference to the function when it is run. Therefore we can take the result of the function definition and assign it directly to our event handler:

```
mc1_mc.onEnterFrame=function _____ () {
    this._x++;
};
```

Of course, the blank is just there for effect. The real way of writing it is as above in the first example. This method is useful when you know you will only be assigning the function one time, to one handler only.

Also note the semi-colon on the end there. This entire block of code is one assignment statement, and therefore should end in a semi-colon, although syntactically it needn't. Function definitions on their own do not need to be ended like that.

Deleting event handlers

One of the great things about event handlers is that they are not written in stone. You can assign them any time you want, assign a different function at any point in time, or get rid of the handler altogether. Say you only want to execute the function once a certain condition is met. You could do something like this:

```
function move() {
    if (this._x<500) {
        this._x++;
    }
}
mc1_mc.onEnterFrame = move;
```

This is what we were stuck with in Flash 5 with clip events. But this is not really the most efficient method. In this example, the move function still checks the value of this._x and compares it to the value 500, once every frame. Not a lot of overhead, but we can be perfectionists. If we know we are completely done with this function, we can just get rid of it. There are a couple of ways to do this, either by deleting the handler or assigning it the value undefined or null. Deleting is a widely accepted method. So we get something like this:

```
function move() {
    if (this._x<500) {
        this._x++;
```

continues overleaf

```
            } else {
                delete this.onEnterFrame;
            }
        }
    mc1_mc.onEnterFrame = move;
```

I should probably make the distinction here that when you delete a handler like this, you are not actually deleting the function that is stored in memory. You are merely deleting the reference to that function that is stored in onEnterFrame. In this case, you still have a reference to the function stored in the variable move. So it can be reassigned at any time.

> *Flash keeps track of functions and how many references point to each function. If you delete the last or only reference to a function stored in memory, Flash should let the operating system know that it no longer needs that space for the function, and that it is free to be used for anything else.*

Changing event handlers

Here's another example of the usefulness of event handlers. In the last example, we wanted our clip to have one behavior until a certain condition was met, then no behavior. But we could just as easily make it have a different behavior at different times. Just assign a different function that makes it do something else. In the following code, we have two functions, moveRight and moveLeft. When the movie clip goes too far right or left, it will swap its onEnterFrame handler for the opposite function. I also sped the motion up a bit so you're not watching the ball crawl across the screen.

```
    function moveRight() {
        this._x+=5;
        if (this._x>500) {
            this.onEnterFrame = moveLeft;
        }
    }
    function moveLeft() {
        this._x-5;
        if (this._x<50) {
            this.onEnterFrame = moveRight;
        }
    }
    mc1_mc.onEnterFrame = moveRight;
```

I'm not at all suggesting that this is the best way to have an object bounce back and forth, but it shows how you can dynamically change event handlers at any time you want to during the movie.

Passing parameters to event handlers

If you have ever used functions before, in any language, you are probably asking right about now, "What about parameters?". Normally when you define a function, you can specify a number of parameters that go inside the parentheses. These can be used to send data to the function when you execute it. The function can then use that data in its statements:

```
function saySomething(message) {
    trace(message);
}
saySomething("I'd like to buy an argument.");
```

So how does this work with event handlers? Well, it doesn't work, directly. First I'll give you the common mistake people make, so you can recognize it and hopefully not do it yourself. You define a function that takes a parameter or two, and then try to assign that function to an event handler.

```
function showCoords(x, y) {
    trace("horiz: "+x+" vert: "+y);
}
mc1_mc.onEnterFrame = showCoords(this._x, this._y);
```

That would be nice, but remember that when you use a function name with the parentheses, the function executes. It doesn't assign a reference. But there is a workaround. Using the direct assignment method, create an unnamed function, and have that function call your function with parameters.

```
function showCoords(x, y) {
    trace("horiz: "+x+" vert: "+y);
}
mc1_mc.onEnterFrame = function() {
    showCoords(this._x, this._y);
};
```

In this example, the unnamed function assigned to onEnterFrame executes. This runs our other function, showCoords(), sending it the parameters.

Event driven programming

All right, now that you're thoroughly convinced that onEnterFrame is the greatest thing since elasticated underwear, let's move on to some of the other available handlers. Here is where we really get into the spirit of event driven programming.

Remember that whatever is in an onEnterFrame event handler function, will be executed many times per second. Here is an example of how this is sometimes used:

```
mc1_mc.onEnterFrame = function() {
    if (buttonStatus == "pressed") {
        // do some stuff here...
    }
};
```

Somewhere else in the movie, there is a button, which when pressed sets the variable buttonStatus to equal the string "pressed". The event handler here checks the status of that variable over and over and over and over, just waiting for it to change. Kind of like a long drive with young children. "Are we there yet? Are we there yet? Are we there yet?"

This is called **polling**. Although we are only running one if statement each frame, you might be amazed at the hit in performance you will take when you have something like this running in your movie. I've had some complex animations that ran just fine on their own. But then I pulled them into an interface that had a couple of pieces of clip event code, which was polling the status of some variable. Suddenly my animation was grinding to a halt. I tracked down the offending loops that were polling for a particular condition and reprogrammed them and all was well again.

Event driven programming operates differently. Instead of checking over and over to see if something has happened yet, we simply set up an event handler, sit back and relax. The program doesn't do anything, and is using minimal CPU time. When an event occurs that it is interested in, it springs back to life and gets to work.

All of the other event handlers we will learn about will operate this way. It's always good to look for ways that these other handlers can be used, rather than polling with onEnterFrame.

Other events

Earlier we mentioned that a movie clip is a listener for the enterFrame event. It knows when the movie has entered a new frame and if it has an appropriate event handler method defined, it will respond to that event by running that function. Well, movie clips are also listeners for another type of events called mouse events. These consist of the events mouseMove, mouseDown, and mouseUp. Although it may be obvious, a mouseMove event occurs whenever you move the mouse, a mouseDown event occurs whenever you press the main mouse button, and mouseUp occurs whenever you release that button. Their respective event handler methods are onMouseMove, onMouseDown, and onMouseUp.

> *Don't get too confused over the difference between, say, mouseMove and onMouseMove. mouseMove is an event. It is what actually happens. onMouseMove is the handler. It is what we do when that event occurs, like saying, "On a mouseMove event, we will do this..." Furthermore, you will never have to type an event name, like mouseMove, mouseDown, enterFrame, etc. These terms only exist to describe the event when talking or writing about it. They are not ActionScript programming key words.*

We can create and assign functions to these handlers in the exact same way we did for onEnterFrame. When the event occurs, the function will be called.

Here we'll assign a couple of functions to the onMouseDown and onMouseUp handlers of a movie clip.

We'll use the shorthand method again, since this is a simple file.

```
mc1_mc.onMouseDown = function() {
    this._xscale = 200;
    this._yscale = 200;
};
mc1_mc.onMouseUp = function() {
    this._xscale = 100;
    this._yscale = 100;
};
```

Remember the almighty this!? Even though we are assigning the function directly to the handler, we still need to specify this, to refer to the object that calls the function.

When you press the mouse button, mc1_mc's onMouseDown handler fires and executes the function assigned to it. This function sets the mc1_mc's x and y scale to 200%.

When you release the button, the function assigned to onMouseUp fires, setting the scales back to 100. You should also notice that this is not like a button where you have to be on top of the movie clip for it to register the click. All movie clips on stage will receive all mouse events no matter where they happen.

Now let's test out the onMouseMove handler. This action fires every time the mouse moves. We'll use the longhand method here, just so you get used to both.

```
function move() {
    this._x = _root._xmouse;
    this._y = _root._ymouse;
}
mc1_mc.onMouseMove = move;
```

I don't think I need to explain this one at all. If you throw in the line,

```
Mouse.hide();
```

...you've just learned how to make a custom cursor for your Flash movies.

Button event handler

In Flash 5, in order to make a movie clip 'draggable', you had to go through a bit of a complex procedure consisting of creating an invisible button inside the movie clip and assigning actions to it that would affect the movie clip it was in. In Flash MX, movie clips themselves can act like buttons. Here are a few new event handlers that apply to both buttons and movie clips:

- onRollOver
- onRollOut
- onPress
- onRelease
- onReleaseOutside

These work exactly the same way as the event handlers we have already seen. The events they handle should be pretty obvious. Let's see how easy it is to create a draggable movie clip.

Since a movie clip can now respond to presses and releases, just like a button, all we need to do is set a function for each handler, to tell it to start dragging and stop dragging. Simple:

```
mc1_mc.onPress = function() {
    this.startDrag();
};
mc1_mc.onRelease = function() {
    this.stopDrag();
};
mc1_mc.onReleaseOutside = function() {
    this.stopDrag();
};
```

I always handle the onReleaseOutside too. This prevents the movie clip from getting 'stuck' to the mouse if you accidentally drag too fast and release it while the cursor is not on the clip.

Since the functions for these two events are exactly the same, we can use another little shorthand trick:

```
mc1_mc.onPress = function() {
    this.startDrag();
};
mc1_mc.onRelease = mc1.onReleaseOutside = function () {
    this.stopDrag();
};
```

This assigns both handlers the same function in one shot.

Notice when you run this file, that the mouse cursor turns into a hand when it is on top of the movie clip, just as if it were a button.

Drag and throw objects

We can even create an extension of drag and drop: drag and throw. This will let the user drag the ball in a certain direction and when he releases it, it will continue to go in that direction. In fact, it will travel at the same speed at which he was dragging when he let go. I think you'll be surprised how easy this is to do, though it will take a few steps to explain.

1. We can start by typing the code we just created above for dragging and dropping.

2. It's important to know whether we are currently dragging the object, or if it is on its own. We can do that with a Boolean variable, which we will call dragging. We set dragging to true when we start dragging the clip, and to false when we release it. In order to keep things tidy, we'll make dragging a property of the clip itself.

```
mc1_mc.onPress = function() {
    this.startDrag();
    this.dragging = true;
};
mc1_mc.onRelease = mc1.onReleaseOutside = function () {
    this.stopDrag();
    this.dragging = false;
};
```

3. We will also need some code to move the object while we're not dragging it. This will happen in an onEnterFrame event handler function. To start with, we just check if the object is being dragged. If not, then we will move it.

```
mc1_mc.onEnterFrame = function() {
```

continues overleaf

```
     if (!this.dragging) {
         this._x += this.xSpeed;
         this._y += this.ySpeed;
     }
};
```

Of course, xSpeed and ySpeed have not been defined yet, so will be evaluated as 0, so we don't see any movement yet. If we set them manually, we can see that the movie clip moves until we click on it, at which point we can drag it around. When we release it, it continues moving at the same speed and in the same direction it was originally going.

```
mc1_mc.xSpeed = 1;
mc1_mc.ySpeed = 1;
```

4. Now we need to define what happens if we are dragging. This will go in an else block after the initial if block. In this case we can ignore the existing speed variables and rewrite them. We know that xSpeed is the number of pixels the clip will move horizontally in one frame. To throw, we just reverse the process when we are dragging. We determine how far we have dragged the object horizontally since the last frame, and assign that value to xSpeed.

```
mc1_mc.onPress = function() {
    this.startDrag();
    this.dragging = true;
};
mc1_mc.onRelease = mc1_mc.onReleaseOutside = function () {
    this.stopDrag();
    this.dragging = false;
};
mc1_mc.onEnterFrame = function() {
    if (!this.dragging) {
        this._x += this.xspeed;
        this._y += this.yspeed;
    } else {
        this.xSpeed = this._x-this.oldx;
        this.ySpeed = this._y-this.oldy;
        this.oldx = this._x;
      this.oldy = this._y;
    }
};
```

It might help to go through this backwards. At the end of the function, we assign the current _x value to a variable called oldx. The next time we go through the function is a fraction of a second later. We have dragged the object slightly, so its _x value is a bit different now. If we subtract the old from the new, we know how much it has actually moved. We assign this value to xSpeed. When we finally release the mouse, it will go back to executing the code to move itself, using the new xSpeed value. Naturally, we will have identical lines for the _y value and ySpeed.

5. The only problems here are that the object may go too fast to capture and then go off screen and be gone. We can fix that with some screen wrapping and friction. First the screen wrap. This means that when the object goes off one side of the screen, it will re-appear on the other side, like a lot of your old video games. All we need to do is test the position and change it if it goes out of range. This would occur directly after we update the object's position.

```
if (this._x>Stage.width) {
   this._x = 0;
} else if (this._x<0) {
   this._x = 550;
}
if (this._y>Stage.height) {
   this._y = 0;
} else if (this._y<0) {
   this._y = 400;
}
```

6. Adding friction is merely reducing the object's speed slightly each frame. The easiest way to do this is to multiply its speed variables by a figure like 0.98 each frame. This fits in nicely just before we add the speed to the position.

```
this.xspeed *= .98;
this.yspeed *= .98;
```

Now, no matter how fast you throw the object, it will always settle down so you can grab it again. In the next chapter, we'll go into adding some more to this. The final code is all in the throwcursor.fla in the **Chapter 6** folder of the CD.

Keyboard event handlers

There are just a couple more event handlers I want to cover. These relate to interacting with the keyboard. Then we'll create something to actually use everything we've covered. But first there is a new concept I need to introduce. That is an event **listener**.

Event listeners

So far, we have been dealing with movie clips, frame activity and mouse activity. All we had to do was create a function and assign it to the movie clips handler for the event we wanted to handle.

With keyboard events, things get just a bit more complicated. Here are the two events for handling keys:

- onKeyDown – fires when you press any key.
- onKeyUp – fires when you release any key.

You're probably getting the hang of this already and may even have your function half written, so let's go ahead, finish it and see what happens...

```
mc1_mc.onKeyDown = function() {
    this._xscale = 200;
    this._yscale = 200;
};
mc1_mc.onKeyUp = function() {
    this._xscale = 100;
    this._yscale = 100;
};
```

This is identical to the code we created for onMouseDown and onMouseUp. So why doesn't anything happen when you run it and press a key? It is because mc1_mc is not a listener for key events.

Earlier we defined what a listener is. Now we need to learn a little more about it. As we said, a listener is simply any object that can receive notification of certain types of events and act on them. We've already seen that movie clips can respond to such events as mouse movement and mouse button presses and releases. That is because, by default, a movie clip is a listener for mouse events. When a mouse event occurs (movement or button press), all movie clips can know about it, and react to it if they have an event handler function for that event. They don't have to respond, but they are able to.

But, a movie clip is not a listener for key events. Whether you tap a key lightly, or pound your fist through the keyboard, mc1_mc will be blissfully unaware. Even if you've assigned it an event handler function for onKeyDown or onKeyUp, it never gets the message, so never executes the function.

So, we need to make our movie clip into a listener for key events. We do this with the command, Key.addListener(object). Every Flash movie has a special object called Key. This object has properties and methods (functions) that keep track of when keys are pressed, which ones were pressed last, which are being pressed now, which special keys are toggled, etc. When you say Key.addListener(mc1_mc), you are telling the Key object that mc1_mc wants to be a listener for key events. Now, whenever a key is pressed or released, mc1 will be duly informed. It's kind of like being on a mailing list. Here, mc1 gets the message and knows when to perform its functions:

```
mc1_mc.onKeyDown = function() {
```

```
        this._xscale = 200;
        this._yscale = 200;
    };
    mc1_mc.onKeyUp = function() {
        this._xscale = 100;
        this._yscale = 100;
    };
    Key.addListener(mc1_mc);
```

Now, things should be working as you expected.

A vital thing to know is that addListener does not only apply to movie clips. Any object can be a listener for almost any kind of event. This means you can create a custom or generic object that can receive and respond to mouse, key and other events. Take this code for example:

```
    myObj = new Object();
    myObj.onMouseMove = function() {
        mc1_mc._x = _root._xmouse;
        mc1_mc._y = _root._ymouse;
    };
    Mouse.addListener(myObj);
```

You can see here that mc1_mc is being pretty passive. It is just being told what to do by myObj, which is now responding to mouse move events. myObj is able to receive and handle these events because we made it into a listener for all mouse events with the Mouse.addListener() command.

Creating a Simple Game

There are other listeners as well, for text fields, components and even the stage. But we've learned all we need in order to create some cool effects with the mouse and keyboard, so let's have some fun with those and create a little game.

The game we create won't be the next best seller. I'm not going to waste time creating fancy graphics or special effects for you to copy and paste. I'd rather have you learn the basic principles of how to use event handlers to control, animate and interact with your graphics. Then it's over to you to make something stunning.

1. This game is going to have some shooting, so first off you can go ahead and create a cross hair to aim with. I just used a vertical and horizontal line, but get creative if you want. Make this into a movie clip named cursor and name the instance cursor_mc.

It's always a good idea to keep your code on a separate layer, so make one now and name that layer **actions** or something similarly descriptive. Click on frame one of the **actions** layer and open the Actions panel. Now I'm going to show you something that will save you hours. In the top right corner of the Actions panel there is a little icon that looks like a pushpin. Click on it. This is the **Pin Current Script** button. Once you press it, the Actions panel will stay pinned to the script that you are working on. You can select other frames, objects, buttons, go many levels deep in the movie, but the script you are working on will always be right there in that window.

A key element of good programming practice is to centralize your code. This means to put all your code in one place rather than spreading it around the movie. All our code will be right in frame one of the Actions layer, which will be pinned to our Actions panel, allowing us to explore the graphic elements of the movie all we want without losing track of our code.

2.   Now, enter this code:

```
Mouse.hide();
cursor_mc.onEnterFrame = function() {
    this._x += (_root._xmouse-this._x)/5;
    this._y += (_root._ymouse-this._y)/5;
};
```

First we hide the mouse so all we see is our cursor_mc. Then we give the cursor an onEnterFrame function to execute. This function is a simple easing equation. It takes the difference between the mouse (even though invisible now) and cursor_mc's current position, divides that by five and adds it to the cursor's position. This gives the cursor a nice smooth movement. (Actually it makes it a little tougher to aim too, adding to the challenge of the game!)

3.   Now of course we need some ammunition. I just drew a simple tiny 4x4 pixel square on the screen and made it into a movie clip named bullet. Make sure you select the **Export for ActionScript** checkbox and keep the same name, bullet for its export identifier. If there is still a bullet on your screen when you are done, delete it. We will be attaching them straight from the Library as needed.

4.   We are going to use the keyboard for a trigger, so we'll need to respond to key events. We'll create a trigger object to capture these events. Then we'll make this object a listener for key events. Here's the code:

```
trigger = new Object();
Key.addListener(trigger);
```

Here we see another advantage to the new event model. In Flash 5, in order to respond to key events, you had to use a movie clip or a button. Often the solution was to put a blank movie clip on the stage and attach some `onClipEvent (keyDown)` code to it. This violates the code centralization principle, and to make things worse, an empty movie clip shows up as a tiny white dot on the stage. Put a few of these on stage with all your other graphic elements, and your code becomes very hard to find.

5. Now, we can assign the function:

```
trigger.onKeyDown = shoot;
```

> Note that you can assign a function before you actually define it, as long as it is defined in the same frame. Flash will automatically read the functions first, no matter where they are in the frame, and they will then be available for any statements that need them. Often it is easier to name and assign your functions first, to get the logical flow of the program, and then go create the functions with the specific code – kind of like making an outline, then filling in the details.

6. Now we can begin to define our function.

```
function shoot() {
    currBullet_mc = _root.attachMovie("bullet", "bullet"+i, i);
    currBullet_mc._x = 275;
    currBullet_mc._y = 400;
    currBullet_mc.onEnterFrame = bulletMove;
    i++;
    if (i>9) {
        i = 0;
    }
}
```

This function first attaches an instance of `bullet` to `_root`. It gives the instance the name "bullet"+i. We add a line in the beginning of the file, setting i to 0. Thus our first bullet will get the name `bullet0`. At the end of the function, i is incremented, so the next time we fire a bullet, it will be `bullet1`. We also use i to set the new clip's depth. It is important to increment the depths of successive bullets, as two movie clips cannot exist on the same depth. Neither can they have the same names if they are on the same timeline. Then we throw a little `if` statement in there. This resets `i` to 0 if it gets over 9, so we will never have more than ten bullets on screen at one time.

We then set a couple of its properties. If we knew the clip's full name, we could use dot notation and say `_root.bullet0._x=275;`. But since the `i` portion will change each time, we need a way to refer to it no matter what `i` is. In addition to dot notation, we can use array notation, putting a string inside the brackets. The string is the name of the object you want to address. The advantage to this method is that the string can be dynamically created. Therefore we can say `_root["bullet"+i]` to refer to the clip whose name is "bullet"+i. However, there is even a better way. It turns out that when you use the `attachMovie` action, it will return a reference to the movie clip you just attached. We assign that to a temporary variable `currBullet_mc` (for current bullet). This lets us set the properties without having to type all those brackets and quotes. It also turns out to be a bit quicker to run. We set its `_x` and `_y` to put it at the bottom center of the screen.

7.   Now we need to give it some motion. We do that with an `onEnterFrame` handler assigned to the clip as follows:

```
currBullet_mc.onEnterFrame = bulletMove;
```

8.   Again, we will assign the function, and then define it. Here's the `bulletMove` function:

```
function bulletMove() {
    if (!this.shot) {
        this.xSpeed = (_root.cursor_mc._x-this._x)/20;
        this.ySpeed = (_root.cursor_mc._y-this._y)/20;
        this.shot = true;
    }
    this._x += this.xSpeed;
    this._y += this.ySpeed;
}
```

This checks a variable called `this.shot`, using the NOT operator, `!`. This is like saying, *if not shot (if shot is zero or does not exist), then do the following...* Since we have not yet defined `shot`, this will evaluate as `true` and the code block executes. This finds the distance from the bullet to the cursor, divides it by twenty and uses this to set an `xSpeed` and `ySpeed`. It then sets `this.shot` to be true. This will prevent this block of code from running again. From there on out, it just adds `xSpeed` and `ySpeed` to the bullet's `_x` and `_y`.

9.   We just want to add one more thing to this function, which is to remove the bullet after it's gone too far, so we don't needlessly calculate its position into eternity. This little line will do that:

```
if (this._y<0) {
```

```
        removeMovieClip(this);
    }
```

This goes right after we set the bullet's _y property. Here is our code thus far:

```
Mouse.hide();
cursor_mc.onEnterFrame = function() {
    this._x += (_root._xmouse-this._x)/5;
    this._y += (_root._ymouse-this._y)/5;
};
trigger = new Object();
Key.addListener(trigger);
trigger.onKeyDown = shoot;
i = 0;
function shoot() {
    currBullet_mc = _root.attachMovie("bullet", "bullet"+i, i);
    currBullet_mc._x = 275;
    currBullet_mc._y = 400;
    currBullet_mc.onEnterFrame = bulletMove;
    i++;
    if (i>9) {
        i = 0;
    }
}
function bulletMove() {
    if (!this.shot) {
        this.xSpeed = (_root.cursor_mc._x-this._x)/20;
        this.ySpeed = (_root.cursor_mc._y-this._y)/20;
        this.shot = true;
    }
    this._x += this.xSpeed;
    this._y += this.ySpeed;
    if (this._y<0) {
        removeMovieClip(this);
    }
}
```

So far, all we know when we hit a key is that **some** key has been hit. It might be nice to know which one. For instance, we could have three separate guns on screen, rather than just one. I mentioned earlier that the Key object has properties to store the identity of they key currently being pressed as well as the last key that was pressed. We'll use the latter. We'll have three guns, controlled by the z, x and c keys on the keyboard, a bit like the old "Missile Command" game of the 70s. We can retrieve the data in one of two ways, as an ASCII value, or a keycode. ASCII values are tied to individual characters, while keycodes are tied to specific keyboard keys. For example, the capital letter 'A' has an ASCII value of 65, and a keycode of 65. The small 'a' is ASCII 97. But since it is still on the same physical key on the keyboard, it still returns a keycode of 65. Also remember that keyboards in different countries may have different layouts and thus return different key codes.

10. We can use a widely available ASCII chart to discover that the values for z, x and c are 122, 120 and 99 respectively. We can set these up as constants in the beginning of the file like so:

```
FIRELEFT = 122;
FIREMID = 120;
FIRERIGHT = 99;
```

11. We now use the following switch statement to test for the value of the key pressed. This is a new feature in Flash MX, which brings it up to speed with most other languages, which have some version of switch. The value we are testing goes in parentheses after the keyword, switch. We then use a series of case statements. Each one uses the word, case, followed by a possible value and a colon. If the value being tested matches this value the following statements will be executed. If not, it will jump to the next case statement and test that.

Note the break statement after each block of code. Once switch finds a match, it will try to execute *all* the following code, even if it's in another case section. Using break causes Flash to jump out of the entire switch statement and continue on from there.

Also note the default section. This is not mandatory, but allows you to set up some actions to run if *no* case matches the value. Here is our new shoot function:

```
function shoot() {
    keyPressed = Key.getAscii();
    switch(keyPressed){
        case FIRELEFT:
            startX = 50;
            break;
        case FIREMID;
            startx = 275:
            break;
        case FIRERIGHT:
            startX = 500;
            break;
        default:
            startX = 0;
    }
    if(startX){
        currBullet_mc = _root.attachMovie("bullet", "bullet"+i, i);
        currBullet_mc._x = startX;
```

```
                    currBullet_mc._y = 400;
                    currBullet_mc.onEnterFrame = bulletMove;
                    i++;
                    if (i>9) {
                        i = 0;
                    }
                }
            }
```

Here we assign the ASCII value of the key pressed to a variable keyPressed. Then we use switch to test it against our pre-defined values, FIRELEFT, FIREMID, FIRERIGHT. If it gets a match, it assigns a numeric value to startX. In the case of no match (some other key pressed), it assigns 0 to startX.

If startX has some non-zero value assigned to it, we then fire a bullet as before.

12. Now we have three functions and a few miscellaneous commands strewn about. It's getting a bit messy. All those miscellaneous commands are only run once at the beginning of the movie, in order to initialize it. So let's pull them all together and put them in a function of their own, called init:

```
function init() {
    Mouse.hide();
    trigger = new Object();
    Key.addListener(trigger);
    trigger.onKeyDown = shoot;
    i = 0;
    FIRELEFT = 122;
    FIREMID = 120;
    FIRERIGHT = 99;
}
```

Now our frame consists of four functions:

```
init()
cursor.onEnterFrame = function()
shoot()
bulletMove()
```

13. If we need to find a certain piece of code, it's pretty logical where it's going to be. Don't forget, though, that our init function will not run all by itself. So we need to add one line, right up at the top:

```
init();
```

14. Now, of course, we need something to shoot! I just made a space ship, and turned it into a movie clip named `ship`. Don't forget to specify that you want to export for ActionScript, again with the name `ship` and delete any instance from the stage to start.

Now let's make a function to create a ship.

```
function createShip() {
    currShip_mc = attachMovie("ship", "ship"+shipCounter,
    ➥shipCounter);
    currShip_mc._x = 0;
    currShip_mc._y = Math.random()*300;
    currShip_mc.speed = Math.random()*10+5;
    currShip_mc.onEnterFrame = shipMove;
    shipCounter++;
}
```

This should all seem pretty familiar to you by now. We've attached a movie clip, set its `_x` and `_y` position, set a variable called `speed`, assigned an `onEnterFrame` function and incremented the variable that we used to name the clip and set its level.

15. We are going to run into a problem here though. Here we are putting our first ship in depth 0, and incrementing from there. We are also putting our first bullet in depth 0, and incrementing from there. Eventually we are going to run into a conflict. Either a bullet will try to go into a depth where there's already a ship, or vice versa. However, since we know that the bullet depths will always be 0-9, we can solve this by starting out our ship levels at 10. This can be done by putting the following line into our `init` function:

```
shipCounter=10;
```

16. Now, if you have been paying close attention, you should be able to predict the next step. We've assigned a function for our ship's `onEnterFrame` handler: `shipMove`. Now we need to define that function. We've already set a random speed for it. We just need to use that speed to control the position of the ship.

```
function shipMove() {
    this._x += this.speed;
}
```

17. OK, we have a function to make a ship. So, how and when do we call this function? We don't want to do it just once, or we'll only have one ship. We don't want to do it on an `onEnterFrame` or within a few seconds we'll be overrun with ships. What we want is to have a ship appear say, every two seconds or so. While this doesn't really have to do with event handling, we'll throw it in here as a bonus (and because we need to, to make the game work!).

Flash MX introduces a much-needed command, `setInterval`. With this, we can tell a function to wait a certain amount of time before executing, and then to execute again every time that interval has passed again. Since this is something we'll need to set up in the beginning of the movie, we'll throw it in the `init` function.

```
setInterval(createShip, 2000);
```

The arguments consist of the function to execute and the interval to wait. Note that we omit the parentheses on the function name here. We just let `setInterval` have a reference to the function itself. The interval is defined in terms of milliseconds. So 2000 is equal to two seconds. Once we run the `init` function, `setInterval` will tell `createShip` to wait two seconds, then execute. It will then run it every two seconds from there on out.

Although we won't use it here, I should mention the companion to `setInterval`, `clearInterval`. There are many cases when you want a function to run at an interval for a while, but eventually stop. We use `clearInterval(intervalID)` to stop that function from executing any further. Where do we get the interval ID? It is returned when you run `setInterval`. Therefore, you would say something like:

```
IntervalID = setInterval(createShip, 2000);
```

Now, say that we only wanted 100 ships to be created, total. We can keep track of the number of ships with our variable, `shipCounter`. Remembering that `shipCounter` starts at 10, when it hits 110 we will have 100 ships. So we would throw a line into the `createShip` function like:

```
if(shipCounter==110){
   clearInterval(shipIntervalID);
};
```

This would stop `createShip` from running again. You might at that point want to set a new interval, in which `createShip` executed every 1.5 rather than 2 seconds, thus speeding up the action. I'll leave such advanced customization up to you!

Here's our code as it stands:

```
init();
function init() {
    Mouse.hide();
    trigger = new Object();
    Key.addListener(trigger);
    trigger.onKeyDown = shoot;
    i = 0;
    FIRELEFT = 122;
    FIREMID = 120;
    FIRERIGHT = 99;
    shipCounter = 10;
    setInterval(createShip, 2000);
}
cursor_mc.onEnterFrame = function() {
    this._x += (_root._xmouse-this._x)/5;
    this._y += (_root._ymouse-this._y)/5;
};
function shoot() {
    keyPressed = Key.getAscii();
    switch(keyPressed) {
        case FIRELEFT:
            startX = 50;
            break;
        case FIREMID:
            startx = 275;
            break;
        case FIRERIGHT:
            startX = 500;
            break;
        default:
            startX = 0;
    }
    if(startX) {
            currBullet_mc = _root.attachMovie("bullet", "bullet"+i, i);
            currBullet_mc._x = startX;
            currBullet_mc._y = 400;
            currBullet_mc.onEnterFrame = bulletMove;
            i++;
            if (i>9) {
                i = 0;
            }
        }
}
```

```
function bulletMove() {
    if (!this.shot) {
        this.xSpeed = (_root.cursor_mc._x-this._x)/20;
        this.ySpeed = (_root.cursor_mc._y-this._y)/20;
        this.shot = true;
    }
    this._x += this.xSpeed;
    this._y += this.ySpeed;
    if (this._y<0) {
        removeMovieClip(this);
    }
}
function createShip() {
    currShip_mc = attachMovie("ship", "ship"+shipCounter,
    ➡shipCounter);
    currShip_mc._x = 0;
    currShip_mc._y = Math.random()*300;
    currShip_mc.speed = Math.random()*10+5;
    currShip_mc.onEnterFrame = shipMove;
    shipCounter++;
}
function shipMove() {
    this._x += this.speed;
}
```

I strongly suggest you take a moment and read through each line of this listing right now, and make sure you know what every command and symbol is, what it is doing and why it is there.

18. OK, one minor flaw in our game is that if we do hit a ship with a bullet, nothing much happens. So we'll throw in a little hit testing just to round things out. In the next chapter we will go much more in depth about how to detect collisions, so we'll just stick with the generic `hitTest` function here, which goes something like this:

```
movieclip1.hitTest(movieclip2).
```

We need to check for a hit constantly, so it's a good candidate for throwing in an `onEnterFrame` code block. Since we already have an `onEnterFrame` handler defined for each ship, that's as good a place as any to check for a hit. There will be up to ten bullets on stage at any one time, and we need to check the ship against each bullet. We can easily do this with a `for` loop, again resorting to array notation to dynamically create each bullet's name. If `hitTest` returns a hit, then we simply remove the bullet and remove the ship. Our `shipMove` function becomes this:

```
function shipMove() {
```

continues overleaf

```
        this._x += this.speed;
        for (test=0; test<10; test++) {
            if (this.hitTest(_root["bullet"+test])) {
                removeMovieClip(_root["bullet"+test]);
                removeMovieClip(this);
            }
        }
    }
```

19. One final thing we should add is an action to remove any ship once it has gone off screen. We'll just use an arbitrary large number to ensure it's well out of the picture, and if so, remove it.

```
function shipMove() {
    this._x += this.speed;
    if(this._x > 700){
        removeMovieClip(this);
    }
    for (test=0; test<10; test++) {
        if (this.hitTest(_root["bullet"+test])) {
            removeMovieClip(_root["bullet"+test]);
            removeMovieClip(this);
        }
    }
}
```

Hopefully this all makes sense to you now (and hopefully your game works now!). It's not the most exciting game in the world, but it does give you some experience in programming event handlers and simple functions. It also gives you a good basic model to program with. Please play around with it and add some new behaviors and functions. You can add as many functions as you like, handle any events you want, make each function as simple or as complex as needed.

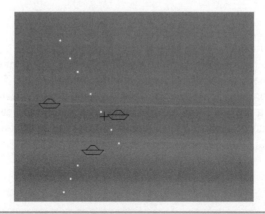

The full code can be found in the **Chapter 6** folder on the CD in `shootemup.fla`.

Watches

The final thing I want to cover here is something totally new to Flash MX, watches. No, not the kind you wear on your wrist. A watch monitors a variable or property, and will call a function when that variable changes. Although it is not actually an event handler, it is similar in that it waits for something to happen, and then performs a function.

Watches are useful in components, such as check boxes. A check box can either be checked or unchecked, which would generally translate into true or false. You don't want a check box to actually do anything until its state is changed. So you add a watch to the variable that holds that state. When it does change, then the function gets called into play and it does something.

Let's go back to our drag and throw experiment and revise it to use a watch. If you remember, we used `onPress` and `onRelease/onReleaseOutside` to start and stop dragging the movie clip. At the same time we set a variable named dragging to `true` or `false`. We are going to watch this variable. When it changes, we change the movie clip's `onEnterFrame` handler to a different function.

First, the syntax for the watch function:

```
object.watch("property", function);
```

- `object` is the object, movie clip or timeline where the variable is located.

- `"property"` is the property or variable itself. Note that this is in the form of a string, not just the variable name.

- `function` is a reference to the function that you want to be executed. `watch` will pass the following parameters to the function:

  - `id` is the name again of the property.

  - `oldval` is the value of the property prior to the change.

  - `newval` is the new, current value.

OK, here is where things get a little interesting. We learned earlier that you cannot supply parameters directly to an event handler function. This fact is emphasized when an event handler is called by Flash, because no parameters are passed to it.

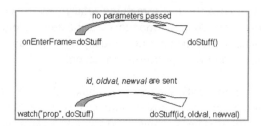

In the case of watch, though, the function is automatically passed three parameters. In the watch statement, we still need only supply a reference – without parentheses. But when we define the function itself, we need to account for the parameters that will be passed to it.

So, here is our watch statement:

```
mc1_mc.watch("dragging", dragHandler);
```

...and here is how we need to begin defining our dragHandler function:

```
function dragHandler(id, oldval, newval){

}
```

Now, we don't need to actually use all these parameters, but we have to define our function with them. In most cases, you may only be concerned with the newval parameter. After all, the new value of the parameter is what we are interested in. That is exactly the case in our example. We know we are always calling the function based on the dragging variable, so we already know what id will be. oldval serves no real purpose to us either.

It is also important to note that, like an event handler function, we use this to refer to the object in question. Inside our dragHandler function, this will refer to mc1_mc.

OK, we know that dragging will be set to true or false, so the value of newval will be delivered to us as true or false. We'll take one course of action if newval is true, and do something else if it is false.

```
function dragHandler(id, oldval, newval) {
    if (newval) {
        this.onEnterFrame = drag;
    } else {
        this.onEnterFrame = move;
```

```
    }
    return newval;
}
```

> *Note the way we simply say* `if(newval)` *...*
>
> *Remember that* `if` *statements always evaluate their contents into* `true` *or* `false`*. Since* `newval` *is already in the format of* `true/false`*, there is no need to do anything further such as comparing it, as in* `if(newval==true)`*. We can use it "straight out of the box." Another important thing to note is that at the end of the actions you take in your watch function, you must add the line* `return newval;` *Although undocumented, it was found that if you omit this line, the variable you passed to the watch function will now become* `undefined`*! In our case, this means that our variable,* `dragging`*, rather than being* `true` *or* `false`*, will be* `undefined`*. Returning* `newval` *handles this.*

So now you see where we are going with this. Rather than having one large function for `onEnterFrame`, which checks the status of the variable dragging many times per second, we break our actions into two different functions. The value of `dragging` is only tested when it actually changes. Thus we have gained some efficiency.

We now only need to define our new functions, `drag` and `move`. These are just the two sections of our original `onEnterFrame` function. Here is the final code for the new throwing code:

```
mc1_mc.onPress = function() {
    this.startDrag();
    this.dragging = true;
};
mc1_mc.onRelease = mc1.onReleaseOutside = function () {
    this.stopDrag();
    this.dragging = false;
};
mc1_mc.watch("dragging", dragHandler);
function dragHandler(id, oldval, newval) {
    if (newval) {
```

249

continues overleaf

```
                this.onEnterFrame = drag;
        } else {
                this.onEnterFrame = move;
        }
        return newval;
}
function move() {
        this.xspeed *= .98;
        this.yspeed *= .98;
        this._x += this.xspeed;
        this._y += this.yspeed;
        if (this._x>550) {
            this._x = 0;
        } else if (this._x<0) {
            this._x = 550;
        }
        if (this._y>400) {
            this._y = 0;
        } else if (this._y<0) {
            this._y = 400;
        }
}
function drag() {
        this.xspeed = this._x-this.oldx;
        this.yspeed = this._y-this.oldy;
        this.oldx = this._x;
        this.oldy = this._y;
}
```

Test that and see that we have recreated our drag and throw program to be fully event driven. You can find it done for you in the `throwcursor_watches.fla` in the **Chapter 6** folder of the CD.

Now before you go trying it and driving yourself crazy, you are not able to set a watch on most of the built-in properties of movie clips, such as _x and _y. The internal methods used to access these properties make them incompatible with the watch function. This is covered in more detail in the Flash MX Reference entry for watch.

There is one last thing I should cover about watches. Similar to the shorthand way of assigning event handler functions, we can use a little shortcut when writing our watch functions. Again, we simply define a nameless function, and include it right in the watch statement.

Instead of using a reference to the function in the statement, we put the function definition there directly (without the name). Here I've separated it a bit to make it clear:

```
mc1_mc.watch("dragging",

function (id, oldval, newval){
    if(newval){
        this.onEnterFrame=drag;
    } else {
        this.onEnterFrame=move;
    }
}
```

And here it is written the way you will usually see it:

```
mc1_mc.watch("dragging", function (id, oldval, newval) {
```

Remember that a function definition without a name returns a reference to that function. This satisfies the requirements for the second argument of `watch`. It doesn't really matter which way you write it. Do whatever is more understandable for you.

Summary

We haven't created anything too amazing in this chapter, but we have learned a new way of using Flash and put some vital tools into our tool belt. You should now know enough about events and handlers, and how to create and use functions, so that you can program some pretty dynamic interactivity into your movies. Although there are several events we didn't touch on (Stage events, TextField and Selection events), these should be no problem for you now, since they work in exactly the same way. In the next several chapters we will be using everything you just learned very extensively, and will be creating some truly impressive effects. Ready?

section 2: ActionScript Interfaces

chapter 7: **Advanced Collision Detection**

In the last chapter, we looked at the possible ways in which the user can interact with the objects on the screen. Now we're going to look at how objects can react to each other through collision detection. A whole chapter on collision detection? Well, we are going to cover a lot of peripheral issues that will enable you to become a collision expert.

In the time that I have been writing tutorials and releasing open source files, many people have sent me back some amazing files they created using the simple principles I gave them. With that in mind, I'm going to steer clear of intricate graphics and really complex files. I'll go through some basic principles so you really understand them, and we'll make a few sample games so you have a good idea of how to apply them. Mix that with a healthy dose of your own imagination and you're off!

hitTest

First we'll cover the simplest of all collision detection methods, `hitTest`. I'm assuming that if you're reading this book, then you may well have used `hitTest` before. At any rate, we used it in the last chapter, but there are a few different versions and ways to use it and I've found that not everyone understands it fully, so let's take a quick run through it and see what it's all about.

First, you should know that there are two distinct ways of using `hitTest`, and the second one has two options. This leaves us with three different methods of using `hitTest`. We'll look at these in order of complexity.

The most basic syntax of `hitTest`, as we saw in the last chapter is:

```
movieClip1_mc.hitTest(movieClip2_mc);
```

This just tests whether two movie clips are colliding or not. It makes absolutely no difference whatsoever which movie clip goes in which position. If the two clips are overlapping, this will return `true`, and if they're not then it will return `false`. Therefore, `hitTest` is almost exclusively used within an `if` statement like so:

```
if (movieClip1_mc.hitTest(movieClip2_mc)) {
    // do something
}
```

Bounding boxes

About the only other important thing you need to know about when using `hitTest` is the **bounding box**, the invisible rectangle that completely encompasses any movie clip. The top of the box corresponds to the top most visible element of the clip, the bottom to the lowest point, and the left and right edges of the box correspond to the furthest left and right points of the clip. If you place a movie clip on the stage and then click on it to select it, you can see a blue outline around it (if you haven't changed the default outlines color). This is the movie clip's bounding box:

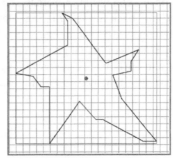

This bounding box is what this most basic form of `hitTest` uses for checking collisions. This makes for a pretty fast and efficient check, but unfortunately can also result in some pretty inaccurate results in many cases. Unless the movie clip in question is a rectangle (in which case the bounding box will fit it perfectly), the bounding box will always cover more area than the actual graphics in the clip itself. Thus, `hitTest` can frequently register a collision when the graphics in the movie clips are obviously still not touching. Here's a typical example of how this can happen:

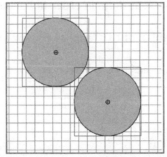

The work-around for this is...well, there really isn't one if you are going to stick to this version of `hitTest`. That's the price you pay for the speed and ease of using this method. For many applications though, it suffices just fine. In the little alien shoot-up game we made in the last chapter, there was enough action going on at a fast enough rate that you wouldn't really notice any small inconsistencies. But imagine a game like Atari's *Asteroids* where objects may be moving around more slowly. You think you're going to ease your ship right up to the edge of an asteroid and suddenly you blow up: 'Hey! I wasn't even close!' you'd complain. So, as you can see, this version of `hitTest` wouldn't be a good solution for that type of situation.

OK, like I said, you've probably used this method before, at least in the last chapter, so we won't waste any more time with examples. Let's move on to the next use of `hitTest`.

Using shapeFlag

Here's the basic syntax for performing a `hitTest` using a `shapeFlag`:

```
movieClip_mc.hitTest(x, y, shapeFlag);
```

I know your eye jumped right to that `shapeFlag` parameter but be patient. Let's read this line from left to right.

First we have `movieClip_mc`, which is obviously the name of the clip we are testing. Notice that we are only testing *one* clip this time. Well, what is the clip hitting (or not)? The answer is just a point. The point is defined by the next two parameters, `x` and `y`. What we are asking here is whether or not the point (x,y) is within the area of the `movieClip_mc`.

At last, we now come to `shapeFlag`. With this parameter we can choose whether or not we want to use the bounding box of the clip. If `shapeFlag` is set to `false` or `0`, the `hitTest` will merely check if the point is within the bounding box of the movie clip. However, if you set `shapeFlag` to `true` or any non-zero numeric value, we now rise above the limitations of bounding boxes, and test whether or not the point is within a visible area of the clip.

OK, this is much more powerful. Using `shapeFlag` as an alternative use of the `hitTest` method is probably most common. In fact, I have rarely, if ever, used this second syntax without also using the `shapeFlag` option.

Now this sounds pretty darn good, but before we think all of our problems are solved, we need to figure out where we are getting these `x` and `y` values from. Remember that the first method we looked at tests a movie clip against another movie clip. We can imitate this by using one clip as the movie clip running the function, and use the `_x` and `_y` properties of the second clip as the `x` and `y` parameters of `hitTest`. We get something like this:

```
movieClip1_mc.hitTest(movieClip2_mc._x, movieClip2_mc._y, true);
```

Now, look at the following image and you'll see the next problem we run into.

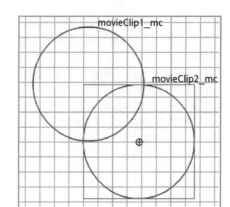

This will not register a hit, because the x and y parameters here refer to the center point of movieClip2_mc, which is *not* within the qualifying hit area.

So, we've jumped out of the frying pan, into the fire, and we're stuck between a rock and a hard place, and yes, mixing metaphors is one method I use to stall. I wish I could give you a final workaround for these two opposite ends of the problem, but I haven't come across a really decent, efficient one (and I've had many discussions about it). This has become a sort of Holy Grail quest in Flash: performing a movie clip to movie clip hit test with shapeFlag. I'm only mentioning this so you know the issue exists and you won't beat your head against the wall thinking that you're missing something obvious. I'll give you a couple of pointers though, to make the best of it:

- The most important point is pretty obvious: whatever method works and looks best is the best way to do it, so test out all the methods.

- In general, if you have a large object and a small object, it is best to use the large object as the clip running the hitTest and the smaller clip providing the X and Y parameters. Since a small object is closer to a point, you can be more accurate.

- If you have an irregular shaped object, particularly if it is large, it's best to call hitTest from this object, since you are interested in the shape of that object's visible area.

- If you have two basically rectangular objects, use the movie clip to movie clip version.

Now that's all there really is to know about hitTest. I now want to jump right into the advanced methods of collision detection, but if you have any confusion on the different varieties of hitTest, play around with the following exercise until you're more confident.

Using the different types of hitTest

1. Open a new movie and make two movie clips called `movieClip1` and `movieClip2`. Make them both irregular shapes and give them instance names of `movieClip1_mc` and `movieClip2_mc` respectively.

2. We're going to use movie clip to movie clip testing first, so put the following code in frame 1 of a new layer called `actions`:

```
movieClip1_mc.onEnterFrame = function() {
    if (this.hitTest(movieClip2_mc)) {
        trace("hit");
    }
};
movieClip2_mc.onEnterFrame = function() {
    this._x = _xmouse;
    this._y = _ymouse;
};
```

3. Test your movie and drag `movieClip2` around. You can see the results of each test in the Output window:

4. Close down your test movie. We'll now try out movie clip to point testing without shapeFlag, so simply substitute the following code in place of the existing code from step 2:

```
movieClip1_mc.onEnterFrame = function() {
    if (this.hitTest(movieClip2_mc._x, movieClip2_mc._y, false)) {
        trace("hit");
    }
};
movieClip2_mc.onEnterFrame = function() {
    this._x = _xmouse;
    this._y = _ymouse;
};
```

5. So that you can see more clearly where Flash registers a hit, delete the fill color from `movieClip2` so that it's just an outline. Now test your movie.

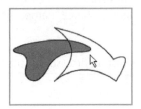 

You can see that a hit isn't registered until the cursor enters the (albeit invisible) bounding box around `movieClip1`.

6. Close down your test movie. Finally, we'll try out the movie clip to point testing, but this time *with* `shapeFlag`. Substitute all the existing code in frame 1 with the following:

```
movieClip1_mc.onEnterFrame = function() {
    if (this.hitTest(movieClip2_mc._x, movieClip2_mc._y, true)) {
        trace("hit");
    }
};
movieClip2_mc.onEnterFrame = function() {
    this._x = _xmouse;
    this._y = _ymouse;
};
```

7. Test your movie. You should be able to drag `movieClip2` around with the mouse and see where the actual collision occurs.

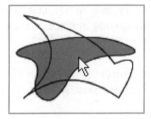 

Playing with each of these methods for a while will give you a good idea what each form of the command does, and which one you will want to use in different situations.

Mathematical collision detection

Although we've now covered all of `hitTest` and seen its power and limitations, don't worry, we're far from through yet. `hitTest` is Flash's built-in collision detection method, but there are some handmade alternatives that can do a much better job for specific tasks.

What are we really looking for when we are checking for collision? Well, collision is when two objects hit each other, or when one object hits another object.

We know there is an object in a particular location. If another object is in the same location, then they are colliding. Say there is a wall at location _x=500. If our object's _x location is higher than 500 then it must be hitting the wall, right? True, as long as you consider the wall has an infinite height, since we haven't bothered to check the _y value. The cool thing is, we don't even have to make a wall. We just say it is there by the value of its position. The easiest thing is to set up a constant in the beginning of a movie and say, `right=500;`. Let's take this further and try it out.

Bouncing ball

1. Open a new movie. While we're at it, let's set up a left wall too. We'll do it in an `init` function just to be neat. Rename the default layer `actions` and type in the following code:

    ```
    init();
    function init() {
        right = 500;
        left = 50;
    }
    ```

2. Now we need to make something collide with our walls. Let's start with a simple ball. Draw a circular ball shape, convert it to a movie clip called `ball`, and give it the instance name `ball_mc`.

3. Next we need to make the ball move. Earlier we used the term **speed**. Here we are going to be a little more technically precise and say **velocity**. Velocity is speed in a certain direction. We'll limit our possible directions to left and right here, so our velocity will be either +speed or -speed. We'll call it `velX`, short for 'velocity along the x-axis'. Let's add this to init:

    ```
    init();
    function init() {
        right = 500;
        left = 50;
        ball_mc. velX = 5;
    }
    ```

4. Now we need a function to move the ball. You might have guessed that we're going to use an `onEnterFrame` handler for this. We'll assign a handler function in the `init` section, and then after that we'll create the `move` function. Add the following to your code:

```
init();
function init() {
      right = 500;
      left = 50;
      ball_mc.velX = 5;
      ball_mc.onEnterFrame = move;
}
function move() {
      this._x += this.velX;
}
```

This takes the velocity and adds it to the _x position. Since `velX = 5`, this function will add 5 to the _x position of the ball on each frame. Test this movie now and you can see that the ball slides off to the right and vanishes. OK, it's time for some collision detection with the wall.

5. If you think back to our earlier hit testing with a point, you'll remember that a shape is larger than the point at which it is located. We need to account for the **thickness** of the object when we test it against the wall. Say our ball has a diameter of 20 pixels. That means that the edge of the ball is going to be 10 pixels away from the center (provided the ball has a central registration point). We can take this into account when we test the position of the ball against the wall. Our code will be something like this:

```
if (this._x>right-(this._width/2)) {
      // then we have a hit
}
```

We'll add this to the `move` function in a moment after we set the ball's position.

Here we are taking the _width property of the `ball` movie clip and dividing it by two. This gives us the distance from the center of the circle to the edge (the radius). Note that this will only work for objects that have a central registration point and have been centered on the x-axis.

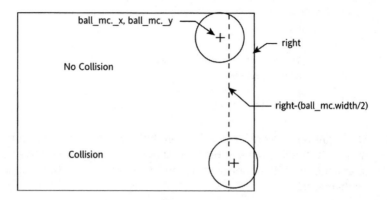

6. OK, so what happens when a ball hits a wall? It bounces. If, as in our case, it is travelling perfectly perpendicular to the surface it hits, it will simply start travelling in the opposite direction. Another way of saying this is that its velocity reverses: our ball has a velocity of +5 right now, so when it hits the wall its velocity will become -5. Rather than hard coding in the -5, we can multiply *whatever* the ball's velocity is by -1, which will give us the reverse velocity. Let's add all this to our code, inside the move function:

```
function move() {
    this._x += this.velX;
    if (this._x>right-(this._width/2)) {
        this.velX *= -1;
    }
}
```

7. Now we can take this code and alter it slightly to create a similar if statement to check for a collision against the left wall. Add this new code to the move function:

```
if (this._x<left+(this._width/2)) {
    this.velX *= -1;
}
```

8. If you need a recap here, here's the code in full so far:

```
init();
function init() {
    right = 500;
    left = 50;
    ball_mc.velX = 5;
    ball_mc.onEnterFrame = move;
}
function move() {
    this._x += this.velX;
```

continues overleaf

```
            if (this._x>right-(this._width/2)) {
                this.velX *= -1;
            }
            if (this._x<left+(this._width/2)) {
                this.velX *= -1;
            }
        }
```

9. You might want to draw some lines on the stage at 50 and 500 on the x-axis so you can see what is happening. Remember that these lines are just graphical elements that have no interaction with the code and action in the movie. All the collision detection is strictly mathematical.

10. Test the movie and you should see the ball bouncing back and forth between the two lines. If your eyes are good though, you'll notice something a bit annoying. The ball actually goes *into* the wall before it bounces:

If you don't see it, either slow down the frame rate of the movie, or jack up the velocity value. If you really threw a ball against a wall, it wouldn't go into the wall and bounce out again. (I'm talking about the usual tennis ball thrown by an ordinary human, not Arnold Schwarzenegger throwing a shot-put). We're going to fix this up now.

11. When we get a hit, we'll know that we are at least a little bit inside the wall, as you can see in the previous screenshot. So, we'll manually replace our ball so that it actually touches the exact edge of the wall. Make the following changes to the move function (the init function stays the same):

```
function move() {
    this._x += this.velX;
    if (this._x>right-(this._width/2)) {
        this.velX *= -1;
        this._x = right-(this._width/2);
```

```
        }
        if (this._x<left+(this._width/2)) {
            this.velX *= -1;
            this._x = left+(this._width/2);
        }
    }
```

12. If you test the movie now, the ball goes into the wall slightly, we register a hit, and the ball is repositioned on the edge of the wall. But, since Flash doesn't update the screen until all this code is completed, we never actually see the ball penetrate the wall, only hitting it. For once, one of the 'inadequacies' of Flash's inner workings has been used to our advantage!

13. Now, I'm going to take a quantum leap and add an entire new dimension to this movie. All I'm doing here is taking the lines containing _x or velX and duplicating them with _y and velY, and also adding two new variables called top and bottom. I've also changed _width to _height. You'll probably also want to draw two more lines on the top and bottom of the stage at (x,50) and (x,350) to display these walls. You should be able to follow this code without too much of a problem:

```
init();
function init() {
    right = 500;
    left = 50;
    top = 50;
    bottom = 350;
    ball_mc.velX = 5;
    ball_mc.velY = 5;
    ball_mc.onEnterFrame = move;
}
function move() {
    this._x += this.velX;
    this._y += this.velY;
    if (this._x>right-(this._width/2)) {
        this.velX *= -1;
        this._x = right-(this._width/2);
    }
    if (this._x<left+(this._width/2)) {
        this.velX *= -1;
        this._x = left+(this._width/2);
    }
    if (this._y>bottom-(this._height/2)) {
        this.velY *= -1;
        this._y = bottom-(this._height/2);
    }
    if (this._y<top+(this._height/2)) {
```

continues overleaf

```
            this.velY *= -1;
            this._y = top+(this._height/2);
        }
    }
```

14. Test the movie. Hey, what the heck? This is starting to look strangely like the old *Pong* game I had when I was a kid. Well, since it's going that way, let's take it a step or two further.

World cup pong

1. Keep the last movie open for this exercise, as we'll use the code as a base. Delete the left and right walls and replace them with paddles. For the paddle, you can just draw a vertical line, whatever length you choose, and convert it into a movie clip called pc (I've added some text to my paddles just to make the screenshot below clearer).

2. Duplicate the pc movie clip and call it player. Drag an instance of both movie clips onto the stage and place them on a new layer called paddles.

3. Give them instance names of pc_mc and player_mc respectively. Manually place pc at (50,200), and player at (500,200). The _y positions aren't quite so important because they'll be updated dynamically in our ActionScript, but we'll start them out in center field.

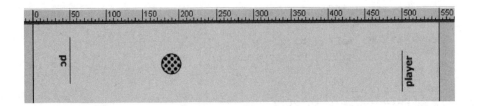

4. We're going to start out by adding some onEnterFrame handlers for the two paddles.

```
init();
function init() {
    RIGHT = 500;
    LEFT = 50;
    TOP = 50;
    BOTTOM = 350;
    ball_mc.velX = 0;
    ball_mc.velY = 0;
    ball_mc.onEnterFrame = move;
    pc_mc.onEnterFrame = pcMove;
```

```
        player_mc.onEnterFrame = playerMove;
}
```

5.   Then we can go ahead and define the functions pcMove and playerMove. pcMove started off as a simple easing equation, so that the pc's paddle is always trying to get to the position of the ball. Then to make it a little tougher, we'll only allow it to move if the ball is moving toward it, (ball_mc.velX<0). player's paddle will simply check if the UP or DOWN cursor keys are being pressed, and if so, move up or down. Both will use distance-based hit checking to make sure they don't go off the playing field.

```
function pcMove() {
    if (ball_mc.velX<0) {
        this._y += (ball_mc._y-this._y)/5;
    }
    if (this._y>bottom-this._height/2) {
        this._y = bottom-this._height/2;
        this.vy = 0;
    }
    if (this._y<top+this._height/2) {
        this._y = top+this._height/2;
        this.vy = 0;
    }
}
function playerMove() {
    if (Key.isDown(Key.UP)) {
        this._y -= 10;
    } else if (Key.isDown(Key.DOWN)) {
        this._y += 10;
    }
    if (this._y>bottom-this._height/2) {
        this._y = bottom-this._height/2;
        this.vy = 0;
    }
    if (this._y<top+this._height/2) {
        this._y = top+this._height/2;
        this.vy = 0;
    }
}
```

6.   You might also notice that I set the initial velocities of the ball to 0. This is so we can decide when and where the game begins. We'll do that by making _root a listener for Key events, and set an onKeyDown event to start the ball moving. Just add these four lines to the init function and then create the serve function at the end of all your code:

```
Key.addListener(_root);
```

continues overleaf

```
    _root.onKeyDown = serve;
    pcServe = true;
    baseSpeed = 10;

    function serve() {
        if (Key.getCode() == Key.SPACE) {
            if (playerServe) {
                ball_mc.velX = -baseSpeed;
                ball_mc.velY = Math.random()*20-10;
                playerServe = false;
            } else if (pcServe) {
                ball_mc.velX = baseSpeed;
                ball_mc.velY = Math.random()*20-10;
                pcServe = false;
            }
        }
    }
```

Now when we start the game, the ball just sits there waiting for you to hit the space bar. Since `pcServe` is true, it will execute the second block, sending the ball hurtling toward player.

7. Now if you test the game, you should have a pretty good Pong game going. One problem though. Try to *miss* the ball: it bounces anyway. Remember, we're not doing any real live collision detection on the paddle, just on the mathematical calculation of the ball's position. Instead of massively changing things though, we're just going to qualify things a little. We're going to make sure that the ball is on the paddle before it bounces.

This means that the ball is lower than the top point of the paddle, but higher than the bottom point. If it's within these two points when it hits `right`, then it's a hit. If the ball is outside, it's a miss. Now we could throw in an old fashioned `hitTest`, but I'll take this opportunity to introduce a new concept and action called `getBounds`. This seems to be one of those sleeper commands. I rarely see it used by others, but I've been warming to it lately. It kind of breaks `hitTest` into its component parts and lets you use what you want.

`getBounds` is a method of the `movieClip` object. When called, it returns an object. That object has four properties that tell us about where the clip is located. Here's how you use it:

boundsObject=movieClip.getBounds(scope);

The `boundsObject` has the following four properties: `xMin`, `xMax`, `yMin`, and `yMax`. These logically correspond to the four edges of the bounding box of the movie clip. But, rather than just telling Flash to calculate what is inside or out of the bounding box, we now have numeric values to work with. We can now mathematically determine our own collisions, taking into account width and so on, as we have been doing with our walls.

The only thing left to define here is the scope parameter. The min and max properties of the returned boundsObject are expressed in terms of pixel units, but in relation to what? That's our scope. Generally you will want to enter _root as the scope, or whatever timeline you are testing your collision on. This will give you the X and Y values of the clip as seen from _root.

If you entered the movie clip itself as the scope, it would return the value of its edges as seen from its own viewpoint. For example, a 100 pixel square movie clip with a central registration point would always return -50 and 50 for its max and min values, no matter where the clip was located on the screen. From its viewpoint, it goes 50 pixels up from the center, 50 pixels down, 50 to the left, and to the right:

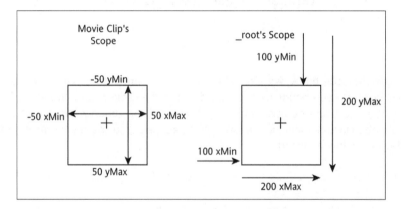

8. This isn't too useful for our purposes here so we'll enter _root. Add this new line inside your move function:

```
function move() {
    this._x += this.velX;
    this._y += this.velY;
    if (this._x>right-(this._width/2)) {
    playerBounds = player_mc.getBounds(_root);
```

Now playerBounds will contain the four properties mentioned previously. The properties we are most interested in are yMin and yMax. If ball_mc._y is between these two after it passes the point defined by right-(this._width/2), then it is hitting the player's paddle:

9. So, we'll add another conditional statement using the logical AND operator (&&). Note that this also takes in to account the width of the ball, so we are not just testing against the center point of the ball. This will give a much more realistic hit.

```
function move() {
    this._x += this.velX;
    this._y += this.velY;
    if (this._x>right-(this._width/2)) {
        playerBounds = player_mc.getBounds(_root);
        upper = playerBounds.yMin - this._height/2;
        lower = playerBounds.yMax + this._height/2;
        if (this._y>upper && this._y<lower) {
            this.velX *= -1;
            this.velY += Math.random()*20 - 10;
            this._x = right-(this._width/2);
        }
    }
}
```

10. Inside the code block, we also add a little randomness to the velY factor. Otherwise, the ball will just keep bouncing back and forth at the same angles. We also increase the speed slightly – just one percent – to keep things getting tougher. Note that we must increase both the current speed, velX, and the baseSpeed, so that at the next serve, the ball will stay at the higher speed.

```
if (this._y>upper && this._y<lower) {
    this.velX *= -1;
    this.velY += Math.random()*20-10;
    this._x = right-(this._width/2);
    baseSpeed *= 1.01;
    this.velX *= 1.01;
}
```

11. Now we know what we will do *if* we hit the paddle, but we have to decide what to do if we miss. What I want to do is reset the ball to the middle of the screen, change the speed and direction randomly, and increase the opponent's score. This will go in an else block:

```
function move() {
    this._x += this.velX;
    this._y += this.velY;
    if (this._x>right-(this._width/2)) {
        playerBounds = player_mc.getBounds(_root);
        if (this._y>playerBounds.yMin && this._y<playerBounds.yMax) {
            this.velX *= -1;
            this._x = right-(this._width/2);
```

```
        } else {
            this._x = 275;
            this._y = 200;
            this.velX = 0;
            this.velY = 0;
            pcScore++;
            playerServe = true;
        }
    }
```

You can make it do anything you want here, but this works fine for me. I've added a dynamic text box over on the left-hand side of the stage with the variable name pcScore. This will give a visual display of how poorly I am doing!

12. Here is the final code for the Pong game:

```
init();
function init() {
    RIGHT = 500;
    LEFT = 50;
    TOP = 50;
    BOTTOM = 350;
    ball_mc.velX = 0;
    ball_mc.velY = 0;
    ball_mc.onEnterFrame = move;
    pc_mc.onEnterFrame = pcMove;
    player_mc.onEnterFrame = playerMove;
    Key.addListener(_root);
    _root.onKeyDown = serve;
    pcServe = true;
    baseSpeed = 10;
}
function move() {
    this._x += this.velX;
```

continues overleaf

```
this._y += this.velY;
if (this._x>right-(this._width/2)) {
    playerBounds = player_mc.getBounds(_root);
    upper = playerBounds.yMin-this._height/2;
    lower = playerBounds.yMax+this._height/2;
    if (this._y>upper && this._y<lower) {
        this.velX *= -1;
        this.velY += Math.random()*20-10;
        this._x = right-(this._width/2);
        baseSpeed *= 1.01;
        this.velX *= 1.01;
    } else {
        this._x = 275;
        this._y = 200;
        this.velX = 0;
        this.velY = 0;
        pcScore++;
        playerServe = true;
    }
}
if (this._x<left+(this._width/2)) {
    pcBounds = pc_mc.getBounds(_root);
    if (this._y>pcBounds.yMin-this._height/2 &&
    ➡this._y<pcBounds.yMax+this._height/2) {
        this.velX *= -1;
        this.velY += Math.random()*20-10;
        this._x = left+(this._width/2);
        baseSpeed *= 1.01;
        this.velX *= 1.01;
    } else {
        this._x = 275;
        this._y = 200;
        this.velX = 0;
        this.velY = 0;
        playerScore++;
        pcServe = true;
    }
}
if (this._y>bottom-(this._height/2)) {
    this.velY *= -1;
    this._y = bottom-(this._height/2);
}
if (this._y<top+(this._height/2)) {
    this.velY *= -1;
    this._y = top+(this._height/2);
```

```
            }
        }
        function pcMove() {
            if (ball_mc.velX<0) {
                this._y += (ball_mc._y-this._y)/5;
            }
            if (this._y>bottom-this._height/2) {
                this._y = bottom-this._height/2;
                this.vy = 0;
            }
            if (this._y<top+this._height/2) {
                this._y = top+this._height/2;
                this.vy = 0;
            }
        }
        function playerMove() {
            if (Key.isDown(Key.UP)) {
                this._y -= 10;
            } else if (Key.isDown(Key.DOWN)) {
                this._y += 10;
            }
            if (this._y>bottom-this._height/2) {
                this._y = bottom-this._height/2;
                this.vy = 0;
            }
            if (this._y<top+this._height/2) {
                this._y = top+this._height/2;
                this.vy = 0;
            }
        }
        function serve() {
            if (Key.getCode() == Key.SPACE) {
                if (playerServe) {
                    ball_mc.velX = -baseSpeed;
                    ball_mc.velY = Math.random()*20-10;
                    playerServe = false;
                } else if (pcServe) {
                    ball_mc.velX = baseSpeed;
                    ball_mc.velY = Math.random()*20-10;
                    pcServe = false;
                }
            }
        }
```

As you can see, I duplicated the above steps for checking against the other paddle, and displaying the player's score in a dynamic text field with the variable name `playerScore`. Go ahead and test out your game.

Feel free to play around with this. The code on the disk has a few little extra goodies, but there are plenty more things you could add to it.

Distance-based movie clip to movie clip collision detection

This is the final type of collision detection we are going to cover. This method is only completely accurate for perfectly circular objects, though you might fake it a bit for something that roughly approximates a circle.

Earlier we looked at the idea that if two objects are in approximately the same position, they can be said to be colliding. Another way of looking at it is if the distance between the two objects is zero. Here we are going to take two circular movie clips and calculate the distance between them. To do that we use Pythagorus' Theorem. This theorem says that if you take the sum of the square of the two short sides of a right-angled triangle, this will equal the square of the long side or hypotenuse. Right, time for a diagram:

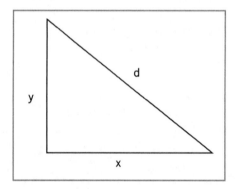

I've labeled the sides x, y, and d. Pythagorus' Theorem says:

$$x^2+y^2=d^2$$

...or in more familiar terms:

```
x*x + y*y = d*d
```

Now if you perform some basic algebra, you come up with (converted to ActionScript):

```
d=Math.sqrt(x*x + y*y);
```

This is saying that if you square both sides, add them together and then take the square root, you get the length of the hypotenuse. Now, let's change our diagram just a bit, and all is revealed:

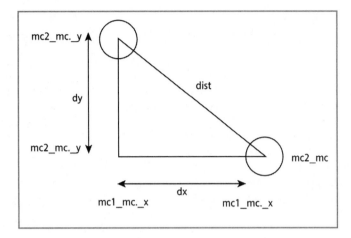

Now we can see that dx is the distance, along the x-axis, between mc1_mc and mc2_mc. dy is the distance along the y-axis and dist is the overall distance between them. Knowing all this, we can make the mental leap to arrive at the following standard code:

```
dx = mc2_mc._x-mc1_mc._x;
dy = mc2_mc._y-mc1_mc._y;
dist = Math.sqrt(dx*dx+dy*dy);
```

Voila! This is another one to tattoo to the back of your hand. OK, OK, just memorize it or write it down, but keep it handy.

Now earlier I said that when the distance between the two movie clips gets to zero, the objects are colliding. But remember in the last Pong exercise, we needed to account for the size of the ball. Well, now we have to account for the sizes of both of the movie clips. If we waited for the distance to become 0, the two balls' center points would have to be precisely located on the exact same pixel in order for a hit to register. That's asking a bit too much.

Last time we just took into account the ball's radius in determining its collision status. Here we do the same thing, but calculate the radius of one ball plus the radius of another ball. If the distance between the balls is less than this figure, we have a hit. The beauty of this method is that it doesn't matter what size the movie clips are, since we are determining the radii dynamically.

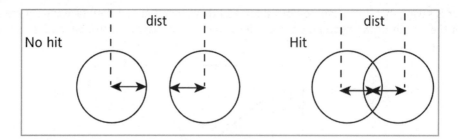

The code to calculate whether a hit has occurred or not is:

```
dx=mc2_mc._x-mc1_mc._x;
dy=mc2_mc._y-mc1_mc._y;
dist=Math.sqrt(dx*dx+dy*dy);
if(dist<mc1_mc._width/2 + mc2_mc._width/2){
    // you have a hit!
}
```

Now, what we do when we find that we do have a hit is another story. Everyone wants to make a file with some spheres shooting around and colliding off of each other. They learn the technique up to where we have arrived at the moment and figure they can reverse the x or y velocity somehow and that'll do the trick. Unfortunately, it's not quite that easy. We'll be getting into some of those reactions in the next chapter. For now, let's just make a quick sample file so that you can see for yourself that it really does work.

This will be another little game framework, somewhat in the vein of Atari's *Asteroids*, though you could turn this into virtually anything you wanted.

Look at the size of that thing

1. Start a new movie. First we'll make a circular shaped movie clip to use (I made mine 100 pixels in diameter). Call it `ball` and check **Export for ActionScript** in its Linkage Properties. Give it the linkage identifier `ball`.

2. Keep a copy of the ball on the stage and give it the instance name `player_mc`.

3. Now we're going to create a bunch of obstacles for our game. These will serve in the asteroid role. We'll do this in an init function as usual, attaching them with a `for` loop. While we're at it, we'll give these obstacles a random position, velocity, and size. Then we'll assign an `onEnterFrame` handler. Whew! That's a productive loop. Add all this to a separate new layer called `actions`:

```
init();
```

```
function init() {
    for (i=0; i<10; i++) {
        ball_mc = attachMovie("ball", "b"+i, i);
        ball_mc._x = Math.random()*550;
        ball_mc._y = Math.random()*400;
        ball_mc.velX = Math.random()*10-5;
        ball_mc.velY = Math.random()*10-5;
        ball_mc._xscale = Math.random()*40+10;
        ball_mc._yscale = Math.random()*40+10;
        ball_mc.onEnterFrame = ballMove;
    }
}
```

4. Now we'll define the function `ballMove`:

```
function ballMove() {
    this._x += this.velX;
    this._y += this.velY;
    if (this._x>550) {
        this._x = 0;
    }
    if (this._y<0) {
        this._x = 550;
    }
    if (this._y>400) {
        this._y = 0;
    }
    if (this._y<0) {
        this._y = 400;
    }
}
```

This should look pretty familiar. It just adds the velocity to the position and checks to see if the ball has gone past the edge of the movie. If so, it wraps the ball back onto the opposite side of the stage. If you prefer, you can modify this so the ball bounces back off the wall, using the exact same code we developed in the previous exercise.

5. Now we create the `player_mc.onEnterFrame` handler. First assign it inside the end of the `init` function:

```
player_mc.onEnterFrame = playerMove;
```

6. Next define the function itself underneath all the current ActionScript. This is a simple ease-to-mouse function, with pretty heavy friction.

```
function playerMove() {
    this._x += (_root._xmouse-this._x)/20;
    this._y += (_root._ymouse-this._y)/20;
}
```

7.   If you test your movie now you'll see a bunch of random circles drifting lazily around the screen, and a large circle trying its best to stick to the mouse. Let's spice this game up by throwing in the collision detection. This is the exact code we just learnt when looking at Pythagorus' Theorem earlier, with the correct instance names added. We'll put this into the ballMove function, right at the end. Now each ball will check itself against player_mc on each frame:

```
dx = player_mc._x-this._x;
dy = player_mc._y-this._y;
dist = Math.sqrt(dx*dx+dy*dy);
if (dist<player_mc._width/2+this._width/2) {
    player_mc._visible = false;
}
```

Our sole reaction is to make player_mc invisible but once a hit is registered, we won't be able to start playing again without restarting the movie. To counteract this, add the following function definition inside the end of the init function to make the player_mc visible again with a simple mouse click:

```
player_mc.onMouseDown = function() {
    this._visible = true;
};
```

8.   That's that. Test your movie and see how long you can stop your ball from popping. Here's the final code to check your file against, and by all means, hack into this and create something cooler!

```
init();
function init() {
    for (i=0; i<10; i++) {
        ball_mc = attachMovie("ball", "b"+i, i);
        ball_mc._x = Math.random()*550;
        ball_mc._y = Math.random()*400;
        ball_mc.velX = Math.random()*10-5;
        ball_mc.velY = Math.random()*10-5;
        ball_mc._xscale = Math.random()*40+10;
        ball_mc._yscale = Math.random()*40+10;
        ball_mc.onEnterFrame = ballMove;
        player_mc.onEnterFrame = playerMove;
        player_mc.onMouseDown = function() {
```

```
                this._visible = true;
            };
        }
    }
    function ballMove() {
        this._x += this.velX;
        this._y += this.velY;
        if (this._x>550) {
            this._x = 0;
        }
        if (this._y<0) {
            this._x = 550;
        }
        if (this._y>400) {
            this._y = 0;
        }
        if (this._y<0) {
            this._y = 400;
        }
        dx = player_mc._x-this._x;
        dy = player_mc._y-this._y;
        dist = Math.sqrt(dx*dx+dy*dy);
        if (dist<player_mc._width/2+this._width/2) {
            player_mc._visible = false;
        }
    }
    function playerMove() {
        this._x += (_root._xmouse-this._x)/20;
        this._y += (_root._ymouse-this._y)/20;
    }
```

Multiple object collision

In the next chapter, we're going to get into some really cool math and physics stuff. I just want to cover one more thing here though. This is a strategy for handling collision detection with large numbers of objects.

So far, we've been testing one object against another object, or one object against several objects. In the alien space ship shoot-up, the ships used a `for` loop to check all the bullets one-by-one. Alternatively, we could have made the bullets check all the space ships one-by-one but that would have required knowledge of how many ships were currently active and what their names were. Not impossible, but the other way was easier.

In the last exercise, we could have turned over the collision detection to the `player` object. It could have used a `for` loop in the same way the ships did, checking for each smaller ball. This would have gone into the `playerMove` function like so:

```
for (i=0; i<10; i++) {
    dx = this._x-_root ["b"+i]._x;
    dy = this._y-_root ["b"+i]._y;
    dist = Math.sqrt (dx*dx+dy*dy);
    if (dist<this._width/2+_root ["b"+i]._width/2) {
        this._visible = false;
    }
}
```

This is a perfectly valid alternative but, still, we've only handled one to one, or one to several. What if we had a bunch of objects moving around and each one had to react to every other object? Well, you could give each one a `for` loop like the above technique, so that every object looped through, checking for a collision with every other object, but this is actually very inefficient. Imagine the following scenario:

You have three objects, A, B, and C. A tests for collision between itself and B, then itself and C; B tests between itself and A, and itself and C; finally, C tests against A and B. So we have:

- A:B
- A:C
- B:A
- B:C
- C:A
- C:B

This makes a total of six tests but that's twice as many as we need. A:B is the same as B:A, A:C the same as C:A, and B:C the same as C:B.

As you increase the amount of objects you are checking it gets worse, always with twice as many tests as you need. So, we need a more efficient way of doing this, a procedure that checks each pair of objects exactly once. Here's the best method I've found to do this. It's fast and clean.

Handling multiple objects in an array

Rather than handle the objects from within themselves using `this`, as we have been doing so far, it now becomes more efficient to handle them externally on the main timeline. The best way to do this is with an array. As we create each object, we add it to the array and then all of our objects are contained in this one array object for easy access and manipulation.

1. Use the movie from the last exercise with the `ball` movie clip in the Library and save it with a different name. Delete all instances from the stage and all of the existing code. Start by adding this code to frame 1 of the `actions` layer:

```
init();
function init() {
    max = 10;
    balls_array = new Array();
    for (n=0; n<max; n++) {
        balls_array[n] = attachMovie("ball", "b"+n, n);
        balls_array[n]._x = Math.random()*550;
        balls_array[n]._y = Math.random()*400;
        balls_array[n].velX = Math.random()*10-5;
        balls_array[n].velY = Math.random()*10-5;
        balls_array[n]._xscale = balls_array[n]._yscale =
        ➥Math.random()*50+30;
    }
}
```

Here we've set up a `max` value that will determine the number of balls we create. We then create an array to store the movie clips in. The loop for attaching the clips is almost identical to the last file, except that it assigns the clip to an array element and accesses it via that element to assign properties. Also, we left off the `onEnterFrame` handler because we'll be controlling the clips externally.

2. Instead, we'll assign an `onEnterFrame` function to `_root`. First add the assignment inside `init` (underneath the line `max = 10;`):

```
_root.onEnterFrame = main;
```

3. Now we can define our `main` function, which is where all the magic is. First we loop through the array to move each ball individually. This is pretty straightforward:

```
function main() {
    for (i=0; i<balls_array.length; i++) {
        balls_array[i]._x += balls_array[i].velX;
        balls_array[i]._y += balls_array[i].velY;
        if (balls[i]_array._x>550) {
            balls[i]_array._x = 0;
        }
        if (balls[i]_array._x<0) {
            balls[i]_array._x = 550;
        }
        if (balls[i]_array._y>400) {
            balls[i]_array._y = 0;
```

279

continues overleaf

```
            }
        if (balls[i]_array._y<0) {
            balls[i]_array._y = 400;
        }
    }
}
```

Look familiar? It should. It's the same code as before, but we're externally accessing the movie clip through the array element it is stored in, rather than internally, using `this`. You can test the movie now and you should have twenty circles floating about randomly. Now for the collision detection...

4. For this step, we are going to use a nested `for` loop. The outer loop will run through each array element (which contains a reference to a clip) and the inner loop will be used to test *that* element against each *subsequent* element in the array. Here's some pseudo code to show how we'll implement this:

```
for (i=0; i<balls_array.length-1; i++) {
    for (j=i+1; j<balls_array.length; j++) {
        // test between balls_array[i] and balls_array[j] here
    }
}
```

If your right hand is getting full, you can tattoo this to your left hand. It's that useful. We'll use our circular/distance-based collision testing code to check if the balls are colliding. If so, we'll remove both balls.

5. To remove them, we need to not only remove the movie clip, but also get rid of its reference in the array. We'll do that with the `array.splice(index, number)` method. This command removes the `number` of elements from the array, starting at `index`. Update your `main` function like so:

```
function main() {
    for (i=0; i<balls_array.length; i++) {
        balls_array[i]._x += balls_array[i].velX;
        balls_array[i]._y += balls_array[i].velY;
        if (balls_array[i]._x>550) {
            balls_array[i]._x = 0;
        }
        if (balls_array[i]._x<0) {
            balls_array[i]._x = 550;
        }
        if (balls_array[i]._y>400) {
            balls_array[i]._y = 0;
        }
```

```
            if (balls_array[i]._y<0) {
                balls_array[i]._y = 400;
            }
        }
        for (i=0; i<balls_array.length-1; i++) {
            for (j=i+1; j<balls_array.length; j++) {
                dx = balls_array[i]._x-balls_array[j]._x;
                dy = balls_array[i]._y-balls_array[j]._y;
                dist = Math.sqrt(dx*dx+dy*dy);
                if (dist<balls_array[i]._width/2+
                ➥balls_array[j]._width/2) {
                    removeMovieClip(balls_array[j]);
                    balls_array.splice(j, 1);
                    removeMovieClip(balls_array[i]);
                    balls_array.splice(i, 1);
                }
            }
        }
    }
```

6.   Lastly, we'll eventually run out of movie clips as they destroy each other so we should provide some way of regenerating them. We'll make an onMouseDown handler at the start of init:

```
_root.onMousedown = createBall;
```

7.   We'll now add this new function underneath all of our existing code:

```
function createBall() {
    ball_mc = attachMovie("ball", "b"+n, n++);
    ball_mc._x = _root._xmouse;
    ball_mc._y = _root._ymouse;
    ball_mc.velX = Math.random()*10-5;
    ball_mc.velY = Math.random()*10-5;
    ball_mc._xscale = Math.random()*50+30;
    ball_mc._yscale = Math.random()*50+30;
    ball_mc.onEnterFrame = ballMove;
    balls_array.push(ball_mc);
}
```

This is pretty similar to the code we used in init to create the original ball movie clips. The main difference is that it assigns the movie clip reference to a temporary variable, assigns all its properties, and then uses array.push to push it into the array.

The wonderful thing about the way we set up our loops in `main` is that we used `balls_array.length` to determine the number of repetitions. The `length` property of the array will be updated as we push and splice objects into and out of the array, so our loops will always loop through the correct amount of times.

8. OK, go ahead and test your movie. If you need a check at this point, here's the complete code:

```
init();
function init() {
    max = 10;
    _root.onEnterFrame = main;
    _root.onMousedown = createBall;
    balls_array = new Array();
    for (n=0; n<max; n++) {
        balls_array[n] = attachMovie("ball", "b"+n, n);
        balls_array[n]._x = Math.random()*550;
        balls_array[n]._y = Math.random()*400;
        balls_array[n].velX = Math.random()*10-5;
        balls_array[n].velY = Math.random()*10-5;
        balls_array[n]._xscale = balls_array[n]._yscale=
        ➡Math.random()*50+30;
    }
}
function main() {
    for (i=0; i<balls_array.length; i++) {
        balls_array[i]._x += balls_array[i].velX;
        balls_array[i]._y += balls_array[i].velY;
        if (balls_array[i]._x>550) {
            balls_array[i]._x = 0;
        }
        if (balls_array[i]._x<0) {
            balls_array[i]._x = 550;
        }
        if (balls_array[i]._y>400) {
            balls_array[i]._y = 0;
        }
        if (balls_array[i]._y<0) {
            balls_array[i]._y = 400;
        }
    }
    for (i=0; i<balls_array.length-1; i++) {
        for (j=i+1; j<balls_array.length; j++) {
            dx = balls_array[i]._x-balls_array[j]._x;
            dy = balls_array[i]._y-balls_array[j]._y;
```

```
                    dist = Math.sqrt(dx*dx+dy*dy);
                    if (dist<balls_array[i]._width/2+
                    ➥balls_array[j]._width/2) {
                        removeMovieClip(balls_array[j]);
                        balls_array.splice(j, 1);
                        removeMovieClip(balls_array[i]);
                        balls_array.splice(i, 1);
                    }
                }
            }
    }
    function createBall() {
        ball_mc = attachMovie("ball", "b"+n, n++);
        ball_mc._x = _root._xmouse;
        ball_mc._y = _root._ymouse;
        ball_mc.velX = Math.random()*10-5;
        ball_mc.velY = Math.random()*10-5;
        ball_mc._xscale = Math.random()*50+30;
        ball_mc._yscale = Math.random()*50+30;
        ball_mc.onEnterFrame = ballMove;
        balls_array.push(ball_mc);
    }
```

9. Save your movie and close it (or play with it for a while, if you like).

Summary

OK, that about covers what we have to say on collision detection. We've covered Flash's built-in collision detection, hitTest, in all its flavors, and seen its power as well as its shortcomings. You now know all there is to know about bounding boxes and shapeFlags.

You also learned all about mathematical collision detection, testing against a flat wall or floor and how to have an object react when it has hit a wall. In addition, we covered the bounds object, so you can use any one part of a movie clip's bounding box for whatever purpose you want.

Then we delved into collision detection between two objects and a very efficient structure to do collision detection against multiple objects.

We've built a pretty complete game and the framework for what could become a couple more. In doing so, we've covered a lot of other areas such as arrays, dynamic object creation and handling and removal. With just what you've learned up to this point, you could probably recreate half the arcade video games of the '70s!

I know you are anxious to get into the heavy-duty stuff. Hopefully you've stuck through these chapters though as you'll need everything you've learned here when you get into the next one. Up next we'll learn some much more advanced math and physics to apply to your movie clips, adding a vast number of new techniques to your repertoire.

section 2: ActionScript Interfaces

chapter 8: Flash Math and Physics

Before beginning this chapter you may want to download `chapter8-final.fla` from www.friendsofed.com/books/studio/flash_mx/code.html

I hope you're looking forward to working through this chapter as much as I was looking forward to writing it, but I strongly advise you to make sure that you're up to speed with the stuff we've covered in the book so far. We're going to speed up from here on out. OK, you've been warned!

> *First, a disclaimer. We'll be delving into various math and physics principles here, and some of what you read may not be entirely in common with what you would read in a physics or math book. Some of the concepts have been simplified for use in Flash: factors are removed from the equations that we're not really concerned with, and definitions may be simplified to the point of heresy. In some cases, I've boldly altered reality in order to get a quick, simple, and believable effect. In short, if you want to learn standard math or physics, you'd be better off with a book dedicated to those fields. If you want to make some cool math and physics effects in Flash, read on...*

Introducing trigonometry

No don't run out of the room screaming! It's not that bad. Seriously though, this is one of the most important subjects you'll need to learn in manipulating movie clips and shapes and it's really not all that difficult. A lot of people say to me "I'd like to do more with ActionScript, but I'm no good with math". I always tell them, "You don't have to be. Flash does all the math for you", and it's true. It's more a matter of thinking logically and visualizing what you need to do. I've learned these techniques and concepts on a casual basis myself, so there is no reason why you can't get it down too.

First of all, what is trigonometry? Simply put, you could say it is the study of triangles. More specifically, it's concerned with the relationship between the angles and the sides of a triangle. We'll deal exclusively with right-angled triangles, those that have one angle of exactly 90°. This is often indicated by a small square in the corner of that angle. (Since we'll be dealing exclusively with right-angled triangles, and it's pretty obvious which one is the right angle, we'll skip the little square.)

A right-angled triangle has some very useful attributes. As we've already seen with Pythagoras' Theorem, the square of the hypotenuse is equal to the sum of the square of the other two sides. See, you already know some trig! But it gets better.

Now we bring up those three little words that you knew you were going to have to tackle eventually: **sin**, **cos**, and **tan**. These merely relate to the ratio of any two sides of the triangle. (By the way, sin is short for sine, cos for cosine, and tan for tangent.) Take the following diagram:

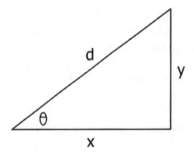

The symbol θ is the Greek letter **theta**, commonly used to indicate an angle. We'll use it to refer to the lower left angle above. x, y, and d refer to the length of the three sides of the triangle. From the viewpoint of θ, y is called the **opposite** side, x is the **adjacent** side and of course d is always the **hypotenuse**.

First let's tackle sin.

sin is defined as the length of the opposite side divided by the hypotenuse. In our case, we can say the sin of θ is equal to y/d. For example, if y is 10 and d is 30, then the ratio is 10/30, or 0.3333...

Each angle will produce a specific ratio for its opposite/hypotenuse. The size of the triangle doesn't matter, just the angle. Take the angle of 30°. It always produces a ratio of 0.5 for its opposite/hypotenuse. Always. So, we say the sin of 30° is 0.5. Therefore if y is 10 and d is 20, the ratio is 0.5 and you know θ is 30°. Or, if you know that θ is 30° and y is 10, then you also know that d must be 20. Finally, if you know that d is 20, then y must be 10.

In other words if you know any two factors, you can figure out the third: you just need to know the ratios that each angle forms. The best bit though is that they all are built into Flash! All you need to say is Math.sin(angle) and it returns the fraction associated with that angle.

Right, let's move on to cos. This is merely the ratio of the adjacent side and the hypotenuse. So we can say in our case, cos θ = x/d.

Finally, tan is the ratio of the opposite over the adjacent. In our triangle, tan θ = y/x.

Now, how do we use these in Flash? Well, one common use is to cause a movie clip to move in a circular path. Circle? I thought we were talking about triangles! Well, take a look at the following diagram:

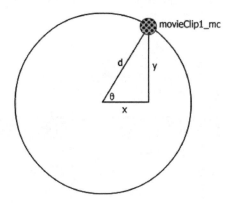

We want movieClip1_mc to move around in a circular motion, performing one complete revolution in a clockwise direction from its current position. Here, d is the radius of the circle and it will never change. Let's say it's 100 and θ is the angle again. Now, at each instant we'll know d and θ, so using sin we can find y, and, using cos, we can find x. The formulas to calculate this would be:

x = sin θ * d
y = cos θ * d

Armed with these values, we can figure out the _x and _y properties of the movie clip. I know you're ready to jump into it and move something around, but there is one more barrier. Flash computes all of its angles for use in Math functions using **radians**, rather than degrees. This is just a different method of slicing the circle up. I don't want to get too sidetracked here, so I'll just say that a radian is about 57.29578 degrees. Wonderful, right? Well, to make it a little easier to remember, a circle is made up of 360 degrees, which is equal to 2π radians. Therefore, 1 radian is π180 degrees. This is generally what we use to convert radians to degrees with. Still got that tattoo needle handy? These might look good just above your left wrist:

```
degrees = radians*180/Math.π
radians = degrees*Math.π/180
```

OK, now that we've got the theory under our belts we can get stuck into some Flash. We'll apply the concepts behind this trigonometry, using ActionScript to make a movie clip move in a perfectly circular motion. If you want to refer to the example file, it's called `circular_motion.fla`.

Circular motion

1. Start a new movie and make a new movie clip. It can contain any graphics you want but don't make it too big though, so that it has plenty of room to move around. Give it the instance name `movieClip1_mc`:

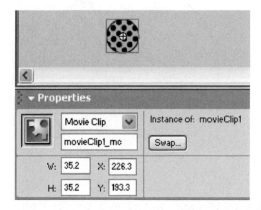

2. Now we'll make an `onEnterFrame` function. The first thing we'll do in it is to increase the angle, `theta`. Add the following code to a new layer called `Actions`:

```
this.onEnterFrame = function() {
    var theta = theta++;
};
```

3. Next we need to convert `theta` to radians. We'll use another variable called `rad` for this:

```
this.onEnterFrame = function() {
    var theta = theta++;
    var rad = theta*(Math.PI/180);
};
```

4. Now if we multiply the cos of `theta` by the radius of the theoretical circle (d=100 in the previous diagram), we'll get our `_x` property. Note that we are going to add 275 to this calculation, as x=275 is the center of the screen (provided your movie's dimensions are still set at the default 550x400 pixels). This will cause the movie clip to travel with a backwards and forwards motion along the x-axis in the center of the screen, not at (0,0), the upper left corner of the stage:

```
this.onEnterFrame = function() {
    var theta = theta++;
    var rad = theta*(Math.PI/180);
    movieClip1_mc._x = (Math.cos(rad)*100)+275;
};
```

5. We then do exactly the same thing to get the `_y` property, using the sin of `theta` multiplied by 100, and then adding 200 to position the movie clip in the center of the screen. Add this to your code:

```
this.onEnterFrame = function() {
    var theta = theta++;
    var rad = theta*Math.PI/180;
    movieClip1_mc._x = Math.cos(rad)*100+275;
    movieClip1_mc._y = Math.sin(rad)*100+200;
};
```

6. If you test your movie now, you'll see your `movieClip1_mc` rotating in a circular motion.

7. To clearly visualize how the code is constraining the movie clip to the theoretical circle, add the following drawing API code to the function:

```
this.onEnterFrame = function() {
    var theta = theta++;
    var rad = theta*Math.PI/180;
    movieClip1_mc._x = Math.cos(rad)*100+275;
    movieClip1_mc._y = Math.sin(rad)*100+200;
    clear();
    lineStyle(1, 0, 100);
    moveTo(275, 200);
    lineTo(movieClip1_mc._x, movieClip1_mc._y);
    lineTo(movieClip1_mc._x, 200);
    lineTo(275, 200);
};
```

This clearly displays the triangle that we're calculating.

There you go. You just used some basic trig to create a motion effect. Not too painful, right? In this example, we knew the angle and one side of the triangle, and used this information to calculate the length of the other sides. We can also do the opposite: if we already know two sides of the triangle, we can find out any of the angles. This is done using the **arc** functions – **arcsin**, **arccos**, and **arctan** (also written asin, acos, and atan). These are simply the opposite functions of sin, cos, and tan. Instead of taking an angle and returning a ratio, they take a ratio and return the angle that would produce that ratio.

By far the most widely used of these is atan. This is very useful for finding the angle between two points, such as two movie clips. We can easily calculate the X and Y distance between the two clips. This can be used to draw the two sides of a right-angled triangle. Remembering that tan is opposite/adjacent, we can see that tan is the only one of the three functions that deals with the two sides and not the hypotenuse. Look at this diagram:

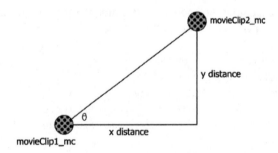

Here we have two movie clips. We can find **x distance** by saying:

```
dx = movieClip2_mc._x - movieClip1_mc._x;
```

and the y distance using:

```
dy = movieClip2_mc._y - movieClip1_mc._y;
```

Now if we get the ratio of dy/dx and take the atan of that ratio, we'll know the angle of θ.

Flash actually gives us two functions to compute atan: `Math.atan(y/x)` and `Math.atan2(y, x)`. The simple atan version takes the ratio of `y/x` itself as its argument. The newer atan2 version takes the individual values of `y` and `x`. I highly recommend you use the atan2 version as this will solve many issues that come up with negative values and angles. Most people use it exclusively.

Don't forget that `Math.atan2`, as with all other Math functions, will return the angle in terms of radians. If you need degrees, it's up to you to convert it.

To round off our introduction to trigonometry, we'll look at how to use `Math.atan2` to perform a very useful function, one that is frequently needed: how to rotate a movie clip to face a certain target.

You looking at me?

This is a quick exercise where we'll make a simple, but very useful, effect: the movie clip will always point at the mouse cursor, dynamically rotating to do this. We'll also make it 'stick' to the mouse. Take a look at `ship.swf` to see the effect in action.

1. Start a brand new movie. First of all we need to make a movie clip that will act as the pointer. Our circular football won't work for this, so create any kind of graphic that is obviously pointing in a certain direction, such as my toy spaceship here. Also, in Flash's coordinate system, 0 degrees is due right and angles increase in a clockwise direction, so whatever you draw, make it initially point to the right. As usual, give it the instance name `movieClip1_mc`:

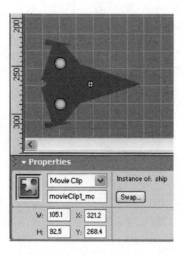

2. Now we need to decide what it's going to point *at*. Since we're building this file from scratch, the only other object currently moving around the screen is the mouse cursor so we'll use this as the target for the movie clip to point towards. So our x distance will be the distance from our clip's _x position to this._xmouse, and the y distance will be the distance between movieClip1_mc._y to this._ymouse. Add a new actions layer and let's set this up like last time in an onEnterFrame function:

```
this.onEnterFrame = function() {
    var dx = this._xmouse-movieClip1_mc._x;
    var dy = this._ymouse-movieClip1_mc._y;
};
```

3. Next we'll calculate the angle between movieClip1 and the mouse, using the Math function atan2:

```
this.onEnterFrame = function() {
    var dx = this._xmouse-movieClip1_mc._x;
    var dy = this._ymouse-movieClip1_mc._y;
    var angle = Math.atan2(dy, dx);
};
```

4. Now we know this angle we can use it to rotate movieClip1. However, we need to remember that the _rotation property of a movie clip is expressed in terms of degrees, not radians. So, we need to add the degree to radian conversion formula that we looked at earlier:

```
this.onEnterFrame = function() {
    var dx = this._xmouse-movieClip1_mc._x;
    var dy = this._ymouse-movieClip1_mc._y;
    var angle = Math.atan2(dy, dx);
    movieClip1_mc._rotation = angle*180/Math.PI;
};
```

5. Test the movie. Your movie clip continuously rotates to point to the mouse cursor.

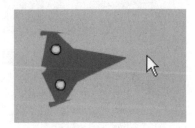

6.   Close down your test movie and let's think about making this *dynamic*. Since the X and Y distances (dx and dy) are constantly being computed, not only can we force the movie clip to always point to the cursor, but we can also make the movie clip continually follow the mouse. Add the small piece of easing code, which should look pretty familiar to you by now.

```
this.onEnterFrame = function() {
    var dx = this._xmouse-movieClip1_mc._x;
    var dy = this._ymouse-movieClip1_mc._y;
    var angle = Math.atan2(dy, dx);
    movieClip1_mc._rotation = angle*180/Math.PI;
    movieClip1_mc._x += (_root._xmouse-movieClip1_mc._x)/10;
    movieClip1_mc._y += (_root._ymouse-movieClip1_mc._y)/10;
};
```

7.   Test the movie again, and watch the movie clip follow the mouse around like a lost puppy. If you can't think of a creative game or effect to make with that...well, I'll just have to try harder.

8.   Save your movie with a suitable name. We'll be using it again later in the chapter.

Motion basics

We've looked at some of the more difficult theory but we'll be using the concepts of trigonometry time and time again, so keep them handy.

So far we've pushed all kinds of things around the screen: ships, bullets, footballs. In each case, we simply changed the _x and/or _y property of the movie clip. By continuously adding the same value to the movie clip's position, frame after frame, we created a smooth uniform motion. We also briefly looked at **velocity**, simplistically defining it as 'speed in a certain direction'. We know that the object has a certain **speed**, say 10 pixels per frame, but what **direction** is it moving in? We can define this direction in terms of an angle. We can say that the object is moving at 15 pixels per frame at 45 degrees.

As a quick note, remember that in Flash, 0 degrees is due right and degrees increase in a clockwise direction:

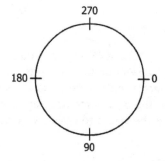

Back in our example, say that the object is moving with a speed of 20 (we'll always be talking in terms of pixels per frame here) and at -35 degrees (this is just 35 degrees moving anti-clockwise in the diagram above). Or, think of a speed of 50 at 180 degrees. The following diagram shows all of these scenarios:

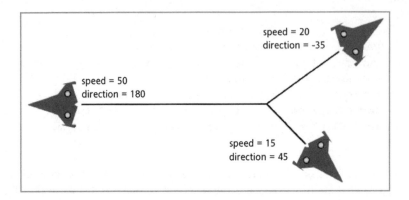

speed = 20
direction = -35

speed = 50
direction = 180

speed = 15
direction = 45

The lines shown are known as **vectors**. They show both the direction and speed at a glance, and therefore the velocity: the longer the line, the higher the speed. You could also think of it in terms of how far the object will travel in one frame.

Now let's go back to the first example. It's moving at 15 ppf (pixels per frame) at 45 degrees. But, in order to accurately represent this motion in Flash, we need to know what value to add to the movie clip's _x and _y property each frame. In other words, we need to know its X and Y velocities. To determine these velocities, we need a way to convert 'speed plus angle' into 'X velocity, Y velocity'. This is where our trig comes in. Take a look at this diagram:

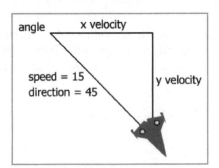

angle   x velocity

speed = 15
direction = 45   y velocity

In one frame, the ship moves 15 pixels, at 45 degrees. You could also say that it moves by X pixels on the x-axis (its X velocity) and y pixels on the y-axis (its Y velocity). Well hey, look at that, we've got a right-angled triangle. In fact it looks almost exactly like the diagram we used to make an object move in a perfect circle. The only difference here is instead of using values to determine an object's position, we're using the values to calculate velocity. The formulas to do this are the same.

```
x_velocity = cos(angle)*speed
y_velocity = sin(angle)*speed
```

In Flash, we'll use `velX` and `velY` to represent the X and Y velocities. Well also need to convert the angle to radians. Here's what it looks like in ActionScript:

```
var angle = 45;
var speed = 15;
var rad = angle*Math.PI/180;
velX = Math.cos(rad)*speed;
velY = Math.sin(rad)*speed;
```

Now we would simply add an `onEnterFrame` function to add the velocities to the position of our ubiquitous `movieClip1` and we're off:

```
movieclip1_mc.onEnterFrame = function() {
    this._x += velX;
    this._y += velY;
};
```

Of course, just having one movie clip moving at a preset speed in a preset direction isn't exactly dynamic. Well, to investigate this method let's continue using the last FLA we made, the mouse-following object (or my toy spaceship). In the last exercise, we used an easing formula to make the movie clip follow the mouse. If the ship were far away from the mouse, it would move quickly and then ease down as it neared the cursor. It might be more realistic in some circumstances to have an object move at a more consistent speed.

Uniform speed

1. Open up the file you were working on in the last exercise. As a quick recap here's the existing code:

```
this.onEnterFrame = function() {
    var dx = this._xmouse-movieClip1_mc._x;
    var dy = this._ymouse-movieClip1_mc._y;
    var angle = Math.atan2(dy, dx);
    movieClip1_mc._rotation = angle*180/Math.PI;
    movieClip1_mc._x += (_root._xmouse-movieClip1_mc._x)/10;
    movieClip1_mc._y += (_root._ymouse-movieClip1_mc._y)/10;
};
```

2. We'll keep the first five lines, which ensures that movieClip1 rotates in the correct direction. Then we just paste in the code we just looked at to calculate the X and Y velocities based on an angle. These will replace the last two lines which move the movie clip, so update your code like so:

```
var speed = 5;
this.onEnterFrame = function() {
    var dx = this._xmouse-movieClip1_mc._x;
    var dy = this._ymouse-movieClip1_mc._y;
    var angle = Math.atan2(dy, dx);
    movieClip1_mc._rotation = angle*180/Math.PI;
    var velX = Math.cos(angle)*speed;
    var velY = Math.sin(angle)*speed;
    movieClip1_mc._x += velX;
    movieClip1_mc._y += velY;
};
```

Notice that I also defined the speed variable to use in the calculations. It is always preferable to first define a variable and then use it in your calculations, as opposed to hard coding in a specific value. If you want to change the value of speed at a later time, it's easy to locate, saving you digging through various code and functions.

3. Test your movie and you'll see that the movie clip follows the mouse with a uniform speed, irrespective of where either one is located on the screen.

However, there's a problem you might notice: when the movie clip reaches the mouse, it actually travels a few pixels beyond it and then turns 180 degrees to face the opposite direction and begin moving again. This happens repeatedly so the arrow flips back and forth. We can fix this with some distance based collision detection. (See, it's all starting to come together!) We just need to compute the overall distance between the movie clip and the mouse. If it's less than a defined distance, we don't move it anymore. This distance should be the same as the overall speed.

4. Add the final code:

```
var speed = 5;
this.onEnterFrame = function() {
    var dx = this._xmouse-movieClip1_mc._x;
    var dy = this._ymouse-movieClip1_mc._y;
    var angle = Math.atan2(dy, dx);
    movieClip1_mc._rotation = angle*180/Math.PI;
    var dist = Math.sqrt(dx*dx+dy*dy);
    if (dist>speed) {
        velX = Math.cos(angle)*speed;
        velY = Math.sin(angle)*speed;
```

```
            movieClip1_mc._x += velX;
            movieClip1_mc._y += velY;
        }
    };
```

5. Test your movie. If the distance between the cursor and the movie clip is greater than `speed`, then the movie clip will move. Otherwise, it just stops and waits.

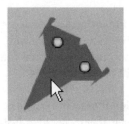

If you wanted something else to occur when the movie clip reaches its destination, such as an explosion or something, you could put the extra code in an `else` block following the `if` block. (You might also want to adjust your movie clip so that the registration point is at the tip of the arrow. Remember that the location of the movie clip is determined by its registration point only. If that's in the middle of the arrow, that's what you'll be testing against.)

6. Save your file and leave it open for the next exercise.

Acceleration

In the last exercise, we looked at velocity that was uniform. In real life, if you hopped in your car and stepped on the gas, you wouldn't instantly start traveling at 55 miles per hour. You start out at zero and step on the gas. After a second, you reach 5 mph, after another second you'd hit 10 mph, and so on. Your speed is increasing by 5 mph in each additional second. This **increase** in speed is known as **acceleration**. In this example, you could say that the acceleration is 5 mph per second, because each second, you are adding 5 mph. Simple enough. Now let's jump right in and apply this to Flash.

Do you want to go faster?

1. Open your movie from the previous exercise (if it isn't still open). Put good old `movieClip1` over on the far left of the stage. Delete all the existing code in the `Actions` layer and add this short piece of code to frame 1:

```
var accel = .05;
```

continues overleaf

```
var velX = 0;
movieClip1_mc.onEnterFrame = function() {
    this._x += velX;
    velX += accel;
};
```

2. Test your movie and watch your movie clip travel from left to right, gradually accelerating as it does so.

This code is quite simple but effective. We continually update the `velX` variable (and therefore the `_x` position of `movieClip1`) with the value of our acceleration variable `accel`. As the code is run through each frame the velocity is incremented and our object accelerates from left to right across the screen.

Now earlier, I defined acceleration as *increasing* speed, and that's how we usually think of it. The *accelerator* in your car makes it move *faster*, right? But we could be a little more accurate and say that acceleration actually *changes* speed. We can be even more accurate and say that acceleration changes *velocity* because as we are about to find out, acceleration always has a direction associated with it.

If the acceleration is in the *same* direction as the existing velocity, it serves to increase that velocity. You're going 30 mph, you step on the gas, you start going at 40 mph.

If the acceleration is in the *opposite* direction to the velocity, it will decrease that velocity. If you're going 30 mph, shift into reverse, and then step on the gas, I guarantee that your forward velocity will be swiftly decreased. If your engine and transmission are still attached to the car and functioning, your velocity will eventually slow to zero and become negative – you'll travel in reverse. Now of course a car isn't made to operate that way, but if you picture an astronaut using a jetpack to control his movement, you might get a better idea of what's happening.

Every force that effects a change on an object's position can be thought of as a form of acceleration on that object. Whether it's a car engine, a rocket booster, gravity, magnetism, wind, it will accelerate the object in a certain direction. Let's take a look at one of these forces and apply it in Flash. We're going to look at simulating the effect of gravity on a movie clip. First, we'll run through a quick exercise to look at the principles behind this, and then we'll move onto a larger project where we'll apply what we've learnt and create an Asteroids game.

Gravity

1. Open up the source file `gravity_base.fla` and take a look at the code in frame 1 of the `actions` layer. This may seem like a lot of code, but there's not a single thing in there that we haven't covered. This is also a good review of what we've learnt so far. Read through it and make sure you know what each line is doing.

   At the moment, you can grab the ball with the mouse and throw it around the screen. The ball's velocity is dampened, gradually decreasing over time. What we're going to do here is add another level of complexity by simulating the effect of gravity on the ball. There will be two forces acting on the ball affecting its motion: friction and gravity.

2. I've already said that gravity, like any other force, acts to accelerate the object in a certain direction. Which direction? Down of course! Since the concepts of **up** and **down** only relate to the y-axis, we can simply think of gravity as adding a certain downward speed to the y velocity, `velY`. This is accomplished with one little line within in the first `if` statement inside the `move` function:

   ```
   function move() {
       if (!this.dragging) {
           this.velY += grav;
           this.velX *= friction;
           this.velY *= friction;
           this._x += this.velX;
           this._y += this.velY;
   ```

3. Naturally we need to go up and define a value for `grav` within our `init` function as well, so let's do just that:

   ```
   grav = 1;
   ```

4. Go ahead and test the movie. Grab the ball with the mouse, give it a good throw, and you'll see how our simple gravity effect impacts on the ball's velocity.

   What is happening here is that `velY` is initially set to 0 since has not been defined (Flash is pretty generous in this respect as many other languages would see this as an error) but then we add 1 to `velY` since `grav = 1`. So, at the start of the movie the ball starts travelling toward the bottom of the screen at a speed of 1. Each successive frame increments `velY` by 1, so the ball accelerates until it hits the bottom of the screen, bounces, and then reverses direction. Here's where the beauty of the code comes in. It's moving upwards because its Y velocity has been reversed (it's now negative).

   So, say that at the point of the bounce, the ball is moving at 20 pixels per second in a downward direction. It bounces and `velY` becomes –20 but `grav` is still adding 1 to `velY` each frame. So soon `velY` is –19, –18, –17, and so on, until it hits zero. Still `grav` is adding 1, always and forever, so the ball moves downward again. This is exactly what occurs when you throw a real object up into the sky.

OK, we've got a lot in our toolbox now. Let's start combining what we've learnt in a full Flash motion-based project. We're going to make an old school Atari *Asteroids* game circa 1979.

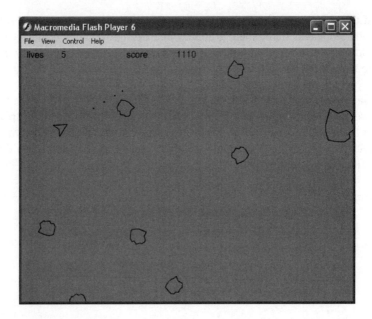

Project #1: Asteroids

First we'll define the exact behavior we want:

- You can rotate the ship clockwise or counter-clockwise with a couple of keys.
- You hit a 'thrust' key and it starts moving in whatever direction it happens to be pointing.
- The longer you thrust, the faster it goes.
- If you turn the ship around and thrust in the opposite direction, it will slow down, eventually stop and go in the opposite direction.
- If you hit another key, it fires a bullet in the direction it is pointing.
- Oh, and there are asteroids floating about. If you hit one, you die.
- If a bullet hits an asteroid, it breaks in two until the pieces are small enough, then they just disappear.

Believe it or not, we have already covered all the knowledge you need to do all of that. We just need to tie together what we learned into a cohesive whole.

1. First, make a very stereotypical asteroid-blasting ship movie clip, export it for ActionScript, using the identifier `ship`. The most important thing to remember is that it must be facing due right.

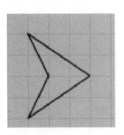 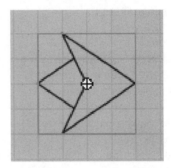

I also made a second frame in this movie clip, showing some flame coming out of the back. This will be used a as a visual indication that the ship is thrusting. Make sure you put a `stop` action on both frames, so that the movie clip doesn't automatically start playing them back and forth.

2. Then make an asteroid, which is just a filled shape a few times larger than the ship. Also export this using the name `asteroid`.

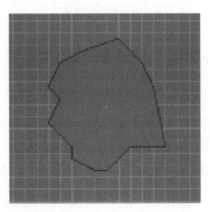

3. Finally make a bullet, exported as `shot`.

4. Make sure you have nothing left on the stage, as we will be attaching all these clips dynamically.

5.   In frame 1, we'll start out with an `init` function. Don't forget to call the function as a first action.

```
init();
function init() {
    // set constants for stage borders
    if (!stageIsSet) {
        LEFT = 0;
        TOP = 0;
        BOTTOM = Stage.height;
        RIGHT = Stage.width;
        stageIsSet = true;
    }
    // how many ships do we start with?
    livesLeft = 5;
    // set how many asteroids to begin with
    maxAst = 3;
    ast_array = new Array();
    // asteroids and shots will be in their own mc's to prevent
    ➥depth conflicts
    createEmptyMovieClip("astField_mc", 0);
    createEmptyMovieClip("shots_mc", 1);
    // create asteroids and ship
    astInit();
    shipInit();
    stop();
}
```

This is pretty well commented, but we'll run through it. First we set the constants for the stage size (RIGHT, LEFT, TOP, BOTTOM). We then set a variable `stageIsSet` to `true`, which prevents us from running this again when the game is restarted.

Then we decide on how many asteroids and how many lives to start out with, and create an array to store the asteroid clips in.

The next two lines are an alternate way to avoid the duplicate depth problems we ran into before. Here we will keep all of our asteroids within one movie clip, and all of our shots in another one. Since the holder clips themselves are on different depths (0 and 1), the asteroid depths will not interfere with the shot depths and vice versa. We just make sure that when we attach our shot and asteroid clips, we attach them to the appropriate holder clip.

We then call a function to initialize our asteroids, and one to initialize the ship. The fact that these are in separate functions means we can simply call them again later when we want to make more asteroids, or reincarnate the ship when it is killed.

Finally, we stop the movie at this frame.

6. Now let's have a look at that `astInit` function:

```
function astInit() {
  // create a number of asteroids
  astIndex = 0;
  while (astIndex<maxAst) {
    createAst();
  }
}
```

All this does is loop through from 0 to however many asteroids we decided to make, and repeatedly runs the function `createAst`, which creates one asteroid. We'll take a quick look at that next.

7. Here is `createAst`:

```
function createAst() {
    // put one asteroid on stage and initialize its properties and
    ➥methods
    ast_mc = astField_mc.attachMovie("asteroid", "ast"+astIndex,
    ➥astIndex++);
    ast_mc._rotation = Math.random()*360;
    ast_mc.velX = Math.random()*6-3;
    ast_mc.velY = Math.random()*6-3;
    ast_mc.onEnterFrame = astMove;
    // push this asteroid onto the asteroid array
    ast_array.push(ast_mc);
    // return a reference to this asteroid
    return ast_mc;
}
```

This attaches an instance of the asteroid clip to the `astField_mc` movie clip. (Remember, they all need to stay in there to avoid depth problems.) Using a temporary variable, `ast_mc`, we randomly rotate it, assign it a velocity and an `onEnterFrame` handler and push it onto the `ast_array` array. It will be useful to store references to all the asteroids in an array so that we can loop through the array to do hit checking.

Finally, we return a reference to the newly created asteroid. Although we ignore that for now in our `astInit` function, it will be useful later.

8. Next up is `shipInit()`:

```
function shipInit() {
```

continues overleaf

```
        // put a ship on stage and initialize its properties and methods
        attachMovie("ship", "ship_mc", 2);
        ship_mc._x = RIGHT/2;
        ship_mc._y = BOTTOM/2;
        ship_mc.velX = 0;
        ship_mc.velY = 0;
        ship_mc.onKeyDown = control;
        ship_mc.onKeyUp = decontrol;
        ship_mc.onEnterFrame = move;
        Key.addListener(ship_mc);
        rotate = 0;
        thrust = 0;
}
```

This attaches an instance of the ship movie clip, giving it the name `ship_mc`. It then positions it, assigns its speed and a few event handler functions, makes it a listener for Key events and sets a couple other variables to 0 – rotate and thrust – just to make sure it's not going anywhere when it appears.

Next we should look at the functions that we assigned to the `onKeyDown` and `onKeyUp` handlers, `control` and `decontrol`.

9. First `control`:

```
function control() {
    // check which key was pressed and control ship accordingly
    switch (Key.getCode()) {
    case Key.LEFT :
        rotate = -1;
        break;
    case Key.RIGHT :
        rotate = 1;
        break;
    case Key.UP :
        thrust = .3;
        ship_mc.gotoAndStop(2);
        break;
    case Key.SPACE :
        shoot();
        break;
    }
}
```

This is a simple switch statement. If LEFT or RIGHT are pressed, it sets the variable, rotate, to −1 or +1.

If UP is being pressed, it sets the thrust variable to .3 (you can change this if you want. I came up with this purely through trial and error – it gave the ship a good feel). Also, here we send the ship to its frame 2 to visually show that it is firing its rockets. We will see in a moment how these rotate and thrust variables are used to control the movement of the ship.

Finally, if SPACE is being pressed, we run the shoot function.

10. That all happens if a button is being pressed. When a button is released, we want to make sure that the ship stops thrusting (and visually shows this), and stops turning (if it was). Simple enough:

```
function decontrol() {
    // no key is pressed, so no thrust or rotation
    rotate = 0;
    thrust = 0;
    ship_mc.gotoAndStop(1);
}
```

11. Continuing on with our ship functions, we had set the onEnterFrame handler to the move function. Let's take a look at that:

```
function move() {
    // rotate ship
    if (rotate) {
        this._rotation += rotate*5;
    }
    // move ship
    if (thrust) {
        // convert rotation to radians
        rad = this._rotation*Math.PI/180;
        // get x and y components of thrust
        this.thrustX = Math.cos(rad)*thrust;
        this.thrustY = Math.sin(rad)*thrust;
        // add thrust to velocity
        this.velX += this.thrustX;
        this.velY += this.thrustY;
    }
    // add velocity to position
    this._x += this.velX;
    this._y += this.velY;
    // perform screen wrapping
    if (this._x>RIGHT) {
        this._x = LEFT;
```

continues overleaf

```
        }
        if (this._x<LEFT) {
            this._x = RIGHT;
        }
        if (this._y>BOTTOM) {
            this._y = TOP;
        }
        if (this._y<TOP) {
            this._y = BOTTOM;
        }
    }
```

Yikes! We'll take it one section at a time:

```
// rotate ship
if (rotate) {
    this._rotation += rotate*5;
}
```

Simple enough. We take our rotate variable, which can be either −1 or +1 depending on which key is pressed, or 0 if no key is pressed. We multiply it times 5, to come up with −5, 0 or +5 and add this to the ship's rotation. Again, 5 was simply a number that worked well after experimenting with different values. You can adjust this to your own tastes. Ideally, you would make this into another constant and define it in the init function, such as ROTATESPEED = 5. I just hardcoded it here to keep the init function as simple as possible during the tutorial.

Next is the toughest section of the move function:

```
// move ship
if (thrust) {
    // convert rotation to radians
    rad = this._rotation*Math.PI/180;
    // get x and y components of thrust
    this.thrustX = Math.cos(rad)*thrust;
    this.thrustY = Math.sin(rad)*thrust;
    // add thrust to velocity
    this.velX += this.thrustX;
    this.velY += this.thrustY;
}
```

If thrust is 0 (UP key not being pressed), this section will be skipped entirely. If it has some value, we have to handle it. First we take the rotation of the ship (degrees) and convert it to radians.

Then we take the thrust value, which lies along the angle the ship is facing, and convert it to its X and Y components, `thrustX` and `thrustY`, using a bit of the trig that you learned earlier in the chapter. This diagram should explain what we are doing here:

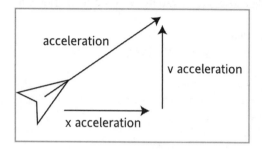

We then just add the thrust, or acceleration, values to the velocities on the X and Y axes. This gives us the new velocity that the ship will be travelling in after applying the thrust in that direction. Note that in the above diagram, if the ship were moving backwards, and you then apply thrust, the acceleration would be in the opposite direction to the motion of the ship, so it would slow down, eventually stop and start going in the opposite direction. Cool. Just what we ordered.

The final section is pretty simple. We just add the current velocity to the current position of the ship and if it has gone off any side of the stage, we stick it back on the opposite side.

```
// add velocity to position
this._x += this.velX;
this._y += this.velY;
// perform screen wrapping
if (this._x>RIGHT) {
    this._x = LEFT;
}
if (this._x<LEFT) {
    this._x = RIGHT;
}
if (this._y>BOTTOM) {
    this._y = TOP;
}
if (this._y<TOP) {
    this._y = BOTTOM;
}
}
```

This is a great time to test your movie, since the ship should now be fully functional. (You'll have a few dysfunctional asteroids parked in the corner. Ignore them for now!) You can use the three arrow keys to rotate and thrust around the screen. It should be pretty darn similar to the original Asteroids game, but feel free to adjust the rotation and thrust variables, as mentioned, to get the exact feel you like.

12. Now let's tackle those lazy asteroids. Here's our astMove function:

```
function astMove() {
    // add velocity to position
    this._x += this.velX;
    this._y += this.velY;
    // perform screen wrapping
    if (this._x>RIGHT) {
        this._x = LEFT;
    } else if (this._x<LEFT) {
        this._x = RIGHT;
    } else if (this._y>BOTTOM) {
        this._y = TOP;
    } else if (this._y<TOP) {
        this._y = BOTTOM;
    }
    // check hitTest against ship_mc
    if (this.hitTest(ship_mc._x, ship_mc._y, true)) {
        // if ship is not already dead, destroy it
        if (!shipDead) {
            destroyShip();
            shipDead = true;
        }
    }
}
```

The first half of this needs no explanation. We simply add the velocity to the position and do the screen wrapping. After that, we have the asteroid do a collision test against the ship:

```
// check hitTest against ship_mc
if (this.hitTest(ship_mc._x, ship_mc._y, true)) {
    // if ship is not already dead, destroy it
    if (!shipDead) {
        destroyShip();
        shipDead = true;
    }
}
```

This does a point to movie clip hitTest, using shapeFlag=true. As you recall, this method has one disadvantage – it will only test the _x, _y point of the ship, which is its center point. Thus, the nose or tail or side of the ship could momentarily slip inside of the asteroid without causing a hit. We could use shapeFlag=false, and test only against the bounding box. However, this would cause the ship to sometimes die when it hadn't touched the ship at all. Of the two alternatives, the second would be likely to annoy me a lot more than the first if I were playing the game. We can't use distance-based collision detection because the clips are odd shaped, not perfectly square or round. We'd have the same problem. You are welcome to try to devise a better solution to this problem, but in my experience these just add a lot of complexity (and processor overhead) to the program. So for this example, we'll bite the bullet and live with the imperfection.

If we do get a hit, we run the function, destroyShip which, among other things, removes the ship movie clip from the stage. I found, however, in developing this program, that even after the movie clip was removed, the coordinates fed into the hitTest would continue to generate a hit for several frames. Therefore, I set a variable, shipDead to true on the first hit, and tested this variable as a prerequisite to running the destroyShip function. This ensures that this is only run once for each collision.

13. Speaking of the destroyShip() function...

```
function destroyShip() {
    // remove ship
    removeMovieClip(ship_mc);
    // update how many lives are left
    livesLeft--;
    // if none, end game.
    if (livesLeft<1) {
        gotoAndStop(2);
    } else {
        // tell it to come back in two seconds
        restoreID = setInterval(restoreShip, 2000);
    }
}
```

This function removes the ship movie clip from the stage and decrements the livesLeft variable.

If livesLeft gets to zero, then we go to frame 2 of the movie and stop there. I set up frame 2 with some text saying "Game Over" and a restart button that sends the movie back to frame 1.

Otherwise, we still have at least one ship left. We dust off setInterval to tell the program to wait two seconds (that's 2000 milliseconds in Flash time) and run the function restoreShip. Note that here we will store an interval ID in the variable restoreID. We only want restoreShip to run one time after the collision, so we will need to clear the interval after it has served its purpose.

14. Segue into `restoreShip`:

```
function restoreShip() {
    // reincarnate ship
    shipInit();
    shipDead = false;
    // make sure this function doesn't run again
    clearInterval(restoreID);
}
```

15. Pretty clear. We run `shipInit` again to put a ship back on stage. We reset `shipDead` to false so that we will be able to destroy it again – if it hits another asteroid. Finally, we clear the interval so we don't repeatedly restore the ship every two seconds (very annoying, if you want to try it out...).

This is another good testing point. Your asteroids should be fully functional now, as well as your ship. You can practice avoiding them, or if you are feeling particularly sadistic, repeatedly crash into them – for testing purposes of course!

16. I also put a dynamic text box on stage and assigned it the variable `livesLeft` so I could have a visual display of my suicidal feats.

Now so far, these asteroids are having all the fun destroying our ship. Time to fight back.

17. We decided above that when we hit the SPACE button, we'd run the function `shoot()`. Time to see it:

```
function shoot() {
    // if we have any ammo left...
    if (numShots<5) {
        numShots++;
        // create one shot and make it move
        shot_mc = shots_mc.attachMovie("shot", "s"+shotIndex,
        ➥shotIndex++);
        shot_mc.onEnterFrame = shotMove;
        // convert ship's rotation to radians
        rad = ship_mc._rotation*Math.PI/180;
        // position shot at ship's nose
        shot_mc._x = ship_mc._x+10*Math.cos(rad);
        shot_mc._y = ship_mc._y+10*Math.sin(rad);
        // determine shot's velocity, adding it to ship's velicity
        shot_mc.velX = 5*Math.cos(rad)+ship_mc.velX;
        shot_mc.velY = 5*Math.sin(rad)+ship_mc.velY;
    }
}
```

Another mouthful. We'll break it down again:

```
function shoot() {
    // if we have any ammo left...
    if (numShots<5) {
        numShots++;
        // create one shot and make it move
        shot_mc = shots_mc.attachMovie("shot", "s"+shotIndex,
        ➥shotIndex++);
        shot_mc.onEnterFrame = shotMove;
```

18. We'll limit the number of shots to five at a time. You can change this if you want. We'll use the variable numShots to keep track of how many shots are active, incrementing it each time we shoot one. If it hits five, we skip the whole function. If it's below five, we attach a shot movie clip to the shots_mc (remember, all shots will go here to avoid depth confusion with the asteroids.) We assign a reference to this movie clip to the temporary variable shot_mc and assign its onEnterFrame handler.

    Now, we don't want the shot firing out of the center of the ship. We want to position it right at the nose of the ship. So we need to find the coordinates of the ship's nose. Well, look at the following diagram:

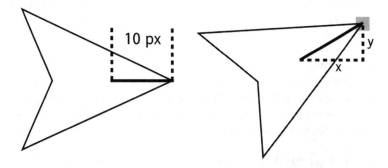

    The ship I made is 20 pixels wide and it's centered on its registration point. So that means it's 10 pixels from center to nose. If I then rotate the ship, it's still 10 pixels from center to nose, but as you can see in the right-hand diagram, we've now formed what should be a very familiar triangle. Given the angle of rotation and the 10-pixel distance, it is now a snap to figure out the x and y values shown there.

```
x = cos(angle) * distance
y = sin(angle)* distance
```

If we add that to the ship's _x and _y positions, we have the exact screen position to place the shot. Here it is in ActionScript:

```
// convert ship's rotation to radians
rad = ship_mc._rotation*Math.PI/180;
// position shot at ship's nose
shot_mc._x = ship_mc._x + (10 * Math.cos(rad));
shot_mc._y = ship_mc._y + (10 * Math.sin(rad));
```

Now we do almost exactly the same thing to determine the shot's velocity. I decided that 5 was a good firing speed. The shot will leave the ship at the same angle as the ship is currently facing. Thus, its X and Y velocities can be broken down into:

```
x velocity = cos(angle)*velocity
y velocity = sin(angle)*velocity
```

Another slight enhancement I made was to add the ship's current velocity to the shot velocity that we just calculated. If you were in a car going 50 miles an hour, and threw a ball out the window – in the same direction the car was moving – at 10 miles an hour, the ball would wind up going at a total speed of 60 miles an hour (We're getting into Einstein's Theory of General Relativity here.-the Flash version of it anyway!). So our code becomes:

```
// determine shot's velocity, adding it to ship's velicity
shot_mc.velX = 5 * Math.cos(rad) + ship_mc.velX;
shot_mc.velY = 5 * Math.sin(rad) + ship_mc.velY;
```

19. OK, we have a shot on the screen and it has velocity. We just need to fill out the shotMove function and we'll be done! However, this function is a doozy. It will do all the work of moving each shot, checking for collision against all asteroids, breaking them up or removing them and keeping score. Whew. For this one, I'm going to build it up little by little rather than dump a page of code on you.

First, let's just get this shot moving:

```
function shotMove() {
    // add velocity to position
    this._x += this.velX;
    this._y += this.velY;
    // if shot is out of range, remove it
    if (this._x>RIGHT || this._x<LEFT || this._y>BOTTOM ||
    ➥this._y<TOP) {
    removeMovieClip(this);
    // update shot count
    if (numShots>0) {
        numShots--;
```

```
            }
        }
    }
```

Here we do the simple task of using velocity to update position. Old hat. Then we see if the shot has gone off the stage. If so, we remove it. Remember we are using the variable numShots to keep track of how many shots are out there. So whenever we remove a shot, we decrement numShots. I also found that sometimes numShots could go into the negative, which would end up allowing more than 5 shots as it was later incremented. Therefore, I test to make sure it is not already at zero before decrementing.

You can test the movie now and the shots will now actually fire. You'll soon notice though, that you are shooting blanks, and the asteroids don't scare so easily.

20. Next, we will loop through the array that contains references to all our asteroid clips, and check for collision on each of them.

```
function shotMove() {
    // add veloicty to position
    this._x += this.velX;
    this._y += this.velY;
    // if shot is out of range, remove it
    if (this._x>RIGHT || this._x<LEFT || this._y>BOTTOM ||
➡this._y<TOP) {
        removeMovieClip(this);
        // update shot count
        if (numShots>0) {
            numShots--;
        }
    }
    // loop through asteroid array, checking for hit
    for (i=0; i<ast_array.length; i++) {
        if (ast_array[i].hitTest(this._x, this._y, true)) {
            // remove shot and update count
            removeMovieClip(this);
            if (numShots>0) {
                numShots--;
            }
            // remove asteroid from stage
            removeMovieClip(ast_array[i]);
            // and remove it from the array
            ast_array.splice(i, 1);
            // if this was the last one, create some new ones
            if (ast_array.length<1) {
                maxAst++;
```

continues overleaf

```
                        astInitID = setInterval(astInit, 2000);
                    }
                }
            }
        }
```

We use ast_array.length as our for loop control, as this will contain the number of asteroids in the array. We test against the shot's _x and _y using shapeFlag=true.

If we get a hit, we remove the shot in the identical manner as above. We then remove the asteroid movie clip from the stage and use ast_array.spice(i, 1) to remove that one element from the array. Take note that this will reduce ast_array.length by one also, which allows our for loop to always loop through the exact number of existing asteroids.

Finally, if ast_array ever reaches zero – all asteroids successfully destroyed, sir – we increase the value of maxAst and create a new batch using astInit. However, we'll put a little two-second delay on running that function by using setInterval. We'll also want to clear that interval, astInitID, so jump back up to astInit and add the clearInterval line to it:

```
function astInit() {
    // create a number of asteroids
    astIndex = 0;
    while (astIndex<maxAst) {
        createAst();
    }
    clearInterval(astInitID);
}
```

Go ahead and test it now, just to make sure it's working. You should be able to shoot your three asteroids and have four appear. Shoot them and five appear. OK, the tide has turned and now the ship has a big advantage over these space rocks. Let's make them a little more persistent.

21. Rather than making them simply disappear with one shot, let's break them up like real asteroids would ...or at least real Atari Asteroids. First we'll need to have two asteroids appear where the hit one was. We'll do this by running the createAst function. Then we'll have to make sure they are both smaller than the original. We'll do this by scaling the movie clips. Here we go...

```
function shotMove() {
    // add veloicty to position
    this._x += this.velX;
    this._y += this.velY;
    // if shot is out of range, remove it
```

```
        if (this._x>RIGHT || this._x<LEFT || this._y>BOTTOM ||
➥this._y<TOP) {
            removeMovieClip(this);
            // update shot count
            if (numShots>0) {
                numShots--;
            }
        }
    }
    // loop through asteroid array, checking for hit
    for (i=0; i<ast_array.length; i++) {
        if (ast_array[i].hitTest(this._x, this._y, true)) {
            // remove shot and update count
            removeMovieClip(this);
            if (numShots>0) {
                numShots--;
            }
            // if asteroid is big enough, break it in two
            if (ast_array[i]._xscale>25) {
                // make this asteroid 1/2 size
                ast_array[i]._xscale /= 2;
                ast_array[i]._yscale /= 2;
                // create a new asteroid, make it same size, same
➥position
                ast_mc = createAst();
                ast_mc._xscale = ast_array[i]._xscale;
                ast_mc._yscale = ast_array[i]._yscale;
                ast_mc._x = ast_array[i]._x;
                ast_mc._y = ast_array[i]._y;
            } else {
                // if asteroid is amall, remove it from the stage
                removeMovieClip(ast_array[i]);
                // and remove it from the array
                ast_array.splice(i, 1);
                // if this was the last one, create some new ones
                if (ast_array.length<1) {
                    maxAst++;
                    astInitID = setInterval(astInit, 2000);
                }
            }
        }
    }
}
```

The first part of that new code is:

```
if (ast_array[i]._xscale>25) {
    // make this asteroid 1/2 size
    ast_array[i]._xscale /= 2;
    ast_array[i]._yscale /= 2;
```

First we check the _xscale of the asteroid just hit. If it is greater than 25, we divide it by two. It will start out at 100. After the first hit, it will be 50. Second hit will make it 25. After that, the if statement will be false, and we'll jump to the else statement, which is the code we already had to remove the asteroid completely.

Now we have made the existing movie clip smaller, we need to add another one, make it the same size as the first and put it in the same position as the first. That's what the second half of the if block does.

```
// create a new asteroid, make it same size, same position
ast_mc = createAst();
ast_mc._xscale = ast_array[i]._xscale;
ast_mc._yscale = ast_array[i]._yscale;
ast_mc._x = ast_array[i]._x;
ast_mc._y = ast_array[i]._y;
```

Remember that the createAst function returns a reference to the asteroid created. Here's where we use that. We assign it to a temporary variable, ast_mc and adjust its _xscale, _yscale, _x and _y to be the same as the one that we just hit. Also remember that createAst assigns each new asteroid a random velocity and rotation, so these two small chunks will appear different and wander off in different directions.

Another thing that createAst does is to push the new asteroid onto the ast_array array, so that it will automatically be checked in future runs through the array for hit testing. It's all coming together now.

Last but not least, we need to know how we're doing overall – a score! I put another dynamic text box up top set to the variable score. We then add one last chunk to our shotMove function. This will do a switch operation based on the _xscale of the asteroid just hit, and assigns a different score to it depending on its size – 100, 50 or 25. This gets added to the total score displayed in the box:

```
function shotMove() {
    // add velocity to position
    this._x += this.velX;
    this._y += this.velY;
    // if shot is out of range, remove it
    if (this._x>RIGHT || this._x<LEFT || this._y>BOTTOM ||
    ➡this._y<TOP) {
        removeMovieClip(this);
```

```
            // update shot count
        if (numShots>0) {
            numShots--;
        }
    }
    // loop through asteroid array, checking for hit
    for (i=0; i<ast_array.length; i++) {
        if (ast_array[i].hitTest(this._x, this._y, true)) {
            // determine score based on asteroid's size (_xscale)
            switch (ast_array[i]._xscale) {
            case 100 :
                score += 10;
                break;
            case 50 :
                score += 50;
                break;
            case 25 :
                score += 100;
                break;
            }
            // remove shot and update count
            removeMovieClip(this);
            if (numShots>0) {
                numShots--;
        }
        // if asteroid is big enough, break it in two
        if (ast_array[i]._xscale>25) {
            // make this asteroid 1/2 size
            ast_array[i]._xscale /= 2;
            ast_array[i]._yscale /= 2;
            // create a new asteroid, make it same size, same position
            ast_mc = createAst();
            ast_mc._xscale = ast_array[i]._xscale;
            ast_mc._yscale = ast_array[i]._yscale;
            ast_mc._x = ast_array[i]._x;
            ast_mc._y = ast_array[i]._y;
        } else {
            // if asteroid is amall, remove it from the stage
            removeMovieClip(ast_array[i]);
            // and remove it from the array
            ast_array.splice(i, 1);
            // if this was the last one, create some new ones
            if (ast_array.length<1) {
                maxAst++;
                astInitID = setInterval(astInit, 2000);
```

continues overleaf

```
                                        }
                                  }
                            }
                      }
                }
```

There we have it. A pretty darned full featured version of Asteroids a la Flash, yet with plenty of room for upgrading and customizing. You might want to have the ship explode when it's hit. This could be done with a tween beginning at the ship's third frame. You'd just have the ship `gotoAndPlay(3)` when it is hit, and before it is removed. You might want to add sounds, using some of the stuff you learn elsewhere in this book. Like the original game, you might want to have an enemy space ship come out to do battle every so often. This would incorporate a lot of what we did in our earlier alien shoot up game.

All of these features will add there own complexity and little problems to deal with as you integrate them into the existing game, but hopefully you've gotten some insight on how you go about addressing these and solving them.

Now, let's learn some more cool Flash Physics.

Springs

In the last couple of files, we got some pretty realistic movement happening. We had things bouncing off walls and floors, falling with realistic gravity, and thrusting through space. There is one more type of motion I'd like to show you: springs, whose particular motion is frequently described as **elasticity**.

Now I know that the idea of spring motion sounds pretty limited, but once you really grasp the concept of how springs work, you will start seeing uses for it all over the place. Springs are basically another form of acceleration. If you had an object on one end of a spring, attached the other end of the spring to a fixed point, then pulled the object away and let it go, the spring would cause the object to accelerate toward the fixed point. This is basically the same as gravity forcing an object downwards, or a rocket thruster pushing an object in a certain direction.

There are a couple of very important things to note about springs:

- A spring generally accelerates towards a specific point. If it passes this point it will slow down, reverse direction, and start accelerating back toward that point again.

- The acceleration is proportional to the distance between the object and the target point.

OK, in English, this second point means that the further away the object is from the point, the stronger the force accelerating it to that point is. You already know this instinctively. If I held one end of a rubber band against your arm and pulled the other end a few inches away, you might look at me a little oddly. You know that if I let go, it wouldn't snap with much force. However, if

I pulled the other end back as far as I could, you'd move your arm away pretty quickly. If I did let go, the band would accelerate quickly enough to hurt.

Right, some illustration is in order. This first diagram shows a (theoretical) spring fully stretched out. The acceleration is at its maximum, let's say +30:

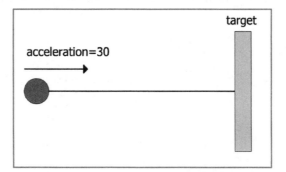

Imagine this in Flash: the object starts moving at 30 pixels per frame. On the next frame it gets a little closer to the target and the spring isn't pulling quite so hard. It adds an acceleration of, say, 20. So now the object will move at 50 pixels per frame. This is an important concept to grasp. The object is *not slowing down* but is still accelerating – going *faster* – but its speed is not increasing at a uniform rate:

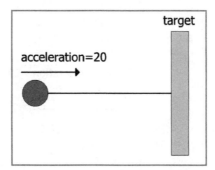

OK, in the next frame, it's right up close to the target. There is hardly any pull on the object at all now, maybe 3. So the velocity finally becomes 53. Note again, that its velocity is not decreasing; it's the rate of acceleration that is declining. The object's velocity is higher than in the previous frame.

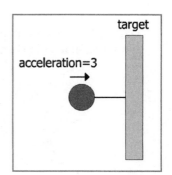

Move onto the next frame. The object is traveling so fast that it goes well beyond the target, like a dog chasing a ball on a frozen lake. Now the target is 'behind' the object. The spring will now be exerting force in the opposite direction, back towards the target. Since the object is a fair distance away from the target now, we know that the acceleration will be fairly strong, enough to cancel out a big chunk of its forward velocity. Say it adds an acceleration of –15. Now our object is *still moving to the right*, but it's slowing down, now with a reduced velocity of only 38:

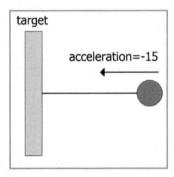

Now it's even further from the target, so the pull will be even stronger. The acceleration is –27, which slows the velocity to just 11. In the next frame the acceleration will be strong enough to overcome what little forward velocity the object has, and will cause it to reverse direction.

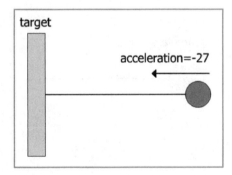

OK, we should start transposing this theory into some ActionScripting, right? Right, let's recreate this spring motion in Flash.

Spring

1. Start a brand new movie and make a movie clip. In my usual flamboyant style, I made a ball with the instance name `ball_mc`. Draw a mark, any kind of simple line, in the center of the screen at (275,y). This will act as a graphical reference for the fixed target point around which our spring motion will be based:

2. Add a new layer called `actions` and in frame 1 define a variable to represent our target point (we'll stick to one dimension/axis for this exercise):

    ```
    var centerX = 275;
    ```

3. Now we need to define a 'springiness' factor or, more specifically, how much acceleration will be applied for any given distance. This is expressed as a fraction. Essentially, we will be taking a fraction of the distance between the object and target point and using that as our value for acceleration. A number of around 0.2 works pretty well, but you can play around with it to get the feel you want. This factor is usually called k. I know it's not very descriptive but, if you use it all the time, you'll get used to it and know instantly what k is. Here's our file so far:

    ```
    var centerX = 275;
    var k = .2;
    ```

4. OK, we've set the stage, now we can yell "Action!" First we need to determine the distance, which is easy enough in one dimension: just subtract `ball_mc._x` from `centerX`. Then we multiply the distance by k to get our value for acceleration, which we'll put into a variable called `accX`. Then we add `accX` to our velocity, `velX`, and finally add the velocity to `ball_mc._x`. We'll add all this beneath the existing two lines in an `onEnterFrame` function like so:

    ```
    onEnterFrame = function () {
        dx = centerX-ball_mc._x;
        accX = dx*k;
    ```

continues overleaf

```
    velX += accX;
    ball_mc._x += velX;
};
```

Here I've separated each individual step for clarity. Some people like to cram every step of a complex function like this into one line, which ends up as:

```
ball_mc._x += velX += (centerX-ball_mc._x)*k;
```

this is perfectly legitimate, but is pretty unreadable. You can adopt your own style and compress as much as you like, as long as it works.

5. If you test the movie, you'll see a pretty good springy object bouncing around the center line. But there's problem: we've made a perfect world without friction or any loss of energy, so our spring will keep on springing forever. Let's add some friction in here, similar to what we did in the drag and throw example in Chapter 6. We'll just multiply the velocity by a fraction like 0.9 on each frame. This will serve to slow the spring down, making this effect much more realistic. Just add this line:

```
var centerX = 275;
var k = .2;
onEnterFrame = function () {
    dx = centerX-ball_mc._x;
    accX = dx*k;
    velX += accX;
    velX *= .9;
    ball_mc._x += velX;
};
```

6. There you go. Test the movie and you've got a pretty realistic one-dimensional spring motion.

It's relatively simple to go on and adapt this file so that you have spring motion on both the x and y-axes. I've done this and made ball_mc draggable in the source file Spring_2_dimensions.fla, if you want to experiment further with this. All the code has been discussed before, so I won't go into any long explanations. If you try it out you can drag and throw the ball, and it will always snap back to the center of the screen – eventually.

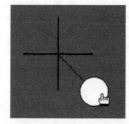

I really do urge you to explore this area further. There is so much that can be done with this simple concept once you fully understand it. Here are some ideas for experimentation:

- Instead of a fixed target point (`centerX`, `centerY`) make the target point moveable. Try using (`this._xmouse`, `this._ymouse`) to define the target's location instead.

- You could make another draggable movie clip called `anchor_mc`. Make the ball spring to (`anchor_mc._x`, `anchor_mc._y`) as the target.

- To show the spring itself, add the following code to the end of the `spring` function, after *ball* is moved to its new position:

```
clear();
lineStyle(1,0,100);
moveTo(centerX, centerY);
lineTo(ball_mc._x, ball_mc._y);
```

- Add some gravity! There's no reason you can't have more than one acceleration force acting on an object. Just add a line `velY += grav;` to the file, and specify a value for `grav` earlier. You'll find that you probably need a much higher value for gravity than you used on previous files. Either do that or you'll have to reduce your `k` quite a bit.

Whew! We've come a long way, and this is the simple stuff. I've got a couple more cool effects to show you yet. Though. I know you'll want to play with some springs for a while, so when you're done with that, we'll continue with some more trigonometry.

Coordinate rotation

Up to this point, we've frequently rotated points, lines, and vectors. Generally we've begun with a radius from a fixed point, and then rotated it to a certain angle. Now that works pretty well, but remember that when we drew our ship or arrow, it always needed to be facing due right (0 degrees) because all our rotations were based on rotating something from an angle of zero.

What if we want to rotate an object around a center point by a certain number of degrees, and that object is located at an angle other than zero degrees? In fact, what if all we know is the x and y coordinates of that object, and we want to rotate it around a center point? Take a look at this:

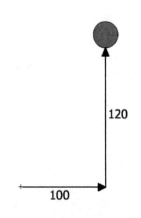

120

100

Here we see that the object is located at x=100, and 120 pixels up from the center point. Now imagine we want to rotate the object by 20 degrees around the center point. We have a problem, because it's not located at zero degrees to start this rotation at. We could use Pythagoras' Theorem to calculate its distance from the center, use atan2 to discover the angle it's at currently, and then add 20 degrees to that and use sin and cos to find out the new X and Y values.

But, this is very long-winded and there's a much more efficient way of doing this – particularly when dealing with multiple objects. Now, I'm going to break from my usual routine here. I'm going to give you a formula without explaining how I came up with it. I'm just going to tell you that it works, you should memorize it, and use it.

When you want to rotate a point (x, y) at a certain angle (angle), this is what you need to use:

```
new_x = x*cos(angle) - y*sin(angle)
new_y = y*cos(angle) + x*sin(angle)
```

I literally have this written out on a piece of paper and taped to the wall above my computer (I don't like tattoos), but I've also got it memorized pretty well now.

> *Note: these aren't some secret formulas I came up with. This is a standard operation used for rotation of coordinates. If you're interested in their derivation, you can look it up in any text on trigonometry and learn step-by-step how the formulas were arrived at. I'm not going to take you through it here as it's a little beyond the scope of our Flash trig applications.*

The next diagram shows the relationship between x, y and new_x, new_y, as well as the angle that we are rotating the object by:

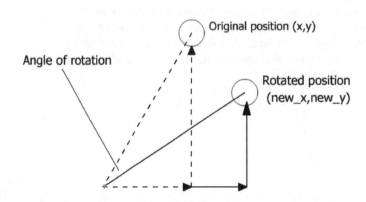

Original position (x,y)

Angle of rotation

Rotated position (new_x,new_y)

Now let's work out how to apply this in Flash.

Ships in flight

1. Open a movie from an earlier exercise in this chapter – you just need a movie clip in your Library, that we can use as objects to rotate. Place three copies at random points on the stage and give them the instance names mc1_mc, mc2_mc and mc3_mc. We'll be rotating them around the center of the stage for now, so draw a graphic at (275, 200) to represent the center point. I'm going for an orbital theme here:

2. Now add a new layer called actions and add the following code to frame 1:

```
init();
function init() {
    cx = 275;
    cy = 200;
    onEnterFrame = rotate;
    var angle = 2;
    rad = angle*Math.PI/180;
    cosAngle = Math.cos(rad);
    sinAngle = Math.sin(rad);
}
```

Let's look at this. Our init function will specify the center point, and set up an onEnterFrame function. We then set an angle to rotate our objects by on each frame, and then naturally convert this to radians. The next couple of lines don't add anything at all to the *functionality* of the program. They do, however, provide a huge amount of *efficiency*. Since we'll need to use the cos and sin of the angle twice during every single frame of the movie, and since it is never going to change, it doesn't make sense to calculate them some 30 or 40 times per second! We'll just do it once at the beginning of the movie, storing the values in the variables cosAngle and sinAngle, and then use those variables throughout the rest of the movie.

3. Now we will create our `rotate` function. This loops through the three movie clips and applies the coordinate rotation formula to their positions:

```
function rotate() {
    for (i=1; i<4; i++) {
        x = this["mc"+i+"_mc"]._x-cx;
        y = this["mc"+i+"_mc"]._y-cy;
        x1 = x*cosAngle-y*sinAngle;
        y1 = y*cosAngle+x*sinAngle;
        this["mc"+i+"_mc"]._x = x1+cx;
        this["mc"+i+"_mc"]._y = y1+cy;
    }
}
```

Note that we always have to decide what we are rotating around – the center point – and we take our measurements from that point. Thus if `mc1_mc` is located at (375,y), this is 100 from the center and that is the X value we use in our calculations. Thus we would subtract the center values, `cx` and `cy`, from the actual coordinates of each movie clip. We then do our rotation, assigning the results to `x1` and `y1`. This gives us the new position of the clip *in relation to the center point*, so we need to add `cx` and `cy` back again to determine our final coordinates.

4. For a final little enhancement, throw in a few line drawing functions so that you can visualize the rotation a little bit better. Here's the final code:

```
init();
function init() {
    cx = 275;
    cy = 200;
    onEnterFrame = rotate;
    var angle = 2;
    rad = angle*Math.PI/180;
    cosAngle = Math.cos(rad);
    sinAngle = Math.sin(rad);
}
function rotate() {
    for (i=1; i<4; i++) {
        x = this["mc"+i+"_mc"]._x-cx;
        y = this["mc"+i+"_mc"]._y-cy;
        x1 = x*cosAngle-y*sinAngle;
        y1 = y*cosAngle+x*sinAngle;
        this["mc"+i+"_mc"]._x = x1+cx;
        this["mc"+i+"_mc"]._y = y1+cy;
        clear();
```

```
        lineStyle(1, 0, 80);
        moveTo(mc1_mc._x, mc1_mc._y);
        lineTo(mc2_mc._x, mc2_mc._y);
        lineTo(mc3_mc._x, mc3_mc._y);
        lineTo(mc1_mc._x, mc1_mc._y);
        moveTo(cx, cy);
        lineTo(mc1_mc._x, mc1_mc._y);
        moveTo(cx, cy);
        lineTo(mc2_mc._x, mc2_mc._y);
        moveTo(cx, cy);
        lineTo(mc3_mc._x, mc3_mc._y);
    }
}
```

5. Go ahead and test your movie and you'll see the movie clips rotating around the central point. If you want to check your file against mine, you can use `coordinate_rotation.fla` in the source files:

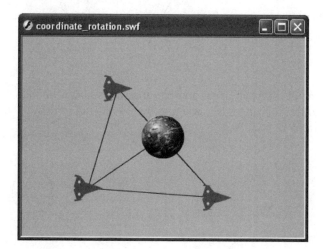

Project#2: Bounce

Our final project is going to incorporate almost everything we've covered so far. Although we won't be introducing any more brand new concepts, we will be combining what we have done to create some whole new effects. With what you have just learned in the last few chapters, there is an almost infinite amount of projects you could create. It's just a matter of thinking of new ways to apply the principles and different ways of combining them. Of course, each *new* thing you learn from here on out just multiplies your repertoire as you find ways to combine it with everything you already know. Anyway, here we go...

So far we have looked at bouncing objects off of straight walls, floors and ceilings. But what happens when a wall is not straight? Say a ball is moving at a 57 degree angle and hits a wall that is at a 32 degree angle. What direction is it going to go and what speed? Well, like I said, we have all the tools to figure that out right now. Take the following diagram:

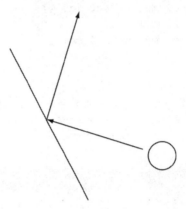

The ball is moving at a certain angle and hits the wall and will bounce off at the angle shown. Now, before you start thinking this is going to be too difficult to possibly understand, take a look at the next diagram:

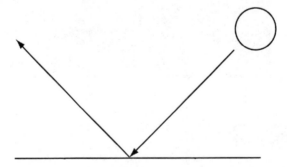

That's an easy one, right? Nothing more than we did in our pong game. You'd simply check if the ball was below the floor, move it so that it rested on the floor, and reverse the Y velocity. Well, those two diagrams are actually the same. I simply rotated the second one to make the floor lie flat. So here is our strategy: we rotate the whole setup to make it flat, do our normal bounce routine, then rotate everything back.

We actually need to rotate not only the ball's X and Y coordinates, but its X and Y velocity (represented by the first arrow in the diagram) as well. (This is chapter8-final.fla on the CD).

1. First make a wall. This is simply a straight horizontal line made into a movie clip, instance called `wall_mc`, and of course, make a ball, called `ball_mc`.

2. Manually rotate the wall, but no more than + or – 90 degrees.

3. Now let's create our `init` function that will give us some gravity, bounce, define our `onEnterFrame` function, and make our ball draggable and throwable.

```
init();
function init() {
    // set some constants
    grav = .5;
    bounce = -.8;
    TOP = 0;
    BOTTOM = Stage.height;
    LEFT = 0;
    RIGHT = Stage.width;
    // our animation function
    onEnterFrame = move;
    // make the ball draggable
    ball_mc.onPress = function() {
        this.startDrag();
        this.dragging = true;
    };
    ball_mc.onRelease = ball_mc.onReleaseOutside=function () {
        this.stopDrag();
        this.dragging = false;
    };
}
```

4. Then we'll define our basic `move` function, without the collision detection.

```
function move() {
    // if we are not dragging the ball
    if (!ball_mc.dragging) {
        // add gravity to the y velocity
        ball_mc.velY += grav;
        // add velocity to the position
        ball_mc._x += ball_mc.velX;
        ball_mc._y += ball_mc.velY;
        // if ball hits any wall, position it at the edge of the
```

continues overleaf

```
➥wall
        // and have it bounce
        if (ball_mc._x<LEFT+ball_mc._width/2) {
            ball_mc._x = LEFT+ball_mc._width/2;
            ball_mc.velX *= bounce;
        } else if (ball_mc._x>RIGHT-ball_mc._width/2) {
            ball_mc._x = RIGHT-ball_mc._width/2;
            ball_mc.velX *= bounce;
        } else if (ball_mc._y<TOP+ball_mc._height/2) {
            ball_mc._y = TOP+ball_mc._height/2;
            ball_mc.velY *= bounce;
        } else if (ball_mc._y>BOTTOM-ball_mc._height/2) {
            ball_mc._y = BOTTOM-ball_mc._height/2;
            ball_mc.velY *= bounce;
        }
    } else {
        // if we ARE dragging the ball
        // velocity = new position - old position
        ball_mc.velX = ball_mc._x-ball_mc.oldx;
        ball_mc.velY = ball_mc._y-ball_mc.oldy;
        // reset old position for next time
        ball_mc.oldx = ball_mc._x;
        ball_mc.oldy = ball_mc._y;
    }
}
```

This is a lot, but all old hat to you now.

5. Since our collision and bouncing code is going to be a bit involved, we'll move it into its own function. Put this line right after you define ball_mc's _x and _y properties.

```
checkWall(wall_mc);
```

6. Now we start to define this function. First, before we get into a whole lot of math, let's just make sure we're somewhere in the neighborhood with a simple hitTest.

```
function checkWall(wall_mc) {
    // first do simple hitTest to see if it's close
    if (wall_mc.hitTest(ball_mc)) {
        ...
    }
}
```

7. By specifying shapeflag as false, we will use the bounding box of the wall only. If it's not in there, we just skip the whole thing. If it is, then we investigate a little further.

8.   Inside the `hitTest`, we first determine our initial X and Y values by subtracting `wall`'s coordinates from `ball`'s. Then we convert `wall`'s `_rotation` (degrees) to radians and set up our `cosAngle` and `sinAngle` variables. Nothing we didn't do in the last file.

```
function checkWall(wall_mc) {
    // first do simple hitTest to see if it's close
    if (wall_mc.hitTest(ball_mc)) {
        // if so, determine ball's x and y position in relation to
        ➥the wall
        x = ball_mc._x-wall_mc._x;
        y = ball_mc._y-wall_mc._y;
        // convert wall's angle to radians and compute cos and sin
        ➥of it
        rad = wall_mc._rotation*Math.PI/180;
        cosAngle = Math.cos(rad);
        sinAngle = Math.sin(rad);
    }
}
```

9.   Now I'm going to introduce a slight alteration to our previous formulas for coordinate rotation. (I know, I said there was nothing new here, but this is only a slight change!) The formulas I gave you were for *adding* an angle to a set of coordinates. In other words, if you supply an angle of 30 degrees, it will rotate it in a positive direction of 30 degrees. But here, say our wall is sitting at 30 degrees, we actually want to rotate it −30 degrees so that it lies flat. Of course we could just supply the same formula the value of −30 instead of +30, but since we are pre-calculating our values for sin and cos, this way is more efficient. The formula for *subtracting* an angle from a set of coordinates is:

```
new_x = cos(angle)*x + sin(angle)*y
new_y = cos(angle)*y - sin(angle)*x
```

10. You see the only thing that has changed is the + and − in the middle! Not so bad after all. So to subtract the wall's angle from the ball's coordinates, we add the next lines:

```
function checkWall(wall_mc) {
    // first do simple hitTest to see if it's close
    if (wall_mc.hitTest(ball_mc)) {
        // if so, determine ball's x and y position in relation to
        ➥the wall
        x = ball_mc._x-wall_mc._x;
        y = ball_mc._y-wall_mc._y;
        // convert wall's angle to radians and compute cos and sin
        ➥of it
        rad = wall_mc._rotation*Math.PI/180;
```

continues overleaf

```
            cosAngle = Math.cos(rad);
            sinAngle = Math.sin(rad);
            // rotate coordinates to align with wall angle
            x1 = cosAngle*x+sinAngle*y;
            y1 = cosAngle*y-sinAngle*x;
        }
    }
```

Now we need to rotate the velocities as well. Think of this as rotating the arrow there on the diagram.

```
function checkWall(wall_mc) {
    // first do simple hitTest to see if it's close
    if (wall_mc.hitTest(ball_mc)) {
        // if so, determine ball's x and y position in relation to
        ➥the wall
        x = ball_mc._x-wall_mc._x;
        y = ball_mc._y-wall_mc._y;
        // convert wall's angle to radians and compute cos and sin
        ➥of it
        rad = wall_mc._rotation*Math.PI/180;
        cosAngle = Math.cos(rad);
        sinAngle = Math.sin(rad);
        // rotate coordinates to align with wall angle
        x1 = cosAngle*x+sinAngle*y;
        y1 = cosAngle*y-sinAngle*x;
        // rotate velocities to align with wall angle
        vx1 = cosAngle*ball_mc.velX+sinAngle*ball_mc.velY;
        vy1 = cosAngle*ball_mc.velY+sinAngle*ball_mc.velX;
    }
}
```

Notice that we don't rotate any actual movie clips. That would be a waste of processor time, since we would be rotating them back before anyone saw them anyway. All of our calculations are purely mathematical here. We have a theoretical flat floor located at (0,0) and a theoretical ball located at *x1, y1*, moving at a theoretical velocity of *vx1, vy1*. All we've done is make a mathematical representation of the second, rotated diagram.

11. Now, all we have to do is apply the simple routine for bouncing off of a flat floor:

   1. See if the ball is below the floor.
   2. If so, move it to be level with the floor.
   3. Reverse its Y velocity.

Since the floor is theoretically located at (0,0,) to take into account the thickness of the ball, we say:

```
if (y1>0-ball_mc._height/2) {
...
}
```

This is the same as earlier:

```
if (ball_mc._y>BOTTOM-ball_mc._height/2){
...
}
```

We're just using our rotated coordinates instead. If not, we skip gracefully to exit. If so, we adjust the position of the ball and reverse the Y velocity. In rotated terms this is:

```
function checkWall(wall_mc) {
    // first do simple hitTest to see if it's close
    if (wall_mc.hitTest(ball_mc)) {
        // if so, determine ball's x and y position in relation to
        ➥the wall
        x = ball_mc._x-wall_mc._x;
        y = ball_mc._y-wall_mc._y;
        // convert wall's angle to radians and compute cos and sin
        ➥of it
        rad = wall_mc._rotation*Math.PI/180;
        cosAngle = Math.cos(rad);
        sinAngle = Math.sin(rad);
        // rotate coordinates to align with wall angle
        x1 = cosAngle*x+sinAngle*y;
        y1 = cosAngle*y-sinAngle*x;
        // rotate velocities to align with wall angle
        vx1 = cosAngle*ball_mc.velX+sinAngle*ball_mc.velY;
        vy1 = cosAngle*ball_mc.velY+sinAngle*ball_mc.velX;
        // check if ball is hitting wall
        if (y1>0-ball_mc._height/2) {
            // do simple bounce calculation, adjusting position of
            ➥ball to align with the edge of wall
            y1 = 0-ball_mc._height/2;
            vy1 *= bounce;
        }
    }
}
```

12. Now we rotate everything back. Now we are *adding* the angle, rather than *subtracting* it, so we go back to the original formula. This goes right in the last if block after `vy1 *= bounce`:

```
x = cosAngle*x1-sinAngle*y1;
y = cosAngle*y1+sinAngle*x1;
```

and the velocities...
```
ball_mc.velX = cosAngle*vx1-sinAngle*vy1;
ball_mc.velY = cosAngle*vy1+sinAngle*vx1;
```

13. Then we add x and y back to wall._x and wall._y to get back into our actual stage position for ball.

```
ball_mc._x = x+wall_mc._x;
ball_mc._y = y+wall_mc._y;
```

That's it! If the ball has actually hit the line, it will now be located precisely *on* the line and its velocity will be such that it will bounce off the line at a realistic angle. Here's the full code for the `checkWall` function:

```
function checkWall(wall_mc) {
    // first do simple hitTest to see if it's close
    if (wall_mc.hitTest(ball_mc)) {
        // if so, determine ball's x and y position in relation to
        ➥the wall
        x = ball_mc._x-wall_mc._x;
        y = ball_mc._y-wall_mc._y;
        // convert wall's angle to radians and compute cos and sin
        ➥of it
        rad = wall_mc._rotation*Math.PI/180;
        cosAngle = Math.cos(rad);
        sinAngle = Math.sin(rad);
        // rotate coordinates to align with wall angle
        x1 = cosAngle*x+sinAngle*y;
        y1 = cosAngle*y-sinAngle*x;
        // rotate velocities to align with wall angle
        vx1 = cosAngle*ball_mc.velX+sinAngle*ball_mc.velY;
        vy1 = cosAngle*ball_mc.velY+sinAngle*ball_mc.velX;
        // check if ball is hitting wall
        if (y1>0-ball_mc._height/2) {
            // do simple bounce calculation, adjusting position of
            ➥ball
            // to align with edge of wall
            y1 = 0-ball_mc._height/2;
```

```
            vy1 *= bounce;
            // rotate coordinates back to original angle
            x = cosAngle*x1-sinAngle*y1;
            y = cosAngle*y1+sinAngle*x1;
            // rotate velocities back to original angle
            ball_mc.velX = cosAngle*vx1-sinAngle*vy1;
            ball_mc.velY = cosAngle*vy1+sinAngle*vx1;
            // adjust wall-relative position to stage position
            ball_mc._x = x+wall_mc._x;
            ball_mc._y = y+wall_mc._y;
        }
    }
}
```

I know you want to see this in action, so go ahead and play with it for a bit.

One thing you might have run into, is that if the ball approaches the underside of the wall, it may suddenly jump up on top of it. This is because we are testing if y1 is simply below the floor. It doesn't matter how much below. We can do a 99% fix on this by adding another condition to that if statement. We know that if the ball is travelling downwards and goes through the wall, the furthest it could possibly travel past the wall is *vy1*, because that's the most it can move in one frame. So if it is further than that much below the wall, it must have come in from the side. So we just make our if statement this:

```
if(y1>0-ball_mc._height/2 && y1<vy1){
...
}
```

OK, now we're going to do a bit more optimization on it. If you read through the sequence, you see that we first do a hitTest, then compute a bunch of values, then run an if statement. But that if statement only uses the values of y1 and vy1. Although we may eventually need x1 and vx1, there's no need to compute them until we determine whether or not they are necessary. So we can move the lines that compute these *inside* the if block. Try it again and see if you notice a speed increase. Here's the final code:

```
function checkWall(wall_mc) {
    // first do simple hitTest to see if it's close
    if (wall_mc.hitTest(ball_mc)) {
        // if so, determine ball's x and y position in relation to
        ➥the wall
        x = ball_mc._x-wall_mc._x;
        y = ball_mc._y-wall_mc._y;
        // convert wall's angle to radians and compute cos and sin
        ➥of it
        rad = wall_mc._rotation*Math.PI/180;
```

continues overleaf

```
           cosAngle = Math.cos(rad);
           sinAngle = Math.sin(rad);
           // rotate y coord and velocity to align with wall angle
           y1 = cosAngle*y-sinAngle*x;
           vy1 = cosAngle*ball_mc.velY+sinAngle*ball_mc.velX;
           // check if ball is hitting wall
           if (y1>0-ball_mc._height/2 && y1<vy1) {
                // rotate x coord and velocity to align with wall angle
                x1 = cosAngle*x+sinAngle*y;
                vx1 = cosAngle*ball_mc.velX+sinAngle*ball_mc.velY;
                // do simple bounce calculation, adjusting position of
                ➥ball
                // to align with edge of wall
                y1 = 0-ball_mc._height/2;
                vy1 *= bounce;
                // rotate coordinates back to original angle
                x = cosAngle*x1-sinAngle*y1;
                y = cosAngle*y1+sinAngle*x1;
                // rotate velocities back to original angle
                ball_mc.velX = cosAngle*vx1-sinAngle*vy1;
                ball_mc.velY = cosAngle*vy1+sinAngle*vx1;
                // adjust wall-relative position to stage position
                ball_mc._x = x+wall_mc._x;
                ball_mc._y = y+wall_mc._y;
           }
      }
}
```

Now we're rocking! Before I leave you, I want to show you the power of what we just did. Make four additional copies of `wall` movie clip on stage. Name the five walls `wall0_mc` through `wall4_mc`. Position them in various locations and rotate them at various degrees. Now go to the `move` function and replace the line that says:

```
checkWall(wall_mc);
```

with:

```
for (i=0; i<5; i++) {
checkWall(_root["wall"+i+"_mc"]);
}
```

This cycles through all the walls, checking them one-by-one for collision, and handling it if so.

OK, over to you. I expect to see a lot of Flash MX pinball machines or "Donkey Kong" type games popping up in the next few months!

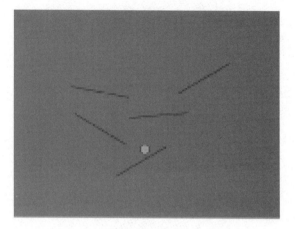

Summary

Wow. We covered a lot in this chapter. Check it out.

You now know the basics of trigonometry:

- Sin
- Cos
- Tan
- How to figure any side or angle of a right triangle, given a minimum amount of data
- How to move a movie clip in a circle
- How to find the distance between any two points or movie clips
- Radians and angles and how to convert them
- How to rotate a movie clip to point at a specific point

In the realm of physics, we covered the basics of motion, including velocity and acceleration – and how to take a particular velocity and its angular direction, and break it down into an X velocity and Y velocity. We also covered springs, which I personally find have almost unlimited potential for cool effects. I'm constantly finding new ways to apply that little tidbit.

Combining some physics and some heavy duty trig, we made an object bounce off a number of angled surfaces – one of the most frequently asked Flash Physics questions.

In building our asteroids game, we pulled almost all of what we learned up to that point into a program which comes extremely close to the original. This shows just how viable your knowledge actually is at this point. You now know enough to really build the framework for some awesome games or applications. Combine that with your own imagination and the rest of the stuff you'll learn in the following chapters – the drawing API, sound, video, etc. and there's no stopping you!

section 2: ActionScript Interfaces

chapter 9: Animation and Interactivity with the Drawing API

In the past, using Flash to create graphics at run-time required at least *some* form of using predefined symbols and manipulating them with code. Sure, you could take a single pixel image in your Library and do some interesting things with it, but you were rather limited in your ability to create useful, dynamic, graphics if you hadn't drawn them manually beforehand. As an example, one of the first experiments many Flash-users attempt is a drawing program, but all quickly learn that only so much can be accomplished with a 100x100 pixel hairline and duplicated movie clips.

Now – hallelujah – with Flash MX, Macromedia has introduced the ability to create graphics at run-time and nothing will ever be the same again (OK, maybe that's a little melodramatic, but at the very least creating dynamic graphics won't ever be the same, and that's what this section is all about).

Using the new drawing API (**Application Programming Interface**) and the new movie clip methods `createEmptyMovieClip` and `createTextField`, Flash users can now code and create anything from buttons and forms, to drawing applications, to entire interfaces without drawing a single graphic beforehand. Don't believe me? Well, it's true, and we'll spend the next few chapters exploring how.

Coded line drawing

Before we get into more complex applications of the drawing API, let's quickly review some of the methods that you explored in chapter 3:

- `lineStyle` sets the visual properties of the line, such as weight, color, and alpha.

- `moveTo` moves the 'pencil' to new coordinates on the stage without drawing a line between them.

- `lineTo` draws a straight line from the pencil's current position to the given coordinates, while `curveTo` creates a curved line to the given anchor point coordinates by curving towards the control point coordinates.

- Finally, `beginFill` and `endFill` act as bookends for the solid color fills in your shapes, and `clear` wipes the canvas clean.

There is only one more command left to explore, but it's a big one: `beginGradientFill`. We'll look into this fun little method later in the chapter.

OK, enough review. Let's work through a short exercise, using the drawing API to draw lines of random color and size.

Chaos lines

In this short exercise, we're going to see how just a few short lines of code can create a quick effect (it's `chaosLines.fla` on the CD).

1. Create a new movie, and rename the default layer `actions`. Open the Actions panel and add the following code to frame 1:

```
pos = {x:0, y:0};
stageWidth = Stage.width;
stageHeight = Stage.height;
```

These three lines initialize some variables for our experiment. First, we create a new object called `pos` that contains the properties `x` and `y`, which will be our changing coordinates throughout the movie. Next we look at the properties of the new `Stage` object and place their values into variables. If we didn't do this at the beginning, these values could change during the course of our experiment and our lines would be drawn outside the stage area.

One thing to note here: when I declare new arrays or objects, I don't use the constructor `new`, but opt for the shorthand. Therefore, a new empty array or an empty object in my code would be, respectively:

```
myArray = [];
myObject {};
```

This will work *exactly* the same as declaring the objects and arrays like this:

```
myArray = new Array();
myObject = new Object();
```

So for our above `pos` declaration in step 1, you *could* write it as:

```
pos = new Object();
pos.x = 0;
pos.y = 0;
```

However, I find it more readable and succinct on one line, especially for objects and arrays with a limited number of indices or properties. Plus, changing the object's name (at least in this instance) requires altering one line, not three. Whichever form you choose, it all comes down to coding style and your own preferences.

I also do not declare variables with `var` unless they appear inside a function, and I only want to set their scope inside that function. That you need to use `var` to declare a variable is a common misconception with Flash. It only makes a difference if used inside a function to limit the variable's scope. Heaven forbid I should type anything extra!

On that note, though I must say that some extra typing *is* required in another area, especially if you opt for shorthand coding, and that is in your code **comments**. For both your own benefit and others', be sure to always comment your code wherever your intentions may be unclear. You'll thank yourself later. (In the code in these chapters, comments are not included, as that is what the accompanying explanatory text is for. You'll find the fully commented FLAs on the accompanying CD.)

2. Now for our line drawing function. Underneath the previous three lines, type:

```
placeLine = function () {
    var thickness = Math.ceil(Math.random()*4);
    var lineColor = Math.floor(Math.random()*16777215);
    this.lineStyle(thickness, lineColor, 80);
    pos.x = Math.random()*stageWidth;
    pos.y = Math.random()*stageHeight;
    this.lineTo(pos.x, pos.y);
};
```

What does this do? Breaking it down, it first sets the `thickness` local variable to a random number between one and four inclusive. `Math.random` will return a floating point number (basically with decimals) between 0 and 1, which we multiply by 4. `Math.ceil` is a rounding method that will round this decimal number up to its nearest integer. Next, `lineColor` is assigned a random color out of the 16 million or so available. `Math.floor` will round that number down to its nearest integer. Finally, the function sets the opacity of the line to 80%. All of this is sent as parameters in the `lineStyle` method.

You might be surprised that you can send the drawing method a base ten integer when it says in the manual that you need to send a hexadecimal value. The reason for this is that when you type `0x` before a hex value in your code, Flash will automatically turn this value into its base 10 equivalent. Try typing `trace(0xFF);` into a blank movie and you'll see that Flash returns 255. So in our code above, `16777215` is the base 10 equivalent of `0xFFFFFF`, which is the color white. By finding a random integer between 0 and 16777215, we are able to pick a random color out of the available color range.

Next in the `placeLine` function, we set new coordinates to move to, finding a random number contained within our stage's dimensions. With this new position set, we draw a line. Note that since we do not use the `moveTo` method again, each time we call this function, the line will be drawn from where the previous line ends. Our pencil remains pressed to the pad.

3.   Here's the last step. Add these two lines:

```
this.onEnterFrame = placeLine;
```

It's a wonderful thing to now be able to dynamically assign handlers! This is one instance where it saves us a few extra steps when we need looping code. In Flash 5, you were forced to create an empty movie clip to run all the code on an `onEnterFrame` event, or you needed to set up a frame loop on the main timeline. Now, we can assign an `onEnterFrame` event handler to the main timeline itself! For every frame of the movie, `placeLine` will be called, giving us a looping action with no fuss.

4.   Go ahead and test the movie to see the drawing API scribble away! Maybe it's not the most beautiful of chaotic creations, but it's pretty nifty with less than ten lines of code and no pre-built graphics:

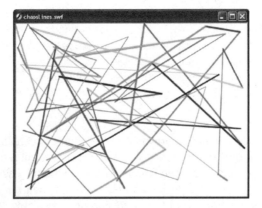

Animating drawings

Scribbles are all well and good, but are hardly the pinnacle of coded animation. Thankfully, the drawing API allows us to do so much more. Since numbers are the only parameters to send to the drawing functions, it's quite easy to create animated drawings in your clips by simply altering the numbers you send each frame. You can also easily alter frame rates for your animations by only calling your drawing functions at set intervals (using the convenient and appropriately named `setInterval`).

The only trick to animating with the drawing API is actually getting the values for your functions in the first place. Let's first create a simple tool that will aid us in this task. This will be a small movie that will allow us to draw line drawings on the stage. Each drawing will represent a single cel of an animation. When we have completed the drawings, we will have a code readout in the Output window of the coordinates needed to recreate the drawings with the drawing API. (Take a look at `API_animation.swf` on the CD.)

Cel generator

1. Create a new movie called `celMaker.fla` and add the following code to the first frame of the default layer:

    ```
    startDraw = function () {
        shapes[shapeNum] = [];
        this.moveTo(this._xmouse, this._ymouse);
        this.onMouseMove = draw;
    };
    stopDraw = function () {
        delete this.onMouseMove;
        shapeNum++;
    };
    draw = function () {
        this.lineTo(this._xmouse, this._ymouse);
        shapes[shapeNum].push(Math.round(this._xmouse)+", "+
        ➥Math.round(this._ymouse));
    };
    ```

    Here we create three quick and dirty functions to handle our drawing. `startDraw` moves the pencil to our current mouse position and sets our `draw` function to occur whenever the mouse is moved. `shapes` is an array that will store our mouse positions.

    `stopDraw` deletes the drawing function from our `onMouseMove` handler and increments our shape count by 1 (each new shape will need a `moveTo` before it).

    `draw` is our actual drawing function that simply uses the `lineTo` method to draw a line. It also places our mouse position into the `shapes` array so that we can play it back later. The string formatting in the `push` parameter is there so that we can plug these values directly into code later on when we copy and paste from the Output window. Basically, an `_x` and `_y` coordinate at (50, 100) will be formatted as a string to look like `50, 100`. When we trace the code at a later step, we can then put this value right into the `lineTo` arguments.

2. Add the following function:

```
listVars = function () {
    code = "shape"+layerNum+" = function() {"+newline;
    code += "    this.clear();"+newline;
    code += "    this.lineStyle(2, 0, 100);"+newline;
    for (var i = 0; i<shapes.length; i++) {
        code += "    this.moveTo("+shapes[i][0]+");"+newline;
        for (var j = 1; j<shapes[i].length; j++) {
            code += "    this.lineTo("+shapes[i][j]+");"+newline;
        }
    }
    code += "}";
    trace(code);
    makeLayer();
};
```

listVars will simply go through our arrays later on and spit out the proper code. I often set up tracing methods such as this to type out all of my long code for me. All the lines actually do here is place our coordinates into strings that are formatted to be copied and pasted directly into the Actions panel. For instance, when we trace the string code at the end of the function, it might send the following to the Output window:

```
shape1 = function() {
    this.clear();
    this.lineStyle(2, 0, 100);
    this.moveTo(50, 100);
    this.lineTo(100, 200);
};
shapes.push("shape1");
```

We will then be able to paste this code into the Script pane of the Actions panel already formatted properly, so no syntax errors will occur. Pretty handy.

3. Add this last function which will create our individual animation cels by dimming out any previous drawings:

```
makeLayer = function () {
    delete layer.onMouseDown;
    delete layer.onMouseUp;
    layer = this.createEmptyMovieClip("layer"+layerNum, layerNum);
    layerNum++;
    layer.lineStyle(2, 0, 100);
    layer.moveTo(150, 100);
    layer.beginFill(0xFFFFFF, 50);
```

```
        layer.lineTo(400, 100);
        layer.lineTo(400, 300);
        layer.lineTo(150, 300);
        layer.lineTo(150, 100);
        layer.endFill();
        shapes = [];
        shapeNum = 0;
        layer.onMouseDown = startDraw;
        layer.onMouseUp = stopDraw;
    };
```

makeLayer is my baby Photoshop function. Every time you finish an animation cel, this will create a new layer on top of your previous cels so you can start a new drawing. Each cel has a 50% opacity fill, so you get a nice onion skinning effect. The function also reinitializes our shapes array (which will hold the drawing's coordinates) and shapeNum, which is a variable that holds the number of shapes drawn on a certain layer. Since we are starting a new layer, this is set back to 0.

4. These last few lines of code start everything rolling:

```
layerNum = 0;
_root.onKeyDown = listVars;
Key.addListener(_root);
makeLayer();
```

Here we initialize our original variables and set up the main movie to listen for a keyPress event. The addListener method is a nice new command that allows objects to receive information on events, even when they were not initially enabled to do so. Movie clips (considering the _root movie to be a glorified movie clip) do not automatically 'hear' key events like keyDown and keyUp but we can add that functionality to certain instances using addListener. Here we've enabled the _root timeline to hear all events associated with the Key object. The final line then creates our first layer and we are good to go!

5. Test the movie. Draw within the animation cel (go outside the borders – live free!), and when you finish it, hit any key to begin drawing a new cel. Your code is output as functions, but we need to set up another movie before we can use them to generate our animation.

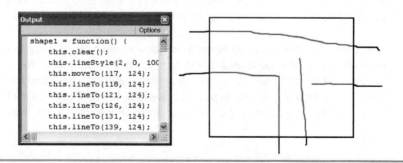

6.   Save your movie and leave it open as we'll be coming back to it very shortly.

Frame-by-frame animation

This is a short exercise where we'll use some drawing API information that will be generated by the `celMaker.swf` to animate some graphics, in this case a rough animated run cycle. We'll use the drawing API to simulate traditional cel (frame-by-frame) animation. Open up `API_animation.swf` (on the CD) to see what we'll be creating with our code:

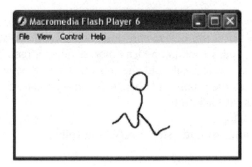

1.   Start a new movie called `API_animation.fla`, and type this code into frame 1 of the default layer:

```
shapes = [];
shapeNum = 0;
drawShapes = function () {
       _root[shapes[shapeNum]]();
       shapeNum = shapeNum+1>shapes.length-1 ? 0 : shapeNum+1;
};
setInterval(drawShapes, 100);
```

This is pretty much all the code we need to type into our new movie. We initialize two variables (and we will store our function names in the array once we know how many we have) and create a function to swap out coded images. `drawShapes` will simply loop through our array and swap out the next image. The speed at which this is done is dictated by our `setInterval` on the next line. Here I've it set to occur every tenth of a second. By changing this number, you can quickly alter your clips' frame rates.

The second line in the `drawShapes` function is an example of using a conditional operator. Basically, this is the same as a single line `if...else` statement. We start the line with a variable, in this case `shapeNum`. We will assign a value to `shapeNum` based on what follows. Next, a condition is checked. In our case, we look to see if `shapeNum+1` is greater than the total number of indices in our `shapes` array. If this statement evaluates to true, then whatever follows the ? symbol is assigned to shapeNum (0, in our example). If the condition evaluates to false, then whatever follows the colon is assigned to shapeNum (shapeNum+1, in our example above). Taking the line in full then, we are incrementing shapeNum until it reaches the end of our shapes array, at which point we loop back to the first index.

2. Go back to the celMaker.fla that you were working on in the last exercise and retest the movie. Create multiple cels of animation, hitting any key between each cel to create a new cel/layer. We're going to animate between each cel, so draw an image that is clearly moving between each state (cel). Here I've drawn four (admittedly rough!) cels of a stick figure in a running cycle:

It's very important that you don't close the Output window when it pops up as we need to keep it there until we're through. One thing to keep in mind while you're drawing is not to rest the pencil for too long, as even the smallest movement will be recorded. The swifter you are when drawing here, the less code there will be later on.

Ah, drawing with the mouse! With more time we could set up something a little more complex that included traditional Bezier curve tools and shape tools for circles and polygons. For now though, this will do fine.

3. Once you've completed your animation cycle, hit any key to output your final cel. The Output window should now have lines and lines of code for you to select and copy. These are all the strings formatted and outputted in the listVars function. Make sure you copy *all* of the code:

4.   Go back into the main timeline of `API_animation.fla` and paste the contents of the clipboard underneath the first `shapes = [];` line of the existing code in the Actions panel. The only thing left to do is insert the names of the cels into our array at the bottom of our code. Our cels are called `shape1`, `shape2`, and so on, in the code you copied from the Output window. Update your array with the appropriate number of cels. I had four, so my amended code now looks like this:

```
shapes = [];

shape1 = function() {
    this.clear();
    this.lineStyle(2, 0, 100);

    [Lots of additional function information]

    this.lineTo(256, 269);
    this.lineTo(255, 269);
    this.lineTo(254, 269);
    this.lineTo(253, 269);
}
shapes.push("shape4");
drawShapes = function() {
    _root[shapes[shapeNum]]();
    shapeNum = shapeNum+1 > shapes.length-1 ? 0 : shapeNum+1;
}
setInterval(drawShapes, 100);
```

If you had more cels, add the appropriate amount to the array. Make sure you only put strings inside the array, and not the functions themselves.

5.   Test your movie to see your coded frame-by-frame animation in action!

Coded tweens

We can see that frame-by-frame animation can be successfully emulated using the drawing API (albeit somewhat simplistically in our example). So what about tweening? Again, if all we're dealing with are numbers, then tweening is a piece of cake. The toughest part is actually coming up with the numbers in the first place.

In this next exercise, I've already done this for you so that we can get straight into the tweening. I showed you one method of generating the numbers in an earlier exercise, and here I've followed a very similar process to generate the numbers for the following curves that we're going to use. I'll leave it to you to explore how you might achieve the same information.

Morphing fruit

What we will attempt to do in the following exercise is create a motion and color tween between two drawing API sketches. Open up apples_oranges.swf (on the CD) and click on the fruit. It morphs, or more accurately tweens, between the apple and orange shapes with each user click. This may not appear particularly advanced at first sight, but what if I told you that this was entirely created with the drawing API, with no graphics on the stage or in the Library?

To begin, let's first create the finished sketches.

1. Create a new movie called apple_oranges.fla. In this movie, we'll be using 100% code, so all the work will take place in the Actions panel. Start by adding the following code to the first frame of the default layer:

    ```
    this.createEmptyMovieClip("drawObj", 0);

    apple = {};
    apple.anchorPoints = [[245,155], [180,50], [245,155], [247,70],
    ➥[265,60], [262,150], [335,130], [354,220], [256,320],
    ➥[163,263], [161,158], [262,150]];
    apple.controlPoints = [[250,50], [150,100], [270,115], [255,70],
    ➥[290,110], [290,109], [373,153], [314,358], [211,357],
    ➥[128,196], [200,118]];
    apple.colors = [[0,0x009900], [2,0x663300], [5,0x990000]];

    orange = {};
    orange.anchorPoints = [[232,152], [192,120], [227,153],
    ➥[307,103], [227,154], [210,154], [260,148], [350,150],
    ➥[380,338], [140,364], [133,175], [210,154]];
    orange.controlPoints = [[212,58], [130,123], [246,102],
    ➥[276,154], [200,104], [230,124], [285,125], [450,204],
    ➥[288,480], [38,263], [178,140]];
    orange.colors = [[0,0x333300], [2,0x335500], [5,0xFF9933]];

    shapes = [apple, orange];
    shapeNum = 0;
    ```

In the first line we create a movie clip to hold our drawings. Then we create two new objects called apple and orange. These both have control points, anchor points, and colors associated with them (and yes, the numbers were all generated by another SWF). For the colors, we are storing the colors and the index positions of the anchor points that the color begins at. We then place these two objects into an array named shapes, and set our current index position to 0, via shapeNum, for the apple.

Now we create a function, aptly called drawShape, that will draw our shapes:

```
drawShape = function (shape) {
    drawObj.clear();
    drawObj.lineStyle(2, 0, 100);
    currentColor = 0;
    drawObj.moveTo(shape.anchorPoints[0][0],shape.anchorPoints[0][1];
    for (var i = 0; i<shape.anchorPoints.length-1; i++) {
        if (shape.colors[currentColor][0] == i) {
            drawObj.endFill();
            drawObj.beginFill(shape.colors[currentColor][1], 100);
            drawObj.moveTo(shape.anchorPoints[i][0],
            ➡shape.anchorPoints[i][1]);
            currentColor++;
        }
        drawObj.curveTo(shape.controlPoints[i][0],
        ➡shape.controlPoints[i][1], shape.anchorPoints[i+1][0],
        ➡shape.anchorPoints[i+1][1]);
    }
};
```

Most of this is fairly straightforward if you understand the arrays above, so let's make sure you're clear on how the referencing works. The variable shape will hold a reference to one of our objects, apple or orange. Therefore, shape.anchorPoints will look at the anchorPoints property of the selected shape. anchorPoints for each object holds a two-dimensional array. Each index position of anchorPoints holds an _x and _y coordinate – the _x value is held in index 0 and the _y value is held in index 1. It follows that if shape is holding our apple object, then shape.anchorPoints[1][1] will look at the _y coordinate of the second index of apple's anchorPoints array, which is 50.

In the drawShape function, we first clear our clip, reset the lineStyle and currentColor variable, and move to our starting position. We run through our entire anchorPoints array for our current object and call the curveTo method for each. The if statement checks to see if we're at the index position where our next color needs to begin. If so, we end the previous fill and begin the new one. I found moving the 'pencil' to the current position after the beginFill call fixed some fill glitches that were present when the command wasn't there.

2.   Now add this final piece of code:

```
clickCatch = function () {
    shapeNum = shapeNum+1>1 ? 0 : shapeNum+1;
    drawShape(shapes[shapeNum]);
};
drawShape(apple);
drawObj.onMouseDown = clickCatch;
```

clickCatch is the function we will call when the mouse is clicked. It increments shapeNum (we use the conditional operator here in case we wish to add additional shapes later on) and calls our drawShape function. We then draw our initial shape and make the drawObj listen for the mouse clicks so it can change its image. Go ahead and test the movie to see the apple and, when you click the mouse, the orange. All this is generated with the above code:

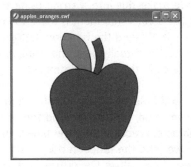 

So, we can draw some fruit with the drawing API. What would be really cool is if we could animate the change. All right then, let's do just that:

3.   Add these lines to the top of your current code, right after the createEmptyMovieClip call:

```
tweenRate = 24;
currentPos = {};
currentPos.controlPoints = [];
currentPos.anchorPoints = [];
currentPos.colors = [];
```

We're simply initializing some variables here. tweenRate is the length of our animation, tied with the frame rate. currentPos will store all the information about what stage our anchor points, control points, and colors are currently at.

4.   Another function submitted for your approval. Place this immediately beneath the drawShape function.

```
convertToRGB = function(c) {
var col = c.toString(16);
while (col.length < 6) {
    col = "0" + col;
}
var r = parseInt(col.substr(0,2), 16);
var g = parseInt(col.substr(2,2), 16);
var b = parseInt(col.substr(4,2), 16);
return {r:r, g:g, b:b}
}
```

Right. `convertToRGB` does exactly what it says. This will accept a color value and return the value for each of the red, green, and blue channels. We'll need these values to tween the colors of the objects.

`c` is the color value sent to the function. We make this into a string using the `toString` method, telling it to convert using base 16. The `while` statement is there to ensure that we have six characters in our string. For instance, if we send the function `255` (pure blue), the string returned by `c.toString(16)` will be `FF`. We actually need the string to read `0000FF` for our hex color, so we add the necessary zeros in the `while` statement.

Next, we extract three substrings from `c`. `r` will hold the red value stored in the first two characters of the string, `g` will hold the green value, in the third and fourth characters of the string, and `b` will hold the final two characters representing the blue value. `parseInt` actually converts a string into a number, so we send the function our substrings, as well as the base of the number system (16). These final values we return in a custom object containing three properties: `r`, `g`, and `b`.

5. This next function is where we will initiate our transformation. Add this code immediately after the `convertToRGB` function:

```
startShift = function (shape) {
    endShape = shape;
    delete drawObj.onMouseDown;
    tweenCount = 0;
    increment = {};
    increment.anchorPoints = [];
    increment.controlPoints = [];
    increment.colors = [];
    for (var i = 0; i<shape.colors.length; i++) {
        var newColor = convertToRGB(shape.colors[i][1]);
        var oldColor = convertToRGB(currentPos.colors[i][1]);
        var r = (oldColor.r - newColor.r)/tweenRate;
        var g = (oldColor.g - newColor.g)/tweenRate;
        var b = (oldColor.b - newColor.b)/tweenRate;
```

```
                    increment.colors.push({r:r, g:g, b:b});
          }
          for (var i = 0; i < shape.anchorPoints.length; i++) {
          var anchor1 = (shape.anchorPoints[i][0] -
          ➥currentPos.anchorPoints[i][0])/tweenRate;
          var anchor2 = (shape.anchorPoints[i][1] -
          ➥currentPos.anchorPoints[i][1])/tweenRate;
          var control1 = (shape.controlPoints[i][0] -
          ➥currentPos.controlPoints[i][0])/tweenRate;
          var control2 = (shape.controlPoints[i][1] -
          ➥currentPos.controlPoints[i][1])/tweenRate;
          increment.anchorPoints.push([anchor1, anchor2]);
          increment.controlPoints.push([control1, control2]);
          }
          drawObj.onEnterFrame = moveLines;
};
```

It's all about the preparation. Well, at least this function is all about the preparation. startShift is sent whichever shape will be our final destination, and we store that value in endShape. We then delete mouseDown so that the user cannot click in mid-transformation (don't worry, we'll put it back in later).

Next, increment is created to store the values we will need to adjust our current shape on each frame. We run through all the colors, control points, and anchor points of the currentPos (we'll take care of establishing currentPos in a moment), find the difference between these values and our destination values, then divide this difference by tweenRate. This will give us the increment value we need to adjust our currentPos by on each frame, to transform from one shape to another. We push these values into the appropriate arrays in our increment object.

The last thing we do is set our object to call the moveLines function every frame. Of course, we'll need to write this function.

6. Place this code directly beneath the previous function:

```
moveLines = function () {
      for (var i = 0; i<endShape.anchorPoints.length; i++) {
            currentPos.controlPoints[i][0] +=
            ➥increment.controlPoints[i][0];
            currentPos.controlPoints[i][1] +=
            ➥increment.controlPoints[i][1];
            currentPos.anchorPoints[i][0] +=
            ➥increment.anchorPoints[i][0];
            currentPos.anchorPoints[i][1] +=
            ➥increment.anchorPoints[i][1];
```

continues overleaf

```
        }
        for (var i = 0; i<endShape.colors.length; i++) {
            var col = convertToRGB(currentPos.colors[i][1]);
            col.r = Math.round(col.r-increment.colors[i].r);
            col.g = Math.round(col.g-increment.colors[i].g);
            col.b = Math.round(col.b-increment.colors[i].b);
            currentPos.colors[i][1] = col.r << 16 | col.g << 8 | col.b;
        }
        drawShape(currentPos);
        tweenCount++;
        if (tweenCount>tweenRate) {
            delete drawObj.onEnterFrame;
            drawobj.onMouseDown = clickCatch;
            drawShape(endShape);
        }
    };
```

This function is what actually takes care of our transformation, though there's not an awful lot to talk about here. It merely adjusts the numbers in our currentPos each frame by the corresponding increment values. Once this is done, it calls drawShape (our drawing function that we wrote way back at the top of the code), and checks to see if this is our final tween frame. If so, it resets everything, stopping the animation and prepares for the next mouse click.

7.   We're almost there. Adjust our drawShape function to deal with our new currentPos object. Update the drawShape function with these new lines (in bold):

```
drawShape = function (shape) {
    drawObj.clear();
    drawObj.lineStyle(2, 0, 100);
    currentColor = 0;
    drawObj.moveTo(shape.anchorPoints[0][0],shape.
    ➥anchorPoints[0][1]);
    for (var i = 0; i<shape.anchorPoints.length-1; i++) {
        if (shape.colors[currentColor][0] == i) {
            drawObj.endFill();
            drawObj.beginFill(shape.colors[currentColor][1], 100);
            currentPos.colors[currentColor] =
            ➥[i, shape.colors[currentColor][1]];
            drawObj.moveTo(shape.anchorPoints[i][0],
            ➥shape.anchorPoints[i][1]);
            currentColor++;
        }
        drawObj.curveTo(shape.controlPoints[i][0],
        ➥shape.controlPoints[i][1], shape.anchorPoints[i+1][0],
```

```
➥shape.anchorPoints[i+1][1]);
    currentPos.controlPoints[i] = [shape.controlPoints[i][0],
    ➥shape.controlPoints[i][1]];
    currentPos.anchorPoints[i] = [shape.anchorPoints[i][0],
    ➥shape.anchorPoints[i][1]];
  }
  currentPos.anchorPoints[i] = [shape.anchorPoints[i][0],
  ➥shape.anchorPoints[i][1]];
};
```

These extra lines store the numbers of our points' current positions so that we can use them in the following frame of our `moveLines` function. Follow the trail and see how these values travel through our movie.

8. Finally, update the `clickCatch` function so that when the user clicks the mouse the tween transformation is triggered. We do this simply by calling `startShift`:

```
clickCatch = function () {
    shapeNum = shapeNum+1>1 ? 0 : shapeNum+1;
    startShift(shapes[shapeNum]);
};
```

9. Now test the movie to see our transforming fruit. Cool!

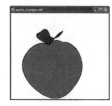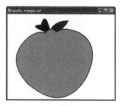

Gradients

So now that we've animated straight lines, curves, and solid fills, it's time we explored the last frontier of the drawing API: gradients. Using gradients, you can create some fairly complex creations with code that would have been impossible to achieve in Flash 5. This is one illustration showing just one of the effects made possible (and created completely) with the drawing API:

Now, as far as gradient creation is concerned, there's an easy way and a not so easy way. The syntax for both is:

```
mcInstance.beginGradientFill(fillType, colors, alphas, ratios,matrix);
```

Wow. Even for the simple type it looks daunting. Let's just jump right in and create a two color linear gradient so we can begin to see how this works (this exercise is `linear_gradients.fla` on the CD).

Linear gradients

1. Create a new movie called `linear_gradients.fla`. In frame 1 of the default layer add this code to draw a square:

    ```
    this.createEmptyMovieClip("square", 0);
    square._x = 270;
    square._y = 200;
    square.moveTo(-100, -100);
    square.lineStyle(2, 0x333333, 100);
    square.lineTo(100, -100);
    square.lineTo(100, 100);
    square.lineTo(-100, 100);
    square.lineTo(-100, -100);
    ```

    This is all pretty straightforward. We create a movie clip called `square` to hold our drawing, then position it at the center of our default movie (270, 200). We then draw a filled shape using `lineTo`. Now onto the color!

2. Above the previous code, type:

    ```
    colors = [0x0000FF, 0xF4620B];
    alphas = [100, 100];
    ratios = [0, 255];
    matrix = {matrixType:"box", x:-100, y:0, w:200, h:200, r:0};
    ```

    This may be a little less straightforward. Still, breaking it down reveals it's not too difficult to set up. First, we define an array of `colors`; in our case this is blue and orange (if you wanted more colors, you'd simply add additional indices to these arrays). In the next line we define an array of the alpha values for each color in the gradient. Then, using the `ratios` array, we specify the points in our gradient where each color is at its maximum value. These values are hexadecimal percentages of the width of our gradient. What we have specified is that the blue color will be at full value at the beginning of our gradient (0% of the gradient's width), and that the orange color will be at full value at the end of our gradient (255, or 100% of the gradient's width). Personally, it would have helped my small math-oriented mind to be able to enter these values as base 10 percents, but we've got the hex percents instead. C'est la vie.

The last line of our variable initialization is to set up matrix. This is a new object containing six properties. The first, matrixType, will always be box. It's the *absence* of matrixType that will be important later. If it's present, though (as it needs to be for the 'easy' type of gradient), it will always be box. We next specify the x and y coordinates of the start of our gradient. I placed the gradient to start at position (-100, 0) in our square clip, which is the left side of our drawn square. w and h are the width and height of our gradient respectively. Since our square is 200x200 pixels, I set the gradient's dimensions to equal those of the square.

Finally I set the rotation (r) of our gradient to be 0 radians. If you do specify a rotation, be aware that it needs to be in radians, so if you wanted the gradient at a 45 degree angle, you'd have to perform a conversion of degrees to radians (radians = degrees*PI/180).

Alright, with these variables set up, let's add the final two lines of code that will fill our square with a linear gradient.

3. Update your code with the following new lines:

```
colors = [0x0000FF, 0xF4620B];
alphas = [100, 100];
ratios = [0, 255];
matrix = {matrixType:"box", x:-100, y:0, w:200, h:200, r:0};
this.createEmptyMovieClip("square", 0);
square._x = 270;
square._y = 200;
square.moveTo(-100, -100);
square.lineStyle(2, 0x333333, 100);
square.beginGradientFill("linear", colors, alphas, ratios, matrix);
square.lineTo(100, -100);
square.lineTo(100, 100);
square.lineTo(-100, 100);
square.lineTo(-100, -100);
square.endFill();
```

4. Test the movie.

5. That's the 'simple' version of the gradient. Try entering other values into the variables to see how the gradient reacts to the changes. Here are a few examples of different linear gradients to try before we move on to the more complex radial type (the code for these are all included as comments in `linear_gradients.fla` on the CD):

Radial gradients

When creating radial gradients the only thing that you need to change is the gradient type 'linear', into 'radial'. That's it. You also need to keep in mind that the x and y properties of the matrix *do not* correspond to the center of the radial gradient. So, to position the hotspot of a gradient in the center of a shape, you might have to do a little bit of simple math. We're going to create a transforming gradient to demonstrate this (take a look at `radial_gradients.swf` on the CD). This gradient is draggable, creating a dynamic radial glow that follows the user's mouse:

1. Create a new movie called `radial_gradients.fla`. Open the Actions panel and add the following code to frame 1 of the default layer:

```
this.createEmptyMovieClip("drawObj", 0);
drawObj._x = 270;
drawObj._y = 200;
drawObj.startSquare = {x:-100, y:-100};
drawObj.squareDim = {w:200, h:200};
```

The first three lines create and set the coordinates of the movie clip. The next two lines create two custom objects as properties of our new `drawObj` movie clip. These hold the x and y starting positions of the drawn square as well as the height and width of the square. We will need all four of these values to create our gradient, which is what we'll do next.

2. Add these lines beneath the previous code:

```
spotlight = {};
spotlight.colors = [0xFF60EC, 0x6F0061];
spotlight.alphas = [100, 100];
spotlight.ratios = [0, 255];
spotlight.matrix = {matrixType:"box", x:drawObj.startSquare.x,
➡y:drawObj.startSquare.y, w:drawObj.squareDim.w,
➡h:drawObj.squareDim.h,
➡r:0};
spotlight.setMatrix = function() {
     this.matrix.x = _root._xmouse+drawObj.startSquare.x-drawObj._x;
     this.matrix.y = _root._ymouse+drawObj.startSquare.y-drawObj._y;
};
```

Here we are creating a custom object to hold the properties of our gradient. This isn't entirely necessary, but it does help to separate gradient types if you use multiple fills in your drawing.

Setting the properties is fairly clear, as it doesn't differ at all from our code in the previous linear gradient example (except we are using variables to set our values). We then add a method that will set the hotspot of our gradient to be under the mouse. Again, using simple math, we take the mouse position, subtract the coordinates of the `drawObj` movie clip and add the starting position of the drawn square. This will effectively offset the starting position of the gradient to the hotspot under the mouse.

3. Continue by adding the following code underneath all the previous lines:

```
drawSquare = function () {
     var right = drawObj.squareDim.w/2;
     var left = -right;
     var bottom = drawObj.squareDim.h/2;
     var top = -bottom;
     drawObj.clear();
     spotlight.setMatrix();
     drawObj.moveTo(left, top);
     drawObj.lineStyle(2, 0x333333, 100);
     drawObj.beginGradientFill("radial", spotlight.colors,
     ➡spotlight.alphas, spotlight.ratios, spotlight.matrix);
     drawObj.lineTo(right, top);
```

continues overleaf

```
                drawObj.lineTo(right, bottom);
                drawObj.lineTo(left, bottom);
                drawObj.endFill();
                updateAfterEvent();
        };
```

Here is our function that will redraw our square each frame. First, we clear the previously drawn square (you need to do this though you might think you are 'drawing over' the previous square). We next call the spotlight object's setMatrix method that we created in the previous step. This will change the matrix values before we redraw the square. The rest of the code is pretty self-explanatory since it's the same square drawing code we've used previously. The only difference is that the values are being set by our earlier variables. We also add an updateAfterEvent to refresh the screen each time the mouse is moved and this code is run, which will prevent the effect from flickering.

4. Finally, let's add the code that will redraw the square whenever the mouse is moved. Type this at the end of all the existing code:

```
drawSquare();
drawObj.onMouseMove = drawSquare;
```

First we call the drawSquare function when the movie starts, then we assign the function to the drawObj's mouseMove event. Test your movie to see this in action:

Note that this will work for a gradient that runs the full width of the square. Once you adjust the width (which will distort the gradient if the width and height are not equal), you'll also need to be play with the setMatrix formulas.

OK, that's one example. How about setting up something that might be useful for future applications?

Dynamic color palette

Here we're going to create a gradient color palette that will allow us to create and edit gradients. Play around with the finished palette (`gradient_palette.swf` on the CD) so you can get an idea of what we're going to create. Adjust the properties of the gradient from radial to linear, and try adding, deleting, and altering colors in the color well. As you play, keep in mind that everything except for the ComboBox component in the upper right of the palette is created dynamically with the drawing API:

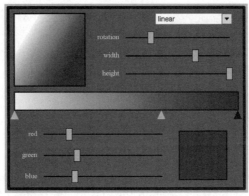

We've started off slow, so let's get stuck in! This exercise is quite long and features some more advanced coding concepts but it's worth it. If you want to compare your file as you go along, you can always refer to the source file `gradient_palette.fla` on the CD. Here we go.

1. Start a new movie. Open your Components panel if it's not currently open (CTRL+F7) and drag out a copy of the **ComboBox** component onto your stage. Now delete it; the component and all of its assets are now stored in the Library, which is exactly where we want them. We'll attach the ComboBox to our stage dynamically in this exercise, and it is the only element of our gradient palette that is pre-built.

2. Create a new movie clip symbol (CTRL+F8) called `colorStopSymbol`. Make sure the **Advanced** options are displayed when you do this, and select **Export for Actionscript**. Flash should then automatically insert the same **Identifier** as the symbol name Click **OK** to accept these options:

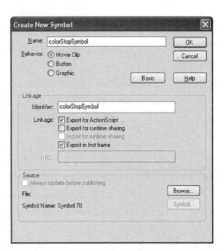

3. Now go ahead and exit Symbol Editing mode to return to the main timeline – we don't need to add anything to our symbol, as this will all be done with ActionScript. We just need a movie clip in the Library that we can extend.

4. Rename the default layer in the main timeline as `actions`. Open the Actions panel and start by adding the following code to frame 1:

```
paletteWidth = 400;
paletteHeight = 300;
gp = this.createEmptyMovieClip("gradientPicker", 0);
gp._x = (Stage.width-paletteWidth)/2;
gp._y = (Stage.height-paletteHeight)/2;
gp.lineStyle(5, 0, 100);
gp.beginFill(0x777777, 100);
gp.lineTo(paletteWidth, 0);
gp.lineTo(paletteWidth, paletteHeight);
gp.lineTo(0, paletteHeight);
gp.endFill();
```

We first set the height and width of our gradient color palette, create the movie clip that will hold that palette, then position the clip to the center of the stage by accessing the properties of the Stage object. Then we use the drawing API to draw a gray box for the palette background. This should all be familiar.

5. Continuing on, add this underneath the previous lines:

```
gradTypes = ["linear", "radial"];
gradNum = 0;
sorter = function (a, b) {
    return a[0]>b[0];
};
setGrad = function () {
    colors = [];
    alphas = [];
    ratios = [];
    stops = [];
    for (var i = 0; i<well.colorStops.length; i++) {
        stops.push([well.colorStops[i]._x, well.colorStops[i]]);
    }
    stops.sort(sorter);
    for (var i = 0; i<stops.length; i++) {
        colors.push(stops[i][1].stopColor);
        alphas.push(100);
        ratios.push(stops[i][1].getValue()*255);
    }
```

```
        sample.drawGrad();
        well.drawGrad();
};
```

This code can get a little confusing since we're referencing objects that haven't been created yet, so bear with me. This is the start of the section of code dealing with the swatches. There will be three in the final movie:

- The **gradient sample** (`sample`) in the upper left of the palette that will preview the gradient result.

- The **gradient well** (`well`), the range bar in the center of the palette, which will hold all of the color stops where we mix and define the gradient.

- The **solid color swatch** (`swatch`) in the lower right of the palette that will display the color of the currently selected color swatch.

In the code above, we first set our two types of gradient (linear or radial) as strings in the `gradTypes` array. We will access these when we set the gradient for the gradient sample. The `gradNum` simply holds the current index of the `gradTypes` array.

We next have a `sorter` function, which will sort through our two-dimensional array. I'll address this in a moment.

The `setGrad` function runs through all the `colorStops` (the little triangles underneath the color well in the screenshot at the start of this exercise) and creates gradient values based on their colors and `_x` positions. It first initializes all the arrays (`colors`, `alphas`, and `ratios`), the purpose of each you should be familiar with now. The `stops` array will hold the `_x` positions of all of our `colorStop` movie clips, as well as references to the clips themselves.

The first `for` loop then runs through each `colorStop` (references to each are stored in `well`'s `colorStops` array, which we set up shortly) and places the `colorStop`'s `_x` position and the object itself into this two-dimensional `stops` array. With that array set, we sort it based on our `sorter` function. We must sort this array because we need to know the order of the `colorStops` based on their current `_x` position. Since the `_x` position order will *not* be the order of creation (additional `colorStops` can be added wherever a user clicks, and these of course can be moved to any position on the well), we need to sort the `colorStops` into an order from the lowest `_x` position to the highest. Therefore, we might read their values for our gradient. It's the `Array.sort` method and our `sorter` function that allow this. The `Array.sort` method accepts a compare method by which to sort by.

The easiest one to use (and I've found the most useful) is one that will sort numbers in order of value:

```
sorter = function(a, b) {
    return a > b
}
```

This pseudo code will sort numbers in ascending order (changing greater than (>) to less than (<) will likewise sort in descending order). a and b represent two adjacent values in our array. Flash will go through the entirety of the array that is sent and 'shuffle' all the values about until they are sorted. To sort an array of multiple dimensions, you simply need to specify in your sorter method which index to sort by. In our palette exercise, we've used the array's first index, which is the colorStop's _x property. This effectively sorts our colorStops in order from the left of the screen to the right.

With the colorStops sorted, we run through our sorted array and place values into our gradient arrays based on the order of the colorStops. Each colorStop has a stopColor property that we push into colors. Each color will be at full opacity (which can be adjusted if you want to later), so we simply push 100 into our alphas array.

Finally, we call the getValue method of our colorStops, which will return a percentage value of where that colorStop sits on the full width of the color well. We multiply this percentage by 255 to get our ratio (remember, ratios are between 0 and 255).

With our arrays filled, we tell our sample and well to go fill themselves (but in a nice way).

6. Next, we write the methods which will actually fill the gradient swatches with color. this.w and this.h are properties of each of our sample, swatch, and well clips (we will assign these values at the end when we actually create the clips) which hold the height and width of the movie clips:

```
drawGrad = function () {
    this.clear();
    this.lineStyle(2, 0, 100);
    if (this == well) {
        type = "linear";
    } else {
        type = gradTypes[gradNum];
    }
    this.beginGradientFill(type, colors, alphas, ratios,
    ➥this.matrix);
    this.moveTo(0, 0);
    this.lineTo(this.w, 0);
    this.lineTo(this.w, this.h);
    this.lineTo(0, this.h);
```

continues overleaf

```
               this.endFill();
       };

       drawSolid = function () {
               this.clear();
               this.lineStyle(2, 0, 100);
               this.beginFill(getSliderValues(), 100);
               this.moveTo(0, 0);
               this.lineTo(this.w, 0);
               this.lineTo(this.w, this.h);
               this.lineTo(0, this.h);
               this.endFill();
       };
```

Both `drawGrad` and `drawSolid` create filled squares, the difference being their fill type. `drawGrad` takes care of both our gradient swatches (`well` and `sample`), while `drawSolid` handles `swatch`. The only things to note are: the `if` statement in `drawGrad`, which handles setting the `gradientType` for `sample` (`well` is always linear); and the `getSliderValues` function in `drawSolid`. This function, which we'll write when we get to our color sliders, will return a hex value based on the color sliders' current position.

7.   Add these lines to finish off our swatches section:

```
       colorSample = function () {
               var w = sample.w*wSlider.getValue()+1;
               var h = sample.h*hSlider.getValue()+1;
               var x = (sample.w-w)/2;
               var y = (sample.h-h)/2;
               sample.matrix = {matrixType:"box", x:x, y:y, w:w, h:h,
               ➥r:rotSlider.getValue()*Math.PI};
               sample.drawGrad();
       };

       colorSwatch = function () {
               swatch.drawSolid();
               well.selected.stopColor = getSliderValues();
               setGrad();
       };

       changeGrad = function () {
               gradNum = gradNum+1>1 ? 0 : gradNum+1;
               sample.drawGrad();
       };
```

The first function here colors our gradient `sample` swatch. The width and height of the gradient are determined by the positions of the `wSlider` and `hSlider` respectively. The sliders' `getValue` method returns a percentage, which we then multiply by the `swatch`'s full width and height (the reason we add 1 to these values is to prevent odd results with our gradient if it has a width or height of less than 1). The `x` and `y` starting point of the gradient is adjusted based on these values (so that the gradient remains centered in the swatch and not offset). We can then populate our matrix object with these values, along with our rotation value that will be a radians value between 0 and pi, and call `sample`'s `drawGrad` method.

`colorSwatch` handles the coloring of our solid filled swatch, which is called every time a color slider is dragged. We first draw the actual swatch itself by using `drawSolid`. We then set the currently selected `colorStop`'s color to the values of our color sliders. We adjust the gradient to match using `setGrad`, then recolor our gradient swatches.

`changeGrad` is the simplest of all (thankfully!). It simply toggles the current gradient type between index 0 and 1, then redraws `sam` to suit. This is called whenever our **ComboBox** is clicked.

We're one third down! Let's keep plowing on.

8.   It's now time to write our `colorStop` code that will handle the little triangular clips underneath our color well (we'll use a capitalized ColorStop when speaking of the Class, and `colorStop` when speaking of instances of the Class). It's a lot of code for such a tiny graphic, but it handles quite a lot. What we will do is create a new Class of MovieClip that holds all of the original properties and methods of the MovieClip, as well as the `ColorStop` properties and methods. Add this underneath all the previous code:

```
ColorStop = function () {
    this.init();
};
ColorStop.prototype = new MovieClip();
ColorStop.prototype.init = function() {
    this._parent.stopDepth++;
    this._parent.colorStops.push(this);
    this.onPress = this.dragMe;
    this.onRelease = this.onReleaseOutside = this.releaseMe;
    this.selectMe();
    setGrad();
};
```

Here's the start of our Class definition, which looks a lot like every other function. You'll notice, that the only thing we do when this function is called is call another function called `init`. `init` is actually a function (or method) that belongs solely to the ColorStop Class itself. If you look down to the `init` method, you will see we increment our depth variable to make way for the next `colorStop` and push the current `colorStop` (the one just created) into our array. We then assign functions to the `colorStop`'s `onPress`, `onRelease`, and `onReleaseOutside` event handlers. These functions (`dragMe` and `releaseMe`) are methods we will create in a moment.

You'll notice that we have attached this `init` method to the `prototype` property of our ColorStop object. The `prototype` is a property of an object that holds all of the other methods and properties of that object. By attaching the `init` method to the `prototype` property of ColorStop, we are ensuring that all `colorStop` instances will be able to use this method without having to duplicate it. Imagine having to duplicate a function for every single instance! Using `prototype`, we don't have to, as every instance will have a reference to it in the `prototype` property.

There's one last line in the above code that we need to address:

```
ColorStop.prototype = new MovieClip();
```

This sets up inheritance for our ColorStop object. By setting its `prototype` property to be a new instance of the MovieClip Class (notice the capitalization), we have caused our ColorStop Class to inherit all of the properties and methods of the MovieClip Class.

9. Immediately after the previous code, type the following:

```
ColorStop.prototype.dragMe = function() {
    this.startDrag(0, 0, this._y, this._parent._width-well._x,
    ➡this._y);
    this.selectMe();
    this.onMouseMove = function() {
        setGrad();
        if (this._ymouse>25) {
            this._parent.selected = null;
            for (var i = 0; i<this._parent.colorStops.length; i++){
                if (this._parent.colorStops[i] == this) {
                    this._parent.colorStops.splice(i, 1);
                    this.removeMovieClip();
                    setGrad();
                    break;
                }
            }
        }
    };
};
```

continues overleaf

```
ColorStop.prototype.releaseMe = function() {
    stopDrag();
    delete this.onMouseMove;
};
```

dragMe has a lot of nesting, but is pretty easy to deal with. It first allows the horizontal drag of the colorStop and calls its selectMe method (which will be created in a moment). It then sets a new function to be called onMouseMove that resets the gradient based on the colorStop movements. Finally, it checks to see as the user is dragging the colorStop whether it is being dragged down off the well. If it is, then it removes the colorStop from the colorStops array and from the stage.

With the releaseMe function, which is called on the colorStop's onRelease and onReleaseOutside events, the clip dragging is stopped and the onMouseMove function created in the method above is deleted.

10. Here's an easy one. Type this after the previous code:

```
ColorStop.prototype.drawMe = function(col) {
    this.clear();
    this.beginFill(col, 100);
    this.lineTo(7, 15);
    this.lineTo(-7, 15);
    this.endFill();
};
```

The drawMe method draws a triangle of the fill color specified in the function call. Note that to draw a triangle, we only need a starting position ((0,0) since that is where the starting position is by default), two sides and an endFill, which automatically closes our shape, drawing the final side of the triangle. So far, so good.

11. Add these three methods to finish off the ColorStop Class:

```
ColorStop.prototype.selectMe = function() {
    for (var i = 0; i<this._parent.colorStops.length; i++) {
        this._parent.colorStops[i].deselectMe();
    }
    this.drawMe(0);
    well.selected = this;
    setSliderValues();
};

ColorStop.prototype.deselectMe = function() {
    this.drawMe(0xCCCCCC);
};
```

```
ColorStop.prototype.getValue = function() {
    return this._x/this._parent._width;
};
```

OK. selectMe first runs through all the colorStops and deselects them (recolors them gray as per the next method). It then redraws the newly selected colorStop with a black fill, places a reference to itself in the selected variable, and sets the color sliders to match its current color. deselectMe simply colors the colorStop a light gray. Finally, getValue will return the position of the current colorStop as a percentage of the width of the well. Breaking it down, if the width of the well is 100, and the current colorStop has an _x value of 50, then getValue will return .5 (50/100). This percentage will be used when determining the ratio of this color in our gradient.

12. To make our colorStop work as an extension of the MovieClip object, we need to do a few more things. Add these lines of code:

```
Object.registerClass("colorStopSymbol", ColorStop);
makeColorStop = function (x, col) {
    well.attachMovie("colorStopSymbol", "h"+well.stopDepth,
    ➥well.stopDepth,{_x:x, _y:well.h, stopColor:col});
};
```

Object.registerClass allows us to associate a symbol stored in the Library with a new Class definition. You will recall the empty movie clip symbol in our Library that we created at the start of this project. Its Linkage identifier is the first parameter of the registerClass method. The second parameter is the name of the Class itself. Now, any time we attach one of these clips to the stage, it will automatically be an instance of the ColorStop Class!

The makeColorStop function is called whenever our color well button is clicked (you'll see this shortly). It only needs one line of code that attaches our empty movie clip to the stage and gives it its initial properties. Our class definition does the rest! Of course, to allow colorStop to inherit the properties and methods of the MovieClip object, we need to set colorStop's prototype property to be a new movie clip. We then register our class with Object, giving it the Linkage ID of our symbol in the Library (colorStopSymbol).

Whew! Half way there and we're not even winded.

13. This next section deals with all of our sliders, which, again, are created entirely with the drawing API. Add this underneath all of the previous code:

```
createSlider = function (instance, label, depth, x, y, height, width,
➥func) {
    this[instance] = gp.createEmptyMovieClip(instance+depth, depth);
```

continues overleaf

```
                    var slider = this[instance];
                    slider._x = x;
                    slider._y = y;
                    slider.createTextField("label", 0, -20, 0, 10, 10);
                    slider.label.autoSize = "right";
                    slider.label.text = label;
                    slider.label.textColor = 0xFFFFFF;
                    slider.label.bold = 1;
                    slider.lineStyle(2, 0, 100);
                    slider.moveTo(0, height/2);
                    slider.lineTo(width, height/2);
                    var s = slider.createEmptyMovieClip("slider", 10);
                    s.lineStyle(1, 0, 100);
                    s.moveTo(-height/4, 0);
                    s.beginFill(0xCCCCCC, 100);
                    s.lineTo(height/4, 0);
                    s.lineTo(height/4, height);
                    s.lineTo(-height/4, height);
                    s.endFill();
                    s.onPress = function() {
                        this.startDrag(0, 0, 0, width, 0);
                        this.onMouseMove = func;
                    };
                    s.range = width;
                    var releaseMe = function () {
                        delete this.onMouseMove;
                        stopDrag();
                    };
                    s.onRelease = s.onReleaseOutside=releaseMe;
                    slider.getValue = function() {
                        return s._x/s.range;
                    };
                    slider.setValue = function(val) {
                        s._x = val/100*s.range;
                    };
                };
```

It's long, but straightforward. We create a new movie clip to hold our slider. We then create a text field for a label, and place it and format it over the next several lines. The drawing API is then called in to draw a horizontal line.

The slider itself is a new movie clip since we want to able to drag it around and check its _x property. The first block of API code is simply drawing a rectangle. The rectangle height is determined by the height variable sent. Its width will be one half of that height. We then set its onPress event to enable the slider to be dragged horizontally.

The function we assign to the onMouseMove event is sent with the initial function call, which allows us to have different sliders with separate functions. There's nothing new with the release methods, but note the two ending methods that set and retrieve the value of the slider. getValue, like the ColorStop.getValue method we created above, returns the _x position of the slider as a percentage of the total width of the slider. setValue simply reverses that, placing the slider at a specific position on the slider range.

14. Here are the final functions for our sliders (yes, final!):

```
getSliderValues = function () {
    var r = redSlider.getValue()*255;
    var g = greenSlider.getValue()*255;
    var b = blueSlider.getValue()*255;
    return r << 16 | g << 8 | b;
};
setSliderValues = function () {
    var hex = well.selected.stopColor.toString(16);
    while (hex.length<6) {
        hex = "0"+hex;
    }
    var r = parseInt(hex.substr(0, 2), 16);
    var g = parseInt(hex.substr(2, 2), 16);
    var b = parseInt(hex.substr(4, 2), 16);
    redSlider.setValue(r/2.55);
    greenSlider.setValue(g/2.55);
    blueSlider.setValue(b/2.55);
    swatch.drawSolid();
};
```

Although we created the functions to get and set the individual slider values, the three color sliders really work together so we create these two functions specifically for them. The first, getSliderValues, retrieves the value of each slider (a percentage), multiplies it by 255, then does some bit shifting to return a hex value.

Bit shifting, not easily explained in a paragraph, shifts our values into proper positions to be added together as a base 10 number and used for our color values. For instance, the base 10 value for yellow is 16776960 and its hex equivalent is FFFF00. The hex value split into three separate color channels gives us 255(FF), 255, and 0 for red, green, and blue respectively. If we start with these three values, how do we get back to a base 10 composite of all three channels? Well, we can use the bitwise left shift operator << to *shift* the values into their proper position. The bitwise left shift operator, which make a lot more sense if you're working in binary, multiplies a number by a specified power of 2. 255<<16 multiplies 255 by 2 raised to the power of 16, which is how far we need to shift the red value for our hex number. If you enter this into a calculator, the operation will return 16711680.

We then perform the same operation on the green value, but multiply it only by 2 raised to the power of 8, and get 65280. We don't need to shift the blue value at all. The bitwise OR operator | adds these numbers together (that's the simplified explanation, but true for our purposes). Our final shifted numbers for 255, 255, 0 are 16711680, 65280, and 0 respectively. Add these together and you get 16776960, the color value for yellow.

Back to the code.

`setSliderValues` does the opposite of `getSliderValues` whenever a `colorStop` is selected (which forces the color swatch to change to show `colorStop`'s color). It first looks at the color value of the selected `colorStop` and changes it into a hex value, adding the extra zeros until we have a string of six characters. It then separates each individual color component and sets the corresponding sliders to match. We created the exact same function in our fruit tweening animation.

We're almost there now, I promise!

15. This next chunk merely creates all of the necessary sliders. To refresh you on what `createSlider`'s arguments are, here's a quick reminder (`instanceName`, `labelText`, `depth`, `_x`, `_y`, `height`, `width`, `functionToBePerformed`). Add this code beneath all the previous lines:

```
createSlider("rotSlider", "rotation", 200, 200, 40, 20, 175,
➡colorSample);
createSlider("wSlider", "width", 201, 200, 70, 20, 175, colorSample);
wSlider.setValue(100);
createSlider("hSlider", "height", 202, 200, 100, 20, 175,
➡colorSample);
hSlider.setValue(100);
createSlider("redSlider", "red", 203, 60, 200, 20, 200, colorSwatch);
createSlider("greenSlider", "green", 204, 60, 235, 20, 200,
➡colorSwatch);
createSlider("blueSlider", "blue", 205, 60, 270, 20, 200,
➡colorSwatch);
```

All we're doing here is calling the `createSlider` function and sending the necessary parameters. Ideally, these values would be altered by changing the initial `paletteWidth` and `paletteHeight` variables located at the top of the code, but that would have meant even more code! I'll leave this up to you if you want to adapt it.

16. Just two blocks of code to go and we're done. All that's left to do is to create the graphics to house all the above functions. Add this first section:

```
well = gp.createEmptyMovieClip("well", 5);
```

continues overleaf

```
well._x = 10;
well._y = 140;
well.w = 380;
well.h = 30;
well.colorStops = [];
well.stopDepth = 0;
makeColorStop(0, 0xFFFFFF);
makeColorStop(well.w, 0x000000);
stopMaker = gp.createEmptyMovieClip("stopMaker", 0);
stopMaker._x = well._x;
stopMaker._y = well._y+well.h;
stopMaker.onPress = function() {
    makeColorStop(this._xmouse, getSliderValues());
};
stopMaker.beginFill(0, 0);
stopMaker.lineTo(well.w, 0);
stopMaker.lineTo(well.w, well.h);
stopMaker.lineTo(0, well.h);
stopMaker.endFill();
```

well will be our gradient well, and here we set up our two initial colorStops. stopMaker is the invisible button that will lie beneath well. Clicking on this will create colorStops. It is important to have this functionality separate from the well itself as the colorStops will have their own onPress events and we don't want them overridden by this invisible button (which is also why we set stopMaker's depth underneath well's).

Notice that on the onPress event we call our makeColorStop function, which attaches an instance of our custom Class on the stage. If you look back at this function, you will see that it accepts two parameters, an _x position and a color. The _x position is determined by the location of the mouse clicks, but the color must be processed. So, instead of sending a color directly, we call our getSliderValues function, which will return a color value based on our three color slider positions.

17. As promised, here's the last section of code:

```
sample = gp.createEmptyMovieClip("sample", 10);
sample._x = 10;
sample._y = 10;
sample.w = 120;
sample.h = 120;
swatch = gp.createEmptyMovieClip("swatch", 15);
swatch._x = 290;
swatch._y = 205;
swatch.w = 80;
swatch.h = 80;
```

377

continues overleaf

```
gradType = gp.attachMovie("FComboBoxSymbol", "gradType", 20);
gradType._x = 250;
gradType._y = 10;
gradType.width = 130;
gradType.addItem("linear");
gradType.addItem("radial");
gradType.setChangeHandler("changeGrad", this);
sample.matrix = {matrixType:"box", x:0, y:0, w:sample.w, h:sample.h,
➥r:0};
well.matrix = {matrixType:"box", x:0, y:0, w:well.w, h:well.h, r:0};
sample.drawGrad = drawGrad;
well.drawGrad = drawGrad;
swatch.drawSolid = drawSolid;
swatch.drawSolid();
setGrad();
```

Here at last are the clips that we've been referring to throughout! sample and swatch come and join well to bask in the fruits of all our work. gradType is our ComboBox (OK, Macromedia did all the work on that one!), which we add our gradient strings to. We give it the changeGrad function to run whenever the ComboBox is clicked on.

Finally, after setting up our original matrices for the gradients, we give them drawGrad methods of their own, and call the drawing methods for all the swatches (setGrad calls both sample.drawGrad and well.drawGrad()).

18. Voila! Test your movie and try the palette out. We've got a fully functional gradient palette with an almost empty Library. Don't you just love the drawing API?

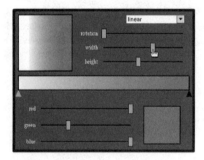 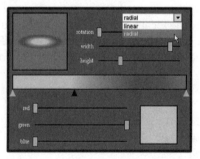

Transformation matrix

Do you remember when I said earlier that there was a simple way to handle gradients and a more complex way? Well, I did. The alternative takes all the same parameters as in the way we've been working with beginGradientFill so far, but differs in the formation of the matrix.

If you look in the Reference panel (**Window > Reference**) for `beginGradientFill`, you'll see the second type of matrix listed as a 3x3 transformation matrix:

OK, let's break this down a bit as it doesn't really give us much more detail. This won't be a lesson in linear algebra but more of a (what is technically known as) 'what-you-need-to-know-to-use-it' exercise. (I'm no math teacher, and I'm sure you'll find many an exhaustive tome dealing with the subject if you want to know more.) Sure, we could talk about identity matrices, inversions, and dot and cross products, but it's really not necessary for our purposes here.

The first thing to know is what exactly a matrix is: a rectangular array of numbers. That's it. A box that stores numbers. It's the structure of the box that's special and allows math to step in and do amazing things. But how does this particular box relate to the properties of a gradient?

Well, basically, if you are just plugging in numbers, you can disregard the third column. (Of course, if you're just plugging in numbers and leaving a static gradient, there's no reason why you couldn't use the first form of the matrix and leave this 3x3 stuff alone. Where the power of this second method comes into play is when we want to transform and animate a gradient, since the 3x3 structure allows for operations to transform the matrix and thus the gradient as well.) The other six properties deal with the translation, scale, and rotation of our gradient.

But how? Well, to transform an existing matrix, we simply multiply it by a matrix containing our transform. If you've never seen an example of matrix multiplication, it looks a lot like this:

$$
\left\{ \begin{array}{ccc} a & b & c \\ d & e & f \\ g & h & i \end{array} \right\} \times \left\{ \begin{array}{ccc} a^1 & b^1 & c^1 \\ d^1 & e^1 & f^1 \\ g^1 & h^1 & i^1 \end{array} \right\} = \left\{ \begin{array}{ccc} a^1a^1+b^1d^1+c^1g^1 & a^1b^1+b^1e^1+c^1h^1 & a^1c^1+b^1f^1+c^1i^1 \\ d^1a^1+e^1d^1+f^1g^1 & d^1b^1+e^1e^1+f^1h^1 & d^1c^1+e^1f^1+f^1i^1 \\ g^1a^1+h^1d^1+i^1g^1 & g^1b^1+h^1e^1+i^1h^1 & g^1c^1+h^1f^1+i^1i^1 \end{array} \right\}
$$

Using this process, you could possibly set up a matrix class that performs that operation for you (that part's just simple math – addition and multiplication) and store the necessary transform matrices that will alter our gradients.

Thankfully – for both you and me – someone has made it easy for us to begin playing with matrix transformations by doing just that. If you have your Flash MX CD handy, check in the **Goodies/Macromedia/Other Samples** folder for a file called `transformmatrix.as`. (Alternatively, you can grab it from this book's CD.) This ActionScript file, written by Christopher Thilgen at Macromedia, holds a matrix class to easily handle the transforms of our gradient matrix. Go ahead and open it up in a text editor to peruse the code.

What the wonderful Mr. Thilgen has provided us with are some methods to help, as he puts it, "simplify the process of building matrices to pass to the Flash MX drawing functions". Thank you, Mr. Thilgen! If you look closely at the code, you'll see what he has done – the class contains scaling, translation, and rotation matrices, and a method called `concat`, which performs our matrix multiplication as shown above.

The transform matrices for our gradient are listed as:

- Translation

$$
\left\{ \begin{array}{ccc} 1 & 0 & 0 \\ 0 & 1 & 0 \\ tx & ty & 1 \end{array} \right\}
$$

- Rotation

$$
\left\{ \begin{array}{ccc} \cos(r) & \sin(r) & 0 \\ -\sin(r) & \cos(r) & 0 \\ 0 & 0 & 1 \end{array} \right\}
$$

- Scale

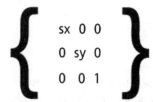

By multiplying these matrices by our original matrix, we can easily transform our gradients to create some fantastic effects.

Let's make a simple sunrise to test out these methods.

Gradient transform 1: sunrise blues

1. Create and save a new movie. Also copy the `transformmatrix.as` file into the same directory as this new movie.

2. Open the Actions panel, and with frame 1 of the default layer selected, type in the following code:

```
#include "transformmatrix.as"

this.createEmptyMovieClip("grad", 1);
colors = [0xDEFFFF, 0x000033];
alphas = [100, 100];
ratios = [0, 255];

matrix = new TransformMatrix();

matrix.rotate(-90);
matrix.scale(400, 550);
matrix.translate(0, 800);

drawGrad = function () {
    matrix.translate(0, -5);
    this.clear();
    this.beginGradientFill("linear", colors, alphas, ratios,
    ➡matrix);
    this.moveTo(0, 0);
    this.lineTo(550, 0);
    this.lineTo(550, 400);
```

continues overleaf

```
            this.lineTo(0, 400);
            this.endFill();
    };

    grad.onEnterFrame = drawGrad;
```

The majority of this code is old hat for you by now. The only unfamiliar lines are those few dealing with the matrix transformations. First, we make a new instance of the matrix object as defined in `transformmatrix.as`. We rotate our new matrix by -90 degrees (the object takes care of the conversion to radians), and scale it to 400x550. Performing this scaling on our original empty matrix will scale it to match the height and width of our default stage.

Though it might be deceptive in this example, remember that when you are performing the scaling operation, you are multiplying the existing scale by your new values, so if you scale by 2, it will double the existing scale.

We then translate our gradient 800 pixels down, enabling us to translate it slowly up each frame, creating our sunrise effect.

3. Go ahead and test the movie. Sit back and relax as the navy blue night turns slowly to day (at 12 fps this is a smooth and gradual change so be patient).

That was short and sweet, but quite simple. How about something a little juicier?

Gradient transform 2: rotation

1. Start a fresh movie (making sure it is in the same directory as the `transformmatrix.as` file). Open the Actions panel and add the following code to frame 1 of the main timeline:

```
#include "transformmatrix.as"

colors = [0xE7D2EC, 0xE7D2EC, 0xE7D2EC];
alphas = [0, 100, 0];
ratios = [128, 192, 255];
gradType = ["radial", "linear"];
gradNum = 0;

drawGrad = function () {
    this.matrix.rotate(this.rot);
    this.clear();
    this.beginGradientFill(gradType[gradNum], colors, alphas, ratios,
    ➥this.matrix);
    this.moveTo(-275, -200);
    this.lineTo(275, -200);
```

```
            this.lineTo(275, 200);
            this.lineTo(-275, 200);
            this.endFill();
    };

    for (i=1; i<5; i++) {
            var grad = _root.createEmptyMovieClip("grad"+i, i);
            grad._x = 275;
            grad._y = 200;
            grad.matrix = new TransformMatrix();
            grad.matrix.scale(200, 400);
            grad.onEnterFrame = drawGrad;
            grad.rot = (i%2>0) ? 5 : -5;
    }

    grad1.matrix.rotate(90);
    grad2.matrix.rotate(90);
    this.onMouseDown = function() {
            gradNum = gradNum+1>1 ? 0 : gradNum+1;
    };
```

Note in the above code that we move all four movie clips to the center of our default stage. We do this since the rotate method rotates around our clip's registration point and I wanted this effect to occur at the center of the stage, not in the upper left corner. I also added an onMouseDown handler to toggle between a linear and radial gradient. Try to predict the effect this will make before you test your movie to see how well you're beginning to understand creating gradients with the drawing API.

If you are unfamiliar with the modulo operator (%), this returns the remainder in the division of your two operands, so 5%2 would return 1 (5 divided by 2 has a remainder of 1). This is a quick way to determine an odd or even number. Any even number divided by two will not have a remainder, whereas an odd number will have a remainder of 1. So by testing for this, we can rotate our alternate clips in different directions.

2. Make the background of your movie black, then test your movie. Remember to click to toggle between the two states:

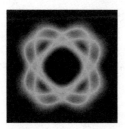 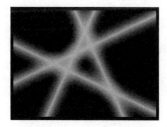

There's one more effect for you to try before we give the transformation matrices a rest (they've been working hard!).

Gradient transform 3: fading gradients

1. Start a new movie and, as usual, check it is saved in the same directory as `transformmatrix.as`. Type the following code in frame 1 of the main timeline:

```
#include "transformmatrix.as"

gradDepth = 1;
grads = [];

makeGrad = function () {
        var grad = this.createEmptyMovieClip("grad"+gradDepth,
        ➥gradDepth);
        grad._x = 275;
        grad._y = 200;
        grad._alpha = 10;
        grad.matrix = new TransformMatrix();
        grad.matrix.scale(5, 10);
        grads.push(grad);
        gradDepth++;
};

colors = [0x000000, 0xFFFFFF, 0x000000, 0xFFFFFF, 0x000000];
alphas = [0, 100, 0, 100, 0];
ratios = [0, 64, 128, 192, 255];

gradType = ["linear", "radial"];
gradNum = 0;

drawGrads = function () {
        for (var i = 0; i<grads.length; i++) {
                var grad = grads[i];
                grad._alpha += 2;
                grad.matrix.scale(1.1, 1.1);
                grad.matrix.rotate(5);
                grad.clear();
                grad.beginGradientFill(gradType[gradNum], colors, alphas,
                ➥ratios,grad.matrix);
                grad.moveTo(-275, -200);
                grad.lineTo(275, -200);
```

```
            grad.lineTo(275, 200);
            grad.lineTo(-275, 200);
            grad.endFill();
            if (grad.matrix.b>2000) {
                grad.removeMovieClip();
                grads.shift();
            }
        }
    };

    this.onEnterFrame = drawGrads;
    this.onMouseDown = function() {
        gradNum = gradNum+1>1 ? 0 : gradNum+1;
    };
    setInterval(this, "makeGrad", 1000);
```

In this code we have we set up a function to create gradients. If you jump to the bottom of the code, you'll see that we use `setInterval` to call this function every 1000 milliseconds. Each gradient will initially be small and faded, then in each `drawGrads` call, it will scale up in size and opacity. When it gets too big for its britches, it's removed.

2. Now make the background of the movie black and test your movie. Be sure to try the linear/radial toggle with the mouse!

 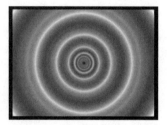

One important note to keep in mind is that gradients are quite processor intensive for Flash, especially those that completely fill the stage (or animate across its entirety). You should keep this in mind as you explore creating gradients and finding new ways to animate them.

These few exercises are just the tip of the iceberg with matrices. You could take this further by applying the transformations of one object onto another, and possibly scaling to match the other object's proportions. Or, perhaps, you could try tweening between two gradients using their transform values. We'll doubtless see those blessed with higher math skills (maybe that's you!) creating some fantastic experiments and effects in the coming months. I'll be looking out for them.

Summary

With these new drawing API methods and a little creativity and application, there's very little that can't be accomplished. The fact is, though, we haven't even begun to see the potential of what can be done with these new commands: dynamic masking, 3D engines, interfaces that intelligently redraw to match the browser, games that generate graphics at run-time, interactive drawing for user application. These are all now possible with the drawing API and some creative invention.

section 2: ActionScript Interfaces

chapter 10: **3D with the drawing API**

I remember when I was but a small lad and my parents took me to the movies to see the latest attempt at 3D film. It was absolutely awful in retrospect, but to my adolescent mind it was an extraordinary experience. I walked out of that cinema in awe and said to my parents, entirely in earnest, "I wish the *real* world was 3D, too!"

My point (other than to suggest I was a slow-minded youth) is that 3D work can easily inspire wonder and amazement, but if its only purpose is to attempt to inspire this wonder and amazement, chances are you'll end up with something like *Jaws 3D*. Like any effect or technique used in site design and animation, 3D should be included to support the content, not simply for eye candy. Keep this fact in mind as you work through these next two chapters, and think about how you might use Flash 3D elements to support and enhance your own designs.

Methods for 3D

Before we get into utilizing the drawing API to create 3D shapes through code, let's quickly take an important look at the alternative methods of incorporating 3D content in your Flash work.

Pre-rendered

This is the easiest method of the lot, if you have the resources. A program like Electric Rain's Swift 3D is dedicated to producing vector images for your Flash movies. Electric Rain also produces plug-ins to export Flash movies from Discreet's 3ds max, NewTek's LightWave, and Softimage. Electric Image's Amorphium Pro also produces Flash output that can be brought directly into your movies. Using these programs and others, you can quickly render stills or multiple frames of animation, and then use ActionScript to manipulate the images inside Flash. Drawbacks of these programs include the cost, of course, but also the file size of the exported movies can be very large at times. Still, these programs enable you to produce images that are simply not possible within the limitations Flash, as we'll discuss shortly.

Approximated illustrations

Believe me, artists were producing 3D imagery long before the invention of the microprocessor. If all you are looking to produce is a static 3D image, then there's no reason why you couldn't make this yourself without the aid of any expensive 3D software. With an image-editing program like Adobe Photoshop you can create faux-3D images that are startlingly real (check out Bert Monroy's web site at **www.bertmonroy.com** to see some fantastic evidence of this). Even within Flash, you can still produce some terrific 3D effects and images using only the drawing tools and knowledge of perspective and lighting.

Real-time 3D

And here's the reason you're reading this chapter in the first place. With a little math (um, or a lot of math), you can create 3D objects at run-time just using code. The drawing API is a big help here since the creation and filling of polygons at run-time is now possible. Though you could work around this in Flash 5 by skewing triangles, it was an imperfect solution as gaps often appeared in objects and the skewing calculations bogged down the processor.

The processing load is still a concern with 3D in Macromedia Flash MX, but there are ways to ease the strain to a certain extent. One way is to avoid attempting to create complete, animated, 3D environments using ActionScript alone. You're not going to make *Halo*, sorry. If you wish to explore fully interactive 3D worlds then look into Flash's big brother, Macromedia Director. Despite debates in the online Flash forums over the relevancy of Director and the equality between the two programs, Director is simply *more powerful* and the 3D capabilities of its latest version can perform astonishing things that are impossible in Flash.

But wait! Before you head off grumbling that you bought the wrong program (we both know that's not true), the benefits of Flash 3D can outweigh those of Shockwave 3D (produced in Director). For one, the Flash Player is simply more ubiquitous than the Shockwave Player. This means that more people will be able to view your Flash 3D content immediately, while they would have to download the relatively larger player to view your Shockwave 3D content. Also, because of the complexity of some of the Shockwave 3D environments, the file sizes are much larger, and sometimes too great for users on slower connections. Until broadband connections are the norm, Flash has the upper hand.

3D concepts reviewed

It's important to review the basic concepts of 3D before we start on the code that will produce our Flash 3D. Now, don't start flipping back through the pages to find where these 3D concepts were discussed initially; they weren't. But, if we're to get to the practical applications of coded, run-time 3D, we have to get started quickly. Because of this, and because friends of ED have already published numerous books with chapters dealing with these concepts (such as Michael Bedar's comprehensive chapter in *Flash 5 ActionScript Studio*), I'm going to work with the assumption that you have at least explored some of these ideas yourself. In this way we can quickly get to the exciting new ground of utilizing the drawing API to extend these standard concepts and methods.

Axes

Your computer screen has two axes, x and y. You use these all the time when accessing the _x, _y, _xscale and _yscale properties of your objects. The x-axis runs horizontally across your screen while the y-axis runs vertically. In 3D, as the name implies, we have a third dimension, represented by the z-axis, which, for us at least, runs perpendicular to the screen. It's the placement of a point on the z-axis that gives us depth, and helps create the illusion of 3D. In our code, a positive value on the z-axis indicates that it is nearer to the viewer.

Vertex

The smallest object in our 3D world is the vertex, which is simply a point in 3D space represented by its three coordinate values of x, y, and z. Vertices are the building blocks of our 3D objects.

Depth

Since we are our outputting to a 2D environment (the computer screen), we need a way to convert our 3D coordinates into 2D space. We do this by adjusting the screen _x and _y properties of our vertices (not to be confused with the vertices' 3D x and y coordinates) based on the vertices' z value. The larger the z value, the closer the vertex is to the viewer, and therefore the farther the vertex is moved away from world center, which serves as our 2D vanishing point. Here's a simple illustration of this process:

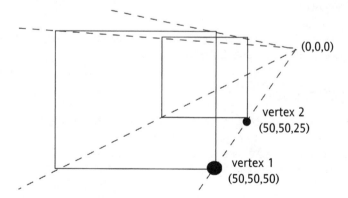

Although vertex 1 and vertex 2 have identical 3D x and y values (remembering that the 3D values are separate from the Flash screen coordinates), their z values differ, so we need to simulate depth between the two points. Vertex 1, having a larger z value, is moved further away from world center, and depth simulation is achieved. The formula we will use to find out *how* we move a vertex from world center is:

```
scale = focalLength/(focalLength-z);
_x = x*scale;
_y = y*scale;
```

`focalLength` represents the distance between the viewer and the screen. Imagine in the above scenario that we set the `focalLength` to 100. For vertex 2, the scale variable will evaluate to approximately 1.33, which will set its Flash `_x` and `_y` properties to -66.5 and 133, respectively. This is the screen distance of the vertex from world center measured in pixels. Vertex 1, with its scale variable evaluating to 2, will have its Flash `_x` and `_y` properties set to −100 and 200, respectively. This sets the vertex's screen coordinates (again, separate from its 3D coordinates) further away from world center. By adjusting `focalLength`, we can increase or decrease this perspective distortion.

Vectors

We'll discuss these further when we get into lighting, but you should at least be aware that a vector is a quantity in our 3D world consisting of a direction and a magnitude. Imagine a theater spotlight shining down from the ceiling on to a soloist on stage. This is a vector as it has a direction that it's pointing in and also has a specific length to its beam.

Matrices

Remember these from the last chapter? Yes, they're back, and this time it's personal (sorry, *Jaws 3D* is still on my mind). Matrices, as you'll recall, are rectangular arrays of numbers. We'll use matrices to help us in transforming our 3D world in much the same way they helped us transform our gradients in the last chapter.

Those are the basic ideas and terms you need to have a firm grasp on, but hey, enough of my yakking! Let's move on and apply these ideas in Flash.

Coding the cube

In this exercise we're going to create the ultimate Flash 3D exercise to demonstrate the concepts we've looked at so far and to give us a base to build on: it's the well-worn but underrated spinning cube.

1. Create a new movie and save it as `spinning_cube_0.fla`. Create a new movie clip symbol with a central registration point called `vertex` and make it a small circle (mine's 12.5 in diameter). In the **Linkage Properties**, check **Export for ActionScript** and give it the identifier name `vertex`.

So now we have the **vertex** symbol in the Library. Eventually, the vertices will only be objects in memory and no longer actual movie clip symbols, but for this exercise we'll utilize them as symbols. Now on to the code.

2. Go back into the main timeline and rename the default layer `actions`. In frame 1 type the following code:

```
this.createEmptyMovieClip("center", 0);
center._x = Stage.width/2;
center._y = Stage.height/2;
focalLength = 400;
```

We've initially created a new movie clip that will hold our 3D world and place it at stage center. We've set our `focalLength` variable (to be used for our depth simulation) to 400.

3. We next create our cube model by defining the vertices. Add this beneath the previous code:

```
cube = {};
cube.vertexList = [];
cube.vertexList.push({x:-50, y:-50, z:50});
cube.vertexList.push({x:50, y:-50, z:50});
cube.vertexList.push({x:50, y:-50, z:-50});
cube.vertexList.push({x:-50, y:-50, z:-50});
cube.vertexList.push({x:-50, y:50, z:50});
cube.vertexList.push({x:50, y:50, z:50});
cube.vertexList.push({x:50, y:50, z:-50});
cube.vertexList.push({x:-50, y:50, z:-50});
vertices = [];
for (i=0; i<cube.vertexList.length; i++) {
    center.attachMovie("vertex", "v"+i, i);
    vertices.push(center["v"+i]);
}
```

`cube` is a new object that we give a single property to: `vertexList`. This will be an array to hold each individual vertex. Over the following eight lines, we push the vertices into the array. Note that each vertex is an individual object made up of three properties: x, y, and

z. Using the length of our array, we place physical vertices (the symbol stored in the Library) on the stage to represent our code vertices. We place a reference to this movie clip in our `vertices` array. Again, this is something we'll dispense with later on as we'll exclusively use the drawing API to produce 3D visuals.

4. Now we need to write the code that will place the vertices in their correct screen positions:

```
render = function (model) {
    for (var i = 0; i<model.vertexList.length; i++) {
        var scale = focalLength/(focalLength-model.vertexList[i].z);
        vertices[i]._x = model.vertexList[i].x*scale;
        vertices[i]._y = model.vertexList[i].y*scale;
    }
};
render(cube);
```

`render` runs through our given model's `vertexList` and sets each vertex's screen position using the depth formula discussed earlier. Finally, we call our function. Go ahead and test the movie to see the result:

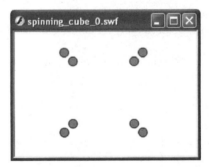

`spinning_cube_0.swf` shows perspective distortion applied to 8 vertices defining a cube. Simulating depth is necessary when attempting to display 3D on a 2D output device like a computer's monitor.

> Note that we are not altering the scale or swapping depths of our vertices as you might expect. This is because we are not attempting to draw perspective spheres as was often seen in Flash 5 experiments, but rather vertices that will define polygons. The vertices themselves do not scale, so we will not apply scaling at this early stage.

Not too impressive yet: the cube isn't spinning so it's difficult to view the vertices' location. We'll change this, at least briefly, with the following function:

5.   Type this directly after the render function:

```
rotateY = function (model, degree) {
    var sin = Math.sin(degree*Math.PI/180);
    var cos = Math.cos(degree*Math.PI/180);
    for (var i = 0; i<model.vertexList.length; i++) {
        var x = cos*model.vertexList[i].x-sin*model.vertexList[i].z;
        var z = cos*model.vertexList[i].z+sin*model.vertexList[i].x;
        model.vertexList[i].z = z;
        model.vertexList[i].x = x;
    }
};
```

This will rotate the vertices of our model about the world's y-axis. We first find the sin and cos of the angle sent (in degrees, so we must convert the number to radians) and then we go through each vertex in our model and move the vertex based on the angle. The formulas for rotation about the axes are established formulas, and to save pages I'll work with the assumption that you accept that they are true.

6.   Finally, replace the last line render(cube); with the following code:

```
center.onEnterFrame = function() {
    rotateY(cube, 3);
    render(cube);
};
```

This final code rotates our cube by 3 degrees about the y-axis and then re-renders it to the screen. Test your movie to view the rotating cube. (If you get some unexpected results here you can check your file against our spinning_cube_0.fla on the CD).

Adding meshlines

The first thing we need to do to more accurately simulate a 3D cube is to join up the vertices of the model with meshlines to create a wireframe. This could be accomplished in Flash 5, but is now far easier in Flash MX as we can use the drawing API.

1.   Save your existing movie as spinning_cube_1.fla. What we'll do now is add some code to our render function in order to draw some lines between our vertices. To do this, we'll need to know which vertices need to be attached to each other. We'll accomplish this by assigning sides to our model made up of selected vertices. Add this code right after the

previous lines that defined the vertices of `cube` (beneath the last line which began `cube.vertexList.push`):

```
cube.side = [];
cube.side.push([0, 1, 2, 3]);
cube.side.push([2, 1, 5, 6]);
cube.side.push([1, 0, 4, 5]);
cube.side.push([5, 4, 7, 6]);
cube.side.push([0, 3, 7, 4]);
cube.side.push([3, 2, 6, 7]);
```

`side` is another array property of our model. Each index consists of four vertices that make up a cube side (try sketching it out from the vertex coordinates to see how these relate). The order that the vertices are placed in each `side` index is very important as you'll see when we come to **backface culling**, which is the process of making invisible any side that isn't facing the viewer (thus saving us from excess processing). We will discuss why in a few pages time. For the time being, just make sure you keep the same order of vertices for each side (the order of sides, however, is of no importance).

2.   We now need to edit our `render` function to actually draw the lines between the vertices. With the sides already defined, this is a fairly straightforward process. The added code is in bold:

```
render = function (model) {
    center.clear();
    center.lineStyle(2, 0, 100);
    for (var i = 0; i<model.vertexList.length; i++) {
        var scale = focalLength/(focalLength-model.vertexList[i].z);
        vertices[i]._x = model.vertexList[i].x*scale;
        vertices[i]._y = model.vertexList[i].y*scale;
    }
    for (var i = 0; i<model.side.length; i++) {
        center.moveTo(vertices[model.side[i][0]]._x,
        ➥vertices[model.side[i][0]]._y);
        for (var j = 1; j<model.side[i].length; j++) {
            center.lineTo(vertices[model.side[i][j]]._x,
            ➥vertices[model.side[i][j]]._y);
        }
        center.lineTo(vertices[model.side[i][0]]._x,
        ➥vertices[model.side[i][0]]._y);
    }
};
```

What we are doing (after clearing and redefining our `lineStyle`) is looping through all of our sides and drawing lines between each vertex. We start by moving our pencil to the vertex at index 0 of our current side. We then draw a line connecting all the remaining vertices on the side, ending by drawing a line back to the initial vertex. Test your movie now to see the drawn meshlines:

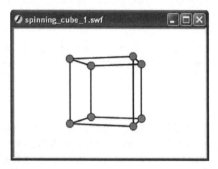

Wireframe lines drawn by the drawing API have been added to help define the edges of our model.

The thing is, now that we've got the meshlines for our model, the vertex movie clips have become a little superfluous. We can get rid of them altogether and make our vertices exist solely in the computer's memory. The only issue we have to deal with here is how to find the x and y screen coordinates of the vertices without being able to look at movie clip `_x` and `_y` properties.

3.   Delete the vertex symbol from your Library, as it's no longer needed. Also delete the following code from your script (these should be lines 23-26 in the Script pane):

```
for (i=0; i<cube.vertexList.length; i++) {
    center.attachMovie("vertex", "v"+i, i);
    vertices.push(center["v"+i]);
}
```

4.   Now update your `render` function like so:

```
render = function (model) {
    center.clear();
    center.lineStyle(2, 0, 100);
    verts2D = [];
    for (var i = 0; i<model.vertexList.length; i++) {
        verts2D[i] = {};
        var scale = focalLength/(focalLength-model.vertexList[i].z);
        verts2D[i].x = model.vertexList[i].x*scale;
        verts2D[i].y = model.vertexList[i].y*scale;
```

continues overleaf

```
        }
        for (var i = 0; i<model.side.length; i++) {
              center.moveTo(verts2D[model.side[i][0]].x,
              ➡verts2D[model.side[i][0]].y);
              for (var j = 1; j<model.side[i].length; j++) {
                    center.lineTo(verts2D[model.side[i][j]].x,
                    ➡verts2D[model.side[i][j]].y);
              }
                    center.lineTo(verts2D[model.side[i][0]].x,
                    ➡verts2D[model.side[i][0]].y);
        }
  };
```

There isn't too much difference. We create a new array called verts2D that stores objects made up of our adjusted screen coordinates. When we loop through our sides and vertices, we look into verts2D for these values. With only a few extra lines (really, we deleted more than we added), we've made our 3D spinning cube exist solely using ActionScript:

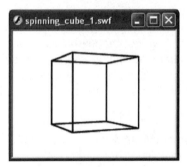

5.   With the movie clip vertices removed, we have a 3D wireframe model spinning about its y-axis completely created using the drawing API.

6.   Save your movie and leave it open, as we'll be modifying it again once we've looked at some more theory.

Transformation matrices

I'd like to discuss another concept here and it concerns how we're handling our transformations. As it is, for each rotation about an axis (even though we only presently have rotation about the y-axis, you can probably surmise the code for the other two axes) we are looping through each vertex and adjusting its coordinates accordingly. Wouldn't it be nice to only have to do this once, after we have calculated all the necessary transformations? Well, we can, and the way to do it is by using matrices.

Although you might not have thought it at the time, each vertex can be described as a matrix too, without requiring us to adjust any code. A vertex with the coordinates (50,30,15) can be written just as easily as:

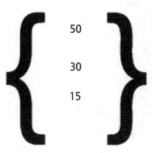

You don't have to change a thing in your code (it's not as if you can format it this way in the ActionScript panel!), just as long as you understand what this matrix means. Um, so what does it mean? Well, you saw how easily we could perform transformations on our gradients using our transforms stored in matrices? Well, we can do the same thing for our 3D transforms.

In our last exercise, for example, in the `rotateY` function the transformation is handled by:

```
x = cos(?)*x - sin(?)*z;
//y = y;
z = cos(?)*z + sin(?)*x;
```

The commented out line was not in our previous code, but I've put it there as a placeholder so you can see where we're going with this.

Now what if I told you that this transform formula could be stored in a transform matrix that we could multiply with our 3D coordinates? What if I told you that these transform matrices could actually be multiplied together, creating a cumulative transform matrix that we would only have to multiply with our coordinates once at the end of our transformations? What if I told you that doing so could save us some processing and aid us in future transformations? What if I keep asking rhetorical questions and never get to show you how this is done? Nah, that'll never happen. The transform matrix for the above code looks like this:

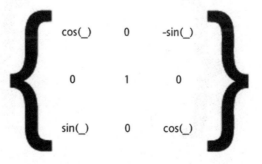

The result of multiplying this 3x3 matrix with our 3x1 coordinate matrix would be another 3x1 matrix:

$$\left\{ \begin{array}{c} \cos(\_)*x + 0* + \text{-}\sin(\_)*z \\[1em] 0*x + 1*y + 0*z \\[1em] \sin(\_)*x + 0*y + \cos(\_)*z \end{array} \right\}$$

Does this look familiar? That's right, it's the same formula as used by our `rotateY` function above! Now you might be thinking that it looks like a lot more work to implement this than its predecessor, but actually, if you set up the formula once (which only consists of simple multiplication and addition), you can use it for all of our transforms, the rest of which look would like this:

- Transformation about the x-axis:

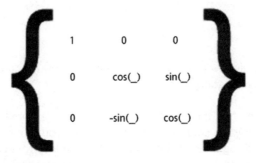

$$\left\{ \begin{array}{ccc} 1 & 0 & 0 \\[1em] 0 & \cos(\_) & \sin(\_) \\[1em] 0 & \text{-}\sin(\_) & \cos(\_) \end{array} \right\}$$

- Transformation about the z-axis:

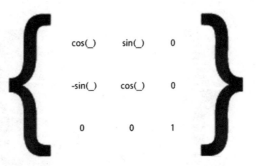

$$\left\{ \begin{array}{ccc} \cos(\_) & \sin(\_) & 0 \\[1em] \text{-}\sin(\_) & \cos(\_) & 0 \\[1em] 0 & 0 & 1 \end{array} \right\}$$

■ Scaling of the object:

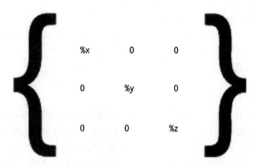

$$\left\{ \begin{matrix} \%x & 0 & 0 \\ 0 & \%y & 0 \\ 0 & 0 & \%z \end{matrix} \right\}$$

Let's incorporate some of these into our code so that we might easily perform these transformations.

Transforming with matrices

1. Still using your movie from the last exercise, save it as `spinning_cube_2.fla`. Then enter this code immediately after our `render` function:

```
rotateX = function (model, degree) {
    var rad = degree*Math.PI/180;
    var sin = Math.sin(rad);
    var cos = Math.cos(rad);
    var matrix = {a:1, b:0, c:0, d:0, e:cos, f:sin, g:0, h:-sin,
    ➡i:cos};
    transform(matrix, model);
};
rotateY = function (model, degree) {
    var rad = degree*Math.PI/180;
    var sin = Math.sin(rad);
    var cos = Math.cos(rad);
    var matrix = {a:cos, b:0, c:-sin, d:0, e:1, f:0, g:sin, h:0,
    ➡i:cos};
    transform(matrix, model);
};
rotateZ = function (model, degree) {
    var rad = degree*Math.PI/180;
    var sin = Math.sin(rad);
    var cos = Math.cos(rad);
    var matrix = {a:cos, b:sin, c:0, d:-sin, e:cos, f:0, g:0, h:0,
    ➡i:1};
    transform(matrix, model);
```

continues overleaf

```
    };
scale = function (model, percent) {
    var rad = degree*Math.PI/180;
    var matrix = {a:percent, b:0, c:0, d:0, e:percent, f:0, g:0, h:0,
    ➥i:percent};
    transform(matrix, model);
};
```

You could easily set these matrices up as linear arrays, but I've chosen to make them objects similar to our gradient transformation matrices from the last chapter so that you can see the relation. After we've made our matrix, we call our `transform` function to add this matrix to our full transform. Let's write this function next.

2. Under the matrix definitions we added in the last step, add the following code:

```
transform = function (matrix, model) {
    if (transformMatrix) {
        var a = matrix.a*transformMatrix.a+matrix.b*transformMatrix.d
        ➥+matrix.c*transformMatrix.g;
        var b = matrix.a*transformMatrix.b+matrix.b*transformMatrix.e
        ➥+matrix.c*transformMatrix.h;
        var c = matrix.a*transformMatrix.c+matrix.b*transformMatrix.f
        ➥+matrix.c*transformMatrix.i;
        var d = matrix.d*transformMatrix.a+matrix.e*transformMatrix.d
        ➥+matrix.f*transformMatrix.g;
        var e = matrix.d*transformMatrix.b+matrix.e*transformMatrix.e
        ➥+matrix.f*transformMatrix.h;
        var f = matrix.d*transformMatrix.c+matrix.e*transformMatrix.f
        ➥+matrix.f*transformMatrix.i;
        var g = matrix.g*transformMatrix.a+matrix.h*transformMatrix.d
        ➥+matrix.i*transformMatrix.g;
        var h = matrix.g*transformMatrix.b+matrix.h*transformMatrix.e
        ➥+matrix.i*transformMatrix.h;
        var i = matrix.g*transformMatrix.c+matrix.h*transformMatrix.f
        ➥+matrix.i*transformMatrix.i;
        transformMatrix = {a:a, b:b, c:c, d:d, e:e, f:f, g:g,
        ➥h:h,i:i};
    } else {
        transformMatrix = matrix;
    }
};
```

Though this might look a bit daunting, this is simply the formula for multiplying a 3x3 matrix by another 3x3 matrix. What we're doing in this function is first checking to see if a transform matrix already exists. If it does, we multiply the two matrices together, thus forming a cumulative matrix of the two (if a transform matrix doesn't yet exist, we create one and set it equal to the matrix sent to the function). The result of this is that we can combine multiple transformations into one matrix *before* we apply it to our vertices. Let's do that now.

3. Add the following bold lines to the `render` function:

```
render = function (model) {
    if (transformMatrix) {
    for (var i = 0; i<model.vertexList.length; i++) {
        var vert = model.vertexList[i];
        var x = transformMatrix.a*vert.x+transformMatrix.b*vert.y
        ➡+transformMatrix.c*vert.z;
        var y = transformMatrix.d*vert.x+transformMatrix.e*vert.y
        ➡+transformMatrix.f*vert.z;
        var z = transformMatrix.g*vert.x+transformMatrix.h*vert.y
        ➡+transformMatrix.i*vert.z;
        vert.x = x;
        vert.y = y;
        vert.z = z;
    }
    delete transformMatrix;
    }
    center.clear();
    center.lineStyle(2, 0, 100);
    verts2D = [];
    for (var i = 0; i<model.vertexList.length; i++) {
        verts2D[i] = {};
        var scale = focalLength/(focalLength-model.vertexList[i].z);
        verts2D[i].x = model.vertexList[i].x*scale;
        verts2D[i].y = model.vertexList[i].y*scale;
    }
    for (var i = 0; i<model.side.length; i++) {
      center.moveTo(verts2D[model.side[i][0]].x,
      ➡verts2D[model.side[i][0]].y);
        for (var j = 1; j<model.side[i].length; j++) {
            center.lineTo(verts2D[model.side[i][j]].x,
            ➡verts2D[model.side[i][j]].y);
        }
    center.lineTo(verts2D[model.side[i][0]].x,
    verts2D[model.side[i][0]].y);
    }
};
```

Finally, before we render the model to the screen, we need to apply our transformations (which are conveniently stored in a single matrix) to our vertices. The extra code is the basic formula for multiplying a 3x3 matrix (our transform) with a 3x1 matrix (each vertex's coordinates). We then delete our transform to ready ourselves for further transformations.

4. To call our new rotation functions, alter the `onEnterFrame` function at the end of our code to read:

```
center.onEnterFrame = function() {
    rotateX(cube, 3);
    rotateY(cube, 6);
    rotateZ(cube, 10);
    render(cube);
};
```

Notice that although we perform three separate transformations, they will not be applied to the model until the `render` function is called, once each frame. Go ahead and test the movie to see the results.

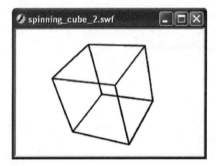

Using 3x3 transformation matrices, the rotation of our wireframe model about all three of its axes is made more efficient.

If you get any unexpected results then you can check your code against mine in `spinning_cube_2.fla` on the CD.

Now we're getting somewhere! Even though all we have is the same old spinning wireframe cube, we're building something that will provide a solid foundation for us to improve on.

Depth sorting

One improvement that will be necessary once we begin filling the models with color is a **depth sorting** or **z-sorting** method. This is a method of placing models or the sides of the cube that are nearer to the viewer *in front of* objects and sides that are further away. Basically, you don't want an object with a z=–200 coordinate to be in front of an object that has a z=50 coordinate. In Flash 5, you needed to swap the depths of your vertex movie clips in order to accomplish this. Now in MX, we can simply create an order to draw in, starting with the sides that are furthest away and working towards the viewer, effectively drawing over the sides that should be behind. This will all be accomplished in our render function, as we'll see in the following exercise.

Filling the sides

1. Save your movie as spinning_cube_3.fla. Update your render function with the following new code:

```
render = function (model) {
    if (transformMatrix) {
        for (var i = 0; i<model.vertexList.length; i++) {
            var vert = model.vertexList[i];
            var x = transformMatrix.a*vert.x+transformMatrix.b*vert.y
            ➥+transformMatrix.c*vert.z;
            var y = transformMatrix.d*vert.x+transformMatrix.e*vert.y
            ➥+transformMatrix.f*vert.z;
            var z = transformMatrix.g*vert.x+transformMatrix.h*vert.y
            ➥+transformMatrix.i*vert.z;
            vert.x = x;
            vert.y = y;
            vert.z = z;
        }
        delete transformMatrix;
    }
    center.clear();
    center.lineStyle(2, 0, 100);
    verts2D = [];
    depthArray = [];
    for (var i = 0; i<model.side.length; i++) {
        var zDepth = 0;
        for (var j = 0; j<model.side[i].length; j++) {
            var whichVert = model.side[i][j];
            if (verts2D[whichVert] == undefined) {
                verts2D[whichVert] = {};
                var scale = focalLength/(focalLength
                ➥-model.vertexList[whichVert].z);
                verts2D[whichVert].x = model.vertexList[whichVert].x
                ➥*scale;
                verts2D[whichVert].y = model.vertexList[whichVert].y
                ➥*scale;
```

continues overleaf

```
            }
            zDepth += model.vertexList[whichVert].z;
        }
        depthArray.push([model.side[i], zDepth]);
    }
    depthArray.sort(function (a, b) { return a[1]>b[1];});
    for (var i = 0; i<depthArray.length; i++) {
        var sideVerts = depthArray[i][0];
        center.moveTo(verts2D[sideVerts[0]].x,verts2D
        ➥ [sideVerts[0]].y);
        center.beginFill(0x666666, 100);
        for (var j = 1; j<sideVerts.length; j++) {
            center.lineTo(verts2D[sideVerts[j]].x,verts2D
            ➥ [sideVerts[j]].y);
        }
        center.lineTo(verts2D[sideVerts[0]].x,verts2D
        ➥ [sideVerts[0]].y);
        center.endFill();
    }
};
```

Wow. That's a lot of changes, but they do quite a lot for us. We've some nested arrays in here that might look a little convoluted, so let's work through it and see what this code is doing.

First, we create a new array called depthArray. This will hold references to our models' sides and the collective z position of each vertex in that side (this will give us a close enough z level for our purposes here). We then loop through each side in our model and convert its vertices into 2D coordinates (which is no different to our previous version) and add each vertex's z value to that side's total zDepth. The if statement is included so that we don't perform any unnecessary conversion operations more than once on a vertex, which would indeed happen since sides share vertices with other sides.

Once the vertices have been converted and the total zDepth of each side is recorded, we place a reference to each side (which holds that side's vertices, remember) and its zDepth into our depthArray, which we promptly sort using a sorting function. We used an almost identical sorting function in the previous chapter, but here we include it directly in the sort arguments instead of calling it externally. Once our depthArray is in the correct order (from the side furthest away through to the nearest side) we loop through it and draw our lines and fills.

The two most confusing variables in the above code might be whichVert and sideVerts, so let's look more closely at these. whichVert holds a single vertex number for a side in the model. So for side[0], which is an array of the numbers [0,1,2,3], whichVert will evaluate to each index on the corresponding iteration of the loop. sideVerts, on the other hand, will hold that full array of vertex numbers. Remember that each index of `depthArray` holds a reference to one of the model's sides and its `zDepth`. By looking at the first index position in a particular index of `depthArray`, we can find that side's list of vertices, which we then place in `sideVerts`.

2.   Test your movie. We now have filled sides! Thanks, drawing API!

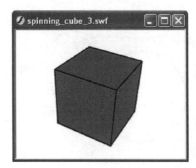

`spinning_cube_3.swf` demonstrates a cube model with solid-filled polygons and visible edges, all created with the drawing API. Depth sorting of each polygon allows for nearer polygon sides to appear in front of further sides. The cube is spun about all three of its axes each frame using 3x3 transformation matrices.

3.   Save your movie and leave it open for the next exercise.

Backface culling

Backface culling, as stated earlier, is simply preventing the rendering of polygons that are turned away from the viewer, saving the computer excess processing work (in fact, it's the polygon's *normal* directed away from the viewer, but unfortunately there's not much time to get into this here). This is desirable most of the time, though you can certainly make this option a toggled state for your models if you so choose. The way to determine if a polygon is facing the viewer or turned away is by examining the **screen** coordinates of its vertices, not the **3D** coordinates, since it's the model's relation to the screen and the viewer that is the important determining factor on whether the polygons can be seen or not. We also need to note if the vertices are in a clockwise or counter-clockwise order. With our method, it is imperative that the vertices are defined for the side in a counter-clockwise order in relation to the object center, in order for them to be seen at the correct angles.

This all sounds a bit confusing, doesn't it? Well, once you get the hang of it, it's pretty easy. Trust me. In fact, explaining it is the most difficult part. The process I use to help me determine the correct order of vertices is to imagine the polygon (or side) to be directly facing me on the *near side of center* before I determine the vertex order. For our cube model, this would mean mentally spinning the cube until each side faced me so that I might see the order for the vertices better.

If I then place the vertices into the `side` array in a counter-clockwise order at the current view, the side will be fully visible to the viewer while on the near side of center. To visualize this better, we'll look at our cube model with three of its sides defined so that the outside of the cube may be seen:

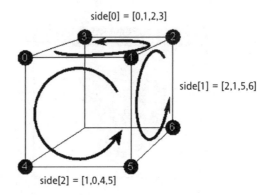

Now although it might appear that we simply have to define all sides in a counter-clockwise order in relation to our view, take a look at the order for our remaining three sides:

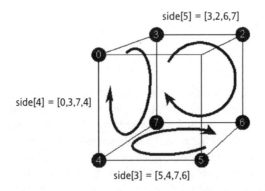

Ah-hah! Clockwise! This is because in this view we *don't* want these sides to be rendered, since they are *inside* the box. It's for this reason that I use the procedure described above, that of mentally spinning the model so that each side faces me before I record the vertex order. If I spin `side[5]` around to face me on the near side of center, then the order of its vertices would indeed be counter-clockwise.

OK, now that we know that whenever a side's vertices are in a clockwise order on the screen it should *not* be rendered, we need a way to determine the order in which the vertices' 2D coordinates are currently seen. (Full credit must go to Pavils Jurjans at **www.jurjans.lv/flash** for his open source code and this fun section).

Rendering only the necessities

1. Resave your movie from the previous exercise as `spinning_cube_4.fla`. Create this new function above the `render` function (really, it doesn't matter too much where you put it in our code but this helps to keep our code more logical and organized):

```
backface = function (x, y) {
    var cax = x[2]-x[0];
    var cay = y[2]-y[0];
    var bcx = x[1]-x[2];
    var bcy = y[1]-y[2];
    return (cax*bcy<cay*bcx);
};
```

What we're going to do is send this function three vertices from a side. Using the screen coordinates of the three vertices in the formula above, we can determine if the vertices run clockwise or counter-clockwise on the screen. All we need really is a `true` or `false`, and so we return just that: `true` if this side is turned away from the viewer, or `false` (i.e. *not* a backface) if the side is turned towards the viewer.

2. To call this function, we add just these few new lines to our growing render function:

```
depthArray.sort(function (a, b) { return a[1]>b[1];});
    for (var i = 0; i<depthArray.length; i++) {
        var sideVerts = depthArray[i][0];
            if (!backface([verts2D[sideVerts[0]].x,
            verts2D[sideVerts[1]].x,
            ➡verts2D[sideVerts[2]].x], [verts2D[sideVerts[0]].y,
            ➡verts2D[sideVerts[1]].y, verts2D[sideVerts[2]].y])) {
            center.moveTo(verts2D[sideVerts[0]].x,
            ➡verts2D[sideVerts[0]].y);
            center.beginFill(0x666666, 100);
            for (var j = 1; j<sideVerts.length; j++) {
                center.lineTo(verts2D[sideVerts[j]].x,
                ➡verts2D[sideVerts[j]].y);
            }
            center.lineTo(verts2D[sideVerts[0]].x,
            ➡verts2D[sideVerts[0]].y);
            center.endFill();
        }
    }
};
```

Now that's a long function call! Really, all we're doing here is nesting our line and fill drawing methods inside a conditional statement that ensures the side is not a backface. If we didn't run through each vertex here in the function call, we would have to do it in the backface function. I think it's a little cleaner this way. We put the first three vertices' x and y coordinates into separate arrays when we call our backface function (look back to that function to see how we access these arrays after they are sent). If the backface function determines that we do *not* have a backface (by returning false), we draw the side.

3. Test the movie. With the z sorting already taken care of, you might be wondering why it doesn't appear to be different:

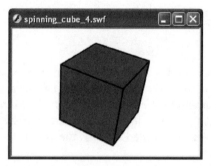

Our spinning cube with backface culling utilized. This prevents the sides that are turned away from the viewer from being needlessly rendered.

4. However, if you go back into the code and change the fill alpha to 0 by updating the beginFill() call to center.beginFill(0x666666, 0);, you'll see that the backface culling has indeed been implemented when you test the movie again:

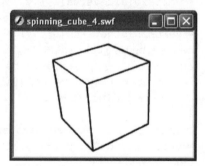

5. Save your movie and leave it open. We're going to be updating it in the next exercise.

Lighting polygons

So far we've got a pretty nifty effect of a solid cube spinning on our stage, but we're missing one important factor necessary for a true 3D illusion: dynamic lighting of our model. To create a more realistic environment we need to provide a light source that will shine on our model and shade the sides based on their angle relative to the light source.

This is where some more advanced math comes into play, and so I'll preface this section by reassuring those who might feel daunted by the coming numbers. Before experimenting in Flash, my post-high school math consisted of doing my taxes and calculating a tip at a restaurant. The formulas we'll be using here are the result of many a night spent at math sites and the kind help of *ahab*, a moderator on the forums at **www.were-here.com**. Some good math-minded friends of mine, Jeff Baldwin and Julie Bellanger, also aided me when the concepts went over my head. My point in saying this, other than to give credit and thanks where due, is to encourage you to use any and all resources at hand to help you, including any books that give you the formulas outright (like this one's about to do). The fantastic Flash work will come by combining these resources with your creativity, not by learning math alone.

Lighting the cube

All right. The first thing we need to add is a light source. We could do this with more variables, but let's make it more object-oriented by making the light its own entity (we'll apply this same concept to the model next chapter).

1. Save your movie as `spinning_cube_5.fla`. Right at the start of your code, immediately before anything else, type:

```
LightSource = function(x, y, z, brightness) {
    this.x = x;
    this.y = y;
    this.z = z;
    his.brightness = brightness;
    this.calcMag = function() {
        this.magnitude =
        ➥Math.sqrt(this.x*this.x+this.y*this.y+this.z*this.z);
    };
    this.calcMag();
};
```

`LightSource` is a constructor function that creates a new light source for our world. As it is, its only properties are position and brightness, which are set on the object's creation (eventually, you'd want to set up methods to change these properties). The method `calcMag` calculates the magnitude of our light (the distance of the light from world center).

We'll need this value later, and it would also need to be recalculated if the x, y, or z properties were changed.

2. To create an instance of a `LightSource`, place the following code after the line `focalLength = 400;` (this is just after the section where we create the **center** movie clip near the start of our code):

```
light = new LightSource(-20000, -20000, 20000, 100);
```

So `light` is now the `LightSource` we use in the scene, and if we need to access any of its properties, we would do so with `light.property`. We've set its position as -20,000 on its x- and y-axes, and 20,000 on its z-axis. This will place it at the front, top, and left of our model, a nice traditional position for lighting. We also set its brightness to 100. Potential improvements on our original `LightSource` object could involve additional methods to alter the brightness or perhaps add color to our light.

We now need a variable in our model that will hold its color. We could easily set this for the whole model, but it might be more beneficial to provide a way to color individual sides or polygons. Let's improve our side property of the model to hold objects containing each side's information, as opposed to just references to the vertex numbers.

3. Alter the six lines that push vertex numbers into our `side` array to read:

```
cube.side = [];
cube.side.push({vertices:[0,1,2,3], sideColor:0x6600CC});
cube.side.push({vertices:[2,1,5,6], sideColor:0x6600CC});
cube.side.push({vertices:[1,0,4,5], sideColor:0x6600CC});
cube.side.push({vertices:[5,4,7,6], sideColor:0x6600CC});
cube.side.push({vertices:[0,3,7,4], sideColor:0x6600CC});
cube.side.push({vertices:[3,2,6,7], sideColor:0x6600CC});
```

Instead of merely inserting numbers into this property, we place objects containing two properties themselves: `vertices` to hold the vertex numbers and `sideColor` to hold the hex value of the side's color.

That takes care of storing our colors. We will have to change a few lines in our `render` function to allow for this new structure, but we'll actually house all the code to determine the light's effect on the color in two other separate functions.

4. Make the following changes to the second half of our `render` function:

```
center.clear();
center.lineStyle(2, 0, 100);
verts2D = [];
depthArray = [];
```

```
            for (var i = 0; i<model.side.length; i++) {
                var zDepth = 0;
                for (var j = 0; j<model.side[i].vertices.length; j++) {
                    var whichVert = model.side[i].vertices[j];
                    if (verts2D[whichVert] == undefined) {
                        verts2D[whichVert] = {};
                        var scale = focalLength/(focalLength-
                        ➡model.vertexList[whichVert].z);
                        verts2D[whichVert].x =
                        ➡model.vertexList[whichVert].x*scale;
                        verts2D[whichVert].y =
                        ➡model.vertexList[whichVert].y*scale;
                    }
                    zDepth += model.vertexList[whichVert].z;
                }
                depthArray.push([model.side[i], zDepth]);
            }
            depthArray.sort(function (a, b) { return a[1]>b[1];});
            for (var i = 0; i<depthArray.length; i++) {
                var sideVerts = depthArray[i][0].vertices;
                if (!backface([verts2D[sideVerts[0]].x,
                ➡verts2D[sideVerts[1]].x,verts2D[sideVerts[2]].x],
                ➡ [verts2D[sideVerts[0]].y,
                ➡verts2D[sideVerts[1]].y, verts2D[sideVerts[2]].y])) {
                    center.moveTo(verts2D[sideVerts[0]].x,
                    ➡verts2D[sideVerts[0]].y);
                    center.beginFill(getSideColor(model,depthArray[i][0])
                    ➡,100);
                    for (var j = 1; j<sideVerts.length; j++) {
                        center.lineTo(verts2D[sideVerts[j]].x,
                        ➡verts2D[sideVerts[j]].y);
                    }
                    center.lineTo(verts2D[sideVerts[0]].x,
                    ➡verts2D[sideVerts[0]].y);
                    center.endFill();
                }
            }
        }
};
```

There's really not too much change here in comparison to what it allows us to do. You can
see that we now have to access the sides' vertices property since that is where the vertex
numbers are stored. Also, instead of providing a fill color in our beginFill method, we
will call a function instead, sending it a reference to our current side (stored in
depthArray[i][0]) and a reference to the model itself. We know that this will return a
color, as that is the required first parameter for beginFill. Let's write this function now.

5. Add this new function, directly below the render function:

```
getSideColor = function (model, side) {
    var col = side.sideColor.toString(16);
    while (col.length < 6) {
        col = "0" + col
    }
    var verts = [model.vertexList[side.vertices[0]],
    ➥model.vertexList[side.vertices[1]],
    ➥model.vertexList[side.vertices[2]]];
    var lightFactor = factorLightAngle(verts);
    var r = parseInt(col.substr(0, 2), 16)*lightFactor;
    var g = parseInt(col.substr(2, 2), 16)*lightFactor;
    var b = parseInt(col.substr(4, 2), 16)*lightFactor;
    return r << 16 | g << 8 | b;
};
```

getSideColor is nearly identical to our convertToRGB function from the last chapter (a more explicit explanation was given there). Most of the function deals with separating our color into its red, green, and blue channels so that we can affect each value individually. The only different lines are those that put our side's first three vertices into a temporary variable array and then send that array to a function called factorLightAngle. By sending the vertices directly (remember, the objects are stored in our model's vertexList), it will be easier for factorLightAngle to deal with the numbers.

There's just one more function to go, the factorLightAngle function, but this is where all the power lies. It's also where the heavy math is waiting, so take a deep breath, and let's dive in!

6. Add these lines immediately beneath the last function:

```
factorLightAngle = function (vertices) {
    var U = [(vertices[0].x-vertices[1].x), (vertices[0].y
    ➥vertices[1].y), (vertices[0].z-vertices[1].z)];
    var V = [(vertices[1].x-vertices[2].x), (vertices[1].y-
    ➥vertices[2].y), (vertices[1].z-vertices[2].z)];
    var p = [((U[1]*V[2])-(U[2]*V[1])), -((U[0]*V[2])-(U[2]*V[0])),
    ➥((U[0]*V[1])-(U[1]*V[0]))];
    var magP = Math.sqrt((p[0]*p[0])+(p[1]*p[1])+(p[2]*p[2]));
    var dP = ((p[0]*light.x)+(p[1]*light.y)+(p[2]*light.z));
    return ((Math.acos(dP/(magP*light.magnitude))/Math.PI)
    ➥*light.brightness/100);
};
```

7. We'll break down what's happening here in just a moment as I'm sure you want to test out all your hard work, so go on and test the movie to see the light shading take effect as your cube spins:

 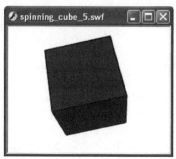 

Dynamic lighting is applied to our spinning cube model, helping to better simulate depth.

Right, let's step back and examine that final section of code. U and V are simply 3D vectors we derive from our vertices (remember, a vector here represents a position and direction in space). You probably do similar things all the time for 2D vectors in your Flash movies, when you subtract one movie clip's _x property from the _x property of another clip (the only difference here being we have an extra dimension to calculate). Once we know U and V, we find the cross product of these two vectors, which is a vector perpendicular to the two vectors used in the operation. In 3D, this vector that is perpendicular to a surface's face is known as the polygon's **normal**. This normal tells us the orientation of the face of the polygon.

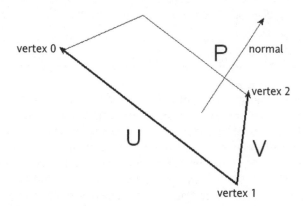

With this vector defined, we can find its relation to our light source and determine how much light it should receive. The formula we use to accomplish this is:

$$\cos(\_) = \frac{u \bullet v}{\|u\|\,\|v\|}$$

NOTE: U and V are here used to signify two vectors and do not relate to the U and V variables used in our above formula.

So what does this mean then? Well, to find the cosine of the angle between our light source and our polygon's normal, we multiply the two vectors together (the dot product, which is the measure of the distance between the two vectors) and then divide this by the product of the length of the two vectors (their magnitudes, or distance from world center).

Another interpretation of this is that some extremely clever and diligent mathematicians worked very hard on this formula, and so who am I to dispute it? I can use it to find the angle at which my light source is hitting my polygon, and that's all that matters to me.

Before we get to the code that utilizes this formula, it's important to understand the nature of the light we have placed in our 3D scene. In 3D software, our light would be akin to a directional light always set to point at world center. This saves us having to orient our light to point at our models when we first place it or if we translate it during an animation. However, because of this, if the light is translated to the world center, it cannot be directed out towards any models so the models would be black and unlit (black because we have no ambient light set in our scene, an adjustment you could make later).

Finally, these are the last three lines of our function. `magP` is the magnitude of our normal, which is basically the polygon's distance from world center (just Pythagoras at work here). `dP` holds the result of the dot product operation, which you can see is just some multiplication and addition of the two vectors' components. Finally we determine the angle by finding the arccosine of our dot product divided by the product of the two vectors' magnitudes. This will give us a value in radians between 0 and pi, so we divide by pi to give us a percentage. We use this to find a percentage of our light's brightness (we divide by 100 again because of the way we set up the brightness value of the light – I wanted to use integers to express this, so we need to divide by one hundred here to return a percentage with this function).

Wow! All that to light our model! You'll be glad to know that we're finished though, so you can take a well-earned break. If however you want to go back over any elements of this exercise (or any of the earlier versions of the spinning cube), all of the source FLAs with fully commented code are on the CD to compare your files against.

In `spinning_cube_final.fla` I've provided text boxes so you may alter the cube's transforms and the light's properties at run-time. I've also added a `translate` function so that your models can be moved from center. Ideally, you'd not incorporate this in the way that I have, (which I've done for brevity's sake). One alternative method is to use 4x4 matrices for our transforms and add a fourth dimension for each vertex. We explore this in the following chapter. Obviously, there is a lot of work that can be done to improve the usefulness and modularity of our code, and this is one of the improvements I would suggest if you wish to develop this further.

Summary

In this chapter we've looked at techniques for rendering 3D elements using the new drawing API. Moving past the wireframes and vertex models of Flash 5, we can now create and manipulate solid shapes that react dynamically to light using ActionScript alone. This opens the door to so many possibilities, but it will take your creativity and ingenuity to utilize these new capabilities in an interesting and useful manner.

In the next chapter we're going to look at ways to incorporate these 3D and drawing methods into Flash interface and game design, but of course this is the tip of the iceberg. Hopefully, the 3D seeds have been planted (and the formulas will be printed!) and you can take these concepts and run with them to places where only your own individual mind can go. I can't wait to see pictures of your trip!

section 2: ActionScript Interfaces

chapter 11: Case Study: SphereCage

Before beginning this chapter, you may want to downlaod `sphereCagecommented.fla` from www.friendsofed.com/books/studio/fash_mx/code.html

In the last two chapters we've been learning about using the drawing API to help create run-time 2D and 3D content for our Flash movies. It's now time we used that knowledge and these new features to actually create some content. In our case, this will be a complete 3D game made exclusively using the drawing API, our ActionScript, and a healthy dose of imagination. Well, I said 'exclusively', but that's only 99% true. One of the terrific advantages of Macromedia Flash MX is that it allows you to quickly and seamlessly bring together your pre-built graphics and code in a user-friendly environment.

My goal, however, was to create a game – graphics, interface, everything – solely using the drawing API in order to illustrate its potential. Sure, in the real world, take advantage of Flash's integration of code and graphics to enhance your games, sites, and applications, whether created in Flash or another program. Here though, in the slightly skewed schoolyard of Flash, let's challenge ourselves by really putting the drawing API to the test. If we do this, I believe you'll leave these chapters fully equipped with the skills, ideas, and code to better tackle your future design challenges.

Before we start work on the game, familiarize yourself with what we'll be creating by opening up `sphere_cage.swf` (on the CD) and playing around with it. Between blocks of the ball, think about what's going on behind the scenes, and how some of it might be constructed (but don't think too long, that ball is harder to hit than you think!).

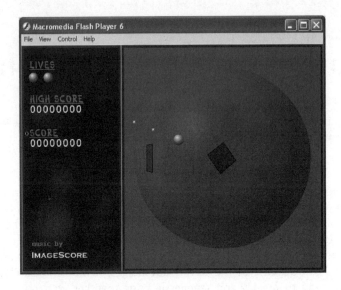

Concept

SphereCage was an idea first conceived about a year ago when I was playing around with a variation of the classic *Breakout* game. In my version, the player was allowed to rotate their paddle by up to 45 degrees and so cause a change in the ball's direction with each deflection. I thought, at the time, that it might be a nice variation (on a variation) to create a Breakout game with all target blocks in the center of a large circle, with the player navigating a paddle about the circumference. I never got around to making it, but as I thought about creating a game for this chapter, it was in the back of my head.

I wanted to use the drawing API for a 3D game, but as I pointed out in the last chapter, Flash's speed with 3D is a bit lacking at times. Sure, you could create a 3D cube, but making an effective 3D game that doesn't grind your computer to a halt is a daunting task.

So I began to think, as you must, about faking some 3D, and using true 3D for the major element of the game: a car racing around a track, a spaceship flying through rings, or a maze seen from the player's point of view. However, none of these excited me and how could I pass a game on to you that I didn't care for myself? I'm a fan of simple yet addictive games, a child of the 1980's eruption of (now classic) arcade games, and I'd rather not memorize 50 different key combinations to throw a punch. To me, *Tetris* is as wonderful as they come, and of course the Granddaddy of simple, addictive games is the Granddaddy of them all: *Pong*.

Why not take that classic and update it using our new skills? Instead of the original 2D back and forth table tennis, we could introduce a third dimension and add a whole new feeling to the game. Suddenly it all came together. The two paddles, the player's and the computer's, would be rendered using our run-time 3D code. The outer sphere and ball itself would be 'fake' 3D, using gradients to simulate depth, though the ball would need to be *moved* in 3D space. We would only need to deal with 9 vertices being transformed (four each for the two paddles and one for the ball, although in the end I decided to add two extra for the ball's trajectory, bringing the total number of vertices to eleven). This would ensure a fast, effective, 3D experience.

This is what I started with, the concept of a ball being hit back and forth between the center and perimeter of a sphere, with the computer's paddle spinning randomly at the center (relieving us the hassle of building an AI). If the ball reached the perimeter, the player would lose a 'life'. Not only could the player maneuver the paddle, they would also able to spin the sphere (and therefore the full 3D world) to see the trajectory of the ball better. The biggest challenge for coding would be determining the angle of deflection as the ball hit the computer's spinning paddle. Everything else would utilize the 3D code we developed in the last chapter. With our concept firmly established, let's get cracking!

The 1%

Before you open Flash, let's take care of the elements we can't create with code. The first is purely aesthetic and so completely optional, but I think it's a nice addition.

Reflection map

If you look at the finished game, you'll see the 'glass sphere' itself has a subtle reflection map overlaying it, adding a touch more realism to the graphic:

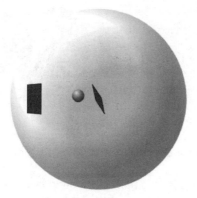

I'll quickly show you how I did this so that you can make your own effect. I used Adobe Photoshop 7.0 for this, but you can use whatever image-editing program you're familiar with, as long as it has a filter similar to Photoshop's **Spherize**. (Or, if you prefer, you can use my finished map included on the CD as reflect.png.)

1. Open up any image you'd like to use for your reflection map. The best images to use are those with a high contrast of light (reflective windows are great). Of course, you can always increase contrast using **Levels** or **Curves**.

2. We'll need a square image eventually, so go ahead and crop your image using the crop tool while holding down SHIFT to constrain proportions. The final image will be so subtle that resolution isn't terribly important here, but as a guide I worked with an image of approximately 500x500 pixels.

3. With your rectangular marquee tool constrained to a perfect square (either set in the options bar or by holding SHIFT), select about 80% of the image from the center outwards, leaving the border of the image unselected:

4. Use **Filters > Distort > Spherize** set at 100%, then deselect.

5. (Make sure your image is on a non-background layer for this next step.) Using the elliptical marquee tool constrained to a perfect circle, select about 50% of your distorted center of the image, again from the center out. With the selection active, click on the **Add Layer Mask** button. You should have the masked center of your image with transparency about the edges.

6. With the mask selected (not the image), go to **Filters > Blur > Gaussian Blur** and blur the mask so that a hard edge can no longer be seen. Use the preview to judge the result before you OK it. Ideally, you want it to be opaque at center, then gradually fade to complete transparency before the mask reaches the hard edge of the spherized section of the image:

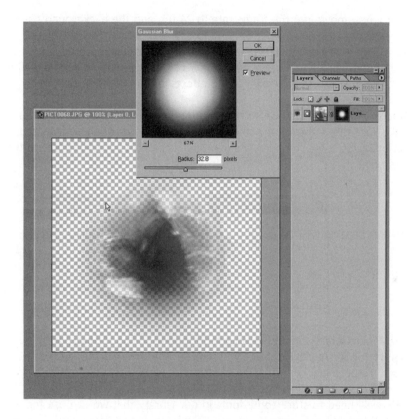

7. Use **Image > Trim** with **Based on Transparent Pixels** selected to get rid of the excess image data. Now go to **Image > Image Size**, and make sure it's set to 72 ppi. I also resampled my image to be 300x300 pixels.

8. Finally, go to **File > Save For Web** and export the image as a **png-24 with transparency**. Close down Photoshop and go into Flash, which we'll be working in for the rest of the chapter.

SphereCage: media

Now that we're in Flash, we begin by importing all of our media (four sounds and the reflection map) so that we may control it with ActionScript.

1.   Start a new movie, set the frame rate to 24 fps, and the background color to **#666666**.

2.   Go to **File > Import to Library** and import your reflection map (`reflect.png`) and the four sound files `blip0.wav`, `blip1.wav`, `blip2.wav`, and `miss.wav` (all included on the CD). Feel free to use your own sound effects instead of those provided.

3.   Drag the reflection map on to the stage and convert it into a movie clip called `reflect`. Make sure the registration point is set for the center of the image and that **Export for ActionScript** is selected with the identifier name `reflect`. Now delete the instance from your stage.

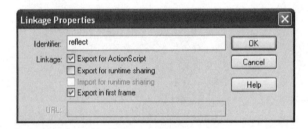

4.   Open your Library and, in the Linkage Properties dialog for each of the four sounds, check **Export for ActionScript** and give them the **Identifier** names `blip0`, `blip1`, `blip2`, and `miss`, respectively.

5.   Next we'll need to store some fonts in our Library that we can use for some dynamically created text fields. I chose two fonts: CosmicTwo for my titles, and Courier New (bold) for my statistics. You can choose any fonts you like, but try to keep your choice for the stats text a monospaced font, as that will allow the numbers to be changed throughout the course of game play without the entire score shifting on the stage and adjusting position due to different character widths. Select **New Font...** from the Library options menu at the top right of your Library. Name your choice for the stats font `statsFont`, and select the font from the **Font** drop down list:

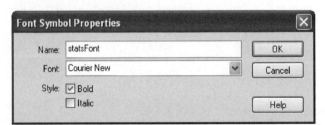

6. Repeat this step, naming your choice for the titles font `statsTitleFont`, selecting an appropriate font.

    I like to use descriptive names for my exported fonts, as something like `Courier New` sitting in the Library tells me very little about how my code uses it. Also, I can change the actual choice of font at any time without worrying about changing linkage names, symbol names, or code.

7. Now, if you've not used exported fonts in Flash MX yet, an additional step is required and that's to export the font from your Library in the same way that you would export your movie clip symbols. Right-click on the font name in the Library, choose **Linkage...**, and check **Export for Actionscript**. Also add an identifier name that corresponds to the symbol name (`statsFont` or `statsTitleFont`). We'll now be able to fill some dynamic text fields with our embedded font.

    We're almost ready to start on the code. However, the last thing we need to do is create our ball. I had originally planned to use Actionscript for this task too, but found that the animation of the ball caused odd effects to occur with the gradient, similar to the shifting pixels of a bitmap. Ah well, so much for the 100% code.

8. Create a new movie clip called `innerBall`. Draw a circle, 35 pixels in diameter, with no outline, and fill it with a white to black radial gradient. Place the hotspot of the gradient at the upper left of the sphere, giving the impression of a light source originating from above and behind your left shoulder. Finally, align the graphic to the exact center of the movie clip.

9. Now create a new movie clip called `ball`. In its Linkage Properties check **Export for ActionScript** and give it the identifier name `ball`. Drag a copy of **innerBall** out of the Library and align it to the exact center of the stage. Give it the instance name `innerBall`:

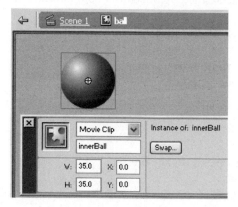

The reason for the nested movie clip is to allow for easier manipulation of the **innerBall** in 3D space. We'll set the outer **ball** movie clip to our 3D world center and throughout the game move the **innerBall** clip, whose registration point (inside **ball**) will always match the world center. This saves us the hassle of having to use an offset variable on each move.

So here we are! A stage without graphics and a Library with ten items – it must be time to code...

The code

I won't lie to you: there's a fair bit of code ahead, so it's best if we take a moment to break down what it is we will be writing so you don't become lost in the script. I've divided the code into four logical sections. Let's take a quick look at what each section will cover.

The SphereCage interface

- Declare the variables for our game
- Create movie clips to house our graphics
- Create sound objects to control the sound effects
- Create and format text fields to hold our score data
- Draw the background graphics

Master Classes

- Create the custom Class `LightSource` to hold our light source information
- Create the custom Class `Model` to hold our 3D model information

Exploring inheritance

- Create `BallModel`, subclass of `Model`, which will hold our ball information
- Create `PlaneModel`, subclass of `Model`, which will hold our paddle information
- Create `PopUp`, subclass of `Model`, which will hold information for our pop-up windows

Game functions and object instantiation

- Create functions to run the overall game
  - Draw foreground graphics
  - Initialize game
  - Keep score
  - Manage sounds
  - Sort depths
  - Update models based on key presses
  - Format pop-ups
- Create object instances of our Classes (paddles, ball and targets)

As you work through the code, refer back to this list from time to time to orient yourself. You might also find it helpful to print out the code from the finished FLA included on the CD. It is heavily commented and might give you additional insight on some of the script.

The SphereCage interface

The first thing that we'll take care of is setting up the elements for our game. We'll create all the necessary movie clips that we'll use later, and also draw the background graphics on the stage.

1. On the main timeline, rename the default layer Actions. All of the code for this game will be placed in the first frame of this layer. Open up the Actions panel and add the following ActionScript:

```
stageHeight = Stage.height;
stageWidth = stageHeight*1.375;
centerX = stageWidth*2/3;
centerY = stageHeight/2;
focalLength = stageHeight;
radius = stageHeight*.4;
radAdj = radius*.8;
planeSize = stageHeight/20;
smoothness = 80;

this.createEmptyMovieClip("backShadow", 1);
this.createEmptyMovieClip("targetMC", 2);
this.attachMovie("ball", "ballMC", 10);
this.createEmptyMovieClip("planeMC", 20);
this.createEmptyMovieClip("paddleMC", 30);
this.createEmptyMovieClip("sphere", 100);
this.createEmptyMovieClip("painting", 150);
this.createEmptyMovieClip("paintMask", 151);
this.createEmptyMovieClip("blip0MC", 250);
this.createEmptyMovieClip("blip1MC", 251);
this.createEmptyMovieClip("blip2MC", 252);
this.createEmptyMovieClip("missMC", 253);
this.attachMovie("reflect", "reflect", 200);
reflect._height = reflect._width=radius*2;
reflect._alpha = 4;

sphere.createEmptyMovieClip("rim", 0);
sphere.createEmptyMovieClip("shadow", 1);
sphere.createEmptyMovieClip("highlight", 2);
targetMC.createEmptyMovieClip("topTarget", 0);
```

427

continues overleaf

```
targetMC.createEmptyMovieClip("bottomTarget", 1);
reflect._x = targetMC._x=ballMC._x=planeMC._x=paddleMC._x=sphere._x=
➥backShadow._x=centerX;
reflect._y = targetMC._y=ballMC._y=planeMC._y=paddleMC._y=sphere._y=
➥backShadow._y=centerY;

blip0 = new Sound(blip0MC);
blip1 = new Sound(blip1MC);
blip2 = new Sound(blip2MC);
miss = new Sound(missMC);
blip0.attachSound("blip0");
blip1.attachSound("blip1");
blip2.attachSound("blip2");
miss.attachSound("miss");
```

There shouldn't be anything too surprising here. We first set a number of variables, including the dimensions of our stage. Notice how everything is based on the stage height, even the stageWidth variable. This means that altering the size of the stage should make everything else in the game change size as well, while maintaining proportion, including font size.

centerX and centerY are the coordinates of our sphere center and also the center of our 3D world. radius is of course the radius of our circle, and radAdj is just a slight offset that is just inside the radius. This offset is where our player's paddle will be located and will serve as the perimeter to be guarded. It gives our sphere the thickness at the edges that you can see in the finished version of the game. Finally, planeSize will be the size of our two paddles, and smoothness dictates the number of lines used to draw our spheres – the higher the number, the smoother the surface. I think a value of 80 gives us all we need.

We then create all the necessary movie clips, and attach our ball and reflection map. We will be referencing a lot of these later with our custom objects. Notice that we set the **reflect** movie clip with an opacity (alpha value) of 4%. If this is too subtle for you, raise the value.

Our **targetMC** (the small 'x' graphics that represent the ball's trajectory) and our **sphereMC** each have movie clips nested within them, so we create those here.

Next, we set the majority of our graphics to the location of centerX and centerY. Rethinking this game now, I'd probably use further nesting (placing all these clips in a parent clip and moving this to centerX and centerY), but this works fine as well.

Finally, we create new Sound objects for each of our sound movie clips, and attach the appropriate sounds from our Library. If you're wondering why we have created movie clips to be referenced by our Sound objects instead of simply using the _root timeline, it is because associating sounds with different timelines allows us to manipulate each sound independently of the others if we wanted to adjust volume or pan. As it happens we don't actually need to with our game, but it is good habit to set up your sounds in this manner in case you wish to add this functionality at a later time.

2. Add this next section of code, which will draw our background:

```
this.lineStyle(10, 0x222222, 100);
this.beginFill(0, 100);
this.lineTo(stageWidth/3, 0);
this.lineTo(stageWidth/3, stageHeight);
this.lineTo(0, stageHeight);
this.lineTo(0, 0);
this.endFill();
this.lineTo(stageWidth, 0);
this.lineTo(stageWidth, stageHeight);
this.lineTo(0, stageHeight);

this.lineStyle(2, 0xEEEEEE, 60);
this.moveTo(0, 0);
this.lineTo(stageWidth/3, 0);
this.lineTo(stageWidth/3, stageHeight);
this.lineTo(0, stageHeight);
this.lineTo(0, 0);
this.lineTo(stageWidth, 0);
this.lineTo(stageWidth, stageHeight);
this.lineTo(0, stageHeight);

paintMask.beginFill(0, 100);
paintMask.moveTo(3, 3);
paintMask.lineTo(stageWidth/3-3, 3);
paintMask.lineTo(stageWidth/3-3, stageHeight-3);
paintMask.lineTo(3, stageHeight-3);
paintMask.endFill();
painting.setMask(paintMask);
```

The first two blocks of code draw our borders (both outer and inner) and the black fill at the left. Notice how I use a thicker border at first, followed by a thinner border at a lower opacity. This gives us a nice effect at the game's edges with little work.

paintMask is a movie clip that will mask our gradient painting, containing it within the black area on the left-hand side. The last line actually sets the mask (though we've yet to draw anything in our **painting** movie clip).

3. Now it's time to prepare our font formatting and add our statistics fields. I have to say that one of my favorite new features of Flash MX is the font formatting control, so I couldn't let this project go by without using it a little:

```
textHeight = stageHeight/20;

statsTitle = new TextFormat();
statsTitle.color = 0x449944;
statsTitle.font = "statsTitleFont";
statsTitle.size = stageHeight*.04;
statsTitle.underline = 1;

stats = new TextFormat();
stats.color = 0xFFFFFF;
stats.font = "statsFont";
stats.size = stageHeight*.05;
stats.bold = 1;

this.createTextField("livesTitleTF", 501, stageWidth/40, textHeight,
➡0, 0);
this.createTextField("highTitleTF", 502, stageWidth/40, textHeight*4,
➡0, 0);
this.createTextField("scoreTitleTF", 503, stageWidth/40, textHeight*7,
➡0, 0);
this.createTextField("highTF", 504, stageWidth/40, textHeight*5,
➡0, 0);
this.createTextField("scoreTF", 505, stageWidth/40, textHeight*8,
➡0, 0);

livesTitleTF.setNewTextFormat(statsTitle);
highTitleTF.setNewTextFormat(statsTitle);
scoreTitleTF.setNewTextFormat(statsTitle);
highTF.setNewTextFormat(stats);
scoreTF.setNewTextFormat(stats);
highTitleTF.embedFonts = scoreTitleTF.embedFonts=
➡livesTitleTF.embedFonts=1;
highTF.embedFonts = scoreTF.embedFonts=1;
highTitleTF.autoSize = scoreTitleTF.autoSize=
➡livesTitleTF.autoSize="left";
highTF.autoSize = scoreTF.autoSize="left";
livesTitleTF.text = "LIVES";
highTitleTF.text = "HIGH SCORE";
scoreTitleTF.text = "SCORE";
highTF.text = "00000000";
```

Cool! Here we create two **TextFormat** objects: stats and statsTitle. We set their size, color, and style, as well as their font (the linkage identifiers from our Library fonts). We then create five text fields, using our stageHeight and stageWidth variables as placement guides.

Now take another look at the code above and notice that we are setting the width and height for each text field to zero. We can do this, because when we come to format the text boxes (near the end of the last section of code) we set their autoSize property to "left", which means that the text field will expand to the right as text is placed in it. This is very handy. You could also use "center" and "right" when needed.

In addition to autoSize, we apply our appropriate TextFormat and make sure to embed the fonts (otherwise the text won't appear in the movie). We conclude by putting the proper strings into the text property of each text field.

4. Go ahead and test your movie to see the background and text that we've created so far. From here on out we won't be able to see any changes on stage until we finish our code.

Master Classes

Now it's time to move on to our 3D objects. In this next section we will create two new Classes that will define these objects in our SphereCage game. This will be our first step in exploring OOP code.

1. The first object to add should come as no surprise since we used it in the previous chapter.

Add this code now:

```
LightSource = function(x, y, z, brightness) {
    this.x = x;
    this.y = y;
    this.z = z;
    this.brightness = brightness;
    this.calcMag();
};

LightSource.prototype.calcMag = function() {
    this.magnitude = Math.sqrt(this.x*this.x+this.y*this.y+this.z*
    ➥this.z)
};
```

This should all be very familiar from the last chapter. We are creating a custom Class to hold the properties and methods for any lights we add to the scene. The only method we add at this time is calcMag, which calculates the light's distance from world center.

2. This next section of code will seem familiar, but with one major difference, so see if you can spot it:

```
Model = function() {
};
Model.prototype.applyTransform = function() {
    if (this.transformMatrix) {
        for (var i = 0; i<this.vertexList.length; i++) {
            var vert = this.vertexList[i];
            var x = this.transformMatrix.a*vert.x+
            ➥this.transformMatrix.b*vert.y+this.transformMatrix.c*
            ➥vert.z+this.transformMatrix.d*vert.w;
            var y = this.transformMatrix.e*vert.x+
            ➥this.transformMatrix.f*vert.y+this.transformMatrix.g*
            ➥vert.z+this.transformMatrix.h*vert.w;
            var z = this.transformMatrix.i*vert.x+
            ➥this.transformMatrix.j*vert.y+this.transformMatrix.k*
            ➥vert.z+this.transformMatrix.l*vert.w;
            vert.x = x;
            vert.y = y;
            vert.z = z;
        }
        delete this.transformMatrix;
    }
};
```

```
Model.prototype.getSideColor = function(side) {
    var verts = [this.vertexList[side.vertices[0]],
    ➥this.vertexList[side.vertices[1]],
    ➥this.vertexList[side.vertices[2]]];
    var lightFactor = this.factorLightAngle(verts);
    var r = side.sideColor.substr(0, 2);
    var g = side.sideColor.substr(2, 2);
    var b = side.sideColor.substr(4, 2);
    r = parseInt(r, 16)*lightFactor;
    g = parseInt(g, 16)*lightFactor;
    b = parseInt(b, 16)*lightFactor;
    return r << 16 | g << 8 | b;
};

Model.prototype.factorLightAngle = function(vertices) {
    var U = [(vertices[0].x-vertices[1].x), (vertices[0].y-
    ➥vertices[1].y), (vertices[0].z-vertices[1].z)];
    var V = [(vertices[1].x-vertices[2].x), (vertices[1].y-
    ➥vertices[2].y), (vertices[1].z-vertices[2].z)];
    var p = [((U[1]*V[2])-(U[2]*V[1])), -((U[0]*V[2])-(U[2]*V[0])),
    ➥((U[0]*V[1])-(U[1]*V[0]))];
    var magP = Math.sqrt((p[0]*p[0])+(p[1]*p[1])+(p[2]*p[2]));
    var dP = ((p[0]*light.x)+(p[1]*light.y)+(p[2]*light.z));
    if (dP>0) {
        dP *= -1;
    }
    return ((Math.acos(dP/(magP*light.magnitude))/Math.PI)*
    ➥light.brightness/100);
};
```

This is the beginning of our custom Model Class. In the last chapter, we used almost exactly the same code for `factorLightAngle` and `getSideColor`, and the `applyTransform` function was actually a part of a larger `render` function, so there's not much new to explain.

What we're doing this time, instead of making generic functions to call in our movie, is making a custom Class to hold all of our main 3D methods. When we need a new model, all we have to do is use the constructor we created above:

```
plane = new Model();
```

That's it! `plane` will then have full use of all of `Model`'s methods, since it will be a model itself, an object instance of the class `Model`. This will make it much easier when we have multiple models on our stage, as opposed to the single 3D cube from last chapter.

To create `Model`'s methods, you can see that we use its `prototype` property, which is the property of every object that holds all of that object's properties and methods. By making `factorLightAngle` a part of `Model`'s `prototype` property, we have made it accessible to every model that we choose to create.

There is another way to add properties and methods to all instances of a Class, which I'll discuss briefly so you might see the difference and the benefits of using the `prototype` property. Try this experiment in a new movie.

Sect frame 1 of the default layer and type the following into the Actions panel:

```
MyClass = function() {
    this.myMethod = function() {};
};
instance1 = new MyClass();
instance2 = new MyClass();
trace(instance1.myMethod);
```

Debug your movie now (**Control > Debug Movie** or CONTROL+SHIFT+ENTER) and press the green play button in your Debugger. Select **level0** in the pane at the top left and click on the "**Variables**" tab below this pane. You should see both `instance1` and `instance2` listed with plus signs to their left. If you expand these instances, you will see they both contain copies of `myMethod`. Your Output window confirms this by returning `[type function]`.

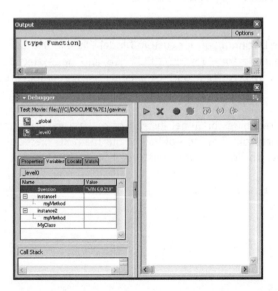

Now go back into your script editor, and change the lines to read:

```
MyClass = function() {};
MyClass.prototype.myMethod = function();
instance1 = new MyClass();
instance2 = new MyClass();
trace(instance1.myMethod);
```

If you debug your movie a second time, you will see that although we have again successfully created two instances of `MyClass`, and our Output window has returned the expected `[type function]`, the `instance1` and `instance2` located in the **Variables** tab DO NOT have plus signs next to them. What's happened?

Well, in the first form of method creation, we are actually attaching the function `myMethod` to every single instance of `MyClass`. We are not assigning a pointer, BUT THE ACTUAL FUNCTION ITSELF. As you can imagine, this means we have multiple copies of the exact same function floating around and taking up memory.

The second form of method creation attaches the method to the `prototype` property instead. This creates only a single copy of the function that can then be accessed by ALL instances. When we call the method (for example, `instance1.myMethod();`), Flash will look first at the instance itself and any local methods we have given it (methods added to a single instance). If it does not find reference to `myMethod`, it will then look to the `prototype` property of the Class. So for any method or property you want repeated across instances, adding these to the `prototype` property makes sense.

You will see an example of adding local properties to an instance in our previous LightSource Class. In the constructor, we add an x, y, z, and brightness property to the newly created instance. Although each instance of a LightSource will contain these properties, the values will differ for each, so we need to make it local to the instance.

If you haven't investigated OOP programming yet, this can hardly be a comprehensive lesson (not if we want to make a whole game!), and in all honesty this is not true OOP anyway. It's Flash OOP, which is a bit of a hybrid, much like the graphics/code Flash environment that I wrote of at the chapter's outset. What I'm hoping for is that this might open some doors for you so that you might see how useful some of the OOP-style coding can be. By its very nature, it contains code within the objects that need it and use it, making for a much cleaner structure to work in. By this I mean that an object controls its own actions and manages its own properties. When the ball moves in our game, the ball itself will control that movement instead of having the paddle do it. If the paddle needs to know the ball's magnitude, it will ask the ball (perhaps, `ball.getMagnitude();`) instead of calculating the value itself. That way, I know that any code that directly alters or manipulates the ball can be found in the ball object itself. Because of this, I've found it's far easier to locate where your scripts go wrong (not that it's always easy to fix them) when you know that objects take care of themselves in this way.

As a final note on the above code, you'll see that our `applyTransform` method (which applies a model's transformation matrix) actually deals with four properties for each vertex: x, y, z, and w. But wait a minute; what's w? In this game we're using 4x4 matrices to transform our models, as opposed to the 3x3 matrices in the last chapter. Using 4x4 matrices allows us to include a `translate` method for our models that we can add to the transformation matrices, which would be impossible in a 3x3 structure. To do this, though, we need to give an extra property to each vertex (you can't multiply a 4x4 matrix by a 3x1, but you can with a 4x1, which is why there is no need to change the value of `vert.w` within the `applyTransform` function since really it's just a placeholder). The value of w will always be 1, but it's a powerful addition, as it will allow us to use the 4x4 matrices.

3. Let's finish off our `Model` Class code:

```
Model.prototype.rotateX = function(degree) {
    var rad = degree*Math.PI/180;
    var sin = Math.sin(rad);
    var cos = Math.cos(rad);
    var matrix = {a:1, b:0, c:0, d:0, e:0, f:cos, g:sin, h:0, i:0,
    ➡j:-sin, k:cos, l:0, m:0, n:0, o:0, p:1};
    this.transform(matrix);
};

Model.prototype.rotateY = function(degree) {
    var rad = degree*Math.PI/180;
    var sin = Math.sin(rad);
    var cos = Math.cos(rad);
    var matrix = {a:cos, b:0, c:-sin, d:0, e:0, f:1, g:0, h:0, i:sin,
    ➡j:0, k:cos, l:0, m:0, n:0, o:0, p:1};
    this.transform(matrix);
};

Model.prototype.translate = function(x, y, z) {
    var matrix = {a:1, b:0, c:0, d:x, e:0, f:1, g:0, h:y, i:0, j:0,
    ➡k:1, l:z, m:0, n:0, o:0, p:1};
    this.transform(matrix);
};

Model.prototype.transform = function(matrix) {
    if (this.transformMatrix) {
        var a = matrix.a*this.transformMatrix.a+matrix.b*
        ➡this.transformMatrix.e+matrix.c*this.transformMatrix.i+
        ➡matrix.d*this.transformMatrix.m;
        var b = matrix.a*this.transformMatrix.b+matrix.b*
        ➡this.transformMatrix.f+matrix.c*this.transformMatrix.j+
```

```
        ➥matrix.d*this.transformMatrix.n;
        var c = matrix.a*this.transformMatrix.c+matrix.b*
        ➥this.transformMatrix.g+matrix.c*this.transformMatrix.k+
        ➥matrix.d*this.transformMatrix.o;
        var d = matrix.a*this.transformMatrix.d+matrix.b*
        ➥this.transformMatrix.h+matrix.c*this.transformMatrix.l+
        ➥matrix.d*this.transformMatrix.p;
        var e = matrix.e*this.transformMatrix.a+matrix.f*
        ➥this.transformMatrix.e+matrix.g*this.transformMatrix.i+
        ➥matrix.h*this.transformMatrix.m;
        var f = matrix.e*this.transformMatrix.b+matrix.f*
        ➥this.transformMatrix.f+matrix.g*this.transformMatrix.j+
        ➥matrix.h*this.transformMatrix.n;
        var g = matrix.e*this.transformMatrix.c+matrix.f*
        ➥this.transformMatrix.g+matrix.g*this.transformMatrix.k+
        ➥matrix.h*this.transformMatrix.o;
        var h = matrix.e*this.transformMatrix.d+matrix.f*
        ➥this.transformMatrix.h+matrix.g*this.transformMatrix.l+
        ➥matrix.h*this.transformMatrix.p;
        var i = matrix.i*this.transformMatrix.a+matrix.j*
        ➥this.transformMatrix.e+matrix.k*this.transformMatrix.i+
        ➥matrix.l*this.transformMatrix.m;
        var j = matrix.i*this.transformMatrix.b+matrix.j*
        ➥this.transformMatrix.f+matrix.k*this.transformMatrix.j+
        ➥matrix.l*this.transformMatrix.n;
        var k = matrix.i*this.transformMatrix.c+matrix.j*
        ➥this.transformMatrix.g+matrix.k*this.transformMatrix.k+
        ➥matrix.l*this.transformMatrix.o;
        var l = matrix.i*this.transformMatrix.d+matrix.j*
        ➥this.transformMatrix.h+matrix.k*this.transformMatrix.l+
        ➥matrix.l*this.transformMatrix.p;
        this.transformMatrix = {a:a, b:b, c:c, d:d, e:e, f:f, g:g,
        ➥h:h, i:i, j:j, k:k, l:l, m:0, n:0, o:0, p:1};
    } else {
        this.transformMatrix = matrix;
    }
};

Model.prototype.render = function() {
    this.applyTransform();
    for (var i = 0; i<this.vertexList.length; i++) {
```

continues overleaf

```
                    var scale = focalLength/(focalLength-this.vertexList[i].z);
                    this.clip[i]._xscale = this.clip[i]._yscale=(scale/4)*
                ➥this.vertexList[i].z+50;
                    this.clip[i]._x = this.vertexList[i].x*scale;
                    this.clip[i]._y = this.vertexList[i].y*scale;
            }
    };
```

Don't be scared, as there isn't actually much new here. `rotateX` and `rotateY` are the same as in the last chapter, although you can see the matrices have the extra values. `translate` is new, but is straightforward if you understand how we're using our matrices. This is the method that will move our ball across the sphere. All we set are the d, h, and l properties of our matrix with our coordinate offset (x, y, z). The `transform` function (as we also used in the previous chapter) is made a bit longer by the extra matrix properties. Looking closely, you'll notice that we don't need to calculate the last row of our matrix, as that will *always* be 0,0,0,1.

With our `render` method, we first apply the model's current transform (we created that method above, remember?), and then loop through its `vertexList` to set the screen coordinates. In truth, this function works for the current game and its structure, but would not be useful in the same form for other projects. The reason for this is that only two of our models actually use this method: our ball and our target. The ball only has one vertex, while the target has two (two mini-targets, each with a single vertex). Because of this, we don't have to worry about sides and color and so on, and really the only reason we loop through vertices at all is because we have two targets.

Other than this, the code does exactly what you'll remember from the cube (the `clip` property in question contains reference to one of **innerBall**, **topTarget**, or **bottomTarget**), with the added line to actually scale the movie clips as they move about the sphere. We didn't need to do this with our cube, but with single vertex models, the physical clip needs to be scaled to simulate depth.

So if only our targets and ball use `render`, what about our two paddles? Ah, observant *and* intuitive – I like that! This will all be revealed in time.

This completes our `Model`, but it hardly takes care of everything we'll need for our 3D world. The thing is, these are the only methods that are needed for *all* the models on our stage.

Exploring inheritance

From this point on the paddles, the ball, and the targets will all have different functionality for us to deal with (actually, our targets are nearly done). So how do we deal with this? One word: **inheritance**. Don't worry if you haven't worked with inheritance before. If you've come this far you already know almost everything you'll need to know.

1. Underneath all of the previous ActionScript, enter the following code and then I'll explain what's going on here (you know the structure by now!):

```
BallModel = function() {
};
BallModel.prototype = new Model();
BallModel.prototype.move = function() {
    var x = this.direction.x*this.velocity;
    var y = this.direction.y*this.velocity;
    var z = this.direction.z*this.velocity;
    this.translate(x, y, z);
    with (this.vertexList[0]) {
        var mag = Math.sqrt(x*x+y*y+z*z);
        if (mag+this.rad>radAdj) {
            if (this.checkPaddle() && !ok2Hit) {
                playBlip(this.velocity);
                ok2Hit = 1;
                updateScore();
                if (this.velocity<6) {
                    this.velocity += .1;
                }
                this.setDirection(-x, -y, -z);
            } else if (!ok2Hit) {
                miss.start();
                killBall();
            }
        } else if (mag-this.rad<10 && ok2Hit) {
            delete ok2Hit;
            playBlip(this.velocity);
            this.checkAngle();
        }
    }
};
```

So what's `BallModel`? Didn't we just create `Model` and talk about how the ball would use its methods? Yes we did, but now we need our ball to go off and do its own thing. The best way to achieve this is by making another Class specifically for the ball, but to make this Class **inherit** the properties and methods from the `Model` Class.

If you've not heard the dog analogy of inheritance before, then it's my privilege to share it with you now. I have a Yorkshire terrier at home named Cassie. Cassie has her own way of doing things, that's for sure, but she has certain methods that are inherent in *all* dogs. She gets excited and wags her tail. She sees a cat or bird and gets territorial. She gets hot and she pants. In programming, you might say that Cassie is an object instance of the `Dog` Class. But this isn't all. Cassie is also covered with hair. She would give birth to live young (if we let her) and nurse them with milk. She is warm blooded. These are all traits she has inherited from the `Mammal` Class. So she actually has `Dog` methods and properties *added* to her initial `Mammal` properties and methods. As you might imagine, you can travel from here up the inheritance chain to `Animal`, `CarbonBasedLifeForm`, and so on.

We will have a ball, an instance of the `BallModel` Class, which is itself a sub-class of `Model`. We have created our first method for `BallModel`, `move`, so you can correctly assume that when we want the ball to move we'll use:

```
ball.move();
```

But, when we want to render the `ball` instance, what will the syntax be? How about:

```
ball.render();
```

Pretty simple, huh? When we use the above line, Flash will look at the instance of `ball` to see if it contains a local method called `render`. It won't, so Flash will then look at `ball`'s Class, which is `BallModel`, for the method. Again, it will be unsuccessful, so Flash will continue searching up the inheritance chain to `Model`, finding the `render` method there.

So why did we separate it out at all? Well, we did this because our paddles and our ball need completely different methods associated with them, but share some common 3D methods of transformation. So, we place the transform methods in a Class, and then create two sub-classes for our paddles and our ball (much like cats and dogs branching off from mammals). To achieve this, we set the `BallModel`'s `prototype` property to be a new instance of the `Model` Class. And there we go; inheritance isn't too tough.

With this addressed, we'd better take a look at the `move` method we wrote in the last section of code. The first thing we do in the method is translate our model based on four variables: the three dimensions of direction (represented by a directional vector) and the `velocity` of the ball. Since the ball is in constant motion, these values don't need to be sent to the method. We multiply our current direction (which will be a unit vector for you math heads) by our current velocity, and then call our `translate` method (defined for the `Model` Class).

After our ball is moved, we need to check its location. We do this by calculating its magnitude, or distance from world center (old Pythagoras at work again). Using this value, we check to see if the ball has reached the perimeter. If this is true, we check to see if the paddle is blocking the hit (using the `checkPaddle` method which we'll define in a moment). If it is, we play the appropriate blip sound (based on the ball's velocity), update the score, increase the ball's velocity slightly, and finally set a variable called `ok2hit`, which is simply a flag to save us from the task of having to adjust the ball back if it overshoots the radius slightly (in which case, the magnitude will cause this condition to be true again in the next frame).

setDirection is a method to set our ball's new direction, which in this case is the opposite of its current direction. It's extremely convenient that we are translating the ball directly back to world center, because our new directional vector (the value stored in ball.direction) is taken straight from our current coordinate. To visualize this, imagine the ball with the coordinates (5,-10,0). To travel to world center, the ball needs to travel by -5 along the x-axis and by 10 on the y-axis. This is a direction, short and sweet, and obtained entirely from its current coordinate. setDirection will take this and make it into a **unit vector**, which we will discuss in a moment.

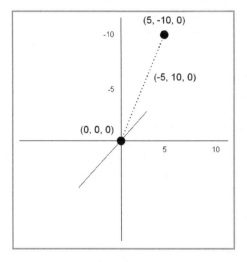

Now, if the paddle *doesn't* block the ball, we call the killBall function and play the miss sound effect.

In the final if statement, we make sure the ball hasn't reached center (or an approximation). If it has, we play the appropriate blip sound and check the current angle of the center plane (the computer's paddle) using the method checkAngle. In this method, we assess the angle of collision between the ball and the plane and deflect the ball in the appropriate direction. But let's not jump ahead of ourselves!

2.   We're now going to add more BallModel methods (this object does the brunt of our game work), so let's keep going on and add the following code to our file:

```
BallModel.prototype.setDirection = function(x, y, z) {
    var mag = Math.sqrt(x*x+y*y+z*z);
    var nD = [x/mag, y/mag, z/mag];
    var dest = [nD[0]*radAdj-this.vertexList[0].x, nD[1]*radAdj-
```

```
        ➥this.vertexList[0].y, nD[2]*radAdj-this.vertexList[0].z];
        mag = Math.sqrt(dest[0]*dest[0]+dest[1]*dest[1]+dest[2]*dest[2]);
        this.direction = {x:dest[0]/mag, y:dest[1]/mag, z:dest[2]/mag};
    };

    BallModel.prototype.checkPaddle = function() {
        var x;
        var y;
        var z;
        var numVertices = paddle.vertexList.length
        for (var i = 0; i< numVertices; i++) {
            x += paddle.vertexList[i].x;
            y += paddle.vertexList[i].y;
            z += paddle.vertexList[i].z;
        }
        x /= numVertices;
        y /= numVertices;
        z /= numVertices;
        x -= this.vertexList[0].x;
        y -= this.vertexList[0].y;
        z -= this.vertexList[0].z;
        var dist = Math.sqrt(x*x+y*y+z*z);
        if (dist<planeSize+this.rad) {
            return true;
        }
        return false;
    };
```

Time to look at the 3D math – it's long overdue in our 3D game programming! setDirection is a method we'll call whenever our ball changes direction, whether at the center or the perimeter. The name is a little misleading, as the intended direction is actually *sent* to this method when called (the x, y, and z arguments). What setDirection does is clean up these numbers into a form we can use. The first two lines turn our directional vector into a unit vector. All this means is that it's a vector with a magnitude of 1 (taking the square root of the sum of the square of each component). To make it a unit vector, all you need to do is divide each component of the vector by the vector's magnitude. With the direction a unit vector, we can control the speed of the ball by altering its velocity, and the direction vector will simply point us in the right direction without affecting speed. This is nD, short for our normalized direction.

Once we find the direction in which we should be heading, we calculate our destination by taking our direction vector and multiplying it by our adjusted radius variable (radAdj), adjusting for our ball's current position offset from world center. (These next few lines won't affect our perimeter checks, but are necessary for when the ball hits the center paddle.) With our destination coordinate found, we normalize this vector once more, and place the values into our ball's `direction` property.

The next method, `checkPaddle`, is called whenever our ball reaches the sphere's perimeter and we need to check if the paddle is blocking the ball. The method finds the center point of the paddle by averaging all of its vertices, then finds the distance between this center and the ball's location. If this distance is less than our `paddleWidth` (which will actually be half the width of our paddle) plus our ball's radius, we register a hit.

OK, this isn't 100% accurate collision detection, but it works just fine for our purposes. If you really want some true math, then read on...

3.   Add the following code and I'll apologize later:

```
BallModel.prototype.checkAngle = function() {
    var vertices = [plane.vertexList[0], plane.vertexList[1],
    ➥plane.vertexList[2]];
    var U = [(vertices[0].x-vertices[1].x), (vertices[0].y-
    ➥vertices[1].y), (vertices[0].z-vertices[1].z)];
    var V = [(vertices[1].x-vertices[2].x), (vertices[1].y-
    ➥vertices[2].y), (vertices[1].z-vertices[2].z)];
    var p = [((U[1]*V[2])-(U[2]*V[1])), -((U[0]*V[2])-(U[2]*V[0])),
    ➥((U[0]*V[1])-(U[1]*V[0]))];
    var magP = Math.sqrt((p[0]*p[0])+(p[1]*p[1])+(p[2]*p[2]));
    p = [p[0]/magP, p[1]/magP, p[2]/magP];
    var b = [-this.direction.x, -this.direction.y,
    ➥-this.direction.z];
    var dP = p[0]*b[0]+p[1]*b[1]+p[2]*b[2];
    var dPxN = [p[0]*dP, p[1]*dP, p[2]*dP];
    b = [dPxN[0]+dPxN[0]-b[0], dPxN[1]+dPxN[1]-b[1], dPxN[2]+dPxN[2]-
    ➥b[2]];
    this.setDirection(b[0], b[1], b[2]);
    setTarget();
};
```

The main idea behind `checkAngle`, and for deflection in general, is that the angle of incidence (the angle at which the ball hits the paddle) is equal to the angle of deflection.

First we use the vertices of our center plane to determine the plane's normal, which we make into a unit vector by dividing it by its magnitude. We've done all this before, and it results in p. For b, we reverse our ball's direction so that we may use it in our formulas. dP is the dot product of our ball's adjusted direction vector and our plane's normal. Remember that the dot product is the measure of the distance between the two vectors, which in this case will basically be the distance from a point on our ball's path to our plane's normal. We can use this distance to determine what the angle and direction would be on the *other* side of the normal.

We next multiply our vector normal by our scalar dot product. This gives us the projection of our vector onto our normal. The ball's new direction will be twice the distance of this projection from our ball's original vector, which we determine in our final b assignment. We send these new values to setDirection so that the vector might be normalized, and then draw our targets in the appropriate locations (we'll add the function that does this very soon).

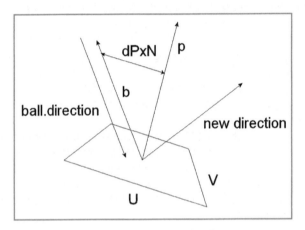

Whew! Those were pretty heavy concepts but it's all downhill from here. The majority of the remaining coding is mostly interface and game initialization that shouldn't be too testing. First, however, we need to finish up our ball Class.

4. Here are the last two methods for our BallModel:

```
BallModel.prototype.rotateDirection = function(axis, degree) {
    var rad = degree*Math.PI/180;
    var sin = Math.sin(rad);
    var cos = Math.cos(rad);
    if (axis == "y") {
        var x = cos*this.direction.x-sin*this.direction.z;
        this.direction.z = cos*this.direction.z+sin*this.direction.x;
        this.direction.x = x;
    } else {
        var z = cos*this.direction.z-sin*this.direction.y;
        this.direction.y = cos*this.direction.y+sin*this.direction.z;
        this.direction.z = z;
    }
};
```

```
BallModel.prototype.reset = function() {
    this.clip[0]._visible = 1;
    this.velocity = 1.5;
    this.vertexList[0] = {x:0, y:0, z:0, w:1};
    this.setDirection(Math.random()-1, Math.random()-.5,
    ➡Math.random());
    setTarget();
};
```

`rotateDirection` is called whenever the player spins the whole 3D world. When this occurs, we not only have to adjust the placement of each object in 3D space, but also the directional vector of the ball itself. Fortunately, this is a pretty easy task to accomplish. Since `ball.direction` is simply a unit vector containing an x, y and z component (its direction is determined by its relation to world center), all we have to do is spin that vector coordinate about the appropriate axis. The code to do this will be familiar if you've done any type of basic 3D in Flash. We also used a similar function at the beginning of our last chapter. We either rotate about the x- or the y-axis (we don't spin about the z-axis in this game), and the formulas to do that are already established, so we won't spend time on them.

Whenever a new round begins (anytime after a player misses a ball), the `reset` method is called. This turns on the visibility of the **innerball** movie clip (stored in the `clip` array), sets its `velocity` back to 1.5, sets a random direction, and sets the ball's coordinates to world center (notice the new w property, which will always be 1). Lastly it sets the target in the appropriate location. This should all be pretty straightforward, except for `setTarget`, which we will code in a moment.

And that's our `BallModel` Class! Remember, that when we create a ball with:

```
ball = new BallModel();
```

...it will not only contain all of the methods of the `BallModel` Class, but also all the properties and methods of the `Model` Class.

5. Our `BallModel` is taken care of. It's now time to define our planes:

```
PlaneModel = function() {
};
PlaneModel.prototype = new Model();
PlaneModel.prototype.render = function() {
    super.applyTransform();
    this.clip.clear();
    this.clip.lineStyle(1, 0, 100);
    var verts2D = [];
    this.zDepth = 0;
```

continues overleaf

```
                    for (var i = 0; i<this.vertexList.length; i++) {
                        var whichVert = this.vertexList[i];
                        verts2D[i] = {};
                        var scale = focalLength/(focalLength-whichVert.z);
                        verts2D[i].x = whichVert.x*scale;
                        verts2D[i].y = whichVert.y*scale;
                        this.zDepth += whichVert.z;
                    }
                    this.clip.moveTo(verts2D[0].x, verts2D[0].y);
                    this.clip.beginFill(this.getSideColor(this.side[0]), 100);
                    for (var j = 1; j<verts2D.length; j++) {
                        this.clip.lineTo(verts2D[j].x, verts2D[j].y);
                    }
                    this.clip.lineTo(verts2D[0].x, verts2D[0].y);
                    this.clip.endFill();
                };
```

You'll be pleased to know that this block of code constitutes the entirety of our `PlaneModel` Class definition. The only method we needed to add for our paddles (which will both be planes) is a rendering method.

Wait a minute! Don't we already have a `render` method defined for the `Model` Class? We do, but think back to the discussion of inheritance chains. When we use `paddle.render`, Flash will first look for a method called `render` in the `PlaneModel` Class. If it finds it there, it will stop looking. Flash will never reach the `Model` Class to see a method of the same name. In this way, we have provided a separate `render` method for our planes, but have allowed the use of `Model`'s remaining methods.

As for what this method does, it first calls the `applyTransform` method of its super class, in this case `Model`. Just as `this` will refer to its own methods, `super` will look at the methods of its super class, which it will find reference to in its `prototype` property (see where we set that in the line before?).

Once the transform is applied, we clear our clip of drawing objects, loop through our vertices, and draw our plane. This is all very similar to our work in the previous chapter, so I won't go into further detail, but you should note the addition of the `zDepth` property. This holds the sum of all the vertices' z coordinates. All we will use this for is to determine whether the plane is located on either the front or the back of the sphere, so further z calculations are unnecessary.

6. There's one final type of model to deal with, and you might not have expected it when playing with game earlier. Add the following:

```
PopUp = function(w, h) {
    this.vertexList = [];
```

```
        this.vertexList.push({x:-w, y:-h, z:20, w:1});
        this.vertexList.push({x:-w, y:h, z:20, w:1});
        this.vertexList.push({x:w, y:h, z:20, w:1});
        this.vertexList.push({x:w, y:-h, z:20, w:1});
        this.vertexList.push({x:-w-15, y:-h-15, z:0, w:1});
        this.vertexList.push({x:-w-15, y:h+15, z:0, w:1});
        this.vertexList.push({x:w+15, y:h+15, z:0, w:1});
        this.vertexList.push({x:w+15, y:-h-15, z:0, w:1});
        this.vertexList.push({x:-w+5, y:-h+5, z:15, w:1});
        this.vertexList.push({x:-w+5, y:h-5, z:15, w:1});
        this.vertexList.push({x:w-5, y:h-5, z:15, w:1});
        this.vertexList.push({x:w-5, y:-h+5, z:15, w:1});
        this.side = [];
        this.side.push({vertices:[0, 1, 2, 3], sideColor:"666666"});
        this.side.push({vertices:[0, 4, 5, 1], sideColor:"888888"});
        this.side.push({vertices:[0, 3, 7, 4], sideColor:"888888"});
        this.side.push({vertices:[7, 3, 2, 6], sideColor:"333333"});
        this.side.push({vertices:[1, 5, 6, 2], sideColor:"333333"});
        this.side.push({vertices:[8, 9, 10, 11], sideColor:"666666"});
        this.side.push({vertices:[0, 8, 9, 1], sideColor:"444444"});
        this.side.push({vertices:[3, 2, 10, 11], sideColor:"777777"});
        this.side.push({vertices:[9, 10, 2, 1], sideColor:"777777"});
        this.side.push({vertices:[0, 3, 11, 8], sideColor:"444444"});
    };
PopUp.prototype = new Model();
```

Yes, the pop-up windows are models as well. Here you can see that the constructor will be sent a width (w) and height (h) variable to customize the size of the pop-up, but I left the bevel size the same. There shouldn't be too much here that you don't recall from the last chapter. Again, notice the extra w property for each vertex so that we might use 4x4 matrices. Also, you will see that I enhanced the 3D lighting of the model by adding my own adjustments to the highlighted and shadowed sides' sideColor.

7. There is only one function for our PopUp model:

```
PopUp.prototype.render = function() {
    this.clip.clear();
    var verts2D = [];
    for (var i = 0; i<this.vertexList.length; i++) {
        var whichVert = this.vertexList[i];
        verts2D[i] = {};
        var scale = focalLength/(focalLength-whichVert.z);
        verts2D[i].x = whichVert.x*scale;
        verts2D[i].y = whichVert.y*scale;
    }
```

continues overleaf

```
                    for (var i = 0; i<this.side.length; i++) {
                        this.clip.moveTo(verts2D[this.side[i].vertices[0]].x,
                        ➡verts2D[this.side[i].vertices[0]].y);
                        this.clip.beginFill(this.getSideColor(this.side[i]), 100);
                        for (var j = 1; j<this.side[i].vertices.length; j++) {
                            this.clip.lineTo(verts2D[this.side[i].vertices[j]].x,
                            ➡verts2D[this.side[i].vertices[j]].y);
                        }
                        this.clip.lineTo(verts2D[this.side[i].vertices[0]].x,
                        ➡verts2D[this.side[i].vertices[0]].y);
                        this.clip.endFill();
                    }
                };
```

That's right, another `render` method! I probably could have consolidated this method with the `PlaneModel`'s render method and made `PopUp` a sub class of `Plane`, but it was only a few extra lines of code, all of which should be old hat to you by now.

Our last piece of object code is an extension of the `Object` object itself:

```
Object.prototype.duplicate = function() {
    var temp = {};
    for (var i in this) {
        temp[i] = this[i];
    }
    return temp;
};
```

There will come a point in the game (when the player spins the 3D world) when we will use this method to duplicate one model's transform matrix. Since Flash stores references to objects and not copies, we will need to make the copies ourselves. I will explain further when we reach that section of code.

Congratulations! We've reached the end of our Flash OOP code and now just have a few `_root` functions to define before we start our game. If you test the movie again now, you'll see absolutely no difference on the stage from when you tested it last. So what was with all that work? It was all **preparation**. With all of our custom Classes defined and set up to take care of their own actions, all that remains are a few housekeeping functions.

Game functions and object instantiation

In this final section we write some functions that take care of general actions that do not deal specifically with individual 3D objects. Some of these include our scorekeeping function, our functions to draw our interface graphics and our function that actually 'runs the game'. Ideally, we'd use Classes and OOP for these as well (perhaps an interface object to run the game and handle its drawing, or a scoreboard object to keep track of the score and lives?). Sometimes, however, making things better, clearer and more object-oriented requires more code and unfortunately we've not got the pages. I encourage you once this is complete to test your understanding of OOP and the concepts we've discussed and experiment with these ideas.

Once these housekeeping functions have been declared, we will create object instances of the Classes we worked so hard on in the previous section, including our ball, paddles and targets. That sounds like a lot to do, so let's get started!

1. This first function will reset the stage at the start of each game:

```
initGame = function () {
    paint();
    scoreTF.text = "00000000";
    lives = 4;
    for (var i = 1; i < lives; i++) {
        var b = this.attachMovie("ball", "ball" + i, 160 + i);
        b._xscale = b._yscale = stageHeight/8;
        b._y = stageHeight/7;
        b._x = (stageWidth/40*(i*2-1)) + b._width/2;
    }
    ball.reset();
    paddleMC.onEnterFrame = frameCode;
};
```

`paint` is the function that draws our random gradient pattern at the left of the interface (we'll write the code for that next). We reset the score to 0 and the total lives to 4. Based on this amount, we attach three balls to our stage (plus the one currently in use gives us 4) to display the lives graphically. We scale and place these balls on the left-hand side (the _x position was determined by just a little trial and error). Finally, we tell our `ball` to reset itself, and set the `onEnterFrame` event for our `paddle` to be a function called `frameCode`. `frameCode` will contain the code that needs to run constantly throughout our game.

2. Here's the `paint` function we just called:

```
paint = function () {
    for (i=0; i<25; i++) {
        var p = painting.createEmptyMovieClip("p"+i, i);
        p._x = Math.random()*(stageWidth/3-0);
        p._y = Math.random()*(stageHeight-stageHeight/4)+
        ➥stageHeight/4;
        var w = Math.random()*50+100;
        var col = Math.ceil(Math.random()*100);
```

continues overleaf

```
            col = col << 8;
            var colors = [col, col];
            var alphas = [50, 0];
            var ratios = [0, 200];
            var matrix = {matrixType:"box", x:-w/2, y:-w/2, w:w, h:w,
            ➥r:0};
            p.beginGradientFill("radial", colors, alphas, ratios,
            ➥matrix);
            p.moveTo(-w/2, -w/2);
            p.lineTo(w/2, -w/2);
            p.lineTo(w/2, w/2);
            p.lineTo(-w/2, w/2);
            p.endFill();
        }
    };
```

This simply loops 25 times and places movie clips in random positions at the left of the interface (masked by the paintMask movie clip). Each clip contains a square shape filled with an opaque green to transparent green radial gradient. You can see for each clip that we set a random position, square size, and tint of green.

3.   Next we write our function to handle the drawing of our glass sphere in the main viewing area of the game on the right of the screen:

```
drawSphereAssets = function (mc, params, center, smoothness) {
    var ang = 360/smoothness;
    var rad = ang*(Math.PI/180);
    mc.moveTo(0, radius);
    var matrix = {a:params.hotspot, b:0, c:0, d:0, e:params.hotspot,
    ➥f:0, g:center.x, h:center.y, i:0};
    mc.beginGradientFill("radial", params.colors, params.alphas,
    ➥params.ratios, matrix);
    for (var i = 1; i<=smoothness; i++) {
        var dx = Math.sin(i*rad)*radius;
        var dy = Math.cos(i*rad)*radius;
        mc.lineTo(dx, dy);
    }
    mc.endFill();
};
```

You'll be able to see better what each of the arguments means when we call the functions later, but basically, this function draws a circle filled with a gradient based on the arguments. By layering different gradients, we'll create our glass sphere. This is a great way to achieve complex effects using just the drawing API and a little experimentation.

Basic trig functions enable us to draw the lines about the circumference of the circle, filling it with a custom gradient defined by the arguments sent. I set this up initially with the 3x3 matrix type, but you could accomplish the same thing with the other gradient matrix type available for `beginGradientFill` (containing the properties `matrixType`, x, y, w, h, and r).

4. Our targets need a couple of functions to control their behavior:

```
setTarget = function () {
    target.vertexList[0].x = (ball.direction.x*radAdj)+
    ➥ball.vertexList[0].x;
    target.vertexList[0].y = (ball.direction.y*radAdj)+
    ➥ball.vertexList[0].y;
    target.vertexList[0].z = (ball.direction.z*radAdj)+
    ➥ball.vertexList[0].z;
    target.vertexList[1].x = (ball.direction.x*radius)+
    ➥ball.vertexList[0].x;
    target.vertexList[1].y = (ball.direction.y*radius)+
    ➥ball.vertexList[0].y;
    target.vertexList[1].z = (ball.direction.z*radius)+
    ➥ball.vertexList[0].z;
    drawTarget();
};
drawTarget = function () {
    for (var i = 0; i<target.clip.length; i++) {
        target.clip[i].clear();
        if (target.vertexList[i].z>0) {
            targetMC.swapDepths(99);
            var col = 0xFFFFFF;
        } else {
            targetMC.swapDepths(2);
            var col = 0x000000;
        }
        target.clip[i].lineStyle(1, col, 100);
        target.clip[i].moveTo(-planeSize/10, -planeSize/10);
        target.clip[i].lineTo(planeSize/10, planeSize/10);
        target.clip[i].moveTo(planeSize/10, -planeSize/10);
        target.clip[i].lineTo(-planeSize/10, planeSize/10);
    }
    target.render();
};
```

I had debated originally whether I would make these methods of a new target Class, but in the end I found it easier to handle them in this manner. `setTarget` sets the 3D coordinate position of the two vertices contained in our target model (an outer and an inner target).

Both vertices are determined by taking the unit vector direction of the ball and multiplying it by a scalar value. The inner target vertex is set approximately at the point where the ball will hit the sphere perimeter (the ball's offset when it begins its journey from center can cause this position to extend pass the perimeter), while the outer target vertex is set a little beyond that point so that the player can better judge the trajectory. We then call our drawTarget method to actually draw and place these targets.

To understand this better, it's good to know how our target object will be set up (which we will do in a moment when we create instances of all of our objects). We have a movie clip called **target** that contains two nested clips called **topTarget** and **bottomTarget**. We set these up at the top of our code. Each clip will contain a cross, an 'X' shape, and represent one of the two vertices of our target model. In this way we can simply draw a cross at the center of the nested clips and move the clips separately in 3D space, which is what we do in this function. The loop goes through both clips, sets the depth either in front of or behind the two planes based on the z property, sets the color to black or white depending on the side of the sphere it is located on, and then draws a simple cross representing the target. Finally, it calls the target's render function to place this at the proper position on the screen.

5. Add these next two functions:

```
sortDepths = function () {
    if (ball.vertexList[0].z>-1) {
        ballMC.swapDepths(25);
    } else {
        ballMC.swapDepths(15);
    }
    if (paddle.zDepth>0) {
        paddle.clip.swapDepths(30);
    } else {
        paddle.clip.swapDepths(10);
    }
};
spinWorld = function (axis, rate) {
    paddle.render();
    plane.render();
    ball.render();
    if (axis == "y") {
        paddle.rotateY(rate);
    } else {
        paddle.rotateX(rate);
    }
    plane.transformMatrix = paddle.transformMatrix.duplicate();
    target.transformMatrix = paddle.transformMatrix.duplicate();
    ball.transformMatrix = paddle.transformMatrix.duplicate();
```

```
            ball.rotateDirection(axis, rate);
            drawTarget();
};
```

sortDepths places our ball and paddle at the appropriate depth based on the side of the sphere they are located on.

spinWorld is called when the player uses the keys to spin the sphere. In that case, all four of our models (plane, paddle, ball, and target) and the ball's direction need to be dealt with.

Our first step is to render each of our models to apply any particular transforms remaining (there shouldn't be, but the extra safe step doesn't affect our game). We then rotate our paddle based on the axis of rotation that is sent to the function. Considering that each of the models' transformation matrices have been cleared in the previous render, the transform needed for each model for the current rotation will be exactly the same. Because of this, we don't need to create the same matrix four times (once for each model). We can use the same transform for all models. Using the duplicate method for objects that we created earlier, we can copy the transform to each model and apply them separately. I feel this is a bit safer than simply copying a reference to the transform matrix object, which is what would occur if we didn't include the duplicate method.

Before we exit the function, we also change our ball's directional vector (remember creating the rotateDirection method? It's all coming together!) and draw our target in its new position.

6. These are three straightforward functions that we call during gameplay:

```
killBall = function () {
    lives--;
    this["ball"+lives].removeMovieClip();
    if (lives == 0) {
        delete paddleMC.onEnterFrame;
        ball.clip[0]._visible = 0;
        gameOverPopUp();
    } else {
        ball.reset();
    }
};
updateScore = function () {
    var score = parseInt(scoreTF.text, 10);
    score += Math.floor(ball.velocity*20);
    score += "";
    while (score.length<8) {
        score = "0"+score;
    }
```

continues overleaf

```
            scoreTF.text = score;
    };
    playBlip = function (velocity) {
        this["blip"+(Math.ceil(velocity/2)-1)].start();
    };
```

killBall, called whenever the player misses the ball, decrements our lives variable and removes one of the corresponding ball graphics. It then checks to see if the player has run out of lives. If so, the game over pop-up window is called (we'll write that code in just a moment). If not, the ball is reset to center.

updateScore takes the text from our scoreTF text field and turns it into a number. parseInt is used so that Flash knows that we want to use numbers of base 10, otherwise it assumes it should use binary. Once we have a number to deal with, we increment it based on the current velocity of the ball. This value is then placed back into the text property of our scoreTF text field, after first ensuring that we have eight digits.

Lastly, playBlip determines the appropriate blip sound to play based on the velocity of the ball: blip0, blip1, or blip2.

7. This next function, which we assigned to paddle's onEnterFrame event, is run every frame to update the game:

```
frameCode = function () {
    if (Key.isDown(65)) {
        spinWorld("y", -paddle.rate);
    } else if (Key.isDown(68)) {
        spinWorld("y", paddle.rate);
    }
    if (Key.isDown(83)) {
        spinWorld("x", -paddle.rate);
    } else if (Key.isDown(87)) {
        spinWorld("x", paddle.rate);
    }
    ball.move();
    plane.rotateX(2);
    plane.rotateY(1);
    if (Key.isDown(Key.RIGHT)) {
        paddle.rotateY(-paddle.rate);
    } else if (Key.isDown(Key.LEFT)) {
        paddle.rotateY(paddle.rate);
    }
    if (Key.isDown(Key.UP)) {
        paddle.rotateX(-paddle.rate);
    } else if (Key.isDown(Key.DOWN)) {
```

```
            paddle.rotateX(paddle.rate);
        }
    plane.render();
    paddle.render();
    ball.render();
    sortDepths();
};
```

This is the one block of code run every frame to call all of the functions and methods that we have created. You can see that the majority of the block deals with looking at which keys are pressed down and then responding accordingly.

The first two if / else statements deal with the A, S, D, and W keys, spinning the world on the appropriate axis if a key is pressed. The code then continues, calling the ball's move method and rotating the plane on two axes. Next we find two more if / else statements to check whether the arrow keys are down, and if true, move the paddle.

Finally, the render method for each model is called, and we sort the depths of our associated clips. That's it! More work on our objects has meant less coding here.

8. The next function (and the one that follows) are long, but relatively simple. Most of the code deals with placing and formatting our text fields in the pop-up windows:

```
startGamePopUp = function () {
    this.createEmptyMovieClip("dim", 200000);
    dim.beginFill(0x656565, 80);
    dim.lineTo(stageWidth, 0);
    dim.lineTo(stageWidth, stageHeight);
    dim.lineTo(0, stageHeight);
    dim.endFill();
    var popUpWidth = stageWidth/4;
    var popUpHeight = stageHeight/4;
    this.createEmptyMovieClip("sg", 200001);
    sg._x = stageWidth/2;
    sg._y = stageHeight/2;
    startGame = new PopUp(popUpWidth, popUpHeight);
    startGame.clip = sg;
    startGame.render();
    sg.createTextField("title", 0, 0, -popUpHeight, 0, 0);
    statsTitle.size = stageHeight/10;
    sg.title.setNewTextFormat(statsTitle);
    sg.title.embedFonts = 1;
    sg.title.autoSize = "center";
    sg.title.text = "SphereCage";
    sg.createTextField("message", 1, -popUpWidth*.9, -popUpHeight*.4,
```

continues overleaf

```
➥popUpWidth*1.8, popUpHeight);
stats.align = "center";
stats.size = stageHeight*.035;
sg.message.setNewTextFormat(stats);
sg.message.embedFonts = 1;
sg.message.wordWrap = 1;
sg.message.text = "use your arrows keys to maneuver the
➥paddle\n\nuse the a, s, d, w keys\nto spin the sphere";
sg.createTextField("replay", 3, 0, popUpHeight*.6, 0, 0);
stats.align = "left";
stats.size = stageHeight*.05;
sg.replay.setNewTextFormat(stats);
sg.replay.embedFonts = 1;
sg.replay.textColor = 0x808080;
sg.replay.autoSize = "center";
sg.replay.text = "click to start";
sg.col = 80;
sg.direction = 1;
sg.onEnterFrame = function() {
    this.col += 5*this.direction;
    if (this.col>254 || this.col<80) {
        this.direction *= -1;
    }
    var r = this.col << 16;
    var g = this.col << 8;
    var b = this.col;
    this.replay.textColor = r | g | b;
};
sg.onPress = function() {
    stats.align = "left";
    dim.removeMovieClip();
    initGame();
    this.removeMovieClip();
};
};
```

I won't go through every line of this code, as it should be fairly self-explanatory. The function creates our initial pop-up window when the game is first loaded. It covers the background with a gray, partially opaque square to 'dim' the interface, and then it creates a new instance of the PopUp Class that we created earlier.

The onEnterFrame we set near the end of the block runs the tween for the coloring of our 'click to start' message, running back and forth between gray and white for the textColor property of our replay text field. The onPress waits for a mouse click from the user. Once this is detected, it removes the dim clip and the pop-up, and calls our `initGame` handler.

9. This is almost the same, but for a different pop-up:

```
gameOverPopUp = function () {
    this.createEmptyMovieClip("dim", 200000);
    dim.beginFill(0x656565, 80);
    dim.lineTo(stageWidth, 0);
    dim.lineTo(stageWidth, stageHeight);
    dim.lineTo(0, stageHeight);
    dim.endFill();
    var popUpWidth = stageWidth/4;
    var popUpHeight = stageHeight/4;
    this.createEmptyMovieClip("gm", 200001);
    gm._x = stageWidth/2;
    gm._y = stageHeight/2;
    gameOver = new PopUp(popUpWidth, popUpHeight);
    gameOver.clip = gm;
    gameOver.render();
    gm.createTextField("title", 0, 0, -popUpHeight*.9, 0, 0);
    gm.title.setNewTextFormat(statsTitle);
    gm.title.embedFonts = 1;
    gm.title.autoSize = "center";
    gm.title.text = "Game Over";
    gm.createTextField("message", 1, 0, -popUpHeight*.2, 0, 0);
    gm.message.setNewTextFormat(stats);
    gm.message.embedFonts = 1;
    gm.message.autoSize = "center";
    gm.createTextField("score", 2, 0, popUpHeight*.1, 0, 0);
    gm.score.setNewTextFormat(stats);
    gm.score.embedFonts = 1;
    gm.score.autoSize = "center";
    var score = parseInt(scoreTF.text, 10);
    gm.score.text = score;
    if (score>parseInt(highTF.text, 10)) {
        gm.message.text = "You made high score!";
        highTF.text = scoreTF.text;
    } else {
        gm.message.text = "You scored:";
    }
    gm.createTextField("replay", 3, 0, popUpHeight*.5, 0, 0);
    gm.replay.setNewTextFormat(stats);
    gm.replay.embedFonts = 1;
    gm.replay.textColor = 0x808080;
    gm.replay.autoSize = "center";
```

continues overleaf

```
        gm.replay.text = "click to play again";
        gm.col = 80;
        gm.direction = 1;
        gm.onEnterFrame = function() {
            this.col += 5*this.direction;
            if (this.col>254 || this.col<80) {
                this.direction *= -1;
            }
            var r = this.col << 16;
            var g = this.col << 8;
            var b = this.col;
            this.replay.textColor = r | g | b;
        };
        gm.onPress = function() {
            dim.removeMovieClip();
            initGame();
            this.removeMovieClip();
        };
    };
```

This is just some different text and formatting for our 'game over' pop-up, but basically the same as our previous function, so we'll keep moving.

10. We're on the home stretch! All of our functions and Classes are defined. Now we simply need to make instances of our objects:

```
paddle = new PlaneModel();
paddle.clip = paddleMC;
paddle.rate = 8;
paddle.vertexList = [];
paddle.vertexList.push({x:-planeSize, y:-planeSize, z:radAdj, w:1});
paddle.vertexList.push({x:-planeSize, y:planeSize, z:radAdj, w:1});
paddle.vertexList.push({x:planeSize, y:planeSize, z:radAdj, w:1});
paddle.vertexList.push({x:planeSize, y:-planeSize, z:radAdj, w:1});
paddle.side = [];
paddle.side.push({vertices:[0, 1, 2, 3], sideColor:"550055"});

plane = new PlaneModel();
plane.clip = planeMC;
plane.vertexList = [];
plane.vertexList.push({x:-planeSize, y:-planeSize, z:0, w:1});
plane.vertexList.push({x:-planeSize, y:planeSize, z:0, w:1});
plane.vertexList.push({x:planeSize, y:planeSize, z:0, w:1});
plane.vertexList.push({x:planeSize, y:-planeSize, z:0, w:1});
plane.side = [];
```

```
plane.side.push({vertices:[0, 1, 2, 3], sideColor:"234523"});

ball = new BallModel();
ball.clip = [ballMC.innerBall];
ball.rad = ballMC._width/2;
ball.vertexList = [];
ball.vertexlist.push({x:0, y:0, z:0, w:1});

target = new Model();
target.clip = [targetMC.topTarget, targetMC.bottomTarget];
target.vertexList = [];
target.vertexList.push({x:0, y:0, z:0, w:1});
target.vertexList.push({x:0, y:0, z:0, w:1});

light = new LightSource(-20000, -20000, 20000, 100);
```

This should all look familiar now, yes? paddle, plane, ball, and target are all object instances of our Classes. We give them all vertexLists full of the vertices, and sides for our planes. Notice that we need to store our ball and target movie clips in an array property because of the way we've set up the code. We wrap it up by creating a new instance of a light source as well.

Only ten more lines and we're done!

11. These next eight lines create our sphere graphics at right:

```
sphereHL = {colors:[0xFFFFFF, 0xFFFFFF], alphas:[20, 0], ratios:[0,
➡225], hotspot:radAdj};
sphereShadow = {colors:[0x000000, 0x000000], alphas:[0, 30],
➡ratios:[100,155], hotspot:radius*3.6};
sphereBackShadow = {colors:[0x090909, 0x000000], alphas:[20, 0],
➡ratios:[80, 140], hotspot:radius*4};
sphereRim = {colors:[0xFFFFFF, 0xFFFFFF], alphas:[0, 2],
➡ratios:[230, 230], hotspot:radius*2};
drawSphereAssets(backShadow, sphereBackShadow, {x:50, y:40},
➡smoothness);
drawSphereAssets(sphere.shadow, sphereShadow, {x:-radius/4,
➡y:-radius/4}, smoothness);
drawSphereAssets(sphere.highlight, sphereHL, {x:-radius/3,
➡y:-radius/3}, smoothness);
drawSphereAssets(sphere.rim, sphereRim, {x:0, y:0}, smoothness);
```

We first create custom objects for our gradients, then we call our drawSphereAssets function that we created. Look back to this function to see how these values relate. sphereHL is the white highlight at the top left of the sphere, and both sphereShadow and `sphereBackShadow` create the shadow at the lower right of the sphere. `sphereRim` is the 'lip' about the rim, giving the sphere its thickness.

12. Can you believe we're down to our last two lines? Add them to your code:

```
paddle.rotateY(45);
startGamePopUp();
```

We rotate the paddle at the start so that it isn't covering the ball and plane at the game's outset.

Finally, `startGamePopUp` is called, drawing our titles pop-up window and setting all of our code in motion!

That's right, it was a bit of coding, but the finished product is a nice and smooth 3D game. Testing on my machine showed that my 24 fps frame rate rarely dropped below 22 fps.

13. Go ahead and test your movie now to see how your work has paid off.

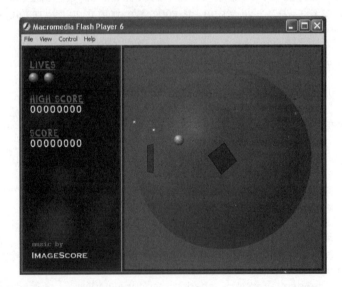

Developing SphereCage further

On the CD, I have included another version of SphereCage with a few additional enhancements. Most notably, a soundtrack has been added (supplied by Imagescore Music) and the ball is 'launched' each round with a gradient special effect. The start of each game features an interface color change and a little bit of 'paddle choreography' which is controlled by the wonderful new `Sound.duration` property. The paddle itself has a lowered opacity so you might see the ball through it. I've also added a pause function for when the player hits the space bar. Finally, and most subtly, I've improved the placement of the trajectory targets so that the inner target is placed right where the ball will hit the sphere perimeter. Open it up to take a look at the code necessary for these improvements.

Of course, there is much you could do to improve the game even further. A splashier opening screen or instructions page, perhaps a shrinking paddle to increase difficulty, or you could incorporate levels by setting a goal for number of deflections each round. You could even use some server-side scripting to create a high score board, or possibly use Flash MX's new Shared objects to save the user's high score information. Without adding anything, you could simply work to incorporate more OOP code into the game, perhaps by first making a Target Class.

Summary

This has been quite a lengthy project, but we've covered a lot of exciting territory, from creating coded graphics to basic Flash OOP and the important concepts of custom Classes and inheritance. You can walk away from this chapter with the knowledge that by using the drawing API and some ingenuity, run-time graphics are now not only possible, but relatively easy to implement as well.

Dynamic masks, cool effects, pop-up windows, full interfaces, 2D and 3D games – the possibilities appear unlimited. Add to this the ability to dynamically create movie clips and text fields, formatting the latter with the new `TextFormat` object, and you have an impressive array of coded tools at your creative disposal.

Have fun with the game and the ideas, but more importantly, have fun with Flash!

section 3: Rich Media

Introduction

When looking at a multitude of different sites on the web, offering all kinds of entertainment, services and information, you may notice a trend towards combinations of these three elements:

- Content you can **see**.

- Content you can **listen** to.

- Content you can both look at and listen to, which also **moves**.

Or more specifically, contemporary sites are frequently combining **images**, **audio**, and **video**, which is exactly what we'll be doing over the course of the next three chapters as we investigate the web site of Flatpack Records, incorporating all of these media:

Hold on, we've seen many books covering this previously, so what's new? Well, for one thing Macromedia Flash MX addresses one of the greatest problems on the web today.

When was the last time you visited a site combining one or more elements of video, audio, or high-quality graphics, and felt instantly satisfied? We know that the Internet has the potential to offer fast and smoothly streamed sound, video, and graphical content, while in reality, there is still some distance to travel before we can all benefit from such a magical experience by downloading content at lightning speed. Part of the problem, of course, is with service providers or our connections, unless you're lucky enough to be using broadband. However, they're not entirely to blame because much of the fault lies, and can you believe this, with... web designers.

When we first realized the creative possibilities of rich media on the web many of us got a little over excited and put together work that, while very impressive on a fast machine using ADSL, alienated the majority of web users who left the site to do something more interesting while it downloaded. Broadband technology is widely available, but the adoption of this technology is nowhere near as widespread as originally hoped, so it's about time that someone built an application that makes rich media experiences available to everyone: this is exactly what Macromedia Flash MX can do.

Over the course of the next three chapters we'll show you how Flash can be used to dynamically load and creatively manipulate the three types of large media file: graphics, video, and audio. This means that instead of loading up a complete web site and all the rich media content simultaneously, necessitating a long download time, Flash can now pull in JPEG images, MP3 music files, and SWFs containing real video, from an external source. This can all be designed to react to user request and will keep the natural flow of the site running like a fresh mountain stream (as opposed to a turgid stagnant canal).

Well, it seems as if we've been dreaming about the possibilities of rich media content for long enough now, so let's look at how this works in Flash MX by examining a real case study web site. As well as examining how the media files can be dynamically called into a movie, we'll also look at how to creatively manipulate these files inside Flash, transforming them into fully interactive features. In many instances, the user won't even realize this has happened as the content is fully incorporated into the overall site design. Finally, as we work through we'll always keep an eye out for techniques that will help you build your site so that it's easily updateable, and how to organize the site and media content to keep it as efficient as possible.

When thinking about a site to create for this case study, we tried to come up with an example site that would cover all the areas we wanted to address, featuring lots of lovely rich media content. After much brainstorming, lo and behold, Flatpack Records was born. While the site is entirely fictional, it could quite easily be the interactive promotional site for a record company. All of the files and media that make up the site are on the CD, and we'll be looking in detail at how they were made and how they combine to form a rich media site.

Open up the completed `flatpackrecords.swf` and take a look around at the various sections. The site is split into **photos**, **video**, and **audio** with individual sub-sections within these. Go ahead and try it all out.

We'll investigate how this works in detail over the next three chapters, and concentrate on keeping the main SWF movie, the base web site, very low in file size by calling and manipulating external media files dynamically. Some of this will make use of elements covered in other parts of this book such as functions and components, so you'll get another chance to practice those, as well as discovering some new multimedia treats along the way.

So, let's go ahead and dive into the entertaining world of Flatpack Records...

section 3: Rich Media Sites

chapter 12: **Dynamic Graphics**

One of the key problems that many people experienced with previous versions of Flash was the difficulty in updating a site's content. You could update text using the `loadVariables` command, but images always needed to be embedded within the Flash SWF. Once you'd made the final Flash movie, the only way to update the embedded images at a later date was to reopen the FLA and edit them there, unless you were using Macromedia Generator and a complex database setup. This lengthy process would cost the client money, and also meant learning how to use Generator and set up a database, which isn't especially ideal.

Now with Macromedia Flash MX all this has changed. JPEG images can be updated as easy as in an HTML page, simply by using the `loadMovie` action. This chapter will investigate the most efficient ways of getting large high-quality graphic files into your web site. I'm going to show you how best to compress a JPEG image, dynamically load it into Flash, and also show several examples of how to use this method in practice, applying techniques such as preloaders and fades.

Optimizing JPEGs

One of my pet hates is the frequency of badly compressed images on the web. It's infuriating to visit a site that is beautifully designed and yet, due to a huge inefficiently compressed JPEG, forces you to wait idly until it is fully loaded. This wastes valuable bandwidth and annoys the user! So then, what is the best way to compress a JPEG? There are no explicitly right or wrong methods, as what may be appropriate for one image may prove awful when applied to another. Personally, I find Macromedia Fireworks is the best compression tool for creating web graphics, although Adobe Photoshop's **Save for Web** option works very well too. However, I find Fireworks generally produces smaller file sizes, and is also much quicker to use.

In the following exercise we'll take a quick look at how to efficiently compress graphics so that they're ready and waiting, fully optimized, for when Flash calls them into the site. We'll be using Macromedia Fireworks MX and if you don't have a copy, you can download a trial version at **www.macromedia.com/software/trial_download**.

If you already favor using Adobe Photoshop (version 5.5 or higher), you'll find that the following exercise is very similar to the **File > Save for Web** procedure.

We won't be using the final image, as this exercise is just a quick introduction to the principles you need to apply to your own graphics, but if you do want to follow along with the exercise, locate a photo image on your hard drive, preferably also containing some text (the source file bracken.psd is in the **images** folder for this chapter on the CD).

Placing the cart columns

If you open up an image in Fireworks, you'll notice that it has a very similar layout to Flash MX, in particular the same drop-down panel layout on the right and the Property inspector at the bottom:

Fireworks has many advanced image manipulation tools, not simply confined to producing JPEGs, but for the purposes of this exercise, we're just going to look at Fireworks' ability to optimize JPEGs for the web (the job that it does best of all).

When you open up an image you'll notice that the document window has four different tabs at the top labeled **Original**, **Preview**, **2-Up**, and **4-Up**. If you click the **2-Up** tab and stretch the document window out you can see two versions of your image, allowing you to compare any changes you make (on the right) with the original source image (on the left):

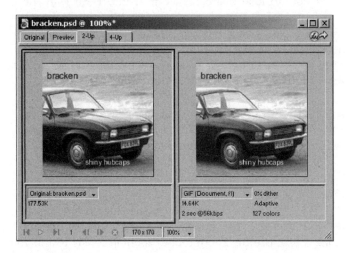

Now let's take a look at optimizing the graphic using the most appropriate compression.

1. Open the **Optimize** panel (**Window > Optimize**) and choose **JPEG** from the Export file format drop-down menu. The JPEG Quality is set to 80% by default, but you can try playing around with the **Quality** slider to see the effect it has on the image in the preview pane.

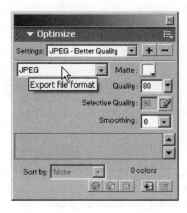

2. Click on the extra options icon at the top right of the Optimize panel and make sure **Sharpen JPEG Edges** is checked.

The two options to note here are **Progressive JPEG** and **Sharpen JPEG Edges**. A progressive JPEG is one that starts to appear before it has fully loaded in. You'll often see HTML pages containing JPEG images that appear to come into focus as they load. At the time of printing, attempts to load a progressive JPEG into Flash with the `loadMovie` command simply don't work. It's important to remember this or you'll have much frustration later on when your image just refuses to appear where it should be! Since Flash *cannot* dynamically load in progressive JPEGs with the `loadMovie` command, it's best to avoid using them for the moment.

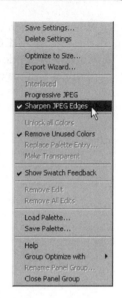

Sharpen JPEG Edges can be quite useful. Using it does admittedly increase the file size, but it also improves images that contain many defined edges. Really, it's a case of experimenting with each JPEG to see what looks best in the preview pane. Sometimes though, it can be best to uncheck this option and boost the **Quality** setting instead. The simple rule is 'try it out'.

3. Whenever you decrease the quality of a JPEG one of the first areas you'll notice deteriorating is text. Use the Zoom tool to zoom in to any text in your image and then try reducing the Quality setting in the Optimize panel. A 'banding' effect becomes apparent (this is with a setting of 30):

Another useful option is **Selective JPEG quality.** This clever feature allows you to select a certain portion of a JPEG and export it at a higher quality than the rest of the image. This feature is especially useful if you have an image containing text.

4. Let's try this feature out. First, make sure you're happy with your overall Quality settings in the Optimize panel, and then select an area of your image that you want to export at a higher quality using the Marquee or Lasso tool. Then go to **Modify > Selective JPEG >**

Save Selection as JPEG Mask to select the required areas (hold down Shift to select more than one area):

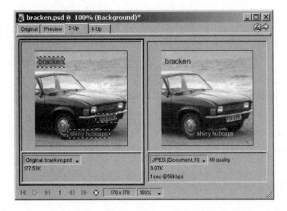

5. The selected area has now been highlighted pink. In the Optimize panel you can now adjust the **Selective Quality** option to achieve the best results. By default it is set to 90%, which is often the best setting for areas such as text. Once you start increasing the JPEG quality above 90% the file size starts jumping up a lot, whereas the visual quality stays about the same.

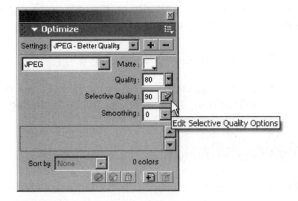

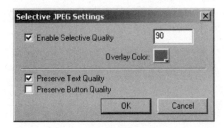

6.   Once you are happy with your image settings go to **File > Export...** and save as **Images Only** (we don't need to worry about any of the HTML settings).

That's it – we're done, and ready to start work in Flash. Obviously, this has been an ultra-quick guide to compressing images for export, but I hope it's given you a good insight into how a few simple steps can make a huge difference in reducing the file size of your image while maintaining an acceptable level of image quality.

Loading JPEGs

JPEGs are loaded into Flash using the same method you would ordinarily use to load in another SWF: with the `loadMovie` command. As with SWFs, you can load in the image to a movie clip instance. So, to load a JPEG into a movie clip instance called `photo` you would use:

```
loadMovie("images/album3.jpg", _root.photo);
```

This loads the JPEG from the **images** folder, located in the same directory as the final SWF on the server, and inserts it into the `photo` instance on the root timeline. Alternatively, if you wanted to load the JPEG onto a different level you would use:

```
loadMovieNum("images/album3.jpg", 2);
```

This would load the same image onto level 2 of the Flash Player. As no movie clip location has been specified for it to load into, it would be positioned at the top left corner of the screen.

Flatpack sleeve designs

Before we get stuck into how we actually made the individual elements that combine to form the album covers, open up `flatpackrecords.swf` on the CD and have a play around to get a feel for the different sections of the site and the structure. Over the course of the next few exercises, I'll show you how the album sleeves section was made, so navigate your way to the sleeve designs area of the site and have a look.

In the following Flatpack Records example I'm going load the JPEG into an instance of a movie clip rather than loading it onto a different level, as this enables us to use the properties of the `MovieClip` object, such as `_alpha`, `_x` and `_y`, in order to manipulate the image.

1.   To begin, let's look at this in action. Open up `flatpackrecords.fla` from the CD and select frame 2 of the **dynamic content** layer:

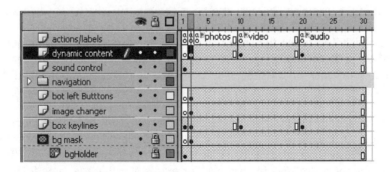

I've placed a movie clip with the instance name `photos` on this frame. When the movie is published, this clip contains the whole photography section of the site.

2.   If you double-click on the `photos` movie clip you'll see that the timeline has two frame labels: **designs** and **bracken**. For this first exercise, we'll be working just within the **designs**

section. Select frame 2 of the **clips** layer and you'll see that there are four blank movie clips with the instance names one, two, three, and four:

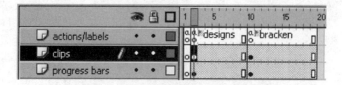

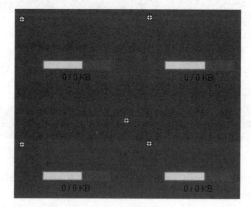

These four movie clips act as containers for the dynamically loaded JPEGs. These will be filled with images of album sleeves as soon as the SWF enters this frame. It's also important to remember that the movie clips all have top left registration points, as the registration point of the incoming JPEG will also be at the top left (exactly as when loading in a SWF).

3.   If you can't wait to see the code that loads in the images, then take a quick look in frame 2 of the **actions/labels** layer. We'll look at it in detail when we've dealt with the other important element of the designs section, the ProgressBar component, as the code handles all of the content.

I hope you can see the logic of naming the clips one, two, and so on. If you look in the Flatpack's **images** folder on the CD you'll see that each of these instance names correlates with the file name of the JPEGs we are bringing in. It's also useful to keep the same file structure on your hard drive as on the server (relative file names). For example, within the same folder as my SWF and HTML file, I have a folder named images, which contains the four album covers. This means that when I test the movie offline, the SWF will still load in the JPEGs exactly as it would if the file was online (albeit somewhat quicker!).

Placing the JPEGs in their own folder is a good practice to get into as it makes them much easier to locate, plus if anyone needs to update the site and upload some new images, they know exactly where to place the images. Also worth noting here is that if a non-Flash user or client needs to upload images regularly, it is a good idea to either limit their read/write access to this folder of the site (via your web site administration – see your host for information on how to do this), or set up their FTP client to access this folder directly.

You've probably also noticed in the last screenshot that there are four ProgressBar components on the stage, one component per image. If you tested the movie online without these components you would notice one of the few problems with dynamically loaded JPEGs: the user has to wait for the images to load into the main SWF. The web audience is used to this at traditional HTML sites, but in the case of HTML sites, there are visual clues indicating that an image is loading such as the status bar at the bottom of the browser window, or an ALT tag in the location of the loading image. However, with Flash there are no visual indicators for the user, just a blank screen with no images and no clues until the external JPEG finally loads. Therefore, to make our movies more usable, the designer needs to build some kind of user feedback elements if a delay is anticipated. To get around this problem we can incorporate small loading movies for each of the incoming JPEG images.

Preloaders

When constructing preloaders in previous versions of Flash, it was necessary to go through the laborious process of building them from scratch, both the graphic elements and the code functionality. Luckily for us, someone was kind enough to create a ProgressBar component for Flash MX, which saves us lots of work. This component isn't included with the installation. To get it you'll need to download the **Flash UI Components Set 2**, available from the Macromedia Exchange at **www.macromedia.com/exchange/flash**. Once you've installed this set, you can access the new components in the usual way from **Windows > Components**:

The ProgressBar component allows you to display both bar graph graphics and information about the file size being loaded in text format. It also allows you to switch off either or both of these if required (there might be some situation where you need an invisible progress bar!):

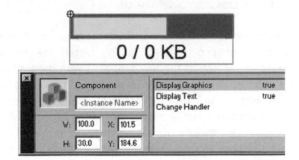

The ProgressBar component has a number of methods that make it very easy to use. In the case of Flatpack Records we'll only use a few of them, but it's definitely worth opening up the **Reference** panel and checking the rest of them out, as many of these methods will allow you to create preloaders, gradual loading, or changing states that occur at defined landmarks of the loading process (such as different graphics at 20%, 40%, and so on).

In the three chapters on the Flatpack site, we'll just use the `setLoadTarget` and `getPercentComplete` methods. Let's take a quick look at each.

setLoadTarget

You may not be surprised to discover that this method tells the ProgressBar which loading file should be monitored. The syntax for this is:

```
progressBar.setLoadTarget(instance or timeline to monitor);
```

For example, here is the code for the instance `progressBar`, which is set to monitor a whole Flash movie timeline:

```
progressBar.setLoadTarget(_root);
```

In our `flatpackrecords.fla`, each image is loaded into a blank movie clip (named earlier as `one`, `two`, `three`, and `four`), which are monitored by four individual ProgressBars on the stage (with instance names `progress1` through to `progress4`):

getPercentComplete

This method allows you to interrogate a ProgressBar, in order to check how much of it has loaded. In practice, this is more akin to a property of the ProgressBar component rather than a method, as it can just be used to check the component. Here's how you can use it to check if something has fully loaded:

```
if(progressBar.getPercentComplete() == 100) {
    _root.gotoAndPlay ("main");
}
```

This method might seem like it has a limited use, but it can be used for changing or transitional stages during the loading (as mentioned earlier), or can be used to start the movie after the majority of the target has loaded (say 60% of an animated movie), while allowing the rest of the movie adequate time to load in during playback.

OK, now that we've seen how to use these basic methods, let's see how they are applied within the Flatpack movie.

Coding the Flatpack designs and photography

In the interests of efficiency and to save repeating code, the ActionScript for loading and preloading the images in the **designs** and **bracken** sections is the same, with the following functions on frame 1 of the **actions/labels** layer of the **photos** movie clip:

```
stop();
function loadImage(loadingTarget, progressBarName, fileName) {
    this.onEnterFrame = function() {
        fadeInc = 10;
        fade = 0;
        loadMovie("images/"+fileName, this[loadingTarget]);
        this[progressBarName].setLoadTarget(this[loadingTarget]);
        this[loadingTarget]._alpha = fade;
        this.onEnterFrame = function() {
            if (this[progressBarName].getPercentComplete() == 100) {
                this[progressBarName]._visible = false;
                this.onEnterFrame = function() {
                    fade += fadeInc;
                    if (fade<=100) {
                        this[loadingTarget]._alpha = fade;
                    } else if (fade>100) {
                        this.onEnterFrame = undefined;
```

continues overleaf

```
                                    _root.count = _root.lastCount;
                                    _root.count++;
                                }
                            };
                        }
                    }
                };
            }
```

We'll go through this in detail, but let's first see what this function is doing in general terms:

- Initializes several variables and sets up the `loadMovie` command and ProgressBars.

- Checks the ProgressBar to see if the image has fully loaded.

- Once it has fully loaded, gradually fades in the image.

Although this function could be broken down into three separate functions, I've left it as one. It should be OK to see the distinct sections as we go through and to see where changes can be made to make it more modular.

Initialization

Here's the first section, which initializes variables, sets up the `loadMovie` and the ProgressBar:

```
function loadImage(loadingTarget, progressBarName, fileName) {
    this.onEnterFrame = function() {
        fadeInc = 10;
        fade = 0;
        loadMovie("images/"+fileName, this[loadingTarget]);
        this[progressBarName].setLoadTarget(this[loadingTarget]);
        this[loadingTarget]._alpha = fade;
```

OK, let's define the parameters which are passed to the function.

- `loadingTarget` is the instance name of the container that the JPEG image will load into.

- `progressBarName` is the instance name of the ProgressBar component that monitors the JPEG loading into the target instance.

- `fileName` is the file name of the JPEG image.

After the initial function definition, an `onEnterFrame` function is set up for `this`, which refers to the **photos** movie clip. As the images will load in sequence, using `this` makes it easier to check if the previous image has finished loading in (this code will be discussed in a moment) and makes referencing levels a little bit easier.

The variables `fadeInc` and `fade` are used later in the function when (surprise, surprise) fading in the image. `fadeInc` represents the amount that is added to the `_alpha` property of the image on each frame, so go ahead and change this to get an alternative fade speed. `fade` simply initializes the `_alpha` value of the `loadingTarget`, as seen in the last line of the section.

The next line of code is the crux of the function as it sets the JPEG loading into the container instance (set by the `loadingTarget` parameter), fetching the file (passed by `fileName`) from the **images** folder on the server. For example, if `bagelboy.jpg` were passed to the function, the `loadMovie` string would be "images/bagelboy.jpg".

This function could be adapted further to add the `.jpg` suffix to the file name...

```
loadMovie("images/"+fileName+".jpg", this[loadingTarget]);
```

...but I've decided against doing so; adding the `.jpg` extension is a force of habit that I could never overcome. If you decide to change the function to save a few keystrokes, make sure that everyone who works with the file is aware that the coded suffix is `.jpg` and not `.jpeg`.

The penultimate line in the above section of code...

```
this[progressBarName].setLoadTarget(this[loadingTarget]);
```

...gives the ProgressBar something to monitor using the component's `setLoadTarget` method. As you can see, it uses the passed in `progressBarName` and `loadingTarget` parameters to good effect.

Has the image loaded?

The second piece of code in the function is thankfully quite short:

```
this.onEnterFrame = function() {
    if (this[progressBarName].getPercentComplete() == 100) {
        this[progressBarName]._visible = false;
```

The first line is set to ensure that the initialization code is not run more than once (it is after all there to initialize our movie), and also enables us to do something else every frame – check if the image has fully loaded.

As with the common method of comparing `getBytesLoaded` to `getBytesTotal`, a check is made every frame to see if the `getPercentComplete` method (the pseudo property we mentioned earlier) of the ProgressBar is equal to 100%. This `onEnterFrame` code will keep running on every frame until the condition becomes true and the image is fully loaded. When this occurs, we hide the ProgressBar and proceed to the next bit of code.

Fading in the image

By this point, the album sleeve image has fully loaded and will be faded in gradually, rather than harshly appearing instantly on the screen. Here's the last section of code:

```
this.onEnterFrame = function() {
    fade += fadeInc;
    if (fade<=100) {
        this[loadingTarget]._alpha = fade;
    } else if (fade>100) {
        this.onEnterFrame = undefined;
        _root.count = _root.lastCount;
        _root.count++;
    }
};
}
}
};
}
```

As you can see, there is a good old `onEnterFrame` event handler to replace the last one, setting up a fading loop. The next line increments the `fade` variable by `fadeInc` (which has been set to 10 in the initialization code), and is followed by a couple of conditionals checking if `fade` is less than, equal to, or greater than 100. In the eventuality that `fade` is less than or equal to 100, the alpha of the image is set to the value of `fade`, producing the desired effect of the image appearing gently. If `fade` is greater than 100 then the `onEnterFrame` is cleared and two variables are changed a little. These variables are used to check the sequence of loading and will be discussed in the next section.

Loading the images in sequence

Providing the user with content, as early as possible, is a simple but very important rule when designing any web site. In this case, if the user has to wait around for four images trying to load in at the same time, they might get bored and leave. A better solution is to load each image in sequence so that the user has something to look at while subsequent content loads. The way to do this is to call the function for each image when the previous image tells it to do so. The code for this is on frame 2 of the **actions/labels** layer (labeled **designs**). It's been organized like this so it is only called when the user navigates to the designs section of the site. Here is the code in full:

```
_root.count = 0;
function storeCount() {
    _root.lastCount = _root.count;
    _root.count = 10;
```

```
        }
    _root.onEnterFrame = function() {
        with (_root.photos) {
            if (_root.count == 0) {
                loadImage("one", "progress1", "album1.jpg");
                storeCount();
            } else if (_root.count == 1) {
                loadImage("two", "progress2", "album2.jpg");
                storeCount();
            } else if (_root.count == 2) {
                loadImage("three", "progress3", "album3.jpg");
                storeCount();
            } else if (_root.count == 3) {
                loadImage("four", "progress4", "album4.jpg");
                storeCount();
            } else if (_root.count == 4) {
                _root.onEnterFrame = undefined;
            }
        }
    };
```

Let's start at the top. The count variable is used to check the progress of the image loading sequence. Setting it to 0 simply initializes it, ready for checking it in the onEnterFrame code. For instance, when count is 0, the first image loading function is called in the onEnterFrame loop. This is then followed by calling the storeCount function. So what does this do? Well, the storeCount function does two things:

- Stores the current value of count in a variable called lastCount.

- Changes the value of count to a neutral value, which happens to be 10.

The reason for doing all this is to fool the onEnterFrame code. If count remained the same and was unchanged, each time the if statements were arrived at, the loadImage function would be recalled, getting us nowhere fast. Setting count to a neutral value means that the onEnterFrame code will run through and do nothing, until it sees a number it recognizes (between 0 and 4).

Before we do this though, we store the value of count in a variable called lastCount. This variable is a safe house for it, until we get the orders to release it. To see when it is released, we must go back to the last bit of code from the last section on fading in the image:

```
    } else if (fade>100) {
        this.onEnterFrame = undefined;
        _root.count = _root.lastCount;
        _root.count++;
    }
```

The penultimate line here releases `count` from `lastCount` and then in the next line, `count` is incremented ready for the `onEnterFrame` code checks, where the whole process will repeat again. Back in the load sequencing code for this section, let's do a quick pseudo code run-through of the `if` statements in the `onEnterFrame` code, with the knowledge that `count` was set to `0` just before this code:

```
if (_root.count == 0) {
//Check to see if count is equal to 0. If true do this

    loadImage("one", "progress1", "album1.jpg");
    //Run loadImage function with set of parameters

    storeCount();
    //Run storeCount function to store current value of count in
    //lastCount variable and then set count to a neutral number
    //(10) so that it won't interfere with anything else in
    //the onEnterFrame code
```

In the `loadImage` function, `fade` becomes greater than 100 and following code is run:

```
_root.count = root.lastCount;
//restore the value of count by setting it to lastCount
//(set as 0)

_root.count++;
//increment count variable so that it equals 1

else if (_root.count == 1) {
//check to see if count is equal to 1 returns true so do this

loadImage("two", "progress2", "album2.jpg");
//Run loadImage function with set of parameters
```

...and so on until:

```
if (_root.count == 4) {
//Check to see if count is equal to 4, returns true, so do this

_root.onEnterFrame = undefined;
//Clear the onEnterFrame code as all images have loaded
```

It is important to know that as the image loading function is doing its thing, the `onEnterFrame` code on this frame is constantly looping, but is ineffectual because none of the conditions are met. This code will keep repeating until `count` is equal to 4 when it is then wiped out.

What this code gives us is sequential loading, much like HTML documents, but far more intelligent. Flash will know here when to load the next image because we tell it when to do so. This provides a smooth loading experience for the user too, keeping them entertained while other content loads. If we don't sequentially load these images, they might try to load in at the same time, meaning that the user must wait for four times longer before anything appears while the images all try to squeeze down the user's connection.

Testing

You can test this movie on your local machine as usual, but the problem is that you can't test simulate how the JPEGs load when online. So, at this stage, it'd be best to upload the file to a server and test it from there. Only by doing this, will you be able to check if all of your links work and your image loading process functions correctly:

If the JPEGs don't appear as you expected, one of the most common mistakes is having an incorrect path or file name. Double-check that you have the same path and file name on the server as you stated in the Flash movie. Another common mistake, especially when developing on a Windows machine and uploading to a UNIX server, is the case of the file name and extension. UNIX is case-sensitive whereas Windows isn't. In general, the best rule to stick to is to use all lower case file names, to use underscore characters for differentiation (and never **ever** use spaces!), and avoid all other special characters. You've been warned!

Random backdrop

On the Flatpack Record site, different image backdrops are loaded in randomly as the user navigates through each of the three main sections. Try this out by moving around the site in `flatpackrecords.swf`. Once you've done so, go back into the main file `flatpackrecords.fla`, and let's look at how this was created.

1. First, there's the **backgroundHolder** movie clip with the instance name bg, located at the top left of the stage (0,0). This, as its name logically suggests, will be the container for the external backdrop images. This movie clip is attached to frame 1 of the **bgHolder** layer on the main timeline.

2. Next, we made a mask layer (called **bg mask**) directly above the **bgHolder** layer and drew masks over the three areas where the random backdrop will display through. As you can see in the following screenshot, the backdrops will display behind the dynamic text and interface on the left, and also the main content window on the right. However, the mask doesn't come into effect until frame 2 to allow for the initial home page to display without the backdrop effect:

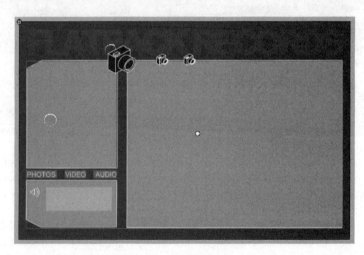

3. Next are a couple of functions that are attached to frame 1 of the **actions/labels** layer, which call up a random JPEG to place in the bg movie clip. These functions are combined into another function which is called up each time the movie enters a new section of the site (this function begins at line 38 in the Actions panel):

```
bgCount = 9;
```

```
function backgroundLoad() {
    fade = -5;
    _root.bg._alpha = fade;
    randBg = Math.round(Math.random()*bgCount+1);
    loadMovie("backdrops/bg"+randBg+".jpg", _root.bg);
}
function backgroundFade() {
    if (_root.bg.getBytesTotal() == _root.bg.getBytesLoaded()) {
        _root.bgCheck.onEnterFrame = function() {
            if (fade<20) {
                fade++;
                _root.bg._alpha = fade;
            } else if (fade>=20) {
                _root.bgCheck.onEnterFrame = undefined;
            }
        };
    }
}
function loadBackground() {
    backgroundLoad();
    backgroundFade();
}
```

The `loadBackground` function is called each time a button is clicked, when the user navigates to a different section (audio, video, or photos), through the `changeButtons` function (located further down the code at line 84 in the same frame).

The first part sets the `_alpha` property of the movie clip that the background will be loaded into (`_root.bg`) to –5. This is set before we load in the background because the imported JPEG inherits the properties of the clip it is loaded into. But, why have we set the value as –5 and not 0? Well, we discovered that even when Flash recognizes that it has loaded the image (using the `getBytesLoaded` method) there is still a delay before the image actually appears on the screen. Setting the alpha to –5 allows time for the image to appear within the SWF before the alpha reaches 0 (any alpha value less than 0 effectively means 0). Setting the alpha to 0 to begin with meant that by the time the image popped up the alpha was already at about 5%, and so the effect of a subtle fade-in was not achieved.

4.   Next is the business end of the function:

```
randBg = Math.round(Math.random()*bgCount)+1;
loadMovie("backdrops/bg" + randBg + ".jpg", _root.bg);
```

This part chooses the random background and loads it into `_root.bg` movie clip (the clip at the top left of the screen). First, a random number between 0 and `bgCount` (initialized at 9) is generated and then 1 is added to it (generating a number between 1 and 10). This is set as `randBg`.

`bgCount` is set up to allow ease of update, but in situations such as this, a string array of file names is usually a better option because it will allow your images to be individually named, and will be easier to update and maintain.

`randBg` is then applied in order to pick a backdrop image (contained in the **backdrops** folder on the CD, named and numbered `bg1.jpg` through to `bg10.jpg`) and place it in `_root.bg`.

5. The next function (`backgroundFade`) fades in the background image, *after* it has loaded. This function first tests to check that the JPEG has loaded using:

```
if (_root.bg.getBytesTotal() == _root.bg.getBytesLoaded()) {
```

If these criteria are met then the script checks that the background hasn't already faded in by 20% and, if not, then it increases the `fade` amount by 1%. We only want the images to have an alpha value of 20% so that they blend comfortably into the background of the site.

```
if (fade<20) {
    fade++;
    _root.bg._alpha = fade;
}
```

So, every time it executes the `onClipEvent(enterframe)` handler it increases the alpha value of the background by 1%. The resulting effect is a nice subtle fade in of a background image. Changing the value of `fade` to increase in larger increments will result in a faster fade, so for instance, if we changed the command `fade++` to `fade +=2`, the fade in would happen at double speed.

The beauty of loading in JPEGs dynamically is that Flash only ever loads in what is needed, whereas in previous versions, if we had wanted such a random choice of images, it would have been necessary to include all nine JPEGs in the SWF, generating a large file size. Plus, we can easily change our backdrops at a later date if we wish, without opening up the FLA and re-exporting an updated version. We simply change the background images in the **backdrops** folder on the server.

Of course, another advantage of loading in the JPEGs dynamically is that you don't need to know anything about Flash to change the images on the site in this way. Anyone with a basic knowledge of how to resize and compress a JPEG and then FTP the files to the server could make changes to the Flash site. In the next section, we'll look at how you can actually design such a setup.

Bracken photo diary

In the photo section of Flatpack Records there's a photo diary of the band *Bracken* (famous throughout the West Country underground). Go into the `flatpackrecords.swf` and navigate to this area (click the **Bracken** button in the photo section) to see what this is:

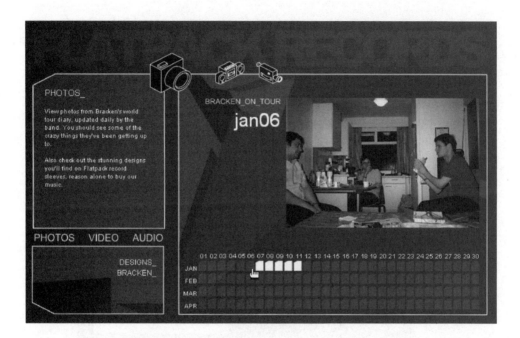

The theory behind this diary is that the band can be given a laptop computer equipped with Fireworks and an FTP program, a digital camera, and take daily snaps of their tour and upload them onto the Flash site. The image manipulation can be made relatively easy as Fireworks can easily be set up with a batch processing function that will resize and export the images to a predefined size and quality. So, even a novice with a small amount of training can update a Flash web site.

To take this even further and, crucially, to make the procedure easier for the band, a basic admin system with a little CGI might be worthwhile. The image and image caption could be inputted from the admin system and the Flash file would simply look to a database for any updates. If this area is one that interests you, refer to **section 4** of this book on dynamic data integration.

How many times have you heard a client say 'Do you think you could make me a simple site that I can update myself?' before they hit you with all the content that's going to be hard work for a web developer, let alone an amateur. Also, we've all seen beautiful sites that have obviously been left in the hands of no one in particular, with text running off into areas you can't access, or buttons that lead nowhere. So, in the next exercise, we'll look at how to create a site (or at least a section of it) that can be easily updated by someone with minimal Flash experience. This will allow you to offer a logical product that's attractive to the client because they only pay out once for the construction, rather than a running fee for the constant updates.

Constructing the photo diary

1. Open the `flatpackrecords.fla` and go into the **photos** movie clip. If you go to the frame labeled **bracken**, you'll see that there is a tour diary set up to dynamically load JPEGs. Here are the graphics that have been drawn up:

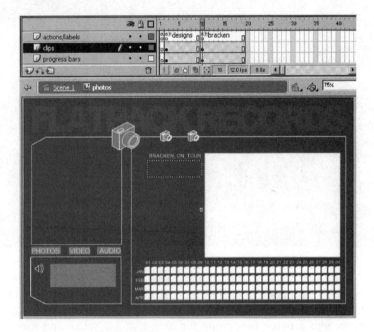

2. We'll start by looking at the content holder movie clip with the instance name `contentholder`, which is the large white rectangle in the screenshot above. As all JPEGs being loaded into this section will have the same dimensions, it's important to note the size of this movie clip (320 x 240 pixels).

3. There is also a dynamic text box (underneath the 'BRACKEN_ON_TOUR' static text), which will respond to the parameter name of the **photomoviebutton** clips (the little white shapes that signify each day). So for example, when the JPEG for January 11th loads up, **jan11** will appear in the text box. We'll look at how to set these parameters in a few moments.

4. Also, it's important at this stage to ensure the font size, type, and color of the dynamic text is to your liking.

Calendar buttons

The rest of the important content in this section is based around the **photomoviebutton** movie clip, which will load in each new image when the user clicks on it. The calendar is made up of just simple static text and many copies of the same photomoviebutton movie clip:

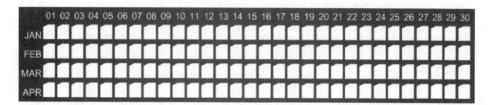

Each of the above icons, corresponding to a different date, sends the appropriate information to the contentholder clip regarding what external file should be loaded, and they also contain the text that is placed in the dynamic text box. We'll take January 6th as our example here.

1. Select the movie clip for January 6th and click on the **Parameters** tab of the Property inspector:

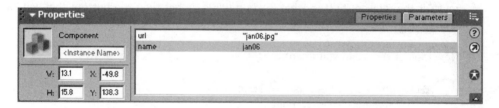

As you can see, the two parameters are url and name. Remember, when referring to an external file i.e. loading up a URL, it needs to be contained within quotation marks because it's the name of a file, not an expression.

2. Now let's have a look inside the guts of this movie clip. Go to the Library and double-click on the photomoviebutton movie clip (it's in the **JPEG** Library folder). You can immediately see that it's pretty simple:

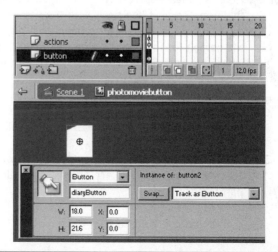

3. There's a button on the stage with the instance name `diaryButton`, and also a small bit of code in the **actions** layer. Open up the actions for this movie clip:

```
if (url == "defaultValue") {
    this._alpha = 20;
} else {
    diaryButton.onRelease = function() {
        _parent.name = name;
        _parent.loadImage("contentholder", "progressBar", url);
    };
}
```

The first statement describes a condition that checks the parameter `url` to see if we have entered anything for this instance of the clip. If the instance has been untouched, Flash automatically fills this parameter with `defaultValue`. If there is no entry for the button, the line `this._alpha=20` then makes the instance of the component more transparent.

So, when the user visits this site, any instance of **photomoviebutton** that has its parameters filled will appear with 100% alpha, but if no information has been entered in that part of the calendar, the button will be transparent. This is a useful trick as you can guide the user towards the relevant buttons that load up JPEGs, rather than the buttons that will have no effect.

4. Now look at the `else` statement:

```
diaryButton.onRelease = function() {
    _parent.name = name;
    _parent.loadImage("contentholder", "progressBar", url);
};
```

Here we make use of both the `url` and `name` variables. After setting the `onRelease` function, the next line deals with the `name` variable. This says that on pressing the button, the text box on the parent timeline will display the value held in the `name` parameter. As the default for these parameters was blank when the component was created, any instance where the parameter hasn't been filled in will cause the text box to simply remain empty.

The next line uses the `loadImage` function that we looked at earlier. The JPEG file name defined in the `url` parameter will load to the location `contentholder` on the parent timeline, and the `progressBar` instance will be set to monitor its loading.

5. In situations like this, you may prefer to switch off the link hand cursor. Flash MX has a command just for this. Try adding the following line to disable the hand cursor for a particular button:

```
myButton.useHandCursor = false;
```

Simply set it back to `true` to switch it back on.

So, that's it for the Bracken photo diary and the whole Flatpack Records photo section as a whole.

Summary

There you have it, we've covered various ways of using JPEGs that dynamically load into the SWF, looking along the way at JPEG optimization for the web all the way through to the final implementation within the Flash site. The methods we've used are quite specific to the Flatpack site, but I hope you can see how they can be easily adapted to suit your own projects' requirements. The great thing about loading JPEGs dynamically is that the main site can load in nice and quick, while the images only ever need to load in as required by the user. With this new functionality we're treated to full malleable images within Flash, combined with the ease of maintenance that a traditional HTML site offers. In the next chapter, we'll apply similar modular thinking and dynamic methods, and investigate how the video content of Flatpack Records was built.

section 3: Rich Media Sites

chapter 13: **Video**

In the previous chapter we looked at the dynamic use of images for our record company site. You'll probably be more familiar with the principles of what we're doing by now, but there are some differences when it comes to incorporating video content in Flash movies. This is partly due to the way that video is manipulated and controlled in Macromedia Flash MX, but we'll also think about what we're used to seeing in current 'video work' and how we can push it beyond our audience's expectations.

To get an idea of some of the things we'll be covering in this chapter, open up the `flatpackrecords.swf` and navigate your way to the video section of the site:

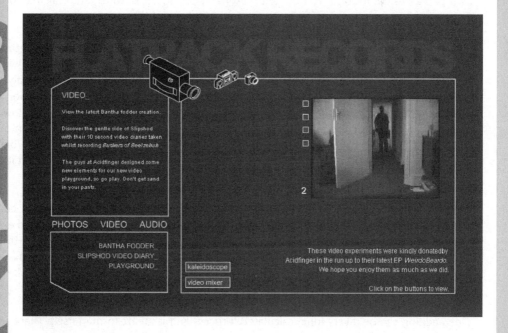

However, before we get too involved in the actual Flatpack video content, we'll go through some important video basics that you'll need for using video in Flash MX.

Digital video basics

Before you have the necessary video files on your machine ready to process for embedding in a Flash movie, it may have originated from varied sources:

- A client has supplied you with raw footage on VHS, DV tape, or even cine film.

- You have shot your own footage.

- You have downloaded or received a video file that needs converting for use in Flash.

It's possible that all the client knows at this early stage is that they want some form of video content on their site. They may already have the source material, as in the first of the three examples above, but before you can start playing with it you'll need to get this onto your trusty desktop machine. There are a number of ways to do this, usually depending on the format of the initial footage.

In the eventuality that the footage is in VHS, S-VHS or tape analog format, you'll need a capture card to digitize the footage. You can get reasonably priced cards, which are available for both PC and Macintosh, providing a suitable quality for video use on the web.

If you receive the footage in a DV format then you can skip the digitizing stage altogether, as you simply need to pull in the footage from the source. Currently, the miniDV format is widely used and has the advantage of being importable with many capture cards and DV-friendly FireWire ports (**www.apple.com/firewire** is a good starting point for more detailed information on this). While other setups may well use different digital tape formats, it's a fact that most low-end DV cameras use and recognize **miniDV**. You can run it from your own desktop, take it into another edit suite if necessary, and even send it to your client to view the quality of footage before you start working with it. Also, if you do have DV capture capability on your camera, then it is always best to take advantage of this and use it, as DV quality footage is superior.

The next stage in getting the video ready is working the footage, and producing an edit that is well suited to the web. Don't be concerned that you must edit in more advanced (and expensive) non-linear editing suites, such as Apple's Final Cut Pro or Adobe Premiere, in order to produce an effective piece of video content. I often prepare footage with Apple's iMovie, which is free with the Macintosh and very simple to use (and for PC users there's also Windows Movie Maker, a free video editing application included with Windows XP).

Video editing can be a very long, calculated, process and is an art form in itself. There's no need for us to go into too much depth here but, as we're specifically interested in *video for the web* in this chapter, here are a few tips and rules of thumb. These are important guides to help you maintain quality throughout the various stages prior to using it in Flash, and will be useful both in your edit and when you come to export your video, as we'll see later on in the chapter.

- Keep your source video edit as uncompressed and 'raw' as you can, exporting the final edit at the maximum frame rate. The compression and frame rate reduction will all be performed separately when importing the video into Flash (or in a dedicated compression application such as Sorenson Squeeze).

- If your video is made up of very quick cuts, be aware that slower frame rates can sometimes affect how this is viewed. A two-second shot, at 6 frames per second, will only contain 12 images after all, which in the grand scale of video isn't an awful lot. It might be useful to do a test export to check this.

- Avoid shots with large patches of fluorescent colors, or even bright primary shades, as these may bleed into each other.

- If you're using video to educate or inform (as opposed to entertain) try to make the point as clearly as possible within the shortest possible time. Grab the attention of the audience quickly, highlighting the important message you wish to convey at the start of the piece and don't prolong it.

- It is best to frame interviews around the head and shoulders of the speaker, rather than using wide shots, as it is easier to read the speaker's expression and relate to the face. If the situation *does* necessitate showing the wider environment (say, the interviewee is walking through their warehouse), start with a wide establishing shot and then cut to a tighter one of the speaker.

- Try to keep effects, filters, and unusual transitions to a minimum. When the frame rate and physical scale of the movie are low, it might not be entirely clear what's going on and, in most cases, the user is more interested in actual subject matter than stylistic touches. Of course, there will be situations (music videos being a great example) where this advice goes out of the window, so it's important to make a judgment of who the audience is and what their expectations may be.

- The soundtrack should be clear and uncluttered so that important elements are not drowned out by extraneous noise or other effects. If the quality of 'location' dialog is no good, consider re-recording it in a 'studio' (i.e. via your computer), even if this means asking your speaker to dub over the original footage.

You may have encountered situations previously where you're exporting to QuickTime from a video editing application, but it is important here to try and forget about all the decisions you would normally have to make regarding quality and compression. This is because Flash optimizes the video on import using the built-in Sorenson Spark codec.

Also, when you have finished the video edit and are ready to create the file for importing to Flash, bear in mind that Flash can import various file formats, but only if you have the appropriate players already installed on your computer. To import the following video file formats you must have QuickTime 4 or higher installed (available from **www.apple.com/quicktime**):

- Audio Video Interleaved (**AVI**)

- Digital Video (**DV**)

- Motion Picture Experts Group (**MPG** or **MPEG**)

- QuickTime Movie (**MOV**)

For users on Windows, DirectX 7 or higher (available at **www.microsoft.com/windows/directx**) must be installed to view these formats:

- Audio Video Interleaved (**AVI**)

- Motion Picture Experts Groups (**MPEG** or **MPG**)

- Windows Media File (**WMV** or **ASF**)

Exporting from QuickTime Pro

OK, so assuming your video has been edited and is now ready to export, let's take a look at how best to export the footage so that it is in an optimum condition, ready for importing into Flash. For this exercise I've exported DV footage from QuickTime Pro, but you should apply the same principles when exporting from other programs, whether it's Premiere, After Effects, iMovie, Windows Movie Maker, or any other editing application.

1. Locate your edited video file, open it up in QuickTime Pro and then choose **File > Export.**

2. In the **Export** drop-down choose to export **Movie as a QuickTime Movie** and click on the **Options...** tab. In the resulting dialog click on **Settings** in the **Video** and apply the following settings:

While this will obviously create a very large file size, we want to export at the best possible quality so that we have maximum control over the video compression settings when we import into Flash. It's very important to always use source video that is as uncompressed as you can get it. If you try and compress the video at this stage you will reduce the effectiveness of Sorenson Spark, Flash's built-in compressor.

Here we have changed the frame rate to match that of the source video. PAL users will import at 25 frames per second and NTSC users at 30 fps, so anything lower than these values will reduce the file size, but also the quality. As discussed above, we don't want to apply any compression, so choose **None** from the **Compressor** drop-down menu and set the **Quality** slider to **Best**.

3. Click on **OK** to accept these compression settings. Next, back in the **Movie Settings** dialog, choose **Size...** from the **Video** tab and check **Use Current Size**:

This keeps the scale (the physical frame dimensions) of the exported movie exactly as they were in the original video. We do this because Flash allows you to reduce the size of the video but not enlarge it when you import it. So, retaining the original dimensions will ensure that we'll have the largest scope for resizing once we're in Flash.

However, it's useful to note here that USB and video capture cards import video at a much lower resolution than digital video. A good rule to apply is to always maintain a ratio of 4:3, irrespective of the resolution of the video.

4. Accept these settings and click on **Settings...** in the **Sound** tab. Make the following changes so that no compression is applied:

Make sure that the **Sample Rate** is set to **44.1 kHz** and **16 bit Stereo**.

5. Once you've made all the required changes, the settings are summarized in the **Movie Settings** dialog:

6. Go ahead and export the video, which will take a few minutes. You now have a QuickTime MOV file ready for use in Flash.

Importing video into Flash

To begin we'll look at how Flash deals with video files in their purest form. After doing this, we'll then move on to look at other methods of controlling the video and how to load up movies dynamically into the Flatpack site in order to keep the main site file size minimized. Remember, it all comes down to our initial brief of designing a navigation that is in itself very small, but capable of loading up a whole gamut of larger files, without affecting the user's experience with long downloads.

Before we get too engrossed in all the possibilities, though, we're going to take a quick look at the process of how to actually import a video into Flash, using the Sorenson Spark quality settings in order to fully optimize the file for playback on the web. If you want to follow along with this section you'll need a video file to practice importing with. (Feel free to use any of your own files, or if you prefer use dummy_bantha_trim.mov on the CD. This is the same quality as the original video except shorter, to keep the file size down). We won't be using this movie later, but it will serve as a good source for learning all the necessary compression techniques.

Optimization with Sorenson Spark

1. Open a new Flash movie. The first thing to do is check that the frame rate of your Flash movie matches that of the video file you're going to import. My original `bantha.mov` was 25 fps.

2. Go to **File > Import** and select a suitable video file. In the following pop-up dialog choose **Embed video in Macromedia Flash document**:

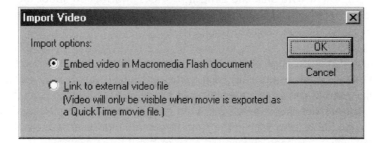

This gives you the option to embed the file into the Flash movie itself or make a link that will refer to a QuickTime file as an external source. However, as this means you then have to export the Flash project as a QuickTime file this is not particularly practical (since far more people use Flash than QuickTime).

3. Once you've chosen to embed the video in the Flash document, you'll see the **Import Video Settings** window where we optimize the video using the Sorenson Spark codec:

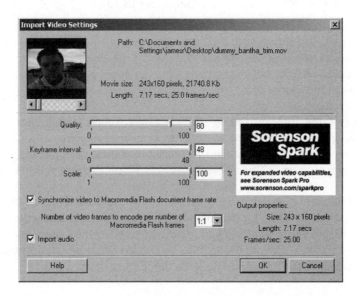

The addition of this codec is one of the most important and significant features of Flash MX. The settings here can be extensively manipulated to match all kinds of source video clips to the needs of your Flash project, and they are very powerful indeed.

We'll take a look at each of these settings as we import our video, beginning with the preview pane in the top left corner. This acts as a thumbnail representation of your movie and is scrollable, allowing you to quickly review the whole content before finally importing.

4. To the right of the preview window, the **Path** shows the location of the movie you're importing. The **Movie Size** and **Length** provides information about the source file (before you've imported and let Sorensen Spark work its magic). As you can see, I kept the original frame rate of the source video (25 fps).

5. The first significant control is the **Quality** slider, which directly affects the quality of the video image. Spark compresses each frame individually and a low setting here will reduce the file size, but this is at the expense of image quality. It may mean there's considerable loss in quality, but this depends partly on the size of the frame. Here is an example of the same video file playing back in the Flash Player. All import settings are the same except for **Quality**, which has been changed in each of these three examples:

Quality set to 100   Quality set to 70   Quality set to 50

As always with Flash design, a balance between quality and download time needs to be achieved, so you need to consider the user's expectations. Are they prepared to wait for high-quality video to begin streaming (or even download) or is the delay time of equal (if not more) importance?

6. The **Keyframe interval** setting stipulates how frequent keyframes occur in the movie. Increasing the number of normal frames in between keyframes increases the amount of compression and makes the file size smaller. However, in sequences with a lot of motion, it's likely that there will be a severe loss in quality if this interval is set too high.

7. The **Scale** setting allows us to reduce the physical dimensions of the video to suit your needs within the Flash movie. Although it is possible to resize videos once they've been imported into Flash, whatever you import is stored in the Library and it is this that makes up the large file size. Knowing this, try to get as close as possible to your required dimensions on import in order to keep the file size down.

Also note again our reason for exporting from the non-linear editing application at the largest possible size. If we had made a QuickTime movie with small dimensions, there's no option to enlarge it once we're in Spark. You'll probably never use the higher settings in **Scale** as the download would be far too large for most connections to handle, but it's good to get into the habit of working like this for when the opportunity does arise.

8. The next setting is based on the **frame rate** of your import:

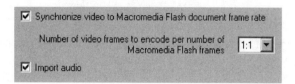

If you keep the first box checked, each frame of the video will be matched to a frame in the Flash timeline. Now, because the Flash default sets up movies that run at 12 fps, if your video was exported at 12 fps, the resulting SWF will play back at the correct speed. But what if your Flash movie was set up to play at 24 fps? Well, if **Synchronize video...** is still checked, the video would match frame for frame on the timeline, but it would be much faster on playback than the original (exactly double speed at 24 fps).

9. However, we're not tied to matching the images like this. If you uncheck the **Synchronize video...** box and look at the option beneath it, we can change the number of video frames to encode per Flash frames in the timeline:

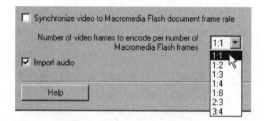

If you were to set a ratio of **1:2** for example, Sorensen would only import every other frame from the video, and each one of these would take up two Flash frames. If in doubt of what to do, it's a pretty good rule of thumb to just make sure the Flash movie runs at the same frame rate as the video by leaving **Synchronize video...** checked.

10. We're also given the choice to **Import audio**, which is pretty self-explanatory. Check this option if you want to maintain the audio from your video clip, otherwise, don't bother because not choosing to include it will keep the file size down. Note that when importing from MPG video files you cannot import the sound anyway and this option won't be available.

11. Finally, in the bottom right corner of the **Import Video Settings** window, the **Output properties** display what the video will import when you hit the **OK** button, and continually update as you change the settings:

Output properties:
Size: 243 x 160 pixels
Length: 7.17 secs
Frames/sec: 25.00

As you can see, there are actually many possibilities of control and compression to consider when importing video files into Flash. Some of these decisions will have been made in the initial footage edit when the video file was exported, but if you keep export settings as close to the original footage as possible (at the same scale and with no compression applied), then you will have more flexibility when you come to importing video into Flash.

This is something you'll pick up and apply to your own work, as we look at more practical examples over the course of the next few exercises.

MX video test

1. If you're happy with all of the settings, go ahead and click **OK** to finally import the video into Flash. When you do you'll be prompted with the following window (although the number of frames will be different if you're not using the same source file as me):

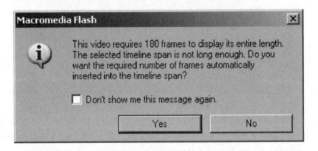

Macromedia Flash

This video requires 180 frames to display its entire length. The selected timeline span is not long enough. Do you want the required number of frames automatically inserted into the timeline span?

☐ Don't show me this message again.

Yes   No

2. Click **Yes** and you should now see the video clip in frame 1 of the main timeline.

3. If the video doesn't fit exactly over the stage, adjust the stage dimensions in the Property inspector so they match the dimensions of the video, and then align the video clip to the center of the stage. Finally, go ahead and test the movie to see it in action:

So that's the basics of using video in Flash MX. I know we've actually done very little with the video but it's a solid start. We've now got a good understanding of how to deal with video in Flash and found that it's actually not that scary.

Another important factor becomes clear if we take a look at what Spark has done to our file size. Even at the same import size of 243 x 160 pixels (identical to the original footage) and the Quality set to 80 (a good recommended balance for web video), the SWF compares very well to the original QuickTime source file:

Name ▲	Size	Type
dummy_bantha_trim.mov	21,741 KB	QuickTime Movie
import_test.fla	1,587 KB	Flash Document
import_test.swf	338 KB	Flash Movie

The SWF file is 338 KB in this case, much smaller than the original QuickTime movie we started with. This should illustrate how your sites can be made more efficient and accessible; it's far more efficient to stream a video in the Flash Player 6 than it is in QuickTime or another plug-in.

It's true that users will need the newest version of the player installed in order to view the video content, but the Flash Player 6 download is only 700 KB for the Mac or 330 KB for PC users. Therefore, this shouldn't put too many people off and these are considerably lower downloads than QuickTime, RealPlayer, or Windows Media Player.

Controlling video in Flash

So we've established that video can be easily imported, but the user will probably expect a little more than a constantly looping video clip. If they were watching it in QuickTime or Windows Media Player, the user would have a full interface of playback and sound control buttons to affect how the video plays back, so let's give it to them here. After all, we want to prove that displaying video in the Flash Player 6 is the better option. This shouldn't be too much of a problem since interactivity is what Flash is all about.

In the next example, we'll look at the video section of the Flatpack Records site, specifically the Banthafodder video with playback controls:

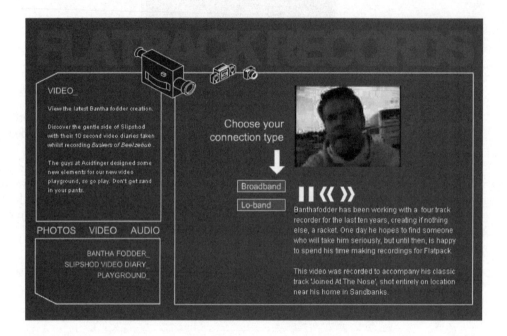

Open up `dummybanthacontroller.fla` to see we started to build the video content while we talk you through it.

Banthacontroller

In this example, we'll look at how to create an interface to control the video with a basic play and pause button – just imagine a broken VCR remote controller! This will be done using one movie clip symbol that is sensitive to the playback state of the video: when the video is paused, a play button will be visible and when the video is playing, a pause button will be visible. Before we examine the actual button in detail, let's take a quick look at some of the basic elements within the movie.

Stage

For what might seem like purely aesthetic reasons at the moment (but will make sense later), the stage has been resized to 180 x 200 pixels. The imported video's dimensions are 180 x 135 pixels, so we've reserved some space on the stage beneath the video to place the play/pause button:

Video

The video clip is imported directly onto frame 2 of the **QT movie** layer. This clip is fully extended over the timeline (giving us 347 frames of pure video). The video starts at frame 2, because we want the user to decide when to start playback, not allow Flash to start playing the video as soon as it's loaded. The user starts playback by pressing the play button in frame 1 of the **buttons** layer, prompted to do so by the welcome text that sits on frame 1 of the **QT movie** layer. Take a look around the timeline to see how this all fits together:

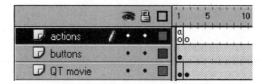

Buttons

The playback control sits on frame 1 of the **buttons** layer. This is a movie clip with the instance name playMov. It's a simple play button, but in conjunction with starting the video playback, it also acts as a pause button when the movie *is* playing. The simplest way to display this graphically is to create a movie clip containing 2 frames with the appropriate symbol graphic on each frame. We've added a play graphic to frame 1 and a pause graphic in frame 2:

Neither really pushes the boundaries of contemporary design, but they're immediately recognizable and functional, which is the main priority when building an interface of course.

Library

As you might expect there is nothing out of the ordinary in here, just the play and pause graphic symbols, the **play-pause** movie clip, and the imported video:

This just lets you see that there's nothing up our sleeves!

Actions

The code for the playMov instance (our play/pause button) is placed on frame 1 of the **actions** layer on the main timeline. Here's the code in full, but we'll look at it in detail below:

```
stop();
playMov.onRelease = function() {
    if (state == "paused") {
        state = "playing";
        play();
        playMov.gotoAndStop(2);
    } else if (state == "playing") {
        state = "paused";
        stop();
        playMov.gotoAndStop(1);
    }
};
playMov.gotoAndStop(1);
state = "paused";
```

OK, let's break it down. This is all relatively simple stuff so it shouldn't cause too many problems. After the `stop` action, there's a chunk of code for the `playMov` button/instance. On the second line, `playMov` is set up to react to a mouse click and, if this occurs, a function is pursued. The first thing to happen is that the flag variable `state` is checked to see if the video is playing or paused. In either eventuality three things happen:

- The value of `state` is changed to its opposite.
- The timeline is stopped or started.
- The visual representation of the button graphic is changed.

So, in the eventuality that the video is paused (`state == "paused"`), the `state` variable is changed to "playing", the video commences playback, and the `playMov` timeline is sent to display the pause graphic at frame 2.

> *Note that in the code above I didn't use the* `_root` *handle for a very good reason. We can usually use* `_root` *to control the main timeline in a Flash file, but in this case we're preparing a SWF that will be loaded into the main Flatpack Records site. So for example, if the complete site loaded in* `banthabroadband.swf` *which contained* `_root` *controls within it, the main site would be affected, not* `banthbroadband.swf`.

The last piece of code above simply closes the function and initializes the movie in pause mode.

That's nearly all the code dealt with. There is one last piece of code to be aware of, which is `gotoAndPlay (2);` parallel to the last frame of the imported video. This makes the movie loop continually unless interrupted by the user. You could also just as easily stop the timeline at this last frame and add a simple 'Play film again?' button before sending the timeline back to the start of the video.

Now you know how it all works go ahead and test the movie. It's simple but effective nonetheless.

There are of course other controls we can use in playing back videos, such as rewind and fast forward, which we'll move on to in the next section.

Creating rewind and fast forward controls

Currently, our video playback is controlled by a kind of toggle switch, but fast forward and rewind work a little differently. When the button is pressed down, the action starts, and it stops when the button is released. Fortunately, we can use Flash MX's new callback scripting capability to make this easier, setting code to activate the manipulation when the button is pressed, and removing the code when the button is released. This is the specific functionality we want to create:

- When the user presses the button begin winding or rewinding.

- When the user releases the button return to normal play.

If you open up the finished banthacontroller2.fla (on the CD) you'll see that there are two extra instances on the timeline, a fast forward and rewind button. They are both placed on the **buttons** layer and assigned an appropriate instance name: rewindMov for the rewind button and forwardMov for the fast forward button:

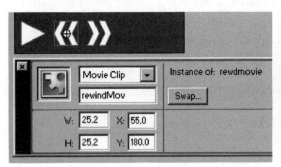 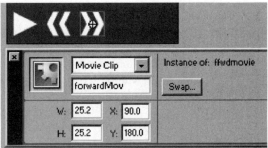

Besides these new additions, the only other changes between this and the dummybanthacontroller.fla we looked at in the last exercise are all on frame 1 of the **actions** layer. Some new functions have been added for each of the two new buttons.

Let's take a look at the additional code for this movie:

```
frameSkip = 10;
stop();
// Play / pause button
playMov.onRelease = function() {
    if (state == "paused") {
        state = "playing";
        play();
        playMov.gotoAndStop(2);
    } else if (state == "playing") {
        state = "paused";
        stop();
        playMov.gotoAndStop(1);
    }
};
// Fast forward button
forwardMov.onPress = function() {
```

```
            forwardMov.onEnterFrame = function() {
                gotoAndPlay(_currentframe+frameSkip);
                };
    };
    forwardMov.onRelease = function() {
        forwardMov.onEnterFrame = undefined;
        state = "playing";
            playMov.gotoAndStop(2);
    };
    // Rewind button
    rewindMov.onPress = function() {
        rewindMov.onEnterFrame = function() {
            if (_currentframe>1) {
                gotoAndPlay(_currentframe-frameSkip);
            }
        };
    };
    rewindMov.onRelease = function() {
        rewindMov.onEnterFrame = undefined;
        if (_currentframe == 1) {
            state = "paused";
            playMov.gotoAndStop(1);
        } else {
            state = "playing";
            playMov.gotoAndStop(2);
        }
    };
    // Initialise
    playMov.gotoAndStop(1);
    state = "paused";
```

The first things you might notice are the extra comments. These are simply there to make the different sections easier to distinguish for both you and me. The first section headed with a comment is the code for the play/pause button, exactly the same as in the previous controller movie we looked at. Above this though, right at the start of the code, is a new variable declaration:

```
    frameSkip = 10;
```

As we're creating fast forward and rewind buttons, we need to tell Flash how many frames to increment or decrement each time. frameSkip is the variable that signifies how many frames to jump, and setting it to 10 gives us a fairly rapid speed. Go ahead and change this value for a different effect and consider the number of total frames in the movie before doing so. We use this variable with our next new piece of code.

```
// Fast forward button
forwardMov.onPress = function() {
    forwardMov.onEnterFrame = function() {
        gotoAndPlay(_currentframe + frameSkip);
    };
};
```

This code gives our fast forward button its functionality. Firstly, it is important to be aware that the fast forwarding activates when the user *presses* the mouse. If you remember from a little earlier, we want to fast forward when the mouse is pressed and resume normal play on release (more on this in a moment).

When forwardMov is pressed, an onEnterFrame function is activated for the instance, telling the timeline to move on rapidly. This sends the playhead to the frame designated by the total of the _currentframe property plus the value of the frameSkip variable. So, having set up this code to run every frame, when the button is released, we need to clear it like so:

```
forwardMov.onRelease = function() {
    forwardMov.onEnterFrame = undefined;
    state = "playing";
    playMov.gotoAndStop(2);
};
```

The first two lines of code clear the onEnterFrame function on the mouse button release, removing all of the frame-skipping code that we previously inserted there.

The next two lines of code should be familiar from the play/pause button code. When the fast forward button is released, the video will proceed to play at normal speed, and these lines simply update the play/pause state and graphic ready for the next press. This might seem an insignificant action, but it certainly saves the frustration of encountering incorrect button states and forcing the user to double press to make something work properly!

Now the fast forward button has been completed, let's move onto the rewind button:

```
// Rewind button
rewindMov.onPress = function() {
    rewindMov.onEnterFrame = function() {
        if (_currentframe>1) {
            gotoAndPlay(_currentframe-frameSkip);
        }
    };
};
```

This should already look familiar from the fast forward button, with one subtle difference – a limit. If you remember from the last movie, when the playhead reaches the last frame of the timeline, it looped back to frame 2. So, if you fast forward past the end of the movie, Flash just returns to frame 2 and continues on playing, allowing unlimited looping.

However, the rewind button will not allow endless rewinding, as the movie will stop when it arrives back at frame 1. It would be easy for us to amend this and make the movie loop in both directions, but the time and space continuum could become confused, and you might just end up back in 1985 like little Marty McFly. Besides, it's something easy for you to go and experiment with.

The `if` statement, therefore, simply checks if the playhead is on or after frame 2 and, if it is, allows rewinding to take place. The next section of code is activated when the mouse is released:

```
rewindMov.onRelease = function() {
    rewindMov.onEnterFrame = undefined;
    if (_currentframe == 1) {
        state = "paused";
        playMov.gotoAndStop(1);
    } else {
        state = "playing";
        playMov.gotoAndStop(2);
    }
};
```

As with the fast forward release code, segments of this will be familiar. The major difference with this code is that there is an `if` statement which takes the position of the playhead and the correct `state` for the play/pause button into consideration. If the playhead is at frame 1, then the play/pause button is set to the paused `state`, and the play graphic is displayed. Otherwise, the play/pause button is set as playing and displays the pause button.

Finally, the actions are completed by the initialization code that was built in the last section:

```
playMov.gotoAndStop(1);
state = "paused";
```

Here's the final movie in action. This will sit there on the server until it's called in to the main site.

We haven't included this is in the final movie but here's another potential use for the `_currentframe` property, a simple scrubber bar for your video, such as you might see in typical video plug-ins that allow you to quickly scan over a whole video file:

If you made a movie clip that was draggable and constrained to the x-axis, it would be a simple case of making the dragging range correlate to the frame on the timeline that the video was currently at. For example, you could use:

```
video_mc._currentframe = dragger_mc._x
```

You might need to use a bit of math so that the top scale of your drag range was the same value as the last frame in your movie, but this shouldn't be too tricky.

Broadband Banthafodder

We've already looked at utilizing progress bars in the last chapter so I won't go into too much depth. However, it's particularly relevant here as we're going to be looking at a large movie in this section – one designed for broadband distribution so the user will probably want an indication of how long they're expected to hang around waiting for it to download.

Open up the source file `banthabroadband.fla` and you'll see the same video we've been working on so far, with relevant changes made and a new layer called **progress bar**:

loading

All the content on frame 1 of each layer has been shunted along to frame 2, to make way for the progress bar. On frame 1 of the new **progress bar** layer is a simple text graphic and the brains behind the operation: a ProgressBar component. This component has the instance name progressBar and a couple of graphic-based parameters, allowing you to switch the progress bar or the text on or off. For now though, we'll leave them both on.

On frame 1 of the **actions** layer is the following code to make progressBar function:

```
stop();
progressBar.setLoadTarget(this);
this.onEnterFrame = function () {
    if (progressBar.getPercentComplete()==100) {
        this.onEnterFrame = undefined;
        this.gotoAndPlay (2);
    }
};
```

Let's run through this code in sections, to see what it does. After the initial frame halt, there is a line of code to tell progressBar which level or target to monitor. As this movie is limited to just one timeline, the progress bar has been set to monitor this.

> Remember that to help avoid complications later on in the site development, try to avoid using _root.

In this case, this means all of this local timeline and therefore all of the bytes. Let's move on to this next section:

```
this.onEnterFrame = function () {
    if (progressBar.getPercentComplete()==100) {
        this.onEnterFrame = undefined;
        this.gotoAndPlay (2);
    }
};
```

The first line of code sets up an action to run on every frame. The if statement then checks to see whether the target assigned to progressBar (namely this, as set in the last bit of code) has fully loaded (is equal to 100%). Next, the getPercentComplete method inherited from the component saves us a considerable amount of calculation work. When the condition is true, the onEnterFrame action is cleared and the playhead is sent to frame 2.

Voila! That's it. If you test the movie now you'll see the same interface and video as last time as the video loads in instantly. You will need to test the file online to check the progress bar.

Flatpack video

Take a look at the main site file `flatpackrecords.fla`. If you remember, there are three areas on the main timeline for photos, videos, and audio. Go to the frame labeled **video** and open up the **video** movie clip on the **dynamic content** layer. You'll see this timeline:

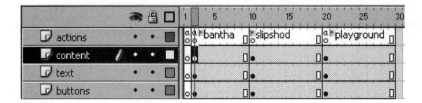

Within here are three states that are accessible from the main navigation system. Each of the **bantha**, **slipshod**, and **playground areas** contain content for the three video sections of the site.

The first element we'll look at is the Banthafodder video. We've made up a good quality download for broadband users and we'll also provide a smaller one for anyone using a normal 56K modem. So, in the **text** layer there is some explanatory text to point this out and, in the **buttons** layer, there are two buttons used to load in either the `banthabroadband.swf` we looked at earlier and a low bandwidth alternative called `banthaloband.swf`:

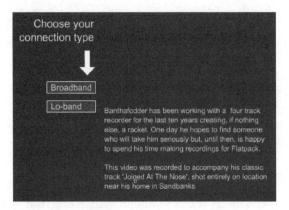

We also added a short description of Banthafodder to inform the user while they wait for the movies to load. Hopefully, by the time they've read the text content, the video will be ready for them to watch.

Dynamically loading Banthafodder video

As we saw in the previous chapter, the principle of loading up media from an external source is pretty straightforward. There are basically three important elements to construct:

- The external media file, in this case the standalone `banthabroadband.swf` we've just made.

- The 'content holder' movie clip, which is the location within the site that the media file is loaded into.

- The main site navigation, which loads the media file into the content holder.

So, let's look in detail at how this was built.

1. First, I wanted to use the broadband version of the Banthafodder video download so I reopened `banthabroadband.fla` to check its stage dimensions. We need to allow sufficient room in the main site for the whole of the SWF. In my case, the `banthabroadband.swf` is 180 x 200 pixels.

2. Back in the `flatpackrecords.fla`, I made a layer called content and in the relevant frame added an empty movie clip with the instance name `contentholder`:

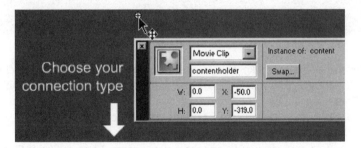

This movie clip has no content at all and is identified on the stage by the small white circle, which signifies the top left corner that the external SWF video will load into.

3. Then all that's left to do is add the necessary ActionScript to load the external movie into the `contentholder` movie clip:

```
broadbandButton.onRelease = function() {
    LoadMovie ("banthabroadbandswf", contentholder);
};
loButton.onRelease = function() {
    loadMovie("banthaloband.swf", contentholder);
};
```

So, the appropriate size SWF will now load into the location `contentholder` whenever either button is pressed.

Testing loading speeds and streaming video

If you test the `flatpackrecords.fla` at this stage, you'll see that it now loads up `banthabroadband.swf`:

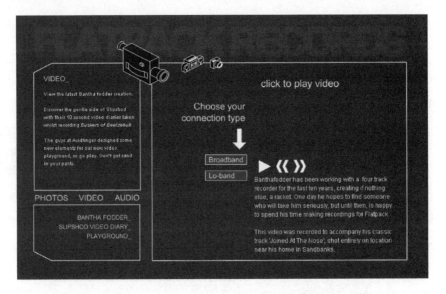

Although testing the movie like this is useful for checking that the functionality is working properly, it doesn't give any indication of how long the user will have to wait for the content to download. There are a few other tools we can use in Flash to give us some more accurate feedback about how the site will really appear when it's on the web.

1. To see how the movie would appear online, go to **View > Show Streaming** in the test movie.

2. This will give you more of an idea of the user's experience, as the movie plays back simulating a modem connection, but you can also use the Bandwidth Profiler (**View > Bandwidth Profiler**) to display the data unloading into the browser. Also check **View > Frame By Frame Graph** is on, as this is the clearest method.

    However, even when you've done all this, although it shows how `flatpackrecords.swf` loads up, `banthabroadband.swf` appears instantly when you click on the broadband button (i.e. you can't view the external source streaming).

3. To do this you need to return to the original `banthabroadband.fla` and test the movie from there. With the Bandwidth Profiler on, we can then see how efficient the load up is for the video.

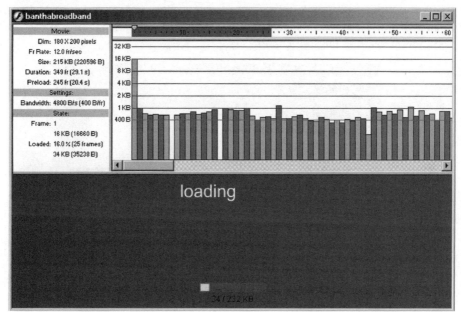

We can see that this file wouldn't stream on a 56K modem, but this is fine anyway as we've included a progress bar. For it to stream, each frame would need to contain less information (i.e. be even more compressed), so it could load up as the user views it. In the Bandwidth Profiler, we can see when a file will stream effectively because the bar graph does not peak above the red line. In the screenshot above, we would need each frame of `banthabroadband.swf` to be below 400B but that's obviously not going to happen. This is academic anyway – we've specifically told the user that this video has been designed for those on a broadband connection.

4. Also note that this depends on the setting chosen in the **Debug** menu for the various types of web connection. I've tested for a 56 KB modem, but you can also make your own settings from the same menu, say, to simulate an ADSL connection as I've done here by going to **Debug > Customize**... and setting it up as follows:

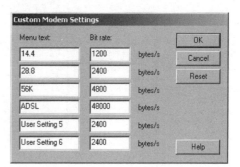

This will naturally change the readings on the Bandwidth Profiler.

5.   So, I then wanted a file that would stream a low-bandwidth version of the same video. The best way to achieve this is to import a lower quality version of the original source video into a new Flash file. I made another movie called `banthaloband.fla` using these Sorensen Spark settings on import:

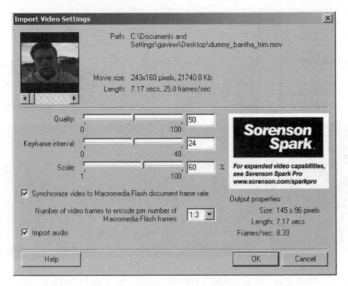

Note that the **Scale**, **Quality**, and **Keyframe interval** have all been drastically reduced to keep each frame of my QuickTime movie as small as possible. The video:Flash ratio has also been adjusted to 1:3.

6.   Now when I test this streaming frame by frame for a 56k Modem, the Bandwidth Profiler looks far healthier:

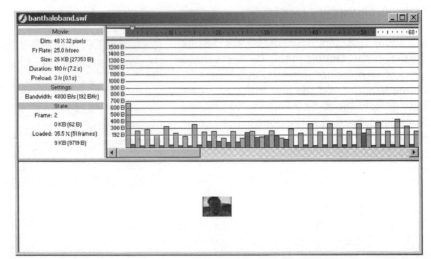

Even though there are a few large blocks towering over the red line, most frames seem to be very small indeed. In fact if you look at the same information in the Streaming Graph layout, you'll see that it averages out pretty much slap bang on the line. Perfect.

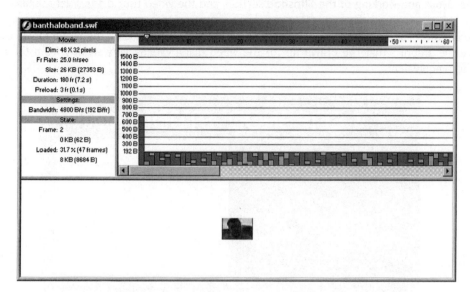

As it's streaming, don't forget you can see what's loaded in (the green bar) and where the playhead is at (the triangular marker). As long as the bar is further ahead than the playhead the movie will stream. In the example above, only 48 frames have loaded but this is not a problem as the playhead is still back at frame 2.

As I now know that `banthaloband.swf` will stream successfully on most modems, there's no need for a progress bar, so I just export it as a standalone SWF. This gets called into the main site when the user requests it by pressing the lo-band button.

Video menu components: the Slipshod tour diary

If you've been through the tour photos section in the last chapter, you should be familiar with the layout and working of the **Slipshod** section, and the video tour diary is very similar.

Still in the `flatpackrecords.fla`, go to the **Slipshod** section inside the **video** movie clip. Here are the graphics that I've drawn up for the video diary, varying very slightly from the previous photo equivalent:

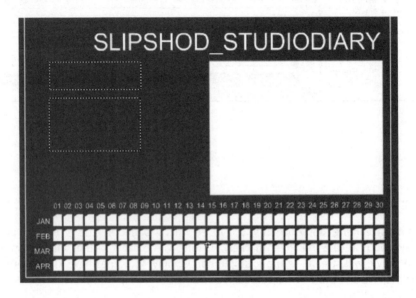

The location that our SWFs will load into is the large white square. This has been given the instance name `contentholder2` to save confusion as we already have another instance name of `contentholder` within the **video** movie clip on the main timeline. Also, as all the pieces of video being loaded into this section have the same dimensions, I made `contentholder2` exactly the same size (240 x 180 pixels).

Note that there are two dynamic fields on the stage. These are used to display the name and description of the SWF. The first field has the variable name `name` and will display the value we set for this variable in the **Paramaters** tab of the Property inspector. The lower text field has been assigned the variable name `description`. Also, an external movie will be called when the component is clicked. So, if you select the **jan11** movie clip, for example, you can see the values it will display and the movie it will load:

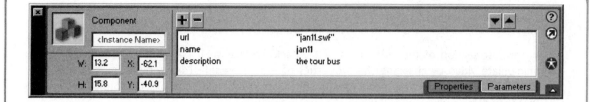

Slipshod SWFs

The SWFs that are loaded into the main site are very simple, basically very similar to the `banthaloband.fla`. They are simply Flash movies with the video imported on to the main timeline and the stage is the same size as the video: 240 x 180 pixels. That's all there is to it.

The scenario I'm imagining is that the band *Slipshod* have gone on tour and a Marketing bod has given them a video camera to make their own tour diary. Each day they shoot a ten-second clip (in most cases this will be made-up of one shot), return to the tour bus, capture the video, and export it to QuickTime. From there it's a relatively simple case of importing the QuickTime movie into Flash and then exporting the standalone SWF. In Flash, the band needs to make sure of three things:

- The SWF is the same size as the `contentholder2` location.

- The export is at the standard Flash 12 fps (the same frame rate as the main site).

- They have named the SWF export according to the date (`jan11.swf`, `jan12.swf`, and so on).

This isn't particularly complicated, even for an average rock band, but as the developer you could even provide them with a `template.fla` and just make sure they always **Save As** and rename the export so it can be recognized by the main site. Each SWF needs uploading to the Flatpack Records site when it's completed. The developer would need to develop an admin area where the band can upload the SWF, and add a caption in a designated form, which are both added to a database. You could then program Flash to call the database for each SWF and the necessary captions for the dynamic text fields.

That's quite a lot to take in at once but the opportunity is most certainly there and all it takes is for a developer to experiment and make this happen. In fact, it'd probably be far trickier making sure the band doesn't trash the equipment than building the actual database and web site.

So, I hope you can see how customized components can be used efficiently to call up movies into the main site. As they're only very short snippets I haven't bothered with controllers or preloaders and as each new movie loads it replaces the last one, so there's no chance of the movie becoming overloaded with unnecessary downloads (i.e. old movies that you've finished watching).

Manipulating video: video playground

In this last section of the video area of Flatpack Records we'll take a fleeting look at how to manipulate video by changing the properties of the `contentholder` movie clip. You may have already used some of these properties in other work but we'll hopefully be able to prove here that they can be just as useful when manipulating video.

First, I thought about a short video piece that was made up of four clips layered over each other but which would only ever display one at a time. This would have worked a little like a mixing desk with several camera sources feeding into it, with all four shots showing the same action but from a different angle. This is a system often used by live TV shows, where a director will sit up in the gallery calling out to the operators when he wants to cut from one live camera to another.

Navigate your way to the **playground** in Flatpack's video area to get an idea of what I'm talking about. The actual separate movie on the CD is `vidmixer.fla`. Although the example here doesn't show four cameras filming one event from different angles (quite the opposite), the principle of live mixing is still there.

1. We started off by filming four pieces of video and embedding them in four small standalone SWFs suitably named `cam1.swf`, `cam2.swf`, `cam3.swf`, and `cam4.swf`. Note that each shot is a different length, but trust me as this adds to the effect.

2. We want this video mixer to be entirely self-contained so this means importing all four videos into the Library of a new Flash document.

> *If you're importing more than one video into your Flash project, but wish to apply the same Sorensen Spark settings to all of the videos, use* **File > Import to Library** *and* SHIFT+Click *to import all the videos simultaneously.*

3. Each of the four videos is then inserted in its own movie clip. So far in this chapter we have imported video directly on to the main timeline rather than a movie clip, but here we're far more interested in affecting the MovieClip object's properties.

4. Take a look at the **cam1** movie clip by double-clicking on it in the Library.

    You'll see the QT video clip is the only content in here, with the top left corner registered to the center of the movie clip at (0,0):

5. Each of the four movie clips was then placed on frame 2 of the **movies** layer on the main timeline (to allow room for a loader bar in frame 1). The decision to overlay all four clips on top of each other in exactly the same position will become clearer when we see how the mixer works.

6. I created a button called **button** and placed four instances on a new layer called **buttons** at frame 2. The four button instances have an instance name of channel1 through to channel4. In this same frame there is also a small dynamic text field below the buttons to tell the user which 'camera' is currently selected:

7. Let's now take a look at the code that controls how the movie clips function. Take a look at the code on frame 2 of the actions layer. The following function sets up the depth swapping:

```
function swapFront(channel) {
```

continues overleaf

```
        stopAllClips(channel);
        this["cam"+channel].swapDepths(1);
        cam = channel;
    }
```

8.   This is called with the following code:

```
channel1.onRelease = function() {
    swapFront("1");
};
channel2.onRelease = function() {
    swapFront("2");
};
channel3.onRelease = function() {
    swapFront("3");
};
channel4.onRelease = function() {
    swapFront("4");
};
// initialize
swapFront ("1");
```

The function performs two operations: it brings the inputted video clip to the front of the stack and sets the dynamic text field cam to the inputted channel.

For the depth swapping, any depth value can be used, as long as the depth level is not already inhabited. In this movie, we are only using the depth level of 1, so all of the clips simply compete for it.

> Remember that the higher the depth level, the further to the front the object will be placed. With this in mind, an object at depth level 3 will obscure another object placed at depth level 1. Also, try not to confuse depth levels with levels used with the loadMovie action.

9.   The rest of the code sets the buttons, and finally initializes the movie, starting it all off with **cam1**. If you were to test the movie with the current code, it would all look swell and dandy. There is just one thing wrong with it, which might not be apparent until the movie is uploaded and tested as part of the final web site online. The problem is that making four videos run simultaneously is not good for the old CPU!

We get around this, of course, by stopping the videos playing while they are in the background. For this, we need a whole new function and need to make a slight adjustment to the `swapFront` function:

```
function stopAllClips(playChannel) {
    cam1.stop();
    cam2.stop();
    cam3.stop();
    cam4.stop();
    this["cam"+playChannel].play();
}
//
function swapFront(channel) {
    stopAllClips(channel);
    //
    this["cam"+channel].swapDepths(1);
    cam = channel;
}
```

Now this looks more like the code in the FLA. The new function simply stops all of the video clips and then restarts the selected channel. Although this might look a little jerky in the ActionScript, the whole process is seamless and invisible to human detection. The `stopAllClips` function is called from within the `swapFront` function, and the channel input is simply passed through it. This means that the button code remains the same, even though the base of the code has changed a little. That's our code finished.

10. Finally we added a ProgressBar component in frame 1 of the main timeline to make Flash wait until the entire project (including the four video clips) has downloaded. Then and only then does Flash move on to frame 2 (containing a `stop ();` action), where all the action takes place.

11. The last job is in the main `flatpackrecords.fla`, where a button has been set to load up the standalone `vidmixer.swf`, just like any other media file.

There are various ways we could have made this: maybe changing the `_alpha` values of each movie clip when the buttons were changed; or creating a four frame loop with each frame showing a different camera. Hopefully, you'll start seeing the versatility of a video contained within its own movie clip so let's finish off by looking at the kaleidoscope toy, which completes the **playground** section and the whole video area of the Flatpack Records web site.

Video kaleidoscope

1. If you open the `kaleidoscope.fla` you'll recognize the (by now very familiar) progress bar on frame 1 and the ubiquitous `stop` actions on frames 1 and 2.

2. On frame 2 there's a movie clip with the instance name `kal`. This holds the entire kaleidoscope effect. I basically wanted to make an example of how video clips can be masked off, reused, and controlled by external sources, so hopefully this little movie sums all these ideas up.

3. Double-click on the **kaleidoscope** movie clip and you'll see that it's made up of four segments. In fact, these are simply four individually named instances (`segment1` through `segment4`) of the same **segment** movie clip, each rotated and positioned so that they form a circle. I've dragged out the original segment with no rotation applied so you can more easily see what's going on here:

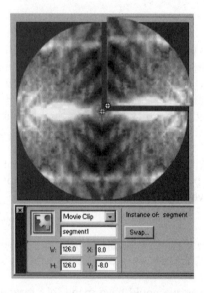

4. Open up the **segment** movie clip and you'll notice that we're dealing with a mask (a quarter-circle shape) covering another movie clip holding a QuickTime video:

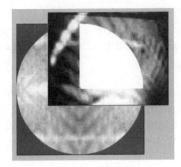

It's particularly relevant to point out that the video clip was centered in the **holder** movie clip so that if I tried rotating it using the Free Transform tool again, it would always do so around the center point so the mask was always covering part of the clip.

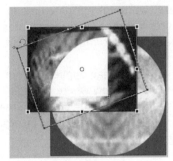

This was so that when we started rotating **holder** using ActionScript the video would always completely fill the mask (i.e. so the circle shape wasn't broken).

5. This script was then added to frame 2 of the **actions** layer on the main timeline:

```
stop();
this.onEnterFrame = function () {
    rotation = 20*(_root._xmouse/_root._ymouse);
    kal.segment1.holder._rotation=rotation;
    kal.segment2.holder._rotation=rotation;
    kal.segment3.holder._rotation=rotation;
    kal.segment4.holder._rotation=rotation;
}
```

The video is made interactive by the sum:

```
20*(_root._xmouse/_root._ymouse);
```

Note that when we previously made SWF files to load into our main site, we balked from using _root. However, in this case we *do* want the video clip to respond to our _root mouse position. In other words, it responds to where the mouse is on the main site, not the kaleidoscope movie itself.

So that's how the kaleidoscope works. As the video constantly runs in a loop and responds to the mouse position, there are many different ways of viewing it, creating all sorts of odd patterns. You could take this further using all sorts of Math functions here, and maybe some of the inertia we looked at earlier in the second section of the book. You could also experiment with a random number element.

Summary

Hopefully we've answered many of your video queries concerning Flash MX. As MX is the first web application to really start incorporating video as a creative tool, rather than leaving it to other third-party applications. It's really worth taking some time to get it right. The main issue for us at the moment is how to create sites incorporating video content but keeping a watchful eye on the crucial file sizes and how to keep the user informed and entertained in the process.

Try to think about how this new knowledge applies to your own designs. Maybe you've always wanted to start using video but never knew where to begin? Well, Flash MX does half the work for you now and then there's really no limit to your own creativity. Apply your newfound coding knowledge from section two with the techniques for incorporating video and you'll be able to create some pretty interesting results.

In the final section of the Flatpack Records site we'll investigate the audio elements, dealing with dynamic loading and manipulation of MP3 files.

section 3: Rich Media

chapter 14: **Audio**

In this last chapter on Flatpack Records we're going to look at the new capability in Macromedia Flash MX to dynamically load MP3 files. In previous versions of Flash, if you wanted to play an MP3 within the SWF you had use one of two methods:

- Import the files to the main FLA prior to publishing (thereby dramatically increasing the final SWF's size).

- Make separate movies containing the MP3 and then use ActionScript to call the SWFs into the main movie.

Thankfully, with Flash MX we no longer need to go through this lengthy process to get sound on to our web site. Flash can call in external MP3 files from the server and load them into the main movie on request. Let's think about what this new capability means in relation to Flatpack Records. One of the main reasons why users visit a record company's site is because they can listen to the latest tracks by their favorite artists. Flatpack Records is no exception (although you might think otherwise when you hear the music).

Ordinarily, if a user wanted to listen to non-embedded audio in a non-Flash MX site they would need to use a plug-in such as RealOne Player or QuickTime, which must also be installed on their machine. If the user is already on our Flatpack Records site, we don't have to concern ourselves over any extra plug-ins as the user must already have the Flash Player 6 in order to view the site, and therefore can hear the audio tracks through this. Any users without the Flash Player 6 would have been advised of this before entering the Flatpack site, and offered a link to the player download area.

MP3 has become an industry standard method of high quality audio compression and is obviously a common format for web users, as the popularity of the many MP3 download sites illustrates. So, we can be very confident that they're ideal for using on our site.

Flash MX has two methods for loading in MP3s: streaming and non-streaming, which we'll now examine in more detail.

Non-streaming audio

Non-streaming basically means that the full MP3 file is downloaded into Flash before any playback begins. This is a good thing if audio quality is your sole consideration and you want to allow the user to listen to the file in full without any interruption to the sound. However, download time is the main issue for most users, and its main disadvantage is that there will be a long delay on ordinary modem connections while the complete file is downloaded. It's this reason that makes non-streamed sounds more appropriate for short sound clips such as button noises as opposed to complete soundtracks.

Non-streamed sounds are also useful for event sounds that will be reused again later in the movie, because they only have to be downloaded once to the user's computer and then stored locally until Flash calls it again.

Streaming audio

Streaming media begins playback during the actual download itself rather than waiting for the whole file to load in before commencing. This is great for longer music tracks, the advantage being that any visitor to your site doesn't have to wait ages for the whole file to load. Playback begins once a connection has been made with the MP3 file and an adequate portion of the file has been buffered in Flash.

The disadvantage with this is that the audio file has to run at the appropriate bit rate, depending on the user's connection speed. So for instance, if your visitor is using a 56k modem connection then they will need to select an MP3 track with a bit rate of approximately 24kbps. Any higher bit rate than this, and your average modem connection will hang up midway through the file transfer while it waits for more data to load in, causing an intermittent stream. This principle is very similar to streaming video in Flash.

As a guide, these are the bit rates you should follow when producing streaming MP3 tracks for your site:

56k	Dual ISDN (128k)	ADSL
24kbps	80kbps	160kbps

These are quite conservative bit rates, as connections are never perfect in the real world, especially on a dial-up modem. So, even though you could theoretically get a connection of 40kbps on a 56k modem, few users would actually be able to sustain this speed for the duration of a four-minute song. On an ADSL connection you could sustain a higher bit rate (around 250kbps), but as 160kbps virtually gives you CD quality, there is little point in going above this level. Even a bit rate of 96kbps is considered near CD quality, while a bit rate of 64kbps provides sound quality similar to that of FM radio.

It's also important to remember that streamed sounds are lost after playback, so if they are required again in the movie they need to be streamed again. They cannot be replayed or reused.

Encoding MP3s using iTunes (Mac only)

There are a number of applications for encoding MP3 files and numerous free encoders on the web for PC users – try searching for 'MP3 encoders' at **http://download.com**. Alternatively, many MP3 encoders for PC users are reviewed and available at **http://tucows.blueyonder.co.uk/mmedia/cdrip95.html**. Fortunately for Mac users, probably the best program to use is one that you most likely already own: **iTunes** (also available as a free download from **www.apple.com/itunes** just in case).

Using iTunes is pretty straightforward and doesn't require much of a tutorial, but we'll quickly go through the basics of converting a track into an MP3 file for your web site. You can convert to MP3 from an AIFF, WAV, or CD track. In this exercise we'll use an AIFF file, though the principle is the same for the other formats.

1. Open up iTunes and go to **Edit > Preferences...**. Click on the **Importing** tab at the top of the **Preferences** dialog and choose **Custom** from the **Configuration** drop-down menu. Then click **OK**.

2. The main options we're concerned with here are the **Bit Rate** and **Sample Rate**. Set the bit rate according to the connection options that you plan to give the user on your site. On the Flatpack Records site for instance, we have 3 different MP3 streaming options for the user to choose from, depending on the speed of their connection: 56k, ISDN, or ADSL. Therefore, if I was now making the MP3 file that would be streamed in after the user selected the 56k option, I would set a bit rate of 24kbps:

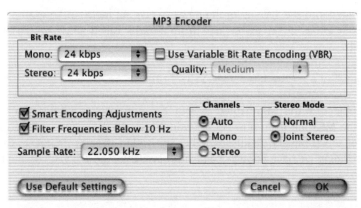

It's very important to set the sample rate correctly because through testing, I've discovered that Flash doesn't like sample rates that exceed 22.050kHz. When I first tried this technique, I used some AIFF tracks with a sample rate of 44.100kHz, which I then encoded in iTunes. As I didn't change the sample rate setting, leaving it as the default **Auto**, I made MP3s with a sample rate also at 44.100kHz. This isn't a problem until Flash tries to dynamically load in the files and play them, at which point you'll get an 'interesting' effect: Flash plays the track back at roughly double speed, which is somewhat annoying. So, to prevent this, we need to set the frequency to 22.050kHz.

Normally you'll want to leave the **Stereo Mode** set to **Joint Stereo**, as this will increase the audio quality of the track without simultaneously increasing the file size, especially if you're using a low bit rate. Joint Stereo allows one channel to carry information that was originally identical across both channels, while the other channel to carries unique information. The science behind this isn't important in this context, just that it generally works a little better at this setting.

3.   Back in iTunes, select **Advanced > Convert to MP3...**. This will then present a window asking you to choose an object to convert. Select a suitable WAV or AIFF file (or CD track) on your machine and proceed to convert the selected track into an MP3 file:

4.   The converted track will now reside in the iTunes Music Library. To prepare the MP3 for Flash, all you need to do is simply drag and drop the track from the iTunes application into the appropriate folder in your web site files. The file will sit there until you call it from Flash.

Loading MP3s into Flash

MP3s are loaded into the SWF using the new `loadSound` method. An example script to load the MP3 file called `friends_on_tv_56.mp3` from a folder called `audio` would be:

```
mySoundObject = new Sound();
mySoundObject.loadSound("audio/friends_on_tv_56.mp3", true);
```

The Sound object (in this case named `mySoundObject`) acts as a holder for the MP3 audio file. To control the MP3 file from now on we would refer to the name `mySoundObject`. The final parameter of the command defines whether the sound streams or not. In this case it is set to `true`, so providing we have enough bandwidth available, the file will commence playback upon loading.

Let's look at how this is used in practice in the Flatpack Records site. To get a feel for this section, open up `flatpackrecords.swf` and have a play around in the audio area.

Flatpack MP3

In the audio section of the main `flatpackrecords.fla`, within the `audio` movie clip, we have a frame labeled `mp3`:

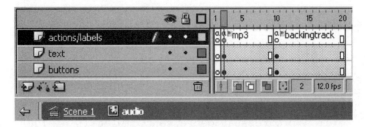

This section contains three tracks by the controversial band *Banthafodder*, with four different download options for each track. I've chosen these options to try and match as accurately as possible the three most popular types of connection speed that users will connect to the site with. The fourth option **160kbps download** gives the user the option of downloading a high quality version of the track, even if they are on a slow connection (so long as they don't mind waiting).

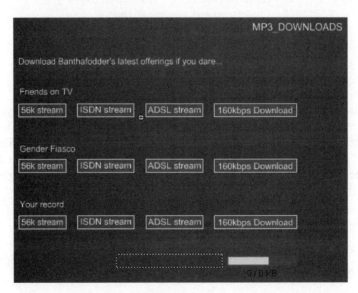

1. Before we look at the code that controls the buttons and loading functions, let's quickly look at the other elements on the stage. There are twelve separate buttons, each with their own instance name, so that we can individually make them call their respective MP3 files.

2.   At the bottom right is a ProgressBar component with the instance name `progressBar`. This will provide the user with feedback on the progress of each audio download or stream. Next to this is a dynamic text box, which is used to relay the current state of the audio files to the user. This box has a variable name of `loadingText` and displays the three possible different states: streaming, downloading, and playing.

3.   There is quite a bit of code to go through here, but none of it is particularly complex. Let's take a look at the first bit of setup code on frame 2 of the **audio** movie clip's **actions/labels** layer:

```
progressBar._visible = false;
//
function progress(loadingTarget) {
    progressBar._visible = true;
    progressBar.setLoadTarget(loadingTarget);
    this.onEnterFrame = function() {
        if ((progressBar.getPercentComplete() == 100) && (playing ==
false)) {
            this.onEnterFrame = undefined;
            loadingTarget.start();
            playing = true;
            progressBar._visible = false;
            if (loadingtext == "downloading") {
                loadingtext = "playing";
            }
        }
    };
}
```

OK, this first function may well be familiar as it is the common progress bar code we've used many times before, but with a few necessary modifications. As before, it is used to monitor the inputted `loadingTarget`, which in this case is an MP3 file loaded through a sound object. The next section runs every frame, checks to see if the `loadingTarget` is fully loaded, and that the audio clip isn't already playing before performing a few actions. Let's check this line by line:

```
this.onEnterFrame = undefined;
```

As we've seen before, this clears the `onEnterFrame` code, saving us unnecessary checks and valuable processor power. After this we have the line:

```
loadingTarget.start ();
```

This simply sets the sound object to play (this is ignored if the sound clip is streaming). Next up is:

```
playing = true;
progressBar._visible = false;
```

These lines change the status of the `playing` flag, and make the ProgressBar component invisible. After all, the file has loaded! We finish this block off with:

```
if (loadingtext == "downloading") {
    loadingtext = "playing";
}
```

These lines simply change the output of the dynamic text box to tell the user that the clip has downloaded fully and has commenced playback.

4. The next two functions set two very similar actions, but are both required to cater for the two different user options of either download or stream:

```
function loadStream(fileName) {
    mp3 = new Sound();
    mp3.stop();
    mp3.loadSound("audio/" + fileName, true);
    stream = true;
    loadingtext = "streaming";
    progress (mp3);
}
function downloadMp3(fileName) {
    mp3 = new Sound();
    mp3.stop();
    mp3.loadSound("audio" + fileName, false);
    stream = false;
    playing = false;
    loadingtext = "downloading";
    progress (mp3);
}
```

Both functions initially set up a new sound object in their respective first lines. The next line, `mp3.stop();` does exactly what you'd expect it to do and stops the sound. You may wonder why we stop it when it hasn't actually started yet. Well, this is because the user may well click on a different button first and already have a sound playing on the `mp3` sound object. This command will therefore stop the previous sound from playing before loading the new MP3 file onto the sound object.

The next lines in the two functions differ from each other: one streams the loaded sound and the other loads it. As we briefly mentioned earlier, the required parameters for the `loadSound` method are:

```
mySoundObject.loadSound (<path/mp3 filename>, <streaming flag>);
```

Given this, the function `loadStream` sets streaming (`true`) and the `downloadMp3` function sets it to `false`. Nice and easy. The next few lines set some variables related to the previous function, before actually calling the `progress` function. The code for the buttons will simply call one of these two functions, and all the required work is called from that function.

5. Let's take a look at the process of what is actually happening in Flash when the user presses one of the buttons:

    1. The button is pressed.

    2. The `loadStream` or `downloadMp3` function is called and the appropriate MP3 file name is passed to it.

    3. The Sound object is initiated.

    4. The Sound object calls an MP3 file and sets the streaming as required.

    5. Dynamic text and other variables are set up.

    6. The `progress` function is called, and is passed the sound object name.

    7. While an MP3 file is loading, the progress bar is functional.

    8. When an MP3 file is fully loaded, the progress bar is hidden.

    So, now we've got this process figured out, it's just a simple matter of coding the buttons to set this functionality running.

6. As you can see, this is all relatively simple. Here is rest of the code in frame 2 of the **audio** movie clip's **actions/labels** layer, which sets up the streaming/downloading functions for each of the buttons:

```
friends56k.onRelease = function() {
    loadStream("friends_on_tv_56.mp3")
};
friendsISDN.onRelease = function() {
    loadStream("friends_on_tv_isdn.mp3");
};
```

```
friendsADSL.onRelease = function() {
    loadStream("friends_on_tv_adsl.mp3");
};
friendsDownload.onRelease = function() {
    downloadMp3("friends_on_tv_adsl.mp3");
};
gender56k.onRelease = function() {
    loadStream("gender_fiasco_56.mp3");
};
genderISDN.onRelease = function() {
    loadStream("gender_fiasco_isdn.mp3");
};
genderADSL.onRelease = function() {
    loadStream("gender_fiasco_adsl.mp3");
};
genderDownload.onRelease = function() {
    downloadMp3("gender_fiasco_adsl.mp3");
};
yrRecord56k.onRelease = function() {
    loadStream("your_record_56.mp3");
};
yrRecordISDN.onRelease = function() {
    loadStream("your_record_isdn.mp3");
};
yrRecordADSL.onRelease = function() {
    loadStream("your_record_adsl.mp3");
};
yrRecordDownload.onRelease = function() {
    downloadMp3("your_record_adsl.mp3");
};
```

As you can see, each button calls one of the two functions, passing a specific file each time. If the user clicks one of the streaming buttons, the dynamic text alongside the progress bar will update to tell the user that the track is streaming:

If the user selects the 160kbps download button, the text changes to 'downloading':

When the file has finished downloading, it begins playing and the text changes again to reflect this:

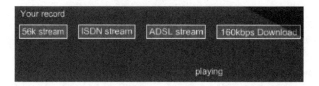

File management

As we have catered for three different user connection possibilities we need three different quality MP3 files for each audio track, all encoded at an appropriate bit rate for the option the user selects. These files need to be labeled logically and placed on the server in a folder that we can target easily from our ActionScript. You can see the organization of the Flatpack files on the CD, which mirrors the file structure you would need to use on the server. If you open the CD in Windows Explorer or a Finder window, you'll see that the MP3 files are all logically named and stored in their own **audio** folder:

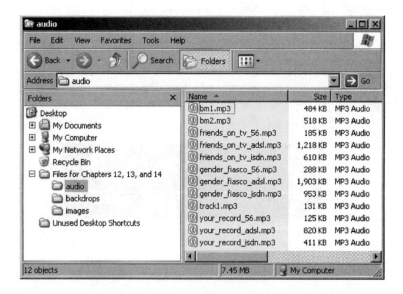

Maintaining this structure is very important as it keeps the site maintainable. If other designers need to update the files at a later date, as you would typically expect at a record label site, they can quickly and easily identify the name and location of the files and which button they relate to in the main interface. If you test this site online you'll see that even the 56K-streamed files are of a reasonable quality, and certainly on a par with streamed Real media files at a similar bandwidth. MP3s really come into their own though, when streamed over higher bandwidths. An ADSL line can easily stream an MP3 of CD quality.

If you've ever downloaded an MP3 file from the web, you'll be aware that you normally expect it to download to your hard drive. Standard downloads often come supplied in ZIP (PC) or SIT (Macintosh) archived formats, which normally force the browser to open the Download Manager or prompt for a save. This is not what happens in the case of Flatpack Records, as the MP3 file is simply loaded before playing in full. Although this might sound a little ungenerous (some things should always be free after all), it's very useful for maintaining the copyright and ownership of a file on the web. Using the Flash Player 6 to playback your music lets the user play or preview the file without ever actually owning it, or worse, making CD quality copies of the material.

If you want to allow the user to download the file (to their hard drive), then use a `getURL` with a `_blank` target to the MP3, ZIP or SIT file.

Backing theme

The final part of Flatpack's audio section contains two different backing tracks for the user to choose from if they so wish. The way the audio works here is slightly different to the MP3 download area we just looked at. In the MP3 download section the audio was played by loading MP3s onto sound objects, which were contained within specific movie clips. Because of this method, when the user leaves that particular section, the sound ceases. This is ideal for an MP3 download section as the user will want the existing audio to stop when they choose another track, but for a backing theme track, the sound runs continuously in the background irrespective of where the user navigates to in the whole site.

If we look back to how we defined the sound object in the previous audio sections, we used this command:

```
mp3 = new Sound();
```

If we changed this to `_root.mp3 = new Sound();` the sound object would be created on the root timeline and would therefore continue to play, even when the user leaves the current movie clip's timeline. Let's see how this works in practice.

1. Back in the audio section of the site (inside the audio movie clip's timeline), go to the frame labeled **backingtrack**:

2. In this section there are two buttons to load in the respective backing track and, again, the familiar ProgressBar component:

3. Also notice the two movie clips beneath the buttons, located in frame 10 of the **marker** and **waveholder** layers. The empty movie clip with the instance name waveholder is used to contain a JPEG image of the waveform that the sound produces (screen grabbed from Macromedia SoundEdit 16). The **slider** movie clip (with the instance name marker) will then travel along the waveform in sync with the music to give the impression of a playhead, just as you would see in a sound editing application:

4. Select frame 10 of the **actions** layer to see how all this works. The ActionScript should already be quite familiar from the previous exercises on Flatpack Records:

```
_root.backing.stop();
marker._visible = false;

function progress(loadingTarget) {
    progressBar._visible = true;
    progressBar.setLoadTarget(loadingTarget);
    this.onEnterFrame = function() {
        if ((progressBar.getPercentComplete() == 100)) {
            this.onEnterFrame = undefined;
            loadingTarget.start(0, 999);
            progressBar._visible = false;
            marker._visible = true;
            marker.onEnterFrame = function() {
```

```
                    this._x = waveholder._x+(waveholder._width*
                 ➡(_root.backing.position)/(_root.backing.duration));
                };
                _root.soundcontrol._visible = true;
                _root.soundPlay = true;
            }
        };
    }


    function playBackingTrack(imageFile, audioFile) {
        _root.backing.stop();
        _root.backing = new Sound();
        loadMovie("images/"+imageFile, waveholder);
        _root.backing.loadSound("audio/"+audioFile, false);
        progress(_root.backing);
    }


    darkTheme.onRelease = function() {
        playBackingTrack("bm_img1.jpg", "bm1.mp3");
    };
    lightTheme.onRelease = function() {
        playBackingTrack("bm_img2.jpg", "bm2.mp3");
    };
```

Looking in the progress function, the line loadingTarget.start(0, 999); simply tells the MP3 to start playing when the track has been fully loaded, and to continue looping for 999 times. That should be long enough for everyone visiting the site.

5. Take a closer look at this section of code, which makes the marker initially appear and then tells it to set up an onEnterFrame event handler:

```
marker._visible = true;
marker.onEnterFrame = function() {
    this._x = waveholder._x+(waveholder._width*
    ➡(_root.backing.position)/(_root.backing.duration));
    };
```

Here, onEnterFrame is using three properties to define the position of the playhead:

- waveholder._width is the same as the width of the waveform JPEG image.

- _root.backing.position is the current position of the audio track.

- _root.backing.duration is the total length of the currently loaded backing track.

The playhead relates to the width of the waveform image in the same way that the `_root.backing.position` relates to the `_root.backing.duration`, or in pseudo code:

playhead._x / waveformwidth = position / duration.

So to get our *playhead._x* position we need to multiply both sides of this equation by *waveformwidth* so that:

*playhead._x = waveformwidth * (position / duration)*

In the actual ActionScript we've used the code below. Note that we added the _x position of the **waveholder** movie clip at the start of the equation:

```
this._x = waveholder._x+(waveholder._width*
➥(_root.backing.position)/(_root.backing.duration));
```

6. The remainder of the code in the progress function relates to the mute button, which we'll look at in detail in a few moments. It simply makes the `soundcontrol` instance visible, allowing the user to switch the sound off and restart it (when pressed again), and sets up the `soundPlay` flag to say that there is sound playing. We'll look at this button in detail in a few moments time. In the meantime, let's finish off looking at what the rest of the code does.

7. Look at the next function called `playBackingTrack`:

```
function playBackingTrack(imageFile, audioFile) {
    _root.backing.stop();
    _root.backing = new Sound();
    loadMovie("images/"+imageFile, waveholder);
    _root.backing.loadSound("audio/"+audioFile, false);
    progress(_root.backing);
}
```

Much of this will already be familiar from previous exercises. The first part stops any background music that might already be playing and defines the `_root.backing` sound object. It's important to do this as if there is already a sound currently playing that is attached to this object – the sound will overlap and make a bit of a mess (or interesting mix depending on your outlook).

8. Next up is the added code that sets up the image loading into `waveholder`. The function ends by calling the `progress` function to make the ProgressBar component work. The code is finally activated when the user clicks on either of the two buttons (with the instance names `darkTheme` and `lightTheme`):

```
darkTheme.onRelease = function() {
```

```
        playBackingTrack("bm_img1.jpg", "bm1.mp3");
};
lightTheme.onRelease = function() {
        playBackingTrack("bm_img2.jpg ", "bm2.mp3");
};
```

9. After looking at how all this was constructed in `flatpackrecords.fla`, go ahead and test the movie to see it in action. The final result is the playhead moving along the waveform in perfect time to the backing soundtrack:

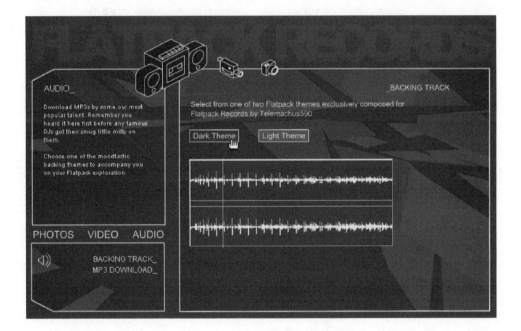

Mute

The sound control button is a toggle switch used to turn the background music on and off.

This symbol (made visible once the background music has loaded – remember the code we just saw?) is a 2-frame movie clip. In frame 1 is a graphic showing that the sound is playing, followed by a graphic showing the sound has been silenced:

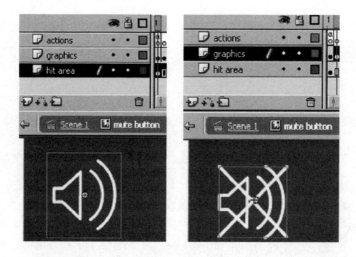

The code controlling the graphics and sound control is all on frame 1 of the root timeline:

```
soundcontrol._visible = false;
soundcontrol.onRelease = function() {
    if (_root.soundPlay == true) {
        _root.backing.stop();
        soundcontrol.gotoAndStop(2);
        _root.soundPlay = false;
    } else if (_root.soundPlay == false) {
        _root.backing.start(0, 999);
        soundcontrol.gotoAndStop(1);
        _root.soundPlay = true;
    }
};
```

You might notice that this code resembles the play/pause button from one of the video exercises in the last chapter. Basically, a conditional is run to check the status of soundPlay (set in the last exercise), and depending on the outcome...

- the sound is halted or started up,
- the movie clip timeline is sent to display the alternative graphic, and
- the `soundPlay` variable is reversed, ready for the next press.

Special attention should be paid to the following code: `_root.backing.start(0,999);`. I challenge anyone to listen to this atrocity 999 times!

A good way to expand on this would be to provide the user with a volume control. This is done with the `setVolume` method and a sound level from 0 to 100 (100 being the default). Here's how to set the sound to half volume:

```
mySoundObject.setVolume(50);
```

We've only touched on what you could do with audio on your site. The download section shows you how easy it is to put high quality MP3 soundtracks on your site that the user can hear streamed. In the backing track we've seen how a sound can be made to run throughout your site, in conjunction with a dynamically loaded JPEG image. Imagine how great a site would be combining these different techniques with some decent music!

Summary

So there you have it, dynamic content loading methods in Flash have suddenly opened up whole new possibilities for site design. The real plus is that the user doesn't need any other plug-ins, so you don't have to worry about whether they prefer using Real player, Windows Media or QuickTime; the ubiquitous Flash plug-in can now do the lot! Not bad for a plug-in that is only 746K on a Mac and a tiny 383K for PC users.

So lets take a look at all the media we have used on the Flatpack record site...

To start with we can load in 10 different backdrops, and had they been stored internally in the FLA, they would add up to 171K. Next, we have the album covers and the photo diary, both containing images that would be updated regularly (in the case of the photo diary, daily). In Flash 5 you'd have to open up the Flash file and re-import each image and then re-export the SWF and upload it. Imagine having to do this everyday for the tour diary – our approach is now much more streamlined. Anyone with a basic knowledge of optimizing JPEGs and uploading can update the site.

In the video section, the Banthafodder video is available for viewing in either a lo or high band format, respectively 264K and 2.2MB, which would bring your main SWF to a slow grind if this made up part of the main site. The video diary works in a similar way to the photo version, with each clip averaging around 150 K. The video mixer is 232K and finally the kaleidoscope SWF comes in at 108K. In total, all the video content has been reduced greatly due to the effectiveness of Sorensen Spark, but still amounts to 2.6 MB.

Finally, as we've just seen, Flash can import MP3s as and when required. If we were to add up all of the MP3 sounds that you can hear in the site they would amount to nearly 8MB. Clearly if you where to put this all into one SWF no one would wait for it to download, and given the content in our example, they'd be sorely disappointed if they had! Now however, the user can decide which MP3s they want to hear from our site and download them accordingly. In previous versions of Flash, if we wanted to import MP3s we would have had to embed them in Flash and encode them as SWFs. This method works, but it means that anyone updating the site needs to have Flash and appropriate knowledge of how to use it – not just an ability to use iTunes!

So to sum up, we have produced an entire site at only 24K, as it contains no images, video or sound when first loaded. The total size of the dynamic media content is 10MB – succinct and succulent!

section 4: Dynamic Data Integration

chapter 15: **Working with external files**

Anyone involved in web development will frequently encounter the need to separate the design of a site from its content. Professional web authoring tools such as Dreamweaver use templates to allow designers to create the building blocks of a web site that can be passed on to subject experts to fill in the content.

The task of separating content from design becomes more awkward when the text that the client needs to change is within an area of a site that uses Flash. Not many companies will have the resources or skills to start playing around with the Flash code and animations even if the developer had been generous enough to supply the source files. The content of a site needs to be updated well after the site designers have washed their hands of the project, and companies who use web design agencies don't want to have to come back to the agency every time they need a paragraph of text changing within their site. Not only would it prove expensive but would also be more time consuming than the client would like, and is a barrier to the frequent updating that many web sites require.

This chapter looks at how content can be stored outside of the Flash movie in easily editable text files, and introduces the methods that can be used to pull data into Flash at run-time. In doing so, we successfully separate content from design, leaving the SWFs as a black box of design, and allowing content to be derived from updateable text files, databases using server side scripting, or XML files.

Here we will concentrate on how to pull text and pictures into your movie from text files containing sets of variables holding the content. The following chapters will show you how to use more extensible and easily editable sources, but for now the text files will suffice to teach you how to load data at run-time.

The text file

Before going any further we need to look at the formatting of the data in the text file in detail. In our first example, it will consist of a single variable name followed by an equals sign, and then the value of the variable. So if you wanted to pass a number into your movie your text file would look something like this:

```
counter=1
```

The simple 'Message of the Day' application we are about to look at only changes the value of one variable, but one text file can contain any number of name and value pairs, each separated by an ampersand:

```
variable1=value1&variable2=value2&variable3=value3
```

The format of the text file is defined by the MIME type 'application/x-www-form-urlencoded', which is a format that is used in a variety of web applications. One common use is for sending the data from an HTML form to a server side script for processing.

To comply with this standard, the values contained in the text file must be encoded so that they do not contain any spaces or other illegal characters. Strict compliance would mean that every non-alphanumeric character would need to be encoded, but Flash is a little more forgiving than some applications and will allow most punctuation and symbols. Characters that must be encoded, though, include the equals sign, the ampersand and spaces. The ampersand must be encoded because it signifies the break between variables and the equals sign because it is used in the variable assignment.

Encoding a character involves replacing the character with a percentage character followed by the hex code for that character. An equals sign becomes '%3D' and an ampersand becomes '%26'. Using this rule a space becomes '%20' but a space can also be expressed as '+'.

So the text:

Energy = mass divided by the speed of light all squared

...becomes either:

Energy%20%3D%20mass%20divided%20by%20speed%20of%20light%20all%20squared

...or:

Energy+%3D+mass+divided+by+speed+of+light+all+squared

To help create properly formatted text files, I have written a small Flash utility that will allow variables and values to be encoded and then copied into a text editor for saving. The Flash file is `encode.fla`, and can be found on the CD in the Chapter 15 folder. To generate an encoded text file, enter the variable name and value pairs one-by-one, pressing **Add Variable** in between each one. Every time **Add Variable** is clicked, the encoded text box will update to include the latest variable added.

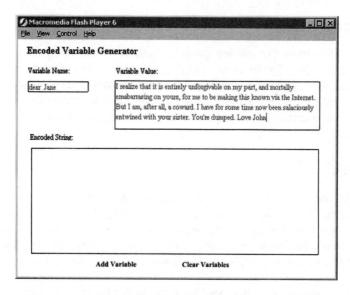

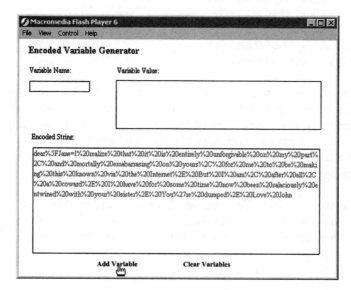

This utility uses the loadVars object, which we will be looking at in the next section, and in particular the toString method, which gives a URL-encoded representation of all the variables contained within the object.

The functions

There are two functions that we are going to look at in this chapter, or more accurately one function and one object. The function loadVariables has been around since Flash version 4 and the object loadVars is new to Flash MX. Both methods work in very similar way but, as you might expect, the loadVars object is more complete and has advantages that are essential for more complex uses. We will start by looking at the loadVariables function, as this is sufficient for the first application.

loadVariables

The most basic application of this function is a Flash movie that can be used within a web site to display a 'Message of the Day'. This movie reads a message from a text file and uses the message to populate a text box in Flash. See dynamictext1.fla in the Chapter 15 folder of the CD. The movie consists of one frame containing a multi-line text box. The text box should be set as dynamic text in the Property inspector and linked to the variable message.

The first frame will contain all the required ActionScript for the application. All that is needed is the following two lines of code:

```
messageURL = "message.txt"
loadVariables(messageURL, _root)
```

In fact, this could be done as a single line if you didn't want to hold the URL inside a variable. In the first line I set a variable as the location of the text file that contains the message to be loaded. I used a variable here so it is easy to edit if I use the movie with files of a different name or where the site layout is different – it saves having to hunt through the code to find any occurrences of the URL. Not a problem with a simple example like this, but more so when we are dealing with more involved applications and multiple text files.

In this case the URL is a simple file name, which indicates that the text file must reside in the same folder as the final SWF file. If you wanted to store all the text for a site in a common folder then this could be changed to point to an URL that is relative to the site root:

```
messageURL = "/text/message.txt"
```

Alternatively, to place the text files in a folder under the folder that contained the final SWF, regardless of whereabouts in the site the files are, you can use a relative URL such as:

```
messageURL = "text/message.txt"
```

Note that there is no forward slash at the beginning of the URL indicating that this is a relative URL. Referencing a text file in the same folder as the final SWF, as we are doing in this example, is the simplest form of relative URL.

The second line of the script does the actual importing. The first argument is the URL of the text file to import and the second argument is the movie to import the variables into. In this case we only have the `_root` movie, and so this is set as the target.

In this example we are just setting one variable so the text file looks like this:

```
message=Hello!+This+is+your+message+of+the+day
```

When the movie is run it loads the variable data, initializes the variable `message` and sets it to the string `Hello!+This+is+your+message+of+the+day`. As we have set the variable name of the text box in the movie to `message` the string is displayed in the text box when the movie is run. So essentially, the message can be changed by simply editing the text file in a basic text editor.

If the movie and text file were uploaded to a web server and the movie was run in a browser there may be a small delay between running the movie and the text being displayed. This is due to the time taken for the Flash movie running on the client machine to request the text file from the web server and download it. We will see later in the chapter the problems this can cause but for a simple application like this it can either be ignored, or to inform the user what is happening the content of the text box, can initially be set to **Loading....** This will be displayed for the time between the movie starting and the variable message being set to a different value when the text file load is completed.

We can extend this application to include an image loaded at run time, defined by a second variable loaded from the text file. To import an image at run time we use the `loadMovie` function with the URL of the image as the first argument, and the movie clip to load the image into as the second argument. This was covered in more detail in Chapter 12.

Alongside the text box in the movie we add a shape converted to a movie clip to act as a placeholder for the image to be loaded into. Using a placeholder in this way gives a visual marker on the stage where the image will appear when the movie is run. This placeholder movie clip is given the name `imgPlace1_mc`. The Flash file is `dynamictext2.fla`. All the ActionScript is still contained in the first frame and becomes:

```
messageURL = "message2.txt"

loadVariables(this.messageURL, _root)
loadMovie(this.photofile, "imgPlace1_mc")
```

The text file `message2.txt` contains:

```
message=Hello!+This+is+your+message+of+the+day&photofile=photo1.jpg
```

The new variable in the text file called `photofile` contains the file name of a JPEG image, this variable is then passed as the first argument to the `loadMovie` function, and the JPEG is displayed in place of our placeholder movie clip.

When you test this movie, don't worry if it doesn't seem to work, this movie is actually unlikely to behave as expected. The message text is displayed as in the previous application but the image is not loaded and the placeholder remains visible.

The reason for this is that the `loadMovie` line of the script will probably be executed before the `loadVariables` line of the script has successfully completed and returned the variables. This is due to the time taken by the Flash movie to request the text file from the server and for the contents of the text file to be downloaded. The time taken will be significantly greater when run on a web site but can still be significant when run locally. The result of this is that when the `loadMovie` line is executed, the variable 'photofile' is empty, and so no image is loaded.

When testing the movie, viewing the variables by selecting **Debug > List Variables** will show that the variable `photofile` is set to `photo1.jpg`. To check the value of the variable when we attempt to load the image, we can insert a couple of trace commands into our code:

```
messageURL = "message2.txt"

loadVariables(this.messageURL, _root)
trace("photofile when loadMovie executed = " + this.photofile)
trace("type of photofile when loadMovie executed = " +
➥typeof(this.photofile))
loadMovie(this.photofile, "imgPlace1_mc")
```

Testing this revised movie will confirm that the `photofile` variable is undefined. Either of the trace commands on its own would be sufficient. Displaying the type of the variable using `typeof` is useful, as it differentiates between the variable not being set (undefined) and the variable being set to an empty string.

> *All variables returned using* `LoadVariables` *or* `LoadVars` *will be strings regardless of their initial value. A variable with a value of* `true` *that you may expect to be Boolean will be a string. This can cause problems if the variable is used in comparison with a Boolean value.*

```
// set this variable as if they had being loaded from an external
➥file

variable1 = "true"

//test value
if (variable1 == true) {
    result = "Match"
}
else {
    result = "No Match"
}
```

> When run, the value of result *will be set to* No Match. *We will use the fact that all variables returned are strings as a way of testing the existence of a variable later in the chapter.*

The problem of the delay in loading variables means that for anything more complicated than the basic 'Message of the Day' application it is better to move away from the loadVariables function and instead use the loadVars object.

loadVars

The loadVars object is new in Flash MX and offers us a solution to the timing problem of the previous application. The load method of the object does the job of the loadVariables function and reads the variables from a specified text file. Instead of these variables being set in a movie clip they are stored within the instance of the loadVars object itself. Going back to our previous application, the loadVariables approach can be replaced by:

```
messageURL = "message2.txt"

myVars_obj = new loadVars()
myVars_obj.load(messageURL)
```

After defining the messageURL variable, we create a new instance of the loadVars object and call it myVars_obj, we then tell this new instance to load the text file by calling the load method with one argument, the URL of the text file.

Testing this code will not display the message or load the photo, but using **Debug > List Variables** will show us what has been done with the content of the text file. The important part of the List Variables output in this case is the myVars_obj section:

```
Variable _level0.myVars_obj = [object #1, class 'LoadVars'] {
    message:"Hello! This is your message of the day",
    photofile:"photo1.jpg"
}
```

This tells us that the two variables contained in the text file – message and photofile – and their values, are now part of the myVars_obj object.

These values can be accessed as if they were properties of the object using standard dot syntax, such as myVars_obj.message.

If the loadVars object already contains a variable of the same name then the existing variable is replaced, but otherwise existing variables remain. This means that one instance can build up a collection of variables by reading the data from a number of text files.

Returning to the problems we faced in the last application, the loadVars object has two built-in ways of checking to see if a file read has completed. The first is the load property, which is set to TRUE when the load operation is completed. The second and more useful is the onLoad event handler, which can be used to call a function when the load operation has completed.

We can use the onLoad event handler to execute any code we want to run immediately after the text file has been loaded. To do this, we assign a function call to the event handler. For our 'Message of the Day' application there is very little code to be called so we use an anonymous function to keep our code close to the event handler:

```
messageURL = "message2.txt"

myVars_obj = new loadVars()
myVars_obj.onLoad = function () {
    loadMovie(myVars_obj.photofile, "imgPlace1_mc")
    message = myVars_obj.message
}

myVars_obj.load(messageURL)
```

We need to do two things when the text file is loaded: import our image and display the message. We load the JPEG movie in place of our placeholder using the same function as before. The difference here is that, because the variables are now contained within the myVars_obj object, the text message isn't automatically displayed. The text box is linked to the value of the variable message in the _root movie, not inside the myVars_obj object. To get round this, we include a line of code to set the _root.message variable equal to the imported message variable.

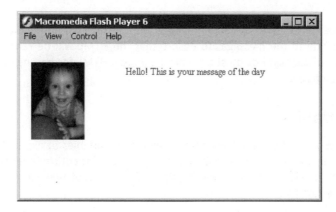

To trap any errors that may happen in the read operation, the onLoad event handler returns a Boolean value that is set to true if the operation is successful, or to false if the operation failed. This value is set automatically and we can modify the callback function assigned to the event handler to use this by adding an argument to the function as shown below: (dynamictext3a.fla):

```
messageURL = "message2a.txt"

myVars = new loadVars()
myVars.onLoad = function (success) {
    if (success) {
        loadMovie(myVars.photofile, "imgPlace1")
        message = myVars.message
    }
    else {
        message = "Error loading message"
    }
}

myVars.load(messageURL)
```

The value of the parameter success is automatically set to the true if the text file read has completed successfully or false if it encountered errors. You can test this by deleting the text file and then testing the movie.

HTML

dynamictext3a.fla also extends the previous application by rendering the imported message as HTML. The new text file contains the following:

```
message=<b>Message+of+the+day</b><br>Hello!+This+is+your+message+of+
➡the+day&photofile=photo1.jpg
```

This gives some control over the appearance of the message within the Flash movie. In this case, it adds a bold title to the message. To ensure that the HTML will be rendered within Flash, the HTML property of our text box must be set to `true`. Any HTML formatting in the message variable will then be rendered.

Multiple variables

In all the above applications the Flash movie knew what variables to expect from the text file and what their names would be. If we really want to give content control over to the text file author rather than the movie author, we need to start thinking about how we can vary the number of variables in the text file.

Updateable marquee

Now we will create a marquee style horizontal scroller that takes any number of single line messages from a text file and displays them one after the other before repeating in a loop.

The text file for this application looks like this (`message3.txt` on the CD):

```
message1=Sales+hit+3+million&message2=New+product+launch+delayed&
➥message3=New+positions+available&message4=Finance+Director+retires&
➥message5=New+catalogue+out+next+month
```

The variables `message1` ... `message5` each contain a message. We could include a variable that contains the number of messages as information for the Flash movie, but dealing with this in the movie instead makes editing the text file easier for the user.

The movie (`dynamictext4.fla`) consists of 25 frames. The first frame is blank except for the actions that read the variables from the text file. The second frame, labeled **offScreen**, contains the text box in its starting position to the right of the movie area. The text box then moves to the center of the movie area using a motion tween before pausing.

1. Open a new Flash project and set the stage size to around 400 by 50 pixels. Then create three layers in a new Flash project, and set them up as shown in this screenshot:

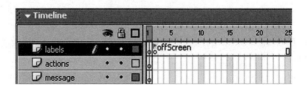

2.   Add the following code to frame 1 of the actions layer. This is essentially the same code that we have been looking at, and is used to set up the variables in a similar way to the previous application.

```
messageURL = "message3.txt"
counter = 1

myVars_obj = new loadVars()
myVars_obj.onLoad = function() {
    gotoAndPlay("offScreen");
}
myVars_obj.load(messageURL)
stop()
```

The variable counter will be used to make up the name of the variable that we are interested in accessing. By appending counter to the end of the word message ("message" + counter), we get the name of the current variable that we wish to display, which in the first case will be message1. We can then increment counter in order to get the name of the next variable in the list.

In this application we are accessing the variables stored within the loadVars object in a slightly different way. Instead of using the dot syntax, we are using the square bracket or array syntax to allow us to include an expression as the variable name.

These two lines are equivalent:

```
myVars_obj["message1"]
```

```
myVars_obj.message1
```

Using the first of these two methods allows us to write:

```
message = myVars_obj["message" + counter]
```

The stop() command ensures that we don't move on until the variables have been loaded, at which point the onLoad handler is invoked. Here we have gotoAndPlay telling the movie that it's time to move on.

3.   Insert a keyframe in frame 2 of the actions layer, and add frames up to frame 24. Then insert the following code into frame 2. By placing the code that handles the setting of the message into frame 2, we have separated the animation of the messages from the loading of the messages from the text file. Doing this makes it easier to see how the animation could be replaced by any number of Flash animation techniques to generate all sorts of message ticker applications.

```
if (typeof(myVars_obj["message" + counter])!="string") {
    counter=1
}

message = myVars_obj["message" + counter]
```

Earlier in the chapter we saw that all variables loaded from a text file will be strings, regardless of their value. This frame uses this information to make sure that there is, in fact, a variable by the name we are asking for by checking to see if it is a string. If not then we need to loop back to the first variable, and so `counter` is set to 1. Once that's sorted we can assign the current variable's string to the `message` variable that will be displayed in our text box.

Using this to test the existence of a variable means we can change the number of messages simply by editing the text file and adding or deleting variables; the number of messages is not coded into the Flash file itself in any way.

4. Now add a keyframe in frame 25 of the actions layer and type this code:

```
counter++
gotoAndPlay("offScreen");
```

Here we complete the loop by just incrementing the counter, and moving back to frame 2.

5. In the message layer add a keyframe in frame 2. Then create a text box a little smaller than the stage like so:

6. Set it as dynamic text with the variable name `message` as in the first applications.

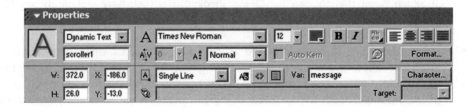

7. Then position it to the left of the stage.

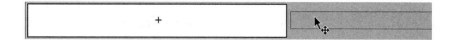

8. Now insert a keyframe at frame 15 of the message layer, move the text box back onto the stage where you want the text to rest and create a motion tween between frames 2 and 15.

9. If you now put a keyframe in frame 25 of the message layer to allow the text to pause, and export the SWFs, you're done in Flash, and your timeline should look something like this:

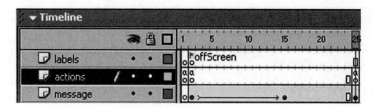

10. Finally, use the encoder I provided to create a set of variables, remembering to name them, `message1`, `message2` etc, and paste the messages into a text file. Save the text file as, `message3.txt` (or whatever file you refer to in your code) in the same folder as you exported your SWF file to.

As with the previous applications the processes introduced here could be used to create any type of rotating message system by applying some more traditional Flash effects to the dynamic text managed by the above code.

This application showed how we could have a text file with an unknown number of variables and display them one at a time. The final two applications build what is the ultimate in content control, a basic web site where not only the content but also the navigation is determined by external text files. For those who love short movies, it is all done in a single frame.

Updateable navigation bar

The first of the two applications looks at building the navigation. For flexibility I have decided on a vertical navbar down the left hand side of the screen giving plenty of room for a large amount of options if required. To give the flexibility we will need for the final application, each navigation element will be an instance of a movie clip.

The movie starts with one instance of the movie clip at the top left of the screen (see `dynamictext5.fla`). The instance of the movie clip is called `mc_navItem1`. The movie will access a text file which has a number of variables, each containing a link title (`menu.txt`).

```
title1=Home&title2=Products&title3=Services&title4=Contact+Us&title5=
➥About+Us
```

The movie will automatically list these titles vertically, irrespective of the number of variables that you put into the text file. So here we go...

1. Start a new Flash project and give it two layers named Actions and Menu. Then create a text box in the top right hand corner.

2. Set the **Var:** to `varTitle`, and the instance to `navtitle`, and the box to **Multiline no wrap**.

3. Now convert it to a movie clip named `mcNavItem`.

4. Now name the instance you have on the stage `mc_navItem1`, and type, **Loading...**, into it.

5. All that's left in Flash is to add the ActionScript to the Actions layer. Just add the code to your file as we go through it. Start by assigning `messageURL` to the name of your text file.

```
messageURL = "menu.txt"
```

6. Now we'll make a function called `setUpMenus`, which uses a similar method to the previous application to check if a variable is set or not. This time we use a `while` loop to move through all the `title1...title5` variables.

```
setUpMenus = function() {
    counter=1

    while (typeof(myNavVars["title"+counter]) == "string") {
```

7. If `counter = 1`, then we are using the movie clip, which is already there. We don't need to make another, or worry about where to put it. So we add the following:

    ```
    if (counter>1) {
    ```

8. On the other hand, in each iteration following this we need to first create a new instance of the navigation item movie clip using the `duplicateMovieClip` method on the first navigation item. The `duplicateMovieClip` function returns a reference to the newly created movie clip. We will store this in a variable so that we can easily access the properties of our new movie clip.

    ```
    var theClip = _root.navItem1.duplicateMovieClip
    ➥ ("navItem"+counter,counter)
    ```

    The movie clip we are duplicating is the first navigation item `_root.navItem1`. We use the counter variable to generate a new instance name for the duplicate clip: `"navItem"+counter`. We also use the value of `counter` to set the depth of the movie clip.

9. We now need to put our new navigation item somewhere; in this case just below the last `navitem` we made. We do this by setting the y coordinates of the new `navitem` (identified by `theClip`) to the y coordinates of the previous `navitem` (identified by `this["navitem"` `+ (counter-1)]`) plus 30:

    ```
        theClip._y = this["navitem"+(counter-1)]._y + 30
    }
    ```

10. We have stored the reference to the current `navitem` in the variable `theClip` only if the movie clip was duplicated from the first the `navitem`, not if it was the first `navitem` itself. We now need to set `theClip` if we are dealing with the first instance.

    ```
    else {
        theClip = _root.navItem1
    }
    ```

11. Now we need to set the text of each of the navigation items:

    ```
    theClip.varTitle = myNavVars["title"+counter]
    ```

12. Then move onto the next item:

    ```
            counter++
        }
    }
    ```

13. Outside of that function, all that's left is to initialize our object:

```
myNavVars = new loadVars()
```

14. Attach the function to the `onLoad` handler, such that it will begin once all the variables have been loaded.

```
myNavVars.onLoad = function() {
    _root.setUpMenus()
}
```

15. Also, of course, load the variables.

```
myNavVars.load(messageURL)
```

Running this movie should generate a vertical navigation bar with each navigation item placed 30 pixels lower than the previous item. You can see the code in full in `dynamictext5.fla`.

Putting it all together

To add the content to our navigation structure we can use what we learnt in the second application of this chapter where we imported a block of text and an image. Instead of fixing the text file that the content is loaded from, we will let the filename be determined by the navigation item that is chosen.

Easily updateable site

The final application (`dynamictext6.fla`) contains the navigation created in the previous application, two dynamic text boxes, one for the section title and one for the content and a placeholder for an image.

1. To start with, open the navigation tools FLA that you just made. To the right of the navigation text box we want a placeholder for the pictures. So draw a rectangle there, convert it to a movie clip named `imgPlace`, and name the instance `imgPlace1`.

2. Then we need another couple of text boxes, one to hold the title of the page, which we'll get from the **Navigation** menu. For this place a smallish sized text box to the right of the image box. Give it the name, `section`, and variable `varSection`. It needs to be multiline, and of course, dynamic text. The other should sit below this and be a lot longer to hold the content, it should be named `maincontent`, and have the variable `varContent`.

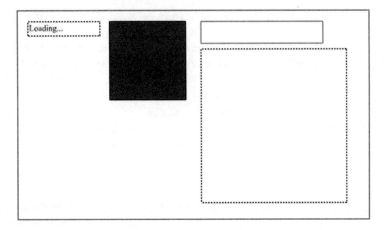

The navigation tools now need to link to something. So in addition to the original variables, it now has these (see `menu2.txt`):

```
content1=section1.txt&content2=section2.txt&content3=section3.txt&
➡content4=section4.txt&content5=section5.txt
```

Each variable, `content1` through to 5, refers to another text file in the same folder as this menu file. Here, `content1` will be the text used when `navItem1` is clicked and so forth. So your `menu2.txt` will need content variables for each title variable you used. Then you will need text files named as declared in your variable, holding the content for your site. For example, `section1.txt` holds the content for our home page:

```
message=Welcome+to+our+new+website<BR><BR>Use+the+navigation+on+the+
➡left+to+navigate+the+site.<BR><BR><B>Have+Fun!!</B>&photofile=
➡section1.jpg
```

Now onto the ActionScript.

3. Under the line...

```
this["navItem"+counter].varTitle = myNavVars["title"+counter],
```

...where you assigned the text to be displayed within each navigation item movie clip, we need to add some code to assign each of these text file links to the navItem movie clips.

In this bit of code we create a new variable, contentFile, within the current navItem movie clip and set its value to the value of the content variable sharing the same counter number as the movie clip. So for example, the first movie clip navItem1 will contain a variable contentFile whose value is equal to myNavVars.content1, which from the text file we are using is section1.txt

```
this["navItem"+counter].contentFile = myNavVars["content"+counter]
```

4. The next section of code uses the onRelease handler for the movie clip to make the navigation item perform the load operation when the user clicks on it.

```
this["navItem"+counter].onRelease = function () {
    _root.varSection = this.varTitle
    if (typeof(this.contentFile) == "string") {
        _root.myContentVars.load(this.contentFile)
    }
}
```

The function sets the content of the section title text box equal to the text of the navigation item itself (root.varSection = this.varTitle), and then if a filename has been set (if (typeof(this.contentFile) == "string")), it instructs the myContentVars instance to load the variables from the text file set in contentFile (root.myContentVars.load(this.contentFile)).

5. Now, at the end of the the setUpMenus function, we need some code to set the initial state of the site by loading the content from the first section:

```
//Start with home page visible
_root.varSection = _root.navItem1.varTitle
_root.myContentVars.load(_root.navItem1.contentFile)
}
```

In full, the new setUpMenus function should look like this:

```
setUpMenus = function() {
    counter=1
    while (typeof(myNavVars["title"+counter]) == "string") {
        if (counter>1) {
            duplicateMovieClip(_root.navItem1,
            ➥"navItem"+counter,counter)
            this["navitem"+counter]._y = this["navitem"+
```

```
            ➥(counter-1)]._y + 30
        }
        this["navItem"+counter].varTitle = myNavVars["title"+counter]
        ➥this["navItem"+counter].contentFile = myNavVars["content"+
        ➥counter] this["navItem"+counter].onRelease = function () {
            _root.varSection = this.varTitle
            if (typeof(this.contentFile) == "string") {
                _root.myContentVars.load(this.contentFile)
            }
        }

        counter++
    }

    //Start with home page visible
    _root.varSection = _root.navItem1.varTitle
    _root.myContentVars.load(_root.navItem1.contentFile)
}
```

6. Finally we need a second instance of the `loadVars` object to read the content variables for the chosen section, placed below the `setUpMenus` function. This second instance, `myContentVars`, is taken directly from the second application of the chapter, except that the names of the variables set by the `onLoad` function are different:

```
myContentVars = new loadVars()
myContentVars.onLoad = function () {
    _root.varContent = myContentVars.message
    loadMovie(myContentVars.photofile, "imgPlace1")
}
```

When this instance is used to read a text file it will set the main content text box, and then load an image from the file specified in the `photofile` variable.

What is really a fairly small piece of code has given a very flexible web site layout, which without much effort could be placed within a graphical site design to generate a good-looking site. The text areas can be moved to fit in with a variety of layouts, and the `loadMovie` function could be used to load in an entirely new background for each section rather than just a small image. The code could also be extended to give multiple pages per section or links to other sites as well as a wider use of images or even rich media all loaded from sources outside of the Flash movie and therefore all editable by users who don't know the first thing about Flash.

Summary

In this chapter we have looked at the two methods that Flash movies can use to import data from text files. We have seen how this imported data can simply be displayed in the form of a message of the day, used in an animation, in the case of our horizontal ticker, or even used to build the navigation for a web site and point to other external resources.

Having shown how much can be done using text files in this way, it is not something that is used very much. Most dynamic applications will not use text files to hold the data to be imported but will use databases. Server side scripting such as PHP or ASP is then used to read the required data from the database and dynamically create the text data that is sent to the Flash file. As far as your Flash movies are concerned they will work in exactly the same way, but instead of the URL pointing to a text file it will be pointing to the server side script that will generate the dynamic content. This is covered in detail in the following chapters.

Server side scripting languages such as PHP can also be used to allow Flash movies to write variables to text files or even to databases in a reversal of what we have covered in this chapter. Flash movies can then take on the role of authoring tools, as well as being just a way of displaying information. In the next chapter you will see how to build a Flash movie that can write text files for use with the message of the day application developed at the beginning of this chapter.

More and more applications are moving beyond the use of text files – whether static or dynamically generated – for transferring data to and from a server, and are using XML instead. XML is overly complicated for the simple applications we built at the beginning of this chapter but for more complex applications it does have a number of advantages. XML does not need to be encoded in the same way that the variables in a text file do, making the XML files themselves a little more readable. XML is also far more structured than a simple list of variables; the data is structured in a tree-like manner, for which Flash provides all the necessary functionality for navigating and extracting the data as required. XML interaction is covered in detail in **Chapter 17**.

section 4: Dynamic Data Integration

chapter 16: Dynamic Flash: PHP

The world is absolutely chock-full of acronyms, isn't it? I'm sure you don't need me to tell you that though, as you only need to look as far as Macromedia and their recent decision to move away from version numbers with the launch of the mysterious sounding Flash MX. There's also HTML, XML, HTTP, and a whole cacophony of other acronyms we're bombarded by on a daily basis.

Well, you'll no doubt be delighted to hear that I'm going to introduce you to yet another acronym in this chapter (stop groaning at the back). **PHP** stands for **PHP: Hypertext Pre-Processor**, and is one of those confusing recursive acronyms where the meaning contains the acronym itself. What's far more interesting though, is that PHP is one of the most powerful server-side scripting languages at your disposal as a web developer.

In this chapter we'll kick off by looking at what PHP is and a little about its history.

History 101

The original PHP language was born in late 1994, when Rasmus Lerdorf put together a collection of Perl scripts to keep a record of visitors to his online resume. These scripts really interested the visitors to his site, and in response he released them into the public domain in 1995 under the moniker 'Personal Home Page Tools'.

The use of PHP grew rapidly, as did the number of developers involved with the PHP project. As I write this sentence we are up to version 4 of PHP, which has access to a large number of third party add-ons, some of which even enable the dynamic generation of SWF files from scratch.

There are several things to note about the PHP engine (the program that actually executes PHP scripts on behalf of the web server).

- It's freely available for anyone who wants to use it, commercially or otherwise.

- It's an **Open Source** project. This means that the source code for the project is freely available, and the upshot of this is that it is under continuous development by people collaborating across the Internet.

- There are many sites around that offer free scripts for you to use – anything from HTML-based bulletin boards and search programs to multiplayer Flash engines (see the Summary section at the end of the chapter for some interesting links).

- It's available on almost every platform you care to think of, including Windows and Unix-based operating systems (such as Mac OSX).

You can find the latest information on PHP at **www.php.net** and **www.zend.com.**

Two servers of Verona

Now, before I let you loose on PHP, we need to cover a few basics, like what on earth a server-side script is, and why you'd want to use one in the first place. In this next section I'll try to answer these questions and teach you more than you ever wanted to know about how all those pretty web pages find their way to your web browser.

OK, if you're looking for a definition of a server-side script, this is as good a one as any:

> *A server-side script is a program that is executed on the server. It can handle information requests and responds by returning the appropriate document or generating a document on the fly, based on certain criteria.*

Basically, a server-side script allows us to do some processing on the server before a document is returned to the web browser. This can be anything from manipulating data files to accessing a database and generating content dynamically. With the help of some diagrams, we can see the process for requesting a file, such as a static web page, and how that process differs when requesting a server-side script.

In a standard client/server setup for the web, a client program (usually a web browser) opens a connection to a server and requests a file. The server then returns the file to the client and the connection is closed. This is the kind of connection we use when requesting HTML files, for example.

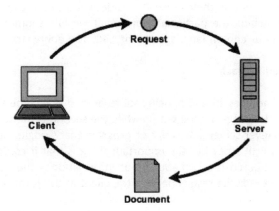

With server-side scripting enabled, the client can request a script file on the server, and the server's response is to execute that script and send back the results as determined by the instructions within the script. This can include fetching data from external sources such as text files or databases.

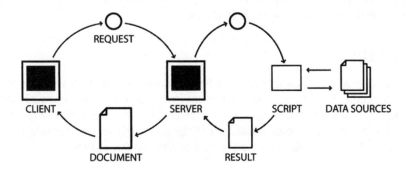

Just to make things a little clearer, let's consider a simple example. I'm sure you're more than familiar with the various search engines that can be used to track down information on the web. My own personal favorite is **www.google.com**, and if you navigate to this site and search on the term 'Macromedia Flash', you'll be redirected to a list of relevant sites. Now this isn't exactly rocket science, but the interesting bit is not the results (at least not at the moment) but the URL down in the address bar of your browser. It should look something like this:

http://www.google.com/search?hl=en&q=Macromedia+Flash

You can break this down into two parts. The first part indicates the page we want to look at, and in this case it's Google's search page:

http://www.google.com/search

This page is actually a script on their server that is designed to search their gargantuan list of web sites for any text matching the particular words that we just submitted. The words have been attached, along with our chosen language, to the URL as a query string that reads:

hl=en&q=Macromedia+Flash

Here we've got two variables, **hl** and **q**, being set to **en** and **Macromedia+Flash** respectively. The first one signifies the language for the search while the second is the search criteria or query, and this is passed to whatever server-side script or program that Google uses to search its databases. In this case, it isn't a PHP script but the important thing is that it *could* have been. So, Google's search script just compared the two sources of information – the user input and the Google database itself – and sends the results back to the client in the form of an HTML page.

The best thing about server-side scripting is that it allows us to create our web content dynamically. We can customize and adapt content to suit the time of day, to reflect different users' preferences, to automatically display a list of the latest news, and to generally keep sites up-to-date – all without having to edit them by hand.

What's more, it isn't just HTML pages that stand to benefit from server-side scripting. We can also write scripts that pass data back to Flash clients, significantly raising the bar on what we can do with them – that's what this chapter is all about.

Installing PHP

For this chapter you will require access to a PHP-enabled web server. If you have your own server then all you need to do is download the relevant installation files from **www.php.net**, where you can also find detailed installation instructions for a variety of setups. Note that there are several different PHP download bundles available with various levels of functionality, but don't let that confuse you – the most basic download should suffice for this chapter!

If you don't have your own server, or don't fancy turning your main computer into one, you should find out from the relevant owner/administrator/technical support staff whether the server you'd like to use already supports PHP, and if not, perhaps you can persuade them to install it for you!

If you don't have a server, then you can download the apache server for free from **www.apache.org**.

PHP in action

In the previous chapter, you mastered the art of loading data into your Flash movies from a specially formatted text file using the new loadVars method. That's all well and good, but at some point we're going to want to update the data in that text file, and as things currently stand, the only way we can do that is to upload a new copy of the text file. While there's nothing inherently wrong with this approach, it could get a little cumbersome if there's a lot of data that needs to be updated – I would imagine that formatting the data as required could become quite a chore after a while, even with the encoder that came with Chapter 15.

Thankfully, help is at hand. Rather than updating the text file manually, we can get special server-side programs to do this for us from information we supply using a Flash or standard HTML form. The best bit about this is that these server-side programs can do all the necessary formatting before it updates the text file. I told you this server-side stuff was cool!

In this section we're going to build a separate Flash movie that we can use to update the text file for one of the applications in the previous chapter. For this we're going to need a PHP script, and since we haven't covered PHP yet, this may seem about as wise as letting me loose in a nuclear power plant with a screwdriver and a jackhammer. All I can say is that you can't do much damage playing around with PHP, and I'll be here to help you along every step of the way.

Recap, cap'n

For those of you who, like me, are more than a little forgetful, I thought it might be useful to go through a brief recap of how the original application from the previous chapter does its stuff.

For the sake of simplicity, and so that this poor old author doesn't get too confused, we're going to be using one of the simpler examples form the last chapter – the Message of the Day application. We'll use the most complex version of this – the one with the HTML text and the photo – but it's still a relatively simple example.

OK, if you remember, the ActionScript code for the example looked like this:

```
messageURL = "message.txt";

myVars = new loadVars();
myVars.onLoad = function(success) {
        if (success) {
                loadMovie(this.photofile, "imgPlace1");
                message = this.message;
        } else {
                message = "Error loading message";
        }
};

myVars.load(messageURL);
```

So, we're dealing with a `message` variable, containing the current message of the day, and a `photofile` variable, specifying the picture that should be loaded into the movie.

Another message of the day

Having got that sorted, we can create a separate movie that can be used to update our text file. Obviously we'll use a PHP script to actually write the new data to the text file (since Flash can't do that on its own), but the Flash movie will act as a nice front-end for the whole application.

1. Create a new movie and recreate the following timeline:

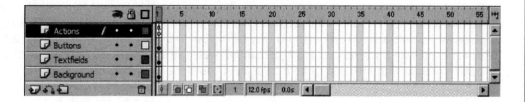

2. On the **Background** layer, draw some graphics and text labels, and add three textfields on the **Textfields** layer so that your stage looks something like this:

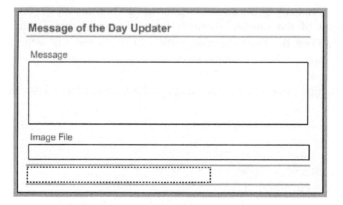

3. The textfields are named `message_txt`, `image_txt`, and `status_txt` from top to bottom.

4. Next, on the **Buttons** layer create some buttons that can be used to load and save the data from/to the text file:

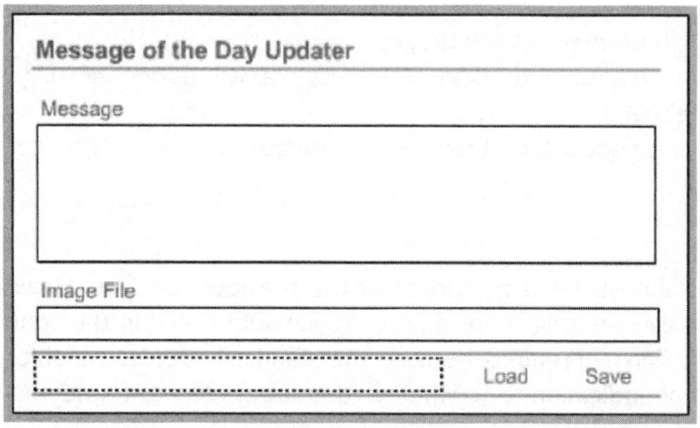

Message of the Day Updater

Message

Image File

Load   Save

As you can see I'm just using simple text buttons here. I've given them instance names of `load_btn` and `save_btn`, and this will allow us to set the event handlers from the frame on the **Actions** layer.

Now we come to the juicy bit, the **Actions** layer. We'll go through this step-by-step so that you know what each bit of ActionScript is for.

The first thing we need to do is to create some `onLoad` event handlers that can be attached to a `loadVars` object. We're actually going to create two separate handlers, as we need to perform different actions depending on whether we're loading or saving the text.

5. First up is the `displayMessage` function, which we'll use when loading the message data straight from the text file:

```
displayMessage = function (success) {
    if (success) {
        message_txt.text = this.message;
        image_txt.text = this.photofile;
        status_txt.text = "Data file loaded";
    } else {
        status_txt.text = "Could not load data file";
    }
};
```

Here you can see that we're checking to see if the operation was a success. If it was, we copy the variables out of the `loadVars` object and into the two text fields, and then set the status text accordingly. If there was a problem, we inform the user through the status text.

6. Moving on to our second event handler, this one will be used when we invoke the PHP script to save the modified data:

```
checkSuccess = function (success) {
    if (success && this.result == "Okay") {
        status_txt.text = "Data saved successfully";
    } else {
        status_txt.text = "An error has occurred";
    }
};
```

This takes almost the same format as the previous function. However, if you look a little closer you can see that there is an extra variable check in the condition section of the `if` statement. This is required because the standard success variable of an `onLoad` handler only gives an indication as to whether the target file was found and loaded. This is fine for simple text files, but it has no way of determining whether the operation inside a server-side script was successful or not.

In order to check this, we'll return a result variable from our script, indicating the overall success or failure of the operation. If this is set to `Okay` then the operation was a success and we set the status text accordingly. If the script could not be found or loaded, or if the operation failed for some reason, then we inform the user via the status text.

7. Now we need to set the `onPress` handlers of our **Load** and **Save** buttons. First is the `load_btn` button, and all we need to do here is set the appropriate `onLoad` event handler (`displayMessage`) and load the text file:

```
load_btn.onRelease = function() {
    dataLoader.onLoad = displayMessage;
    dataLoader.load("message.txt");
};
```

Note that we haven't created the `dataLoader` object yet – that comes in the next step – but it is the `loadVars` object that we will use to load all our data and invoke the PHP script.

8. The `save_btn` button is a little more complicated in that we have to copy the variables from our textfields into the `dataLoader` object. We can then proceed to set the event handler and invoke the PHP script:

```
save_btn.onRelease = function() {
    dataLoader.message = _root.message_txt.text;
    dataLoader.photofile = _root.image_txt.text;

    dataLoader.onLoad = checkSuccess;
    dataLoader.sendAndLoad("update.php", dataLoader, "POST");
```

```
};
```

If you haven't encountered the `sendAndLoad` method before, it basically allows us to send data to a server-side script and then read the information returned.

9. The last smidge of ActionScript we need is the following, which creates the `dataLoader` object that we've just been using:

```
dataLoader = new loadVars();
```

That's it for the Flash movie. It's quite a simple movie really, but deceptively so as it's the PHP script that does all the work.

10. Since we haven't covered any PHP yet, I'm just going to list the whole script here. I'll make a few small clarifications at the end, but you should be able to follow what's going on from the comments. Enter this using a plain text editor such as Notepad and save it as `update.php`. Make sure that your text editor doesn't add its own file extension, and if it does remove it – it's not welcome here:

```php
<?
// update.php
// Flash MX Studio - Steve Webster

// Data file name
$datafile = "message.txt";

// Create data string for message
$data = "&message=" . urlencode($HTTP_POST_VARS['message']);

// Add photofile variable to data string
$data . = "&photofile=" .x urlencode($HTTP_POST_VARS['photofile']);

// Open data file in write mode
$file = @fopen($datafile, 'w');

// If file not opened...
if (!$file) {
  // Report error and exit
  print "&result=Fail";
  exit;
}

// Write data string to file and close
fwrite($file, $data);
fclose($file);
```

continues overleaf

```
// Report success to Flash
print "&result=Okay";

?>
```

This script basically overwrites the current contents of the data file with the variable values sent from the Flash movie. If the script is unable to open the data file in write mode then an error message is sent back to the Flash movie and the script is aborted. Otherwise, the data is overwritten as planned.

11. That's it. All you need to do now is to upload the new HTML, SWF, `message.txt`, and PHP files to your web server in the same directory and load the new movie.

> *Remember that if you try to load from the movie when there are no values attached to the variables in the text file, you will receive an error because of the way that this has been set up.*

If you find you are having problems writing to the data file then you may need to set the file permissions for that file to allow the PHP script to open it in write mode. This is done using a command called CHMOD that is built into most FTP clients, and you can find a good tutorial on this subject at **www.phpforflash.com**.

PHP for the masses

In this section we're going to cover a little basic ground on the PHP language. Don't worry if the thought of this makes you go weak at the knees – PHP is actually a lot like ActionScript so learning the basics shouldn't be too painful. This section is not a complete guide to PHP, as we just don't have the space here to cover even a fraction of the language. By the end of this chapter, you should be able to create your own basic scripts, but if you really want that PHP Guru status, then you need to get yourself a book dedicated to the subject. It just so happens that I've written such a book for friends of ED, you lucky people you! The book is called Foundation PHP for Flash, and it guides you through the finer points of using PHP with Flash to produce dynamic content in your movies.

Right, enough of the blatant plug, on with the show.

PHP files are essentially just ASCII (or plain text) files, just like HTML documents, so the first thing you're going to need is a decent editor. A lot of people are happy to code their PHP script using

Notepad or BBEdit, but I must confess to being a huge fan of EditPlus. This is a commercial editor that includes syntax highlighting for many server-side languages, including PHP.

Let's take a look at a simple PHP script. Type the following into a blank document, save the file as `hello_world.php` and upload it to your web server:

```php
<?
    print "Hello World!";
?>
```

To see it in action, you now just need to open your browser and call up the address of the file, which will be something like:

http://www.somewhere.com/path/to/hello_world.php

The following should now appear in your browser:

OK, so now for a quick run-down of the structure of this simple script:

- The first and last lines contain matching `<?` and `?>` tags. These tell the server that everything in between these tags should be interpreted as PHP code, and processed by the PHP engine, rather than just being sent back to the browser and interpreted there. You can put any number of these tag pairs in a page and intersperse them with, for example, HTML or XML code, but for our purposes in this chapter we'll only ever use one set, so you don't need to worry about this.

- Within these tags we have a single line of code, which is actually pretty self-explanatory. As you'd expect, the command `print` simply outputs its argument to the browser – in this case, the string `Hello World!`

The results of all PHP print statements are sent to the browser consecutively, so multiple print statements will still only generate one page of output.

```
<?
  for ($count = 0; $count < 10; $count++) {
    print "Hello, world!<br>";
  }
?>
```

This is a simple PHP `for` loop that looks very much like its ActionScript counterpart and behaves in exactly the same way. All this code does is print out the string `Hello, world!` ten times with a <br> tag between each line. The reason that we have to use the <br> tag rather than a new line character is that the browser interprets the output as HTML, and so we must format our output using HTML tags.

PHP uses variables in a similar way to Flash, in that PHP is a loosely typed language. In other words, this means that any variable can contain any type of data, and that the data type may be temporarily converted on-the-fly depending on the context in which it is used. However, unlike ActionScript, in PHP we distinguish a variable name by the use of the dollar symbol $. In the last example, we set a variable `$count` to 0, and then looped around, incrementing it each time. As you can see, the structure of the language is remarkably like ActionScript at this level.

There are a number of areas where PHP and ActionScript differ, and one of those is in the way that strings are concatenated. When we want to join two strings in ActionScript, we use the + operator. However, in PHP the + operator is strictly for mathematical operations, and the . (dot) operator is used instead:

```
$myVar = "Hello, " . "world!";
```

Now that we have a handle on the basics, let's start looking at how we can put this to use.

Creating a simple e-mail application

I don't know about you, but I think it's about time we do something with all this new knowledge we've picked up over the course of the chapter so far. What we're going to do in this section is to use that knowledge to build a fully functional Flash application that would be a useful addition to almost any web site.

"What is this fabulous application?" I hear you ask. Well, we're going to build a Flash feedback system that will take information from a Flash form and send it to a designated e-mail address. We're going to throw a few extras into this application too, so that it's not just your run-of-the-mill form mailer, and we're going to spend some time doing a spot of planning for our application. Before we get that far, here's a glimpse at what we're aiming at.

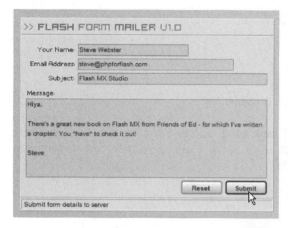

In order to build this rather funky application, we're going to need to go through several stages. The first thing we need to do is to design a nice button component that we can use to build the user interface for our form. We'll then look at the ActionScript needed to run the whole show, before finally moving on to the PHP script that'll do the hard work.

Designer application

Before we move on any further, we need to actually plan the application. This involves sketching out what we want the application to do, and looking at how we might go about making it do those things using the tools available to us. The design stage is one of, if not the most, critical stage in developing an application. The traditional mantra goes something like this:

> *If your design doesn't work on paper, then it won't work, period.*

This is a bit of a throwback to traditional software engineering practices, but is just as true for web-based Flash applications. If you don't know where you're going (i.e. you don't plan your application properly), how can you ever hope to get there?

Enough of the lecture stuff, on with the design. The fundamental aim of our application is to take data from our Flash movie (i.e. data which has been entered by the user) and send it to a designated e-mail address. Sounds simple enough, huh? Well, it is, and yet it isn't. Going into a little more depth, these are the features that I think would be useful for our application. It should:

- Have the ability to handle as many different textfields as required with little or no modification of the code.

■   Keep the user informed at all times.

■   Handle errors in an intelligent way.

■   Make use of reusable components where possible.

■   Last, but by no means least, it should look good. Strictly speaking, this shouldn't be a primary goal for our application, but since we're Flash developers we undoubtedly appreciate the finer looking things in life.

Now we're getting somewhere.

Funky button component ahoy

Before we get into the thick of building the Flash movie, we need to make a swanky button component that we can use to build part of the user interface. Since components were covered back in Chapter 4 (you did read that chapter, right?) you shouldn't have too many problems following me. The CD also contains two additional chapters on components and don't forget that you can always check with the source files for this chapter if you get lost at any point.

At this point, I should just mention that we're not going to be doing anything particularly fancy with this component, and that includes not adding it to the Component panel in the Flash MX authoring environment.

1.   OK, first thing's first. Create a new movie and save it as `formmailer.fla`. Inside this movie, create a new movie clip called `FSimpleButton` and arrange the timeline so that it looks something like this:

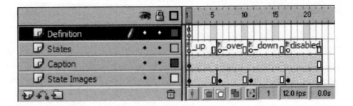

Our component uses a new feature of Flash MX to achieve its button-like actions, and the **_up**, **_over**, and **_down** frame labels play an integral part in this. It is also possible to have a **_hit** frame to define the hit area of the button, though we're not using that here.

When a movie clip has an `onPress` or `onRelease` event handler assigned to it then it behaves like a button and will automatically show the appropriate frame from the above.

This saves us a little bit of coding so I decided to use it here, though we will have to implement the disabled state manually since that isn't part of a standard button.

2. While we're here, let's get the graphics out of the way. If you're following my example then you can copy the graphics from the following screenshot. If you're going it on your own then go ahead and create whatever graphics you want for each state on the **State Images** layer.

3. Finally, add a dynamic text field to frame 1 of the **Caption** layer with an instance name of `caption_txt`. Don't worry about text color (we'll deal with that in the ActionScript code in a moment) but set the text field to center justified, ensuring that it covers the whole width of the button.

4. With all that done, we're finally ready to move onto the code that'll make our button dance. The first thing we need to do here is to create our new button class, which we'll call `FSimpleButton`. Add the following code to frame 1 of the **Definitions** layer:

```
#initclip 1

// Constructor
FSimpleButton = function(){
    // Initialise component
    this.init();
};

// Inherit from MovieClip object
FSimpleButton.prototype = new MovieClip();

// Register component class
Object.registerClass("FSimpleButton", FSimpleButton);
```

This should all look pretty familiar to you, as this is almost exactly the same way the Tool Tip component started out in Chapter 4. I won't dwell on this anymore, but if you're stumped then flick back and have a look at that chapter.

5. Before we go any further we need to define some component parameters for our component. Right-click on our movie clip in the Library, select **Component Definition...** from the menu and create the parameters you see in the following screenshot.

Name	Variable	Value	Type
Button Caption	captionText		String
Caption Color [Enabled]	captionColor	#000000	Color
Caption Color [Disabled]	captionDisabledColor	#999999	Color
onClick Handler	clickHandler		String
Show Hand Cursor	showHand	false	Boolean
Status Text	statusText		String
Status Variable	statusVar	statusText	String

6. The next thing we want to do is to define our `init` method, which will be called when a new instance of our component is created and sets up the component ready for use:

```
// Initialise component
FSimpleButton.prototype.init = function(){
    // Set caption text and color
    this.caption_txt.text = this.captionText;
    this.caption_txt.textColor = this.captionColor;

    // Setup cursor and disable tabbing
    this.useHandCursor = this.showHand;
    this.tabEnabled = false;

    // Set event handlers
    this.onRollOut = this.myRollOut;
    this.onRollOver = this.myRollOver;
    this.onPress = this.myPress;
    this.onRelease = this.myRelease;
    this.onDragOut = this.myDragOut;
    this.onDragOver = this.myDragOver;
    this.onReleaseOutside = this.myReleaseOutside;
};
```

You can see here that we're setting the text and text color of the `caption_txt` textfield. The variables used for this are among the component parameters that we set in the previous step.

Next up, we set the cursor according to the `showHand` component parameter, and then disable our button from receiving input focus using the TAB key. I've done this because I think that nasty yellow focus rectangle spoils the design of the application, but it's up to you if you keep this in or not.

Finally, we set the mouse-related event handlers for our component, and since we're inheriting from the `MovieClip` object we've got quite a few to play with. We won't actually use all of the ones set here, but I've included them just in case you wanted to do something a little different with your button component.

7. We now move on to create the event handlers that we've just mentioned. The first group we need to deal with are the onRollOut and onRollOver handlers, and we're going to use these to set a status variable on the parent timeline:

```
FSimpleButton.prototype.myRollOut = function() {
    this._parent[this.statusVar] = _global.oldStatusText;
};

FSimpleButton.prototype.myRollOver = function() {
    _global.oldStatusText = this._parent[this.statusVar];
    this._parent[this.statusVar] = this.statusText;
};
```

The status variable is specified as another of our component parameters, as is the actual status text. We'll use the global variable oldStatusText to store and retrieve the previous status text. The reason for this will become apparent when we move on to the Flash movie proper.

8. Moving on to the onPress and onRelease handlers, you can see from the code below that the former is actually unused at present. This is one of those 'included just in case' event handlers I mentioned earlier, and would be useful if you wanted to expand the functionality of the component.

```
FSimpleButton.prototype.myPress = function() {
};

FSimpleButton.prototype.myRelease = function() {
    // Execute callback
    this._parent[this.clickHandler](this);
};
```

The onRelease handler, on the other hand, is probably the most important event handler of all in our component. It is this handler that calls the function specified in the clickHandler component parameter.

You'll notice here that we're passing a reference for the current object to the callback function. This is useful if you have a single callback function for several buttons and need to determine which button initiated the callback. We won't actually use this in our application, but it's a useful feature to have nonetheless.

9. There is only one event handler left that's actually implemented, and that's onDragOut.

```
FSimpleButton.prototype.myDragOut = function() {
    this.gotoAndStop("_up");
};
```

I've used this to correct a small quirk in the way that buttons operate in Flash. In most common operating systems, when you hold your mouse over a button and then drag the mouse outside, the button returns to its 'up' state, indicating that releasing the button now will not count as a button press. In Flash, however, the button will remain in its _down state. To correct this, all I've done is to send the button back to the _up frame when the mouse is dragged outside of the button area. It's up to you whether you want to implement this or not, but I like to keep things consistent.

10. The remaining event handlers are not implemented:

```
FSimpleButton.prototype.myDragOver = function() {
};

FSimpleButton.prototype.myReleaseOutside = function() {
};
```

11. The final thing we need to do for our component is to create some methods to allow us to enable and disable the button from outside of the component. This is where the _disabled frame comes into play:

```
FSimpleButton.prototype.disable = function() {
    this.caption_txt.textColor = this.captionDisabledColor;
    this.gotoAndStop("disabled");
    this.enabled = false;
};
```

You can see that all we're doing here is changing the color of the caption text to that specified in the captionDisabledColor component parameter, moving to the disabled frame, and disabling the component. While the component is disabled, no events will be processed and it will remain on the designated frame.

12. Here's the next method:

```
FSimpleButton.prototype.enable = function(){
    this.enabled = true;
    this.gotoAndStop("_up");
    this.caption_txt.textColor = this.captionColor;
};
```

The enable method simply reverses the changes made in the disable method, enabling the button, moving it back to the _up frame, and resetting the caption text color.

13. I've also thrown in an `isEnabled` method, which will allow the button state to be determined. Again, this is another feature that we won't be using in our application, but could prove handy in another:

```
// Public: isEnabled
FSimpleButton.prototype.isEnabled = function(){
    return this.enabled;
};

#endinitclip

stop();
```

That completes our component definition and it's now ready to be used. If you haven't already done so, rename the component in the Library to `FSimpleButton` and set its linkage as follows:

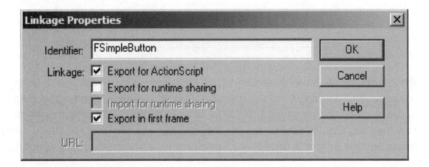

Da Flash Moo-Vee

Now we've got the design out of the way, and a shiny new button component ready to go, we can start to build up the Flash movie side of the application. We'll kick off with the graphical side and then move onto the ActionScript code a little later.

1. If you're still editing the button component then return to the main stage. Our application is only going to have a single frame so we don't need to worry too much about the timeline, but for the sake of clarity I've split my movie up onto 4 layers: **Actions**, **Buttons**, **Textfields** and **Background**.

Use the **Background** layer to create whatever kind of background graphics you want for your application. If you do deviate from the example I've given then you'll probably want to play with a few of the color values mentioned later in this section.

2. On the **Textfields** layer, add the `input` text fields from which you want to gather information. Since I'm working on a simple feedback form, my stage now looks like this:

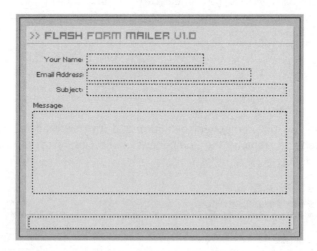

These text fields have instance names of `name_txt`, `email_txt`, `subject_txt`, and `message_txt` working from the top down. I've also added an extra text field at the bottom of the stage to display status text to the user. In addition to giving this an instance name of `status_txt`, I've associated it with the variable `statusText`, as this is more convenient for setting the contents of the text field from within our button component.

3. On the **Buttons** layer, drag two instances of our **FSimpleButton** component from the Library onto the stage and give them the instance names `resetBtn` and `submitBtn`. These are going to be our buttons to reset and submit the form, and you should set the parameters of these two buttons as follows:

resetBtn:

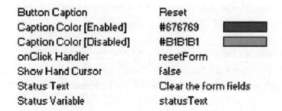

submitBtn:

Button Caption	Submit	
Caption Color [Enabled]	#676769	▉
Caption Color [Disabled]	#B1B1B1	▉
onClick Handler	submitForm	
Show Hand Cursor	false	
Status Text	Submit form details to server	
Status Variable	statusText	

We'll create the resetForm and submitForm functions in the next step. That's it for the non-code section of this movie. Just to make sure you're still on track, your stage should now look something like this:

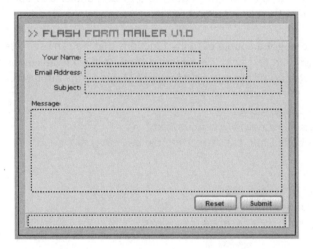

Yours may not look exactly the same as this as I've added a live preview to the button component that I didn't tell you about. This updates the caption to that specified in the component parameters. If you want to have a go at doing this yourself then Chapter 4 has details on creating live previews for components. Otherwise, feel free to take apart the livePreview.fla file on the CD.

With the graphical elements of our application sorted, we need to turn our attention to the ActionScript code on the **Actions** layer. This is where all the real work is going to be done, from sending the user input to the PHP script, through to creating and displaying the message box shown in the original screenshots of the application.

4. The first thing we need to do is add a small extension to the loadVars object. This will allow us to clear all variables out of the object so that a form can be submitted more than once without fear of it 'remembering' any information from the previous submission.

```
loadVars.prototype.clear = function() {
    for (element in this) {
        if (typeof(this[element]) != "function") {
            delete this[element];
        }
    }
};
```

I actually found it hard to believe that this isn't a standard method of the loadVars object, but it appears that Macromedia decided we didn't need anything like that. Still, at least they gave us the ability to extend the functionality ourselves.

As you can see, we're using a for...in loop to go through each element of the loadVars object and remove anything that is not a function. We need to check that what we're about to delete isn't a function since both the onLoad handler and our new clear method will be included in the elements processed.

5. Next up we've got a couple of utility functions that we can use to set and fetch the text for the status_txt text field. I've included these so it's a relatively simple task to change the name or location of the text field in which status text is displayed:

```
// Set status text
setStatus = function(statusText) {
    _root.status_txt.text = statusText;
};
```

```
// Fetch status text
getStatus = function() {
    return _root.status_txt.text;
};
```

In order to help the user identify which text field, if any, currently has input focus, we'll use some of the event handlers of the new TextField object to change the background color of a text field when input focus is received and lost. This will also allow us to set the status text accordingly.

6. We'll actually set the onSetFocus and onKillFocus event handlers for each text field later, but for now we're just going to create the functions themselves.

```
// Focus handler for form fields
setFocusHandler = function () {
    // Set status text
    setStatus(this.statusText);

    // Highlight field
```

```
        this.backgroundColor = 0xCACED5;
};
```

7. The `setFocusHandler` function will be called whenever a text field receives input focus. It sets the status text to the `statusText` property (which we'll set up later) of the text field that called the event handler, and changes the background color of the text field to a darker color:

```
// Kill Focus handler for form fields
killFocusHandler = function() {
    // Clear status
    setStatus("");

    // Lose field highlight
    this.backgroundColor = 0xDEE0E4;
};
```

The `killFocusHandler` is called whenever a text field loses focus. It clears the status text and sets the background color back to the original.

Having got that sorted, we need to address the problem of click-happy users that go around clicking buttons when they aren't supposed to. For example, there's no point hitting the Reset button if the form is already empty, and we don't want them hitting the Submit button until they've filled out all of the form fields. Rather than coding the button functions to check that the required functions have been met before proceeding, we're going to enable/disable the buttons depending on the status of the form. In order to accomplish this we're going to employ another of the `TextField`'s event handlers: `onChanged`.

8. As with the above event handlers, we'll set the `onChanged` handler for each text field a little later, but we'll define the function here:

```
// Changed handler for form fields
changedHandler = function() {
    var submitCheck = true;
    var resetCheck = false;

    for (var count = 0; count < textFields.length; count++) {
        if (_root[textFields[count]].length == 0) {
            submitCheck = false;
        } else {
            resetCheck = true;
        }
    }

    if (submitCheck) {
```

continues overleaf

```
            submitBtn.enable();
        } else {
            submitBtn.disable();
        }

        if (resetCheck) {
            resetBtn.enable();
        } else {
            resetBtn.disable();
        }
    };
```

This code actually requires a little faith on your part since it refers to an array, textFields, which we haven't created yet. For now it is enough to say that it contains the instance names of each of our input text fields. All the above code does is loop through each of our text fields and check to see if any text has been entered. If we find a text field that is empty, then we want to disable the Submit button, and if we find a text field that is not empty, then we want to enable the Reset button.

Notice here that we're using the length property of the TextField object itself to determine whether any data has been entered. According to Macromedia this produces the same result as using TextField.text.length, but is actually a little bit faster. It's also less for us to type, so everybody wins!

9. We now need to create a function to disable the form. We'll use this when the form is being submitted so that the user can't play around with either the text fields or the buttons:

```
// Function to disable form fields and buttons
disableForm = function() {
    // Disable all form fields
    for(var count = 0; count < textFields.length; count++) {
        _root[textFields[count]].selectable = false;
        _root[textFields[count]].border = false;
    }

    // Disable submit and reset buttons
    submitBtn.disable();
    resetBtn.disable();
};
```

By setting the selectable property for each text field to false, we prevent them receiving input focus. We also remove the border of the text field as a visual cue to the user that they are disabled, and disable the buttons while we're at it too!

10. Next up we need to create the resetForm and submitForm functions that we mentioned earlier:

```
// Function to reset form to initial state
resetForm = function() {
    // Clear status text
    setStatus("");
    _global.oldStatusText = "";

    // Clear and enable textfields
    for(var count = 0; count < textFields.length; count++) {
        _root[textFields[count]].selectable = true;
        _root[textFields[count]].border = true;
        _root[textFields[count]].text = "";
    }

    // Disable buttons
    resetBtn.disable();
    submitBtn.disable();
};
```

This function clears the status text and then sets about enabling and clearing all of the text fields. Since the textfields are all going to be empty, we know that both buttons should be disabled. Unfortunately, the onChanged event for a text field is only fired when the user changes the value, meaning that we have to set the button states manually.

11. Now for the submitForm function:

```
// Function to submit form data to the server
submitForm = function() {
    // Disable form fields & buttons
    disableForm();

    // Clear dataHandler data...
    dataHandler.clear();

    // Load data into dataHandler...
    for (var count = 0; count < textFields.length; count++) {
    dataHandler[textFields[count]] = _root[textFields[count]].text;
    }

    // Send data to PHP script and set status text
    dataHandler.sendAndLoad("simplemailer.php", dataHandler,
    ➡"POST");
    setStatus("Contacting server...please wait!");
```

continues overleaf

```
};
```

The first thing we do here is to disable the form using the function we constructed earlier. Next we clear all data out of the `dataHandler` object (which is an instance of `loadVars` that we'll create later) using the new `clear` method we implemented right at the start of this section. We then need to move all the data from the various text fields into the `dataHandler` object, before using the `sendAndLoad` method to invoke our PHP script and send the data using the `POST` method. Finally, we set the status text to keep the user informed as to what's happening.

Moving on, we come to the last of our functions. Before you start to jump about in elation, this one's a little longer than the functions we've encountered before. Having said that, there's nothing in here that you haven't covered so far in this book, so you should be OK! The purpose of the function is to create the message box to inform the user as to the success or failure of the `sendAndLoad` operation. We'll do this using a combination of the drawing API, the ability to create movie clips and text fields dynamically, and our trusty button component.

12. So, the first thing we need to do is to create a movie clip for the message box:

```
// Popup message box function
messageBox = function(message) {
    var maxWidth = 200;
    var msgBox_mc = _root.createEmptyMovieClip("msgBox_mc", 0);
```

Note that we've added a `message` parameter for the function, which will be the text displayed in the message box. We've also defined another variable here, `maxWidth`, which is used to determine the width of the message box (the height is determined by the amount of text) and can be changed according to your personal taste... or just because you feel like it.

13. The next thing we need to do is to create our text field to actually display the text, and set its properties accordingly.

```
msgBox_mc.createTextField("body_txt", 1, 5, 5, maxWidth - 10,
➥10);
msgBox_mc.body_txt.multiline = true;
msgBox_mc.body_txt.autoSize = true;
msgBox_mc.body_txt.wordWrap = true;
msgBox_mc.body_txt.selectable = false;
msgBox_mc.body_txt.textColor = 0x676767;
msgBox_mc.body_txt.text = message;
```

We've given the new text field a 5-pixel border from the edge of our movie clip, and set the initial height to 10. We've then set the text field up so that it will expand vertically depending on how much text there is to display.

14. We then create a `TextFormat` object so that we can specify the font color and size of our textfield:

```
var format = new TextFormat();
format.align = "left";
format.font = "_sans";
format.size = 10;

msgBox_mc.body_txt.setTextFormat(format);

var currentHeight = msgBox_mc.body_txt.textHeight + 10;
```

Once that's done we can determine the height of the textfield using the `textHeight` property. We'll use this to determine where to place our button and, ultimately, where to draw the boundaries of the message box, taking into account our 5-pixel border.

15. So, the next step is to actually add an instance of our button component:

```
var closeBtn = msgBox_mc.attachMovie("FSimpleButton", "closeBtn",
➥0);
closeBtn._x = (maxWidth - closeBtn._width) / 2;
closeBtn._y = currentHeight;
closeBtn.captionText = "Close";
closeBtn.showHand = false;
closeBtn.captionColor = 0x676769;
closeBtn.init();
closeBtn.onRelease = function() {
    resetForm();
    this._parent.removeMovieClip();
};
```

The button is centered horizontally and set up to remove the message box movie clip when the button is released.

16. Finally, we're ready to draw the boundaries and fill in the message box movie clip. The first thing we need to add is the height of the button, plus a 5 pixel border, onto our `currentHeight` variable to determine the total height of the movie:

```
currentHeight += closeBtn._height + 5;
```

17. With that done, we position the message box movie clip so that is it centered about the stage and is drawn:

```
msgBox_mc._x = (Stage.width - maxWidth) / 2;
msgBox_mc._y = (Stage.height - currentHeight) / 2;

msgBox_mc.moveTo(0, currentHeight);
msgBox_mc.lineStyle(1, 0xF5F6F8, 100);
msgBox_mc.beginFill(0xEBECF0, 75);

msgBox_mc.lineTo(0, 0);
msgBox_mc.lineTo(maxWidth, 0);
msgBox_mc.lineStyle(1, 0xC2C2C4, 100);
msgBox_mc.lineTo(maxWidth, currentHeight);
msgBox_mc.lineTo(0, currentHeight);

msgBox_mc.endFill();
};
```

Using the drawing API, we draw a raised-bevel edge around the movie clip and fill it with a nice light green at 75% alpha. You'll be glad to know that that concludes our messageBox function.

18. That's all of our functions out of the way. Next we need to create the dataHandler object and set up its onLoad event handler to call the messageBox function we've just created, using a different message depending on whether the operation was a success or failure:

```
// Create data handler and set onLoad event handler
dataHandler = new LoadVars();
dataHandler.onLoad = function(success) {
    if (success) {
        messageBox("Your data has been mailed by the server. Thank
        ➥you for your feedback, and someone will be in touch with
        ➥you shortly regarding your query");
    } else {
        messageBox("You data was not able to be sent due to a
        ➥problem on the server. Please try again later!");
    }
}
```

19. All that remains for us to do now is to create the textFields array and associated status strings, and initialize the textfields:

```
// Array of textfield names and status strings
textFields = new Array("name_txt", "email_txt", "subject_txt",
```

```
➥"message_txt");

statusStrings = new Array("Enter your name here", "You should enter
your email address here", "This is the subject of your email", "Enter
➥the main body of your message here");

// For each textfield
for (count = 0; count < textFields.length; count++) {
    // Set properties
    textField_txt = this[textFields[count]];
    textField_txt.border = true;
    textField_txt.borderColor = 0xB1B1B1;
    textField_txt.background = true;
    textField_txt.backgroundColor = 0xDEE0E4;
    textField_txt.onSetFocus = setFocusHandler;
    textField_txt.onKillFocus = killFocusHandler;
    textField_txt.onChanged = changedHandler;
    textField_txt.statusText = statusStrings[count];
}
```

This should all be pretty self-explanatory. We've already created the text fields and the event handlers, so all we're doing here is to set the properties and event handlers of each text field. The one line that does deserve special attention is the last one, where we're storing the status text for a given text field as a property of the text field itself. It seems like many moons ago, but we used this property in the setFocusHandler function to set the status text.

20. Oops, nearly forgot something. Initially both buttons are enabled, and we don't want them to be. In this case, a simple call to the changedHandler function will do the trick:

```
// Set initial button states and halt movie
changedHandler();
stop();
```

That's it. That's all the ActionScript code necessary to get our application up and running. If you go ahead and test it now, you should see the fruit of your labor in all its glory. Submitting the form at this stage produces a failure message box, as the PHP script doesn't actually exist yet. It's also worth noting that if you're testing the application inside the Flash authoring environment, the message box will not appear at the center of your movie. The reason for this is that, in the authoring environment, the Stage object is the whole of the test window, and then some, and this throws off the positioning code in the messageBox function. If you test the application in a browser window everything should be OK!

And Now for something completely PHP

OK, we're entering the final straight now and it's time to take a look at the PHP script that will do most of the hard work in our application. We'll go through this step-by-step, and everything here should be familiar from the PHP primer earlier in the chapter. If you feel unsure at any stage, just flip back and refer to this earlier section. Having said that, there isn't a great deal to the PHP script for this application because a lot of the work is being done in the Flash movie. All we need to do here is to create the message body from a list of the variables passed to the PHP script and then send the e-mail using the mail function.

1. Open up your text editor and save the file as `simplemailer.php`. The first thing we need is our opening PHP tag. We'll also set up the recipient e-mail address while we're at it:

    ```
    <?php
    // simplemailer.php
    // Flash MX Studio - Steve Webster

    // Set recipient for email
    $recipient = "you@yourisp.com";
    ```

    You can see a few comments in this code section and, as with ActionScript, it's always a good idea to comment your code fully; you never know when you might need to understand it again.

    Moving on, we need to deal with a small quirk of the loadVars object. When using the send and sendAndLoad methods, the onLoad event handler and our new clear method will be sent along with any other data in the object. Since one of our stated objectives for this application was to make it as flexible as possible with regards to the number of variables it could handle, we're going to use a loop to add each and every variable sent from the Flash movie to the body of the e-mail.

2. In order to prevent the aforementioned quirk from throwing a spanner into our finely oiled machine, we simply delete the variables associated with the methods concerned:

    ```
    // Remove methods from data...
    unset($HTTP_POST_VARS['onLoad']);
    unset($HTTP_POST_VARS['clear']);
    ```

    We're accomplishing this using the unset function to remove (i.e. delete) the appropriate elements of the HTTP_POST_VARS array. This array holds all of the variables that were sent to the PHP scripting using the POST method.

3. With that mean old quirk removed, we're almost ready to start looping through the remaining variables in the array. Before we get there though, we need to set up a variable to hold our message body:

```
// Setup body text
$body = "The following information was submitted...\n\n";
```

We set this up with some initial text that will appear at the top of the e-mail.

4. Now we can deal with the remaining variables. We'll loop through all of the elements of the HTTP_POST_VARS array, adding them to our $body variable as we go:

```
// Add each key/value pair to the body text
foreach($HTTP_POST_VARS as $key => $value) {
    $key = substr($key, 0, -4);
    $body .= "$key: $value\n";
}
```

You can see that we do this using a foreach loop. This is similar to a for...in loop in ActionScript, which we used earlier on in the new clear method for the loadVars object. In the above example, each iteration of the loop sees the key (variable name) and value for the next array element extracted and stored in the $key and $value variables respectively.

Once this is done, we use the substr function to chop off the _txt extension that all our variable names currently have. This isn't exactly a necessary step, but it seemed a little pointless including this extension in the e-mail so we strip it out. In PHP, the substr function works a little differently to its ActionScript counterpart in that we can specify a negative value for the end point of the substring. If this is the case, the substring is formed from the start index to n characters from the end of the original string. Translated into English, this line of code would read:

> *Take all the characters in* $key, *from position* 0 *to* 4 *characters from the end of the string, and store the result in the* $key *variable.*

We then append the current key and value onto the $body variable and move on to the next array element.

The next thing we need to do is build a proper **From:** address for the e-mail. We're actually going to make it appear as though the e-mail was sent from the person filling out the form, rather than by the PHP script, using the name and e-mail details supplied. The correct format for a **From:** field of an e-mail is:

```
"Name" <email@whatever.com>
```

5. So, go ahead and build a string that looks like this for our e-mail:

```
// Set from address
$from = $HTTP_POST_VARS['name_txt'] . " <" .
➡$HTTP_POST_VARS['email_txt'] . ">";
```

6. All that's left to do is to set the subject of our e-mail and call the `mail` function, which is built in to PHP, to actually send the whole lot off:

```
// Set subject for email
$subject = $HTTP_POST_VARS['subject_txt'];

// Send email
mail($recipient, $subject, $body, "From: $from");

?>
```

7. That's all there is to this application. Publish the Flash movie and upload the HTML and SWF file, along with our newly created PHP script, to your web server and test.

Trouble and strife

If you're having problems getting the PHP script to work properly, there are a few things you should check:

- First and foremost you should check that your PHP script is not generating any errors. You can do this by typing in the URL for the script directly into your web browser and appending the necessary variables:

  http://.../simplemailer.php?name_txt=Bob&email_txt=...

- The latest version of PHP actually suppresses error messages by default, so if you still get no joy then try adding the following code to the top of the script (just below the opening PHP tag):

  ```
  error_reporting(E_ALL ^ E_NOTICE);
  ```

  If you find any errors, go through your script and correct them. If you're still unsure, simply copy the script supplied on the CD that came with this book.

- Check that your web host actually supports PHP script running on their servers. I know this sounds pretty obvious, but you'd be surprised at how many support e-mails I've received asking why a particular application isn't working, only to find out the host doesn't support PHP.

- Some hosts require PHP script to have a different file extension such as `php3`, `php4`, or `phtml`. Again, this is something you should check with your hosting company.

- If the script appears to be running fine but you're not receiving any e-mails, get hold of your hosting company and check that they allow use of the `mail` function on their servers. I've yet to come across a hosting company that doesn't actually allow this, but it *is* a configuration option for PHP and so should be checked.

- As a final port of call you can always send a quick e-mail to the nice support people at **support@friendsofed.com**.

Where to go from here

With the application finished, I thought I'd give you a few pointers on some extra features that would be really useful for this application.

Response e-mail

The first great addition I could think of was to expand the PHP script to send an e-mail to the person filling out the form, thanking them for taking the time to give their feedback or whatever. This is a really personal touch, and is fairly easy to implement.

Select recipient

It could also be useful to allow the user to select a recipient for a particular e-mail. For example, you could use a combo box component to list various departments within your company as recipients. Each selection would have an e-mail address associated with it, which would be passed to the PHP script.

There are a few other things that you could do with this application, but I'll let your minds wander on their own.

Summary

Well, that's it then! We've covered some massive ground in this chapter and, if nothing else, you've now got a shiny new Flash form mailer that you can bolt onto your web sites. Hopefully though, you'll have picked up some PHP knowledge along the way, and should feel comfortable writing simple scripts of your very own.

We started off discussing server-side scripts in general, looking particularly at how they compare to 'normal' document requests and what they can be useful for. We then moved on to look at

PHP in particular, digging up a bit of background information in the process, before diving head first into a working Flash/PHP application. With the 'Baptism of Code' out of the way, we then started to look at the basic elements of the PHP language and how we can use them to build our scripts. This section was fairly brief, but gave a decent insight into the PHP language. Finally, we used the knowledge gleaned in the earlier sections of this chapter to build a bona fide useful application: a Flash/PHP form mailer.

To give you an idea of what you can accomplish with your new-found knowledge, it would require only a little work to turn the last application we developed into a tell-a-friend system. All you really need is to have the destination e-mail address passed to the PHP script from the Flash movie, though a few more modifications would be desirable.

Another idea may be to combine both of the main applications presented in this chapter to create a Flash-based guestbook application that e-mails you when a new entry is made. This is a little more complex, however, but you have all the information required at your fingertips.

If you are interested in developing more complex Flash applications using PHP then I'd suggest you pick up a copy of my Foundation PHP for Flash book and we can continue the journey together. If you want more information on this book, then check out the friends of ED web site at **www.friendsofed.com.** I also mentioned earlier that I'd give you some interesting links to check out in relation to PHP scripts, so here you go:

> **www.hotscripts.com**
> This is one of the largest script repositories on the web, and it has a huge section dedicated to PHP.

> **http://php.resourceindex.com**
> This site is similar to the previous one, which a huge categorized list of PHP scripts.

> **www.evilwalrus.com**
> The Evil Walrus site is packed full of articles and scripts, and has an active subscriber community to boot.

That's just about it from me. If this chapter has got you hooked into the possibilities of combining server-side scripting with Flash, then not only have I done what I set out to do, but you should grab hold of your seat because you're about to get a second portion... this time with Macromedia with XML.

section 4: Dynamic Data Integration

chapter 17: XML

In all likelihood, you already have a pretty good idea of what XML is and what it does. It's been around for a little while now, and has rapidly matured into a popular technology wherever the exchange of data between applications or tiers is involved. There are numerous introductions to XML on the web and in books, but with the increasing importance of separating content from style, we thought you might appreciate a refresher before we look at some applications of XML in Flash MX.

With a strange old mystic/Yoda approach to explaining what XML is, let's start with an orange. If asked to describe the parts that constitute an orange we might say something like:

```
'Pips, Peel, Pith, Skin, Segments, Little bubbles of
juice.'
```

Did we miss anything? It might not be perfect but that sounds roughly like an orange to me, even if 'little bubbles' isn't exactly the correct biological term for the bits that hold the juice. However, if we gave this description to Mork (an alien from a planet called Ork), it wouldn't really tell him all that much would it? Where do these segments go? Are the pips embedded in the skin? This list of components tells him nothing about the structure of an orange. A better description would be:

```
'Skin surounding pith which covers a number of segments
containing pips and little bubbles that hold the juice.'
```

Now Mork has a much better idea of what an orange is all about. This is fairly similar to what XML does; it takes data and structures it in such a way so it's understandable to anyone, namely applications or architectures that process the data.

What is XML?

XML stands for e**X**tensible **M**arkup **L**anguage, but it's not a programming language per se. It's a *markup* language, concerned with the description and structuring of information. Markup languages have been used for a long time in printing, and traditionally consist of symbols added to content in order to describe the required layout on the page. You almost certainly use HTML regularly, doing essentially the same thing for the web. XML is different from HTML because HTML can include styling information as well as descriptive and structural information. Obviously, having different types of information within the same document can get a bit messy, which is why XML concerns itself only with description and structure, while the styling is left to an external document.

Tags and elements

The symbols we use to convey this information are referred to as **tags**. There are opening tags, such as the bold tag <b> in HTML, indicating that formatting should begin here; and closing tags which, in bold's case would be </b>, indicating that bold formatting should stop here. Anything written between these tags will be made bold and is known as the **content**. The two tags along with the content between them forms an **element**. In addition to these there are also tags that hold no information, such as the line break tag <br/>, known as an empty element.

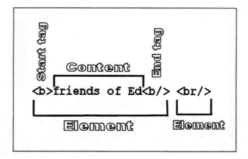

HTML is a language with a well-defined set of tags that you can use to style web pages. As we said, XML is more about description and structure, and we can define any tags that we might want to use in our files to be as descriptive as we like about the subject. For instance, going back to our orange anecdote, we might define the description and structure of an orange like this:

```
<orange>
    <peel>
        <pith>
            <segment>
                <pip/>
                <little bubbles of juice/>
            </segment>
            <segment>
                <pip/>
```

```
            <little bubbles of juice/>
    </pith>
  </peel>
</orange>
```

Here we have a language that explains that an `<orange>` consists of `<peel>`, which contains `<pith>`, surrounding a number of segments (in this case only two) which hold pips and bubbles of juice. We could also very easily add more segments below the existing ones. In this way, XML is extensible because we can extend the structure or add new descriptions, depending on our requirements. You could even perhaps have some segments without pips, and this would still be OK.

Attributes

We can add yet more data to our XML by using **attributes**. These are essentially pairs of names and values associated with an element. The syntax looks like this:

```
<tagname attributename='value'>
```

So if we wanted to add some more information to our peel tag; say we wanted to signify that it is colored orange, the start tag would become:

```
<peel color='orange'>
```

The empty tags can be altered in a similar fashion:

```
<pip color='magnolia'/>
```

Single (‘) or double quotes (“) work equally well as long as you are consistent, ending any single quote with a single and vice versa. You can have as many attributes as you like inside a tag, as long as each element name is different and every one has a value, even if it's just an empty string like ' '.

Why use attributes when a bit of content would do?

Few of the numerous XML tutorials seem to completely agree on when and where to use attributes instead of content. Why have we used an attribute to explain that the peel is orange when we could quite easily have added `<color>` orange `</color>`, as an element within the `<peel>` element?

The essential thinking behind attributes is that they provide us with **meta data**. Meta, as every good student knows, comes from the Greek word for 'with', 'behind', 'after', or most appropriately in this case, 'about'. It is meant to provide us with data about data. But, the definition of what meta data is depends entirely on your point of view. For instance, as a passenger on an airplane, the details of how to actually fly the plane are of no importance to you. As long as it gets you where you're going, at the time that you want to get there, you're happy. In this situation that data is simply meta data. However, to the pilots who have to fly the plane this is **data**, as without it they wouldn't be able to do their job. So, you can use attributes to separate different types of data. If we were writing XML for flying a plane we could insert any technical details as attributes, and then use elements to describe destinations, routes, and times.

Other developers have more personal reasons for using one or the other. Your decision could be as simple as finding one easier to use than the other, or that one looks better than the other. Most of the arguments boil down to personal preference.

Nodes

Elements are nodes, but to complicate matters, not all nodes are elements. As far as we are interested in them, Flash recognizes two node types: **element nodes** and **text nodes**. Element nodes are used to structure data by holding other nodes. They can be used to supply information in the form of attributes. Text nodes contain character data (strings of letters) only. So, in the document `<color> orange </color>`, `color` is an element node, while `orange` is a text node, and `orange` is a child node of the element node. We'll get onto child nodes in a moment.

Declarations

Before we start writing our XML we need a line to inform the parser (the program that is reading the XML, which is Flash in our case), what it's looking at. So, at the beginning of your XML you should include the line:

```
<?xml version='1.0'?>
```

This simply tells the parser which version of XML you are using. If you wish you can also define the text encoding by adding `encoding='ISO-8859-1'` after the version. (`ISO-8859-1` indicates the Latin-1/West European character set, which is the default.)

Comments

Comments are also part of XML and are totally ignored by Flash. For this reason they are a useful way to comment the grammar itself but it's a good idea to remove these before finishing your project as they are sent to the Flash client and do take up bandwidth. The syntax looks like this:

```
<!-- This is a comment -->
```

Well-formed XML

In order for an XML document to be understood by the Flash client it must be well-formed. Saying that XML is well-formed is simply another way of saying that it is syntactically correct. There are some strict grammatical rules for creating XML, some of which are implicit in what we have just discussed, and others which are not.

First, all XML documents must have a **root element**. Essentially, the whole document must be contained inside a single element known as the **root node**. So, this example below is OK:

```
<?xml version='1.0'?>
<!-- members of The Beatles -->
<Beatles>
     <member>Lennon</member>
     <member>Ringo</member>
     <member>McCartney</member>
     <member>Harrison</member>
</Beatles>
```

However, this example is invalid because the <member> </member> tags need to be contained within a parent node:

```
<?xml version='1.0'?>
<!-- members of The Beatles -->
<member>Lennon</member>
<member>Ringo</member>
<member>McCartney</member>
<member>Harrison</member>
```

Error message

If you try to load an XML file in your browser that is not well-formed, it will tell you that the XML cannot be displayed along with the reason why. For example, if we were to open the invalid XML from above in our browser, we would get this output:

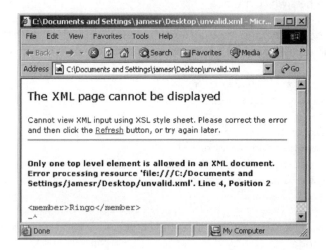

You'll receive a message that the **XML page cannot be displayed**, including a reason for your error. Flash cannot parse XML that is not well-formed, so be careful when creating your XML.

Nesting

When elements are sitting inside of other elements, it is known as nesting. If a start tag appears before another start tag is closed it is referred to as the child node of that node, and must close before its parent. In HTML it is OK to disobey this rule, making this example OK:

```
<b>
    some bold text
    <i>
        some bold italic text
</b>
    some italic text
    </i>
```

However, to reproduce this in XML we would need to write:

```
<b>
    some bold text
    <i>
        some bold italic text
```

```
        </i>
    </b>
    <i>
        some italic text
    </i>
```

Another place where HTML often fails the well-formed XML test is with tags that open and never close:

```
A statement like this<br> would be confusing<br> to an XML parser<br>
```

In XML, the `<br>` tags signify the beginning of a node that contains other nodes. An empty node tag must have a slash before the end bracket: `<br/>`. So the example below is fine:

```
This<br>would be a fine substitute</br>
```

This difference makes it much easier for a parser to make sense of a document. It can attach every childless node and text node that it finds to the current node. When it finds the start tag for a node with children, it starts attaching child nodes to that node. It attaches every node that it finds to the node with children until it finds that node's end tag.

White space

You may have noticed that we put most nodes on their own lines and then indent when nesting occurs. We call these spaces and line breaks **white space**. White space is often used to increase the readability of a file but not intended to affect its behavior. Although, strictly speaking, it is a text node, it is often useful to ignore it. The Flash parser provides the `ignoreWhite` flag which, when set to `true`, causes any extra spaces and line breaks to be ignored.

Naming

Node names must begin with a letter or an underscore, and be made up of letters, numbers, underscores, dashes, and periods, but *not spaces*. Also it *cannot* begin with XML.

```
<thisTagIsFine> <_this_one_is_2> <2Many re@$ons why this one fails/>
<xml wouldn't underst@nd th$s either>
```

You should also note that XML is case-sensitive. So, if you open a tag named `<Tag>`, it will not close with `</tag>` or `</TAG>`, as these are entirely different element names as far as XML is concerned. This would therefore mean that your XML would be incorrectly nested.

As you can see, there are very few rules. Hopefully you've got the impression that the rules that do exist are there to keep things simple.

Styling XML content

Now we know a little bit about XML, its purpose and how to construct a basic XML document. Let's now go one stage further and apply some style to our XML, but it would be pretty useful to know how to apply some sort of style to it.

Default style sheet

Remember back in Chapter 5 when we created the `pictures.xml` file and opened it in our browser?

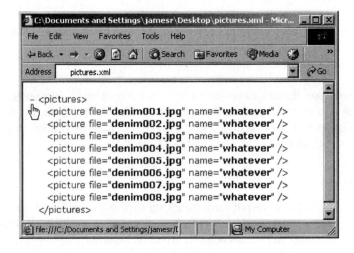

When we opened the document, we didn't specify any particular style for how we wanted the information to be displayed, so the XML parser that's used with the browser used a default style sheet to 'pretty print' the XML document as a hierarchical tree view.

If we wanted to give the document a style of our own choice, we need to create an external **style sheet** and reference the style sheet inside the XML document that we want the style(s) applied to.

Attaching style sheets to XML documents

No doubt you're familiar with **Cascading Style Sheets** if you've used HTML to any extent. With HTML, we can place our Cascading Style Sheet information inside the `<style>` `</style>` tags, like this:

```
<html>
    <head>
```

```
        <style>
            div {background-color:white;color:darkblue;};
        </style>
    </head>
    <div>Some Text</div>
</html>
```

In a browser, the above HTML will simply give you 'Some Text' in a dark blue font, on a white background.

In XML, we must create a separate document for our style preferences, and then reference the separate document inside the XML file. So, let's use the XML that we just used to describe the Beatles.

1. Type the following XML into a text file and save it as `beatles.xml`:

```
<?xml version='1.0'?>
<!-- members of The Beatles -->
<Beatles>
    <member>Lennon</member>
    <member>Ringo</member>
    <member>McCartney</member>
    <member>Harrison</member>
</Beatles>
```

2. We'll now create our style sheet – type the following into a text file and save it as `1a.css` in the same directory as the XML file.

```
member { display: block;}
```

So, we now have the document we want our styles applied to, as well as the separate document containing our style preference. The final thing to do is reference the CSS file inside the XML.

3. To associate an XML document with a CSS document, we simply add a processing instruction to the XML document in the form:

```
<?xml-stylesheet type="text/css" href="1a.css" ?>
```

This should be added immediately after the XML declaration or `<!DOCTYTPE>` declaration. So, using the style sheet we just created, our declaration would look like this:

```
<?xml version='1.0'?>
<?xml-stylesheet type="text/css" href="1a.css" ?>
```

Add the highlighted line of code to your `beatles.xml` file and save it as `beatlesWithStyle.xml`. When you open the file in your browser, rather than using the default style sheet, you'll see an output like this:

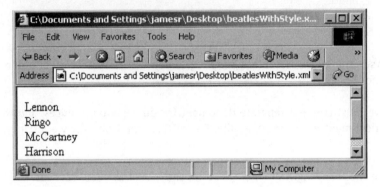

We can enhance the style of our XML document by adding preferences to our style sheet. For instance, type the following code into a text file and save it as `1b.css` in the same directory as your XML file:

```
member
{
    display: block;
    background-color: green;
    color: yellow;
    font-family: Arial;
    font-style: italic;
    text-align: right;
    font-size: large;}
```

You need to change your XML stylesheet declaration to read:

```
<?xml-stylesheet type="text/css" href="1b.css" ?>
```

Note that we're now referencing `1b.css` with the new style preferences rather than `1a.css`. Your result will now look like the screenshot on the following page.

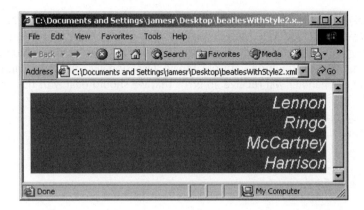

In terms of style, this is a decent improvement from where we started with the default style sheet view. At least there is now a division of information – an important requirement, especially when working with more complex XML documents and structures. The more style and division of information you need, the more complex your style sheet will be.

Valid XML

This isn't something that you should have to worry too much about. Essentially there are ways to set further rules for your XML beyond the syntactical so that you can define exactly which tags are expected to appear in your XML documents. For instance, if you had a system in which your XML described the components of a car, you might set a rule that meant `<seat/>` elements must always be within a `<car>` node. At the same time, you might want the car file to be invalid if it contains any tags from our orange file. XML Schemas and, previously, DTDs (Document Type Definitions) are the technologies used to execute XML validation. They validate whether the XML you create is not only well formed, but also valid and makes sense in the context in which it is used. XML validation is a complex technique and way beyond the scope of this chapter, so let's now get back to looking at how we can use XML with Flash.

Accessing XML from Flash

After you've made your XML file you'll probably want to use it in your Flash movie. The first thing you have to do is create an object to hold and access it. Nine times out of ten you'll probably want to tell the parser to ignore any white space that you might have put in your file:

```
//create the object
var myXML = new XML();

//ignore white space
myXML.ignoreWhite = true;
```

As it may take a while to load the XML file, Flash lets us overwrite an event handler, which allows us to know when our XML file has completed loading. Very often it makes sense for our movie to do nothing while the file loads. It is likely that the way we handle its completion is to go to another frame and continue on with our movie. Occasionally something will be wrong with our XML file and the handler will receive an error that we should deal with (it's good form):

```
myXML.ignoreWhite = true;
myXML.onLoad = function(success) {
    if (success) {
        gotoAndPlay("someFrame");
    } else {
        trace("failure loading xml file");
    }
};
```

The last step in getting our XML file into our Flash movie is to actually load it. We save this until last because we want the object to know how to handle the file before it actually asks for it:

```
//load the file
myXML.load("someFile.xml");
```

When we have all of our information it's likely that we will want to access it. From any node in an XML object, the following ten properties can access every piece of information in the document:

- childNodes is used to find the array of nested nodes.

- attributes points to an object that holds the properties of a node.

- nextSibling is used to find the next node in the array.

- previousSibling is used to find the previous node in the array.

- parentNode is used to move up the hierarchy.

- lastChild points to the last node in the array of childNodes.

- firstChild points to the first node in the array of childNodes.

- nodeName tells us the name of the node such as 'message' or 'NAVIGATION'.

- nodeType tells us whether the node is a markup element or text.

- nodeValue tells us what the text is in the case of a text element.

It's important to know where you are starting. The XML object actually represents the whole document, which means that the root node of any file that you write will actually be represented as a child of the XML object. Because an XML document must have one and only one root node it is fairly easy to find it. The following three statements evaluate to the root node of the XML object myXML:

```
var rootNode = myXML.firstChild;
var rootNode = myXML.lastChild;
var rootNode = myXML.childNodes[0];
```

Something to remember while you are traversing the XML object is that it's not necessary to do it all at once. Though it is certainly possible to write one line of code to find any piece of data in the object, it is not always a good idea. As you become more comfortable with the XML object, denser statements will become easier to understand. However, as a beginner it will be much less frustrating if you try to keep it as simple as possible:

```
//this line of code is difficult to understand
someTextField = myXML.firstNode.childNodes[i].firstChild.nodeValue;

//while these are clearer
var rootNode = myXML.firstNode;
var messageArray = rootNode.childNodes;
var messageNode = messageArray [i];
var textNode = messageNode.firstChild;
someTextField = textNode.nodeValue;
```

Updateable marquee revisited

One of the nice features of XML is that it is readable. You might remember the following line from the first time you made an updateable marquee way back in Chapter 15 (this is from message3.txt in the CD's chapter 15 folder):

```
message1=Sales+hit+3+million&message2=New+product+launch+delayed&
➡message3=New+positions+available&message4=Finance+Director+retires&
➡message5=New+catalogue+out+next+month
```

We are going to take the same marquee and modify it. Instead of receiving its data from message3.txt, it will come from message3.xml, which will look like this:

```
<messagelist>
    <message> Sales hit 3 million </message>
    <message> New product launch delayed </message>
    <message> New positions available </message>
```

```
            <message> Finance Director retires </message>
            <message> New catalogue out next month </message>
        </messagelist>
```

This is so much prettier, and so much easier to organize.

1. Open the `dynamicText4.fla` file that we used in Chapter 15 and resave it as `marquee_revisited.fla`. Open up the actions on frame 1 of the main timeline and edit the `messageURL` to point to `message3.xml` (all of these files are in this chapter's folder on the CD):

    ```
    // the location of our XML file
    var messageURL = "message3.xml";
    ```

2. Change the `counter` to begin at 0. This is because we are going to be using an array and the first element of an array is number 0.

    ```
    // the index of the message node that we will display
    var counter = 0;
    ```

3. Change `myVars_obj` from a `loadVars` object to an XML object:

    ```
    // the Flash representation of our XML document
    var myVars_obj = new XML();
    ```

4. Next, add a line telling the XML parser to ignore any white space:

    ```
    //ignore the spaces we added to make the file human-readable
    myVars_obj.ignoreWhite = true;
    ```

5. Leave the rest of the existing code on the first frame as it is. It should still look like this:

    ```
    myVars_obj.onLoad = function() {
        gotoAndPlay("offScreen");
    };

    myVars_obj.load(messageURL);
    stop();
    ```

6. Now go to frame 2 of the **actions** layer and delete all the existing code. First, create a variable to hold the root node of our document and then create another variable to hold the children nodes of the root:

    ```
    //the root node is the messagelist node. It will be the first
    ➥//(and only) node in the XML document
    ```

```
var rootNode = myVars_obj.firstChild;

//the nodes that we are interested in are the children of the root
➥//node. This is the array that holds all the message nodes.
var messageArray = rootNode.childNodes;
```

7. Add the following code to make sure that counter has the number of one of our message nodes. If the counter has gone too far, then set it back to 0.

```
//if we've gone through all of our messages then start over
if (counter>=messageArray.length) {
        counter = 0;
}
```

8. Create a variable to hold the message node itself:

```
//get the current message node from the array of message nodes
var messageNode = messageArray[counter];
```

9. Recall that any bit of text that isn't an element node in our XML document is a text node. Use the following code to get the text node from inside the message node:

```
//get the text node in the current message node
var textNode = messageNode.firstChild;
```

10. Here's the last piece of code. Set the message to the text inside the text node:

```
//set the marquee to the value of the text node in the current
//message node.
message = textNode.nodeValue;
```

11. Finally, make sure that message3.xml (included on the CD) is in the same directory on your hard drive as this marquee_revisited.fla and test the movie.

There are no other changes necessary. This should work exactly the same as the previous marquee example in Chapter 15, with the dynamic text sliding in from the right-hand side of the screen. The difference here though is obviously the source information we have used.

We're now going to move on and tackle something a little more complicated, using some PHP to help us this time.

Dynamic XML driven content

Many of us spend a lot of time organizing our web sites. Normally we have a pretty good idea of how our navigation should work, but how we organize our categories and how we view them are often in the same piece of content, which can make maintenance a nightmare. By separating the organization from presentation, we can easily change the way our information is accessed. We can do this without going back into and modifying our Flash client (or Flash clients).

Here's an example of what a simple organization might look like:

```
<? xml version='1.0' encoding='ISO-8859-1' ?>
<NAVIGATION>
    <FILE name='contents' extension='php'/>
    <FILE name='browser' extension='swf'/>
    <FILE name='browser' extension='fla'/>
    <FILE name='index' extension='php'/>

    <CATEGORY name='resume'>
    <FILE name='resume' extension='html'/>
    </CATEGORY>

    <CATEGORY name='portfolio'>

    <CATEGORY name='studentWork'>
        <FILE name='caffeine' extension='swf'/>
        <FILE name='lust' extension='swf'/>
        <FILE name='lust2' extension='jpg'/>
        <FILE name='duchamp' extension='swf'/>
        <FILE name='beer' extension='swf'/>
        <FILE name='korea' extension='jpg'/>
        <FILE name='malevich' extension='swf'/>
    </CATEGORY >

    <CATEGORY name='professionalWork'>

        <CATEGORY name='webWork'>
        <FILE name='rhino' extension='swf'/>
        <FILE name='tokyo' extension='swf'/>
        </CATEGORY >

        <CATEGORY name='printWork'>
        <FILE name='tecn' extension='jpg'/>
        <FILE name='vao' extension='jpg'/>
        </CATEGORY >
```

```
          </CATEGORY >

          </CATEGORY >
     </NAVIGATION >
```

There is a **resume** category with a resume document in it and there is a **portfolio** category, which is broken into two sub-categories: **studentWork** and **professionalWork**. It's easy to imagine that this navigation would extend to cover almost any organizational structure. In this case, it describes a set of folders and files like this:

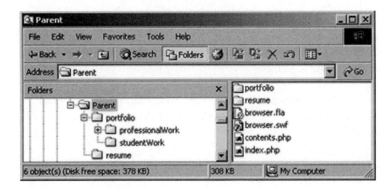

Creating a browser in Flash with PHP and XML

The really great thing about this XML document is that it can be generated automatically with a PHP script running on the server. The PHP will look at the contents of your directory and based on your files and directories, it will generate a representative XML document. Flash will ask the server for a PHP file but instead of getting a whole bunch of code, it will get a document that the code created. All you have to do is copy a new file into a category (directory) and the script serves up an updated navigation. Add an **experiments** directory with all your questionable projects and the next time you ask for the navigation structure it's represented. The server does all the work of updating your web site.

In order to make your PHP scripts work you are going to need access to a server that can run PHP. If you don't have an online server available you can set up your own machine as a server, getting everything you need from **www.apache.org** and **www.php.net**. You can still write fake PHP script by writing a text file that contains the XML document. You can just copy the simple organization XML from the start of this section into a file named `contents.php` (this file is also on the CD).

1. Open up a text editor to start setting up our PHP. Let's start by looking at the PHP script that creates the navigation document:

```php
<?php
     //tell our client that it's receiving XML
     header("Content-Type: text/xml");

     //tell the parser that it is receiving XML. This lets us
   ➥//look at it in an Explorer window
     echo "<?xml version=\"1.0\" encoding=\"ISO-8859-1\" ?> ";

     //get the time on the server
     $time = time();
     //print the starting tag for our root node
     echo "<NAVIGATION>";

     //"." Represents the current directory on servers
     //this function will print everything inside our root node
     printFileStructure(".");

     //print the ending tag of our root node
     echo "</NAVIGATION>";
```

In the first part of our script we've told the client that it's receiving XML and we've told the parser what kind of XML. Then we printed a NAVIGATION node with the file structure of the current directory (".") in it.

2. Next we add the function responsible for writing the representative XML. If we can open the directory represented by the $inDir path, then write it before going through each element (directory or file) in the current directory:

```php
function printFileStructure($inDir)
{
     //if we are able to open the directory at the specified
     //path then we will write its contents
     if ($currentDirectory = opendir($inDir))
     {
          //go through each file and sub-directory in the
          //directory
          while ($dirElement = readdir($currentDirectory))
          {
```

3.   We then need to determine the path to the current directory element, and if the current element is a file, then write a FILE node:

```
//build the path to each contained element by adding
➡//a slash followed by its name to the end of the path

$pathToElement = $inDir . "/" . $dirElement;

//deal with files differently from the directories
if (is_file($pathToElement))
{
```

4.   Separate the file name from the file extension:

```
//determine the position of the dot in the file name
$dotposition = strpos($dirElement, ".");

//the characters before the dot are the file name
$filename = substr($dirElement, 0, $dotposition);

//the characters after the dot are the extension
$extension = substr($dirElement, 1 + $dotposition);
```

5.   Then we need to write the actual node, including the file information:

```
    echo "<FILE name=\"$filename\" extension=\"$extension\" />";
}
```

6.   We make sure the directory isn't the one that we are already in ("."),or the one that we just came from (".."), then we print the starting tag for our category node:

```
    else if($dirElement != "." && $dirElement != "..")
    {

    //open a CATEGORY node to store any sub-CATEGORY
    //nodes and file nodes in
        echo "<CATEGORY name=\"$dirElement\">";

        //call the funtion we wrote to fill in all the
        //subdirectories
        printFileStructure($pathToElement);

        //close the CATEGORY node
        echo "</CATEGORY>";
    }
```

continues overleaf

```
        }

    closedir($currentDirectory);
        }
    }
    php?>
```

All the function does is go through each file in the directory and then writes some useful information about each file to a node. When it comes across a directory, it calls a function to handle it. It recursively calls itself as it digs through the directories giving us an automatically valid listing of our current directory and every directory inside of it.

Now we can write our Flash browser (`browser.fla` on the CD).

7.   Start a new movie and save it as `browser.fla`. Begin by adding the following three things to the stage: two ListBox components and a dynamic text field. We'll give one ListBox the instance name `directories` and the other one `files`. Also, set the text field to display the variable `path` (so you need to give the text field this variable name in the Property inspector). We'll use directories to display a collapsible hierarchical view of the directory structure that we are browsing. The `files` ListBox will list the files located in the directory that is selected in the `directories` ListBox. The `path` text field will display the path from the root directory to the directory that is selected in the `directories` ListBox, just like Windows Explorer.

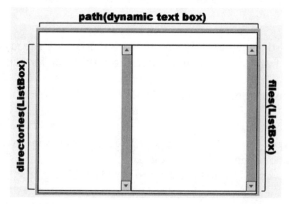

8.   Now we'll move on to the code. The first thing we do is set up our XML object. We create the object, tell it to ignore white space, and what to do when it has loaded an XML document by defining a function. The function adds an entry to our `directories` ListBox

that represents the root of our document. It then tells directories that the new entry is selected. Add this to frame 1 of the default layer:

```
//create new XML object
var fileStructDoc = new XML();
//tell our XML object to ignore any whitespace
fileStructDoc.ignoreWhite = true;

//write a handler to deal with our XML document once we get it
fileStructDoc.onLoad = function( success) {
    if( success) {
        //store the root of the XML document
        var docRoot = fileStructDoc.firstChild;

        //add an entry to our directory list representing the root
        directories.addItem('root', docRoot);

        //tell directories to select the root entry
        directories.setSelectedIndex(0);
    } else {

        //handle failure
        trace('failure: fileStructDoc.onLoad');
    }
};
```

9. We have a little bit of initializing to do for our directories ListBox before we can expect it to behave:

```
//set up a function to handle user input when it happens
directories.setChangeHandler('handleDirectoriesSelection');
function handleDirectoriesSelection(component) {
    var item = component.getSelectedItem().data;
    var index = component.getSelectedIndex();

    //close open directories, open closed directories
    toggleDirectory(item, index);

    //display files from selected directory in 'files' ListBox
    displayFiles(item);

    //update the path of our new directory
    updatePath(item);
}
```

10. We tell `fileStructDoc` to load `contents.php`. The `onLoad` script that we've just written will get called after it's loaded:

```
fileStructDoc.load('contents.php');
```

11. We add the functionality to both open closed directories and close those that are already open in order to handle user interaction:

```
function toggleDirectory(item, index) {
    //isOpen is an attribute that we add when we open a
➥//directory. It will be null to start
    if (item.attributes.isOpen == 'true') {

        //user must click twice in order to close a directory
        if (lastDirectorySelected == item) {
            closeDirectory(item, index);
        }
    } else {
        openDirectory(item, index);
    }

    //keep track of user's last selection
    lastDirectorySelected = item;
}
```

12. Next add the functionality that will handle opening the directories with the `openDirectory` function:

```
function openDirectory(item, index) {
    item.attributes.isOpen = 'true';
    for (var i = 0; i<item.childNodes.length; i++) {
        var node = item.childNodes[i];
        var name = node.attributes.name;
```

13. Now we add category nodes to the `directories` ListBox, indenting the label based on how deep in the structure it is. The `for` loop in the function starts at the level of the node from the `item.childNodes` array. It then goes to its parent node, then the parent node of that node. It continues up until it finds the root node that will be named NAVIGATION. On each iteration it indents the entry that will be added: the deeper the node, the more indented the entry.

```
if (node.nodeName == 'CATEGORY') {
    //go up until we find the root
    for (var tempNode = item.childNodes[i];tempNode.nodeName !=
➥'NAVIGATION'; tempNode = tempNode.parentNode) {
        //indent the entry
```

```
            name = ' ' + name;
        }
```

14. Here we place our node in the next position in the directories ListBox:

```
                index++;
                directories.addItemAt(index, name, node);
            }
        }
    }
```

15. Surprisingly enough we now add the code for closing the directories to the `closeDirectory` function:

```
function closeDirectory(item, index) {
    item.attributes.isOpen = 'false';
```

16. First, go through each item that is a subcategory of the one being closed:

```
        for(var i = 0; item == item.childNodes[i].parentNode; i++) {
            var node = item.childNodes[i];
            var name = node.attributes.name;
```

17. Then, remove any subcategories before removing the category by recursively calling `closeDirectory`:

```
            if(node.attributes.isOpen == 'true') {
                closeDirectory( node, index + 1)
            }
            directories.removeItemAt(index + 1);
        }
    }
```

18. We now do our bit of initializing to our `files` ListBox in a function to handle user input when it occurs:

```
files.setChangeHandler('handleFilesSelection');
function handleFilesSelection(component) {
    var item = component.getSelectedItem().data;
    updatePath(item.parentNode);
    var name = item.attributes.name;
    var extension = item.attributes.extension;
    url = path + name + '.' + extension;
    getURL(url, '_blank');
```

```
    }
```

We could handle the files in any way. We could load JPGs and SWFs into the current movie, or load XML documents into another XML object and handle those but, for simplicity, we are loading all files into a new browser window.

19. We need to write a function to handle the adding of any files that might exist in a given category:

```
function displayFiles(item) {
```

20. Start with a clean slate...

```
    files.removeAll();
```

...go through any of the nodes we've received...

```
    for( var i = 0; i < item.childNodes.length; i++) {
        var node = item.childNodes[i];
        var name = node.attributes.name;
        var extension = node.attributes.extension;
```

...and add it to the `files` ListBox if it's a file:

```
        if (node.nodeName == 'FILE') {
            files.addItem(name + '.' + extension, node);
        }
    }
}
```

21. Finally, we need a function to keep track of the path of the selected directory from the directory we are currently in. The `for` loop in the function acts in the same manner as the indenting code we've already added in step 13. It starts at the level of the selected node, and then goes up until it finds the root node. With each node that it comes across, it builds the path from the root to the selected element.

```
function updatePath(selectedNode) {
    //first clear the path
    path = '';

    //go up until we find the root
    for (var tempNode = selectedNode; tempNode.nodeName !=
    ➡'NAVIGATION'; tempNode = tempNode.parentNode) {
//prepend the parent root name and a slash to the front
        ➡//of the path
```

```
        path = tempNode.attributes.name + '/' + path;
    }
}
```

We're done! Your Flash movie should look something like this:

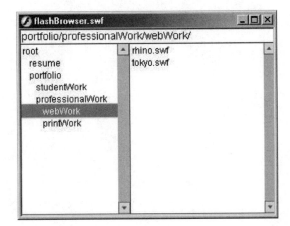

Of course, your movie will display the contents of your computer's folders instead. Just remember to run it from your server and not just play the Flash movie so that the PHP will work. You can obviously tidy this up and tailor it to your specific needs. After you do this though, you'll never have to touch it again. The only things you'll ever need to do to maintain this content is to add or remove a directory and add or remove a file.

Summary

Assuming that you didn't get lost in the code, you may be scratching your head thinking 'That's it?' Well, that is it. That's the whole point. It's a set of half a dozen or so rules applied to any markup language that you feel like inventing. Its simplicity is its greatest strength, making it extremely flexible. The most important thing XML does is separate the different content from the design. The more content you have, the more maintainability becomes an issue and by separating your application into sensible parts (such as presentation, logic, and information), you guarantee a maximum level of maintainability and scalability.

section 4: Dynamic Data Integration

chapter 18: **Flash, ColdFusion and Remoting**

ColdFusion is another server-side scripting language serving a similar purpose to that of PHP.

> *If you've skipped* Chapter 16 *then you should certainly take a look at the section headed 'Two servers of Verona' to get an idea of what server-side scripting does.*

There are in fact a fair number of server-side languages around including: ASP, ASP.Net, Java Server Pages and Perl, but we've chosen to cover PHP and ColdFusion in this book. PHP was included because of its popularity, excellent performance, and well, the fact that it's free. ColdFusion on the other hand is not free at all. In fact, at the time of writing, the Enterprise version of ColdFusion will set you back $4999.00. Although you can get the professional version for $799.00, it's still a big jump from nothing, so I suppose we must have a good reason.

ColdFusion (CF) is Macromedia's solution for the application server market. Developing applications with CF provides the developer with several benefits. It provides for a rapid application development (RAD) environment, which allows the developer to easily develop and deploy web applications. The reason for this is that CF uses a tag based markup language similar to HTML. It can be argued that whatever is lost with the purchase of a CF license can be gained in terms of development time. Applications built using CF usually take much less time, which ultimately saves the developer (or company) money. CF is very easy to learn and it doesn't take long to start taking advantage of all the power and functionality that it offers. Therefore, CF applications can usually be developed faster than their ASP and PHP counterparts.

Macromedia ColdFusion MX now ships with the Flash Remoting components that serve as a layer of communications between Flash MX and the server. The Remoting components are not currently available for PHP, which means that some of the older methods will need to be utilized.

Getting started with ColdFusion

A trial version of ColdFusion MX can be downloaded from the Macromedia web site at **www.macromedia.com/software/trial_download**. The trial will expire after 30 days and revert to single IP mode, which means that the CF server will be accessible from a single IP address allowing the developer to test their applications. CF MX can be installed on servers running Unix, Linux, and Windows. It also integrates very well with both IIS and Apache web servers. CF MX now has a stand alone web server that can be used for development and testing purposes. When taking applications to a production environment it is recommended to use one of the web servers mentioned above. CF is relatively a breeze to set up and it won't take long before you're ready to start coding your own applications.

> *Note that if you are using the trial version of ColdFusion MX for the purposes of this chapter, you need to reboot your machine after installation before you can actually open the CF Administrator and begin to work.*

To begin coding your CF applications you can use a simple text editor that ships with many different operating systems. Just make sure to save your files with the CFC extension for CF templates and CFC for CF components. CFCs will be introduced later in the chapter when we cover the application itself. There are several Integrated Development Environments (IDEs) available such as Macromedia's ColdFusion Studio and Dreamweaver MX. These programs make developing CF applications much easier by providing code hints and help files that explain what different CF tags do. Let's take a brief look at the CF syntax and what it can do here.

The basics

Writing CF code is really no more complicated than writing HTML once you've got the basics down. The following example will introduce you to some CF tags and their syntax (the application at the end of the chapter will go into further detail). It's just a matter of learning the tags and their attributes and away you go into the world of building robust web applications. For starters we'll take a quick look at some basic CF tags and explain what they do. While we don't have enough time to cover all the tags, we'll get started with some of the most important ones so feel free to expand on what you learn here. There are many great CF books on the market and I would highly recommend taking a look at a couple of them if you're interested in broadening your CF skills.

First, we'll look at setting and outputting variables to the page. Variables are an important piece of programming and can be used to store integers, strings, arrays, and structures. To set a variable in ColdFusion we use the `<cfset>` tag:

```
<cfset variables.subject = "Flash Remoting">
```

We have created a variable named `subject` that contains the value `"Flash Remoting"`. Now that we've set the variable, we can call it using the `<cfoutput>` tags. These tags tell CF to interpret anything enclosed within # signs as variables.

```
<cfoutput>#variables.subject#</cfoutput>
```

This will output the value of the `subject` variable to the page. CF has many different variable scopes available, some of which include:

- variables (local)
- form
- URL
- client
- cookie
- session

It's good practice to scope your variables, as this will enable your applications to run faster and make debugging easier. If a scope is not provided, CF will have to look through all of the available scopes to see that the variable exists. Also, when debugging your applications it's good to know that the variable comes from a form or URL, instead of looking in the template for the variable.

Let's take a look at a simple template that demonstrates setting and outputting a variable to the page. You can create the file in a simple text editor, but be sure to save it with a CFM extension. We'll call it `welcome.cfm`.

```
<html>
<head>
<title>CF Example</title>
</head>
<body>

<!--- set the variable --->
<cfset subject="Flash Remoting">

<!--- output the variable --->
<cfoutput>
```

```
Welcome to the world of #variables.subject#
</cfoutput>

</body>
</html>
```

> Note: CF variables are not case sensitive as in most programming languages. For example, CF interprets "subject" exactly the same as "Subject".

Now you just need to browse to your local web server running CF and access this page, i.e. **http://localhost/examples/welcome.cfm**. You should see 'Welcome to the world of Flash Remoting' displayed on the page but first, just a quick note about the comments in the code above. As you already know, HTML comments look like `<!-- my comment here -->`. These can still be used within CF templates, but CF comments are sometimes preferred. These take the syntax of `<!--- my CF comment here --->` (note the use of three hyphens instead of two). The advantage of using CF comments is that they will not be visible on the page if the user decides to **View Source**. They are only accessible on the server-side when looking through the code. A very handy feature indeed!

With any programming language, there needs to be the ability to make decisions based on some sort of logic. This is where the `<cfif>` tag becomes useful. This tag enables developers to handle specific tasks such as a situation where the user makes a certain selection or certain results are expected:

```
<cfset variables.product = "ColdFusion">

<cfif variables.product eq "Flash">
Macromedia Flash was chosen.
<cfelseif variables.product eq "ColdFusion">
Macromedia ColdFusion was chosen.
<cfelse>
No selection was made.
</cfif>
```

If you were to create a template and access it through your browser you would get the result: 'Macromedia ColdFusion was chosen'. You can see if you play around with the product variable that different results can be generated.

There are many, tags and functions within the ColdFusion development environment. If you can think of something that needs to be done, there is probably a CF tag or function that will do it. If not, you can definitely write your own to handle the job. The following example should be relatively simple to understand with a basic knowledge of the CF syntax.

Message of the day using ColdFusion

We'll briefly review the 'Message of the Day' exercise that we made in Chapter 16, but this time it'll be converted to ColdFusion format. Most aspects of the Flash file will stay the same except for the reference to update.php will be changed to update.cfm. Therefore the onRelease method for the save button will look like this:

```
save_btn.onRelease = function() {
     dataLoader.message = _root.message_txt.text;
     dataLoader.photofile = _root.image_txt.text;
     dataLoader.onLoad = checkSuccess;
     dataLoader.sendAndLoad("update.cfm", dataLoader, "POST");
};
```

So, the actual Flash movie will function the same and the changes will be invisible to the user. The server-side logic is the part that will change since we'll be sending the variables to CF, in our case update.cfm. Let's take a look at the necessary CF code that will take the form variables passed from Flash and save them to a text file on the server.

```
<cfsetting enablecfoutputonly="yes">
```

The <cfsetting> tag is used to tell CF not to print anything on the page except for anything included within the <cfoutput> tags. This will prevent any extra spaces and line feeds from showing up on the page. Flash tends to be picky about white space, so it's good practice to remove it.

```
<cfset path="c:\inetpub\wwwroot\">
<cfset datafile="message2a.txt">
```

These variables simple set the directory path on the server as well as the name of the file we'll be creating. Be sure to update the path reference to wherever you'll be placing these files on your server.

```
<cfparam name="form.message" default="">
<cfparam name="form.photofile" default="">

<cfset data = "&message=" & urlencodedformat(form.message)>
<cfset data = data & "&photofile=" &
urlencodedformat(form.photofile)>
```

Next we set some default values for the form fields in case they don't get passed to the page. This isn't necessary for the application to work, but it helps in preventing any errors from being thrown if the page is accessed directly through the web browser. The `data` variable is used to store the variables from Flash, which are encoded using the `urlencodedformat` function. It's good to note that there are many CF functions available to the developer. These functions can be found in the CF documentation included during the install, assuming a default installation.

```
<cffile action="write" file="#path#message2a.txt" output="#data#">
```

Once we've built our data variable from the information passed from Flash, we can write a file on the server and store this information in it. `<cffile>` is an extremely powerful CF tag that allows developers to read, write, update, and delete files on the fly. The file is stored in the directory we specified earlier and is named `message2a.txt`. Of course, the `data` variable is used to store the information from Flash in the text file.

```
<cfoutput>&result=Okay&</cfoutput>
```

Finally, we output the result to the page, which is then loaded into Flash. A status message is then displayed to the user letting them know that file was successfully saved. Once the file has been saved they can click the "load" button and load the information from `message2a.txt`.

Flash Remoting

Flash MX has taken a big leap forward in catering for Flash developers. The integration of Flash with application servers has become even tighter. Also, Macromedia have released an exciting new feature for integration: the Flash Remoting service. Flash Remoting allows developers to take advantage of passing complex data to and from the server (CF in our case). Now, recordsets and custom objects can be passed between Flash and CF with ease. Flash Remoting is not limited to just CF and is available for such platforms as JRUN, .NET, and J2EE application servers.

The Flash Remoting service has to be one of the most exciting new features for Flash developers who want to take advantage of dynamic content. It allows the developer to make direct calls to CF or any application server running the service. This is also a two-way communication process where data can be sent from Flash to the server. This provides a new and improved way of communicating with the server as opposed to older methods such as `getURL` and `loadVariables`. These older methods are by no means obsolete, but the preferred method for transferring complex information is via Flash Remoting. The process is very intuitive and provides a way to create reusable components on the server-side as well.

For example, let's say you want to build an authentication scheme that can be deployed in different situations. All you would need to do is build the necessary front-end components, and a back-end component that checks the database to see if the user is valid. These components could then be reused in future applications, without having to write them again from scratch.

The process of communication between Flash and the server is done via the **Flash gateway**, the server-side component of Flash Remoting. The Flash gateway passes data to and from the server and can handle complex data such as objects and recordsets. Recordsets can only be passed from the server to Flash, but are valuable in that they are well structured and help maximize bandwidth efficiency. The ability to send recordsets directly from CF to Flash minimizes any unnecessary data transmissions.

Flash Remoting transfers data between Flash and the server via the **Action Message Format** (AMF). AMF is transferred over HTTP and provides a more effective and efficient means of communication. This diagram demonstrates the communication process between Flash and the application server:

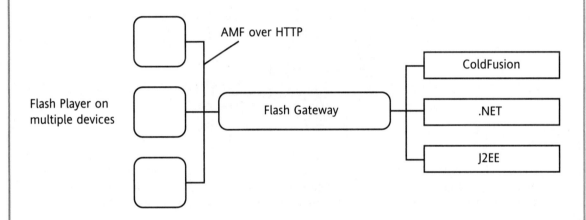

This communication process is performed with a new set of ActionScript classes that are installed with Flash Remoting. These classes include:

- **NetServices** serves as an abstract layer to **NetConnection** and provides a means of communication with the Flash gateway.

- **NetConnection** creates a two-way connection between Flash and remote services.

- **NetDebug** serves as a method to debug Flash applications and works in conjunction with the **NetConnect Debugger**.

- **RecordSet** handles recordset objects returned from the application server and provides different methods of accessing and manipulating recordset data.

- **DataGlue** provides a way of binding RecordSet objects to Flash UI components such as the ListBox component.

These classes contain many methods for accessing and manipulating data. The following figure displays the available methods for each of these classes:

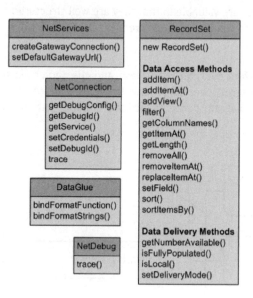

For detailed information on the methods of the Flash Remoting classes, be sure to view the ActionScript reference in Flash MX (**Window > Reference**). We'll take a closer look at the structure of the code when walking through the personal management application in the next section.

Setting yourself up for Remoting

You'll need the Flash Remoting components, as we'll be using them in the following application. They can be downloaded from **www.macromedia.com/software/flash/flashremoting**. Installing these components provides you with the necessary ActionScript classes and documentation to learn about the different classes and their methods. Once these are installed along with ColdFusion MX, you'll be ready to start developing the PMA application.

PMA contacts application

The purpose of this application is to provide a real world example that focuses on Flash/CF integration. This will be titled the PMA (Personal Management Application) and will serve as a way to manage contacts and their information through a web browser. We're not only limited to a web browser because the Flash movie could easily be packaged into a stand alone projector file. The PMA will demonstrate the power of Flash and ColdFusion MX by allowing users to maintain a database of contacts as well as specific information about them. This will be tied into a

Microsoft Access database for testing and demonstration purposes. Flash MX components will be used to enhance the user's experience while ColdFusion components (CFCs) will be leveraged on the server-side. This is a perfect example of how to utilize and integrate these exciting new technologies.

> *You should note however, that to use this database you'll need to work on a computer with Microsoft Access installed.*

The database

To build a fully functional application, users should have the ability to add new contacts along with the ability to update and delete existing contacts. Flash will serve as the user interface layer that displays the contact's information and allows the user to interact with the interface. Interaction may simply be selecting a contact from a ListBox or clicking a PushButton to perform a certain action. ColdFusion will handle the application logic that queries the database and handles the necessary server-side components.

The key to creating a dynamic web application is to make sure the data structure is in place. Take a moment to look at the `pma.mdb` database file that is included with the source files and open the **Contacts** table. This table will store contact information such as first name, last name, address, email, and so on. Here's the data structure for the contacts table:

id	first_name	last_name	email	address	city	state	zip	phone	notes
2	Mr	T	sucka@fool.com	111 pity da fool lane	san francisco	ca	32456	076-156-245	test
3	He	Man	adam@greyskull.co.dk	1 Castle Greyskull	Copenhagen	ga	29445	867-451-523	test
4	Micheal	Knight	knight@rider.org	785 Cheddarstrasse	Dresden	tx	75223	256-788-340	test
(AutoNumber)									

The **id** field will serve as the primary key for each contact record and will be used extensively when passing information between Flash and ColdFusion. The id will come in handy when making updates to the contacts or deleting a contact.

1.   Save the `pma.mdb` database on your hard drive.

2.   Before any communication can exist, a data source name (DSN) needs to be created in the ColdFusion Administrator. Open up the Administrator by pointing your browser to **http://localhost/cfide/administrator/index.cfm**.

3.   After logging into the CF Administrator, click on the **Data Sources** link (under **Data & Services**) and add your DSN, which is `pma`. Be sure to specify the **Microsoft Access** from

the **Driver** drop-down menu and then click on **Add**. In the following dialog, specify where the database file is located on the server:

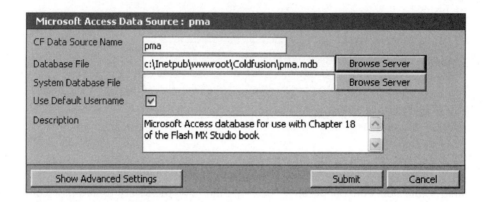

4. In this application we'll be referencing pma as the DSN using a template. Open up your preferred text editor and type in:

```
<cfset request.dsn = "pma">
```

5. Now name it Application.cfm and save it in a new folder called pma in your root directory.

You can change this folder name to something else if you prefer, but, if you do, make sure that the Application.cfm template is updated to reflect this folder name change. This template merely sets a request scoped variable called request.dsn, which is accessed through the CFCs. The purpose of setting this variable in Application.cfm is to provide a global variable that can be changed in one place without having to update the rest of the code in the application. All of the queries in the application reference this variable, which points to our pma.mdb database file.

If you intend to simply run the files provided on the CD rather than building them from scratch, make sure that you unzip the files contained in pma.zip into a sub-directory of your web root. For the PMA to run out-of-the-box, the files should be placed in a directory called pma directly beneath your web root. The directory structure can be changed, but the ActionScript code will need to be modified to point to the new location. We'll take a look into this shortly.

6. If you don't want to modify the ActionScript, then you should set up the PMA's directory structure like this:

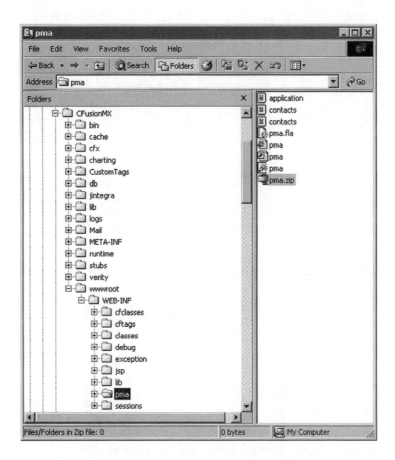

The components

The PMA consists mainly of components that either ship with Flash MX or can be downloaded from the Macromedia Exchange for Flash at **www.macromedia.com/exchange/flash**. We'll be using the PushButton, ListBox, and ScrollBar components that all ship with Flash MX, but we'll also be using the Calendar and MessageBox components from the Flash UI Components Set 2, so you'll need to grab this set from the Exchange.

All of these components provide increased functionality and prevent the developer from reinventing the wheel. This saves the developer many hours of work when developing applications. As we begin to look through the application, you'll become more familiar with these components and the code that is used to control them. Right, let's get started!

The Flash movie

1.   Start a new movie, save it as `pma.fla`, and set up your timeline like so:

2.   On the **background** layer draw up some nice sections to lay our components on, similar to this:

The small white box will hold the data window (a MessageBox component) containing a list of contacts. The calendar will go in the bottom left corner of the larger white section, and the right-hand side is reserved for the input controls and buttons.

3.   The **nav button** layer simply holds a link to the contacts application, which could be added to at some point in the future if we wanted to add more applications. In my version this is placed in the top left corner of the interface:

4. The **static text** layer should include all the static text and box graphics to map out the user interface, selected in the image below:

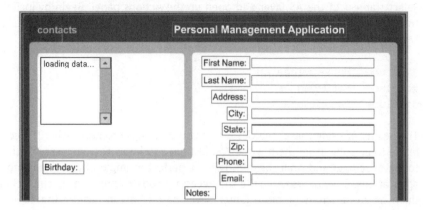

5. The **dynamic text** layer consists of a number of input text fields positioned on the right-hand side of the stage. These are single line input text boxes given the variable names `first_name`, `last_name`, `address`, `city`, `state`, `zip`, `phone`, and `email` respectively. Underneath the **Notes:** heading, add a multiple line input text field with the instance name `notes`.

6. Finally, we just need to add the components:

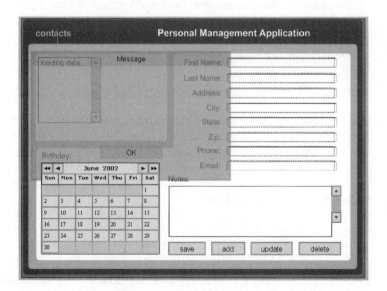

Now that's the graphical elements of the site set up, we'll move on to the code.

Initializing the application

1. Select frame 1 of the **AS** layer and open up the Actions panel. Begin by including the files that contain the Flash Remoting classes we discussed earlier. These are provided by Macromedia as part of the Flash Remoting install:

```
#include "NetServices.as"
#include "NetDebug.as"
#include "DataGlue.as"
```

The beauty of using these includes is that you don't have to know what the code looks like inside to actually make them work. You just need to know the necessary methods available to the developer and what they do. This is a perfect example of creating component-based applications. Developers can write the necessary code to perform specific actions and pass them on to designers or more junior developers who can include the code and call the necessary methods. I'm not promoting laziness by any means, but it does illustrate that code can be encapsulated into components where the implementation is separated from the interface, meaning that the inner workings don't need to be understood as long as the public methods can be accessed and the expected results returned.

> The `NetDebug.as` file is not necessary for this application to run correctly. It is mainly used with the NetConnect Debugger (**Window > NetConnection Debugger**) as an aid to the debugging process. Once the application is ready for production this line can be removed or commented out to conserve file size (though it isn't much).

Now that the necessary Flash Remoting classes have been included it's time to initialize the application. This is one of the most important parts of the process since the connection to the Flash gateway needs to be established before we can start communicating with the server. The following steps will go through the code required to initialize the PMA.

2. Start by adding the `inited` variable:

```
if (inited == null) {
    inited = true;
```

This is used simply to make sure that the code contained in the `if` statement is only run once. After the code has initially run, `inited` is set to `true`, and the code will not run again unless the browser is refreshed or the user leaves the PMA and comes back. This is good practice, and isn't a huge necessity in this application since there's only one frame, but it would be very useful in a movie that loops back to the first frame several times over since we wouldn't want the PMA to be initialized repeatedly.

3. Now we need to add a few lines of code to set the properties for some of the components on the stage:

```
// disable the save clip since it won't be accessible
// until the user decides to add a new contact
save_mc.setEnabled(false);

// set the size of the contacts ListBox
contacts_mc.setSize(200, 120);

// set the height of the scroller
notes_scroller_mc.setSize(79);
```

4. Here we need to handle the initial connection to the Flash gateway. The default gateway URL, for testing purposes, will run on `localhost`:

```
NetServices.setDefaultGatewayUrl("http://localhost/
➥flashservices/gateway");
```

Once the PMA is taken to a production environment this address will need to be changed to the domain name or IP address of the hosting server. The purpose of this security measure is to prevent external applications from making calls to services that exist on the local server. The `createGatewayConnection` method actually makes the connection to the gateway and waits for any services to be called. When the contacts service is called it is stored in an object, which will be referenced later when calling the service methods.

5. First create the gateway connection object, and then create the contacts service object which points to our contacts CFC:

```
var gw = NetServices.createGatewayConnection();
var contacts_service = gw.getService("pma.contacts", this);
```

The service name is a reference to the CFC being called. Therefore, `pma.contacts` corresponds with the `contacts.cfc` component stored in the `pma` directory (we'll make this component shortly). The `pma` directory resides directly beneath the web root and can be called this way. If the directory structure changes, then the service calls need to be changed to reflect this. For example, if your `pma` directory is stored under `\wwwroot\flashremoting\pma\contacts.cfc` your call to this service should be `flashremoting.pma.contacts`. This is similar to importing and referencing Java packages in the Java programming language. We simply replace \ with . (period).

6.   Finally, call the `getAllContacts` method of the CFC, which returns a recordset of all contacts from the database:

```
contacts_service.getAllContacts();
}
```

Getting contacts

Now that the service objects have been declared we can call different methods when necessary. As the application has been initialized we need to make our first call to `contacts_service.getAllContacts`. This statement is calling the `getAllContacts` method in the `contacts.cfc` component we're going to make, and is used to pull the list of contacts into Flash. Here's an overview of the communication process between Flash and ColdFusion:

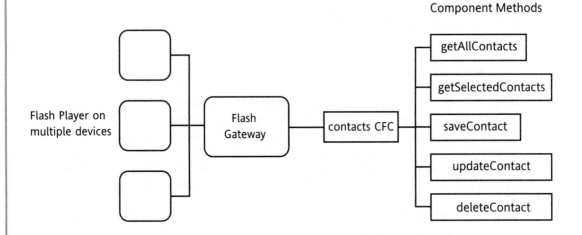

The `contacts.cfc` component will basically be a ColdFusion template with a new type of structure. Several methods reside in the component while the only one currently being accessed is `getAllContacts`.

1.   Open your text editor and save the file as `contacts.cfc`. Start by adding the following code:

```
<cfcomponent name="contacts">

<!--- retrieve all contacts to send to flash and populate
➥listbox --->
```

```
<cffunction name="getAllContacts" access="remote">
<cfquery datasource="#request.dsn#" name="get_all_contacts">
select id, first_name, last_name from contacts
order by last_name asc;
</cfquery>
<cfreturn get_all_contacts />
</cffunction>


<!--- you'll stick the other component methods here --->

</cfcomponent>
```

The CFC has a different structure than a typical CF template with the <cfcomponent> tag specifying the name of the component. As we add further functions they will reside within this tag.

Component methods are set with the <cffunction> tag and if results are being returned the <cfreturn> tag is used. In this case, we make a query to grab all first names, last names, and ids from the contacts table. This recordset is then returned to Flash via the <cfreturn> tag. The access attribute of the <cffunction> tag must be set to "remote" to allow access from the Flash gateway. If this attribute is not set, the method will not allow access to the application. For more information on access attributes, dig into the ColdFusion MX documentation.

So, Flash makes the service request, CF queries the database and returns the results. Now what? Every service call has a result method that handles data or performs an action when a response is received from CF. Since we initially called the getAllContacts service from Flash, the results are then sent to getAllContacts_Result. All response methods are labeled using the service name with _Result appended to it.

2. Back in the pma.fla movie, go back into the actions on frame 1 of the **AS** layer. We now need to add the getAllContacts_Result method to handle the results from CF, and populate the ListBox at the top left corner of the stage:

```
function getAllContacts_Result(records) {
    // place the recordset in the ListBox and format the display
    DataGlue.bindFormatStrings (contacts_mc, records,
    ➥"#last_name#, #first_name#", "#id#");
    // handle which record is selected in the ListBox
    if (contact_index == undefined) {
        contacts_mc.setSelectedIndex(0);
    } else {
        contacts_mc.setSelectedIndex(contact_index);
    }
}
```

The recordset is passed from CF, through the Flash gateway, and will be handled by the `result` method. Now we need to find a way to populate the ListBox component with this information. This is where the `DataGlue` class (which we included initially) comes in handy. It definitely simplifies the process by allowing us to specify which fields will be used for display in the ListBox while setting a value for each field. The `DataGlue.bindFormatStrings` method requires the following four parameters:

- The instance name of the ListBox, `contacts_mc` in our case.

- The recordset object passed from CF.

- The column names to display (surrounded by # signs).

- The data value for each record (surrounded by # signs).

When this method fires it will do the necessary data parsing and populate the ListBox with our desired results.

Adding user interaction

Up until this point there has been no user interaction. Well, this is all about to change. There are several options the user has and we're about to cover each of them. Also, the order of methods listed in the ActionScript code does not matter. These methods sit in `_level0` of the movie and simply wait to be called. The PMA is structured to allow the user to interact with it how they want and we'll take care of the logic meaning the user can delete an entry before adding a new one, or update an entry before adding a new one. However, they cannot delete an entry without first receiving a confirmation message asking them if they want to do so. The logic will be in place to prevent user error and provide a flexible environment.

Since the ListBox has been populated with contacts, we'll take it from here. When the PMA is initialized, the code sets the first entry in the ListBox to be selected. This is referred to as a change handler. A change handler method is called whenever the ListBox changes state. For our ListBox we've specified the change handler as `getSelectedContact`. We set the change handlers for various components in the Property inspector, but here's our ListBox as an example:

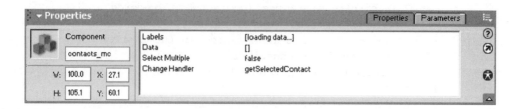

Selecting contacts

1. The `getSelectedContact` method is called each time a contact is selected from the ListBox. Add this next function to ask CF for the contact's information:

```
function getSelectedContact() {
    // if the save button is enabled go ahead and disable it
    if(save_mc.getEnabled()) {
        save_mc.setEnabled(false);
    }
```

   We check to see if the **save** button has been enabled and disable it if it has. This is just a fail safe to prevent the **save** confirmation box from popping up, which is what will happen when the button is clicked.

2. We now need to retrieve the unique id of the contact from the ListBox using the `getValue` method, and then pass it to the proper CFC method:

```
    // get the id of the selected contact
    var id = contacts_mc.getValue();
    // create an object and store the id to pass to CF
    var o = new Object();
    o.id = id;
    // set the contact index variable so we know where
    // to position the ListBox when it's refreshed after
    //updating
    contact_index = contacts_mc.getSelectedIndex();
    contacts_service.getSelectedContact(o);
}
```

3. For consistency's sake, we then call the CFC method `getSelectedContact` back in the `contacts.cfc` file. This method basically queries the contacts table and pulls the contact's info based on the id. The code is very straightforward and is listed below. This should be placed underneath the `getAllContacts` function we created earlier:

```
<!--- retrieve the selected contact and return it to flash --->
<cffunction name="getSelectedContact" access="remote">
<cfargument name="id" default="0" required="true" />
<cfquery datasource="#request.dsn#" name="get_selected_contact">
➡select first_name, last_name, address, city, state, zip, email,
➡phone, notes, birth_date from contacts
➡where id=#flash.id#;
</cfquery>
<cfreturn get_selected_contact />
```

continues overleaf

```
</cffunction>
```

The id is set as a required field using the `<cfargument>` tag in the CFC. It's also assigned a default value of `0` just to prevent an error if an id isn't passed. Once the contact's information is queried from the database it is returned to Flash through the gateway using the `<cfreturn>` tag.

As mentioned earlier we use the `_Result` method to take care of handling the server's response. Here we set up the `getSelectedContact_Result` method to take the data passed from the server and place the corresponding values into the input text fields for display.

4. Returning to the Flash movie, we first make reference to the record using the `getItemAt` method. Since there is only one record being returned we access the `0` index:

```
function getSelectedContact_Result(records) {
    // since only record is being returned we access it at the 0
    //index
    var curr_record = records.getItemAt (0);
```

5. The reference to this record is stored in the `curr_record` variable. We can now access the contact data passed from CF and place them into our text fields on the stage:

```
    // set the values of the dynamic text fields on the stage
    first_name = curr_record.first_name;
    last_name = curr_record.last_name;
    address = curr_record.address;
    city = curr_record.city;
    state = curr_record.state;
    zip = curr_record.zip;
    email = curr_record.email;
    phone = curr_record.phone;
    notes.text = curr_record.notes;
    // set the birth date on the calendar
    calendar_mc.setSelectedItem(curr_record.birth_date);
    // we also have to tell the calendar what month to advance
    //to
    calendar_mc.setDisplayedMonth(curr_record.birth_date);
}
```

The text fields are set as input text fields so dynamic data can be displayed and modified if necessary. Since they are input text fields, as opposed to dynamic text, the user will be able to modify the contact information and update the record. The `notes` text field has been assigned an instance name so that it can be referenced by the ScrollBar component. This is a little different in previous versions of Flash where the only way to access a text field was through its variable name. Assigning instance names to text fields is new to Flash MX and allows the developer more control to dynamically access methods and properties of the field. The ScrollBar component simply needs to be assigned a target text field name to function properly. Once the target has been assigned, the ScrollBar will dynamically change depending on how much content has extended vertically past the viewable area. The target text field can be assigned in the Property inspector for the ScrollBar component.

This `getSelectedContact` method is called each time a selection is made from the ListBox and the entire process will repeat. It's definitely redundant, and not particularly efficient to grab the contact's information each time their name is selected in the ListBox. This is for demonstration purposes only and I urge you to improve on this functionality. Consider saving all records to a Local Shared Object on the user's machine and pulling the information from there. This will reduce strain on the server as well as making access times faster since data will be read locally. Obviously there will need to be some synchronization in place to make sure the local data coincides with the server data.

Adding contacts

The next section of the PMA we'll look at is the functionality to add contacts to the database. Our **add** button is a PushButton component that calls the `addConfirm` click handler method whenever it's pressed:

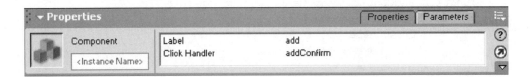

We will now create the `addConfirm` method we set as the click handler. If the button is pressed, a message needs to be displayed, instructing the user on how to add a new contact. They can either proceed or cancel and return to the PMA.

1. Begin by displaying the message clip by setting the MessageBox component's visibility to 1, which should be turned off by default in the movie. Also, set the size and message of the clip as I've done here:

    ```
    function addConfirm() {

        message_mc._visible = 1;
        message_mc.setSize(200, 150);
        message_mc.setMessage("Please fill out the form and click
        ➥\"save\" to add the new contact.");
    ```

2. Next, set the buttons and their width in the MessageBox using a button array to store the names of the PushButtons in the MessageBox. Then we call the `setButtons` and `setButtonWidth` methods to dynamically set and scale the buttons.

```
var buttons = ["Okay", "Cancel"];
message_mc.setButtons(buttons);
message_mc.setButtonWidth(60);
```

3. Finally, define the close handler method:

```
message_mc.setCloseHandler("addContact");
}
```

Here, several properties (such as the size of the box) and the message are then set. Being able to set these properties dynamically is very useful, as we'll be able to utilize the MessageBox component for other confirmation messages throughout the application. The last line of code in the above block sets the close handler of the MessageBox, which is triggered whenever the box is closed. Obviously we don't want anything to happen if the **cancel** button is clicked so we'll need to accommodate this in our `addContact` method.

4. If the **OK** button is clicked we need to clear the form fields and enable the **save** button so the user can proceed to add the new contact information.

```
function addContact(component, buttonIndex) {
    if (buttonIndex == 0) {
        first_name = "";
        last_name = "";
        address = "";
        city = "";
        state = "";
        zip = "";
        email = "";
        phone = "";
        notes.text = "";
        save_mc.setEnabled(true);
    }
}
```

Since the **OK** button has the 0 index in the array, we determine if it was clicked and proceed by clearing the form fields, before making the **save** button selectable. Otherwise, nothing happens and the user is returned to the PMA.

5. Now the input fields have been cleared and the **save** button has been enabled, the user is allowed to create the new entry. The user must fill out all the fields before proceeding and in our case we'll use a simple validation method that checks to see if everything is filled out:

```
function validateFields() {
    if (first_name != '' && last_name != '' && address != '' &&
    ➥city != '' && state != '' && zip != '' && email != '' &&
    ➥phone != '' && notes.text != '' &&
    ➥calendar_mc.getSelectedItem()) {
        return true;
    }
}
```

This is a very basic method that simply checks to see if any data exists in the fields and that the contact's birth date has been selected. Of course, the validation could be much more thorough but it's suffices for our purposes here. Once again, if you want to take this application further, feel free to expand on this method and create a validation scheme that fits your needs. The `validateFields` method returns `true` if the form passes validation.

6. Now we can use this in conjunction with a `saveContact` method, which will be called when the user clicks the **save** button, to save the new contacts information to the database:

```
function saveContact() {
    if (validateFields()) {
```

7. As the user has now filled in all of the fields, create the object of the new contact to pass to CF:

```
        var o = new Object();
        o.first_name = first_name;
        o.last_name = last_name;
        o.address = address;
        o.city = city;
        o.state = state;
        o.zip = zip;
        o.email = email;
        o.phone = phone;
        o.notes = notes.text;
        o.birth_date = birth_date;
```

8. Each time a date is selected on the calendar we call the `getBirthDate` change handler which sets the `birth_date` variable. Send it to the `saveContact` CFC through the Flash gateway:

```
        contacts_service.saveContact(o);
    } else {
```

9. If they haven't filled in all the fields, we'll tell them using the same message box we used earlier. This is done in the same way as in the `addConfirm` function:

```
message_mc._visible = 1;
// set the size and message of the clip
message_mc.setSize(200, 150);
message_mc.setMessage("Please be sure to fill out all
➥fields.");
// set the buttons and their width in the MessageBox
var buttons = ["Okay"];
message_mc.setButtons(buttons);
message_mc.setButtonWidth(60);
```

10. Now we just need to reset the close handler method if it's been set:

```
message_mc.setCloseHandler(null);
        }
    }
```

11. Let's move back to the text editor holding our ColdFusion functions and create the CFC responsible for grabbing the information from the object and inserting it into the database, which we just called in the `saveContact` function. Type in the following code:

```
<!--- save contact info --->
<cffunction name="saveContact" access="remote">
<cfquery datasource="#request.dsn#" name="add_contact">
insert into contacts(first_name, last_name, address, city, state,
➥zip,email, phone, notes, birth_date)
➥values('#flash.first_name#', '#flash.last_name#',
➥'#flash.address#', '#flash.city#', '#flash.state#',
➥'#flash.zip#', '#flash.email#', '#flash.phone#',
➥'#flash.notes#', #createodbcdate(flash.birth_date)#);
</cfquery>
<cfreturn 1 />
</cffunction>
```

If you're at all familiar with CF and variable scopes then you'll be glad to know that the Flash variable scope exists in ColdFusion MX. When accessing data passed from Flash, it can be referenced as `flash.yourvariablename`. This is how we access the data passed from Flash and include it in our `insert` statement. After the `insert` has successfully finished we then return a success flag back to Flash. This flag simply has a value of `1` and will be passed back to the `saveContact_Result` method.

12. This method should display a success message to the user if the insert was successful. We'll start by checking to see if the insert was successful and then, if true, proceed by displaying a success message to the user. Add this to your existing actions in your Flash movie:

```
function saveContact_Result(success) {
    if(success) {
        message_mc._visible = 1;
        message_mc.setSize(200, 150);
        message_mc.setMessage("The new contact was added
        ➥successfully.");
        // set the buttons and their width in the MessageBox
        var buttons = ["Okay"];
        message_mc.setButtons(buttons);
        message_mc.setButtonWidth(60);
        // reset the close handler method in case it was already
        // set
        message_mc.setCloseHandler(null);
```

13. At the same time we then make a call to our initial getAllContacts method, which will update the ListBox with our new contact:

```
        contacts_service.getAllContacts();
    }
}
```

Updating contacts

So, we've created the functionality to view and add contacts to the application, but we still need to be able to update a contact's information, just in case it changes. When a contact has been selected from the ListBox their information is displayed in the movie. The user needs to be able to modify the contact's information and update the record. This is done by clicking the **update** button, which calls the updateContact method.

1. To do this we first need the updateContact function to send the updated contact information to CF:

```
function updateContact() {
    // make sure that a contact is selected
    if (contacts_mc.getValue()) {
        // create an object that will be passed to CF for the
        //update
        var o = new Object();
        o.id = contacts_mc.getValue();
```

```
            o.first_name = first_name;
            o.last_name = last_name;
            o.address = address;
            o.city = city;
            o.state = state;
            o.zip = zip;
            o.email = email
            o.phone = phone;
            o.notes = notes.text;
            // handle the birth date
            // the birth_date variable is set with the getBirthDate
            //method
            o.birth_date = birth_date;
            // call the updateContact service
            contacts_service.updateContact(o);
        }
    }
```

As you can see, this method is similar to `saveContact` except that we check if the ListBox is selected because we don't want to allow the method to fire if no contact has been selected. The contact's record id is also passed to CF so it knows which record to update in the database. The id is stored in a data object along with other contact information. This object is then passed to the `updateContact` method of our CFC.

2. We create the `updateContact` CFC method to take the parameters passed from Flash, update the database, and send a success flag back to Flash:

```
<!--- save existing contact info --->
<cffunction name="updateContact" access="remote">
<cfquery datasource="#request.dsn#" name="save_contact">
update contactsset first_name="#flash.first_name#",
➥last_name="#flash.last_name#", address="#flash.address#",
➥city="#flash.city#", state="#flash.state#", zip="#flash.zip#",
➥email="#flash.email#", phone="#flash.phone#",
➥notes="#flash.notes#",
birth_date=#createodbcdate(flash.birth_date)#
where id=#flash.id#;
</cfquery>
<cfreturn 1 />
</cffunction>
```

3. Back in the Flash movie, the `updateContact_Result` method proceeds by displaying a success message to the user via the MessageBox component in a very similar way to the `saveContact_Result` function:

```
function updateContact_Result(success) {
    // if the update is sucessful do the following
    if (success) {
    // refresh the contact ListBox after update
        contacts_service.getAllContacts();
        // display message to user that the update was successful
        message_mc._visible = 1;
        message_mc.setSize(200, 150);
        message_mc.setMessage("The contact was updated
        ➥successfully.");
        // set the buttons and their width in the messagebox
        var buttons = ["Okay"];
        message_mc.setButtons(buttons);
        message_mc.setButtonWidth(60);
        // reset the close handler method in case it was already set
        message_mc.setCloseHandler(null);
    }
}
```

Once again the getAllContacts method is called to update the ListBox in case the contact's information has changed. So now we can view, add, and update contact information and you're probably asking 'Are we about done yet?' Well, there's one last piece of the pie and then I promise you we'll have a full-blown PMA.

Delete contacts

The PMA would not be complete without the ability to delete contacts from the database. You can probably take a wild guess at how we're going to accomplish this but let's go ahead and look through the code. First off, a contact needs to be selected from the ListBox before we can do anything. Then when the **delete** button is clicked, we call the deleteConfirm method.

1. First we check if a contact is selected. If it isn't we need to display a message asking the user to do so:

```
function deleteConfirm() {
    if (contacts_mc.getValue()) {
        message_mc._visible = 1;
        message_mc.setSize(200, 150);
        message_mc.setMessage("Are you sure you want to delete
        ➥the selected entry?");
        var buttons = ["Okay", "Cancel"];
        message_mc.setButtons(buttons);
        message_mc.setButtonWidth(60);
```

```
        message_mc.setCloseHandler("deleteContact");
    }
}
```

2. If the deletion is confirmed we can proceed and delete the contact. We check to see if the **OK** button was pressed using its 0 index as before. Then, we need to pass the id to ColdFusion. This is stored in an object and passed to the deleteContact method of the contacts CFC.

```
function deleteContact(component, buttonIndex) {
    if (buttonIndex == 0) {
        // set the object to pass to CF
        var o = new Object();
        o.id = contacts_mc.getValue();
        contacts_service.deleteContact(o);
    }
}
```

3. As for the CF counterpart, we just need a basic delete query that purges the record from the database. Once completed, the success flag is passed from CF, through the Flash gateway, and back to the deleteContact_Result method:

```
<!--- delete contact from the database --->
<cffunction name="deleteContact" access="remote">
<cfquery datasource="#request.dsn#" name="delete_contact">
delete from contacts
where id=#flash.id#;
</cfquery>
<cfreturn 1 />
</cffunction>
</cfcomponent>
```

4. This function is again, very similar to the other result functions:

```
function deleteContact_Result(success) {
    // delete the contact index since this index is no longer
    //valid
    delete contact_index;
        // if the delete is sucessful do the following
        if (success) {
        // display message to user that the delete was
        //successful
        message_mc._visible = 1;
        message_mc.setSize(200, 150);
        message_mc.setMessage("The contact was deleted
```

```
➡successfully.");
var buttons = ["Okay"];
message_mc.setButtons(buttons);
message_mc.setButtonWidth(60);
message_mc.setCloseHandler(null);
contacts_service.getAllContacts();
        }
    }
```

Once again a status message is displayed and the contacts ListBox is updated with the revised contacts list. I'm sure you could very easily update these confirmation functions to inform the user when the requests are unsuccessful.

Summary

By now the communication process should make much more sense and you should feel more comfortable with Flash Remoting. It may seem overwhelming at first, but the process is very intuitive and improved from the older methods of communication. There are many methods and properties available with the new Flash components so become familiar with them. They can help simplify and expedite your development efforts along with bringing increased functionality to your applications.

I hope you feel more comfortable with what Flash can provide as the presentation layer for interacting with application servers. The integration between Flash and ColdFusion MX is tight, and this will only increase in the not too distant future. Take what you've learned here and build upon it to create unique user experiences with these exciting new technologies. The future is looking good for Flash/CF integration.

Index

The index is arranged hierarchically, in alphabetical order, with symbols preceding the letter A. Many second-level entries also occur as first-level entries. This is to ensure that users will find the information they require however they choose to search for it.

Notes

Notes

Notes

Notes

friends of ED writes books for you. Any suggestions, or ideas about how you want information given in your ideal book will be studied by our team.

Your comments are valued by friends of ED.

For technical support please contact support@friendsofed.com.

Freephone in USA	800.873.9769
Fax	312.893.8001
UK contact: Tel:	0121.258.8858
Fax:	0121.258.8868

Registration Code: 02684KL8ZZ4X9801

Flash MX Studio - Registration Card

Name ....

Address ....

City ....State/Region ....

Country ....Postcode/Zip ....

E-mail ....

Profession: design student ☐ freelance designer ☐
part of an agency ☐ inhouse designer ☐
other (please specify) ....

Age: Under 20 ☐ 20-25 ☐ 25-30 ☐ 30-40 ☐ over 40 ☐

Do you use: mac ☐ pc ☐ both ☐

How did you hear about this book?..

Book review (name)..

Advertisement (name) ....

Recommendation ....

Catalog ....

Other ....

Where did you buy this book? ....

Bookstore (name) ....City................................

Computer Store (name)...

Mail Order..

Other...

How did you rate the overall content of this book?
Excellent ☐ Good ☐
Average ☐ Poor ☐

What applications/technologies do you intend to learn in the near future?...
....

What did you find most useful about this book? ....
....

What did you find the least useful about this book? ....
....

Please add any additional comments ....
....

What other subjects will you buy a computer book on soon?
....
....

What is the best computer book you have used this year?
....

Note: This information will only be used to keep you updated about new friends of ED titles and will not be used for any other purpose or passed to any other third party.

friendsof

DESIGNER TO DESIGNER™

NB. If you post the bounce back card below in the UK, please send it to:

friends of ED Ltd.,
30 Lincoln Road,
Olton,
Birmingham.
B27 6PA

BUSINESS REPLY MAIL
FIRST CLASS   PERMIT #64   CHICAGO, IL

POSTAGE WILL BE PAID BY ADDRESSEE

**friends of ED,
29 S. La Salle St.
Suite 520
Chicago Il 60603-USA**